ST. MAR
ST. MARY
OF MARYLAND
IY, MARYLAND 20686
W9-CCV-750

History,
Historians,
and the
Dynamics of Change

WILLIAM A. GREEN

HISTORY, HISTORIANS, AND THE DYNAMICS OF CHANGE

 PRAEGER

Westport, Connecticut
London

Library of Congress Cataloging-in-Publication Data

Green, William A., 1935-
    History, historians, and the dynamics of change / William A.
    Green.
        p.   cm.
    ISBN 0-275-93901-4. — ISBN 0-275-93902-2 (pbk.)
    1. History—Methodology.   2. Social change.   I. Title.
D16.G78   1993
902—dc20   92-26023

British Library Cataloguing in Publication Data is available.

Copyright © 1993 by William A. Green

All rights reserved. No portion of this book may be
reproduced, by any process or technique, without the
express written consent of the publisher.

Library of Congress Catalog Card Number: 92-26023
ISBN: 0-275-93901-4
        0-275-93902-2 (pbk.)

First published in 1993

Praeger Publishers, 88 Post Road West, Westport, CT 06881
An imprint of Greenwood Publishing Group, Inc.

Printed in the United States of America

The paper used in this book complies with the
Permanent Paper Standard issued by the National
Information Standards Organization (Z39.48-1984).

10 9 8 7 6 5 4 3 2 1

To my parents

Contents

Introduction ix

Part I HISTORY AND THE HISTORIAN 1

 1. History: The Elusive Quarry 3

 2. The Framework of History 17

Part II THE DYNAMICS OF HISTORICAL CHANGE:
    EUROPE 33

 Introduction: Search for a Governing Dynamic 35

 3. The Commercial Model 39

 4. The Demographic Model 59

 5. The Marxian Dynamic 83

 6. Weber, Sombart, and the Spirit of Capitalism 107

Part III THE DYNAMICS OF HISTORICAL CHANGE:
    WORLD HISTORY 127

 Introduction: The Global Perspective 129

 7. World-System Analysis 143

 8. Environmental History 167

Part IV SUMMATION 191

 9. The Continuing Pursuit of Order 193

Bibliography 213

Index 255

Introduction

This is a book about history and about some of the great historians of our century. It was undertaken to relieve a void in my own historical training. The book is presented in hope that it will illuminate aspects of the historian's enterprise for others. It is addressed to reasonably sophisticated undergraduate and graduate students as well as others who seek insight into the structure of historical knowledge and the theoretical formulations upon which contemporary historians base their work. It is hoped that the book will have value for history faculty at various academic levels—for people like myself who emerged from years of formal university education with little training in the structure of history, the history of historical writing, or the philosophy of history.

The book emerged by way of diversion. I was engaged in preliminary reading on a project involving the economic integration of the Atlantic world in the early modern period. To my distress, I discovered that I was operating without any well-formulated understanding about how change occurred at the macrohistorical level, and I was chagrined to find that many of the historians I was reading were no better informed than I. My research focused on the "transitional" period between what we have defined as the Middle Ages and early modern times. If the Western world was in transition, then there had to be some extraordinary dynamic at work in European civilization. But what was it? Different historians had entirely different opinions on the topic, and all too many demonstrated no consistency in their analyses, offering one type of causal explanation for one set of changes and a second for others without ever attempting to integrate those explanations into an over-arching model for change. My confusion led to frustration; with some reluctance, I set aside my main project—ever so briefly, of course—in order to inform myself, as best I could, about the prevailing theories of change that should, or could, guide a historian studying the period between the Middle Ages and the Industrial

Revolution. In time, this diversion became a passion, and the original project came to rest in a file drawer.

The book is divided into three main parts, plus a summary. The first introduces readers to the many pitfalls of historical writing and to questions about what we can and should learn from the past. While it emphasizes the limitations of our discipline, it attempts to alert readers to the importance of sound theory. One of the most important and least debated aspects of historical theory is periodization. Chapter 2 discusses the importance of periodization and the historical evolution of our current mode of periodization. It raises the question, which is revived in the final chapter, whether the prevailing mode should be overhauled.

Part II of the book addresses the chief theories that historians in this century have used to explain the process of change in European history. Part III extends the range of theoretical concern to world history. Part IV draws together many threads that emerge throughout the work and offers recommendations on specific theoretical issues. The book consistently draws its examples and seeks reference points from the period between the eleventh and eighteenth centuries, chiefly in Europe.

I am grateful to the Rockefeller Foundation and to the American Philosophical Society for support of my research. Holy Cross College, once again, has provided me time and resources to pursue serious study and writing. I am very grateful to my wife, Karin, for her continuing encouragement and understanding. Two outstanding students, Kathleen Hamel and Richard Wareing, offered me vital help on Marxist historiography and the demographic school of historians, respectively. My special thanks are owed to Ellyn McNeil, who has generously given many hours on the word processor and provided invaluable assistance in the compilation of bibliography.

In hope that this book conveys a sense of the pleasure as well as the mystery of learning, that it offers some wisdom, some stimulation, and some good judgment, I dedicate it to my parents, whose wisdom, stimulation, judgment, and love have been among the abiding treasures of my life.

Part I

History and the Historian

1

History: The Elusive Quarry

Those who cannot remember the past are condemned to repeat it.
George Santayana

This maxim from the pen of George Santayana boasts an ancient pedigree. The greatest of the classical Greek historians, Thucydides, considered history a guide to conduct, a medium by which thoughtful men could acquire wisdom through example. For Christian writers of the Middle Ages, history revealed God's truths. Voltaire, the eighteenth-century philosopher-historian, contended that knowledge of the past enabled the living to escape the errors of the dead. More recently, England's leading military historian asserted that history "shows us what to *avoid*" even if it cannot teach us what to do.[1] For all such thinkers, history is profoundly useful. It provides a rational ordering of human experience. It satisfies humankind's insatiable need to know whence we have come. For the deeply initiated, it affords the capacity for intelligent prediction.

Such optimism, though comforting, requires qualification. What happens in history, happens once. Each historical event involves a vast array of human and physical factors that cannot be reproduced in the same combination a second time. No historian can account for the totality of forces that have influenced past events, nor are historians able to test hypotheses in the way that physical scientists can endlessly re-run the same laboratory experiment under controlled conditions. Since historians cannot verify their private interpretations of past events, their work is always subject to attack by other scholars possessing contrary evidence, additional evidence, or a different range of vision.

In view of the kaleidoscopic diversity of educated historical opinion, one must be cautious about Santayana's maxim. Historians perpetually engage in the search for truth, but what they seek is an endlessly elusive quarry. Different people perceive the "logic" of history in different ways, and different perceptions occasion different conclusions concerning what constitutes appropriate human conduct. In spite of these uncertainties, historians continue to encounter the past with a driving will to reduce it to manageable order, to harness its spirit, and to reconstruct relationships—in effect, to wrench order from chaos and afford meaning to the human experience. The purpose of this first chapter is to examine major problems in the structure of historical studies and to identify the most notorious pitfalls that all serious students must encounter in reading and writing about the past.

SUBJECTIVITY

Every historian is a prisoner of his or her own time, language, and culture. "It is impossible," wrote Gerhard Benecke, "for anyone living today to hear early music with the ears of those who first heard it, and it is idle to pretend otherwise."[2] When we examine earlier forms of agriculture or industry or early social institutions, we advance upon them with an elaborate body of preconceptions derived from our contemporary understanding of these things. This breeds *anachronism* in history, the imposition of ideas or conditions upon past peoples who could neither have shared those ideas nor recognized such conditions. Because we live in a highly complex and diverse economic society, we are inclined to foist modern economic incentives on earlier peoples. We often assume, for example, that medieval traders possessed a degree of economic sophistication that, in reality, was beyond their understanding and inconsistent with their collective mindset, as indeed we presume that such traders had options and choices of which they were certainly ignorant. It is only with the greatest of effort that twentieth-century students can comprehend a pre-industrial value system that allowed hospitals to be adorned with valuable pieces of art while they suffered chronic shortages of beds. The time warp is inescapable. However we try, we cannot cross the barriers of value and perception that separate us from our distant progenitors.

The values we share in our own time will be reflected in the type of history we write. During the nineteenth century, a time of ardent nationalism in Europe, diplomatic and military history enjoyed wide acclaim. In the late twentieth century, social history commands center stage. Traditional military history with its emphasis on human valor and the nobility of arms has virtually slipped from sight. Diplomats and statesmen of the last century who meticulously preserved their personal papers and correspondence in the certain knowledge that historians would one day comb them for every nuance would be appalled to discover that many of today's scholars are at least as interested in scattered scraps of information bearing witness to the lives of uneducated handloom weavers or rebellious peasants.

When historians view the past from the underside of society, the history they write may bear little resemblance to that of historians who take an elitist perspective. Until recently, intellectual history involved the study of great thinkers, but in response to the remarkable achievements of cultural anthropologists and in keeping with our growing collectivist mentality, intellectual historians have begun to concentrate on the study of mass movements and of the myths and symbols that have provided unity and coherence to popular culture. In the past, histories of the Italian Renaissance, like those of modern European empires, have concentrated on elite populations, their problems and their creative endeavors. The very concept of "the Renaissance" might not have occurred to historians had they persistently viewed the culture of Italy in the fifteenth and sixteenth centuries from the democratic perspective of the masses.

Subjectivity is most evident in our use, or abuse, of language. Governments come and go; economies experience episodes of prosperity and depression. In perceiving these changes, we commonly ascribe biological properties to them. Civilizations "decay" and "die." Nations become "sick" and "degenerate." Yet, argues the sociologist Robert Nisbet, "No one has ever seen a civilization die."[3] Such expressions are metaphorical.[4] They are also imprecise and misleading. Hayden White, an eminent philosopher of history, contends that historical writing is "an essentially *poetic* act."[5] History, he declares, is a product of philosophy—of the historian's own personal mindset, not of objective reality. It is created by historians who give expression to their poetic presuppositions through strategically chosen literary devices.

The idea that history is the mythological creation of historians is a central theme of modern structuralist thought. From their beginnings in

France in the 1960s, structuralist thinkers have extended their intellectual influence throughout the West. They challenge the very premises upon which historians presume to draw conclusions from so-called objective facts, denying the possibility that the real life of the past is capable of being comprehended or described. The past is but an "infinite regress of distorted representations," they argue, and historians must face up to the "artifices they employ" to give shape and substance to their work.[6]

Most historians reject the extreme implications of structuralist assertions. If history is to survive as an academic discipline, historians cannot abandon their empirical tradition. But, as the structuralists correctly observe, neither can historians escape the subjectivity of language. In order to communicate ideas above the most primitive level, historians must employ abstract generalizations. Expressions like feudalism, mercantilism, capitalism, bourgeoisie, the Scientific Revolution, the Renaissance, the Enlightenment, and the Middle Ages are grandiose abstractions created by scholars to provide common denominators for understanding. For all their utility, however, such terms offer wide latitude for misinterpretation. Social patterns in different periods and in different countries—even in separate sections of the same country—have been so varied that we can only employ the same general words for them at the risk of misapprehending reality.[7] This situation intensifies as historians gather distance either in time or cultural context from the object of their investigation. Occidental scholars writing on the Orient commonly impose conceptual patterns embedded in the abstract language of the West upon cultural patterns in which those patterns fit awkwardly or not at all. The problem is similar, if not so grave, for scholars who translate the life of eleventh-century Europe into the idiom of the twentieth century.

Even if we could agree on terminology, our problems would not be resolved. Many of the most common generalizations in history have assumed heavy ideological overtones. Marxist historians not only impart different meanings to the words "feudalism" and "capitalism" than non-Marxists, but the words themselves, like terms such as "bourgeoisie" and "proletariat," have become ideologically charged. When historians approach the past with personal lexicons of socially weighted terms, they carry a theory of history concealed in their vocabularies.

THEORY IN HISTORY

All historical theory is rife with subjectivity, but history as a study of society cannot proceed without theory. The raw material of the historian remains an atomized mass of assorted facts until it is screened and organized for the purpose of testing a hypothesis. Any hypothesis, however weakly formulated, represents some over-arching idea, some theory. It is theory that gives shape to history, just as it is the historian with his biased intellectual baggage and his particular orientation to the past who gives shape to theory. Only the most naive writers can still claim, as did the leading French medievalist of the late nineteenth century, "Tis not I who speaks, but History, which speaks through me."[8]

No large body of scholars has been more immune to the theoretical properties of their discipline than historians.[9] The main reason for this is the historian's preoccupation with unique phenomena. As a conscious practice, most historians work inductively—that is, they reason from the specific to the general. Having identified a subject for investigation, they plunge into the archives, turn over immense quantities of data in response to their hypotheses (which are often vaguely formulated), and then presume to draw conclusions based on this evidence. Because they concentrate on the singularity of each historical experience, they have no reason to develop elaborate methodological strategies for identifying uniformities in human behavior that might transcend the time and place of their particular studies.

This practice contrasts rather sharply with the approach of economists, sociologists, or political scientists. Such social scientists might agree that every event is unique, but they would probably add that no event is unique in all ways. Human beings are essentially what they have been for centuries, and it is reasonable, therefore, to suppose that similar stimuli operating upon people of similar disposition under similar conditions will, in all probability, generate similar forms of conduct. In daily life, this type of reasoning lends wisdom to the ordinary citizen. But in academic life, it has been the province of social scientists, not historians, to seek out regularities in human conduct as a basis for establishing laws of behavior that facilitate prediction. Of late, sociologists, anthropologists, and economists have invaded the historians' domain in increasing numbers, bringing with them a rich theoretical tradition and a diverse assortment of research methods initially designed to study contemporary society. Although such methods do not lend themselves to all, or even to most, historical questions, the emphasis that social scientists place on theory and their concurrent criticism of the theoretical confusion exhibited by traditional historians has, at long last, awakened the latter to the theoretical implications of their own work.

MODELLING

The most important contribution of social science to history is the analytical model. Models are explicit theoretical representations of the structure and function of social phenomena. As abstract mental constructs, they serve the student of society in the way that physical models serve engineers and architects. Just as urban architects build balsa wood models to represent networks of buildings, avenues, and subways, social scientists create conceptual models to aid them in explaining the structural relationships that give coherence to a social system, to its specific elements, or to whole congeries of social systems. The very term "social system" is an abstract concept. It presumes the existence of regularity and order over a particular body of people inhabiting a specific geographic space. A model of a social system attempts to delineate the complex nature of that social order, to comprehend its hierarchies, to identify linkages between critical elements, and to explain how the system experiences change. A famous example of this is Karl Marx's model of the nineteenth-century capitalist system. Marx defined the functional relationships of that system and identified the means by which it underwent change. But no model, whether the Marxian model or any other, provides a mirror image of reality. All models are approximations. All are born in the intuitive intelligence of their creators. None can possibly incorporate all the facts of history that bear upon social structure. But they can assist us in identifying categories, comprehending relationships, and perceiving historical processes with greater clarity.

Some historical work is particularly suited to modelling. Models are used most frequently and successfully in treating well-defined, fairly cir-cumscribed problems where the data base is strong, but they are also use-ful in macrohistorical studies that examine the process of change across broad fronts. Not every historian will choose to create or choose to use explicit theoretical models. Nor should they. Humanist historians who prize the artistic qualities of their discipline and view the writing of history as the gradual unfolding of a story would consider the explicit declaration of theory and method associated with model building an intolerable intru-sion upon good historical literature. This does not relieve such historians from considerations of social theory. Wherever the guiding theory of a work of history is not stated explicitly, it will manifest itself implicitly. Only by being alert to the theoretical implications of their scholarship can historians avoid the embarrassment of unwittingly incorporating several antagonistic theoretical positions in a single work.

If a concern for theory is essential to the historian, so too is an awareness of the limits of theory. Theory in history is derived both *deductively* and *inductively*. The deductive process involves reasoning from the general to the specific in that one draws conclusions concerning specific phenomena from general propositions. Inductive reasoning operates in reverse, drawing general conclusions from specific information. Deductive historical theory is most evident among philosophers of history in the tradition of Vico, Croce, Spengler, and Toynbee.[10] These thinkers have purported to explain the course of human history in sweeping cyclical or other terms although, by and large, their works often exhibit little basis in empirical research and no important bearing on historical reality. In contrast to such deductive theorists, most practicing historians perceive themselves as inductive scholars who closely examine their evidence before attempting to refine their theories. Nevertheless, *inductive reasoning cannot function independently of deduction.* Every historian approaches his or her evidence with an assortment of prejudices or presuppositions already intact. These presuppositions can be considered proto-theories, vague orientations consciously or unconsciously held, that await refinement and confirmation through the research process. At some point in that process, induction blends imperceptibly with deduction. Precepts are affirmed, and they serve as organizing principles for the assembly and sorting of additional data. Karl Marx performed a prodigious amount of detailed empirical research on his model of the capitalist economy, but it is impossible to determine from his work where induction ends and deduction begins. Elias Tuma claims that Marx's grand theory of history was essentially formulated *before* he pursued his extensive research and that his empirical studies merely brought "his model closer to reality than if he kept it an abstract theory."[11]

If Tuma is correct, Marx was operating in a manner not unlike that of modern social scientists. As a rule, they propound a general theory, draw a working hypothesis from the theory, then test the hypothesis through empirical research (the theory-hypothesis-data method). The risks of such a method are obvious. The existence of a firm guiding theory, deductively derived, will dispose the researcher, consciously or not, to select evidence that confirms his hypothesis. At the same time, he may be prone to overlook, perhaps even conceal, evidence that contradicts his theoretical position. For social scientists who focus on contemporary problems, the perils of manipulating or ignoring data are relatively great as a result of the public nature of much of their evidence, not to mention their need to achieve a certain level of predictability. For historians, research data is usually more private. They deal with events already passed for which no public test of predictability is possible. Most historians would agree that an unscrupulous or dogmatic researcher can find some evidence to support any theoretical proposition, however bizarre.

The noted Cambridge historian and historiographer, Geoffrey Elton, believes that the theory-hypothesis-data method when employed by historians merely reduces history to "a repository of examples selected or distorted to buttress [a theoretical] scheme."[12] Elton's criticism belies his preference for the inductive approach; but as we have observed, there can be no purely inductive process. The historian cannot approach his evidence without some underlying hypothesis, however vague, or without some personal values that will govern his analysis of data. Whether explicitly declared or implicitly held, deductive reasoning is an inextricable element of all historical analysis. The differences in orientation between Elton and the social scientists are differences of degree. Does the open, social-scientific declaration of theoretical premises produce a more or a less prejudicial approach to empirical research in history than an implicitly theoretical, more clearly inductive process?

Certainly Elton is justified in his claim that historians who engage in modelling are prone to *reify* their abstractions. Reification is the mental process by which abstract concepts are given the property of reality. One might contend, for example, that people's advocacy of the "rights of man" during the French Revolution was a product of the Enlightenment. Yet the Enlightenment had no power of production, no ability to give or to take. The Enlightenment is an organizing principle, an intellectual abstraction that seeks to encompass within a single term a congeries of eighteenth-century orientations and ideas. Abstractions are not realities. The writings of Thomas Paine or of Jean-Jacques Rousseau may have stimulated advocacy of the rights of man, but to give that power to the Enlightenment is to reify an abstraction.

Theoretical models should be seen as analytical tools. They should be tested against the facts and reshaped and revised to meet the demands of conflicting evidence. Since no model can accommodate all the contradictory facts of history, there is a limit to which anyone can revise his theory without undermining its logical integrity. When that point is reached, scholars are often tempted to advance from declaring their models merely "the best reasonable means" of explaining an aspect of human behavior to identifying their models with reality itself.

TELEOLOGY

The most troublesome pitfall for historians, particularly those engaged in formal modelling, is the teleological trap. A teleological explanation is one that assigns meaning to historical events in terms of the implications they might have for other events that follow them in chronological time. Stated differently, teleological explanations attribute significance to persons, institutions, or events in terms of some destiny toward which the historian believes history has moved or is moving. Again, we can take our example from Marx. The orthodox Marxian concept of history declares that human society must pass in stages from one level of development to another en route to a classless communist society. A common criticism of Marxist historiography, precisely the one expressed by Elton, is that Marxists are prone to judge the significance of all historical events exclusively in terms of the bearing they might have upon this preconceived evolutionary process.

Most teleological explanations are not occasioned by grand theory but by methodological strategies or by the methodological blunders that historians are often unaware they are committing. Because we know that the French Revolution erupted in 1789, we are prone to examine all events during the preceding era in terms of the effect they might have had upon the outbreak of the revolt. Clearly, in treating eighteenth-century France, our approach to the collection and classification of evidence as well as our analysis of the evidence we collect has been of a different order from what it would have been had we remained ignorant of 1789. Because we know what happened, we scrutinize with special care those developments that appear to have had bearing upon the revolution while neglecting those that did not. It is important to keep in mind, however, that the people who lived in France in 1780 and 1785 could not have known that a revolution would occur at the end of the decade. They thought their thoughts, made their choices, and took their actions in utter innocence of the impending event. As historians, should we weigh their motives and actions in terms of their own perceptions of the world they lived in, or should we shape their history in terms of the cataclysm that ultimately befell them?

We should do neither exclusively. A reasonable balance must be struck, but even those scholars who are genuinely committed to achieving such balance slip unawares into teleological traps, ascribing motives to the actions of human beings in light of historical knowledge that we possess but that the actors themselves could not have had. The creators of historical models, knowing how history has evolved, are particularly prone to weave taut teleological webs of causal interaction. It is all too easy to start at the end and work history backwards to the beginning, subordinating all things to the acknowledged end. In reality, people live their history from the beginning in perfect ignorance of the ends toward which they are moving.

FREE WILL VERSUS DETERMINISM

Because theoretical models emphasize social forces and regularities in human behavior, they tend to sublimate the free will of individuals. This is particularly true of macrohistorical models in which the role of individuals is swallowed up and rendered insignificant by the tidal flow of vast historical forces. The importance of individuals in shaping events lies at the heart of much of the antagonism between humanistic history and social science. Have figures like Luther or Columbus made a difference in the grand march of human affairs? Would their exploits, however notable, have been performed by someone else had they never seen the light of day? Before Luther, the unity of the Christian Church had been repeatedly threatened but never shattered.[13] Is it the case, then, that Luther's particular personality and genius were critical in determining when and how the ultimate fissure in Christianity occurred? Had Columbus not landed in the West Indies in 1492, others would shortly have discovered the New World. But would they have claimed it for Spain? And without the alluvial wealth of America, could Spain have sustained its position as Europe's greatest power in the second half of the sixteenth century? In similar fashion, it is reasonable to question whether German unification under the monarchical principle would have been conceivable as early as 1871 without Bismarck. Could the Nazi Party have gained and sustained power in Germany without Hitler? Could a successful revolution by the Bolsheviks in Russian have occurred without Lenin?

These questions are impossible to answer, but our sensibilities tell us that the will of specific individuals has made an important difference in history. How much difference? Perfect free will does not exist. The exercise of freedom is always qualified by the contextual conditions in which one has his being—the value system one embraces, the countervailing wills of people with whom one engages, and the particular circumstances in which one's life takes place.[14] Do individuals influence the course of history only in the short run, hastening or retarding processes that must inevitably come to pass? All historians grapple with this problem, and the conclusions they reach will influence the way they write history. But the scale of the problem itself obliges sober scholars to mediate cautiously between the role of individual actors and the power of the social forces that enveloped them.

Historians acknowledge the importance of individual will to the extent that they allow for *contingency*. Except for confirmed determinists, historians generally presume that what has happened in history (in the short term, at least) need not have happened, at least it need not have happened in the way that it did or at the time that it did. The importance of contingency in history is manifestly evident in controversies such as the one that probes the origins of World War I. Provoked by the war guilt clause of the Versailles treaty, which attributed all responsibility for the outbreak of the "Great War" to Germany and its allies, historians of many nations have repeatedly re-examined the causes of the war and the relative responsibility of the participating great powers. Their numerous efforts generally pivot on the assumption that this universal catastrophe—one that shredded the world order, facilitated the Bolshevik Revolution, and set the stage for a second, more costly world conflict—might have been avoided, localized, or moderated by the action of individuals. With few exceptions, studies of the origins of the war have focused on political and diplomatic figures.[15] It is the abiding characteristic of diplomatic history to view the past in terms of the contingencies confronted by statesmen. Every phase of the prewar drama is examined in light of the options available to the chief actors, and the assumption underlying this mode of analysis is that wiser or different individuals might have pursued a different course and thereby altered the destiny of humankind.[16]

Do we, at the end of the twentieth century, possess the power to preserve this planet, or are we led by inexorable forces to contaminate our living space through multiple forms of pollution or, even worse, to terminate history in nuclear holocaust? How much can the will of individuals affect these ultimate questions? We may never know with certainty, but there is reason to believe that groups of people as well as individual leaders consistently take rational actions on the basis of perceived dangers or discomforts, adjusting their behavior to avoid the impact of negative forces. Such adjustments usually befuddle the predictions of social scientists and occasion public rebuke of their work.[17]

The repeated inexactitude of social scientific predictions tempts humanistic historians to condemn the theoretical and methodological pretensions of their social science colleagues. But the shortcomings of social science should have only the most sobering implications for historians. Most social scientists work in broad daylight. The utility of their theories and the relevance of their calculations are perpetually being tested by contemporary behavior. Yet, despite their easy access to vast amounts of relatively reliable data and their intimate acquaintance with contemporary individuals and institutions, social scientists have great difficulty determining the laws of motion that govern contemporary society. How, then, can historians, who are frequently oblivious to theoretical and methodological principles and who write history by the seats of their pants, presume to unravel the more complex and difficult problems of the past with any degree of accuracy? Willard Quine has written of the natural sciences, "all is tentative, all admits to revision."[18] His point is doubly true for history. There is good history and bad history, good theory and bad theory. But there is no history without theory, and good history depends upon good theory.[19]

NOTES

1. B. H. Liddell Hart, *Why Don't We Learn from History?* (New York, 1971), p. 15.

2. Foreword to Hermann Kellenbenz, *The Rise of the European Economy* (New York, 1976), ix.

3. Robert A. Nisbet, *Social Change and History: Aspects of the Western Theory of Development* (New York, 1969), p. 3. For the most part, Nisbet is correct. However, in the case of American Indians, one might argue that within a single lifetime it was possible to witness the decay and virtual disappearance of a distinct culture.

4. Nisbet's point is well taken, although there are some cases, like North American Indian civilization, for which such language would not be wildly metaphorical.

5. Hayden White, *Metahistory: The Historical Imagination in Nineteenth-century Europe* (Baltimore and London, 1973), x.

6. In a highly controversial structuralist-Marxist analysis of pre-capitalist economic patterns, two British authors have resisted any involvement with empirical data in their attempt to evaluate Marxist concepts. See Barry Hindess and Paul Q. Hirst, *Pre-Capitalist Modes of Production* (London, 1975). Succinct statements on the impact of structuralist thinking in history appear in a symposium published in *History Workshop*, vols. 5–8 (1978–1979): see articles by Richard Johnson, Gavin Williams, Keith McClelland, Simon Clarke, and the editors themselves. Quoted phrases in the text of this book are taken from vol. 6 (1978): 2. For a stinging counterattack against the structuralist critique of empiricism, see E. P. Thompson, *The Poverty of Theory and Other Essays* (New York and London, 1978).

7. See Alfred Cobban's review of Charles Tilly, *The Vendée* (1964) in *History and Theory* 5 (1966): 201. For a fuller treatment of this problem and the historiography of the French Revolution, see Cobban, *The Social Interpretation of the French Revolution* (Cambridge, 1971), pp. 17–21.

8. Fustel de Coulanges, quoted in Harold T. Parker, "Some Concluding Observations," in Parker and Georg G. Iggers, eds., *International Handbook of Historical Studies: Contemporary Research and Theory* (Westport, Conn., 1979), p. 421.

9. In selecting insightful works from leading historians of the last two centuries for his excellent anthology, *Varieties of History from Voltaire to the Present* (Cleveland, 1956), Fritz Stern discovered that even the great historians have been "reluctant to articulate their views about history" or to identify their presuppositions. Many renowned historians, including Tocqueville and Maitland, had to be omitted from the anthology because at no place in their works had they left explicit statements of the essence of their historical thought. See Stern's introductory essay to the volume, p. 15.

10. For a general overview of these philosophers of history, see Joseph Maier, "Cyclical Theories," in Werner I. Cahnman and Alvin Boskoff, eds., *Sociology and History: Theory and Research* (New York, 1964), pp. 47–57.

11. Elias H. Tuma, *Economic History and the Social Sciences: Problems of Methodology* (Berkeley and Los Angeles, 1971), pp. 174–175.

12. G. R. Elton, *The Practice of History* (New York, 1967), p. 36.

13. We have the immediate pre-Reformation examples of Wyclif, Hus, the Waldensians, and the Albigensians.

14. Gordon Leff, *History and Social Theory* (University, Ala., 1969), pp. 35–37.

15. One important exception is Marc Ferro's *The Great War 1914–1918* (London, 1973), which explains developments in broad sociological terms.

16. In a witty and insightful assessment of his long life as a diplomatic historian, A. J. P. Taylor emphasized the importance of accident (the ultimate contingency) in history as an offset to *"les forces profondes."* A war between Germany and much of the rest of Europe was likely in the early twentieth century, he wrote, but "the actual war that broke out in 1914 would not have occurred as it did if Archduke Franz Ferdinand had not gone to Sarajevo on June 28 or even if his chauffeur had not taken a wrong turning." A. J. P. Taylor, "Accident Prone, or What Happened Next," *Journal of Modern History* 49 (1977): 1–18.

17. A classic example of this is a *Wall Street Journal* article entitled "Why Demographers Are Wrong Almost as Often as Economists," 29 January, 1985, p. 35.

18. Willard V. Quine, "The Scope and Language of Science," *British Journal for the Philosophy of Science* 8 (1957): 17, quoted in Peter D. McClelland, *Causal Explanation and Model Building in History, Economics, and the New Economic History* (Ithaca, 1975), p. 21.

19. The need for historians to cultivate a keener awareness of the theoretical foundations of their work should involve them in closer liaison with social science disciplines that are already steeped in theory. So argues Gareth Stedman Jones. However, he adds, historians should not consider these disciplines academic department stores where pre-tailored concepts can be secured to meet any specific requirement. This will only render them dependent. Much social science theory is inappropriate to history, and the indiscriminate shopper will likely wind up with theoretical merchandise that members of the dispensing discipline no longer prize. The time has come for historians to participate more fully in the formulation of the theoretical precepts that undergird their own studies: "theoretical work . . . is too important to be subcontracted to others." Gareth

Stedman Jones, "From Historical Sociology to Theoretical History," *British Journal of Sociology* 27 (1976): 295. This is an extremely valuable article on the relationship between sociology and history. Also see Raphael Samuel and Gareth Stedman Jones, "Sociology and History," *History Workshop* 1 (1976): 4–8.

2

The Framework of History

Two aspects of theory are particularly important for historians: propulsion and periodization. The first concerns the forces that promote change. The second involves mental architecture: the chronological framework within which we set our history. Since all periodization presumes a theory of change, these are linked theoretical properties.

Despite its importance, periodization may be the least scrutinized theoretical component of history. Scholars assert that history constitutes a seamless garment, but they cannot render the past intelligible until they subdivide it into manageable and coherent units of time. Periodization operates at two levels: individual and institutional. Individually, each writer chooses the chronological parameters for his or her work of history. Whether that work covers ten years or ten centuries, its beginning and ending dates are chosen because they coincide with significant watersheds that set the era of the study apart, provide it a composite character, and enable the writer to focus on particular aspects of the human experience. At the institutional level, historians in the Western world have adopted a tripartite form of periodization that separates the past into three vast compartments—ancient history, medieval history, and modern history—with epochal breaks at roughly A.D. 500 and A.D. 1500. These compartments are further subdivided for convenience and manageability. The Middle Ages are divided three ways—early, central, and later—with breaks around A.D. 1000 and A.D. 1300. The modern epoch is split into early and late modern, with a break falling at the end of the eighteenth century.

This chapter will concentrate on institutional periodization. When, why, how, and by whom was tripartite periodization adopted? What are its implications for historical thinking and writing?

Although periodization is founded on disciplined concepts of continuity and change, change occurs at different rates in different areas of human experience. It occurs quickly in politics, slowly in systems of value.[1] All aspects of human activity are interrelated: technology is affected by what happens in politics; religion is influenced by what happens in science. But the internal rhythms of science and religion, of politics and technology are different. Our judgment on periodization depends, therefore, upon the *priorities* we assign to different areas of human endeavor. For Hegel, history was the dialectical evolution of the *absolute idea*; for Marx, it was the dialectical unfolding of *modes of production*. For both, the structure of the model used to explain the process of change—the dialectic—was similar; but Hegel and Marx emphasized different aspects of human experience, and their periodization reflected those differences.[2]

Periodization is profoundly affected by social orientation. Should we emphasize a top-down or a bottom-up approach to past societies? Until recently, historians have focused on elite groups, and the circa 1500 medieval/modern watershed is partly a result of that. Were we to examine European history in terms of the longevity, labors, physical circumstances, and mentalities of ordinary men and women, we might conclude, as one French historian has done, that the dawn of a new epoch in Europe did not arrive until the eighteenth century.[3]

Any division of time, however meaningful, will cut and separate important on-going historical processes. The treatment accorded the bubonic plague by different groups of historians serves as a case in point. Descending upon Europe in the 1340s, the Black Death recurred continuously in pandemic proportions, remaining Europe's leading killer until the eighteenth century. Human devastation was heaviest in the early period, but the demographic, social, and psychological impact of the plague was profoundly felt for several centuries. Historians of the Middle Ages give it great attention. Scholars of the modern world frequently neglect it. The latters' time clock generally commences around 1500. They break into the epidemiological cycle at midstream, and with some exceptions they are largely oblivious to its monumental societal ramifications.

All periodization is arbitrary. All periodization is flawed. But some forms of periodization are more arbitrary and more flawed than others. More than any other aspect of historical theory, periodization resists change. Once firmly drawn and widely accepted, period frontiers can become intellectual straightjackets that profoundly affect our habits of mind—the way we retain images, make associations, and perceive the beginning, middle, and ending of things. Powerful vested interests inevitably arise to perpetuate accepted practices. Nowhere is the rigidifying power of periodization more evident than in the modern university. We staff departments of history, organize graduate training, and structure undergraduate curricula largely in terms of tripartite periodization. Textbooks reinforce this pattern,[4] and professional journals scrupulously adhere to standard epochal frontiers.[5] Faculty carefully partition the historical terrain to avoid intruding upon places and periods that "belong" to their colleagues. As a result, standard periods have become self-contained entities. Writers and publishers, teachers and students regard them as immutable features of the intellectual landscape, and this influences the way issues are identified and emphases applied.

In the main, two conceptual approaches have been used to justify period frontiers: (1) an *aggregate* approach, and (2) a *leading sector* approach. Aggregate theory identifies converging developments in several areas of human activity. Leading sector arguments focus upon one overwhelming source of change that exercises decisive pulling power on all others. Those advancing an aggregate view might contend that within several decades of 1500 the Ptolemaic perception of the universe was undermined; printing and gunpowder assumed wide importance; Columbus discovered America; the Portuguese opened a sea route to the Indies; the Protestant Reformation erupted; Constantinople fell to the Turks; and the monarchies of France, Spain, and England were consolidated. Together, it is argued, these events wrenched Western man sufficiently from the continuities of an earlier time to merit the establishment of an epochal frontier.

A proponent of the leading sector concept might argue instead that the discovery of America with its alluvial wealth; its effect upon the European power structure; its extraordinary impact on the intercontinental transfer of diseases, plants, and animals; and its influence on Europeans' perception of the physical world, philosophy, and religion catapulted the whole of Western society from one set of norms toward another. Both examples are *episodic* views of periodization wherein a single chance event (e.g., the discovery of America) or the coincidental convergence of many discrete happenings produced exceptional change in human affairs.

An alternative to the episodic approach is one that focuses on *process*. Adam Smith believed that commercial forces were the main engine driving history and that historians should identify major watersheds at climactic points in an evolving international division of labor. Other scholars contend that the rhythmic action of demographic forces has constituted so dynamic an engine of change that epochal divisions can be measured by the ebb and flow of population. Marxists declare that economic affairs dominated and determined all others and that history proceeded from epoch to epoch according to a precise and predictable dialectical process based on modes of production.

If propulsion and periodization are linked theoretical properties, then our periodization should be governed in large measure by our understanding of the forces that drive the historical process. In subsequent chapters, the theories of change currently used by historians will be examined in some detail. Each will be assessed in terms of its compatibility with standard tripartite periodization. In this chapter, however, my objective is to determine how Western tripartite periodization took shape. That, in itself, is an object lesson in the subjective and theoretical character of history.

EARLY CHRISTIAN PERIODIZATION

Medieval chroniclers demonstrated familiarity with several concepts of periodization, all extrapolated from Holy Scripture or other religious writings. The Book of Daniel envisioned a world order of four universal monarchies. The fourth of these, "dreadful and terrible, and strong exceedingly," was expected to give way to a new dominion of glory (a fifth age) in which all people, nations, and languages would be everlastingly united [Daniel (7:14)]. The four universal monarchies were commonly identified with Assyria, Persia, Greece, and Rome.

After the Christianization of the Roman Empire, Rome was viewed increasingly as God's instrument for universal proselytization. Orosius's *Seven Books of Histories against the Pagans* (early fifth century) endorsed the four-monarchy concept, linking Rome with the sacred history of Christianity. Germanic invasions of the Roman Empire were explained as God's means of carrying the Gospel of Christ to all peoples. A century later, Cassiodorus contended that the fourth and final universal monarchy, Rome, was being perpetuated by the Germans. This view persisted through the Middle Ages: the Holy Roman Empire of the German Nation was a continuation of the early Roman Empire and a central force in the sacred history of Christianity. It was destined to survive to the end of the world.[6] That end was near. The decline of Roman political power since the early Caesars and the withering of towns and trade after the fifth century seemed mere confirmation to many Christians that they lived in the final years of a weary and senile world whose end would be accomplished by the second coming of Christ.

Another widely approved periodization was extrapolated from biblical texts during the first centuries of the Christian era. It contemplated six ages of history in geometric symmetry with the six days of creation:

1. From creation to the flood
2. From the flood to Abraham
3. From Abraham to David
4. From David to the Babylonian captivity
5. From captivity to the birth of Christ
6. From the birth of Christ to the second coming.

As a rule, Christian scholars who wrote general surveys of "world history" began with a summary of holy scripture from Genesis through the New Testament, then proceeded to narrate, in greater detail, the events of the sixth age. The exceptional regularity of this scheme gained reinforcement from St. Matthew's gospel, where it is declared that fourteen generations separated Abraham from David, David from the Babylonian captivity, and the captivity from the birth of Christ [Matthew (1:17)]. The seventh glorious age, the gathering of the elect in an eternal sabbath, was expected to commence with the second coming.[7]

INTERVENTION OF THE HUMANISTS

Early Christian concepts of historical periodization encountered no sustained challenge until the fourteenth century, when Italian humanists made the first major revision. Annoyed by German claims to Roman succession and inspired by the growing wealth and power of their own states, Italian humanists launched a relentless attack on the centuries that stretched between the collapse of Rome and their own time. For Italians, Rome was the ancestral civilization. Like no other Europeans, Italian humanists expressed a near-tribal pride in the accomplishments of their classical forebears. They drew sharp distinctions between the cultural magnificence of Roman civilization and the "barbarous darkness" that followed the Empire's demise. Having resisted the overlordship of Germanic Holy Roman emperors since the eleventh century, Italians firmly rejected the moral foundations upon which that overlordship rested—that is, the Germans' claim to be legitimate successors to the emperors of Rome.

Italian humanists did not inaugurate modern tripartite periodization. That would not happen for several centuries. They did create the forward epochal frontier of the tripartite scheme, and they laid important conceptual groundwork for the backward parameter. In his *History of the Florentine People,* a work in twelve books that provided a model for other humanist scholars, Leonardo Bruni (d. 1444) insisted that the Roman Empire fell under the onslaught of barbarian invaders. It was never revived, neither in Italy nor Germany. When the long succession of northern incursions into Italy finally subsided, Italians began a remarkable recovery, which by the fourteenth century had produced numerous flourishing and powerful city-states.[8] Flavio Biondo's history of Europe from the fifth to the fifteenth century (published 1439–1453) emphatically declared that the Roman Empire fell in A.D. 412. He lamented that fall, but like Bruni and other Italian humanist historians, he took consolation in the rise of the new Italy whose great cities, he thought, had restored to the peninsula its lost dignity.[9]

For Italy's secular historians, the fifth-century fall of the Roman Empire was *the* watershed event in the history of Western mankind. Bruni and Biondo assumed the view of Petrarch that from the fifth century to their own day Europe had been enveloped by darkness. All three were passionately committed to recovering the lustre of an earlier age, but none of them developed the concept of a third, modern age.

IMPACT OF THE REFORMATION

The achievements of Italy's humanist historians were blunted in upcoming centuries by the Protestant Reformation. The greatest of the northern humanists, Erasmus, insisted that purity of religion depended upon purity of good letters and that purity of letters had subsided in Europe with the demise of the classical writers and the early Church fathers.[10] His view furnished intellectual fodder for Lutherans. By the 1520s Lutheran writers were identifying the fifth-century collapse of both classical literature and evangelical Christianity with the beginning of the thousand-year reign of the papal antichrist. Rejecting the secular orientation of Italian humanists, Lutherans reaffirmed the union between history and theology. God was directly involved in human affairs, and the chief function of historians was to identify His interventions and to interpret their meaning. At the same time, Lutheran historians agreed with Italian humanists that the millennium from the fifth through the fifteenth century was a period of cultural darkness. For them, however, it was religious corruption, not the Germanic invasions of Italy, that occasioned the darkness. Protestant reform offered the world one last chance at redemption. Time was short. "We clutch at a tiny last corner of the world," wrote the Lutheran Andreas Musculus in 1561; "it is certain that the end of the world is on our doorstep, for Luther has preceded the second coming of Christ as John went before the first."[11]

Lutheran writers generally adhered to the four-monarchy plan.[12] Outside Germany, however, the four-monarchy concept came under attack. Jean Bodin, the French humanist-historian, rejected it on the same grounds as the Italians. The notion that Germans had assumed the mantle of Roman authority and perpetuated the Empire for a thousand years was, for Bodin, a monumental fiction. Growing knowledge about the empires of Asia rendered consideration of a universal Roman Empire (or any other universal empire) futile.[13] Bodin urged historians to abandon religious mythology in order to focus attention on explaining, in a purely secular manner, the ebb and flow of civilizations and the rise and fall of great political states.[14]

As long as religious issues dominated social consciousness, a religious ordering of historical time was likely to prevail. That dominance waned in the seventeenth century. Even the last of the so-called religious wars—the Thirty Years War—was driven less by religious loyalties and more by the political opportunism of secular rulers bent on consolidating territorial states. Those states enjoyed greatly enhanced power in the seventeenth century. Tax revenues increased; trade expanded; mercantile empires were formed; and centralized bureaucracies assumed greater control over a host of social institutions. Historians adjusted their thinking accordingly. Greater attention was given to scientific and technological developments and to the oceanic discoveries of the fifteenth and sixteenth centuries that wrought changes in the conduct of trade, the distribution of power, and the spatial orientation of Europeans toward the world at large. Protestants considered the Reformation a momentous epochal event, and by the end of the Thirty Years War, Catholics conceded that the rupture of Western Christianity, now permanent, represented a major break in historical continuity.[15] New terms had already crept into the common language of

Europeans identifying the millennium following the fall of Rome: *media tempestas* (1469), *media tempore* (1531), *media aetas* (1518), and *medium aevum* (1604).[16] By the late seventeenth century, all of the ingredients for tripartite periodization were at hand.

EIGHTEENTH-CENTURY ADOPTION OF TRIPARTITE PERIODIZATION

The scholar who first assembled the pieces was a German philologist, Christof Keller, commonly called Cellarius (1638–1707). Author of numerous linguistic and geographical studies, Cellarius composed a brief overview of ancient history in 1675, following it the next year with a work entitled *Nucleus of Middle History between Ancient and Modern*. Thereafter, he published a more extensive treatise on the Middle Ages and another on modern Europe.

Cellarius's chief historical publications passed through at least eight editions, but the tripartite model he adopted gained ground very slowly.[17] Early eighteenth-century scholars generally accepted the fall of Rome as an epochal frontier, but many of them acknowledged no other break. All that preceded the fall of Rome was ancient history; all that followed was modern. This was the understanding that prevailed at Oxford and Cambridge in the 1720s when George I established the Regius Chairs of Modern History.[18]

Enlightenment rationalism intensified the hostility of eighteenth-century intellectuals to the Church, to superstition, to willfull ignorance, and to constraints artificially imposed upon individual human freedom and rationality—all of which were thought to be characteristic features of the millenium following the fall of Rome. Voltaire's well-known prejudice against the so-called Middle Ages was shared by the most noteworthy of British historians, David Hume, William Robertson, and Edward Gibbon.[19] The latter's luxuriant seven-volume *Decline and Fall of the Roman Empire* (1776–1788) combined formidable criticism of medieval Christianity, deep skepticism concerning human nature, and an Enlightenment optimism that man could bring order and coherence to his life through the exercise of reason. For Gibbon, the fall of Rome represented "the triumph of barbarism and religion." That fall, he thought, was "the greatest, perhaps, and the most awful scene in the history of mankind," the baleful consequence of the slow decay of ancient virtues.[20] Gibbon's history comprises two nearly equal parts—the history of Rome to 476, and the ensuing ten centuries to the fall of Constantinople in 1453. It was entirely compatible with tripartite periodization. In fact, all the grand historians of the eighteenth century, including Bolingbroke and Muratori, distinguished between ancient, medieval, and modern times. They were, however, imprecise about dating those epochs.

Precision was a concern of the first distinguished body of academic historians, established at the University of Göttingen in the eighteenth century. History was not a primary branch of learning in European universities, but Göttingen, founded in 1737, became an exception.[21] Johann Christoph Gatterer, who assumed the Chair in history in 1759, had an extraordinary range of historical interests and, for his time, exceptional historical vision.[22] What, he asked, are the determining forces that give unity to the experience of all peoples on this planet? In terms of the entire human experience, how should historical time be marked out?

Gatterer began his periodization with the creation. He identified four great epochs in the history of the world: (1) the age of creation, which included the era of the flood; (2) the age of the founding of nations, including Assyrian, Persian, and Roman nations; (3) the age of the *völkerwanderung,* beginning with the fifth-century movements of Germans and Slavs and continuing thereafter with the conquests of Moslems and Mongols; and (4) the age that commenced with the discovery of America.[23]

If we delete from Gatterer's scheme the one element that reflects literal acceptance of Old Testament scripture—namely, the age of creation—we are left with a tripartite structure not dissimilar from that of Cellarius. Gatterer and his colleagues pursued a universal form of history in which the chief overriding factor since 1500 was the unparalleled dominance of Europe in world affairs. Göttingen historians advocated the primacy of politics, insisting that the central theme of European history in the three centuries after 1492 was the rise of the great powers and the formation of the modern states system. It was this, above all else, that rendered Europe's experience unique and gave Western peoples the vigor, direction, and material prowess to dominate the remaining quarters of the globe.

THE CREATION OF THE RENAISSANCE

Thus far, no mention has been made of the Renaissance. Nor did historians of the eighteenth century have any perception of a distinct segment of time, a general European experience, that might be designated "the Renaissance." As an organizing abstraction, "the Middle Ages" had already taken shape. It was the creation of a second abstraction, "the Renaissance," that put the final seal on Western man's collective conceptualization of the thousand-year period following the fall of Rome.

The modern concept of the Renaissance is largely the gift of Jacob Burckhardt, the eminent Swiss scholar whose *Civilization of the Renaissance in Italy* (1860) constitutes a major historiographical event. Numerous eighteenth-century writers, including Voltaire, had taken humanists at their word and accepted their view that the revival of classical learning represented an intellectual revolution of the first magnitude. But not until Burckhardt did that revolution transcend the realm of artistic and literary achievement.

Burckhardt transformed the Renaissance idea into a comprehensive revolution in the civilization of Italy, a revolution that radiated its light across much of Western Europe and drew the final curtain on the Middle Ages. The revival of classical learning was a necessary but insufficient explanation for the Italian Renaissance, Burckhardt contended. Writers and artists of the ancient world merely provided the guidelines, the models, that this virile society elected to pursue in its effort to shed the "fantastic bonds of the Middle Ages."[24]

Italy's development of a unique civic life uniting noblemen and burghers in societies that rewarded wealth, not birth, encouraged the assertion of human individuality. Dynamic individualism became the touchstone of Italian life. Individualism inspired the discovery of beauty in nature. It stimulated investigation of the wider reaches of the globe, and it rendered Italians increasingly secular. Medieval civilization reached its highest development in France; it never achieved a comfortable fit in Italy. After the fourteenth century, Italians rebelled against it and created a new, modern civilization.[25]

Burckhardt's vision pervaded historical thinking through the late nineteenth century, and it remains today, with numerous corrections and revisions, the basis of our understanding of the Renaissance. Burckhardt's vision of the Renaissance was elitist. His emphasis on Italian individuality resonated with the sense of rugged individualism expressed by Western Europe's expanding bourgeoisie.[26] Although he emphatically distinguished between medieval and modern civilization, Burckhardt did not attempt to create a distinct epoch in human history called "the Renaissance."[27] Rather, he affirmed the Renaissance as a breakwater between medieval and modern times. It was the first flowering of modernity, a bulwark of the tripartite formula.

HISTORY AS AN ACADEMIC DISCIPLINE

Burckhardt's contribution is doubly important because it was during the halcyon years of his interpretive revolution that history came of age in the universities of Britain, France, and the United States. Before 1873, only two persons were formally teaching history at Cambridge University. History was an adjunct of philosophy and politics.[28] A decade later, only twenty people were fully engaged in university-level history teaching in the United States.[29] Thereafter, the discipline expanded rapidly. National associations of historians were formed, and national journals of history quickly made their appearance.[30] A surge in the publication of monographs generated growing demand for collaborative syntheses. The most famous of these—possibly the most influential collaborative work ever to appear in Western historiography—was the twelve-volume *Cambridge Modern History,* which commenced publication in 1902.

Responsibility for orchestrating this massive history fell to Lord Acton, Regius Professor at Cambridge, who declared that Western historical continuity had sustained an abrupt break around 1500:

The modern age did not proceed from the medieval by normal succession, with outward tokens of legitimate descent. Unheralded, it founded a new order of things, under a law of innovation, sapping the ancient reign of continuity. In those days Columbus subverted the notions of the world, and reversed the conditions of production, wealth, and power; in those days Machiavelli released government from the restraint of law; Erasmus diverted the current of ancient learning from profane into Christian channels; Luther broke the chain of authority and tradition at the strongest link; and Copernicus erected an invincible power that set for ever the mark of progress upon the time that was to come. . . . It was an awakening of new life; the world revolved in a different orbit, determined by influences unknown before. After many ages persuaded of the headlong decline and impending dissolution of society, and governed by usage and the will of masters who were in their graves, the sixteenth century went forth armed for untried experience, and ready to watch with hopefulness a prospect of incalculable change.[31]

In succeeding decades, the *Cambridge Modern History* became a reservoir of information for graduate students, a quarry mined by innumerable college professors for class lectures, and an inspiration for writers of single-volume college textbooks.[32] The periodization established in that history was affirmed in subsequent series of similar magnitude and influence: the *Cambridge Medieval History* (eight volumes, 1911–1936) and the *Cambridge Ancient History* (twelve volumes, 1923–1939). Tripartite periodization has continued to dominate the Western conceptualization of historical time ever since.

Should it?

Historical orientations have changed since Lord Acton initiated the *Cambridge Modern History*. Egalitarianism has triumphed over elitism. Social history has taken prominence over political history. Religious divisions have lost their sting under ecumenical pressures, and great religious movements, like the Reformation, are now thought to have been as much a consequence of economic and social forces as of spiritual or intellectual strivings. Less attention is given to the ideas of great thinkers of the past, more to the mentalities of "the people." New areas of study have arisen—for example, women's history and the history of the family. If we view history from the perspective of women or of common folk, the era around 1500 has little to distinguish it. Not until industrialization, we are told, did patterns of life for common people change significantly in Europe. Between 1500 and 1800 annual per capita income could not have increased by more than 0.2 to 0.3 percent. Yet, in the early nineteenth century, per capita income was growing at a rate of 0.5 to 0.7 percent per annum, and by the mid-nineteenth century, that rate had risen to 1.2 percent.[33]

The few scholars who have written on periodization in recent decades have rejected 1500 as a suitable watershed in European history. In their view, a period break around 1500 severs the vital continuity of European life from the tenth to the eighteenth century.[34] In defense of their position, it can be argued that the Industrial Revolution of the eighteenth century constitutes the great economic and technical divide in Western history. The unprecedented modern surge in population began in the eighteenth century, and the democratic revolutions of the late eighteenth century probably outweigh any comparable experiences of the fifteenth or sixteenth centuries.

Still, the circa 1500 watershed has much to recommend it. It may be the product of episodic thinking, and clearly some of the episodes that gave it significance have faded in historical importance. At the same time, new historical significance has been attached to the most prominent event of this era: the European discovery of America. For Lord Acton, this was a major geographical revelation that eventually altered political balances in Europe and provided a virgin arena for Western economic development. Recent scholarship has emphasized the connection between European exploitation of America, the rise of Western capitalism, and the establishment of a Western world hegemony. Many contemporary scholars consider capitalism the very essence of modernity. Equally important is the work of Alfred Crosby, who has disclosed the startling inter-hemispheric transfers of flora, fauna, and disease that transformed life on this planet in the wake of the Columbian voyages.[35]

Whether circa 1500 can hold up as a pivotal watershed era or whether it should give way to some other divide is an issue that concerns us in this book. If circa 1500 holds up, its success will not hinge upon historical accident, the result of some untoward event or events that befell Western people, broke essential continuities, and altered their orientations. The Europeans' discovery of America may have been accidental to the extent that in 1492 Columbus initiated a wholly different venture—a westward crossing to Asia. Nevertheless, his participation in overseas exploration was part of a long process that involved politics, economics, technology, and a host of other elements in a broad historical context. The same might be said for the eighteenth century. The simultaneous occurrence of the industrial, demographic, and democratic revolutions was not accidental or mere coincidence. These revolutions were integrated aspects of a complex historical process.

For historians, the overriding issue is fathoming the nature of that process: determining how change occurred, what the chief engines of change were, and how various engines of change, primary and secondary, were interwoven to generate significant events. When this is achieved, it will be possible to identify with greater confidence those protracted "moments" in history when old continuities dissolved and new continuities were formed.

NOTES

1. George Duby, "L'Histoire des systèmes de valuers," *History and Theory* 11 (1972): 15–25.

2. The internal structure of Roman history has been periodized in response to political phenomena, but one distinguished ancient historian contends that emphasis upon other aspects of Roman life would have occasioned a different order of periodization. M. I. Finley, "Generalizations in Ancient History," in Louis Gottschalk, ed., *Generalization in the Writing of History* (Chicago and London, 1963), p. 24.

3. Emmanuel Le Roy Ladurie, "Motionless History," *Social Science History* 1 (1977): 131–134.

4. One of the leading texts in modern history, now in its seventh edition, delivers the standard view: "In general, it is agreed that modern times began in Europe about the year 1500. Modern times were preceded by a period of 1000 years called the Middle Ages, which set in about A.D. 500, and which were in turn preceded by another 1000 years of classical Greco-Roman civilization." See R. R. Palmer and Joel Colton, *A History of the Modern World* (New York, 7th ed., 1992), p. 12.

5. For example, *Medieval Studies* or the *Journal of Medieval History* rarely, if ever, step beyond 1500, and the *International Medieval Bibliography* has fixed parameters (500–1500). The same concern for period frontiers applies to the modern history journals. Journals having universal scope (e.g., *American Historical Review*) commonly divide their book review sections into ancient, medieval, modern.

6. Ernst Breisach, *Historiography: Ancient, Medieval, and Modern* (Chicago, 1983), pp. 86, 89, 104, 143–144.

7. This concept was favored by St. Augustine, Venerable Bede, and numerous writers of the medieval chronicles. Denys Hay, *Annalists and Historians: Western Historiography from the VIIIth to the XVIIIth Century* (London, 1977), p. 28.

8. Donald J. Wilcox, *The Development of Florentine Humanist Historiography in the Fifteenth Century* (Cambridge, Mass., 1969), pp. 11–12.

9. For an analysis of Biondo's work, see Denys Hay, "Flavio Biondo and the Middle Ages," *Proceedings of the British Academy* 45 (1959): 97–128.

10. Wallace K. Ferguson, *The Renaissance in Historical Thought* (Boston, 1948), p. 44.

11. Quoted in Gerald Strauss, *Luther's House of Learning: Indoctrination of the Young in the German Reformation* (Baltimore, 1978), p. 82.

12. Johann Philip of Schleiden's universal history, *On the Four World Empires*, passed through sixty-five editions and provided a staple of Lutheran education for several generations. At least three other historians of note in the sixteenth century— Wimpheling, *Epitome of German History*; Nauclerus, *Memorabilia*; and Aventius, *Bavarian Chronicle*—adopted the four-monarchy plan. See Breisach, *Historiography*, p. 163. Luther himself was inconsistent in his use of periodization. See John M. Headley, *Luther's View of Church History* (New Haven, 1963). The four-monarchy plan actually persisted among many German writers until the end of the eighteenth century despite repeated and devastating assaults upon its legitimacy by both German scholars and foreign luminaries, including Voltaire.

13. Bodin's great work, published in 1566, effectively dismantled the theoretical supports of the four-monarchy scheme. Jean Bodin, *Method for the Easy Comprehension of History*, trans. Beatrice Reynolds (New York, 1945), p. 292.

14. Bodin provided a model for several French historians of the sixteenth century, including Louis Le Roy, Nicholas Vignier, and Henri Voison de La Popelinière. George Huppert contends that Vignier was probably the first author of universal history who did not view the coming of Christ as an epochal event. See Huppert, *The Idea of Perfect History: Historical Erudition and Historical Philosophy in Renaissance France* (Urbana, 1970), pp. 88ff.

15. Hubert Jedin et al., *History of the Church*: vol. 5, *Reformation and Counter Reformation* (New York, 1980), p. 644.

16. George L. Burr, "How the Middle Ages Got Their Name," *American Historical Review* 20 (1914–1915): 813–814. Also see Ferguson, *The Renaissance in Historical Thought*, pp. 73–74.

17. Cellarius's role has too often been exaggerated and his merits as a historian unnecessarily demeaned by those who object to the tripartite mode of periodization. In a widely read passage, Geoffrey Barraclough referred contemptuously to Cellarius as "a very indifferent German scholar." He attributed to this "mediocre" scholar the discovery of the idea of the Middle Ages, contending that Cellarius "fitted it, like a straight-jacket over all future historical thought." See Barraclough, *History in a Changing World* (Oxford, 1955), pp. 54–56. In reality, Cellarius neither created the Middle Ages nor coined the term. He was simply the first well-published writer to gather together in a single conceptual package the many threads of a tripartite division that had been accumulating since the fifteenth century.

18. Herbert Butterfield, *Man on His Past: The Study of the History of Historical Scholarship* (Cambridge, 1955), p. 46. Also see G. P. Gooch, "The Cambridge Chair of Modern History," in Gooch, ed., *Studies in Modern History* (Freeport, N.Y., 1968; reprint of 1931 ed.), pp. 289–325.

19. Hume (1711–1776), an economist, philosopher, and essayist, produced an eight-volume *History of England*. His comparison of Anglo-Saxon history with the battles of kites and crows resonates with Voltaire's comment that the early Middle Ages required as little attention as the ramblings of wolves and bears. Hume perceived the millennium before the Renaissance as a profoundly depressing one when humankind wallowed in barbarism and superstition. Robertson (1721–1793), the historian of Scotland, shared this negative view, though he perceived the Middle Ages—at least in their later stages—as preparation for the flowering of civilization in sixteenth-century Europe. For an analysis of the work of both authors, see J. B. Black, *The Art of History: A Study of Four Great Historians of the Eighteenth Century* (New York, 1926). J. H. Brumfitt's *Voltaire, Historian* (London, 1958) remains a valuable and comprehensive analysis of Voltaire's purposes and method.

20. Edward Gibbon, *The Decline and Fall of the Roman Empire*, vol. 7 (London, 1909), p. 308; David P. Jordan, *Gibbon and His Roman Empire* (Urbana, 1971), pp. 70–122, 183–190, 213–230.

21. Charles E. McClelland, *State, Society, and University in Germany 1700–1914* (Cambridge, 1980), pp. 3, 39–42.

22. Peter Hanns Reill, "History and Hermeneutics in the *Aufklärung*: The Thought of Johann Christof Gatterer," *Journal of Modern History* 45 (1973): 27–28.

23. For a detailed exposition of Gatterer's periodization, see Peter Hanns Reill, *The German Enlightenment and the Rise of Historicism* (Berkeley and Los Angeles, 1975), pp. 77–80.

24. Jacob Burckhardt, *The Civilization of the Renaissance in Italy*, trans. S. G. C. Middlemore (London, 1944), p. 107.

25. The Burckhardt thesis had few foreshadowings. Art historians had long used the term "Renaissance" to denote a style of art, but historians of society at large ignored the wider implications of the word. Five years before the appearance of Burckhardt's study, Jules Michelet (1798–1874) completed the seventh volume of his monumental *Histoire de France*, which, with some originality, he chose to title *Renaissance*. But the Renaissance of Michelet was essentially a French phenomenon. He took a very negative view of Italian society in the fourteenth and fifteenth centuries.

26. In the English-speaking world, Burckhardt's vision was effectively confirmed and elaborated by John Addington Symonds, who produced a seven-volume, highly readable masterwork, *Renaissance in Italy* (1875–1886), filling in the roughly sketched terrain of the Burckhardt treatise.

27. Efforts by later scholars to denominate the Renaissance as a separate transitional period between the medieval and modern times have failed to gain acceptance. The most notable attempt was made by Wallace Ferguson, who strongly advocated the concept of the Renaissance as a period of transition. His article, "The Interpretation of the Renaissance: Suggestions for a Synthesis," *Journal of the History of Ideas* 12 (1951): 483–495, preceded a full treatment of this view in Ferguson, *Europe in Transition, 1300–1520* (Boston, 1962).

28. G. Kitson Clark, "A Hundred Years of the Teaching of History at Cambridge, 1873–1973," *Historical Journal* 16 (1973): 541.

29. Arthur S. Link, "The American Historical Association, 1884–1984: Retrospect and Prospect," *American Historical Review* 90 (1985): 2.

30. *Revue Historique* in 1876, *English Historical Review* in 1886, and *American Historical Review* in 1895. Germans were well ahead of the pack. *Historishe Zeitschrift,* the model professional journal, had been established in 1859. For development of the French historical profession, see William R. Keylor, *Academy and Community: The Foundation of the French Historical Profession* (Cambridge, Mass., 1973), pp. 60, 219. Doris Goldstein, "The Organizational Development of the British Historical Profession, 1884–1921," *Bulletin of Historical Research* 55 (1982): 180–193.

31. Lord Acton, *Essays in the Liberal Interpretation of History,* ed. William H. McNeill (Chicago and London, 1967), p. 304. Acton died shortly before the first volume appeared, but he firmly affixed his stamp to the project. Contributors to the *Cambridge Modern History* echoed Acton's aggregate and impressionistic vision. Introducing the series, Mandell Creighton, Anglican bishop, a professor of ecclesiastical history at Cambridge and the first editor of *English Historical Review,* referred to the "extraordinary change of mental attitude" that distinguished the sixteenth from the fifteenth century. For commentary on Creighton and his reliance upon Acton, see Doris Goldstein, "The Origins and Early Years of *The English Historical Review,*" *English Historical Review* 101 (1986): 3–11. Repeatedly, contributors to the first volume of the *Cambridge History* identified the advent of modernity with the growth of nation-states, of individualism, of capitalism, and of secular attitudes.

32. The distinguished historian and historiographer, G. P. Gooch, summed up early twentieth-century opinion of the *Cambridge Modern History*: it was, he wrote, "beyond comparison the best survey of the modern world in any language." Gooch, *History and Historians in the Nineteenth Century* (London, 1913), p. 390.

33. Paul Bairoch, "Europe's Gross National Product: 1800–1975," *Journal of European Economic History* 5 (1976): 276–279.

34. Barraclough, *History in a Changing World,* pp. 54–63; Dietrich Gerhard, "Periodization in European History," *American Historical Review* 61 (1956): 903; Gerhard, *Old Europe: A Study of Continuity, 1000–1800* (New York, 1981), p. 139; William A. Green, "Periodization in European and World History," *Journal of World History* 3 (1992): 13–53.

35. Alfred W. Crosby, Jr., *The Columbian Exchange: Biological and Cultural Consequences of 1492* (Westport, Conn., 1972).

Part II

The Dynamics of Historical Change: Europe

Introduction:
Search for a Governing Dynamic

This section of the book will examine four engines of change employed by historians in our time. In keeping with the priorities of the twentieth century, three of them—the commercial, demographic, and Marxian explanations—are materialist. The fourth, which advocates the religious roots of change, was conceived in response to materialist models, particularly the Marxist one.

The most influential historians and social scientists of this century have identified modernity with the rise of capitalism. Fashioned to create wealth, capitalism transformed the physical structure of Europe, its social psychology, institutional patterns, and outreach to the wider world. All explanatory models in this section of the book concentrate on the advent of capitalism. They are exclusively concerned with Europe and chiefly focused on historical developments during the late Middle Ages and early modern period.

Historians may agree that capitalism is virtually synonymous with modernity, but they do not agree in detail on how capitalism, as a historical abstraction, should be defined. Some are content to define it as the use of mobile property for the purpose of achieving profits. Yet, under so limited a definition, almost all forms of market activity qualify as capitalist. Marxists deny that merchants and markets necessarily indicate the presence of capitalism; for them, capitalism is a mode of production, not a process of exchange. Some insist that capitalism involves high adventure and speculation. Dismissing this, Max Weber contends that reckless speculation is an impediment to capitalism, and that capitalism involves the application of reason, discipline, and sober calculation in business enterprise.

Many scholars hold the opinion that numerous preconditions had to exist before capitalism could be consolidated in European society. First, there had to be an accumulation of capital available for investment by private individuals; second, there had to be a class of propertyless wage workers available for hire. Other preconditions include the need for security in commercial transactions, both physical security for traders and legal security for their property. Some would insist that capitalism could not emerge until business techniques and banking facilities had matured or until there was substantial demand for moveable goods in the marketplace. At some point, it becomes difficult to discern between the preconditions for capitalism and capitalism itself.

How a scholar defines capitalism dictates when he or she thinks it took hold in Europe. Henri Pirenne, a leading figure of the commercial school, identified the presence of capitalism in the merchant community of the twelfth century. Max Weber thought it emerged in the sixteenth century, and the Marxists advocate a seventeenth- and eighteenth-century transition.

Perhaps the term "capitalism," being so diversely employed, has ceased to have value. Fernand Braudel, a leading expert on the rise of capitalism, confronted that possibility, then drew back. If you throw the term out the door, it comes in the window, he argued. It is ambiguous. It is used indiscriminately. It is laden with controversies, past and present. Any use of it for the pre-industrial world may be anachronistic. But we are stuck with it.[1]

Each of the explanations offered in this section is introduced by its theoretical founding father: for the commercial school, Adam Smith; for the demographic school, Thomas Malthus; for the Marxian school, Karl Marx. It can hardly be said that either Sombart or Weber founded schools of history, but their influence was widespread, and they will speak for themselves on the religious origins of capitalism. Smith, Marx, Weber, and Sombart reacted strongly to political and economic stimuli in their own lives. Smith advocated laissez-faire economics in reaction against eighteenth-century mercantilism. In the political struggles of the twentieth century, his approach has been judged highly complimentary to capitalism. Marx reacted against the harsh and exploitative character of mid-nineteenth century capitalism, and of course his work provided the intellectual foundations for modern communism. Responding to the particular needs of Germany at the end of the nineteenth century, Sombart and Weber expressed opposition to laissez-faire capitalism and vehement hostility to the materialist determinism of Karl Marx.

Part II commences with an examination of the commercial dynamic. This mode of explanation is presented as persuasively as possible. Unlike the other chapters, Chapter 3 contains no criticism of the explanatory formula under discussion. The reason is not that I am partial to the commercial explanation. Rather, all other schools of thought—demographic, Marxian, and Weberian—take many of their cues from the commercial dynamic. In developing their own lines of argument, they provide appropriate criticism of it. Apart from affording a clear assessment of the commercial interpretation, Chapter 3 attempts to introduce the salient historical issues that provide the nucleus for debate in succeeding chapters.

Readers will discover that every mode of interpretation identifies particular centuries or parts of centuries as being significant watersheds in the history of Europe. The period around A.D. 1000 is especially significant for both the commercial and demographic schools because it is possible to date aggregate economic growth and secular population growth from that time. The fourteenth century is a critical time for historians of the Marxian and demographic schools. Both argue that Europe confronted a grievous crisis in that century. The sixteenth century is critical for Weber. It is also significant for both the demographic and commercial schools because economic and population growth was renewed after the long hiatus associated with the plague.

The Black Death is an event of major importance in these chapters. Some proponents of the demographic explanation have been tempted to integrate it into the rhythm of their model. Others have considered it an exogenous force. It cannot be ignored, and the reader of these chapters may conclude that none of the explanations offered in Part II accommodate it effectively.

Three modes of explanation identify the specific trajectory of history through time. The commercial mode is linear and progressive. Human affairs evolve continually from the less complex to the more complex. The demographic mode posits a homeostatic equilibrium in which every flow is followed by an ebb, every growth by a subsidence. Marxian analysis is progressive and millennial. Progress is achieved by stages, and the nature of each stage is determined by the inexorable operation of the dialectic.

Some things are noticeably absent in these chapters. No one introduces God as an active force in history. Sombart and Weber argue that religious impulses drive human affairs, but both of them distinguish between God and religious belief. Race and heredity form a part of Sombart's explanation, but his only. Geography as a factor in history is manifestly important only to the commercial school.

I conclude this introduction with a word about language. Among the many abstract terms that suffer from ambiguity of meaning, the word "feudal" is one of the most problematic. For many professional medievalists, the word connotes a relationship between a lord and his vassal by which each party pledges to exercise responsibility to the other in a particular way. Marxist historians use the term to define a mode of production that existed in medieval Europe. In either case, the word is an abstraction intended to facilitate communication between historians concerning a body of similar, though not identical, practices. Marxists take no offense when non-Marxists use the term "feudal" to identify vassalage relationships. Non-Marxists have been very prickly on the matter. Like "capitalism," the word "feudal" has its ambiguities. We shall simply have to live with them.

NOTE

1. Fernand Braudel, *Civilization and Capitalism, 15th–18th Century*: vol. 2, *The Wheels of Commerce* (New York, 1982), p. 231.

3

The Commercial Model

Capital was the solvent of the Middle Ages and the engine of modern progress. So declared the first edition of the *Cambridge Modern History*.[1] This pillar of scholarship embodied the commercial view of historical change in classical form. It determined that early medieval Europe was a "natural economy" comprised of self-sustaining, rural communities that, with few exceptions, produced a narrow range of coarse goods for local consumption. Beginning in the eleventh century, this economy was transformed, expanded, and refined by the unrelenting pressure of commercial forces. Long-distance trade emanating from the Mediterranean altered social habits, cultivated new tastes, and laid the institutional foundations for modern capitalism. From the Dark Ages to the Industrial Revolution, commerce was the primary engine of change in European life.

The commercial explanation for the rise of the modern world is the oldest and most firmly rooted body of concepts employed by scholars. It embodies a linear, progressivist concept of human development and provides economic girding for what Herbert Butterfield called the Whig interpretation of history, the notion that history is the record of man's relentless progress toward liberty.[2] Its main theoretical foundations were elegantly and abundantly set forth in Adam Smith's *Wealth of Nations*, first published in 1776. Professional historians have painstakingly assembled documentary and other evidence to flesh out Smith's theory. In recent years, the theoretical structure has been reworked and revised by the British economist Sir John Hicks.

Writers of the commercial school share several assumptions about human nature and human history. Human beings have always been motivated primarily by self-interest. They are naturally acquisitive. They prefer more goods to fewer, and wherever incentives exist, they will strive to improve their material well-being. Economic forces are the primary, though not the only, factors governing the direction of history. Significant changes in the material circumstances of life trigger changes elsewhere. It is assumed, for example, that human refinement, manners, and good taste are directly linked to the accumulation of property. Abbé Raynal made the point two centuries ago when he argued that "commercial states have civilized all others."[3] Propelled by an innate "propensity to truck, barter, and exchange one thing for another,"[4] men and women have achieved a steadily expanding division of labor. Progressive division of labor both elevates and renders more complex all aspects of human endeavor.

Adam Smith believed that the mode by which people achieve subsistence determines the character of their social order. Humankind, he declared, had passed (or was passing) through a hierarchy of four distinct historical stages differentiated by their relative social complexity. The most primitive, the hunting stage, was characteristic of early man and of some contemporary Indian tribes of North America. The second, a herding stage, was historically evident among Arab tribesmen, Mongols, and the Germans who invaded and undermined the Roman Empire. The third, an agricultural stage, involved the establishment of settled societies like those of Europe in the central Middle Ages. The fourth and highest level was the commercial stage to which Western Europe had ascended in recent centuries.

Germanic invaders of the Roman Empire introduced massive disorder, Smith wrote. Communications broke down; cities shrivelled; buildings, monuments, river ports, and roadways fell into disrepair. Even Rome, its aqueducts cut, saw its population shrink from a half million to 50,000 in the mid-sixth century. By the time St. Benedict withdrew to Monte Casino to establish a rigorous monastic order, circa 529, barbarian darkness had settled across the western continent. All lands were divided among a few great proprietors who, by recourse to laws of primogeniture[5] and entail,[6] deliberately prevented the subdivision of their estates.

> Every great landlord was a sort of petty prince. His tenants were his subjects. He was their judge, and in some respects their legislator in peace, and their leader in war. He made war according to his own discretion, frequently against his neighbours, and sometimes against his sovereign. The security of a landed estate, therefore, the protection which its owner could afford to those who dwelt on it, depended upon its greatness. To divide it was to ruin it, and to expose every part of it to be oppressed and swallowed up by the incursions of its neighbours.[7]

Preoccupied with the defense or extension of their territories, great landlords were not great improvers. Neither were the servile occupiers of the land who lacked both leadership and incentive. In the absence of towns or foreign commerce, whatever surpluses landlords extracted from their tenants had to be consumed "in rustick hospitality at home." If the lord's agricultural surplus enabled him to maintain a thousand men, he had no means of exploiting that surplus other than by maintaining a thousand men, all of whom being supported by his largesse were compelled to obey his commands.

Security was the critical need of all persons in this state of life. The desire for security eventually encouraged lesser landlords to enter feudal contracts with greater lords as, indeed, the greater lords established similar arrangements with the king. Occurring between the ninth and eleventh centuries, these developments provided greater security and tranquility to Western Europe, but lingering violence between lords and the prevailing absence of economic incentives rendered the early medieval economy incapable of growth.

Growth waited upon commercial towns. If economic growth depended upon an expanding division of labor, as writers of the commercial school contend, significant division of labor could not occur in the absence of active and reliable markets. The few concentrations of population that existed in early medieval Europe did not have a commercial character. Lacking merchants and artisans, they were little more than places of residence for bishops, great lords, and their numerous retainers.

The most influential medievalist of the twentieth century, Henri Pirenne, adopted Adam Smith's views on the central importance of towns, trade, and the division of labor. Pirenne's explicit commercial ori-

entation so profoundly shaped the views of two generations of medievalists that most textbooks used in English and American universities from
the 1930s through the 1960s boldly embraced his market-driven division-
of-labor model, even to the point of borrowing his anecdotes.[8] Pirenne
rejected Smith's baleful characterization of the Germanic invasions, but he
adopted Smith's argument on towns. Prior to the appearance of Pirenne's
celebrated *Mahomet et Charlemagne* (1937), only a few scholars had
challenged the conventional cataclysmic explanation for the end of the
ancient world. One of them was Fustel de Coulanges, a nineteenth-
century historian who provided evidence that German invaders had not
undertaken wholesale dismantling of Roman institutions.[9] After World
War I, sensitivity was running high in Germany concerning assertions of
barbarism, both past and present; in 1924 a German scholar, Alfons
Dopsch, produced an influential, though exaggerated, work emphasizing
the continuity between Roman and German Europe.[10] Dopsch argued that
Germans who invaded the Roman Empire were vastly more civilized than
conventional wisdom allowed, that they attempted to preserve, not to destroy, the structure of imperial government and trade, and that significant
institutional continuity was preserved through the early Middle Ages,
providing a basis for cultural and economic revival in the eleventh century.

Pirenne concurred with Dopsch. Germans, he argued, had attempted to
perpetuate Roman civil institutions, trade relations with the East, and
classical culture. Despite disorders associated with the German migra-
tions, the unity of the Mediterranean had been preserved well beyond the
fifth century. It was the Arab expansion of the seventh century, Pirenne
believed, that divided the Mediterranean by planting hostile Moslem forces
in the Levant, across North Africa, in Sicily, and throughout Iberia to the
summits of the Pyrenees. Apart from a thin thread of exchange between a
few Italo-Byzantine towns and the Orthodox East, Christian communication via the inland sea was destroyed. The Western Mediterranean became
a Moslem lake, and Christian settlements along its northern shore were
perpetually harassed and pillaged. Overwhelmed by successive disasters,
West Europeans turned inward, away from the sea, to the cold and
forested North. Trade, towns, and the merchant class disappeared;
seignorialism became entrenched; and cultural refinement all but vanished.
The Middle Ages did not commence with barbarian invasions, Pirenne
concluded. They began with Charlemagne. His coronation in 800 represented a symbolic break with the past. The essential quality of ancient
civilization—its Mediterranean character—had been rejected. All that remained of the Roman Empire was the Byzantine state at Constantinople.

The Carolingian West, isolated and impoverished, had begun its inexorable slide toward Europe's cultural nadir.

For writers of the commercial school, the existence of a primitive "natural economy" in a rich, temperate region of the earth was a negation of man's natural acquisitive instincts. It could be explained only by great social catastrophe like the barbarian invasions, or as Pirenne would have it, by the Moslem conquests. To discover how and why Europe recovered from the Dark Ages, it would be necessary to determine why the barbarian invasions or the Moslem conquests of the seventh century had plunged Western Christendom into such profound economic and cultural stagnation. For Pirenne, the answer was clear. The negation of Mediterranean influences and the collapse of long-distance trade were responsible. Revival could only occur through the renewal of commerce from Mediterranean sources.

This revival was achieved at the expense of powerful vested interests. The Christian Church sanctioned prevailing economic structures. Its vast estates dwarfed those of individual noblemen; its members constituted a tiny literate elite; and its ascetic ideals were precisely suited to an agrarian culture. God, the Church taught, had planted man on earth to work out his salvation. To seek profits or to devote energy to the accumulation of worldly goods was deplored as the sin of avarice. Those who inherited wealth were expected to make generous distributions of their riches, preferably through Christian charity. Usury[11] was forbidden; the concept of a "just price"[12] was supported. European culture had become so intensely anticommercial, Pirenne argued, that it could be jolted from its introverted stupor only by the action of some strong external force. Long-distance trade provided that force.

Proponents of the commercial argument for change have consistently recognized the importance of navigable water. No waters have better served the interest of traders than those of the Mediterranean. Sir John Hicks determined that the best explanation for the divergence between European and Asian history is "the fact that European civilization has passed through a city-state phase." The reason is geographical: "The city-state of Europe is a gift of the Mediterranean." Rich in "crannies, islands, promontories, and valleys . . . which have been readily defensible, the Mediterranean," Hicks declares, "is incomparable."[13]

Hicks sketched out a theoretical model of the city-state. That model is too elaborate to reproduce here, but a few fragments may help clarify some of the theoretical underpinnings of the commercial explanation.

When two communities having different resource endowments produce surpluses of different kinds, mutual advantage is gained by both communities if each of them exchanges its form of surplus for that of the other. At the outset of such exchanges, merchants may enjoy high profits, but as the volume of trade grows, the rate of profit diminishes. The reason is twofold. Merchants have to offer higher prices to stimulate a larger output of surplus from producers. Second, by the natural order of supply and demand, a steady increase in the supply of a commodity tends to depress its market price. Facing diminishing returns, merchants will attempt to expand their range of trade, opening new markets or encouraging the development of new commodities in the older market. They will also attempt to reduce *transaction costs,* the costs of conducting business, so that despite falling margins between buying and selling prices, the profitability of trade will remain the same or nearly the same.

Among other things, reducing transaction costs involves creating legal and quasi-legal institutions to protect the property of traders, to guarantee contracts, to facilitate the settling of disputes, and to provide for special arrangements such as the insuring of trade goods. Legal structures appropriate to an agrarian economy are not suited to a commercial one. The rulers of large regional states comprised of great landed estates are unlikely, at first, to appreciate the needs of merchants or to adopt readily the legal institutions needed to protect trade.

It is here that the city-state structure is superior. The European city-state was by its nature a trading community. Its political leadership was involved in trade, and traders enjoyed social prominence. In contrast to large regional states, independent city-states could shape their legal and institutional structures to provide security for the private property of traders. The legal institutions of different city-states may not have been identical, but they were sufficiently similar that security and commercial facilities were provided to merchants operating between city-states. Hicks concluded that the city-state structure, having the ability to facilitate a diversity of trade and to provide institutional securities to such trade, offered an exceptional means of extending trade into backward regions of the continent.

COMMERCIAL REVOLUTION OF THE TOWNS

Among the Italian city-states, Venice led the way. Situated on sandy islands at the head of the Adriatic, the town was protected by water from mainland powers, far removed from Moslem predators, and politically linked with the Byzantine Empire.[14] At first the community merely exchanged fish and salt for landside agricultural provisions. But townsmen quickly diversified their commodity base and cultivated new markets, extending their mercantile interests up the Po Valley and over the Alps. By the eleventh century, Venice had become the principal maritime supplier of Constantinople. Genoa and Pisa followed its example. Having been periodically sacked by Moslem corsairs, they counter-attacked during the early eleventh century, seized Saracen ports in Sicily and Sardinia, then carried their battle to the coast of North Africa. This Christian resurgence anticipated the Crusades, a movement that would monumentally advance the commercial interests of Italian cities during the next two centuries. Italian merchants conveyed waves of troops as well as pilgrims to the Holy Land, supplied them, and secured weighty economic concessions in the bargain. Eastern trade to Europe flourished, and other Mediterranean communities, like Marseilles and Barcelona, hastened to join it. By the thirteenth century, the inland sea from Gibraltar to the Levant was dominated by Christian fleets.

Both Genoa and Venice established maritime empires in Eastern waters. Colonies were planted in the Black Sea, and Genoese ships sailed on the Caspian. Italian overlords developed large plantations on Crete, Cyprus, and other Eastern islands, producing sugar with slaves imported from the Crimea and Africa.[15] In order to pay for Eastern luxuries, the West developed export industries. The Lombard Plain produced grain and wine for overseas sale, and cities throughout northern Italy initiated the manufacture of linens, woolens, and silks. In time, the commercial vitality of the Mediterranean spread over the alpine passes into Germany and up the Rhone Valley to France.

In transalpine Europe, concentrations of population were gradually transformed into commercial towns by the catalytic action of long-distance traders. So argued Pirenne. Hardy adventurers, bearing a limited assortment of goods, appeared in the environs of castles (bourgs) or other formidable structures located at critical intersections of communication, particularly river crossings. Their activities drew the attention of rural artisans, and in time, growing commercial communities established their own suburbs (faubourgs, or outside bourgs) with the blessing of local lords. As towns grew, walls were extended to secure each additional suburb.

The Flemish lowlands, cut by great rivers and adjacent to the sea, enjoyed an industrial renaissance in the tenth century. An ancient woolens industry predating the Roman conquest existed in the valley of the Scheldt, where lush meadows sustained great numbers of sheep. Although Viking raiders of the ninth century destroyed the few important settlements specializing in the sale of woolens, the Flemish industry swiftly recovered, supplementing its own wool supplies with a superior product imported from England. Originally a rural enterprise, clothmaking was gradually concentrated in a growing number of industrial towns. By the twelfth century, Flemish woolens, distinguished above all others by their soft texture and brilliant colors, were being sold in the Baltic by German traders and throughout the Mediterranean by Italians.[16]

Towns grew in Europe because they conferred some benefit on everyone. Commercial towns expanded the division of labor and revolutionized the operation of agricultural estates. New business techniques evolved in the towns, laying the foundations for modern commercial capitalism. Towns provided a haven for serfs fleeing from rural estates.[17] Some serfs became artisans, more of them proletarians. By the fourteenth century, intense class battles were occurring in major industrial towns between impoverished proletarians and the manufacturing elite. Substantial towns introduced a new and complicating element in the long-standing power struggle between kings and nobles. In the main, kings and urban elites consummated alliances of convenience at the long-term expense of the nobility. Trade promoted the restoration of Roman Law and satisfied the material demands of the great courts for unprecedented indulgence in luxury expenditures.

COMMERCE AND THE DECLINE OF FEUDALISM

The revival of long-distance trade and the introduction of a money economy freed Europe's great landlords from the necessity of expending their agricultural surpluses on retainers. Adam Smith made the point emphatically:

> what all the violence of the feudal institutions could never have effected, the silent and insensible operation of foreign commerce and manufactures gradually brought about. These gradually furnished the great proprietors with something for which they could exchange the whole surplus produce of their lands, and which they could consume themselves without sharing it either with tenants or retainers. All for ourselves, and nothing for other people, seems, in every age of the world, to have been the vile maxim of the masters of mankind. As soon, therefore, as they could find a method of consuming the whole value of their rents themselves, they had no disposition to share them with any other persons. For a pair of diamond buckles perhaps, or for something as frivolous and useless, they exchanged the maintenance . . . of a thousand men for a

year, and with it the whole weight and authority which it could give them. . . . Thus, for the gratification of the most childish, the meanest and the most sordid of all vanities, they gradually bartered their whole power and authority.[18]

Whether the landlords truly bartered their whole power and authority is an issue to which we will return in subsequent chapters. Suffice it to say, life on the estates changed for tenants as well as lords. Towns created new markets for agricultural products, offering rural serfs the incentive to exchange their meager surpluses for money. By earning money in the marketplace, serfs were able to meet obligations to their lords through money payments rather than payments in kind. In time, many lords commuted the labor services of their serfs in favor of rents. Serfs had long been obliged to perform coerced labor at critical seasons on their lord's demesne.[19] With the rise of towns and a money economy, the lords could release serfs from labor obligations in exchange for money payments, shifting the full burden of marketing manorial surpluses onto the peasants. By the end of the thirteenth century, relatively few large landlords in northwestern Europe were directly engaged in agriculture. Instead, they farmed out their demesnes to third parties or rented demesne lands in small parcels to their own serfs. They had become landowners living on rents. In different ways, the rise of towns, commerce, and a money economy had increased the freedom of both lords and peasants.

THE EVOLUTION OF BUSINESS TECHNIQUES

The growing business acumen of Europeans receives admiring attention from economic historians of the commercial school. Beginning with the tenth century, they argue, the improvement of business methods systematically absorbed Western Europe into the money economy. Innovations in the instruments of credit most dramatically fostered the extension of trade. If capital was to be employed to generate greater wealth, it had to be transferred from those who hoarded it or expended it thriftlessly to those who wished to employ it to make money. In the tenth century, Italians developed *commenda,* a plan whereby a party not directly engaged in trade could advance money to a person conducting trade—generally foreign trade—in return for a portion of the profits of that commerce. An Italian merchant might engage any number of people in contracts of *commenda,* large and small, to expand his cargo and increase his potential for profit. Apart from facilitating trade, *commenda* enabled rich men, craftsmen, even widows with a small savings to invest their money in the activities of traders with a clear expectation of gain.[20]

The most pervasive problem for long-distance merchants was physical insecurity. It was risky to carry large sums of metallic coin. Individual lords, motivated by short-term advantage, often pillaged the property of traders or charged ruinous tolls for rights of passage. Moreover, the perpetual shortage of gold and silver depressed commercial activity. The bill of exchange, developed either at Genoa or Florence, was created to relieve both of these difficulties. One of the most important instruments in business history, the bill of exchange enabled a buyer of goods in one country to pay for his purchases through a promissory note, which the seller could redeem in his own city.[21] Non-negotiable bills of exchange were widely employed by the fourteenth century, and at the end of the Middle Ages they were discounted and circulated as negotiable instruments among parties altogether unassociated with the original transaction. In this sense, they became a substitute for cash, expanding the money supply as well as the volume of trade.

COMMERCE AND THE TRANSFORMATION OF POLITICAL STRUCTURES

The rise of commercial towns produced major adjustments in the political structure of Europe. It enhanced the power of great princes while reducing the relative strength of the Church and nobility. There was a natural alliance between secular princes and the urban bourgeoisie. The growth of a money economy liberated monarchs from restraints associated with traditional forms of feudal tenure. It accelerated changes in military organization, and it altered relationships between kings and nobles, empowering the former at the expense of the latter. The grant of fiefs in return for service became obsolete by the fourteenth century. Instead, princes granted incomes—money fiefs—to vassals who pledged their homage and performed essential public services. By the fifteenth century, retainers were offering their loyalty to princes under contracts of indenture whereby they served a lord for a specific period in return for an agreed sum. Armies that fought the Hundred Years War were raised in large measure through indenture. As the institutions of chivalry disappeared, the growing cash nexus permitted kings to hire mercenary armies and keep them in the field for longer periods. The pervasive use of metallic money facilitated tax collection; larger, more reliable revenue enabled powerful rulers to exploit fourteenth-century innovations in weaponry, particularly gunpowder and cannons.[22] The medieval warrior had brought his own weapons and armor into battle. By the fifteenth century royal arsenals had begun to appear, and in the sixteenth century the Spanish government began furnishing uniform weapons. The growing size of royal armies and fleets made it increasingly difficult for feudal lords to defy their kings. At the same time, large royal armies increased the problems of supply. Only the great merchants could organize provisioning on a scale required by ambitious monarchs.

The alliance between royalty and the urban bourgeoisie is evident in the revival of Roman Law. Customary law with its insistence on the principles of conditional property had satisfied the needs of a feudal agrarian society. It did not accommodate the political ambitions of kings, nor did it satisfy townsmen and traders who required firm assurances for the rights of private property. Roman civil law admitted the concept of absolute private property. Roman public law justified the absolute authority of the sovereign. The diffusion of Roman civic and public law across Europe in the final centuries of the Middle Ages betokened the converging interests of rising monarchs and the merchant class. The relative position of the nobility declined.[23]

COMMERCE AND CULTURAL SOPHISTICATION

The growth of trade, towns, and urban manufactures went hand in hand with the development of manners and high society. The rich were the best customers of the merchant class; indeed, the consumer demands of the wealthy elite, particularly royalty, substantially enhanced the growth of commerce and the prosperity of traders. Werner Sombart, a renowned German sociologist-historian, argued that the luxury spending of the great courts constituted a fundamental impetus to the growth of modern capitalism. The first extravagant court, he observed, was established under papal rule at Avignon in the fourteenth century. Ecclesiastical princes and noblemen with "no vocation other than that of serving the court's interest" kept the company of clever, witty, and beautiful women who gave court life its distinguishing sensuous and erotic quality.[24] In the age of the Renaissance this papal extravaganza moved to Rome, where the court of Paul II (1464–1471) exceeded all others in magnificence. Secular courts sprang up in Milan, Ferrara, Naples, and elsewhere. Across the Alps, Francis I (1515–1547) inaugurated the first elaborate French court, gathering around him "ladies of noble birth who before then had pined away behind the gray walls of their ancient castles."[25] Other European courts became slavish examples of the French. Castiglione's *Book of the Courtier* instructed contemporaries in the style, etiquette, dress, and other requirements of princely life. This book passed through a hundred editions by 1600. The demand for luxuries was immense, and whole cities rose up in service to princely courts—Naples, Sombart noted, "was never anything but the residence of a prince," and Paris and London owed much of their populations to people engaged directly or indirectly in service to the royal courts.[26] Under Louis XIV, Versailles provided the ultimate example of a social system that exalted monarchy and employed the nobility as expensive ornamentation. Courtly life may have indulged the aristocratic elite, but it transferred wealth to the bourgeoisie, partly in return for the supply of luxuries and partly through the indebtedness that kings and noblemen incurred to merchants in order to pay for their luxuries.

OLD WORLD EXPANSION

Expansion was the watchword of commercial society. In no sphere is the impact of commerce more evident than in the world-wide extension of European power and influence. As commercial firms grew in size they extended their interests into new, more profitable forms of business. Trade and investment required geographical outreach: old territories were exploited more thoroughly; new lands were opened to trade; and the tentacles of European commercial society began to wrap around a shrinking planet. As a matter of course, successful trading houses engaged in banking, securing the deposits of creditors and lending money under concealed interest arrangements. Italian firms dominated medieval banking, dispersing their agents throughout Europe and the Mediterranean. In the fourteenth century, the Peruzzi house of Florence had branches in other Italian cities, Sardinia, Sicily, Cyprus, the Balearics, Tunis, Bruges, Paris, and London.[27] Bankers became tax collectors for the Church as well as for European princes. Successful firms sold maritime insurance and organized manufacture in various industries. When trade floundered in one area, they transferred investments elsewhere. The Genoese lost most of their Eastern colonies to the Turks in the middle years of the fifteenth century, but by that time they had already cultivated new fields for investment in the Western Mediterranean.[28] After 1462 they gained the right to farm the great alum mines discovered at Tolfa, near Rome.[29] Having lost access to the slave trade of the East, they tried to acquire black slaves from North Africa; they sought Malagueta pepper from the west coast of Africa; and they cultivated a silk trade in Grenada before and after its reconquest by Spanish Christians. They financed fruit growing in Andalusia, mercury production in Castile, and iron mining in Biscay. With Genoese financing, the Portuguese colonized Madeira and the Azores, introducing sugar culture from the Mediterranean.[30] This spirit of enterprise, as well as the new focus on Atlantic opportunities, was evident in the young Genoese mariner, Christopher Columbus, who left the Aegean in 1451, ventured to Madeira, then shipped from West Africa to Iceland before launching his great trans-oceanic voyages of discovery.

The energy of Italians in the trans-Mediterranean and north-south trades was matched in the North Sea and Baltic by a remarkable expansion of German commercial power. By the twelfth century, Cologne led a field of developing cities in the Rhine Valley—the main axis of the north-south trade. These Rhenish and Westphalian towns served as nuclei from which German burghers launched an unprecedented eastward urban migration, planting towns beyond the Elbe and along the Baltic coast in lands devoid of urban life. Lubeck, Danzig, Riga, and Reval are only the most noted eastern cities established in the late twelfth or thirteenth centuries by parties of German merchants with the approval of great Slavonic princes.

This eastward migration, coinciding with a similar movement of German agriculturists into the lightly populated East Elbian plain, consolidated German control of the sea approaches to Novgorod, the principal Russian emporium for the fur trade. Unlike West German cities from which they sprang, these eastern towns had no Church heritage. They were, from their founding, organized and dominated by burghers engaged in long-distance trade. A century before the Hanseatic League was formed, the towns that would ultimately constitute it were informally united through interlocking family connections and mutual self-interest.

THE ESTABLISHMENT OF CAPITALISM

Had Western Europe become capitalist? Pirenne, for one, had no doubt of it. Only those completely blinded by preconceived ideas, he thought, could deny the importance and influence of commercial capitalism in Europe by as early as the twelfth century.[31] In the late Middle Ages, Europe was knitted together by a hierarchy of increasingly efficient markets. Village folk sold their small surpluses at local market towns; townsmen traded those goods at regional markets; and large-scale traders accumulated surpluses from regional markets to exchange for scarce or exotic goods at the great fairs. International fairs, originating in the eleventh century, were an enormous asset to long-distance traders. The celebrated Champagne fairs, held four times a year for nearly three centuries, provided a convenient meeting point for the exchange of Mediterranean and Flemish goods. The great fairs became financial markets. Debts incurred in trades not related to the exchange of goods at a particular fair could, nevertheless, be settled there. All obstacles to trade were met and surmounted. By the thirteenth century, Italian business practices were more sophisticated than those of Byzantium, and moral anxiety over such concerns as avarice and usury was fading fast. In the sixteenth century, traders in the Eastern Mediterranean generally accepted the superiority of Italian mechanics, metallurgy, and weaponry.[32] Lynn White, a historian of technology, declares that by 1500 Europe's industrial skill as well as its industrial capacity exceeded that of any world culture.[33] In the language of the *Cambridge Modern History,* capitalism "swept away local exclusiveness." It broke down ancient restrictions, overtook industry, and gave powerful impetus to the formation of national monarchies.[34]

Even the most ardent advocate of the commercial model acknowledges that the expansion of trade and the progressive evolution of inter-regional division of labor did not continue unabated throughout European history. In the fourteenth century, economic growth subsided. The Flemish cloth industry, ravaged by labor strife, suffered decline, and an alarming number of Italian banking firms collapsed. German traders, concerned by general trends, established the Hanseatic League to defend and consolidate their interests. Famine descended between 1315 and 1317, and in 1346–1347 the Black Death began its inexorable migration from the Middle East. During the next five years plague devoured up to a third of the European population. Plague was complicated by strife. In 1337, the English and French began their Hundred Years War, laying waste a large part of France. Political anarchy reigned over much of Germany. Although the Italian states retained some of their vigor, the fourteenth century was for most of Europe a time of despair, anguish, and economic stagnation.

Despite these setbacks the essential ingredients of a dynamic new economy were in place in Europe. The Italians had taught others efficient methods of conducting business. The Flemish, having pioneered in the cloth industry, had passed their methods to the English, who at long last were utilizing their immense herds as the basis for a highly successful export industry in finished woolens. When the ravages of plague and war subsided, Europeans possessed the material and commercial instruments required for rapid economic recovery. The opening of mines in Germany, Bohemia, and Hungary after 1450, made possible by improved pumping, extracting, and smelting techniques, rapidly expanded the trade in minerals. Silver production in Europe increased fivefold between 1450 and 1530.[35] French wine, salt, fruits, and linen; Scandinavian timber, iron, and forest products; Russian fur; Spanish wool; Roman alum; German minerals; Dutch herrings—these and innumerable other products were traded in growing volume across Europe. The flow of Baltic grain to the West, though not terribly large, permitted the transfer of manpower from farm to workshop in critical industrial areas, particularly the Lowlands. Most important, the opening of a direct sea route to India and the discovery of the Western hemisphere suddenly expanded the international division of labor and offered unprecedented opportunities for profit.

NEW WORLD EXPANSION

European exploitation of America provides emphatic evidence of the power of commerce and the deepening alliance between monarchs and merchants. From the start, Europe's monarchs asserted administrative authority over the process of overseas expansion. Prince Henry the Navigator pursued his explorations of West Africa and initiated colonization of the Atlantic islands under dispensation from the Portuguese Crown.[36] Shortly after the discovery of America, Spanish monarchs asserted supreme authority over the process of colonization, centralizing all American trade at Seville. The fact that events in America outran the superintending power of Madrid or that regulations issued in Spain were neglected in the Indies was more a function of distance and time than of disregard for the monarchy. The Crown was universally perceived as the fount of privilege, the ultimate authority that any aspirant to high position must conciliate. When the French and English launched exploring or colonizing probes during the sixteenth century, they too acted under patent or charter from the Crown.

How were these overseas probes to be financed? Being aware that American bullion strikes enriched the Spanish Crown, English and French monarchs were prepared to support endeavors to find alluvial wealth or to discover a northwest passage to India. But their resources fell short of costs. Money had to be raised from merchants or courtiers or syndicates of the two. London became the propaganda center for every variety of English "venture." Its merchants were clearly the principal underwriters of overseas endeavors,[37] and in France, overseas adventures, slave trading, and colonization were almost exclusively the province of merchants residing in the coastal cities.[38]

Colonization required prodigious capital resources, and trans-Atlantic investment accelerated the evolution of capitalist institutions. The planting of colonies was always speculative: not only was it big business, but it was a form of big business that required a generous investment of capital as well as considerable lead time before investments could bear fruit. In contrast to routine European trading, the establishment of colonial positions involved the construction of port facilities, forts, villages, and all the physical paraphernalia of permanent habitation. Both the costs and the risks of such ventures were high, and investors required commercial institutions that would attract abundant capital while permitting an equitable sharing of the greater risks of long-distance operations.

Existing business structures did not fulfill all these requirements. In northwestern Europe, the concept of incorporation had not advanced beyond the regulated company, a form of merchant guild by which an association of merchants was granted a royal charter giving it monopoly trading rights in a particular area. The regulated company was akin to a privileged chamber of commerce representing multiple forms of business ownership. It was not a unified company with a single mode of ownership. To meet the exceptional requirements of overseas expansion, Europeans developed the joint stock company, an institution that accepted capital investments from a large number of shareholders in order to minimize risks and conduct business under a single unified directorship.[39] Although early English joint stock companies—the Muscovy Company, the Virginia Company, the Hudson's Bay Company, and the East India Company—possessed vestigial remains of earlier forms of business operations, they were formative structures that laid the groundwork for subsequent monuments of Western capitalism such as the Bank of England.[40]

CONCLUSION

Commerce had drawn Europe from the dismal quiet of the Dark Ages to the conquest of world markets. Europe's experience was unique. Only once in world history has such a natural evolutionary transformation from agrarian backwardness to dynamic urban capitalism occurred. All subsequent breakthroughs to modern capitalism have been, in one degree or another, force-fed by the pressure and example of Europeans. In Europe, man's natural acquisitiveness was aided by a temperate climate, rich soils, and natural highways of communication. Rent by numerous navigable rivers and surrounded by seas, the continent afforded relatively easy movement of men and trade goods, even in times of primitive technology.

It was, however, the Mediterranean that provided the economic well-spring for Western Europe, first in Roman times and later in the tenth and eleventh centuries when Italian city-states began their illustrious career as purveyors of products and culture to backward fellow Christians across the Alps. What transformed Venice from a shabby community of fishermen to the great port of Christian Europe was trade. Venice's example ignited similar strivings elsewhere in Italy. In trans-Alpine Europe, a keen acquisitive outlook was belatedly and slowly aroused by merchants who tramped from region to region, huddling in the shadow of great stone fortresses. Gradually, trade increased the use of money; the money economy gave life to towns; and towns became catalysts of change across the countryside. By 1600, the center of economic power and cultural influence had passed from Italy to northwestern Europe. Spain may have been the great political power of the period, but the Low Countries were the nucleus of an expanding commercial world. Antwerp, the great emporium of the sixteenth century, gave place after 1585 to Amsterdam. Both stood at the maritime crossroads of Europe, opposite Great Britain, halfway between the Baltic ports and Iberia, at the terminus of rivers that drained Eastern France and Germany. The explosion of wealth was evident in European ports; in the vast growth of shipping; in the size and character of armies, navies, and bureaucracies; and in conspicuous expenditure on country houses and royal palaces.

Commerce was the engine that drove every momentous change in European life. It facilitated the rise of monarchical power while it eroded the power of the Church and the ascetic principles upon which the Church relied. Every obstacle to the expansion of trade was met and overcome by new devices, new technology, or new modes of business organization. By the sixteenth century, desire for profit had occasioned the great maritime discoveries, the establishment of trans-oceanic colonies, and the extension of European commercial activity to the far reaches of the world. European culture had become distinguished above all other world cultures by its superior arms and marine technology, by its commitment to the development and use of machinery, by its sophisticated business methods, and by its self-confident bravado. The instruments as well as the mentalities of modern capitalism had triumphed, and European society, the master of an advancing world-wide division of labor, was marching inexorably toward its eighteenth-century Industrial Revolution. For all its diversity, the culture of Europe was fundamentally the product of commerce.

NOTES

1. William Cunningham, "Economic Change," in *The Cambridge Modern History:* vol. 1, *The Renaissance* (Cambridge, 1902), pp. 494, 497, 500.

2. Herbert Butterfield, *The Whig Interpretation of History* (London, 1931). This was the viewpoint of countless series histories and university textbooks during the first six decades of the century. Textbooks like Carl Stephenson's widely read *Medieval History* (New York, 1935) and Sidney Painter's *History of the Middle Ages* (New York, 1952) pursued that approach, and volumes of the influential *Rise of Modern Europe* series, edited by William Langer, were unabashedly market oriented. See, for example, Edward P. Cheyney, *The Dawn of a New Era 1250–1453* (New York, 1936).

3. Abbé Guillaume-Thomas Raynal, *Histoire philosophique et politique des établissemens et du commerce des Européens dans les deux Indes,* vol. 1 (Geneva, 1782), p. 4. The French wording is as follows: "*les peuples qui ont poli tous les autres, ont été commercans.*"

4. Adam Smith, *An Inquiry into the Nature and Causes of the Wealth of Nations,* vol. 1 (1776; Oxford, 1976), p. 25.

5. A law of inheritance by which the entire real estate of a deceased person passes to the eldest son.

6. A legal settlement by which the inheritance of a landed estate is limited to an unalterable succession of heirs. Entail prevents the person currently enjoying landlord rights from bequeathing the property at his or her pleasure.

7. Smith, *Wealth of Nations,* vol. 1, p. 383.

8. Pirenne's commercial orientation is delineated in *Medieval Cities: Their Origins and the Revival of Trade* (Princeton, 1925) and *Economic and Social History of Medieval Europe* (London, 1937).

9. Fustel de Coulanges, *Histoire des institutions politiques de l'ancienne France* (Paris, 1975). This work is discussed in Bryce Lyon, *Henri Pirenne: A Biographical and Intellectual Study* (Gent, 1974), p. 443.

10. Alfons Dopsch, *Wirschaftliche und Soziale Grundlagen der Europäischen Kulturentwicklung* (Vienna, 1923–1924), 2 vols. The work has been condensed in English translation, *The Economic and Social Foundations of European Civilizations* (London, 1937).

11. In modern times, usury involves the taking of exorbitant interest on a loan. In the Middle Ages, any interest taken on a loan was considered usury.

12. In theory, the "just price" of a product should be equal to the cost of the materials and labor required in its making; in practice, it was perceived as fair market price.

13. Hicks observed that the inland Sea of Japan was relatively small and that the lands around it did not generate the variety of natural resources of the Mediterranean. The coastline of India, largely unbroken, provided less attractive opportunities for trade. Only the South China Sea linking Indo-China, Indonesia, and the Philippines offered conditions approaching those of the Mediterranean. Hicks did not speculate on why this area had been less productive of active commercial city-states than the Mediterranean. Sir John Hicks, *A Theory of Economic History* (Oxford, 1969), pp. 138–139.

14. Before the eleventh century, a number of south Italian towns (Naples, Gaeta, Amalfi, Solerno, and Bari) as well as Venice recognized the emperor at Constantinople.

15. Fernand Braudel, *The Mediterranean and the Mediterranean World in the Age of Philip II,* vol. 1, trans. Sian Reynolds (New York, 1972), p. 115.

16. Braudel contends that the urban population of Flanders and Brabant was about 50 percent by 1400. The proportion of townspeople for Western and Central Europe by the end of the eighteenth century was only 20–25 percent. Fernand Braudel, *Capitalism and Material Life 1400–1800* (New York, 1975), p. 376.

17. It was a common medieval expression that the air of the city made one free. If a runaway serf was able to escape capture for one year and a day, he or she was granted freedom.

18. Smith, *Wealth of Nations,* vol. 1, pp. 418–419.

19. Demesne was the land of a manor held by and worked in behalf of the lord. Nondemesne lands were distributed to serfs who worked those lands for their own maintenance.

20. Pirenne, *Economic and Social History,* p. 18.

21. Herbert Heaton offered an example of a bill of exchange: "I, A.B. (Genoese importer), have accepted from you, C.D. (Alexandrian exporter), goods to the value of *xyz* pounds of Genoese money, and I promise to pay to you in Alexandria, in bezants of Alexandria, *pq* bezants to the pound, before (a certain date)." Heaton continued: "This bill was sent to C.D. He sold it for bezants to some Alexandrian importer (E.F.) who owed pounds to G.H., an exporter in Genoa. E.F. sent the bill to G.H., who presented it to A.B. and collected pounds. Thus two debts between two remote towns were settled with one document and two local transfers of money." Herbert Heaton, *Economic History of Europe* (New York, 1948), pp. 177–178.

22. Carlo M. Cipolla, *Guns, Sails and Empires: Technological Innovation and the Early Phases of European Expansion, 1400–1700* (New York, 1965), pp. 24–26.

23. It might be argued that nobles were compensated for their diminished influence by the establishment of private property rights over lands distributed to their antecedents under the usufruct conditions of fiefdom.

24. Werner Sombart, *Luxury and Capitalism* (Ann Arbor, 1967), p. 52. This work was first published in German in 1913.

25. Ibid., p. 3.

26. Ibid., pp. 22–28.

27. Gerald A. J. Hodgett, *A Social and Economic History of Medieval Europe* (London, 1972), pp. 67–68.

28. Ruth Pike, *Enterprise and Adventure: The Genoese in Seville and the Opening of the New World* (Ithaca, 1966), pp. 6–9, 17–19, 145–147.

29. Alum was a vital chemical used in the woolen industry. Western supplies had come from Phocaea near Smyrna, but the Turks gained control of the eastern mines in 1455 and imposed weighty taxes on the product. The Tolfa concession was, therefore, a valuable asset to the Genoese.

30. Robert Lopez, "Market Expansion: The Case of Genoa," *Journal of Economic History* 24 (1964): 456–462.

31. Pirenne, *Economic and Social History,* pp. 160–168.

32. Braudel, *The Mediterranean,* vol. 2, pp. 799–800; Carlo Cipolla, *Before the Industrial Revolution: European Society and Economy, 1000–1700* (New York, 1976), p. 207.

33. Lynn White, Jr., *Medieval Technology and Social Change* (Oxford and New York, 1962), pp. 128–129.

34. Cunningham, "Economic Change," pp. 494–500.

35. Heaton, *Economic History*, p. 232.

36. Charles Verlinden, *The Beginnings of Modern Colonization* (Ithaca, 1970), pp. 204–209.

37. Theodore K. Rabb, "Investment in English Overseas Enterprise, 1575–1630," *Economic History Review*, 2d ser., 19 (1966): 70–81.

38. Gabriel Debien, *Les Engagés pour les Antilles (1634–1715)* (Paris, 1952), pp. 38–39. Attempts by the French Crown to encourage the participation of nobles were rejected on grounds that commerce was a socially degrading activity. See Guy Richard, *Noblesse d'affaires au XVIIIe siècle* (Paris, 1974).

39. Italians had developed prototypes of the joint stock company to administer imperial holdings in the Eastern Mediterranean in the fourteenth century. E. L. J. Coornaert, "European Economic Institutions and the New World: The Chartered Companies," in E. E. Rich and C. H. Wilson, eds., *The Cambridge Economic History of Europe*, vol. 4 (Cambridge, 1967), p. 221.

40. K. G. Davies, *The Royal African Company* (London, 1957), pp. 24–33.

4

The Demographic Model

Although the commercial explanation enjoyed absolute dominance among Western historians during the first half of this century, that dominance was challenged in the decades after World War II. Medievalists led the charge. For all its appeal, the linear and progressive commercial model failed to explain the unevenness of medieval economic life. Despite expanding markets and increasing division of labor, things did not "grow bigger and better from generation to generation": indeed, wrote M. M. Postan, there was "no continuous ascent from barbaric primitivity . . . to the glorious efflorescence of the renaissance." As we have seen, the fourteenth and fifteenth centuries were a time of commercial failure, bankruptcy, and retrenchment. Markets shrivelled, and the international division of labor was thrust into reverse. If market activity and the money economy were unable to counter Europe's fourteenth-century tailspin, then perhaps commercial forces had not been primarily responsible for the growth that occurred earlier.[1]

Historians have lavished attention on markets and money, but most of the medieval economy was not involved in long-distance trade. Inter-regional commerce does not account for some of the most significant changes in a fundamentally agricultural society: the rise of new villages; the increase in crops, animals, and men in agriculture during the thirteenth century; or the disappearance of villages and the decline of agricultural production in the fourteenth and fifteenth centuries. Nor can expanding trade or the "rise of the money economy" account adequately for the commutation of the serfs' labor services or for the elimination of serfdom itself. Postan demonstrated that commutation was not a continuous and progressive process. The typical chronology of lord-serf relations in England was a change from labor services to money rents in the twelfth century, a return to labor services in the thirteenth century, and a wave of commutations in the fourteenth and fifteenth centuries. Serfdom had ended in Western Europe by the sixteenth century. Labor services were commuted first in those regions of England that were least commercial, not in trading districts adjacent to London.[2]

In the early modern period as well, Europe's vital signs were irregular. The sixteenth century was a time of commercial and demographic expansion, the seventeenth one of stagnation. In Eastern Europe, the growth of long-distance trade and the expansion of the international division of labor neither increased human freedom, stimulated urban life, nor enhanced the general well-being. Instead, the rise of international commerce proved socially regressive. From the Baltic to the Black Sea, peasants who for centuries had enjoyed relative freedom were systematically reduced to serfdom upon the advent of large-scale inter-regional trade in the fifteenth and sixteenth centuries. In Poland, agricultural ownership became concentrated in the hands of great lords; peasants were confined to survival-sized plots; artisanal groups withered; interior towns declined; and the few large manufactories that arose employed serf labor.[3]

Because the linear commercial model seemed ill-equipped to accommodate these realities, scholars have sought alternative theories of change more sensitive to the unevenness of material life in Europe. For some, the celebrated essays on population of the English parson, Thomas Robert Malthus (1766–1834), provided inspiration. Malthus challenged Adam Smith's trade-based division-of-labor model, arguing that material progress was possible only within the narrowest limits. Likewise, he rejected the optimistic speculations of French revolutionaries and Enlightenment philosophers concerning the perfectibility of man and of society. History was not a linear account of human progress. The material existence of humankind had ebbed and flowed like ocean tides. Every surge to the fore was followed by a retreat, albeit this ceaseless oscillation occurred around a slowly rising trend of material wealth. The key to understanding the historical process was not commerce. It was population pressure.

Malthus determined that stable agrarian societies having fixed land resources and limited technological skill confronted upper limits, or ceilings, to population size. These ceilings were determined by the maximum amount of food that could be drawn from the land at a particular time. Malthus offered two fundamental postulates: first, that food is necessary for human survival; second, that passion between the sexes is both necessary and enduring. He observed, however, that the procreative power occasioned by human passion is vastly greater than the power of the land to supply subsistence. When unchecked, population naturally increases geometrically (1–2–4–8–16–32), while subsistence increases only arithmetically (1–2–3–4–5–6). Using these ratios and assuming that humans could double the bounty of their lands every twenty-five years, Malthus determined that without checks the natural growth of population would be 315 times greater than the growth of the food supply over a period of three centuries.[4]

Such imbalance is inconceivable. In reality, observed Malthus, population is kept in homeostatic balance with food supply by the operation of preventive and positive checks. Preventive checks were voluntary actions taken to control fertility. They included contraception, celibacy, late age of marriage for women (a practice peculiar to European society), the delay of property transfers between generations, and out-migration. Preventive checks alone had never preserved a stable equilibrium between population and subsistence, Malthus believed. Given natural passion between the sexes, population rose whenever subsistence was ample, and rising population ultimately placed excessive pressure on food resources, ensnaring the masses of humankind in subsistence crises. Such crises triggered positive checks (famine, epidemic disease, and war over scarce resources), sharply increasing mortality. When the painful operation of these checks finally restored equilibrium between population and food supplies, a new cycle of growth and subsidence would commence. With each succeeding cycle, population ceilings drifted upward. This drift was made possible by agricultural and technological innovations introduced under the pressure of successive crises.

The Malthusian model was highly pessimistic. For all historical time, the lives of common people had oscillated between mere sufficiency and extreme misery. Humankind was capable of moderating the severity of overpopulation by exercising "moral restraint," but the inexorable logic of the Malthusian principle insured that the upward drift of material progress would be painfully slow and erratic.

Although numerous refinements and adjustments have been made to Malthus's theory, his principle of population continues to provide an intellectual cornerstone for modern historical demography. Malthus worked under enormous handicap. He had no reliable population statistics. Nineteenth-century Britain became the world's leader in recording demographic information, but the country's first national census was not taken until several years after Malthus's essay appeared. Not until 1838 did the law require public registration of births, deaths, and the causes of all deaths. In the absence of such records it is extremely difficult, if not impossible, for historical demographers to determine with certainty the relative importance of fertility and mortality in producing demographic change. Thomas McKeown, a renowned demographer, doubts that we will ever have an acceptable interpretation for the modern rise of population.[5] Yet McKeown's work concentrates on the last three centuries, a period for which vital statistics are relatively abundant! What about the twelfth or fourteenth or sixteenth centuries? For them, wrote Michael Flinn, we must resort to "hypothesizing on an heroic scale."[6]

THE POPULATION HISTORY OF EUROPE

It is ironic that the demographic explanation for historical change has been most persuasively advocated by scholars focusing on the Middle Ages and the early modern era. We will never know the actual population figures for Europe (or for even the smallest regions of Europe) in the Middle Ages, but the relative simplicity of medieval life enables us to draw some conclusions about the ebb and flow of population and material life. J. C. Russell estimated the population of western and central Europe to have been 9 million in A.D. 500. At that date, the whole Mediterranean basin from Iberia and Morocco eastward to Syria may have supported 35 million people.[7] In A.D. 541, bubonic plague entered the inland sea from East Africa, killing up to a third of the Mediterranean population. The weakened Byzantine government was unable to achieve Justinian's goal of restoring the Roman Empire, and the decimation of stable populations in North Africa enhanced the seventh-century conquest of Arabs, whose nomadic habits rendered them less vulnerable to plague. Northern Europe was largely spared the effects of the ancient plague. By A.D. 1000, the gradual recovery of Mediterranean populations and the slow demographic advance of transalpine peoples provided all Europe a total population estimated in the range of 36 to 38.5 million.[8]

After A.D. 1000, Europe's population expanded. On a graph, this upward movement would show a saw-tooth configuration, indicating sharp short-term fluctuations, yet the overall direction of demographic change was unmistakably upward. During three centuries, total population may have doubled, reaching as much as 74–78 million by 1300. Some historians think this growth slowed in the thirteenth century and stopped around 1270; others believe that growth continued at reduced rate until the 1340s. In the late 1340s bubonic plague swept over Europe, producing catastrophic loss of life. Initial mortality may have been a third of the population, but successive recurrences of plague increased losses.[9] By 1410, England may have lost half of its pre-plague population, and similar losses occurred elsewhere in Europe. At some point in the later fifteenth century, population growth resumed. Precisely when this recovery began and how it was staggered across Europe is disputed, but once under way, the recovery continued vigorously through the sixteenth century.

In the seventeenth century population retreated once again, but in the absence of universal catastrophe on the scale of plague, the retreat was uneven and comparatively modest. The Iberian countries suffered significant decreases in the seventeenth century; population declined in Italy in the first half of the century; it stagnated in France. In German-speaking Europe where the Thirty Years War occasioned widespread devastation, population fell as much as 40 percent. Growth continued in England and the Netherlands during the first half of the seventeenth century, then stabilized for another hundred years.

By 1750, population growth had, once again, resumed almost everywhere in Europe. Growth has continued to the present day (see Figure 4.1). Europe's population was about 140 million in 1750. It rose to around 180 million in 1800, to 390 million by 1900, and it is expected to reach 700 million by 2000.[10]

Figure 4.1
European Population Growth, A.D. 100–2000 (Estimated)

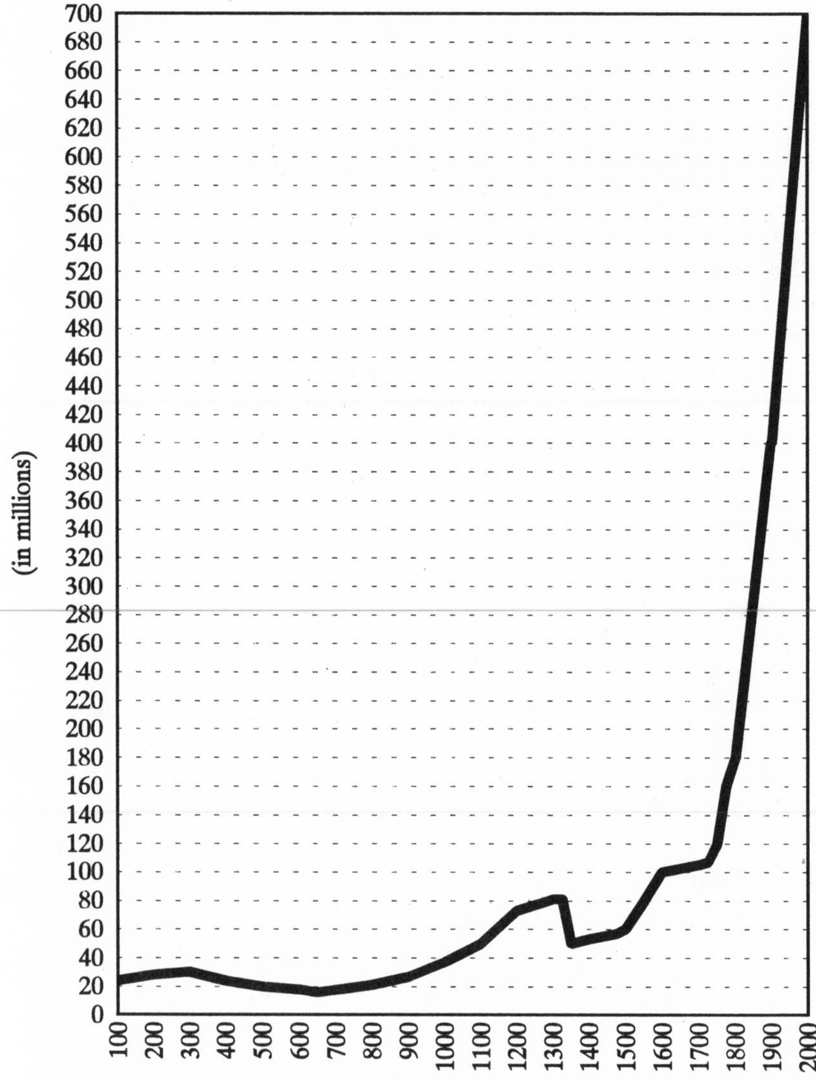

Sources: Colin McEvedy and Richard Jones, *Atlas of World Population History* (Harmondsworth, 1978), p. 19; Roger Mols, S. J., "Population in Europe 1500–1700," in Carlo M. Cipolla, ed., *The Fontana Economic History of Europe:* vol. 2, *The Sixteenth and Seventeenth Centuries* (Glasgow, 1974); J. C. Russell, "Population in Europe 500–1500," in Carlo M. Cipolla, ed., *The Fontana Economic History of Europe:* vol. 1, *The Middle Ages* (London, 1972).

Can a pattern be discerned in these figures? Arguing in the affirmative, D. B. Grigg has identified the following population trends since A.D. 1000.[11]

Years	Trend
1000–1100	Increase
1100–1200	High Growth
1200–1300	Growth Rate Cooling
1300–1347	Stagnation
1347–1450	Decline
1450–1600	Growth
1600–1740	Stagnation in Northern Europe
	Decline in Southern Europe
1740–	Growth

For neo-Malthusian historians, the two cycles of growth and subsidence—1000–1450; 1450–1740—represent Malthusian rhythm writ large. In agricultural societies, rising population imposes pressure on land resources, requiring the progressive fragmentation of arable land into smaller and smaller parcels. By the simple action of supply and demand, landlords are able to extract higher rents from their tenants. The number of landless people grows, and those having no land or too little land must obtain their livelihood (or part of it) through wage labor. When the number of wage workers competing for employment grows, wage levels fall. Food costs rise both as a reflection of increasing land values and as a response to intensified demand by an expanding population. Because people are compelled to spend a larger share of their wealth on daily sustenance, they have fewer resources to expend on manufactures. Therefore, in periods of growing population pressure, the terms of trade run against industry and in favor of landlords.

When a population ceiling is reached and the land is unable to sustain the demands placed upon it, a self-correcting mechanism is triggered, and all the trends are reversed. Land empties out. Marginal lands occupied under a regime of high pressure are abandoned; land values fall; rents fall; and the terms of trade begin to favor industry. Wages rise, and bargaining power passes from the landlord to the tenant and from the employer to the wage earner. To the extent that political power is based upon economic power, the power of landlords is increased in times of high population pressure and compromised in times of population decline.

THE DEMOGRAPHIC MODEL AND THE MIDDLE AGES

Neo-Malthusians contend that European history after A.D. 1000 offers a vindication of Malthus. The upward trajectory of population after the year 1000 was possible because Europe's abundant virgin land permitted the establishment of new villages and new settlements. Population grew, but yields from the land did not increase significantly.[12] Medieval farmers were not profit maximizers, and it stands to reason that the ready availability of land during the eleventh and twelfth centuries discouraged technological innovation. As the land gradually filled with people and population pressure mounted, pasture was converted into arable, reducing the numbers of grazing animals and limiting the availability of manure. Increasingly, marginal agricultural lands were brought under the plow, but such lands were particularly subject to the law of diminishing returns. In brief time, poorer lands punished the men who worked them with failing crops and cattle disease.

Symptoms of overpopulation were abundantly evident by the fourteenth century. Land was being subdivided through inheritance and fragmented through exchange into smaller and smaller holdings. Despite intense cultivation, the land could not produce enough food to supply an expanding population. As demand for land increased, so did its price. Rents rose; wages fell. Landlessness increased, and with it, banditry, vagrancy, and pauperism. Food prices soared, trapping people in a wage-price scissors and leaving them vulnerable to any type of natural disaster. All that was needed was some combination of adverse circumstances—a few years of drought or crop disease—to set off a crisis. Occasional bad harvests in the late thirteenth century sent preliminary shock waves across the continent. These were mere portents of the disaster that befell England in 1317–1319 or southern France in 1335–1347 when failing crops produced severe famine. With the arrival of bubonic plague in the 1340s, a society already experiencing a Malthusian check suffered demographic catastrophe.

Plague relieved pressure on the land, and the whole bundle of social and economic trends surged into reverse. Food prices fell; wages rose. Great landlords, who in the thirteenth century had benefitted from high rents and low wages, found themselves hard-pressed to obtain suitable tenants to occupy their properties. Exploiting their advantage, tenants demanded and received lower rents and long-term leases. At the abbey of

Saint-Germain-des-Prés, rents averaged 84 deniers per arpent from 1360 to 1400, 56 deniers from 1422 to 1461, and 31 deniers from 1461 to 1483.[13] Leases of twenty and forty years' duration became common, and a few estates, like Chertsy Abbey in England, granted leases for 200 and 300 years![14] The most enterprising peasants seized the opportunity to purchase customary or freehold property as well as to lease demesne land. During preceding centuries, a growing disparity had emerged in the size of holdings occupied by peasants. The dislocations of plague enabled prosperous and vigorous peasants who preserved their health to accumulate extensive land holdings. By the sixteenth century, many of these rich peasants—so-called kulaks—had become country gentlemen.

Changing demographic conditions in the late fourteenth and fifteenth centuries also served the poorer peasants by reversing bargaining power between employers and workers. Food had become cheap; labor dear. When the lords enacted laws to keep peasants bound to the land and their wages low, peasants rebelled. The most dramatic example of this is the celebrated Peasant's Revolt in England in 1381. In the chaotic period following the fall of Rome, peasants had sacrificed their personal freedom in exchange for the protection of feudal lords. This situation no longer applied, and lords who insisted upon extracting onerous obligations were viewed as mere exploiters. Peasants were highly mobile. Since their possessions were few, they were able to assemble their modest belongings and be on the high road in a matter of minutes. Landlords who resisted the reasonable demands of peasants risked losing their services altogether, and by the fifteenth century, there was no shortage of competing landlords willing to hire them. In these conditions, the constraints of serfdom, which for centuries had bound individuals to the soil, were peeled away across Western Europe.

These developments prompted a sea-change in political power relationships. The end of serfdom and the assertion of greater independence by leading elements of the peasantry weakened the relative power of the landed nobility. A diminished nobility was less capable of resisting the attempts of Europe's monarchs to consolidate their power through the extension of royal taxation and the expansion of royal bureaucracies, royal armies, and royal courts. It is no accident that the monarchs of England, France, and Spain consolidated their power at the end of the first great Malthusian cycle.

In formulating the demographic model, neo-Malthusian historians have not ignored the growth of markets, towns, and manufactures; nor are they insensitive to the importance of division of labor. Being pre-modern historians for the most part, they view the subject of economic growth differently from their modernist colleagues. Modern economists and economic historians have distinguished two categories of wealth—per capita (individual) and aggregate (collective)—observing that increases in the production of aggregate wealth need not generate an increase in per capita wealth if the number of individuals who must share the aggregate product grows at a rate faster than aggregate production itself. For this reason, economists determine that *real* economic growth occurs only when a society experiences sustained increases in *both aggregate and per capita wealth.*

This definition has little relevance for European society during most of the pre-industrial age. Because medieval people had no inclination to maximize profits and because they experienced no technological or structural changes far-reaching enough to revolutionize production, economic output in medieval society depended overwhelmingly on the number of labor inputs—that is, on the number of people working. Rising population meant rising aggregate output. Yet, as Malthus observed, rising population also meant reduced average income per capita. In spite of this, argue neo-Malthusian historians, long-term demographically driven oscillations did not occur around a fixed axis. In other words, when a population reversal occurred, it did not return the European economy to the place it had been prior to the last long-term surge of population growth. Long periods of rising population—which is to say, long periods of aggregate economic growth—generated important structural changes in society, even though such changes occurred at an almost glacial rate. The rise of markets offers a case in point.

In England, rural markets were established in profusion during the thirteenth century. These markets, held at specific locations once a week, did not initiate exchange among villagers. Village trade had always existed. Formal markets, established by local lords, merely regularized and regulated rural trade when it become apparent that such trade was large enough to benefit from formalization. Often, rural markets served as collection centers from which raw materials were funneled into market towns and thence to the long-distance trade. For this reason, advocates of the commercial model have long contended that it was the rise of long-distance trade that stimulated the establishment and growth of rural markets. Not so, writes R. H. Britnell: it was population growth that prompted the founding of rural markets by promoting division of labor and stimulating local demand for manufactures, services, and foodstuffs. Economic specialization requires a significant density of population. As population pressure mounted and increasing numbers of people suffered from landlessness or from insufficiency of land for family maintenance, their sustenance had to be achieved through specialized wage work: for example, threshing, thatching, ditching, carting, or employment in trades. Moreover, population growth naturally increased the absolute number of craftsmen who served the community—the smiths, millers, tailors, carpenters, potters, tanners, clothworkers—and, of course, these people depended upon the sale of their goods or services to buy food and raw materials.[15] Rural markets provided the necessary vehicle for exchange. Like towns, however, markets were sensitive to population trends, and population decline in the fourteenth and fifteenth centuries caused the contraction of market activity, a falling-off of long-distance trade, and the shrinkage of towns.

THE DEMOGRAPHIC MODEL
AND EARLY MODERN EUROPE

The decades around 1500 witnessed a quickening of activity. Among other things, there was new buoyancy in long-distance trades. The great discoveries permitted direct trade to the Orient as well as the founding of colonies in the New World. Neo-Malthusians consider this renewed vigor highly predictable. Population growth had resumed in the late fifteenth century, initiating this vitality. The transportation and business infrastructure so carefully delineated by scholars of the commercial school was already in place by the late fifteenth century. Moreover, legal recognition of individual property rights by many European governments enabled enterprising persons to pursue economic gain with greater security. These developments permitted a swifter acceleration of aggregate economic growth when the growth of population resumed.

Of course, Europe was riding to a fall. Aggregate growth in the sixteenth century occasioned a revival of towns and trade, but this was offset by higher rents, higher food costs, and lower wages—in effect, by declining per capita wealth. Europe was being drawn toward another Malthusian trap, and by the century's end, Spain, Europe's greatest political power, was enduring repeated famines. In fact, much of Mediterranean Europe was confronting a grain crisis by 1600.[16] Only England and the northern Netherlands escaped a Malthusian check in the seventeenth century. There, population growth continued through the first half of the century and remained stable during the second half. The ramifications of these developments for international politics were profound. Spain began its long and tortured decline as a great power; Italy's economic and strategic importance withered; and the center of European political and economic power passed from the Mediterranean to northwest Europe.

Exponents of the demographic model, Douglas North and Robert Paul Thomas, explain why England and the Netherlands escaped the seventeenth-century Malthusian trap and emerged as Europe's economic nucleus. During the growth surge of the sixteenth century, rising aggregate demand for goods and services reduced the transaction costs borne by Europe's leading merchants. As noted in the previous chapter, transaction costs are the expenses incurred in acquiring information about markets, in negotiating commercial exchanges, and in enforcing compliance with business contracts. Although per capita incomes fell in agriculture, incomes rose in the trading sector as a result of declining transaction costs. Only those countries that earned a substantial part of their income through trade could increase population levels and concurrently enjoy both aggregate and per capita economic growth.[17]

Britain and the Netherlands were Europe's leading commercial countries. By the seventeenth century, England possessed a large uninterrupted national market; its urban growth was second only to that of the Netherlands; and institutional factors favored the expansion of commerce. The Netherlands already possessed a capital market and a long history of trading activity. The material interests of Dutch society were manifestly connected to international trade, and laws governing property rights reflected that fact. New business procedures had reduced transaction costs, and innovations in agriculture had integrated the countryside in a mutually beneficial relationship with the cities.

It was different in Europe's agrarian regions. In his study of Languedoc, the rural province stretching across Mediterranean France from the Rhone to the Pyrenees, Emmanuel Le Roy Ladurie bore witness to successive demographic cycles, what he called the "immense respiration of a social structure." At the end of the medieval cycle of expansion and contraction, Languedoc experienced vigorous population growth. With some irregularity, population climbed steeply until about 1570, then leveled off. Production levels were low and production per capita grew slowly. As farm land was subdivided, people struggled more and more to make ends meet. By 1680, there was no slack left in the system. Demographic growth ceased, and for the first time in two centuries, Languedoc sustained long-term decline. It was a decline, writes Le Roy Ladurie,

> provoked not so much by the repeated famines—which were perhaps less serious than in the center and in the north of France—as by joblessness and poverty; by chronic undernourishment; by the

low standard of living which favored the spread of epidemics; by the primitive sanitary conditions of the poor; and—very accessorily—by emigration, late marriages, and even a little birth control.[18]

Le Roy Ladurie does not contend that population pressure was the sole engine driving provincial affairs or that the timing of great demographic cycles was consistent across Europe. Political dictates from Paris, tax laws, religious disputes, warfare, changing trends in regional and international trade: these and other forces affected the lives and the livelihoods of Languedoc's peasants. Each of these forces had some bearing on provincial fertility rates. As for timing, vigorous population growth began later in Languedoc than elsewhere during the second great Malthusian "respiration," and the Malthusian check arrived later. Population sometimes stabilized at a low level even though the prospects for growth were abundant. This was true of Languedoc in the final decades of the first great cycle, 1470–1500. All that was needed was a catalyst—a series of good harvests—to trigger the mechanism. Once the mechanism was operative, however, the cycle moved inexorably along its course despite the action of secondary forces—that is, tax laws or political conflicts—that might delay or accelerate the process. In Languedoc, as in other agrarian regions, the ultimate constraints upon human affairs, the parameters that determined what was possible and what was not, were demographic.

Ironically, the demographic rhythm identified by Malthus lost its predictive value during his own lifetime. "Malthus was a clear-headed theoretician of traditional societies," wrote Le Roy Ladurie, "but he was a prophet of the past."[19] From one cycle to another, the cumulative upward drift of technical knowledge, physical and social infrastructure, financial institutions, and business acumen finally equipped Europeans—particularly northwest Europeans—with the ability to increase per capita production dramatically. Beginning in the eighteenth century, the productive, social, and institutional changes that we identify as the Industrial Revolution gave rise to an unprecedented and sustained increase in the rate of economic growth, both aggregate and per capita. A few statistics graphically demonstrate the degree to which rising per capita production outdistanced the growth of population, even at a time when population was growing at an unprecedented rate. During the three centuries from 1500 to 1800, the average annual increase of gross national product (GNP) per capita could not have exceeded 0.2–0.3 percent. In the early nineteenth century—the beginning phase of the Industrial Revolution—annual per capita income for all of Europe was growing at a rate of 0.5–0.7 percent. Between 1830 and 1910, the annual rate of growth of GNP per capita was 1.98 percent in the industrialized European countries. Over the same period, population grew at an annual rate of 0.82 percent per year.[20]

By the nineteenth century, Europe had surmounted the Malthusian trap: aggregate growth no longer dictated per capita impoverishment. Enjoying backward vision, it is much easier for us to identify this breakthrough than it was for contemporaries. Neither Adam Smith nor Malthus, two acute observers of the contemporary scene, were aware that they were living through the early stages of the Industrial Revolution, perhaps the greatest watershed since the Agricultural Revolution, B.C. 8000–3500!

Demographic forces are a factor in the interpretation of late modern history. However, the model conceived by Malthus and refined by neo-Malthusians has little utility for the history of Western society since the Industrial Revolution. Whether it is still suitable for the study of pre-industrial societies of the Third World where rising population, overstrained resources, and shrinking productivity impede development is a matter for debate.[21]

CHALLENGING THE DEMOGRAPHIC MODEL: THE ROLE OF PLAGUE

The integrity of the demographic model as a macrohistorical mode of explanation depends upon the ability of its practitioners to demonstrate that the two great Malthusian checks of the fourteenth and seventeenth centuries were predictable crises in a recurring pattern of growth and sub-sidence. The two crises were dissimilar in important respects. The four-teenth-century crisis was a universal catastrophe of the first magnitude, and its effects lingered in Europe for at least a century and a quarter. The seventeenth-century crisis was briefer; it was less severe, and it did not have a uniform result.[22] For this reason, many historians deny that the so-called crisis of the seventeenth century was prompted by demographic pressures. Some argue, for example, that Spain's decline in the seven-teenth century was a result of injudiciously assumed political commit-ments that overextended the national economy. Others contend that the collapse of population in seventeenth-century Germany was a conse-quence of the last great religious war and that religious warfare in Europe was not prompted primarily by population pressure.

Most historians concede that Europe confronted population pressure in the fourteenth century. Advocates of the demographic model generally agree that famines in the early fourteenth century constitute evidence that a positive check was under way. There is disagreement on the role of the Black Death. Postan separated the fourteenth-century famines from the Black Death, deliberately minimizing the importance of plague in the operation of the late-medieval Malthusian check.

> The Black Death could perhaps be regarded as a biological catastrophe; yet it is doubtful whether the Black Death, even if taken in conjunction with other great epidemics of the fourteenth century, could by itself account for the population trend of the later Middle Ages. . . . [S]igns of falling trends appear before the Black Death and do not disappear after the direct effects of the great pestilences should no longer have been felt.[23]

Other historians link famine with plague, sometimes explicitly, sometimes vaguely. Famine, argue North and Thomas, "set the stage for disease" and often accompanied it. Echoing such sentiments, Le Roy Ladurie referred to the Black Death as a "holocaust of the undernourished."[24]

Because plague coincided in time with what neo-Malthusians perceive as a positive check and because it occasioned enormous loss of life over an extended period, the relationship between the check and the plague must be clarified. Malthus argued that a positive check could take the form of famine, epidemic disease, war over scarce resources, or some combination of the three. If excessive demographic pressure begot famine in the fourteenth century, did famine, in turn, beget plague?

Plague entered Europe from the Black Sea port of Caffa where a Mongol army, laying siege to the city, had been overcome by the disease in 1346. Striking swiftly at Constantinople, plague progressively extended its deadly presence around the continent, reaching England in 1348 and the Baltic by 1350. Devastation was not confined to Europe. From the 1320s, plague had worked its way along the trade routes of Central Asia. China was hard hit. One authority contends that the population of China may have declined from around 125 million to 90 million by the 1390s.[25] The leading scholar of plague in the Middle East believes that by the early fifteenth century that region may have lost more than a third of its population.[26] North Africa and much of Eurasia experienced plague in the fourteenth century. Yet only a few of the victimized areas had suffered famine in the period preceding the pandemic.

In the mid-1960s, Jean Meuvret contended that there was no simple or necessary cause-effect relationship between famine and epidemic disease.[27] His position was affirmed by Jean-Noel Biraben in a monumental study of the plague. Biraben showed that although bubonic plague often followed famine, there were numerous cases in which famine followed plague and others in which plague was altogether unaccompanied by famine or famine by plague. He concluded that in the case of the Black Death there was no cause other than the disease itself that could have brought about plague.[28] There may have been a relationship between famine and plague, he writes, but it was not because famine aggravated the virulence of plague; rather, it was because plague, after striking, induced famine as a result of the violent interruption of agriculture and the disorganization of the economy. In all the abundant recent literature on plague, there is no direct linkage established between malnutrition and plague.[29]

If Biraben's views are correct, the unparalleled demographic blowout of the fourteenth and fifteenth centuries was not related to famine or to population pressure. Rather, demographic collapse was occasioned by an extraordinary and unpredictable epidemic that would have befallen Europe whether population was at, above, or below its presumed ceiling.

Minimizing the role of plague and maximizing the effects of demographic rhythm, Postan argued that Europe was already experiencing a Malthusian check before the onset of plague and that plague does not explain protracted demographic stagnation at the end of the Middle Ages. Others would disagree. One historian of plague considers the fourteenth-century pandemic "the worst disaster that has ever befallen mankind."[30] For the modern United States to sustain a demographic tragedy of similar proportions, 75 million people would have to die of disease in a few years' time. That is more than 200 times the number of U.S. troops killed in World War II. Yet, despite the incomprehensible scale of such a disaster, scholars believe that the recurrent nature of plague, not the initial die-off, was its most devastating feature. Writing about the early modern era, a time when the worst ravages of plague had eased, Michael Flinn asserted the following:

> The key to population growth or decline in early modern Europe lay, beyond doubt, both in the ebb and flow of epidemic tides of particularly infectious diseases and in the secular shifts of endemic levels of diseases. Of all the infectious diseases taking part in these processes bubonic plague was the preeminent arbiter of population growth rates. Until the middle of the seventeenth century this terrifying disease was seldom absent on an epidemic scale from any part of Europe for much more than a decade and was mostly present permanently at a low endemic level, at least in the great cities. More than any other single factor, the comings and goings of bubonic

plague determined whether and where population would grow, stagnate, or decline.[31]

In fairness to neo-Malthusian historians, fourteenth-century Europe may have undergone a population reversal had plague never occurred. It is hardly possible, however, that a fourteenth-century crisis uncomplicated by plague would have been as grave as the disaster that actually befell the continent. It stands to reason that without so devastating and recurring a force as plague, less arable land would have been abandoned. Rents would have held up better, and wages would have risen less. The nobility would have remained stronger, the kings weaker, and the ability of the peasants to throw off serfdom and acquire property rights would certainly have been jeopardized. Presumably, these altered social and economic relationships would have occasioned different responses to the stimulus of population growth whenever growth resumed. If, as Biraben contends, the plague pandemic was a chance epidemiological episode, only partially if at all related to the state of subsistence in Europe, then plague profoundly exaggerated any medieval Malthusian check.

This conclusion raises doubt about the general utility of the demographic model. Historians of Europe have identified only two macro-historical cycles. The apparent symmetry and universality of the medieval cycle may only be a reflection of distortions occasioned by plague. As for the second cycle, 1470/1500–1750, it lacks both symmetry and universality, and many historians remain dubious about the demographic roots of the so-called crisis of the seventeenth century.

CHALLENGING THE DEMOGRAPHIC MODEL: POPULATION AND INNOVATION

One of the sternest critics of the neo-Malthusian argument, Ester Boserup, acknowledges that population pressure has been vitally important to human development, but she rejects the neo-Malthusian concept of predictable, recurring cycles of growth and subsidence.[32] Rather, argues Boserup, a gradually rising population has been the normal condition for humankind throughout history. Historians of the pre-industrial West should not view rising population as a harbinger of famine and privation. Rising population has been the chief engine of technological innovation; in turn, technological innovation has consistently raised population ceilings and permitted a consistent upward trend in population figures. If Europe suffered dramatic demographic reversals over the last two thousand years, the explanation must be sought in unpredictable incursions of disease, not in Malthusian checks.

For a thousand years, writes Boserup, Europe lagged behind China in technology. Why? Because China had sufficient population to sustain a relatively high level of technology. Europe did not. When the population of a society is small, it is difficult to effect economies of scale. Specialization (division of labor) is rendered problematical, and the creation and maintenance of collective capital assets (bridges, walls, dikes) is harder to achieve and more costly for each of the people being served. Higher levels of technology, like degrees of specialization, require high densities of population.

At no time was pre-industrial Europe overpopulated. If anything, it was underpopulated, writes Boserup. As population density increased, declining supplies of land and other resources stimulated people to discover more efficient means of utilizing existing resources. Either by invention or by the borrowing of new technologies, Europeans found ways to enhance productivity. In Roman times, much of Western and Central Europe was cultivated by means of long fallow. Long fallow involved burning off a bit of bush or forest, planting and replanting the land as long as it remained fertile, then moving on to do the same in another place. Suited only to a thin population, this system allowed lands to lie fallow for five or more years. By the eighth century, a two-field short fallow was being used across Western Europe; subsequently, in densely populated areas, the more sophisticated three-field system replaced it. By the nineteenth century, fallow had been abandoned altogether.[33] Each adjustment involved the adoption of innovations and new technology to accommodate the needs of a larger population. Whereas the only tool needed for long fallow was the hoe, short fallow required the plough. Long fallow permitted tribal tenure systems; short fallow necessitated systems of secure tenure in which permanent investments in land and water supply could be guaranteed. It was in Tuscany and the Low Countries, both densely populated districts, that Europeans first developed intensive systems of agriculture.[34] Likewise, in Tuscany and the Low Countries sophisticated systems of trade and industry first developed.

Boserup's thesis on the relationship between population size and technology raises many questions. Why, for example, did population pressure in Europe produce innovation and advancing technology when rising population did not evoke equivalent innovations elsewhere in the world? At the same time, Boserup's analysis directs us back to a debate among historical demographers. If, as Malthus argued, passion between the sexes naturally produced overpopulation, what was the principal mechanism of population control? Was it the positive check generating high mortality, or the preventive check achieving fertility control?[35] Neo-Malthusian historians place their chief emphasis on positive checks. Yet we know that West Europeans adopted social patterns to control fertility. Most West European families were nuclear. Marriage usually involved the creation of a new household, and marriage could not occur until the economic base for a new household existed. By the seventeenth century, the average age of first marriage for women was 26 years, and between two-fifths and three-fifths of women of childbearing age (ages 15–44) were unmarried.[36] Not surprisingly, Boserup would observe, this unique marriage pattern was present in densely inhabited Tuscany as early as the fourteenth century. Scholars like Boserup are prone to emphasize fertility control. Fertility-lowering adjustments in family structure and marriage customs, like adjustments in fallow, are perceived as innovative responses to population pressure that precluded the necessity for positive checks.

CONCLUSION

Both Boserup and the neo-Malthusians consider population pressure the chief propellant of historical change in pre-industrial Europe, but they draw opposite conclusions concerning the nature of the changes wrought. The neo-Malthusians consider high pressure a portent of subsistence crises, demographic decline, and aggregate economic stagnation. Boserup deems high population pressure a vital goad to technological innovation and, as a consequence, to further population growth. Both views are deterministic: a particular condition, it is inferred, produces a particular result. In Boserup's case, it is not clear that Europeans consistently responded to high population density with new technologies. In fact, many of the most revolutionary technological innovations in European history occurred during periods of low population pressure. Notable examples are the fifteenth-century introductions of printing, gunpowder, and navigational instruments as well as the development of the superior sailing ships that enabled Europeans to establish maritime hegemony throughout the world. Even when new technologies emerged in Europe, their diffusion tended to be painfully slow before the nineteenth century. Likewise, changes in cultural values and social customs that were capable of relieving population pressure were adopted slowly. Among all areas of human experience, the slowest to change is our system of values.[37]

As for neo-Malthusian theory, it is clear that there are close historical correlations between the movement of population, prices, wages, and rents, and it is reasonable to deduce that in pre-industrial times an equilibrating mechanism like that discerned by Malthus generally kept population in line with subsistence. At best, however, such a mechanism would have worked asymmetrically. Fertility, mortality, and the material and social conditions of daily life were organically interconnected. If fertility and mortality shaped the circumstances of community life, they were also influenced by them. In such an interactive relationship, it is difficult to discern where the driving force resided, if indeed it resided in the same place throughout historical time. Different communities behaved differently. Some communities lived perpetually on the edge of Malthusian crises: marriage was early, living standards low, and there was little land per head. Elsewhere, communities maintained marriage and inheritance patterns that preserved a wide margin over subsistence.[38] For some, the prevailing vital force was mortality; for others, fertility.

An equilibrating model like that conceived by Malthus provides important explanatory power, especially for early agrarian societies. Does it offer predictive power? The expansion-contraction mechanism was always vulnerable to distortion from random exogenous forces such as epidemics or geographical discoveries that might accelerate or reverse prevailing trends. This may have been the case during the fourteenth and fifteenth centuries when plague intensified what neo-Malthusians have considered a predictable subsistence crisis. Similarly, the unforeseen introduction of New World food crops to Europe (potatoes, maize, and tomatoes, to mention a few) might have moderated the so-called crisis of the seventeenth century by increasing yields on European farms. By elevating the Malthusian model to a macrohistorical level, have neo-Malthusians stretched the predictive power of the principle of population beyond the limit of its utility?

NOTES

1. M. M. Postan, *Essays in Medieval Agriculture and the General Problems of the Medieval Economy* (Cambridge, 1973), pp. 41, 196.

2. M. M. Postan, "The Chronology of Labour Services," first published in 1937, reprinted in *Essays in Medieval Agriculture*, p. 90.

3. These developments occurred after Poland had become heavily involved with the West in the exchange of grain for finished products. Marian Malowist, "Poland, Russia and Western Trade in the Fifteenth and Sixteenth Centuries," *Past and Present* 13 (1958): 26–39; "The Economic and Social Development of the Baltic Countries from the Fifteenth to the Sixteenth Centuries," *Economic History Review*, 2d ser., 12 (1959): 117–189.

4. Thomas Robert Malthus, *An Essay on the Principle of Population*, ed. Philip Appleman (1798; New York, 1976), p. 23.

5. Thomas McKeown, *The Modern Rise of Population* (New York, 1976), p. 17.

6. Michael Flinn, *The European Demographic System, 1500–1820* (Baltimore, 1981), p. 1.

7. J. C. Russell, "Population in Europe 500–1500," in Carlo M. Cipolla, ed., *The Fontana Economic History of Europe*, vol. 1 (London, 1972), p. 39.

8. The 36 million figure appears in Colin McEvedy and Richard Jones, *Atlas of World Population History* (Harmondsworth, 1978). J. C. Russell, "Population in Europe 500–1500," offers 38.5.

9. Spain, for example, suffered sixteen recurrences of plague between 1362 and 1497. Rural England fared somewhat better, but London had twenty recurrences during the fifteenth century.

10. This modern surge of population in Europe has been mirrored elsewhere in the world. In 1750 world population may have been 750 million. Humankind reached one billion around 1830, two billion in the 1930s, three billion by 1960, four billion in 1975. Currently, world population is around five billion, and it is expected to reach 6.2 billion by the year 2000. McKeown, *Modern Rise of Population*, p. 1; Richard Gardner, "Bush, the U.N., and Too Many People," *New York Times*, 22 September 1989.

11. D. B. Grigg, *Population Growth and Agrarian Change: An Historical Perspective* (Cambridge, 1980), pp. 7, 64, 65, 281.

12. In England, the average gross yield of food grains per grain of seed sown was about 3.7 in the early thirteenth century, perhaps 4.7 in the fifteenth century. Yields only doubled in midland and southern England between 1200 and 1820. Carlo Cipolla, *Before the Industrial Revolution: European Society and Economy, 1000–1700* (New York, 1976), pp. 119–120; Grigg, *Population Growth and Agrarian Change*, p. 36. The best record of yields in medieval Europe is analyzed in J. Z. Titow, *Winchester Yields: A Study in Medieval Agricultural Productivity* (Cambridge, 1972).

13. Karl F. Helleiner, "The Population of Europe from the Black Death to the Eve of the Vital Revolution," in E. E. Rich and C. H. Wilson, eds., *The Cambridge Economic History of Europe*, vol. 4 (Cambridge, 1967), p. 14.

14. Gerald A. J. Hodgett, *A Social and Economic History of Medieval Europe* (London, 1972), p. 206.

15. For a stimulating discussion of early rural markets, see R. H. Britnell, "The Proliferation of Markets in England, 1200–1349," *Economic History Review* 34 (1981): 209–221.

16. Fernand Braudel, *The Mediterranean and the Mediterranean World in the Age of Philip II*, vol. 1, trans. Sian Reynolds (New York, 1972), pp. 588–606.

17. Douglas C. North and Robert Paul Thomas, *The Rise of the Western World: A New Economic History* (Cambridge, 1973), pp. 93–113.

18. Emmanuel Le Roy Ladurie, *The Peasants of Languedoc* (Urbana, 1974), p. 295.

19. Ibid., p. 311.

20. Paul Bairoch, "Europe's Gross National Product: 1800–1975," *Journal of European Economic History* 5 (1976): 275–282.

21. In the 1970s, world population was rising at a rate of 2.05 percent a year, and few countries in the underdeveloped world had a rate below 2 percent. The significance of this becomes apparent when we acknowledge that in the century between 1750 and 1850 the population of England and Wales nearly tripled, albeit the average increase per

year was only about 1 percent. A 3 percent rate of growth will produce a thousandfold increase in population in two centuries.

22. Most scholarly literature on the "crisis of the seventeenth century" subordinates demographic factors among a host of other causes of crisis. See articles by E. J. Hobsbawm and H. R. Trevor-Roper in Trevor Aston, ed., *Crisis in Europe, 1560–1660* (New York, 1967). Theodore K. Rabb's analytical treatise on the crisis of the seventeenth century devotes little attention to demographic forces: *The Struggle for Stability in Early Modern Europe* (New York, 1975).

23. Postan, *Essays in Medieval Agriculture*, p. 12.

24. North and Thomas, *Rise of the Western World*, p. 72; Le Roy Ladurie, *Peasants of Languedoc*, p. 13. Charles Frederic Mullett offers a similar view. Having observed that Europeans had undergone a number of famine years, he argued: "The Black Death thus attacked a population wholly susceptible to the bubonic plague." *The Bubonic Plague in England: An Essay in the History of Preventive Medicine* (Lexington, 1956), p. 13.

25. Robert S. Gottfried, *The Black Death: Natural and Human Disaster in Modern Europe* (New York, 1983), pp. 34–36.

26. Michael W. Dols, *The Black Death in the Middle East* (Princeton, 1977), p. 223.

27. Jean Meuvret, "Demographic Crises in France from the Sixteenth to the Eighteenth Century," in D. V. Glass and D. E. C. Eversley, eds., *Population in History* (Chicago, 1965), pp. 510–513.

28. Jean-Noel Biraben, *Les hommes et la peste en France et dans les pays européens et méditerranéens*, vol. 1 (Paris, 1975), pp. 148–154. Plague is primarily a disease of rodents, not humans. The bacillus, *Pasteurella pestis*, lives in the bloodstream of warm-blooded animals, particularly rodents, more than 200 species of which are susceptible to the disease. The disease organism is transmitted from rodent to rodent by the flea, especially the flea *Xenopsylla cheopis*. When fleas draw blood from a host infected by the disease organism, the bacilli multiply in the gullet of the flea, sometimes blocking the digestive tract. Such "blocked" fleas become ravenously hungry. In their desperate attempt to feed, they regurgitate bacteria into the bloodstream of their host. When a diseased rat dies, his fleas migrate to other rats, progressively devastating the rat community. When, through such decimation, insufficient rodent hosts are available, the fleas migrate to other warm-blooded creatures, including man, thereby transmitting plague to the human population. Because fleas stray little distance from their hosts and because rat populations travel very slowly, plague epidemics will, as a rule, spread only if infected rats and fleas are transported from region to region. Grain is a favorite food of the black rat, and the *Xenopsylla cheopis* breeds best in the debris of cereal grains; consequently, grain transports were a major means of spreading contagion. At the same time, infection could be dispersed by the transfer of flea-infected cotton, wool, hides, or furs. For clear and brief descriptions of the etiology of plague, see Robert S. Gottfried, *Epidemic Disease in Fifteenth Century England* (New Brunswick, 1978), pp. 58–63; John T. Alexander, *Bubonic Plague in Early Modern Russia: Public Health and Urban Disaster* (Baltimore, 1980), pp. 2–12; L. Fabian Hirst, *The Conquest of Plague: A Study of the Evolution of Epidemiology* (Oxford, 1953), pp. 28–31, 266–271.

29. John D. Post makes the point firmly: "The clinical evidence . . . indicates no biological interaction between plague bacillus and nutritional levels." "Famine, Mortality, and Epidemic Disease in the Process of Modernization," *Economic History*

Review, 2d ser., 29 (1976): 37. D. B. Grigg confirms the point, observing that medical science currently demonstrates that it is difficult to trace any causal link between disease and hunger. *Population Growth and Agrarian Change: An Historical Perspective* (Cambridge, 1980), p. 13.

30. Dols, *Black Death in the Middle East,* vii.

31. Flinn, *The European Demographic System,* p. 55.

32. Ester Boserup, *The Conditions of Agricultural Growth* (London, 1965); *Population and Technological Change: A Study of Long-Term Trends* (Chicago, 1981).

33. Soil-enriching fodder crops were being sown on lands that in former times would have been left fallow.

34. According to Ester Boserup,

In the eleventh century, draining, irrigation, and other investments needed for intense agriculture were undertaken in northern Italy, and dikes and polders were built in the Netherlands as early as the tenth century. In the fourteenth and fifteenth centuries, fallow in these densely populated areas was replaced by fodder crops for domestic animals and by industrial crops. In most other parts of Western and Central Europe, similar changes had to await the wave of population increase in the eighteenth and nineteenth centuries.

Ester Boserup, *Population and Technological Change: A Study of Long-Term Trends* (Chicago, 1981), p. 103.

35. For most of modern history, scholars have held that population regulation was primarily a function of high mortality. See, for example, Carlo Cipolla, *Economic History of World Population* (Baltimore, 1962), pp. 76–77. An emphatic defense of the role of fertility control is made in Roger S. Schofield, "Through a Glass Darkly: *The Population History of England* as an Experiment in History," in Robert I. Rotberg and Theodore K. Rabb, eds., *Population and Economy: Population and History from the Traditional to the Modern World* (Cambridge, 1986).

36. Flinn, *European Demographic System,* p. 27; E. A. Wrigley, *Population and History,* (New York, 1969), p. 90.

37. Georges Duby, "L'Histoire des systèmes de valuers," *History and Theory* 11 (1972): 15–25.

38. H. J. Habbakuk, *Population Growth and Economic Development since 1750* (Leicester, 1972), pp. 17–20; Michael Anderson, "Historical Demography after *The Population History of England,*" in Rotberg and Rabb, eds., *Population and Economy,* pp. 41–44.

5

The Marxian Dynamic

Marxist historians dismiss the neo-Malthusian model. Subsistence crises were not occasioned by inexorable Malthusian forces. They were not even necessary. The crisis of the fourteenth century was brought about by *an exploitative system of feudal class relations* that permitted lords to consume conspicuously and to fight interminably while it precluded technological and organizational changes in agriculture that would have generated ample food for an expanding population. The neo-Malthusian model may account for alternating booms and slumps in aggregate economic activity, but it offers little or no illumination about how a new social order, like capitalism, takes its rise within an old social structure.

Marxists consider the commercial model to be no better. In its tendency to conceive history as no more than the progressive evolution of efficient markets, the commercial model muffles the heartbeat of the historical process. Adam Smith and Henri Pirenne saw merchants, markets, and commercial towns as external agents that persistently and systematically pulled a primitive economy toward ever-expanding levels of technological and institutional complexity. Their approach was compellingly simple, but it leads to the anachronistic imposition of modern bourgeois mentalities upon medieval peoples—and, argue the Marxists, it fails to discern that traders and townsmen, far from being external agents of change, were conservators of an abiding social structure.

More than any other thinker, Karl Marx has fashioned the intellectual landscape of modern historical scholarship. Marxists and non-Marxists alike have adopted his historical vocabulary, his categories of analysis, and his emphasis upon social and economic forces. To the extent that historians identify the modern age with capitalism, they reflect the Marxian view that capitalism constitutes a distinct social structure whose existence, from its advent to its demise, represents a major historical epoch. One of the most influential thinkers of our time, Michel Foucault, describes the impact of Marx:

> It is impossible at the present time to write history without using a whole range of concepts directly or indirectly linked to Marx's thought and situating one's self within a horizon of thought which has been defined and described by Marx. One might even wonder what difference there could ultimately be between being a historian and being a Marxist.[1]

Marxism is more than a theory of history. It is a revolutionary ideology—a purposeful, progressivist, even millenarian political philosophy. While interpreting history, Marxists have sought to change the world. Their politics have been informed by their theory of history, and their theory has always been sensitive to the changing demands of contemporary politics. Particular Marxist orientations became official doctrine in the Soviet Union after 1917, and during much of the Cold War, the Soviet position provided a common ideological denominator for communist activists throughout the world. For better or for worse, Marxist intellectuals were drawn into alliance with Moscow. They were dedicated to the destruction of capitalism; they had high hopes for the Soviet experiment; and all too often they served as apologists for its shortcomings. In the West, Marxist scholars were always subject to the criticism that their identity with Moscow or their affiliation with local communist parties compromised their intellectual integrity. None of Britain's distinguished Marxist historians—and there have been many— chose to focus his or her studies on the twentieth century, where a scholar's intellectual integrity and ideological loyalties might be brought into conflict with his or her political attachment to the Soviet Union or to the Party.[2]

If the Cold War imposed constraints upon Marxist theoreticians, it also generated critical scrutiny of Marxist theory by non-Marxist journalists and scholars. Each element of the Marxist canon was tested empirically. As errors or inconsistencies were exposed, Marxist historians adjusted their models and redirected their emphases. The revisions undertaken by innumerable Marxist scholars have been anything but uniform; consequently, the intellectual landscape of modern historical Marxism has become bewilderingly diverse. Marxist theory continues to divide Marxist historians from non-Marxists, and the nuances of theory separate one brand of Marxist from another.

All Marxism derives from a common source: the corpus of Karl Marx's written work. It is important, therefore, that we examine Marx briefly in the hope of understanding something of his objectives, his achievements, his shortcomings, and his relationship with Friedrich Engels, his co-author, intellectual companion, and survivor. Marx's attention swung alternately between philosophy and activism. Professor Robert Daniels discerned five distinct periods in his forty-year working life.[3] From 1841 to 1847, Marx made a philosophical migration from idealistic Hegelianism to materialism, focusing on economic conditions, class struggle, the role of the proletariat, and the concept of an ideal communist society. The years 1847–1852 were years of activism: participation in the revolutionary events of 1848, and co-authorship with Engels of *The Communist Manifesto.* With revolutionary movements in retreat across Europe after 1852, Marx repaired to the British Museum, where he undertook his greatest work, *Capital,* a three-volume exegesis upon the structure of capitalism, in particular British capitalism. From the mid-1860s to 1872, Marx devoted increasing energy to political activism, to the International Workingmen's Association, and during 1870, to the revolution in France. After 1872 his creative energies declined. He died in 1883.

Marx studied mature capitalism. His occasional forays into earlier historical periods were undertaken primarily to shed light on the origins and development of capitalism. Our knowledge of his historical periodization and our understanding of his concept of historical dynamics in the precapitalist era derive from limited, often sketchy, writings or by way of analogy from his detailed analysis of capitalism. At the root of Marx's theory are several cardinal principles. Most important, he was a doctrinaire materialist. People must eat and be sheltered before they can contemplate God, he argued: life is not determined by consciousness; consciousness is determined by the rigors of life. Two key concepts derive from his materialism: mode of production and class struggle. Unlike historians of the commercial school who focus on the distribution of scarce resources, Marx concentrated on production. That which distinguished one form of society from another was the mode by which wealth was produced. For Marx, history constituted the progressive journey of humankind through successive modes of production. The motor of change within each mode of production was class struggle, and the process by which change occurred was dialectic.

In his most compact and most oft-quoted theoretical statement on the dynamics of historical change,[4] Marx declared that mode of production, the system of work and of social relations by which material wealth is generated, "determines the general character of the social, political and spiritual processes of life." In other words, legal and political institutions as well as religious, family, and educational practices represent a social superstructure that is erected upon and derived from the economic base of society. This *base-superstructure* model constitutes an extreme example of economic determinism, or economism. Although it was modified by Marx in other writings, twentieth-century Marxists continue to debate the primacy, or at least the degree of primacy, of the economic base.

Each social structure, argued Marx, harbors internal contradictions that manifest themselves in *class relations*. The relationship that different groups of people experience to the process of production and the degree to which they possess productive forms of property determines, in the main, their class identity. In every society some people exercise control over the productive process, extracting ample surpluses for their pleasure. Others acquire relatively little surplus. They are repressed, restrained, or victimized by the productive process, and at some point they unite in opposition to it. The struggle of antagonistic classes over the appropriation of surplus provides the driving force of history.

Class struggle is played out through the predictable operation of "scientific dialectics." Each social structure generates within itself the seeds of its own destruction. In Marxian terms, the dominant class within a mode of production provokes opposition from less advantaged classes. The struggle between opposing classes ultimately leads to revolution and to the displacement of the old dominant class by a successor. That displacement does not occur, however, until the productive forces of the old order have become mature or until the material base for a new dominant order has developed "in the womb of the old society." When a new dominant class takes hold, it gives rise to the opposition of hostile classes. Struggle ensues, and in time that dominant class is replaced by yet another successor. By this means, history, propelled by class struggle, advances through successive modes of production.

In his Preface to *A Contribution to the Critique of Political Economy* (1859), Marx explained the transition from one mode of production to another in economistic terms. Incremental changes in productive technology or changes in the resources used in the productive process gradually undermine the close correspondence between the dominant class and the productive process, thereby rendering the dominant class vulnerable to revolution. In recent centuries, for example, there has been gradual change from the use of hand tools to machines as well as a change from organic sources of energy (e.g., timber) to inorganic sources (e.g., coal, petroleum). The increasing use of machines and inorganic sources of energy powerfully enhanced the prospects of the bourgeoisie in the productive process.

This enhancement occurred at the expense of an older dominant class, the nobility, whose economic roots were embedded in a fading productive order based upon hand tools and organic sources of energy. Because outmoded property relations and outmoded political power relations inhibited the full realization of the new productive order, the class representatives of that incipient order, the bourgeoisie, rose up, seized political power, and consolidated their command over the economy. In this way, one social structure, feudalism, was displaced by another, capitalism. For Marx, the French Revolution of 1789 was a classic transitional episode in which the bourgeoisie forcibly asserted its class control over the new productive system that had developed "in the womb" of the old.

"In broad outlines, " Marx declared, "we can designate the Asiatic, the ancient, the feudal, and the modern bourgeois [capitalist] methods of production as so many epochs." In other words, history was divisible into four stages, each distinguished by its mode of production. Under capitalism, Marx wrote, society was becoming divided into two great hostile classes: the bourgeoisie and the proletariat. When, in accordance with the dialectic, the inevitable proletarian revolution arrived, capitalism would give way to communism, a social structure in which private property was forbidden and wealth was equally divided. Under communism, social classes would cease to exist because class divisions, based on property, could not arise when private property had been abolished and material resources had been equally distributed. Without classes, there could be no class struggle. The new dominant order, communism, would not generate internal contradictions. The dialectical process of historical change would end. The millennium would have arrived.

This is a highly simplified and conservative synopsis of Marx's theory of history. In fact, it is somewhat presumptuous, if not flatly incorrect, to assert that Marx had a single theory of history. His published works, written over forty years, are replete with contradictions, ambiguities of language, and downright obfuscation. Some of the contradictions can be explained by Marx's changing orientations over time; some of them result from the publication of notes that Marx used in his own intellectual development—what he called "clarifying my own ideas."[5] Contradictions in Marx's philosophy are all the more difficult to reconcile because he was given to the use of strident and dogmatic language. In his Preface to the first German edition of *Capital*, for example, Marx claimed to have discovered "the natural laws of capitalist production . . . working with iron necessity towards inevitable results."

The kind of scientism suggested by this passage was even more characteristic of Engels than of Marx. A constant intellectual companion, Engels enjoyed his most productive years after 1872 when Marx's creative energies flagged. It was he, not Marx, who provided a systematic elaboration of dialectical philosophy. Engels rendered the dialectic process highly mechanistic and extended it beyond the realm of human history to encompass the natural world and the process of evolution. Engels's mechanistic emphasis was widely adopted by European Marxists after the Russian Revolution.[6]

In our time, a small academic industry has arisen, probing the depths of Marx's own scholarship, attempting to fathom his "real" intentions, trying to reconcile inconsistencies and to provide meaningful definitions for critical terms. No scholar has difficulty finding quotations from Marx to legitimate his or her particular analysis. On critical interpretive matters, however, the scholars remain in disarray. Clearly, the gospel according to Karl Marx will continue to be interpreted as variously as those of Matthew, Mark, Luke, and John.

ECONOMIC DETERMINISM

At the root of the interpretive muddle is determinism. In Marx's base-superstructure model, do the technical and material foundations of production dictate and determine all else in the social structure? Or do elements of the superstructure—religious tenets, legal traditions, social and political practices—influence, moderate, or even direct aspects of the economic base? If an organic two-way relationship does persist between base and superstructure, what are the dynamics of that relationship? Are they the same in all societies? Or does each historical situation dictate a different dynamic? If it does, can Marxist theory be predictive? If Marxism is not predictive, what do we make of Engels's scientism or Marx's claim to have discovered a natural law that works "with iron necessity towards inevitable results?"

Marx himself did more to confuse than to clarify the issue. Take, for example, a single passage in his 1859 Preface:

> At a certain stage of their development, the material *forces of production* in society come in conflict with the existing *relations of production*, or—what is but a legal expression of the same thing— with the property relations within which they had been at work before. From forms of development of the forces of production these relations turn into their fetters. Then comes the period of social revolution. With the change of the economic foundation the entire immense superstructure is more or less rapidly transformed. [emphasis added]

Apart from the sheer difficulty of this language, Marx never explicitly defined what he meant by "forces of production" or "relations of production." The passage appears to contend that changes wrought in the material circumstances of production (forces of production) evoke and intensify contradictions in the social order (relations of production), ultimately giving rise to social revolution. This interpretation has encouraged many scholars to emphasize economic determinism and the absolute primacy of the economic base.[7]

Theoretically, Marx probably preferred this approach. It accorded with his concept of the future transition from capitalism to communism. Yet he was not able to reconcile his economistic model with past events, most notably the transition from feudalism to capitalism. The historical chapters of *Capital* I and III invert the base-superstructure model, contending that the development of capitalist forces of production (the economic base) was a by-product of the prior establishment of capitalist relations of production—that is, business institutions, authority structures, market facilities, and property relations—which had demonstrated their ability to generate larger material surpluses.[8]

The issue of determinism spills over into every aspect of Marxian historiography. Obvious questions arise concerning Marx's periodization and his theory of progressive historical stages. Must all countries pass through the same, or similar, stages of historical development? Does the movement of peoples through history always involve a unilinear progression from a slave mode of production to a feudal mode of production to a capitalist mode to communism? In his Preface to the first edition of *Capital* I, Marx observed that "the country that is more developed industrially only shows, to the less developed, the image of its own future," a statement that has consistently been used to afirm a unilinear progressivist view of history. Yet, just as stridently, Marx denied having authored a "historiophilosophical theory of the general path every people is fated to tread."[9]

What about human agency in history? Since Marxism is both a revolutionary creed and a theory of history, Marxists have attempted to reconcile economic determinism with voluntarism. What historical role do revolutionary activists play? If the course of history is predetermined, can political activism be of any utility? Marx was more, rather than less, inclined to affirm the value of human agency in determining the course of history. His followers, beginning with Engels, generally encouraged activism as a means of hastening the course of events, albeit with an important qualifier. Political activism, it was stressed, can only be meaningful when it functions in accordance with the natural laws of history. It cannot alter the general direction of history.

CLASS STRUGGLE ANALYSIS

Modern Marxist historians who resist or reject the rigorous economism of the base-superstructure model have generally adopted class struggle as the thematic centerpiece of their work. But class struggle analysis presents its own problems, some practical, some philosophical. Neither Marx nor Engels ever provided a systematic exposition of the concept of class even though Marx's discovery of the "proletariat" prompted his studies of capitalism and inspired his claim that the "history of all hitherto existing society is the history of class struggles."[10] Is class rooted in economic structure, as the base-superstructure model assumes? Conventional economistic Marxists affirm the model: social consciousness derives from social being, and social being is framed by the material circumstances of the mode of production. This seemingly straightforward proposition can be a problem for the historian. How does a historian, working with evidence that is several centuries old, distinguish one class from another? Is occupation a sufficient criterion of class?

This question was addressed in the first systematic investigation of the American class structure undertaken from an explicitly Marxian perspective.[11] Erik Olin Wright and a team of researchers discovered that occupational status was *not* a sufficient criterion of class. In contemporary society at least, occupation would be a highly misleading determinant of class. The research team, working with live subjects, found it necessary to conduct a survey of those subjects in order to validate their class position. If the team had been forced to define the subjects' class by occupational category, it would have misclassified up to 45 percent of the people in the survey![12] Considering the difficulties in discerning class distinctions encountered by contemporary researchers, how can historians hope to achieve a finely tuned understanding of bygone class structures? Because historians rarely have the opportunity to survey living subjects, they are compelled to rely upon the type of empirical data—census records, tax lists, occupational status—that Wright et al. found highly misleading.[13]

Among the philosophical issues raised by class struggle analysis is the problem of anachronism. In recent years, historians have come to realize that the Marxian concept of class, particularly as it relates to class consciousness and class identity, is historically specific *only* to an urban, industrial society. Urban proletarians may have developed an acute sense of class. But peasants living in agrarian societies never possessed strong class identity.[14] Is it possible for people to act together in specifically class ways if they are not conscious of their class identity? Is class struggle a meaningful engine of historical change in epochs that predate the evolution of modern class consciousness?

All of these questions have been examined by E. P. Thompson, a free-spirited English Marxist historian. His masterwork, *The Making of the English Working Class* (1963), demonstrated that genuine class identity only emerged among British workers during the decades between 1780 and 1832. Thompson rejected economic determinism in the formation of class, and he lamented that Marx, Engels, and most Marxists since them had unduly saddled themselves with static models and misguided assertions about iron "laws" of history. Class is not a thing. It is not the automatic by-product of mode of production. It is not a mathematically defined body of people standing in a particular relation to the means of production. Nor can it be defined or discerned by theoretical formulas. Production relations (including occupational status) provide coloration and tonality to the class experience, but class is, above all, a fluid, constantly changing "*historical* phenomenon" experienced by men and women who share the pleasures and the penalties of a common cultural context:

> If we stop history at a given point, then there are no classes but simply a multitude of individuals with a multitude of experiences. But if we watch these men over an adequate period of social change,

we observe patterns in their relationships, their ideas, and their institutions. Class is defined by men as they live their own history, and, in the end, this is its only definition.[15]

As for the problem of anachronism, Thompson offers the following:

To put it bluntly: classes do not exist as separate entities, look around, find an enemy class, and then start to struggle. On the contrary, people find themselves in a society structured in determined ways (crucially, but not exclusively, in productive relations), they experience exploitation (or the need to maintain power over those whom they exploit), they identify points of antagonistic interest, they commence to struggle around these issues and in the process of struggling they discover themselves as classes, they come to know this discovery as class-consciousness. Class and class-consciousness are always the last, not the first stage in the historical process.[16]

In effect, class struggle *can* antedate class consciousness in the sense that exploitative human relationships occasion antagonism between social groups, producing conflicts that are structured in class ways even before self-conscious class formations have arisen.

Thompson has thrown down the gauntlet to Marxist historians and to non-Marxist historians alike. In order to fathom class in a bygone society, the historian must achieve profound intimacy with a bewildering array of people, of groups, of attitudes and beliefs; the historian must mediate between the vocal and the silent, between the advocates of causes and the faceless multitudes whose collective inner will can be discerned only by their actions. Combining empirical research with patience, perception, and "historical logic," he or she must attempt to comprehend how culture has comingled with the material circumstances of life to produce class, and how class (consciously or unconsciously) has served to resist or to promote change.

Thompson's work reset the battleground upon which Marxists contest points of theory and methodology. Economic determinists, even those of moderate disposition, reacted strongly to Thompson's "culturalism," insisting that he gave insufficient attention to the deep structural phenomena that have shaped human attitudes and behavior. Would the English working class have evolved as it did had there been no Industrial Revolution?

At another level, structuralists, following the lead of the French Marxist, Louis Althusser, reject all historical empiricism, especially that of

Thompson, insisting that real history is unknowable and that attempts to fathom the inner consciousness of earlier peoples can only lead to false consciousness and misunderstanding. Since the past is inaccessible, argue the structuralists, theoretical knowledge is the only true knowledge. For Marxism in particular, true theory is discernable only through a critical reading of Marx that discards teleological argumentation and logical inconsistencies. In sum, theory is not an aid to historical understanding. Theory is history.

WHAT IS A MARXIST HISTORIAN?

Considering these sharply divergent viewpoints, how does one define "the Marxist historian"? Some Marxist historians continue to pursue orthodox historical materialism, utilizing an economically determined base-superstructure model while periodizing history in accordance with changing modes of production. Others (like Thompson) deny the paramount directing influence of economic forces and give equal or near-equal weight to superstructural elements in determining the character of social formations. Some self-proclaimed Marxist historians avoid direct encounter with the base-superstructure model although they acknowledge the primacy of material forces. Some pay little heed either to mode of production or to class struggle while, at the same time, they emphasize exploitative social relationships. Some reject empiricism in any form, deriving an understanding of the past through the systematic elaboration of theory. These latter, the structuralists, offer little of value to historians save a sobering reminder of the dangers and limitations of their discipline. Marxists of every stamp share a vocabulary bequeathed them by Marx, but they define common terms differently, causing confusion in their own ranks and bewilderment outside them. Marxists do employ common designations for historical periods, though many would deny Marx's theory of progressive stages, and they do focus scholarly attention upon two epochs—the feudal and capitalist periods. But disagreement abounds concerning when and why the epochal transition from feudalism to capitalism occurred. In its manifold diversity, historical Marxism constitutes a contemporary school of thought only to the extent that its practitioners share some ideological orientations to the past. What is a Marxist historian? It is someone who, in professing to be a Marxist historian, can justify his or her claim by adherence, however small, to some aspect of Marx's historical theory.[17]

THE TRANSITION FROM FEUDALISM TO CAPITALISM

Despite the ahistorical negativism of the structuralists, Marxist historians have been compelled to reconcile their theories of history with the actual record of history. Otherwise, they could never hope to earn the respect of non-Marxist historians or achieve the conversion of others to their points of view. The central problematic for Marxist historians has always been the rise of capitalism. In keeping with Marx's theory of historical stages, how, when, where, and by what agency did the transition from a feudal mode of production to the capitalist mode of production occur? Marx did not undertake a systematic analysis of the internal dynamics of the feudal mode of production; in fact, not until the appearance of Maurice Dobb's *Studies in the Development of Capitalism* (1946) did a Marxist scholar attempt to explain, in comprehensive detail, the process of transition from feudalism to capitalism.[18] Dobb's work evoked an electrifying debate, attracting contributions from leading Marxist luminaries around the world. While agreement on many aspects of theory and interpretation emerged, the debate exposed vital areas of disagreement that continue to divide Marxist writers. What follows in this chapter is an attempt to identify the critical issues raised in that controversy, the main points of consensus, and the chief areas of dispute.

Dobb adopted the logic of the 1859 Preface: Marx's emphasis on the primacy of economic forces, on the dialectical process, on the concept that change occurs through class conflict, on the view that class conflict derives from contradictions within the dominant mode of production, and on Marx's assertion that the transition from one epoch to another must ultimately be consummated by the revolutionary action of a new dominant class. Having subscribed to the proposition that the feudal mode of production must give way to capitalism, Dobb and his allies developed precise definitions for both feudalism and capitalism. Feudalism, Dobb declared, was virtually identical to serfdom. In the feudal mode of production, unfree producers remained attached to the land but in possession of their own primitive tools. They were compelled, independently of their own volition, to render payments to their overlords in the form of labor, dues, money, or goods in kind. The precise nature of the payment was not critical. That payments involved the forced extraction of surplus above that required to sustain the lives of unfree producers was critical. Extractions were made possible by the military, juridical, and political power exercised by the feudal elite.

In the capitalist mode of production, it is argued, ownership of the means of production (e.g., tools, factories, raw materials, sources of energy) is concentrated in the hands of a relatively small class, the bourgeoisie. The rest of society, lacking ownership of the means of production, is obliged to sell its labor as a commodity in order to earn a livelihood. The bourgeoisie acquires the productive labor of the proletariat through freely undertaken wage contracts, not by compulsion, legal or otherwise. The surplus generated by the productive system, above that required to sustain the mere existence of the proletariat, accrues to the bourgeoisie.

Marxists readily appreciate that history does not offer a succession of "pure" modes of production. Nevertheless, each prevailing mode has its own "law of motion." In the feudal mode, the prime mover was the ceaseless struggle between lords and peasants over feudal rent. As the nobles' revenue requirements increased, they extracted ever-expanding levels of surplus from their peasants. Concurrently, the peasants strove to increase the amount of surplus retained by them. Feudal lords did not behave like modern commercial agribusinessmen, minimizing costs and maximizing efficiency. Little or no thought was given to estate management. Feudal properties were the source of social prestige and political and military power. A lord enhanced his prestige and power by expanding his holdings and enlarging the number of his dependents. The former was chiefly accomplished by warfare, the latter by subinfeudation, a process by which the number of vassals owing fealty to a lord was increased. Combined with the natural enlargement of noble families, subinfeudation increased the parasitic class that had to be sustained from the surplus product of serf labor. The Crusades added additional burdens upon the servile class, and the growth of markets multiplied the lords' opportunity for conspicuous consumption. To satisfy their numerous indulgences, the nobles consistently intensified their squeeze on the serfs.

The agrarian economy upon which this burden fell was primitive. Innovations in the productive process were relatively few, and the geographical dispersion of innovation was slow. After three centuries of population growth, land for new settlements was exhausted in Western Europe, and many villages barely survived on inferior soils. At the same time, market activity created greater social stratification among servile producers. The better-off peasants sold more of their surplus at market, acquired more estate land for their own use, and hired the wage labor of poorer peasants. As the lords' demand for revenue increased, the richer peasants objected vehemently to increased demands on their small surpluses. Their antagonism was powerfully reinforced by despairing poor peasants who were driven to (or beyond) the margin of subsistence by the lords' increasing demands for rent. By the fourteenth century, the lords could not extract more and the serfs could not provide more. The feudal mode was in crisis.

Beleaguered peasants fled the manors in increasing numbers. With the onset of the Black Death, labor shortages multiplied. The lords, in their so-called feudal reaction, tried to restore discipline through draconian legislation. Peasant revolts—the Jacquerie in France, peasant rebellion in England in 1381, and risings in Germany, Spain and the Low Countries—were decided in favor of the lords, but demographic realities, the empowered bargaining position of the peasants, and the need of lords to make concessions to retain ample estate labor conspired, over time, to free the peasants from bondage.

Before the end of the fifteenth century, peasants were no longer attached to the soil. Many were still obligated to grind their grain at the lord's mill, to pay entry fines, and to remain subject to the jurisdiction of manorial courts, but the disciplinary prerogatives of the lords had eroded. The feudal order, wrote Dobb, had disintegrated in many ways:

> The ranks of the old nobility were thinned and divided; and the smaller estates, lacking sufficient labour-services, had taken to leasing or to wage-labour as soon as the increase of population and in particular of the ranks of the poorer peasantry had made labour cheap again. Merchants were buying land; estates were being mortgaged; and a *kulak* class of improving peasant farmers were becoming serious competitors in local markets and as rural employers of labour.[19]

THE AWKWARD CENTURIES: 1500–1700

If we accept Dobb's contention that the feudal mode of production was roughly identical to serfdom, then the feudal mode of production was moribund by the fifteenth century. The capitalist mode of production, as defined by Dobb, did not take hold in Europe until the seventeenth century at the earliest, and then only in England. How do Marxist historians categorize the awkward period between 1500 and 1700? Paul Sweezy, an American Marxist, suggested that the period be redefined as a time of "pre-capitalist commodity production," a distinct but lesser stage of historical development lodged between the greater epochs of feudalism and capitalism.[20] Dobb rejected any modification of Marx's stages theory, arguing that Europe was feudal until, by the revolutionary action of the bourgeoisie, it became capitalist. In response to Sweezy, Dobb posed a critical question: what was the ruling class of the awkward centuries, 1500–1700?[21] He answered the question. The ruling class in the sixteenth and seventeenth centuries was the traditional feudal nobility, and the monarchical state in Europe continued to serve as the political instrument of feudal rule.

In *Studies in the Development of Capitalism*, Dobb had tried, within reason, to keep faith with the base-superstructure model. Sweezy's challenge exposed the model's fragility. How long can a superstructure, shorn of its economic base, sustain its independent existence before the logic of the base-superstructure model is undermined? A century? Two centuries? Sensing his weakness, Dobb redirected the focus of attention from judicious economism and mode of production to class. Feudalism persisted from the fifteenth through the seventeenth century *because Europe continued to be ruled by the feudal class.*

Class struggle analysis has increasingly dominated historical explanation among Marxists. Louis Althusser, the structuralist theoretician, observed that the "political regime of the absolute monarchy [was] only the new political form needed for the maintenance of feudal domination and exploitation in the period of development of a commodity economy."[22] Pursuing this idea, Perry Anderson published *Lineages of the Absolutist State* (1974), contending that absolutism, the leading political medium of the early modern period, was essentially the "redeployed and recharged apparatus of feudal domination." It was designed to keep the peasant masses back in their traditional social position despite any gains they had made through their release from serfdom.[23] When the class power of the feudal lords was threatened by the dissolution of serfdom, the nobility deliberately reposed their power with a centralized, militarized monarchy whose "permanent political function was the repression of the peasant and plebeian masses at the foot of the social hierarchy."[24]

The absolutist state was feudalism writ large, argues Anderson. It was a machine built for war. The rationale for feudal warfare was the maximization of power, prestige, and wealth. Land was the chief object of conflict, and the ceaseless squeeze on peasant resources provided nobles the material means to fight. In the absolutist state, these conditions persisted. War was perpetual. Land was the chief object of struggle; tax systems were created to support armies; and the peasants were squeezed to provide the means to fight. Other attributes of the absolutist system further advanced the interests of the nobility. Royal bureaucracies provided public offices to members of the nobility. Such offices were used to stabilize or recoup fortunes, "a kind of monetarized caricature of investiture in a fief."[25] Tax systems were a form of centralized feudal rent. The lords were exempt from many taxes, while tax burdens weighed heavily on commoners. Even the weakening of vassalage relations worked to the lords' advantage. Under the original fief system, land holding by leading members of the nobility and their vassals had been conditional upon service. With the growth of Roman Law and its concept of absolute private property—a condition that conferred primary benefit upon the bourgeoisie—the lords were able to assume unqualified property rights in their estates.

From the beginning of historical Marxism, the length of time between the decline of feudalism and rise of capitalism has been an awkward historical problem. Engels addressed the question. Like Anderson, he attributed the length of the transition to the rise of absolutism, but his conclusions were sharply different from those of Anderson. The class representatives of feudalism and capitalism (the nobility and the bourgeoisie) were stalemated for two centuries, wrote Engels: they were balanced and offset by absolutist monarchs who exercised independence from both classes and mediated between them.[26] Using the same triad, Robert Brenner, a Marxist economic historian, considers absolutist kings the competitors of the nobility, not their protectors and not the mediators between them and the bourgeoisie.[27] Brenner's position bears resemblance to that of the commercial school, whose authors have considered the alliance between kings and the bourgeoisie to have been a means of advancing capitalism and undermining the nobility.

There is something to say for and against each of these arguments. Anderson's position seems least tenable. He declared it his intention to integrate history with theory, but his historical chapters are replete with evidence that could be used to support an opposite conclusion. Did the nobles of Europe consider the absolutist kings their protectors or the usurpers of their traditional powers? There were numerous armed struggles between the nobles and kings, the Fronde being only the most famous, and noble-dominated regional estates across Europe bitterly resisted the grant of taxes to monarchs. In seventeenth-century France, the monarchy responded to this resistance by drawing up to 38 percent of its income from the sale of offices. To whom were the bulk of these offices sold? To wealthy members of the bourgeoisie. There was a massive absorption of the bourgeoisie into the fabric of the absolutist state by the system of purchase. Anderson himself declares that the purchase of offices was so profitable an investment of capital for members of the bourgeoisie that money was diverted from manufacturing and mercantile ventures into collusion with absolutism. For whom, then, was absolutism a shield? The bourgeoisie or the nobility? And what portion of the nobility—those people owning estates and assuming the appearance of a feudal class—were actually of bourgeois origin?

This confusion of classes and class-consciousness constitutes a serious problem for Marxist historians. It would seem that real actors on the world's historical stage frequently failed to recognize what latter-day historians would perceive as their class interest. Nor did they consistently act in conformity with it. Edward Thompson alluded to this in *The Making of the English Working Class,* cautioning that whenever class is presumed to be a fixed condition in which people stand in some relation to the means of production, writers are all too disposed to describe class-consciousness "not as it is, but as it ought to be."[28]

THE ADVENT OF CAPITALISM

It is one thing to argue, as Dobb and Anderson have, that in spite of the erosion of feudal economic structures, feudal class power was preserved in England through the seventeenth century and in France and other continental states through the eighteenth century. It is another thing to identify clearly the economic processes by which a capitalist mode of production came into being. Before capitalism could take hold, three conditions had to be met, argue the Marxists. First, laborers had to be separated from the means of production so that labor itself could become a commodity for sale in the market. Second, capital—real money power—had to accumulate in unprecedented volume, and these accumulated resources had to be invested in revised methods of production. Third, when new productive relations had matured in the "womb" of the old system, the representatives of the new order had to rise up in revolutionary action to assert their class control over political, social, and economic institutions. Since the transition to capitalism occurred first in England, most historical attention has been directed to the English experience.

In order to create a free market in industrial labor, working people had to be displaced from the land. Also, agricultural productivity had to rise in order that displaced workers could be fed. In England, this was achieved in two ways. There was an unparalleled growth in the number of aggrandizing peasant farmers, the so-called kulaks, who amassed power and property at the expense of less successful peasants and who were, in a great many cases, assimilated into the gentry. Kulaks consolidated village lands. Their successes were recorded at the expense of poor peasants who lost land and became propertyless, or near propertyless, agricultural wage workers—a rural proletariat. At the same time, class struggle was under way between the traditional manor lords and their peasants, the former using whatever weapons they still possessed, including entry fines, to pry peasants off their customary plots in the open fields so that those lands could be reorganized and consolidated for more efficient and profitable production. Although major agrarian risings erupted over these matters during the sixteenth century—the northern revolt of the 1530s and Ket's Rebellion of 1549—the power of the landlords prevailed. Much of England's pasture land was consolidated, and arable farming assumed a pattern whereby great landowners subdivided their acreage into large tenant farms, which were leased on long-term contracts to "capitalist" farmers. In turn, the tenant farmers hired agricultural proletarians as wage laborers. By 1700, Robert Brenner observes, 70 to 75 percent of the cultivable land of England was controlled by large landowners. Capitalist relations were evolving on the land; excess proletarians were being displaced to the towns; and the productivity of English agriculture, having become more adaptable to technological innovation and capital inputs, was rising.[29]

The accumulation of capital is the second prerequisite for the transition to capitalism. There is no doubt that money capital had been accumulating for centuries. The histories of Venice, Genoa, Bruges, Antwerp, and a host of other cities bear ample evidence to this. Marx himself declared that European plundering of the New World and the East Indies was the "chief momenta of primitive accumulation." The problem for Marxists is not whether capital was accumulating, but how to define the class role played by the merchants who fostered this accumulation. Marx himself insisted that the replacement of one mode of production by another does not depend on commerce. It depends on the nature of the old mode of production. Each mode of production generates within itself the contradictions that give rise to antagonistic class struggles. In the feudal mode of production, the struggle over rent created a dialectical confrontation between landlords and peasants.

In this confrontation, where did the ever-rising bourgeoisie stand? What role is to be given to the long-distance merchants heralded by Pirenne and the commercial school as an external element that broke into the natural agrarian economy of the Middle Ages and precipitated its destruction? Marxist writers reject Pirenne. Long-distance merchants were not external to the feudal economy, they argue. Far from precipitating the destruction of the system, great merchants sought to preserve it.

The Marxists' argument derives from their emphasis on production. Merchants were engaged in distribution, in conveying articles for sale from one place to another. They did not change the structure of production. They did not alter the character of the articles sold. They earned profits through arbitrage, taking advantage of price differentials prevailing between markets that were distant from one another. The great long-distance merchants formed merchant guilds in medieval towns, and their merchant guilds generally dominated the various craft guilds. In time, leading merchants assumed control over the organization of production. They acquired contracts from distant buyers to deliver specific goods that were fabricated in their towns; they set the craft guildsmen, their fellow-townsmen, to work producing those goods; and ultimately they became de facto employers of the craft guildsmen because they controlled the access to raw materials and the markets for finished goods. The effect of this process was to proletarianize craft guildsmen.

The merchants' activities went further still. They initiated the practice of putting-out; that is, they distributed some forms of industrial work, like wool spinning, to rural people who performed labor in their cottages with raw materials supplied them by the merchants. Putting-out permitted merchants to enlarge the scope of their operations, to evade guild restrictions in the towns, and to obtain labor at a price below that paid to town workers. All the same, neither putting-out nor the merchants' exercise of hegemony over craft guildsmen altered the prevailing mode of production. The prevailing system of petty commodity production remained intact. Only the administration of it was altered. It terms of production, the merchants were not a revolutionary class.

Nor were they revolutionary in social and political terms. From the earliest days, merchants were parasites of the landlord class. They supplied the nobility with consumables and credits, and they lived off the lords' largesse. At no time did they attack the feudal structure. Often, they demonstrated solidarity with the lords in their struggles against the peasants. The goal of long-distance merchants was not to endanger the system but to "muscle in" on the privileged position of the lordly class. Indeed, wrote Dobb, the merchant bourgeoisie, far from being a progressive force for change in history, retarded the development of capitalism as a mode of production.[30]

That retardation was occasioned by commercial monopolies. In the sixteenth and seventeenth centuries, the time when absolutist aspirations excited monarchies across Western Europe, merchants and kings achieved a symbiotic relationship. Great merchants made loans to royalty and engaged in contracts to equip their armies and supply their courts. In exchange, they received monopoly rights over every manner of trade. In England, there was the fifteenth-century Company of Merchant Adventurers, a group of merchants having the exclusive privilege of trading cloth to the Low Countries. A parade of chartered monopolies followed: in 1553, the Russia Company; in 1555, the Africa Company; in 1577, the Spanish Company; in 1600, the East India Company. These are but a few. Monopoly restricted major trading opportunities to a privileged few, and it stifled developmental changes in the structure of production.

Since Marxist historians characterize privileged merchants as parasites and allies of the feudal elite, they must, to fulfill the logic of the dialectic, specify some other bourgeois element to serve as class antagonist to the feudal establishment. In accord with Marxist theory, that class antagonist would, at a decisive moment, rise up, seize power, and set in place the social and political apparatus of a capitalist mode of production. The chief candidate for this role was the enterprising artisan. Marx thought the new mode of production would take hold when commerce was subordinated to production. That would happen when artisans stopped producing merely for local consumption and began, as employers of wage labor, to produce for a larger national or international market. The basis of their earning power would not depend upon monopoly privileges in the distribution of goods but in greater efficiency and higher levels of productivity in the production of goods. This, Marx considered, was the "really revolutionary way," a way that subordinated commerce to production. In practice, however, Marxist scholars have had difficulty demonstrating that the capitalist mode of production emerged via the artisans in this "really revolutionary way." On the other hand, there is ample evidence that the great merchants, despite their monopolies, accelerated progress toward what Marxists define as the capitalist mode of production.

The great discoveries and the opening of direct trade with the East evoked enormous demands for capital investment, for shipping, and for the supply of vital commodities in intercontinental trade. The exploding size of royal armies required the services of large-scale suppliers of weapons. Mines were being driven much deeper, at far greater cost. In England, the first paper mills, cannon factories, and sugar refineries were established in the sixteenth century, each of them requiring relatively high capital investment. There is little likelihood that these industries could have evolved so successfully had the state not provided them with secure contracts and protection from foreign competition. Artisans—even extraordinary artisans—could not expand their operations quickly enough to accommodate the rising scale of demand or to meet the need for regularity and uniformity in the output of armaments. For commerce to become subordinate to production in the "really revolutionary way," production had to become more profitable. Increased profitability could only be achieved through industrial innovation, but even by the early eighteenth century Europe's industrial technology was essentially what it had been in the fifteenth century. In the early eighteenth century, the normal pattern of manufacturing involved a host of tiny shops operated by individual artisans. If the great merchants did not revolutionize production, they did at least coordinate and direct the production of these artisans. The effect of this was to increase output, heighten demand, and encourage a level of consumerism that set the stage for technical innovation at the end of the eighteenth century. Even when Europe entered the Industrial Revolution, utilizing what Marxists would agree was a capitalist mode of production, the industrial innovators were no more likely to emerge from the artisan class than from merchant communities.[31]

THE REVOLUTIONARY SEIZURE OF POWER

The Marxian thesis that representatives of a new mode of production would finalize the process of transition by taking revolutionary action against defenders of the old economic structure has generated intense debate in recent decades. Encouraged by the work of Georges Lefebvre in France[32] and Christopher Hill in England,[33] Marxists ardently adopted the English Civil War, 1642–1649, and the French Revolution, 1789, as critical watersheds when the bourgeoisie forcibly asserted its primacy in society. In his original thesis, Hill conceived the English Civil War as a confrontation between two well-defined and self-conscious class entities, the bourgeoisie and the aristocracy, the former representing trading and industrial interests in the towns as well as yeomen and lesser gentry (kulaks) who were determined to wrest power from the feudal elite and advance the interests of capitalism. The monarchy, allied with the feudal elite, enjoyed the support of the great monopolistic merchants. Marxist historians considered Hill's work the opening gambit in a constructive debate on mode of production in the seventeenth century and on the class configuration of English society. Non-Marxists considered it a call to arms, and in the years that followed they dismantled it piece by piece.[34] We cannot probe these debates here. Suffice it to say, Hill was obliged to modify his position, ultimately affirming only that the Civil War established conditions that were more favorable to capitalism than those that persisted in England before 1642. The debate on the French Revolution has been at least as intense and, on balance, somewhat less baleful to the Marxian position, although in the French case as well the more strident early assertions of Marxist writers have been systematically discredited.[35]

CONCLUSION

The contribution of Marxists to modern historical scholarship can hardly be exaggerated. Marx's identification of modernity with capitalism has taken root across the spectrum of historical opinion, and the specific categories of analysis employed by Marxist scholars, especially the concepts of class and class struggle, have been widely adopted in the profession. No mode of interpretation has been more provocative of debate, either within or without the ranks of the converted. No form of theory has taken so many tangents or offered such kaleidoscopic variation. That Marxism has been a seedbed for both sympathetic and antithetic modes of historical interpretation is a testament to the compelling force of many of its most fundamental propositions.

NOTES

1. Quoted in Jeffrey Weeks, "Foucault for Historians," *History Workshop Journal* 14 (1982): 108.

2. This does not mean that some scholars did not defy the Party. When the British Communist Party refused to condemn the Soviet invasion of Hungary in 1956, three of the leading socialist historians in Britain—Rodney Hilton, Christopher Hill, and E. P. Thompson—resigned from the Party. Two other renowned historians stayed in: Maurice Dobb and Eric Hobsbawm. Harvey J. Kaye, *The British Marxist Historians* (New York, 1984), p. 17.

3. Robert V. Daniels, "Marxian Theories of Historical Dynamics," in Werner J. Cahnman and Alvin Boskoff, eds., *Sociology and History: Theory and Research* (New York, 1964), p. 63.

4. Marx's "Preface" to his *Contribution to the Critique of Political Economy* (New York, 1904; first published, 1859).

5. David McLellan, *Karl Marx: His Life and Thought* (New York, 1973), p. 305.

6. Daniels, "Marxian Theories," p. 72.

7. G. A. Cohen, *Karl Marx's Theory of History: A Defense* (Princeton, 1978), p. 165.

8. Jon Elster, *Making Sense of Marx* (Cambridge, 1985), p. 285.

9. These points are succinctly argued in Tom Bottomore, ed., *A Dictionary of Marxist Thought* (Cambridge, Mass., 1983), pp. 117–119.

10. This statement appeared in the early portion of Marx and Engels's *Manifesto of the Communist Party,* which was published in February 1848. For the original text of the *Manifesto* and a comprehensive introduction to it, see Howard J. Laski, *Howard J. Laski on the Communist Manifesto* (New York, 1967).

11. Erik Olin Wright, Cynthia Costello, David Hachen, and Joey Sprague, "The American Class Structure," *American Sociological Review* 47 (1982): 709.

12. Ibid., p. 719.

13. Numerous scholars have attacked the conventional Marxist position that the French Revolution was a "bourgeois" revolution by demonstrating that the French bourgeoisie was a congeries of highly diverse groups whose attitudes toward the revolution were widely varied. See, for example, Alfred Cobban, *The Social Interpretation of the French Revolution* (Cambridge, 1964), and George V. Taylor, "Non-Capitalist Wealth and the French Revolution," *American Historical Review* 72 (1967): 486–496.

14. A distinguished French sociologist-historian, Roland Mousnier, initiated a major debate in the early 1970s by declaring that the concept of class was inappropriate to pre-industrial Europe. Rather, he argued, Europeans were stratified by a hierarchy of "orders" based upon the dignity that society attached to particular social functions. For his argument on Europe as a "society of orders," see Roland Mousnier, *Social Hierarchies, 1450 to the Present*, trans. Peter Evans (New York, 1973).

15. E. P. Thompson, *The Making of the English Working Class* (New York, 1966), p. 11.

16. Quoted in Kaye, *British Marxist Historians*, p. 201.

17. Paul Hirst, a structuralist, makes the point well: "There is no such thing as 'orthodox Marxism.' All 'orthodoxies'—Kautsky's, Lukacs', Stalin's—are particular theoretical constructions culled out of the possibilities within the complex whole of Marx and Engel's discourse." He says much the same thing about structuralism. See Paul Hirst, "The Necessity of Theory," *Economy and Society* 8 (1979): 420, 443.

18. Maurice Dobb was a leading Marxist theoretician in England. Between 1924 and 1967, he was lecturer, then reader in economics at Cambridge University, where he provided guidance to several generations of young communists and communist sympathizers.

19. Maurice Dobb, *Studies in the Development of Capitalism* (New York, 1984), p. 65.

20. Paul Sweezy, "A Critique," in Rodney Hilton et al., *The Transition from Feudalism to Capitalism* (London, 1978), p. 51.

21. Maurice Dobb, "A Reply," in Hilton et al., *The Transition from Feudalism to Capitalism*, p. 62.

22. Quoted in Perry Anderson, *Lineages of the Absolutist State* (London, 1974), pp. 18–19.

23. Ibid., p. 18.

24. Ibid., p. 19.

25. Ibid., p. 33.

26. Friedrich Engels, *Origin of the Family*, Kerr edition (Chicago, 1902), p. 209.

27. Robert Brenner, "Agrarian Class Structure and Economic Development in Pre-Industrial Europe," *Past and Present* 70 (1976): 63-73.

28. Thompson, *The Making*, p. 10.

29. Brenner, "Agrarian Class Structure," pp. 61–62.

30. Dobb, *Studies*, p. 122.

31. J-F. Bergier, "The Industrial Bourgeoisie and the Rise of the Working Class 1700–1914," in Carlo Cipolla, ed., *The Fontana Economic History of Europe*, vol. 3 (Glasgow, 1973), pp. 408–412.

32. Georges Lefebvre, *The Coming of the French Revolution, 1789*, trans. R. R. Palmer (Princeton, 1947).

33. Christopher Hill, *The English Revolution, 1640* (London, 1955). This essay was first published in 1940 in a three-essay collection.

34. The protracted debate involving Christopher Hill, R. H. Tawney, H. R. Trevor-Roper, Lawrence Stone, and others occupied two decades. J. H. Hexter's "Storm over the Gentry," *Encounter* (May 1958), reproduced in his *Reappraisals in History* (Evanston, 1962) and Perez Zagorin's "The Social Interpretation of the English Revolution," *Journal of Economic History* 19 (1959): 376–401, capped the controversy in a fashion inimical to the interpretive interests of Marxists. For an overview of historiography on the issue, see R. C. Richardson, *The Debate on the English Revolution* (New York, 1977).

35. Many of the most important scholarly contributions to the debate have been collected in a book designed for students. See Ralph W. Greenlaw, ed., *The Social Origins of the French Revolution: The Debate on the Role of the Middle Classes* (Lexington, 1975). William Doyle, *Origins of the French Revolution* (New York, 1980), provides an excellent summary of the state of the question. For an evaluation of Marxist writings on the 1789 experience, see G. Ellis, "The 'Marxist Interpretation' of the French Revolution," *English Historical Review* 93 (1978): 353–376.

6

Weber, Sombart, and the Spirit of Capitalism

Two world-renowned German sociologists, Max Weber (1864–1920) and Werner Sombart (1863–1941), vehemently affirmed Marx's belief that capitalism constituted a distinct social formation in Western history. For them, the advent of capitalism marked the beginning of modern history. All of their historical work was devoted to understanding capitalist culture, its spiritual essence and the particular qualities of Western culture that promoted and sustained its existence. Like Marx, Sombart and Weber grew progressively estranged from the capitalist system, although the level of their estrangement never approached that of Marx. Both deplored the alienation that working people suffered under mature capitalist production, and both lamented the erosion of individual heroism and creativity within bureaucratic capitalist states. Unlike Marx, however, they rejected economic determinism and monocausality. While they admitted that the relative importance of economic factors had increased in modern times, they insisted that history was not the product of impersonal material forces. It was driven by the interaction of numerous forces, some economic, some not. But all such forces were set in motion by ideas—in particular, religious ideas.

In the medieval seedbed where capitalism took root, economic stimuli were powerfully influenced by religion. Weber and Sombart studied the world of religious ideas, contending that spiritual forces were crucial to creating the cultural climate that promoted capitalism. Weber was better disciplined and more profound than Sombart. But it was Sombart who first probed the inner logic of capitalism, arguing that the "spirit" of capitalism called the substance of capitalism into being. Sombart remained a competitor, interlocutor, and foil for his more famous colleague, and together they challenged the theoretical postulates of Adam Smith, Karl Marx, and their respective academic partisans.

Weber, in particular, contended that neither Marx, Smith, nor the schools of historical explanation they fostered fully appreciated the distinctive character of Western capitalism. Yes, capitalism involved private appropriation of the means of production; yes, it involved a money economy and a search for profit through market exchanges; yes, it comprehended the use of free wage labor drawn from a propertyless population that had only its labor to sell; and, of course, it was driven by individual economic self-interest. But capitalism, as a social structure, a culture, a comprehensive code of conduct, is more than these, Weber insisted. Capitalism transcends the free exercise of acquisitive instincts under market conditions. Ardent acquisitiveness has been evident in most social systems since the beginning of recorded time. There is no shortage of examples, East and West, of avaricial entrepreneurs exploiting private property to achieve high profits. Yet only in Europe and only in the sixteenth century was there a breakthrough to capitalism as a distinctive civilization, as a way of life.

Although Weber and Sombart advocated different reasons for the emergence of capitalism, their intense focus on the question was inspired by heated academic debates in imperial Germany. The Germans had experienced industrial capitalism differently from other West Europeans. In England, the Industrial Revolution unfolded gradually but steadily over the eighteenth and nineteenth centuries. In Germany, industrialization descended abruptly in the second half of the nineteenth century. Germany did not undergo a successful bourgeois revolution; consequently, the German middle class exercised substantially less political and cultural influence than its counterpart in France, Belgium, or Britain. Because British industrial capitalism emerged slowly as a natural evolutionary growth, most Britons took it for granted: in fact, the scholarly community in England devoted little attention to capitalism as a distinct social system.

In Germany, on the other hand, rapid and belated industrialization commanded the attention of the nation's social thinkers. Germany's new industrial order was founded at precisely the time that a German nation was being unified under Prussian leadership. New circumstances demanded new policies. In order to cope with the multiple dimensions of the new national order, it was deemed important that scholars fathom the character of capitalism, probe its origins, and identify the principles that sustained it.

Having assumed this charge, German academics became divided on a host of theoretical issues.[1] Among them was the question whether all human beings, in their economic pursuits, exhibited the same motives and behavior. Beginning with Adam Smith, Britain's classical economists had advanced this position, arguing that "economic man" was universally propelled by individual self-interest and the desire to maximize his or her material advantage. The best societal means of achieving maximum economic efficiency was to permit the greatest measure of individual economic freedom. This orientation was well suited to Great Britain, a self-conscious and centuries-old national state whose modern industrial growth had occurred over many generations.

It was not suited to Germany. There, social scientists constituting the German Historical School condemned the classical tradition as unduly abstract, unverified by inductive historical research, and thereby both ahistorical and falsely universal. They found it ethically and pragmatically repellant. It was, many Germans argued, an utterly materialist orientation, indifferent to the special requirements of particular cultures. It failed to acknowledge that in some times and some places individual economic behavior could be significantly constrained by ethical or other non-economic imperatives. More pragmatically, argued the Germans, the laissez-faire component of the classical tradition did not meet the special needs of a newly unified national state in which infant industries required protection and the swift progress of industrialization evoked calls for government interference to protect workers and unravel the worst problems created by rapid economic expansion.

SOMBART: THE SPIRIT OF CAPITALISM

In 1902 Sombart published his two-volume *Modern Capitalism* purporting to show how capitalism had emerged in Europe.[2] He divided European economic development into chronological stages, beginning with "traditional societies" in which people were the sum of all things.

They accepted what was handed down to them; their economic activity was calculated to satisfy natural wants and to achieve self-sufficiency. Leisure was prized over accumulation. By the sixteenth century, traditional economies were giving way to early capitalism (merchant capitalism), and in the nineteenth century early capitalism was supplanted by "high" capitalism (industrial and financial capitalism). Throughout the centuries, human values determined what was acceptable economic conduct, and those values were shaped by an on-going dialectical struggle between opposing principles: a traditional principle and an acquisitive principle. The traditional principle held that people should engage in economic activity only to satisfy fixed needs. The acquisitive principle urged that people pursue unlimited acquisition. Over the last six centuries, the acquisitive principle, embodying the "spirit of capitalism," steadily gained ascendancy over the traditional principle.

The rise of the capitalist spirit was a necessary, though not sufficient, condition for the triumph of capitalism, Sombart thought. He identified a host of political and material forces that promoted changes in production and exchange. The growth of the modern state with its demand for military hardware, troops, and luxury goods stimulated organizational changes in the economy. The introduction of precious metals from America after 1492 increased the money supply and heightened the rate of circulation. There were numerous technological inventions as well as innovations in commercial institutions and business techniques that accelerated economic change. But all material adjustments were preceded by and integrated through an evolving capitalist spirit.

What was this capitalist spirit? It had two dimensions, Sombart thought: on one side, it was dynamic, adventuresome, enterprising, and driven by a ruthless greed for riches; on the other, it was calculating and rational. Neither dimension alone could produce the capitalist spirit or initiate a capitalist order. The capitalist spirit could only be produced when its two components were united. Where did this union first arise? With the Jews, declared Sombart.

SOMBART: ETHNICITY AND CAPITALISM

Sombart's identification of the Jews with early capitalism first appeared in his book *The German Economy in the Nineteenth Century,* which was published the year after *Modern Capitalism.* Together, these works achieve important unity. *The German Economy* amplifies hints in the earlier work that Sombart was becoming hostile to the capitalist system, and the book embodies Sombart's first resort to hereditary and racial explanations for historical developments. Jews had a special propensity for capitalism, he argued. Jewish character demonstrated selfishness and powerful will. Jews were sober. Their family structure was tight, and this permitted the ready transfer of property from one generation to another. Jews had an exceptional capacity for abstract thought, a facility that enhanced their appreciation of the abstraction, money. By the dictates of heredity, they were the ultimate traders. Their religion was highly rational and legalistic. Because the Old Testament did not discourage the accumulation of riches, Jews never formulated an ideal of poverty. Christians did. The New Testament was replete with ominous warnings against laying up earthly treasure and serving two masters: alas, "it is easier for a camel to pass through a needle's eye than for a rich man to enter the kingdom of God."[3] The Book of Deuteronomy enjoined Jews to observe one code of commercial conduct in dealing with one another, and another code, less scrupulous, in treating with Gentiles. This applied to the practice of usury. Christians were formally and universally forbidden to engage in usury; Jews were forbidden usurious undertakings with other Jews. But Jews were free to practice usury in contracts with Christians. Because Jews living in Christian Europe were excluded from traditional modes of advancement, from high state office, or from the dignities of the Church, the only avenue of advancement open to them was the accumulation of wealth. Christian kings and merchants consistently repaired to them for loans of money—at interest, of course. In Venice, Holland, Frankfurt, and many other places where Jews arrived in large numbers, business activity burgeoned. By religion, by temperament, and by circumstance, Jews were particularly fitted to be early agents of the capitalist spirit and educators to those who would follow their example.

In books written before World War I—*The Jews and Modern Capitalism* (1911) and *The Quintessence of Capitalism* (1913)—Sombart emphasized the importance of race and heredity in influencing the course of history. All Europeans had the qualities necessary for capitalism, he contended, but those qualities flourished in different peoples in different ways and to different degrees. Among Europe's ancient tribes, some, like the Celts and Goths, were "under-inclined" by their heredity toward capitalism. Others were "over-inclined." Sombart divided the latter into two categories consistent with the two components of the capitalist spirit. There were the adventurous, enterprising "Heroic peoples" who demonstrated their ruthless acquisitiveness through a special talent for "forcible, all-conquering undertakings on a large scale." These included the Romans and several Germanic peoples: Normans, Lombards, Saxons, and

Franks. The second group, the "Trading peoples," exhibited special gifts of rationality. They exercised this quality in conducting "successful business by peaceful contract-making, by diplomacy and by clever calculation." Among the "Trading peoples" were Scots (descended from Frisians), Florentines (descended from Etruscans and Greeks), and Jews. The latter were, from the first, he wrote, "a pure trading people."[4]

Sombart lamented the ascendancy of trade over heroism in modern capitalism. Man was no longer the measure of all things. Dynamism, enterprise, and adventure had fallen prey to the barren power of rationality. Economic activity was governed by cold reason. Profit had become the only objective. Wealth was not being generated to serve human interests. Everything was sacrificed to the "Moloch" of work. Human beings had become degraded faceless cogs in a productive machine committed to accumulation—accumulation for the sake of accumulation: "all the higher instincts of heart and mind [were] crushed out by devotion to business."[5] In the evolving mentality of Werner Sombart, all the ingredients for what would later become a Nazi worldview were in place before World War I: a sentimental tribalism, a contempt for high capitalism, an emphasis on heredity and race, and an inclination to blame Jews for perceived misdirections in German society.[6]

Sombart has been described as a "weathercock for the creative winds of his age."[7] During his long and colorful career, he passed through at least three distinct phases—from sentimental conservatism, to social democracy, to the advocacy of racialism. Sombart served as a stimulus, sometimes an outrageous stimulus, to the steadier, more systematic Max Weber. For twenty years, he and Weber exchanged ideas as well as critical volleys. Although their books on the rise of modern capitalism located the origins of the capitalist spirit in religious communities, they differed fundamentally on which religious communities embodied it. Scholars often contend that Weber's historical sociology was a direct response to the extreme economism of Marx. In some ways, it was. More emphatically, however, Weber responded to the work of Sombart, a professional colleague with whom he shared similar intellectual roots and orientations but highly dissimilar fruits.

WEBER: THE SPIRIT OF CAPITALISM

Max Weber published his famous work, *The Protestant Ethic and the Spirit of Capitalism*, in 1904–1905 as a two-part article in the *Archiv für Sozialwissenschaft und Sozialpolitik*, a journal for which he served as an editor. The work gave ample evidence of Sombart's influence. Both men considered modern capitalism an epoch-forming and unique historical phenomenon. For both, the spirit of capitalism was paramount in generating the institutional structures of capitalism. That spirit was rooted in religious ideas, and it had a rational dimension. Both considered the capitalist spirit a necessary, but not sufficient, condition for the rise of capitalism. At the same time, Weber rejected Sombart's main conclusions. He denied his argument on the Jews,[8] and he set aside the immediate value of using heredity as a causal explanation in history. Weber did not disavow a hereditary explanation. On the contrary, he admitted that he too was "inclined to think the importance of biological heredity very great," but there was, at his time of writing, no way of knowing either how or to what extent heredity produced different behavior in different races or national groups.[9]

Weber addressed his main criticism to Sombart's two-dimensional concept of the capitalist spirit. According to Weber, Sombart mistook the origins of capitalism because he misrepresented the capitalist mentality. The modern spirit of capitalism has a single dimension. It is exclusively rational, not, as Sombart argued, rational in part. Weber agreed with Sombart that capitalism displaced traditionalism, a condition in which workers, even to some extent businessmen, preferred shorter working hours and more leisure, seeking only to earn enough money to preserve the mode of living to which they had grown accustomed. In traditional society, it served no purpose for an employer to double his worker's pay in hope of stimulating an increased yield. The hired man would work only half as long, earn the same pay, and thereby obtain more leisure. What Weber sought to explain was how this traditional ethos was displaced by a calculating and rational orientation to work, one in which profits were maximized, risks were minimized, idle leisure was despised, and the accumulation of personal wealth was perceived as a duty.

Sombart's dualistic notion of the spirit of capitalism did not help. Enterprise, bold adventure, and the ruthless search for riches—the heroic side of the Sombartian concept—are not especially modern, and they have nothing to do with the transition from traditionalism to capitalism, Weber argued. As the embodiment of rationality in economic activity, capitalism relies on systematic business enterprise that yields consistent profit through careful planning, honest exchange, and repeatable performance. Capitalism is not well served by high adventurism, spoilation, or rapine— the type of avaricial self-interest that propelled Cortez and Pizzaro.[10] High-stakes speculation may, on occasion, exhibit capitalistic qualities, but speculative economic behavior does not produce a culture of capitalism. The two dimensions of Sombart's capitalist spirit were contradictory. The bold adventurer and the calculating profit-maximizer were utterly dissimilar types. To envision their union as achieving the consummation of the capitalist spirit was, to Weber, empirically untenable. Only half of Sombart's analysis was correct, his recognition that capitalism involves the application of rational calculation to economic activity.

Like Sombart, Weber asserted that an array of preconditions was necessary before the capitalist spirit could breathe life into a capitalist economy. These included an entrepreneurial organization of capital whereby business and family accounts would be kept separate; a free labor market; a system of calculable law that offered protection to private property; unrestricted (or minimally restricted) markets in goods and services; and rational technology. A vital facilitating medium through which these and other preconditions evolved was the bureaucratic state. Served by professional administrators and professional jurists, it supplanted the highly personal feudal or patrimonial state. The bureaucratic state pacified large areas, eliminated barriers to trade, standardized currencies, provided the means for reliable banking institutions and dependable courts of law, and increased the demand for goods and services by raising armies and expending large sums on luxuries. However, material development and bureaucratic government, by themselves, did not produce capitalism. In China, elaborate Confucian bureaucratic regimes had functioned for centuries, maintaining armies, enjoying relatively high technology, and exercising strong demand in the marketplace without achieving the transition to capitalism. Something more was needed: namely, a capitalist spirit, an ethos, that could integrate and consolidate the preconditions for capitalism into the reality of modern rational capitalism. For both Weber and Sombart, that spirit was a precondition *for* as well as an abiding condition *of* modern capitalism.

The capitalist spirit was superbly and succinctly expressed in the writings of Benjamin Franklin, Weber contended. Weber quoted Franklin at length:

> Remember, that *time* is money. He that can earn ten shillings a day by his labour, and goes abroad, or sits idle, one half of that day, though he spends but sixpence during his diversion or idleness, ought not to reckon *that* the only expense; he has really spent, or rather thrown away, five shillings besides.
> Remember, that *credit* is money.

Remember, that money is of the prolific, generating nature. Money can beget money, and its offspring can beget more, and so on.

The most trifling actions that affect a man's credit are to be regarded. The sound of your hammer at five in the morning, or eight at night, heard by a creditor, makes him easy six months longer.[11]

Franklin enjoined his readers to be attentive to opportunity costs; to keep exact accounts; to maximize profits; to resist all temptation to squander time or capital; to exhibit honesty, punctuality, and commercial dependability; and to be ever vigilant in enlarging capital. Acquisition was the "ultimate purpose" of life. Making money was not merely a virtue; it was a duty. Franklin's advice was more than plain talk to aspiring tradesmen, Weber argued. He was expressing an "ethos," a comprehensive orientation to living, and any infraction of his tenets constituted "forgetfulness of duty."

Franklin's values were different from those of entrepreneurs in China, Babylon, or ancient and medieval Europe. The latter may have exhibited commercial daring; some, especially medieval Christians, would have accumulated their riches at the peril of their souls. But Ben Franklin had no fear for his soul. On the contrary, utilitarian honesty, punctuality, frugality, and industry were doubly enriching because they pleased God while they assured other mortals of one's credit and credibility. Weber not only denied Sombart's assumption that daring speculation and ruthless acquisition constituted a critical component of modern capitalism, but he also contended that any exercise of irrationality or unscrupulousness in the conduct of business was anathema to its spirit. Dishonesty (or even the appearance of dishonesty) in commercial dealings as well as the exercise of dual standards of commercial behavior (a characteristic that Sombart attributed to Jews) were impediments to regular, reliable, and repeatable trade. The ethos of modern capitalism is not to be found in the unrestrained pursuit of gain; it is found in the rational tempering of such impulses in order that renewable, continuous, secure business profit can be assured.

Where did Franklin, in particular, and the modern world, in general, acquire this ethos? Was it, as Marx would have argued, a part of the ideal superstructure that merely reflected conditions prevailing in the economic base of society? Hardly, wrote Weber. Ben Franklin lived in colonial Pennsylvania where money was scarce and barter was common, where there were no large enterprises, and where banking was rudimentary. For Franklin, *ideas* offered guidance for economic practice, not the reverse.

Was the ethos expressed by Franklin simply a product of Occidental rationality? Yes and no, thought Weber. Rationalism comprehends a world of different things, and Occidental rationality has evolved under differing timetables in different places.[12] The task before Weber was to locate the particular source of rationalism expressed in the worldview of Benjamin Franklin.

WEBER: CALVINISM AND CAPITALISM

Weber found the rationalism he sought in the Protestant Reformation. Virtually all Protestants adopted the concept of *the Calling,* a belief that individuals could glorify God by conducting their lives admirably and meeting their obligations fully in this world.[13] It was Calvinism, however, that was chiefly instrumental in forming the capitalist spirit. John Calvin (1509–1564), lawyer, theologian, and father of Puritanism, acknowledged that God was both omnipotent and omniscient. Therefore, he reasoned, not only has God the power to offer salvation, but He knows who will be saved and who will be damned before they are born. To assert that an individual, once born, can alter his or her fate is to assume that the dictates of God can be modified by mere mortals. The individual cannot help himself. The intercession of priests, the sacraments, stained glass, religious statuary—all the sensuous accents of the Catholic Church—offer nothing but sentimental illusion.

In practice, Calvin's doctrine of predestination was all but impossible for his followers to sustain. Because people became obsessed with the question of whether or not they were among the elect, the principle of predestination had to be moderated in pastoral practice. Calvinist pastors enjoined their flocks to glorify God, to consider themselves among the elect, and to fight all doubts about their salvation as if such doubts were temptations of the devil. They embraced worldly activity, demonstrating to themselves and to one another their worthiness. According to Calvin, punctilious conduct may not have had any effect upon an individual's ultimate fate, but it did, in daily practice, provide personal reassurance. It was, as Weber argues, an indispensable "sign" of election—"the technical means, not of purchasing salvation, but of getting rid of the fear of damnation."[14]

Highly ascetic, Calvinists renounced popular amusements on the Sabbath or frivolities like dancing or card playing or theatre. Vanity and ostentation, whether in clothing or decoration, were repudiated as idolatry of the flesh. The accumulation of wealth was considered objectionable only if it tempted the flesh to excess or bred idleness, but if wealth was acquired in the performance of duty, if its accumulation could be seen as a means of glorifying God (as in the parable of the talents),[15] it was both permissible and encouraged.

Wealth is seductive, Weber observed. Medieval monasteries that began with the best ascetic intentions often succumbed to worldly temptations once they had accumulated wealth. This would happen to Calvinists as well, but not before the asceticism that regulated economic behavior in the full flush of Calvinist religiosity was transformed into a sober economic virtue. Calvinists transformed what earlier generations had considered vices into Christian virtues. They renounced idleness; rendered labor a spiritual enterprise; encouraged thrift, diligence, and sobriety in daily life; and identified honest profit-taking as a duty to God. Economic accumulation was encouraged within the bounds of correct moral conduct. While this was most evident in the bourgeois businessman, it manifested itself as well in "sober, conscientious, and unusually industrious workmen, who clung to their work as to a life purpose willed by God."[16] When, after time, the religious veneer was peeled away, what remained of worldly asceticism was rational economic conduct founded on the concept of a Calling. This was the wellspring of Ben Franklin's worldview. It was the key ingredient in the rise of modern European capitalism.

Weber recognized that capitalism may have arisen at another time without the inspiration of aescetic Protestantism. It would never have arisen unless economic, demographic, technological, and monetary preconditions were in place. But, he concluded, in the particular experience of sixteenth-century Europe, Calvinism provided the spiritual spark that ignited material tinder that had been accumulating there throughout the late Middle Ages.

THE WEBER THESIS REFUTED

From the moment of its publication, Weber's essay aroused intense debate. The Marxists, Pirenne, Sombart, and a host of other luminaries rejected his thesis. It would be fruitless to identify more than a few participants in the controversy. Debate has persisted at differing levels of intensity for nearly a century. Almost every historian concerned with early modern Europe has taken some position on Weber's work. Many, perhaps most, have oversimplified his thesis, assuming that Weber believed that ascetic Protestantism was the prime cause of capitalism and that the presence of the former necessarily produced the latter. As we have seen,

Weber's argument was more subtle and more moderate than that. It was no surprise to him that the advent of Calvinism in places like Hungary and Scotland did not inspire the rise of capitalism. Yet many of his critics used the example of places like Hungary or Scotland to discredit his thesis. Historians working on the Netherlands, Rhineland Germany, and Switzerland found no apparent connection between Calvinist religious practice and capitalism. Others demonstrated that Calvinists were as idle as Catholics, that they were as opposed to usury as Catholics and just as hostile to an economic ethos baldly committed to material accumulation.[17]

Weber's critics have challenged him at many levels. Some have derided his advocacy of Calvinism. Others have dismissed his emphasis on the role of ideas, insisting that ideas are derivative of material conditions. Still others have challenged his use of statistics and the factual data employed to support his thesis.[18] Some challenges to Weber arise obliquely, not directly. This is the case with Theodore Rabb, a student of the English merchant class in the sixteenth and seventeenth centuries. Rabb discovered that during the early years of English expansion, whether in exploration, the founding of colonies, slave trading, or piracy, investors—many of them Calvinists—exhibited precious little of the sober rationality identified by Weber as being genuinely capitalist. A lottery mentality prevailed in England, and investors referred to their overseas enterprises, quite appropriately, as "ventures" or "adventures." Men dreamed of great windfalls, eldorados, and they recklessly poured capital into scores of ill-conceived and ill-fated projects. Rabb describes the mood of those years as "irrational and emotional," moved by international competition, national animosities, and zenophobia—an approach quite at odds with the cautious capitalism of the nineteenth and twentieth centuries or the sober, systematic capitalism described by Weber.[19]

Sombart considered Calvinists the least likely religious community to evoke a capitalist spirit. Calvinists were "inimical to acquisitiveness." They were hostile to grandeur in art, decoration, and clothing, and their behavior had the effect of repressing demand in the marketplace. Even Catholics were more likely candidates to raise the capitalist spirit. Early Church fathers may have advocated poverty, Sombart continued, but Thomas Aquinas, uniting Pauline and Augustinian doctrines of love and legalism, established an ethical system based on the rationalization of life. Reason should regulate the world and control the passions, Thomas thought. He deplored idleness. He taught industry, frugality, and honesty: indeed, commercial honesty in Europe owed much to Church teaching.[20] As for Ben Franklin, he was antedated by a host of writers who advocated virtually identical doctrines. Sombart quoted at length from a fifteenth-century Florentine, Leon Battista Alberti, whose book *I Libri della Famiglia* offered homilies advocating thrift, industry, and frugality very similar to those of Franklin. Such doctrines appeared in numerous works throughout the centuries, among them Daniel Defoe's *The Complete English Tradesman* (1727). Defoe, Sombart observed, was among Franklin's favorite authors.[21]

R. H. Tawney, the renowned English economic historian, was sympathetic to some aspects of Weber's work and critical of others.[22] Tawney agreed that the sixteenth century was a watershed in Western history and that the Reformation was a vital factor in Europe's transition to capitalism. But, with Sombart, Tawney believed that Weber overstated the uniqueness as well as the importance of the Protestant concept of the Calling. He undervalued the extent to which the rationalizing impulse of the Calvinists was foreshadowed by Roman Catholic schoolmen, and he failed to appreciate the degree to which changing social and economic needs gave rise to the Reformation and its abiding religious mentalities. Tawney acknowledged the existence of a rationalizing, ascetic Protestant ethic, and he agreed that Calvin provided the first systematic body of religious teaching to recognize and applaud economic virtues. But neither the Protestant ethic nor Calvin's teachings manifested themselves until economic and political change had created a congenial environment for them. Calvinism did not trigger the rise of capitalism. Rather, the existing apparatus of capitalism adopted Calvinism as religious reinforcement. For Tawney, the Protestant ethic was an intellectual capstone, a moral justification for cultural adjustments that were rooted in and advanced by material forces. In this sense, it was more an effect than a cause of historical change.

Marxists have been sterner critics than Tawney, yet their orientation differs in degree, not in kind. Religion is an element of the superstructure, they argue. Its biases reflect those of the prevailing productive system, a productive system that serves the interest of a particular dominant class. In late medieval Europe, the small but growing bourgeoisie struggled against the forces of feudalism. Because Roman Catholicism was the ally of feudalism, the class interest of the urban bourgeoisie could only be advanced by undermining Catholic authority. Luther pierced the Church's armor, but it was Calvin who provided an ideological structure highly accommodating to the class interests of the bourgeoisie. Does the rapid spread of Calvinism through the urban centers of France, the Low Countries, and England not suggest a convergence of interests? A bourgeoisie that was already engaged in the systematic accumulation of capital was naturally attracted to Calvinism, and Calvinist divines, eager to please their audiences, shaped their messages in a language the bourgeoisie was pleased to hear.

WEBER ANSWERS HIS CRITICS

Weber was not chastened by early criticism of his work. When his essay was republished in 1920, he changed nothing of substance and added a hundred pages of densely argued notes responding point by point to his numerous critics. Neither side in the controversy could generate absolute empirical proof, nor could the matter be resolved easily by routine causal analysis. In determining historical causation, historians attempt to evaluate the importance of forces that bear upon a particular event by asking: if A had not occurred, would B have happened anyway? Or, if A had not occurred, would something akin to B have happened, albeit in significantly modified form?[23] In the case of Weber's thesis, if condition A (the Protestant Reformation) had not occurred, would result B (capitalism) have come about anyway?

Demonstrating the causal relationship between two events is less problematic than ascertaining the causal relationship between belief and action.[24] To achieve the latter, historians require evidence of the independent existence of a belief prior to its implementation in action. This is rarely possible. Normally, we observe actions; we assume the existence of the beliefs that motivate those actions; then we verify the motive power of the beliefs by referring to actions that are consistent with them. The explanation becomes circular, and the further we retreat in historical time, the more we are compelled to rely on actions to provide insight into attitudes.

At no point did Weber declare that capitalism could only have arisen as a result of the Reformation. Nor did he consider religious factors exclusively responsible for the capitalist spirit. But he did contend that in the experience of Europe, Protestant religious forces powerfully affected the "qualitative formation and the quantitative expansion" of the capitalist spirit.[25] In the absence of Protestantism, capitalism would have been delayed, altered, or possibly even precluded, Weber thought. Shortly before he died, he commented on the relative role of material interests (economic forces) and ideas in historical causation: "Interests (material and ideal) not ideas directly determine man's action. But the world views, which were created by ideas, have very often acted as the switches that channeled the dynamics of the interests."[26] Weber always gave precedence to the switches. In so doing, he took the most difficult historiographical approach.

History, Weber knew, was infinitely multidimensional and complex. In searching for the causes of an event, historians identify critical antecedent factors related to that event. Those factors are integrated into an organic formula that weighs the importance of each factor in relation to others and ascertains when various factors entered the process and at what velocity they achieved an impact. Too much of one factor, too little of another, or a different velocity of impact would alter the formula and produce a different historical outcome. Considering the numerous factors at play in the rise of capitalism, how could any scholar hope to get it right? The historian's only recourse, thought Weber, was to seek a higher level of insight.

For him, that higher level involved religion. Before the onset of modern industrial capitalism, religion provided the pervasive medium through which all institutions received validation. This was as true of the Occident as the Orient. Even Tawney readily admitted that medieval Europe was a Church-civilization, that until the sixteenth century religion enveloped all forms of human activity and that governance, law, social comportment, and transactions in the marketplace had to be justified "at the bar of religion."[27] During most of Western history, the Church was better organized for the conduct of politics than secular governments. The Church first developed bureaucratic institutions of government, and the Church set down the model for courtly life.[28] Before the advent of modernity, the forces producing change in society were critically linked to religion, Weber contended.

But how could he confirm his thesis? Only, he thought, by comparative study of other great civilizations. It was only through comparative analysis that one could discover the truly distinctive attributes of Western culture that might have triggered (or, at least, not have impeded) the rise of rational capitalism. Those who asserted that Western capitalism arose naturally through the progressive action of material forces invariably assigned special causal significance to specific factors: to the rise of markets, to the growth of state power, to technical innovation, and so forth. All such material forces were at work in other great world civilizations. Yet those civilizations did not develop rational capitalism. Until Western scholars undertook systematic comparisons of Western and non-Western cultures, they could not know what experiences those cultures shared, what they did not share, and what weight should be given to their differences. Causal analysis of the rise of European capitalism that excluded the comparative dimension was purely speculative.

Weber responded to his own mandate. Suspecting that the chief obstacle to rational capitalism in non-Western cultures was ideological, he pursued a daunting program of research in comparative religious sociology, studying Judaism, Hinduism, Buddhism, Confucianism, Taoism, and Islam.[29] He found what he was looking for, as historians generally do. Having examined the interaction of non-Western religions and non-Western cultures, Weber concluded that the chief impediment that those civilizations encountered in achieving rational capitalism lay in the realm of religion. In India, for example, the caste restrictions of Hinduism restricted gain-seeking for millions of people. Caste has imposed monumental obstacles to the free and open interaction of peoples in the workplace or the market. In the West, a religiously inspired worldview conducive to rational capitalism arose. Outside the West, it did not.[30]

CONCLUSION

Both Sombart and Weber placed highest priority on the formative influence of religious ideas. Sombart considered Weber's concentration on Calvinism entirely myopic, and this aspect of Weber's work continues to evoke heaviest criticism. One of his most sympathetic latter-day defenders, Randall Collins, excuses his "error." Having died prematurely, Collins noted, Weber was never able to complete his studies. The last stop on his projected intellectual journey through the world's great religions was to have been ancient and medieval Christianity. Had Weber concluded that enterprise or had he had access to the works of the professional medievalists in the twentieth century, he would have discovered the revolutionary and rationalizing forces at work in the late-medieval Roman Church.[31]

Weber always contended that capitalism could not emerge until critical structural supports were in place: rationalizing technology, free labor, unrestricted markets, entrepreneurial use of capital. Equally, Weber acknowledged the importance of the bureaucratic state as the preserver of order and the provider of legal security to merchants. These preconditions were in place in the High Middle Ages, writes Collins, and the institution most responsible for advancing them was the Roman Catholic Church. The Papacy was the first bureaucratic state. It operated under formal rules, kept careful records, separated individuals from offices, and instituted recruitment on the basis of talent. Also, it advanced the concept of citizenship. The Pope was chosen by election; cathedral chapters elected their own bishops, monasteries their abbots. The concept of citizenship within a community offset the Church's authoritarian tendencies, fostered calculable law, and provided the clergy with rights from below as well as rights from above.

In economic matters, the Church fostered rationality and entrepreneurial behavior. With the onset of a second wave of monastic orders in the twelfth century—Cistercians, Augustinians, and various crusading orders—monasteries became the most efficient economic units ever to have existed in Europe. Cistercian monasteries maintained factories, often hydraulically powered; they used their capital assets with entrepreneurial aplomb; and they plowed their profits back into the institution. In the secular economy, capital was immobilized for want of promising areas for investment, but among the religious orders capital moved freely. The Roman Church possessed up to a third of the property in Europe. It was clearly the most dynamic, most modernizing sector of the medieval economy. Collins contends, rather dubiously one might argue, that the premodern merchant capitalism of Venice, Genoa, and Florence left no lasting impact on European institutions, whereas the capitalistic practices of the monastic orders laid the groundwork for rational capitalism in Northern Europe.[32]

Weber would have come to this view had he lived longer, Collins believes. Already, at the end of his life, he was gravitating in this direction. Collins thinks that too much attention has been bestowed on *The Protestant Ethic and the Spirit of Capitalism,* Weber's first and most dramatic work, and too little on his last, *General Economic History,* which brings together a full theory of the rise of capitalism. There, Weber remained committed to the proposition that religious ideas were critical in the emergence of rational capitalism in the West. However, at no point in the latter work did he refer to the doctrine of predestination, which figured so heavily in his *Protestant Ethic.* Weber, it seems, was migrating toward the position held by Sombart, Tawney, and many others, that the Church of Rome foretokened the rationalizing impulse that the *Protestant Ethic* had attributed specifically to Calvinism.

Whether a longer-lived Max Weber would have modified his thesis, adopting a more broadly Christian explanation for the spirit of capitalism, we will never know. Nor is it that important. Although Weber may have explained the rise of rational capitalism too exclusively in terms of one Christian sect, he—and to a lesser degree, Sombart—remained committed to the proposition that the roots of Western capitalism must be sought in the realm of religious ideas. Weber did more than intensify debate on the origins of capitalism, he raised the question beyond the confines of Western Europe, challenging serious scholars to view the issue not merely as a problem for European history but as a problem in world history.

NOTES

1. These theoretical disagreements are well presented in Gordon Marshall, *In Search of the Spirit of Capitalism: An Essay on Max Weber's Protestant Ethic Thesis* (New York, 1982), pp. 25–30.

2. Although this work has not been translated into English, a book-length synthesis of it was written by Frederick L. Nussbaum, *A History of the Economic Institutions of Modern Europe: An Introduction to Der Moderne Kapitalismus of Werner Sombart* (New York, 1935).

3. Matthew 19:24.

4. Werner Sombart, *The Quintessence of Capitalism* (New York, 1967), p. 217.

5. Ibid., p. 181.

6. In 1934, one year after the Nazis came to power, Sombart published *Deutscher Socialismus,* a stridently anti-liberal, anti-capitalist, anti-Marxist appeal for collective German national socialist renewal. His work was academic and sophisticated, by no means a piece of party propaganda, but his worldview was, by 1934, largely in harmony with the philosophical orientations of the Nazi regime. The work was translated into English by Karl F. Geiser as *A New Social Philosophy* (Princeton, 1937).

7. Arthur Mitzman, *Sociology and Estrangement: Three Sociologists of Imperial Germany* (New York, 1973), p. 136. As early as 1902, Sombart began to feel estrangement from the Germany that embraced capitalism. In his youth, Sombart had supported the German Historical School's concern to preserve the artisan class and to forestall social revolution within the growing urban proletariat. His early work reflected the School's rejection of British economic models and its desire to achieve German solutions to German problems. By 1890, Sombart had changed his mind. Renouncing the sentimental conservatism of the Historical School, he declared himself in favor of the factory system. Any attempt to save cottage industries and the artisan class was futile and backward-looking, he argued. Industrial capitalism and the factory system would generate wealth in far greater abundance than older productive processes, thereby permitting the lower orders—if they were politically organized—to achieve higher incomes and better public health and education. Capitalism should be seen as a positive force in European history, albeit not a permanent force. With Marx, Sombart argued that socialism would follow capitalism, but he resisted Marx's materialism. Material forces were moving society toward socialism. But human beings, by the exercise of their collective will, were also moving society toward a new, progressive order.

It was during his social democratic phase, the 1890s, that Sombart developed supreme confidence in voluntarism, in the collective will, in the "spirit" that directed human affairs. His confidence deepened over time. Concurrently, however, his faith in the utility of industrial capitalism as a vehicle for uplifting the people diminished. At the end of his life, Sombart had come to share much common ground with the Nazis.

8. Weber's views on this were tightly summed up in his *General Economic History* (New York, 1927), pp. 358–361.

9. Max Weber, *The Protestant Ethic and the Spirit of Capitalism,* trans. Talcott Parsons (1904–1905; New York, 1958), p. 30.

10. Weber, *General Economic History,* p. 356.

11. Weber, *The Protestant Ethic,* pp. 48–50.

12. For example, the rationalization of private law reached its apogee in late Roman antiquity, and its medieval renaissance was most successful in the Catholic countries of Southern Europe, not in the North where capitalism took hold.

13. Weber, *The Protestant Ethic,* pp. 80–81. Even the least capitalistic of the Protestant sects made some contribution in this regard. Luther was conservative, authoritarian, and unsympathetic to capitalist conduct. He condemned usury, material acquisitiveness, and social climbing, yet Lutheranism, like other Protestant persuasions, adopted the concept of the Calling.

14. Weber, *The Protestant Ethic,* p. 115.

15. Matthew 25:14–30.

16. Weber, *The Protestant Ethic,* p. 177.

17. Ephraim Fischoff, "The Protestant Ethic and the Spirit of Capitalism: The History of a Controversy," in S. N. Eisenstadt, ed., *The Protestant Ethic and Modernization: A Comparative View* (New York, 1968), pp. 77–78.

18. Perhaps the most stinging rebuke of Weber's methodology and use of statistics is by a Swedish scholar, Kurt Samuelsson. See Kurt Samuelsson, *Religion and Economic Action,* trans. E. G. French (London, 1961). A segment of Samuelsson's work appears in Robert W. Green, ed., *The Weber Thesis Controversy* (Lexington, 1973), pp. 106–136, a book designed to provide students with the main lines of the Weber debate.

19. Theodore K. Rabb, "The Expansion of Europe and the Spirit of Capitalism," *Historical Journal* 17 (1974): 675–689.

20. Werner Sombart, *The Quintessence of Capitalism: A Study of the History and Psychology of the Modern Business Man,* trans. M. Epstein (1915; New York, 1967), pp. 238–248, 269.

21. Sombart, *The Quintessence of Capitalism,* p. 116.

22. R. H. Tawney, *Religion and the Rise of Capitalism* (New York, 1926).

23. Reinhard Bendix makes this point in the context of Weber's work. See Reinhard Bendix, *Max Weber: An Intellectual Portrait* (New York, 1960), p. 103.

24. For an engaging discussion of methodological issues, see Marshall, *In Search of the Spirit of Capitalism,* pp. 65–68, 149–150. See also Elias H. Tuma, *Economic History and the Social Sciences: Problems of Methodology* (Berkeley, 1971), pp. 117, 176, 204–207.

25. Weber, *The Protestant Ethic,* p. 91.

26. Quoted in Wolfgang Schluchter, *The Rise of Western Rationalism: Max Weber's Developmental History,* trans. Guenther Roth (Berkeley, 1981), p. 25.

27. Tawney, *Religion and the Rise of Capitalism,* p. 4.

28. This argument was made early by Sombart in *Luxury and Capitalism* (1913; Ann Arbor, 1967), pp. 2–4.

29. This enterprise was not entirely completed. Works on Judaism, the religions of India, and the religions of China have been published separately in English. They were

incorporated, with his essays on the Protestant ethic, in his *Gesammelte Aufsätze zur Religionssoziologie* (Tübingen, 1920–1921), 3 vols. Weber did not complete his work on Islam.

30. Weber, *General Economic History*, pp. 313–314, 356–369.

31. Randall Collins, *Weberian Sociological Theory* (New York, 1986), p. 9.

32. Ibid., pp. 45–48.

Part III

The Dynamics of Historical Change: World History

Introduction:
The Global Perspective

In the 1970s, two distinct but highly compatible approaches to the study of history came to maturity: world-system analysis and environmental history. The first of these offered an explicit model that explained the rise and development of capitalism through exploitative relationships established between Western Europe and the wider world during the sixteenth century. World-system analysis was a logical extension of dependency theory, a theory that emerged after World War II in Latin America among development specialists who were disillusioned by the growing disparity between rich nations and poor and by the universal failure of modernization strategies. The second approach, environmental history, received powerful impetus from a United Nations Conference on the Human Environment held in Stockholm in 1971. The report of that conference, *Only One Earth*,[1] grimly alerted readers to the abuse that humans had wrought upon their environment, poisoning air and sea, destroying tens of thousands of species, depleting fisheries, laying waste the forests, encouraging the deserts, and generally endangering the long-term survival of human life on this planet.

Unlike world-system analysis, environmental history offered no over-arching theory of change; rather, it united under one umbrella a host of specialties concerned with climate, population, disease, food, fuel, natural resources, and natural disasters. Environmentalists expressed concern that conventional history, being preoccupied with human affairs, considered nature a constant, a vast and stable theatrical stage upon which human actors played out their drama. This was not the case, they argued. Natural forces are perpetually changing; man and nature have always interacted. If twentieth-century man is capable of devastating nature to such an extent that human life on this planet might become unsustainable, earlier man was a prisoner of changing natural forces, and much of his history was determined by them.

World-system analysis and environmental history are global in scope. The world-system integrates continents through economic interdependence. Environmental historians demonstrate that pollutants observe no frontiers, that the destruction of tropical forest has serious implications for people in temperate countries, that global cooling or global warming affects everyone, and that human or animal diseases that arise in one sector of the globe generally spread to others. Both modes of analysis consider the discovery of America and the biological and botanical merger of hemispheres watershed events of the first magnitude. A leading environmental historian, Donald Worster, urges that Columbus's landfall in the Bahamas and Neal Armstrong's landing on the moon mark off a distinct era in world history.[2]

World-system historians and environmental historians are either openly hostile to capitalism or exceedingly wary of it. With their intellectual roots embedded in Marxism, world-system theorists deplore the unequal distribution of wealth occasioned by capitalism. Environmentalists are alarmed by capitalism's reckless obsession with economic growth and by the extravagant rate at which capitalist societies have consumed the world's resources. Raymond Dasmann divides the world's inhabitants into ecosphere people and biosphere people. The former have the capacity to survive for centuries or longer on the resources of a single ecosystem or on adjacent or related ecosystems. They sustain life without seriously depleting the biological context of the environment upon which they depend. Biosphere people—those deemed more civilized, more sophisticated, more involved in complex divisions of labor—are dependent on world trade, a trade that widely distributes resources drawn from innumerable regional ecosystems.[3] Despite the laying waste (or, perhaps, because of the laying waste) of one regional ecosystem after another, the most powerful biosphere people may, for a time, achieve a very high material standard of living. But persistent and improvident extraction will eventually deplete the world's resources and its biological variety to the extent that the rich and powerful will be unable to sustain their extravagance and the poor will be condemned to wretchedness and desolation.

Historians of both orientations focus heavily on extraction. Environmental historians are alarmed by the growing extractive impulse of powerful biosphere peoples; world-system scholars have attempted to identify the economic linkages through which that extractive process has evolved. There is little doubt, argue the environmentalists, that population pressure and industrial capitalism have rendered thousands of regional ecosystems vulnerable to destruction. This development has been fueled primarily by Western capitalism. Almost every innovation in production, every sophisticated technology, and every development in transportation during the last century or more has been inspired by the demands of capitalist economic culture.[4]

The impulse behind the development of environmental history is clear. Our world is in crisis. If humankind is to survive on this planet, men and women must become conscious of the complex natural and biological relationships that shape the biosphere upon which our future depends. To appreciate our present difficulties and to map coherent strategies for survival, we must understand more about mankind's earlier interactions—for good and for evil—with the natural world. The impulse underlying the development of world-system analysis is less obvious. Therefore, the remainder of this introduction will focus on the changing worldviews and political and economic conditions that gave rise to what is clearly the fastest-growing and most fashionable theory of history treated in this book.

As power relationships change, so do historical orientations. In the early twentieth century, Western historians assumed that Europe would continue to shape the world in its own image, exercising hegemonic power in accordance with the balance of forces prevailing in the North Atlantic. Today, this attitude seems outrageously arrogant. In the context of the time, it was by no means unreasonable.

European power reached its zenith in 1914. All of Africa, save Ethiopia and Liberia, had been absorbed into European empires.[5] The Red Sea and the Persian Gulf were British lakes. Except for Siam (Thailand), all of southern Asia from Aden to Singapore answered to British power. Indonesia was Dutch; Indo-China was French; the Philippines were American; Central Asia and Siberia were Russian; China, while preserving a tenuous independence, had been dissected by Europeans into economic spheres of influence. In the East, only Japan enjoyed real independence.

Australia and New Zealand were self-governing dominions of the British Empire, and the islands of the Pacific, like those of the Atlantic and Indian oceans, were administered by Europeans.[6] Although formally independent states occupied most of Latin America, those states were economic dependencies—"informal colonies"—of the United States and Great Britain. The United States, a transatlantic extension of European material and intellectual culture, had taken its place among the great powers at the end of the nineteenth century. In a famous poem in 1898, Rudyard Kipling welcomed Americans to the inner circle, urging them to "Take up the White Man's burden," to share with Europeans the responsibility to lead the "silent sullen peoples" slowly "toward the light." It was a world ordered and ruled by Europeans and their American offspring, and it was perfectly natural for historians to conclude that any culture capable of exercising such universal predominance was intrinsically superior to those over which it held sway. There was every reason to assume that European culture, in its several variants, would gradually, systematically, subvert all others.

History was written accordingly. Africans, Native Americans, and Aboriginals were considered "people without history."[7] For example, what passed for the history of Africa was the history of European conquest, European competition, and European enterprise in "the Dark Continent." Builders of empire—Prince Henry the Navigator, Columbus, Cortez, Robert Clive, and the American pioneers—were lionized in Western historical literature and fiction.

World War II ended the European era. European countries suffered massive physical damage and unprecedented loss of life. Germany was subdivided; European Russia was devastated; France was humiliated; Britain, although victorious, was exhausted. Having sustained no domestic destruction and having suffered relatively few casualties, the United states of America, still a stronghold of Western culture, emerged as world hegemon. Yet in spite of its position as nucleus of world capitalism, America's hegemony was not deemed secure. Americans believed themselves and their Western capitalist allies imperiled by revolutionary communism, an ideology sustained and promoted in Moscow.

The Cold War, begun in 1947, was an intense ideological struggle fought throughout Eurasia, Africa, and Latin America. It coincided in time with the reluctant, often forced, withdrawal of war-worn European states from their overseas colonies. Beginning with Britain's necessitous grant of independence to India in 1947, the pace of decolonization exceeded anything the Europeans could have imagined. France was driven from Indo-China in 1954; Britain granted independence to Ghana in 1957, and this act was followed throughout French, British, and Belgian Africa by a rush of successful independence movements. European officers who had enrolled in their colonial services at the end of World War II expecting to pursue lifetime careers in African or Asian administration had, by the mid-1960s, returned to Europe to seek other careers. The colonial world had become the Third World, and in the context of the Cold War, the Third World had become an extended battleground for the conflicting ideologies of East and West.

New political circumstances demanded new historical orientations. Prewar assumptions were in tatters. It was no longer useful to focus on Europe's gifts to the world. Alas, the history of Africa had to be a history of Africans, not the history of Europeans in Africa. If the West was to appeal to Third World peoples, it must know them for what they were; it must attempt to comprehend their aspirations and appreciate their historical and cultural contributions. Decades earlier, Max Weber had been a lonely voice urging greater attention to world history. Now, new voices, beginning with William McNeill and L. S. Stavrianos, pioneered the study of world history, deliberately broadening our historical canvas beyond its traditional cultural-centric focus on Western civilization.[8] We live in a "global village," they argued, and our ability to function effectively with our neighbors depends in large measure upon our ability to understand their history and to appreciate our mutual interdependence.

The writers of world history founded their work on an old intellectual abstraction—the distinct and autonomous "civilization." Their chief engine of change was "diffusion," a process by which great autonomous civilizations dispersed their special skills, products, organization, and culture, like the concentric outward movement of ripples created by pebbles tossed into placid water. Such diffusion, they argued, compromised and seduced barbaric peoples on the periphery of the great civilizations. Converging cultural ripples emanating from various distinct civilizations generated action and reaction, borrowing, change, and adjustment between civilizations.[9]

Diffusion became a guiding principle in reshaping the postwar world. In the global village, few countries were rich; many were poor. The poor were considered particularly vulnerable to communist penetration, to political attachment to Moscow, and to permanent alienation from the capitalist West. In the interest of capitalism as well as in the interest of humanity, it was deemed imperative that the rich nations assist the poor in achieving economic development. All regions of the world had been underdeveloped at one time or another, it was argued. It was only in modern times that the West had outdistanced other regions in terms of industrial production, communications, education, political sophistication, public health, and a host of other attributes. The waning European empires had devised strategies for the development of their colonies, but those strategies were set for the long term, and they were predicated on the assumption that colonies should, for the most part, generate whatever income was necessary to underwrite their own development. The Cold War and decolonization created a new sense of urgency about development. If development was to be accelerated, it would require the rapid diffusion of modernism from advanced societies to backward areas. But what strategies, what plans, what theoretical models were to be employed?

The first wave of theorists to attack the postwar development problem, social scientists of the modernization school, were grounded in functionalist theory. Devised by the American sociologist Talcott Parsons, functionalist theory regarded human society as similar to a biological organism. All parts were interdependent, and each part contributed a special function vital to the survival of the whole. In human society, there were four vital functions. The first, the adaptation of society to its environment, was performed by the economy. Goal attainment, the second function, was undertaken by government. The third, the integration of key institutions, was provided through religious and legal structure. The fourth, the preservation of social values over time (what Parsons labeled "latency") was performed by the family and by educational institutions. Functioning together, these vital parts achieved "homeostatic equilibrium," a balanced and uniform state. If change occurred in one social institution, other institutions would change in response to it, thereby reducing tension and preserving equilibrium. Such a system was constantly moving, constantly accommodating, constantly adjusting.[10]

Members of the modernization school were equally attracted to evolutionary theory. Like nineteenth-century Positivists, they believed that human society was perpetually and irreversibly moving from a primitive to an advanced condition. Because Western culture represented the highest state of social and material development, backward societies were bound to emulate it. They could not resist it. Pockets of modernism already existed throughout the Third World, particularly in the cities, yet the countryside in most underdeveloped countries remained bound to tradition, sometimes in quasi-subsistence agricultural villages, sometimes on feudal-type latifundia. The goal of most modernization theorists was to integrate divergent social sectors of the same underdeveloped polity so that the process of homeostatic equilibrium could more rapidly achieve an evolutionary upward adjustment. This, they assumed, would be accomplished most swiftly by the emergence of a commercial and industrial bourgeoisie, a class that would diffuse the cultural requisites of modernism among fellow nationals.

Different theorists offered different formulas for modernization depending upon their personal orientations, their academic disciplines, and the geographical regions they studied.[11] One notable prescription was that of W. W. Rostow.[12] An economist, Rostow discerned five distinct stages in economic development. In ascending order, they were traditional society, precondition for takeoff, takeoff, drive to maturity, and mass-consumption society. A country entered the second stage, precondition for takeoff, when capitalist activity had initiated new industries and expanded domestic markets. Notwithstanding such progress, however, an underdeveloped country could not achieve takeoff into sustained economic growth until it raised its annual rate of productive investment to at least 10 percent of national income. Without it, Rostow argued, annual surpluses would be soaked up by population growth. Investment capital could come from a variety of sources: from redistribution of national income through taxation or confiscation; from borrowing; from foreign trade that paid for the importation of essential technology; or from direct foreign investment. There was at least one other source: foreign aid from the industrialized nations. Recognizing the importance of a high reinvestment rate in underdeveloped countries, the United States and other Western governments contributed millions of dollars and thousands of technicians to enhance Third World infrastructures and establish local industries.

Among Third World peoples, Latin Americans have produced a particularly large and creative literature on development. The problem of underdevelopment has especially rankled intellectuals and nationalists in Latin America because their countries, having been politically independent since the early nineteenth century, have made relatively little economic progress compared to the nations of North America. These matters were addressed in a manifesto by the United Nations Economic Commission for Latin America (ECLA) in 1950.[13] The Commission identified a growing structural problem in the world economy. An international division of labor had arisen between the industrialized countries of the North Atlantic and non-industrialized states elsewhere in the world. The industrial nations formed the center, or nucleus, of the world economy, while the rest constituted a dispersed periphery engaged in the production of primary goods—food and raw materials. The terms of trade were highly unfavorable to the periphery. Although, ideally, all parties would benefit from maximizing production and consumption, unrestrained competition in world markets would occasion a dramatic shift of income to the industrialized center. The Commission determined that Latin American countries, in their earlier history, had unwisely foregone the opportunity to establish manufactures capable of satisfying domestic needs. Instead, they chose to rely on the export of primary products, thereby perpetuating, even enhancing, the social influence and political power of feudal oligarchies. The time had come to redeem that error.

ECLA proposed a comprehensive strategy to encourage the development of industries in Latin America that would supply domestic consumer needs without attempting to compete in overseas markets, at least not right away. This import substitution strategy required that fledgling local industries receive tariff protection until they were fully competitive with foreign importers. While this was happening, the usual export of primary products would supply some of the income needed to pay for the importation of industrial machinery and other capital goods. Latin American governments were urged to support this program in the expectation that it would produce a larger, more powerful and progressive nationalist bourgeoisie, which would not only combat feudalism and traditionalism but encourage democracy.

The ECLA strategy failed. Import substitution did not eliminate Latin America's dependency on foreign industrial suppliers. It simply shifted that dependency from consumer goods to capital goods. Moreover, local markets for manufactured goods did not expand once basic needs were satisfied. Primary exports had fallen off in the excitement over industrialization, and by the 1960s Latin American countries were suffering severe balance-of-payments problems and pervasive economic stagnation.

Modernization theory, the optimistic intellectual product of the world's wealthy societies, had been discredited. Diffusion had not worked—indeed, despite external influences and assistance, the gap between rich and poor nations everywhere was widening, not closing. By the 1960s, modernization theory was being upstaged by a more pessimistic and radical attitude toward Third World development: dependency theory.

The most radical, influential, and controversial dependency theorist was the American-educated German national, André Gunder Frank.[14] In 1967 he combined several powerful essays into a single book, *Capitalism and Underdevelopment in Latin America*, challenging every precept, principle, and presumption of the modernization school. According to Frank, ECLA got one thing right. The world was structurally divided into a capitalist center and a dependent periphery. But this division was much older than ECLA had presumed, and it was not subject to reform by the strategies ECLA had proposed. In fact, it was not subject to reform at all. At no time in their history had Latin American states had the opportunity to industrialize, as ECLA had supposed. The structural division of the world into center and periphery began in the sixteenth century when Europeans initiated the expropriation of surplus from their far-flung colonies. Colonial surplus had helped to generate economic development in Europe while, simultaneously, it had created underdevelopment in the periphery. By placing innumerable restrictions upon manufacture and trade, European metropoles acquired monopoly rights over vital economic functions. Key manufactures and services were preserved for metropolitan businesses while the colonies were deliberately restricted to the production of raw materials.

The development of the center and the underdevelopment of the periphery were two sides of the same coin, argued Frank. It is futile to contend, as members of the modernization school have done, that development and underdevelopment are relative conditions, that one merely represents more development than the other. Development and underdevelopment are not products of different economic systems; they do not represent different stages of economic growth within the same system. Although they have distinct forms, those distinctions must persist because the very existence of underdevelopment derives from the existence of development.

One by one, Frank dismissed the premises of the modernization school. Functionalist theory presumed the existence of homeostatic equilibrium, the tendency of a social system to strive for balance between separate elements of the same social structure. Frank's center-periphery concept presumed a world-scale social structure that was predicated on the permanent existence of disequilibrium between the developed metropole and the underdeveloped periphery. Evolutionary theory was a fiction. The Third World, Frank contended, was stuck in permanent subjection to the industrialized nations. Moreover, the inclination of modernization theorists to focus their analyses on individual national units was myopic, Frank thought. Underdevelopment was a global problem. All nations of the Third World suffered from the same general condition. They were all structurally tied to the developed, metropolitan center. Well-meaning modernization programs that tinkered with social and economic problems within the separate underdeveloped states had no chance of success because they did not address the universal structural condition that produced underdevelopment.

Issues that concerned members of the modernization school were often trivial, Frank thought. How much could it matter whether a country in Latin America or Africa divided its politicians into parties and held free elections? What difference could it make in the overall scheme of things if there was less rather than more political instability in peripheral states?

Frank denied the claim of sociologists that countries in Latin America were backward because they had dual social and economic systems: feudalism in the countryside and capitalism in the cities. The villain of the modernization school, feudalism, was not feudalism at all! What passed for feudalism in a country like Brazil was, in reality, a product of world capitalism, Frank wrote. No part of any Latin American economy was feudal: all of it—right down to the smallest Indian village—was integrated into a single world system of capitalism. As for the hopes that moderniz-ers placed on the development of a national bourgeoisie, Frank demurred. There was no possibility that a national bourgeoisie would be "independent enough" to lead a real national liberation movement or "progressive enough to destroy the capitalist structure of underdevelop-ment at home."[15] The Latin American bourgeoisie remained a thoroughly compromised tool of foreign industry, he argued. Its interests were shaped by its relations with foreign economic forces, and its members used high government office to spawn policies that perpetuated social, political, and economic underdevelopment.

This was not new. In its earliest days, the independence movement in Latin America was advanced by exporters of raw materials who sought to increase their exports to the British industrial market. Political indepen-dence only intensified economic dependency. During the nineteenth cen-tury, sectors of the Latin American bourgeoisie involved in marketing raw materials challenged and defeated the more industrial-oriented bourgeoisie in a series of civil wars. Liberal reforms in the nineteenth century were not simply a result of ideological enlightenment: they permitted an increase in the production and export of primary products. Even in the late twentieth century, the Latin American bourgeoisie links itself to the metropole as a junior partner, endorsing policies that increase the economic subjugation of their nations.[16]

In Frank's opinion, the strategies of the modernization school almost always left countries worse off than before. Rostow's concept of stages of economic growth had no bearing on realities in the Third World. It was futile to expect peripheral countries to repeat the growth experience of modern developed nations. Having achieved development by exploiting a colonial periphery, countries of the center continued to prosper by pro-longing their exploitative advantage. In a complex global system in which development and underdevelopment, dominance and dependency, were integral elements of a single historical process, dependent communities could not expect benignly to repeat the development experience of the central dominant states. The system required a center and a periphery. The center already existed, and it jealously guarded its privileges. Rostow's formula for modernization would only compound the problems of the Third World. If peripheral countries obtained the means to reinvest more than 10 percent of their national income by borrowing money from great metropolitan financial institutions or by encouraging private investment by large metropolitan corporations, they would only be transferring more surplus from the periphery to the center and thereby increasing the level of their dependency. The only way to change the system was to get rid of it. The only way to get rid of it was through armed revolution.

Frank's theory provoked criticism from both right and left. The right, highly ill-disposed to revolution, accused him of indulging too much in ideology and too little in empirical research. Marxists were mortified. Frank was a proponent of revolution, and he worked within an intellectual context—dependency—that had acquired strong Marxist associations. But he violated the most sacred principles of Marxism. His motor of history was not conflict between classes. Although class was not unimportant, class struggles were integrated in and subsumed by a conflict between geographical regions of the world, between center and periphery. Frank's economic structure was not fundamentally defined by mode of production. Production was meaningful only in the context of exchange relations. In fact, Frank disregarded what Marxist scholars had identified as numerous pre-capitalist modes of production in Latin America. Although such modes might appear to exist, he argued, all productive structures in the region were enveloped by capitalism.

Frank's orientation was particularly disturbing to conventional Marxists who adhered to the proposition that society must evolve through successive economic stages based on mode of production. For them, historical theory served a specific teleological purpose: to provide a guide to revolutionary action. Frank advocated revolution. But, in the absence of class analysis, who did Frank presume would form his revolutionary cadre? Who would serve as his rank and file?[17]

In spite of, perhaps because of, the controversial nature of his views, Frank raised the level and the range of debate. Latin American Marxists, like members of the modernization school, had focused their efforts on individual polities. Frank concentrated upon a world-scale economic system, arguing that underdevelopment is the product of a long historical process. No progress in modernization could be made, he argued, until the historical and structural character of underdevelopment was understood.

Although Frank rooted his theory in history, he made no claim to be a historian, and he readily admitted to the empirical thinness of his historical work. His first concern was Third World development; his intended audience was the people who were striving to achieve it. Still, his concept of the "development of underdevelopment" immediately aroused interest among historians, particularly radical Third World historians for whom similar ideas had been gestating for several decades.[18] In 1972, the radical West Indian scholar Walter Rodney published *How Europe Underdeveloped Africa*, transferring some of the themes of dependency analysis to Africa, where it has since taken root.[19] The ultimate payoff emerged two years later in Immanuel Wallerstein's *Modern World System*, a comprehensive historical theory of the emergence and development of the modern capitalist world.[20] Wallerstein's world-system analysis, an elaboration of Frank's theory, quickly took large sectors of the history profession by storm.

NOTES

1. Barbara Ward and René Dubos, *Only One Earth: The Care and Maintenance of a Small Planet* (New York, 1972).

2. Donald Worster, "The Vulnerable Earth: Toward a Planetary History," in Donald Worster, ed., *The Ends of the Earth: Perspectives on Modern Environmental History* (New York, 1988), p. 4.

3. Raymond F. Dasmann, "Toward a Biosphere Consciousness," in Worster, ed., *The Ends of the Earth*, pp. 277–278.

4. Worster, "The Vulnerable Earth," p. 15.

5. Having barely escaped Italian conquest in the 1890s, Ethiopia succumbed to Mussolini's invasion in 1935; Liberia was, in reality, an economic colony of the United States.

6. In purely territorial terms, the European sway was extended by the defeat of the Ottoman Empire in World War I. Britain and France assumed imperial control over all Arab lands between the Mediterranean and the Persian Gulf.

7. With some sarcasm, Eric Wolf titled his book on the interaction of Europeans with peoples of the wider world as follows: *Europe and the People without History* (Berkeley, 1982).

8. William H. McNeill, *The Rise of the West: A History of the Human Community* (Chicago, 1963); L. S. Stavrianos, *A Global History of Man* (Boston, 1962).

9. William H. McNeill, "Organizing Concepts for World History," *Review* 10 (1986): 211–229.

10. For an overview of the theories adopted by the modernization school, see Alvin Y. So, *Social Change and Development: Modernization, Dependency, and World-System Theories* (Newbury Park, 1990), pp. 17–37.

11. Political scientists emphasized the values of Western democracy—constitutional legitimacy, multiparty systems, and competitive electoral politics. Sociologists, being concerned about political instability, sought to reduce the stress of adjusting from tradi-

tional to modern cultural norms. Economists proposed various strategies to stimulate capital accumulation and market development.

12. W. W. Rostow, *The Stages of Economic Growth: A Non-Communist Manifesto* (Cambridge, 1960).

13. The Commission operated under leadership of Raul Prebisch, an economist, academic, and former director-general of the Central Bank of Argentina. Raul Prebisch, *The Economic Development of Latin America and Its Principal Problems* (New York, 1950).

14. For an introduction to the extensive literature on dependency, see Roland H. Chilcote, "Dependency: A Critical Synthesis of the Literature," *Latin American Perspectives* 1 (1974): 3–29. His edited work, *Dependency and Marxism: Toward a Resolution of the Debate* (Boulder, 1982) brings analysis of the literature further. Also see So, *Social Change and Development*, pp. 91–165.

15. André Gunder Frank, *Capitalism and Underdevelopment in Latin America: Historical Studies of Chile and Brazil* (New York, 1967), xii.

16. André Gunder Frank, *Lumpenbourgeoisie: Lumpendevelopment, Dependence, Class and Politics in Latin America* (New York, 1972), pp. 3–16.

17. Among Marxists, Frank's greatest sin was his effect upon the revolutionary movement. He has been accused of confusing and dividing Marxists across the southern continent. In Marxist theory, class interest should provide the medium through which revolutionary sentiment is galvanized. For example, a class-based revolutionary strategy could set peasants, workers, the petite bourgeoisie, and the industrial bourgeoisie against feudal interests as a preliminary step toward the ultimate socialist revolution. In this context, conventional Marxists might, as an interim step, support the development of a national bourgeoisie. But Frank confounded such class-based strategies, arguing that the structure of dependency had penetrated to the core of Latin American society, corrupting local interests, distorting class interests, and inspiring complicity with foreign capitalist forces at every level.

18. At a December 1986 conference, "South Asia and World Capitalism," held at Tufts University and attended by many of the world's leading South Asian historians, I was astonished by the degree to which the idiom of world-system analysis had penetrated the Asian field.

19. For a striking example of the influence of dependency analysis in African history, see Joseph Inikori's "Introduction" in Inikori, ed., *Forced Migration: The Impact of the Export Slave Trade on African Societies* (New York, 1982).

20. Immanuel Wallerstein, *The Modern World-System I: Capitalist Agriculture and the Origins of the European World-Economy in the Sixteenth Century* (New York, 1974). This is the first of four volumes treating the course of modern history.

7

World-System Analysis

World-system analysis links the rise of capitalism to Europe's overseas expansion in the sixteenth century. It approaches history from the outside in, from the periphery to the center, demonstrating the momentous effect that frontier lands have had on the development of wealth and culture in the metropolis. It is new to the extent that it consolidates within a single comprehensive historical formulation a number of theories that have accumulated in historical literature over many decades.

Americans were the first modern scholars earnestly to address their history from the outside in. A century ago, American history was written from the perspective of the eastern seaboard. Emphasis was placed upon the impact of European influences on the original colonies and the outward dispersal of those influences toward the frontier. In 1893, Frederick Jackson Turner delivered a paper before the American Historical Association revolutionizing historical orientations in the United States. His essay, "The Significance of the Frontier in American History," scorned the "exclusive attention" paid by American historians to

European influences, arguing instead that the frontier, not the Atlantic coast, had "furnished the forces dominating American character."[1] The advance of the frontier had reduced dependence on Britain; it had nurtured "the formation of a composite nationality" among ethnically diverse European immigrants; and most important, the frontier had encouraged individualism and promoted democracy. It was the frontier that shaped the American personality, its coarseness, its inquisitiveness, its inventiveness, its capacity to find expedients, its restless energy, its firm grasp of material things. As well, it discouraged artistic accomplishments, permitted lax business honor, and gave rise to a comparatively low civic spirit, which manifested itself in the spoils system, disreputable currency schemes, and wildcat banking. The underlying dynamic of American history was to be found on the periphery. Initiatives arose there. The frontier generated its own momentum, and that momentum was unstoppable. No treaties, no administrative regulation, no Washington politicians could halt the inexorable march of the westward migrants. The frontier acted; the center reacted.

EUROPE'S GREAT FRONTIER

Considered the most influential thesis in American history, the Turner thesis has had detractors as well as defenders.[2] Among its most ardent defenders was Walter Prescott Webb, a distinguished historian of the American West, who in the years following World War II expanded Turner's thesis to embrace the entire Atlantic basin. Webb lamented that the frontier thesis had been confined to the history of North America. European and Latin American historians had all but ignored it. Yet Europe, too, had had its frontier, wrote Webb. Not only was it a much larger frontier than that of the United States, it was the greatest frontier in history, almost as influential in forming the institutions of Europe as the American frontier had been in shaping those of the United States. Opened by Columbus and the explorers who followed him, it encompassed the entire Western hemisphere in the sixteenth century, expanding thereafter to include Australia, New Zealand, and other regions of the Eastern hemisphere.

Webb used the word "metropolis" to define Europe—a densely populated, small region, a "cultural center holding within it everything pertaining to Western civilization."[3] The Americas, Europe's initial frontier, were a "vast and vacant land without culture,"[4] five to six times the size of the metropolis and capable of producing every conceivable material asset.

European exploitation of these assets gave rise to modern capitalism and precipitated a four-century economic boom unprecedented in human history .

America was a one-time windfall. There are no more Americas left, no more rich and vacant lands. By 1950, Europe's 450-year frontier had closed. The experience of that frontier constituted an utterly abnormal phase in the regular course of historical development. The modern age, beginning with Columbus, did not flow from preceding history as a natural evolution. It emerged boldly under the conditions of economic boom generated by unparalleled and unexpected territorial acquisition.

Advocating what he called the boom hypothesis—"the most naked reality of the modern age"—Webb examined the three classic ingredients of economic productivity—land, labor, and capital—in the context of Europe's frontier experience. He accepted William Graham Sumner's contention that the "ratio of population to land . . . determines what are the possibilities of human development or the limits of what men can attain in civilization and comfort."[5] When Columbus set sail, the population/land ratio in the European metropolis was 26.7 people per square mile. With the addition of 20 million square miles of "fabulously rich [American] land practically devoid of population," that ratio fell to less than 5 persons per square mile. Not until the 1930s would the population/land ratio for Europe and its "great frontier" return to that of Columbus's day.[6]

The metropolis fully exploited the capital assets of its frontier. Between 1492 and 1930, the value of gold and silver in the metropolis rose by over 18,000 percent.[7] The frontier "hung like a horn of plenty over the Metropolis," emptying upon it "an avalanche of wealth beyond human comprehension": coffee, cocoa, sugar, forest products, furs, cotton, maize, hides, tobacco, rubber—not to mention quinine, a drug derived from Peruvian bark that protected Europeans from malaria and enabled them to conquer sub-Saharan Africa.[8]

Webb's simplistic concept of capitalism would have chagrined Max Weber. He defined capitalism merely as a cultural complex involving a striving for profit. Because there was so little wealth for Europeans to strive for, capitalism did not emerge as a general cultural phenomenon before the sixteenth century, he thought. The great frontier changed all that, supplying the gold, silver, and space necessary for a capitalist economy. No one benefitted more than businessmen, Webb contended. Pursuing the arguments of Earl J. Hamilton,[9] Webb observed that bullion flows from the frontier to the metropolis produced price inflation in the sixteenth century. In Europe, commodity prices rose at a much sharper rate than rents or wages, giving advantage to the sellers of "things." Between 1500 and 1700, prices in France increased by 101 percent, wages by only 35.8 percent. A similar situation prevailed in England. Landlords and laborers were losing advantage; entrepreneurs were gaining. There was never a time in history so accommodating to the businessman, the speculator, and the profiteer. The century from 1550 to 1650 was a golden age, declared John Maynard Keynes: it was the time when modern capitalism was born.[10] Capitalism had waited upon opportunity. When the great frontier provided that opportunity, capitalism took hold.

The frontier imposed its stamp upon human values and public institutions as well. If the frontier inculcated in North Americans a strong sense of individualism and a predisposition for democracy, it also inspired a respect for hard work. Walter Prescott Webb may never have read Max Weber, but like Weber, he seized upon Benjamin Franklin as the human embodiment of a particular set of values—the values of the frontier, not the values of European-based Calvinism, as Weber had contended. When Franklin addressed his American audience through *Poor Richard's Almanack,* delivering homely maxims like "God helps them that help themselves" or "God gives all things to industry" or "Early to bed and early to rise makes a man healthy, wealthy, and wise," he was expressing the folk wisdom of a people who had learned such lessons through prolonged encounter with the frontier. Although metropolitan governments and metropolitan peoples may have been the main beneficiaries of the opening of the great frontier, the dynamic forces that drove the historical process and shaped the character of Western civilization after 1500 emerged on the periphery.

Webb's orientation was reinforced by an Oxford-educated Trinidadian scholar, Eric Eustace Williams, who shocked his English mentors and aroused intense controversy by contending, most persuasively, that plantation colonies in the British West Indies generated the capital that underwrote the English Industrial Revolution. His book, *Capitalism and Slavery* (1944), offered the quintessential outside-in argument. It rooted the origins of one of the two most significant events in human history (the other being the Agricultural Revolution, B.C. 8000–3500) on the colonial periphery of Europe's world economy.

Williams defied conventional historical wisdom. The Industrial Revolution began in England in the eighteenth century, spread to Belgium and northern France in the early nineteenth century, thence to Central Europe and the United States. Since Arnold Toynbee first gave expression to the abstraction, "the Industrial Revolution," historians have sought its origins in the special conditions of Europe and the particular genius of Europeans. Because Britain experienced the only unassisted industrial revolution (all follower states had a British model to emulate), the tendency of historians has been to ask "Why was England first?" and to seek the particular combination of forces within England that propelled the nation's economy toward industrialization.[11] Economic historians generally recognize the importance of colonial trade in the evolution of the British economy, but as a rule they consider internal trade to have been more important than overseas trade in the eighteenth century. Even the late Ralph Davis, a specialist in early English trade and author of *The Rise of the Atlantic Economies,* concluded that colonial economies were merely "subsidiary to" and an "enhancement of" the internal economies of the individual European states.[12]

At the time of its publication, *Capitalism and Slavery* received little attention from scholars. What attention it did get was mainly hostile. In the 1950s, however, colonial independence movements produced a highly receptive audience for Williams's point of view. His work embraced the salient historical issues of the postwar world: racism, slavery, the origins of industrialization, and the evolution of a world order divided between rich and poor.[13]

Williams observed that the opening of the Americas vastly increased world trade. For Britain, that trade was chiefly triangular, linking Africa and plantation America with the Mother Country. Trade in African slaves was "the mainspring" that set "every wheel in motion."[14] By 1750, there was hardly a trading or manufacturing town not connected with the slave trade. The British West India colonies, alone, represented nearly one-seventh of Britain's total overseas trade between 1714 and 1773.[15] Every Englishman with ten slaves in the West Indies gave employment to four workers in England; moreover, the West Indies were the commercial partners of North American colonists who exported fish, timber, grains, farm animals, vegetables, and assorted other primary products to the plantations to sustain the slaves. At home, Bristol's trade with the West Indies was worth double that of its other overseas commerce. Liverpool owed its success as a port to the slave trade. Lodged in Lancashire, the nuclear region of the Industrial Revolution, Liverpool called the industry of Lancashire into existence, not the reverse. Williams gave numerous examples of individual entrepreneurs who, having accumulated capital in the slave trade, in slave holding, in ship building, or in industries supplying the slave trade and the slave plantations, invested their earnings in Britain's infant industries. It was capital earned from the West Indian trade, he noted, that financed James Watt and the steam engine.[16]

In the 1960s, Williams's argument garnered powerful support from Richard Sheridan, an assiduous American economic historian who demonstrated that tropical American plantations yielded large capital surpluses for investment in Britain.[17] In the final years of the eighteenth century, West Indian property earned between 8 and 10 percent of the income of Great Britain, Sheridan argued.[18] Like Williams, he used selected examples to show that the richest colonial planters invested enormous sums in British government securities, the factorage business, shipping, and industry.[19] In the main, however, Sheridan, like Williams, offered little comparative data on the relative importance of West Indian capital in stimulating particular areas of British industry. Both have relied on the general argument that trade begets trade, that earnings produce investment, and that the slave colonies, as a center of trade and a source of savings, provided the necessary impetus to launch the English Industrial Revolution.[20] Scholars in the Third World have embraced the Williams-Sheridan position. In the First World, most historians have continued to seek the origins of modern industrialization in forces internal to Europe.[21]

THE WORLD-SYSTEM

The most expansive history from the outside-in, a work that integrates provocative studies like those of Webb and Williams with modern dependency theory, is Immanuel Wallerstein's multi-volume treatise on the modern world-system. Wallerstein's model is the most influential to appear in recent decades. It is certainly among the most controversial. A sociologist by training, Wallerstein has founded a "school" of history, a scholarly journal, and an institute to facilitate world-system research.[22] His historical orientation, like that of Eric Williams, has been most warmly embraced in the Third World. Third World scholars continue to seek explanations for their dependency, for their poverty, for the decimation of local institutions, traditional values, and collective self-esteem. The world-system model identifies a long-standing exploitative relationship that assigns moral culpability to the West and sanctions righteous indignation in the wider world. It appeals, therefore, at both polemical and professional levels.

In the remainder of this chapter, it will be possible only to present Wallerstein's general theory, the main lines of his analysis, and a brief critique of his work. I will focus exclusively on his first volume, *The Modern World-System I: Capitalist Agriculture and the Origins of the European World-Economy in the Sixteenth Century* (1974). Here, in dealing with the transition from the medieval to the modern world, Wallerstein offers an explicit presentation of theory and a systematic response to key historical questions.

What is the subject to be studied? The creation of the modern world, a complex process involving the rise of capitalism. How important is it? Wallerstein considers it equivalent in importance to the Agricultural Revolution. How should such a study be organized? Not country by country, but as a comprehensive, integrated historical experience involving Europe and the entire Western hemisphere. Social change can be fathomed only in social systems, Wallerstein argues. National states do not constitute social systems, even though they may be important components of social systems. To understand the rise and development of the capitalist world, one must study the capitalist social system as a whole—the modern world-system.

How do we define the modern world-system? It is an economic, not a political, phenomenon. Historically, it functioned through an exploitative division of labor that permitted West Europeans to extract surplus wealth from Eastern Europe and America to fuel their breakthrough to capitalism. Systemically, it involved a division of the Atlantic basin into three concentric hierarchical tiers distinguished by their products and by their modes of production: northwestern Europe was the commercial and industrial core; central and southern Europe constituted a dependent semiperiphery; Europe east of the River Elbe and most of the American colonies formed a dependent periphery engaged in the production of primary products. The system was driven by the desire for profit. Its efficient functioning required the use of free wage labor at the core, tenantry and share-cropping in the semiperiphery, and coerced labor in the periphery. All three zones were integrated through trade, and trade was dominated by merchants of the core. These are the main elements of the world-system. Each will be treated in greater detail later.

Wallerstein chose the term "world-system" because it transcended any juridically defined political unit. As his title indicates, he also used the term "world-economy" to refer specifically to economic aspects of the world-system.[23] The modern world-system encompassed a congeries of nations, city-states, and empires bound together by economic forces. Before the advent of modern world-economy, there were others—Roman, Persian, Chinese—but each of these became coequal with a political empire. Although such empires were capable of guaranteeing economic flows from the periphery to the center through the regulation of trade and tribute, they required bureaucracies at the center and repressive military forces at the perimeter. Both absorbed profits. The distinguishing characteristic of the modern world-system is that it thrived and expanded in the Atlantic basin without a central political structure. In fact, argues Wallerstein, it thrived and expanded *because* it lacked a central political structure. Capitalism and modern science provided the structure.

Capitalism did not impel Europeans to launch their overseas empires. *Capitalism was a product of European expansion.* It was the discovery and colonization of the New World, writes Wallerstein, that saved Europe from collapsing into anarchy. Late-medieval Europe was in crisis. In the three centuries before 1300, the continent had experienced geographic, commercial, and demographic expansion. Between 1300 and 1450, what had expanded contracted. To explain this contraction, Wallerstein combines three theoretical lines of argument. First, he accepts the neo-Malthusian theory of cyclical economic trends treated in Chapter 4 of this book, arguing that population, having grown beyond the capacity of land and technology to sustain it, suffered decline. Second, he takes up the Marxist argument, examined in Chapter 5, that a thousand years of surplus extraction in the feudal mode of production had produced impasse. The lords wanted more, but the peasants were unwilling and unable to produce more. Third, he accepts the climatic argument that a fall in average temperatures reduced soil productivity in Europe. The crisis of feudalism, he argues, resulted from a conjuncture of these three conditions. There was only one way for Europe to escape economic contraction and social chaos: to expand overseas.[24]

Expansion was the first and most critical requirement for the formation of a capitalist world-system. There were two others: (1) the establishment of differing methods of production in the three zones of the world-economy; (2) the development of strong state machineries in the European core states.

The first of these insured greater efficiency in the production of staple foods and minerals across several climatic zones. In much of tropical and subtropical America where native populations were thin or nonexistent, European masters imposed slave labor.[25] Slave labor was needed in situations where open land resources required a rigid disciplining of workers to achieve efficient plantation production. Slave labor was possible in America because Africa was willing to supply the slaves. East of the Elbe, the capitalist world-economy called into being a "second serfdom," what Wallerstein prefers to call coerced cash-crop labor. In the semiperiphery, share-cropping was widely adopted. Because population/land ratios in Southern Europe were generally higher than in Eastern Europe, the amount of coercion required to stimulate agricultural production there was lower. In the northwest European core, high population density, intensive farming practices, and urban manufacturing all conspired to encourage the use of competitive free labor.

In describing the effect of capital transfers between the New World and the Old, Wallerstein uses the same sources[26] and much the same argument as Walter Prescott Webb. American bullion stimulated inflation, and inflation, unaccompanied by a comparable rise in real wages, generated a profit windfall for the manufacturers and sellers of "things." Wallerstein takes Webb's argument a step further. Different European workers responded differently to inflation. In old industrial centers where workers enjoyed strength (e.g., Flanders and northern Italy), wages tended to keep pace with inflation. Where workers possessed little power or solidarity (e.g., Spain) wages lagged far behind prices. In Holland and England, a middle position prevailed: relative wages fell, but not catastrophically. On balance, the sixteenth century witnessed both a reduction of income for workers and a redistribution of manufacturing investment within Europe. Manufacturers were ill-disposed to invest in low-wage countries like Spain because low wages impaired purchasing power and thereby depressed regional markets. Entrepreneurs steered away from high-wage areas like Venice because wages absorbed too much of their profits. It was the mid-range countries, notably England and Holland, that offered optimal conditions for industrial investment. During the sixteenth century, it was these countries that established their position at the core of the capitalist world-economy.

Despite differences in labor control and apparent differences in modes of production across the several tiers of the capitalist world-economy, the whole system was capitalist, argues Wallerstein. The argument is identical to the one advocated by André Gunder Frank for twentieth-century Latin America. No large region produced exclusively for a local economy. All labor forms were calculated to produce the largest quantity of goods in the most efficient manner for a world market, and the governing principle of that market was capitalist.[27] The Caribbean slave holder, the Polish seigneur, and the Dutch manufacturer were all capitalists, for the exploitative pressures that each of them exerted upon their laborers were dictated by the demand-supply curve of the world market. There is little doubt, adds Wallerstein, that the capitalist world-economy had established a unified market: in 1500, the price gap between the Christian Mediterranean and Eastern Europe was around 6 to 1; by 1750, it was 2 to 1.[28]

THE WORLD-SYSTEM AND THE STATES SYSTEM

The rise of capitalism and the development of powerful states at the European core were mutually reinforcing phenomena. Strong states were necessary to ensure the preservation of order, control of the seas, and efficient exploitation of colonial lands. A plurality of states at the core was equally important; otherwise, the world-economy might become a world-empire. The principal preoccupation of any state is self-preservation. In the case of empire states, self-preservation involves either the repression or the accommodation of all sectors of the imperial polity. Both are expensive. The latter is generally achieved by insuring that the wealth of the empire is dispersed with some degree of equity to all parts of the imperial community. Economic efficiency is thereby sacrificed to political necessity. In the case of the capitalist world-system, a plurality of strong states at the core of the world-economy insured inter-state competition at the core. This competition promoted more efficient distribution of production functions and capital flows throughout the system, and it inspired a more thorough exploitation of the periphery in the interest of preserving the competitive edge of the core states. Capitalism has flourished, writes Wallerstein, "precisely because the world-economy has had within its bounds not one but a multiplicity of political systems.[29]

For Wallerstein, that which determined whether a country would become a powerful core state was its ability to establish a secure bourgeoisie dedicated to commercial and industrial enterprise. England and Holland did it. Spain did not. France held a middle ground. Geography as well as politics (one might even say, politics as a function of geography) played a decisive role. The overriding political issue of the sixteenth century was the conflict for imperial pre-eminence in Europe between the houses of Habsburg (Spain, Austria) and Valois (France). They competed for the title of Holy Roman Emperor; they fought numerous wars for control of Italy; and they remained hostile and belligerent well into the seventeenth century, mutually exhausting one another while succumbing to a succession of royal bankruptcies. The Spanish government paid out its American silver to support war and to purchase the manufactures of the Low Countries, offering little inducement for the development of its own domestic industries. When, in the interest of imperial religious solidarity, Catholic Spain attempted to discipline its Calvinist-ridden estates in the Low Countries, rebellion erupted there, destroying the prosperity of Flanders and establishing an independent economic power of the first magnitude in the Netherlands. The United Netherlands became the quintessentially bourgeois state.

England outdistanced France as a core state. The reason lies partly in geography. With no part of the country more than 75 miles from the sea, England was decidedly maritime. She enjoyed the benefits of cheap water transport. Like the Netherlands, the country could serve as a half-way station for trades linking the Baltic and Mediterranean; and, of course, England stood opposite the great river estuaries of the Meuse and the Rhine, which carried trade goods to and from the continental interior. With the growth of New World trades, England and the Netherlands concentrated on the sea. By contrast, France was both a maritime and a continental state. The kingdom had three natural geopolitical zones: the northwest, looking outward to the Atlantic; the northeastern Rhenish area; and the south. In the great imperial struggle with Spain, the latter two took precedence. The French nobility preserved its pre-eminence while the French bourgeoisie was seduced into seeking status enhancement through the purchase of royal offices. In England the aristocracy and gentry readily took to commerce, occasioning the embourgeoisement of power. In France, on the other hand, the bourgeoisie was feudalized. Dutch and English capitalists undersold French competitors in domestic as well as foreign markets. French shipbuilding and French trade fell behind, and the country relied increasingly on the production of goods for which it held a historic edge—luxuries, especially silk—when the sale of cheaper goods in wider markets would have provided a firmer industrial base. In the new capitalist world-economy, France was able to preserve advantage over Spain and Germany, but the English and Dutch achieved advantage over all.

HOW THE WORLD-SYSTEM FUNCTIONED

The sixteenth-century capitalist world-system had a specific geographical dimension. Its size was limited principally by the speed at which communication could occur between its most widely separated components.[30] Whenever technological developments increased the speed of communications, the world-system was capable of expanding. As Wallerstein conceived it, the world-system was highly self-contained. If the sixteenth-century capitalist world-system had been cut off from all external regions of the world, it would have continued to function in essentially the same way.[31]

In response to changing geopolitical and resource factors, the relative position of all entities within the capitalist world-system was subject to change. Individual components were able to rise in status, say from peripheral to semiperipheral status, or to fall a notch. Wallerstein's concept of a semiperiphery, a third tier in the world hierarchy, is a major innovation upon Frank's bimodal (metropolis-satellite) theory of dependency. While each tier is only an abstract category—a convenient mental vehicle—the concept of the semiperiphery offers slack to the world-system and facilitates our understanding of how structural change occurs. The middle layer interacted with both core and periphery; it considered itself superior to the periphery; and it indulged (albeit less fully than the core) in the exploitation of the periphery. Consequently, the semi-periphery deflected some of the political heat that peripheral communities would otherwise have directed exclusively upon the core.

Although Wallerstein suggests several ways in which states can rise within the world-system,[32] his system is biased in favor of stability. Division of labor within the world-system is both functional and geographical. The most complex tasks requiring the highest skill levels and the heaviest capitalization have been reserved for the core. Because the system rewards these tasks at a higher rate than the less skilled tasks performed in the periphery, the tendency of the system has been to perpetuate the prevailing geographical maldistribution of wealth—indeed, to intensify it.[33]

Wallerstein has produced an elaborate division of labor model, although it is one that differs in subtlety and complexity from that of Adam Smith and later-day historians of the commercial school. Wallerstein does not assume that commercial growth and an expanding international division of labor will uniformly generate higher levels of economic prosperity and greater cultural enrichment. The world-system division of labor may have multiplied the world's wealth, but it distributed it unequally. In Poland and other regions east of the Elbe, for example, the advent of large-scale international trade led to a monocultural economy based on grain exports to the West, the demise of the regional bourgeoisie, the decline of handicrafts, the withering of towns, the impoverishment of cultural life, and the growth of serfdom—the "second serfdom." Having consolidated their land holdings and intensified their exploitation of labor, Polish lords aggrandized in their own behalf the profits of international trade. Meanwhile, Poland became a peripheral country from which surplus was drained to the northwest European core.

Like André Gunder Frank, Wallerstein challenged conventional Marxist analysis. Marxists generally attempt to explain the transition from feudalism to capitalism within the geographical confines of Western Europe, ordinarily focusing on the operation of historical forces within single sovereign states. Class differentiation was thought to be dictated by local productive forces, and differing modes of production—whether feudal or capitalist—represented different stages of development toward socialism. Wallerstein subsumes all such differences within a single vast world-system, declaring the whole enterprise to be capitalist. As an engine of change, class struggle has been replaced by interaction and struggle between geographical regions of the world-system.

Wallerstein devotes little attention to demographic forces, except as a partial explanation for the crisis of the late Middle Ages. Although he recognizes that the core states were Protestant and the semiperipheral states Catholic, he dismisses Weber's theory of the Calvinist roots of capitalism without engaging it. In his view, religious ideas are highly malleable and, in the sixteenth century, they were marshalled to reinforce specific social and economic interests. Along with many of Weber's critics, Wallerstein thinks the great German sociologist could just as easily have written a book entitled "The Catholic Ethic and the Spirit of Capitalism."

CHALLENGES TO THE WORLD-SYSTEM MODEL

The world-system model may be weakest at its point of inception. Wallerstein provides an eclectic blending of the arguments of neo-Malthusians, Marxists, and a noted climatic determinist to explain why Europeans expanded overseas and established the capitalist world-system. Late medieval Europe was in crisis, he says, and that crisis was the result of three conditions: a Malthusian demographic crisis; a crisis in the feudal mode of production; and a climatic reversal. Since the issue of climate will be addressed in the next chapter, we need only consider the former two explanations here.

How grave was the crisis in Europe when overseas expansion came to the continent's rescue? Plague had swept away up to 33 percent of the population in the years around 1350, and recurring epidemics had kept the population well below its late-thirteenth-century level until the sixteenth century. By the time Prince Henry the Navigator launched the Portuguese overseas explorations, population pressure had eased all across Europe. As for the Marxist contention that class conflict between lords and serfs had reached an impasse, that too had subsided with the demographic blowout of the plague. If there was a feudal crisis after 1450, it involved the decline of the lords' bargaining power and the consequent emancipation of the serfs. Population decline might have occasioned a fall in the volume of international trade, with the effect that some commercial towns were weakened, but per capita income for working people—and that represents the vast majority of Europeans—rose in the fifteenth century.[34]

By presenting an unduly gloomy picture of the state of Europe in 1450 and by urging that without overseas expansion the continent would have succumbed to anarchy and fratricidal war, Wallerstein is guilty of highly tactical argumentation. Because he exaggerates the peril of Europe's situation, he unduly enhances the importance of the remedy employed to escape it—the discovery and colonization of America.

Explaining Europe's thrust overseas, Wallerstein contends that above all, Europeans needed more abundant food supplies (calories) and fuel. This has become a popular line of argument, and it would be futile to contend that Europeans—or anyone else in the fifteenth century—would not have benefited from greater food. But were Europeans driven by the exigencies of hunger into overseas exploration and colonization? Falling population since 1350 had reduced pressure on the land. The least productive lands had been taken out of cultivation; Baltic grain was beginning to arrive in northwestern Europe in sufficient quantity to permit English landlords to transform arable land into grazing land; and increasing numbers of workers in the Lowlands were leaving agriculture in favor of industry. Even after the Americas were discovered, there was no inordinant rush to bring the new lands into cultivation. North America lay vacant for a century. The Portuguese held a claim to Brazil for over thirty years before they initiated formal settlement there.[35] When settlement was undertaken, the reason was not to supply food to European markets but to prevent another European power from claiming the region.

Having exaggerated the ills of Europe in the fifteenth century, Wallerstein is compelled to ask why Portugal was the agent that extricated Christendom from want and chaos. Why would one of the weakest, poorest, and most peripheral kingdoms step forward to save the continent? Because, argues Wallerstein, Portugal's location adjacent to vital ocean currents made it easier for her to undertake exploration and because "she alone of the European states maximized will and possibility."[36] The currents had always been there, even in 1300 when population pressure was at its peak and the need for new lands was greatest. As for maximizing will and possibility, that may be a clever turn of phrase, but it is not an explanation.

The problem is that Wallerstein cannot draw a logical connection between his analysis of Europe's needs and Portugal's action. The question "Why Portugal?" is not new. It has long perplexed historians and given rise to elaborate myths about a far-sighted royal prince, Henry the Navigator, who steered his tiny impoverished country along a steady course of Atlantic exploration. It is more probable that Henry and his compatriots took greater interest in Morocco than the Atlantic, in knight-errantry and plundering Moors than commerce, and in personal conquest rather than the satisfaction of Europe's broad social needs.[37] In sum, Wallerstein does not offer a convincing argument about the historical forces that initiated the capitalist world-system.

In fairness, however, the central importance of Wallerstein's work rests on the operation of the world-system, not on its inception. The strength of the model hinges on two overriding hypotheses: (1) that American wealth was a necessary prerequisite for the breakthrough to capitalism in Europe; (2) that division of labor in the world-economy consistently favored the core at the expense of the periphery. If the first of these propositions is true, why did American metals circulate so quickly to parts of Europe beyond Spain unless, of course, they were attracted there by production? In the main, America's precious metals were converted to coin, not hoarded or used for religious ornamentation. The latter usage would have been consistent with the priorities of a precapitalist economy in which the volume of commercial exchange was limited. Since the highest priority for silver and gold in Europe was for use as a circulating medium, would that not imply that the society exercising that priority possessed an active exchange economy?

When does an exchange economy become active enough to be declared capitalist? Wallerstein does not say. In fact, he does not define capitalism as an economic phenomenon, institution, or way of life apart from his world-system. Like Webb, Wallerstein sees capitalism as a striving for profit within a cultural complex; unlike Webb, he provides elaborate definition of that complex. Yet the world-system did not take shape immediately upon the opening of the Americas. It was a half-century from the first settlements in Hispaniola to the discovery of silver loads in Mexico and Peru. The major American plantation crops were not developed until the late sixteenth and seventeenth centuries.[38] Are we to assume that the advent of capitalism awaited the slow consolidation of the Atlantic system of trade and empire?

Fernand Braudel thought not. The great distance between Europe and America and the long turnaround time for investors meant that only large-scale capitalists could have managed trade with America.[39] If America's precious metals were an important factor in European development, it was because Europe was ready to exploit them.[40] Had America offered no bullion, Europe would have discovered other outlets and secured other spoils, Braudel argued.[41] Ironically, Europeans may have been better off focusing on the East, where complex commercial networks and sophisticated infrastructures rendered wealth more accessible.[42] Many of Wallerstein's critics would reverse his outside-in ordering of history: it was not the exploitation of American bullion that created a vibrant European exchange economy; it was a vibrant European exchange economy that gave rise to a particular exploitation of America's resources.

There is no point in denying that American bullion oiled the productive process and accelerated the rate of circulation in Europe. But who benefited from it, and by how much? Spain, the immediate imperial profiteer of American mineral wealth, derived very little long-term economic benefit. In fact, it has been repeatedly argued that American bullion was the undoing of the Spanish economy. It permitted the Spanish to purchase desired manufactures from the northwest European countries while neglecting the development of the country's domestic industries. A Venetian ambassador to Madrid once observed that American treasure fell on Spain like rain on a roof—"it poures on her and it flows away."[43] Since most of it flowed to the manufacturing economies of the Northwest, it has been assumed that the Dutch and English were the real beneficiaries of Spain's American mines.

This assumption ignores one of the principal uses to which Spain's American bullion was put. Silver enabled Spain to pursue a century of warfare, much of it against the Protestant states of northwestern Europe. Warfare is a form of negative productivity. If, in the sixteenth century, warfare obliged the so-called core states, in their defense, to expend a large portion of their resources unproductively, should it not be concluded that one of the principal contributions of American bullion to the European world-economy was that it permitted a semiperipheral country, Spain, to misappropriate the continent's human and physical resources? The capitalist states of the core, against whom Spain directed its attacks, may have become capitalist not because of surplus extraction from America, but in spite of it.[44]

Did a world-scale division of labor consistently favor the core? Was the capitalist world-system enhanced by using free labor at the core and coerced labor in the periphery? Robert Brenner, a Marxist critic of world-system analysis, thinks not. In both cases, he uses Poland to illustrate his point. The imposition of an oppressive coerced labor regime in Poland, he argues, did not enhance the long-term growth of the core states. Nor can

Poland's feudal mode of production be considered an integral part of the capitalist system. It was because Polish lords persisted in a feudal mode and resisted capitalist development that Poland impeded rather than advanced economic growth in the core. In a manner typical of the feudal mode, Polish nobles made no effort to improve productive processes or to maximize their profits. They merely sustained their dominance and acquired Western luxuries by squeezing increasing levels of absolute surplus labor from the serfs. Without technical innovation, the non-capitalist Polish economy was unable to export more than 7 percent of its total grain product. When a genuine capitalist agriculture arose in the West, Polish grain became increasingly uncompetitive; exports from the Baltic fell; and the terms of trade began to run against the core and in favor of the periphery.[45]

Poland constitutes a problem for all the models treated in this book. The trade-based division-of-labor model assumes that increasing commercial exchange and international division of labor will, of necessity, generate higher levels of prosperity, social diversity, and human freedom. That happened in the West; it did not happen in Poland. According to demographic theorists, the fifteenth century should have been a favorable time for peasants, a period of trial for landowners. This was not the case in Poland. Moreover, the Polish experience does not fulfill the expectations of conventional Marxist analysis. Internal inconsistencies and class struggle within the feudal mode of production in Poland did not unhinge the oppressive system there in spite of a low population/land ratio. In Poland, the feudal system gathered strength from the same forces that are supposed to have destroyed it in the West. If Brenner's attack on Wallerstein's analysis of the East European periphery is reliable, then none of the models presented in this book satisfactorily explain why East Elbian Europe developed in the manner that it did.

Many historians bristle at Wallerstein's methodology. Even those with a high tolerance for grand social-science theorizing are frequently irritated by Wallerstein's penchant for reification and his tendency to engage in teleological explanation. There is little sense of contingency in his history, little coincidence, little blind luck, no accidents that send events lurching in unexpected directions. All things are linked and everything happens purposefully, as in the case of Portugal's rescue of a hungry and fratricidal Europe. The world-system is an abstract organizing concept, as are each of the hierarchical tiers within it; yet at one point or another Wallerstein affords them a conscious and deliberate will of their own. In summing up his world-system, he declares: "the capitalist world-economy was built on a worldwide division of labor in which various zones of this economy . . . were assigned specific economic roles, developed different class structures, used consequently different modes of labor control, and profited unequally from the workings of the system."[46] Did the capitalist world-system "assign" economic roles to the zones? Because states, zones, continents, and social classes are among the chief actors in Wallerstein's history, reification is difficult to avoid. Usually, Wallerstein keeps his language in check, but the abiding impression one garners from repeated readings of his work is that the world-system is not simply an organizing abstraction that reflects reality but a reality with a capacity for organization.

CONCLUSION

Wallerstein lifts the rise of capitalist modernity out of the parochial context of Western Europe. Employing the dependency theory of André Gunder Frank and building upon the historical insight of scholars like Webb and Williams, he has conceived a highly useful model to explain the organic relationship between diverse political and geographical entities in the modern world. Although the world-system he describes is conflictive and exploitative, the dynamic he employs is not Marxist. It is an elaborate division-of-labor model, driven by commerce and the desire for profit. Divisions within the model are determined by geography and resources, not by social class. If there is abiding tension within the system, it is an inter-regional, not inter-class, tension. Production distinctions are not ignored. They are critical to the operation of the model insofar as the world-system demands the use of free labor in the core and coerced labor in the periphery. Distinctions between the slave, the feudal, and the capitalist modes of production are acknowledged, but they are not given central importance because the whole system is defined by its dominant mode: capitalism.

Because the world-system is three-tiered, it has considerable flexibility. Peripheral countries can ascend to the semiperiphery, core countries can fall to the semiperiphery, and so on. The original structure was set in place by the exploitation of America's alluvial wealth. Bullion flows from America stimulated a price revolution in Europe, triggering a geographical division of labor that determined which states became the core, which the semiperiphery, and which the periphery. A plurality of sovereign states in the industrial core kept the system competitive and efficient, precluding the merger of the world-economy with a world-empire.

The model is more successful in explaining how early modern capitalism functioned over time and space than it is in explaining how capitalism came into being. Having followed Webb's lead in linking the advent of capitalism to the discovery and exploitation of America, Wallerstein drew too sharp a distinction between Europe, desperate and hungry, in the fifteenth century and Europe, saved by overseas expansion, in the later sixteenth. Virtually all scholars agree that the colonization of America significantly advanced the economic prospects of Europe, but many would deny that Europe's rapid economic and demographic growth during the sixteenth century—or for that matter, its transition to capitalism—hinged so profoundly upon the exploitation of the New World.

NOTES

1. Printed in Turner's *The Frontier in American History* (New York, 1920).

2. The debate on the Turner thesis has been the subject of two compilations for use in American history courses. See Ray Billington, ed., *The Frontier Thesis: Valid Interpretation of American History?* (Huntington, 1977) and George Roger Taylor, *The Turner Thesis Concerning the Role of the Frontier in American History* (Boston, 1956).

3. Walter Prescott Webb, *The Great Frontier* (Boston, 1952), p. 8.

4. Webb's language and orientation would give great offense in the 1990s. For him, the Americas and Australia were "the empty lands" without culture. Native populations were disregarded.

5. William Graham Sumner, "Earth-Hunger or the Philosophy of Land Grabbing," in Albert G. Keller, ed., *Earth-Hunger and Other Essays* (New Haven, 1913), p. 31, quoted in Webb, *The Great Frontier*, p. 17.

6. Webb, *The Great Frontier*, pp. 17–18. Webb was a woefully imprecise statistician. It must be granted that the discovery of the New World favorably altered the population/land ratio for Europeans, but Webb calculated the whole of the Western hemisphere as an immediate windfall. In fact, the windfall was realized one region at a time as Indian empires were subdued or European settlements pressed upon the wilderness. At no point did Webb include the native population of the Western hemisphere in his calculations. A great portion of the Americas (North America, Brazil, the Argentine) were sparsely populated. Very little of America was vacant; some of it—Central America and Peru—was rather densely inhabited. Despite the crude character of his calculations, his overall point is not invalidated by these statistical deficiencies.

7. Webb used the figures of Michel Chevalier, *Remarks on the Production of the Precious Metals and on the Depreciation of Gold* (London, 1853). Values would have been estimated in nineteenth-century American dollars.

8. Webb, *The Great Frontier*, p. 20.

9. Earl J. Hamilton, "American Treasure and the Rise of Capitalism (1500–1700)," *Economica* 9 (1929): 338–357.

10. Webb quotes Keynes to this effect; see *The Great Frontier*, p. 177.

11. N. F. R. Crafts, "Industrial Revolution in England and France: Some Thoughts on the Question, 'Why was England First?' " *Economic History Review* 30 (1977): 429–441. Special attention has been paid to technological innovation, to the substitution of inorganic (coal) for organic (wood) sources of energy, to trade and to capital accumulation, to demographic growth and the pressure of demand in the marketplace, to government institutions, to the degree of state regulation of industry, to guild structures, to the particular character of English society, to the flexibility of English law, and to the special advantages of England's geography. For a review of the historiography of the Industrial Revolution, see R. M. Hartwell, ed., *The Causes of the Industrial Revolution in England* (London, 1967).

12. Ralph Davis, *The Rise of the Atlantic Economies* (Ithaca, 1973), xiii.

13. There were, in fact, several theses lodged in *Capitalism and Slavery*: that black slavery generated racism, not the reverse; that slavery, the slave trade, and the slave plantations produced the capital that financed the Industrial Revolution; and that mature industrial capitalism, having arisen through the suffering of slaves, turned on slavery and destroyed it when the interests of capitalism were best served by free labor and free trade. Economic necessity produced slavery; economic necessity, not Christian philanthropy, ended it. In all their dealings in the wider world, Williams thought, the metropolitan peoples have consistently served themselves at the expense of others. Each of Williams's theses has been the subject of intense controversy, none more than his claim that the slave system underwrote the Industrial Revolution. For the most recent compilation of scholarly exchanges on Williams's work, see Barbara L. Solow and Stanley L. Engerman, eds., *British Capitalism and Caribbean Slavery: The Legacy of Eric Williams* (Cambridge, 1987).

14. Eric Williams, *Capitalism and Slavery* (Chapel Hill, 1944), p. 51.

15. Ibid., p. 58.

16. Ibid., pp. 102, 126–127.

17. Richard B. Sheridan, *Sugar and Slavery: An Economic History of the British West Indies, 1623–1775* (Baltimore, 1974) and "The Plantation Revolution and the Industrial Revolution, 1625–1775," *Caribbean Studies* 9 (1969): 5–25. Recent support has been forthcoming from Barbara Solow, "Caribbean Slavery and British Growth: The Eric Williams Hypothesis," *Journal of Development Economics* 17 (1985): 99–115.

18. Richard B. Sheridan, "The Wealth of Jamaica in the Eighteenth Century," *Economic History Review* 18 (1965): 292–311.

19. Richard B. Sheridan, "Simon Taylor, Sugar Tycoon of Jamaica, 1740–1813," *Agricultural History* 45 (1971): 285–296; "Planters and Merchants: The Oliver Family of Antigua and London, 1716–1784," *Business History* 13 (1971): 104–116.

20. Sheridan's conclusions on the profitability of the colonies were challenged by Robert Paul Thomas, who, through cost-benefit analysis of data generated largely by Sheridan, concluded that the eighteenth-century West India colonies were not profitable and that Britain would have gained more by investing its wealth elsewhere. Philip Coelho reached a similar conclusion. See Robert Paul Thomas, "The Sugar Colonies of the Old Empire: Profit or Loss for Great Britain?" *Economic History Review* 21 (1968): 30–45; Philip Coelho, "The Profitability of Imperialism: The British Experi-

ence in the West Indies, 1768–1772," *Explorations in Economic History* 10 (1973): 253–280. Sheridan responded: "The Wealth of Jamaica in the Eighteenth Century: A Rejoinder," *Economic History Review* 21 (1968): 46–61. Using figures provided in secondary sources, Stanley Engerman determined that the slave trade contributed only about 1 percent to national income in Britain and that the sum of profits from the slave trade and from West Indian plantations—if calculated on the most generous basis— would have been less than 5 percent of British income in an early year of the Industrial Revolution. This is not sufficient to sustain Williams's or Sheridan's conclusions. Stanley L. Engerman, "The Slave Trade and British Capital Formation in the Eighteenth Century: A Comment on the Williams Thesis," *Business History Review* 46 (1972): 430–443.

21. Recent work, whether for England or the continent, has followed true to form. See for example, Rondo Cameron, "A New View of European Industrialization," *Economic History Review* 38 (1985): 1–23; A. E. Musson, "Industrial Motive Power in the United Kingdom, 1800–70," *Economic History Review* 29 (1976): 415–439; Thomas C. Cochran, "The Business Revolution," *American Historical Review* 79 (1974): 1449–1466; J. F. Gaski, "The Causes of the Industrial Revolution: A Brief 'Single Factor' Argument," *Journal of European Economic History* 11 (1982): 227–233.

22. The Fernand Braudel Center for the Study of Economies, Historical Systems, and Civilization is located at the State University of New York at Binghamton. The Center publishes the quarterly journal, *Review*.

23. The two terms are almost interchangeable. Still, they are not synonymous. Non-economic links between component parts of a world-system, especially cultural links, render a world-system something more than a world-economy.

24. Immanuel Wallerstein, *The Modern World-System I: Capitalist Agriculture and the Origins of the European World-Economy in the Sixteenth Century* (New York, 1974), pp. 37–38.

25. Where Indian labor was available, coercion took the form of *encomienda*, whereby a Spanish settler gained the right to use the services of a prescribed body of Indians who were to provide him personal services, goods, or a combination of these.

26. Earl J. Hamilton, "American Treasure and Andalusian Prices, 1503–1660," *Journal of Economic and Business History* 1 (1928): 1–35; "American Treasure and the Rise of Capitalism," *Economica* 9 (1929): 338–357; "Prices and Progress: Prices as a Factor in Business Growth," *Journal of Economic History* 12 (1952): 325–349. John Maynard Keynes, *A Treatise on Money*, vol. 2 (New York, 1930), pp. 154–164.

27. Wallerstein, *World-System I*, pp. 92–93.

28. Ibid., p. 70.

29. Ibid., p. 348.

30. Wallerstein argued that a world-system would not be larger than the distance that could be covered in forty to sixty days by the best means of transport. *World-System I*, p. 17.

31. This, of course, is a non-testable, counter-factual hypothesis. It is not possible for historians to separate the sixteenth-century world-system from regions external to it—in effect, to remove all consideration of contacts between Asia, the Middle East, Africa (except for a few coastal enclaves), and the capitalist world-system in order to determine whether that system could have operated in much the same fashion.

32. For a brief exposition of this, see Alvin Y. So, *Social Change and Development*, pp. 180–184.

33. Wallerstein, *World-System I*, p. 350.

34. Wallerstein recognizes this elsewhere in his book; see *World-System I*, p. 80.

35. Davis, *The Rise of the Atlantic Economies*, p. 172.

36. Wallerstein, *World-System I*, p. 51.

37. Among the leading scholars of the age of discovery, J. H. Parry argued that Portugal had desperate need of gold. Portugal struck no gold coins between 1383 and 1435. Even silver coinage was uncommon. The kingdom's copper coinage was seriously debased, and inflation raged. Parry also emphasized the knight-errantry of the Portuguese. See his *Discovery of the Sea* (Berkeley and Los Angeles, 1981), pp. 84, 90–94. Vitorino Magãlhaes Godino, like Wallerstein, presents a shopping-basket approach to Portuguese motives for discovery. But gold stands at the top of his list and receives primary emphasis in his analysis. See his *L'économie de l'empire portugais aux XVe et XVIe siècles* (Paris, 1969).

38. Chief among them was sugar. In 1570, there were only 60 sugar mills in Brazil; this rose to about 120 by 1585. Alexander Marchant, *From Barter to Slavery: The Economic Relations of Portuguese and Indians in the Settlement of Brazil, 1500–1580* (Baltimore, 1942), p. 125. Frédéric Mauro claims that there were 235 mills in Brazil by 1628. See his *Le Portugal et L'Atlantique au XVIIe siècle, 1570–1670* (Paris, 1960), p. 195. A plantation economy in sugar was not launched in the Caribbean until the 1640s. Tobacco took hold in North America around 1620.

39. Fernand Braudel, *The Mediterranean and the Mediterranean World in the Age of Philip II*, vol. 1 (New York, 1972), p. 377.

40. Pierre Vilar observed that strong money (gold and silver) never streams into a system unless it is attracted there by production. Money is a commodity, exchanged in the marketplace for other commodities. Vilar is highly critical of the Hamilton-Keynes thesis upon which Wallerstein rests his argument for capital accumulation in Europe. Pierre Vilar, "Problems of the Formation of Capitalism," *Past and Present* 10 (1956): 15–38.

41. It would have exploited more fully its own silver loads. John Davy contends that by 1460 the European bullion famine had run its course. Hitherto intractable European silver deposits had become commercially exploitable in the fifteenth century by the introduction of new technology, and between 1450 and 1530 European silver output may have increased fivefold. John Davy, "The Great Bullion Famine of the Fifteenth Century," *Past and Present* 79 (1978): 3–54.

42. Braudel, *The Mediterranean*, vol. 2, p. 679. The single decisive factor in Europe's swift development was not American silver, argued Braudel. It was "the restless energy of the West."

43. Carlo M. Cipolla, *Guns, Sails and Empires: Technological Innovation and the Early Phases of European Expansion 1400–1700* (New York, 1965), p. 36.

44. Analyzing the silver question in terms of a Marxian concept of surplus value, Dennis Flynn observes that Marx considered surplus value to be created in the process of production, not circulation. The surplus that accrued to Spain from its control of American mines must be measured in terms of the differential between the value expended in producing bullion and the value obtained from the bullion when it was exchanged for commodities or services in the European marketplace. When an exchange occurred between Spaniards and members of another community in which silver was

traded for industrial manufactures, that exchange was voluntary and, one must presume, in the interest of both parties. The surplus value that accrued to the Spanish because they controlled the production of American silver was not attached to the silver itself, an object of exchange. Consequently, surplus value was not passed on to Spain's trading partners in the process of circulation. It was retained by the Spanish, who acquired it in the original act of production. The Spanish chose to use it to sustain a century of warfare. Dennis Flynn, "Early Capitalism Despite New World Bullion: An Anti-Wallerstein Interpretation of Imperial Spain," paper delivered at meetings of the Social Science Historical Association, Washington, D.C., 1983.

45. Robert Brenner, "The Origins of Capitalist Development: A Critique of Neo-Smithian Marxism," *New Left Review* 104 (1977): 68–73. Brenner's criticism, whatever its merits, does not challenge Wallerstein's proposition that Western Europe needed foodstuffs from the East to release its own productive forces and that Polish grain imports permitted the launching of a modern capitalist economy in the sixteenth century. In response to Brenner's criticism, it could be argued that the introduction of capitalism into sixteenth-century Poland was altogether unlikely and that without coercion peasants would have eaten up their surpluses, allowing for no important export of grain.

46. Wallerstein, *World-System I*, p. 162.

8

Environmental History

Environmental history has flourished under crisis. During the century before World War II, scattered voices warned that the earth's resources were being despoiled, that greater efforts at conservation and greater caution in the use of toxic substances were essential if humankind was to preserve its natural heritage. Hiroshima demonstrated the ability of humans to destroy as well as to befoul their habitat, and nuclear contamination was added to a growing list of perils. In 1948, two American environmentalists issued sober judgments on past and present behavior. Fairfield Osborn declared that over the last century, the story of the United States regarding "the use of forests, grasslands, wildlife and water sources [was] the most violent and most destructive of any . . . in the long history of civilization."[1] William Vogt concurred: "By excessive breeding and abuse of the land mankind has backed itself into an ecological trap. By a lopsided use of applied science it has been living on promissory notes. Now, all over the world, the notes are falling due."[2]

Rachel Carson argued that the promissory notes of applied science often promised nothing short of ecological cataclysm. In its attempt to enhance the quality of human life through the production of synthetic insecticides, the chemical industry had poisoned animal, bird, and marine life and was endangering humans through the progressive accumulation of toxic substances in the food chain. While insect pests were quickly developing resistance to one chemical agent after another, other forms of life were being jeopardized so seriously that we could, in the not too distant future, witness a "silent spring" in which birds no longer sang, bees no longer pollinated the apple blossoms, and fishermen, themselves grown weak, no longer waded into fishless streams.[3]

A report on world environment commissioned by the secretary-general of the United Nations in 1971 gave every indication that a doomsday scenario was entirely possible if humankind did not exercise more "careful husbandry" of its "thin and fragile" environment .[4] The 152 experts[5] who advised Barbara Ward and René Dubos, the report's authors, had little difficulty agreeing on factual evidence relating to the global environment, but their opinions diverged widely on how those facts should be interpreted, what priorities should be established, and where the burden of ecological probity must rest. Can that burden be shared without prejudice? Having done most to create an environmental crisis, will the industrialized nations try to impede industrialization among the poor nations? At the same time, can industrialization proceed in the Third World without causing irreversible ecological damage? All agree that environmental degradation is a global problem that must be addressed globally.

At the root of the environmental controversy is the conflict over first principles. What is humankind's role in the natural order? Genesis informs us that God gave man "dominion over the fish of the sea, the birds of the air, and the cattle, and over all the wild animals and all the creatures that crawl on the ground." Man has behaved accordingly, striding the earth as its landlord, determining where to till and where to drill, which landscapes to protect, which to transform, what forms of life to preserve, what forms to sacrifice, and in whose interest the tilling, the drilling, and the preserving are to be undertaken. Ward and Dubos do not deny humans their proprietary function; rather, they urge upon them the burden of stewardship, the responsibility to serve as trustees, to protect and preserve our natural patrimony for generations unborn. Most theoretical ecologists hold a different view. For them, humankind is the most elevated of the species, but no more significant than other elements of our natural ecosystem. Some favor a systematic process of deindustrialization to save the planet; others fear that no measures sufficient to save the earth are likely to be taken in a world suffused with greed.

James Lovelock, a British scientist, disagrees with both orientations. Stewardship is important, he declares, but if the survival of intelligent life on this planet were to depend solely upon the benevolent trusteeship of human beings, our situation would surely be lost. At the same time, there is no need for panic, no need to deindustrialize, no need to despair. Instead, Lovelock offers the Gaia hypothesis. Gaia, mother earth, is perceived as a complex and self-regulating organism that reacts to chemical and other threats to its well-being in compensatory ways that preserve homeostatic equilibrium and ensure that life is sustained. Lovelock states the concept graphically: "the entire range of living matter on Earth, from whales to viruses, and from oaks to algae, could be regarded as constituting a single living entity, capable of manipulating the Earth's atmosphere to suit its overall needs and endowed with faculties and powers far beyond those of its constituent parts."[6]

Life began on earth about 3.5 billion years ago. Yet despite the changing output of heat from the sun and changing surface properties of the earth, the planet's climate has remained remarkably stable. The earth's atmosphere continues to give evidence of extraordinary homeostasis.[7] We need not ban aerosol sprays in a frenzy of fear over a depleted ozone layer. When Krakatoa erupted in 1895, the volcanic effluent spewed into the stratosphere was sufficient to deplete the ozone by 30 percent. This amounts to twice the depletion that might occur if the 1979 rate of chlorofluorocarbon emissions were continued to the year 2010. Although numerous natural forces have continually filled the stratosphere with ozone-depleting chemicals, natural compensation has been achieved through the self-regulating capabilities of the earth. In light of modern industrial growth and the rise of population, human vigilance has become increasingly important. The earth's vital organs reside between latitudes 45 degrees north and 45 degrees south, especially in the tropical forests and the inshore waters of the continental shelves. It is here that reckless human action could do irremediable damage.[8] Humans must be the stewards of their environment, but their stewardship is merely a complement to the natural, self-regulating properties of Gaia. Humans cannot destroy the life-sustaining capability of the earth, argues Lovelock, but they can render the planet incapable of supporting their own form of life.[9]

Whatever views diverse groups of environmentalists may take of man's role in the natural order, all of them concur that humans are integral elements of the ecosystem, reactive to modifications within it and capable of dramatically altering its character. Mankind's planetary environment should no longer be viewed as a stable backdrop against which the drama of human history is played. The environment is and always has been a major player. Sadly, it is only the surging crisis of the twentieth century that alerts us, as historians, to the pervasive importance of environmental factors in the human experience.

Environmental history is distinguished by a particular orientation to the past, an orientation that integrates people with nature and exposes the impact upon human affairs of numerous forces that are beyond the control or beyond the immediate understanding of men and women. It encompasses climate, disease, natural disaster, and the ecological effects of displaced plants and animals. It treats the ecological implications of various forms of agriculture and industry; it examines the altering ratios of humans to the land and of humans to other species, and it considers the effect of these changing ratios upon all forms of life in the ecosystem. Environmental history catalogues our judicious exploitation and our reckless befouling of the global habitat. It informs us of our place within the natural order; it alerts us to the precarious state of our existence; and it identifies the tortured and tortuous roadways that have brought us to our current predicament.

Many older works of scholarship anticipate the concerns of modern environmental historians. Among them are the writings of Frederick Jackson Turner and Walter Prescott Webb, scholars mentioned in the previous chapter. These frontier historians identified the changes wrought by humans in a vast continental ecosphere.[10] French historians of the *Annales* school were the first well-defined body of scholars who self-consciously affirmed the significance of mankind's dynamic encounter with its environment. The signature, *Annales*, derives from the title of a scholarly journal founded in 1929 by Marc Bloch and Lucien Febvre in protest against the prevailing orthodoxy of event-oriented narrative history that focused almost exclusively on political, diplomatic, and military topics.[11] *Annalistes* advocated "total history," a more comprehensive and human history that would study societies as wholes, eliminating barriers between academic disciplines while creating a single "science of man."[12] *Annales* historians are noted for their creative methodologies, not for any overriding theory of change. Working generally in the pre-industrial era, they have concentrated on underlying structures, the great institutions and social formations that have stabilized the human condition. In the process, they have demonstrated considerable concern for the interplay between customs, values, and the material environment. In this regard, they have foretokened the work of environmental historians.[13]

The most ambitious venture by an *Annaliste* into environmental history is Fernand Braudel's luxuriant work, *The Mediterranean and the Mediterranean World in the Age of Philip II* (1946). This triumph in "total history" is divided into three parts, each part being concerned with different structural phenomena and different rates of change. The first examines structures of great duration—the *longue durée*—in which change occurs almost imperceptibly over as much as a thousand years. Topics include geography, climate, and the interaction of humans with both. Part two concerns trends, cycles, and rhythms of medium duration—say, fifty or a hundred years—involving such matters as economic systems, demography, and modes of warfare. Part three treats events of short duration, *l'histoire événementielle*—what Braudel disdainfully described as brief, rapid fluctuations, momentary outbursts, mere surface disturbances that are explicable only in terms of the deeper forces of medium or long duration.[14]

The most persistent criticism of Braudel's work is that he was not able to achieve harmonious integration between the three planes of his study, between durable phenomena and rapidly changing human events.[15] The most persistent criticism of *Annales* scholars in general is their tendency to view history as a natural science in which vast impersonal forces of long and medium duration rule out the possibility that individual human beings make their own history.

Environmental historians confront similar problems. They too work with vast, impersonal, often inanimate forces, and they do it, very often, in the more complex context of modern times. Equally committed to holism, they must penetrate numerous disciplines: geology (the aging of the planet), climatology, soil chemistry, plant biology, geography (the restructuring of past landscapes), and ecology (the interaction between different organisms and between organisms and their physical environment). In its human dimension, environmental history is intimately linked to anthropology, to the role of nature in shaping culture (and vice versa), as well as to aesthetics, ethics, and religion, fields that shed light on the way in which humans perceive and value nature.[16] Despite the formidable range of their interests, environmental historians are less inclined than *Annalistes* to dismiss the importance of the history of events (*l'histoire événementielle*) or to deny individual human beings a role in deciding their own destiny. Much of the impetus for the development of environmental history derives from the gathering crisis over human survival. Without intelligent human stewardship at the everyday level of politics, diplomacy, and military affairs, the men and women of planet earth may be approaching the end of their history.

It is one thing to know what must be done to achieve holistic environmental history. It is another thing to do it—to master and reconcile so many diverse historical forces. The field is relatively young. Environmental history has produced no single study of Braudelian scale and no universal theoretical model that accommodates all past experience. It may never do so. Yet a number of theoretical models have been proposed for various segments of the field,[17] and scholars working in those areas have produced important hypotheses concerning the forces that promote change. This chapter will concentrate on two environmental factors— climate and disease—indicating the extent to which they may have influenced historical development on a macrohistorical scale.

CLIMATE AND HISTORY

Some of the most distinguished historians of our time have made far-reaching claims concerning the importance of climate. Having observed the similarity of long-term demographic rhythm in regions as widely separated as Europe and China, Braudel declared that in all probability the universal factor providing unity to world history was climate.[18] In *Commercial Revolution of the Middle Ages, 950–1350* (1971), Yale University historian Robert Lopez suggested that climatic variation was a primary cause of major developments in the ancient world.

The cyclical flows and ebbs of disease and famine, which can be observed over multisecular periods, seem to be connected with certain "pulsations" of climate. . . . Less long and sharp than the great prehistoric alterations of glacial and interglacial periods, these pulsations have brought about, in historical time, slow yet telling changes in the average temperature and humidity of the earth. Scattered but consistent evidence indicates that the last centuries of antiquity and the first ones of the early Middle Ages were especially cold and wet. This might not in itself have been disastrous for the normally warm and dry Mediterranean world, but it made the traditional techniques of dry farming less successful and accelerated the already advanced process of erosion. It was a great shock for Rome, in the fifth century, to be sacked by the Ostrogoths, but the slow degradation of the surrounding countryside, which preceded those dramatic events, was a greater economic catastrophe. Campania was turning into a stony wilderness, Etruria into a malarial swampland. Some other regions were less affected by soil exhaustion and endemic disease, but none was spared by the dramatic succession of "pestilences" which ravaged the Greco-Roman world over and again, from the year 180 to the mid-sixth century. These periodical epidemic outbursts were probably caused by several agents, but the greatest killer undoubtedly was the bubonic plague. There have been only two multisecular periods in recorded history when the plague, normally confined to some pockets in the Far East, repeatedly spread over the Eurasian continent: the one we have just mentioned, and the stretch between the mid-fourteenth century and the mid-seventeenth. It is probably not an accident that both periods coincided with a cold and wet pulsation of the climate.[19]

The pulsations of climate to which Lopez refers are associated in Europe with westerly winds that encircle polar regions of the globe. When the westerlies extend into lower latitudes, cold years become colder and harvest failures occur with greater frequency. The final centuries of the ancient period were relatively cold, as Lopez contended, but at the beginning of the ninth century, Europe experienced a warming trend that lasted about four hundred years. The fourteenth century opened wet and cool, and for about two hundred years thereafter weather appears to have been highly variant. By the sixteenth century, Europe was sliding into an extended cold phase, the Little Ice Age, circa 1550–circa 1850.

Climate does not change abruptly, nor do changes occur simultaneously in all regions of a large country or continent. During the Ice Age when glaciers up to two miles thick covered much of North America, average annual temperatures were only five degrees centigrade lower than they are today and, according to some climatologists, winters were no more severe.[20] In the last five thousand years, the earth's climate has remained remarkably constant. It is probable that world temperature has fluctuated within a range of plus or minus two degrees centigrade and that rainfall fluctuations have not exceeded 5 percent.[21] Nevertheless, small changes in mean temperature can have significant impact along the climatic margins, the cold and dry limits of agriculture, if those changes are extended over a considerable period of time. A decrease of one degree centigrade (1.8 degrees fahrenheit) in average temperature in Iceland reduces growing degree days by 27 percent.[22] In the warm years of the late ninth and tenth centuries, Vikings settled Iceland and Greenland. Eric the Red's Greenland colony numbered 3,000 people working 280 farms. With a shift of the westerlies in the twelfth and thirteenth centuries, the Greenland settlements had to be abandoned, and Icelandic sagas, which for centuries had made no mention of pack ice, began recording massive ice flows that gripped the island in winter. Farms retreated lower into the valleys of Norway, and by the fifteenth century dozens of vineyards that had flourished in England were given up.[23]

Two types of evidence permit us to reconstruct climate history. One is derived from natural materials, field data; the other is the human record. Among the former, tree rings, ice cores from glaciers and from arctic ice-sheets, and cores of sediment from ancient lake beds provide year-by-year weather information. The analysis of marine organisms buried in the ocean floor, the layering of stalagmites, and radiocarbon dating provide further information. Records 125,000 years old can be gathered from pollen fossils in lake beds or peat deposits. Most of our knowledge of post–Ice Age climatic history before 1950 was derived from pollen analysis. This type of evidence can be correlated with data gathered from human sources. Although readings from meteorological instruments (if only crude ones) provide the most reliable information, sagas, chronicles, and diaries frequently offer direct observations of meteorological events. Finally, "proxy data" provides weather-related information from continuous records of such things as price series for grains and other vital foodstuffs, crop-yield ratios, and the dates when harvests were taken.[24]

In relating climate and history, we must distinguish between random and non-random phenomena. The random intervention of weather in human affairs (e.g., the "Protestant winds" that dispersed the Spanish Armada) may be important, but such intervention is unpredictable and unsustained. Climatic explanation at a deeper level requires that we correlate long-term climatic shifts with significant human developments: demographic changes, modifications in economic behavior, crises of disease, or the rise and fall of great states—the type of phenomena treated in the foregoing quotation from Lopez.

Climatic shifts occur on varying scales. The coming of the Ice Age was an event of enormous proportion; the Little Ice Age, although significant for human history, was comparatively minor. There are even lesser "trends"—warm or cool phases lasting ten to fifty years—and, of course, there are random climatic episodes that obscure definitional distinctions between "climate" and "weather." This group includes volcanic eruptions that distribute sun-shielding dust throughout the stratosphere, lowering temperatures at the earth's surface and reducing crop yields for two or three years.

John Post studied such an episode, the explosion in 1815 of the East Indian volcano Tomboro, which in combination with other volcanic activity precipitated what he called the last great subsistence crisis in the Western world, 1816–1817. Summer temperatures were among the lowest in recorded history; crops failed; hunger and disease, vagrancy and social disorder increased; and European governments responded with repressive measures. Historians have commonly explained the distress of these years by reference to economic dislocations occasioned by the Napoleonic wars, but Post emphasizes the environmental variable. Further, he encourages scholars to take account of similar climatic episodes for eight other three- to five-year periods in modern European history when veils of volcanic dust and economic depression coincided.[25]

Consideration of climate as the critical engine of historical change began in earnest with the work of Gustaf Utterström. In a celebrated article, Utterström declared that over the last millennium periods of prosperity and population growth in Europe occurred during warm climatic intervals. Furthermore, the late medieval crisis and the crisis of the seventeenth century could be explained in large part, he thought, by climatic change.[26] Utterström's argument is circumstantial. In pre-modern Europe, most people were engaged in agriculture, and agriculture was fundamentally dependent upon weather. Braudel made the same point: 80 to 95 percent of people in pre-industrial European societies "lived from the land and from nothing else. The rhythm, quality and deficiency of harvests ordered all material life."[27] These arguments were sufficient to convince Wallerstein. Citing Utterström, he declared climatic change to be one of the three forces that impelled fifteenth- and sixteenth-century Europeans to surmount their difficulties through overseas colonization.

In 1979, conferences of scholars were held in Britain and the United States to explore the relationship between climate and history. Each conference inspired the publication of a scholarly volume.[28] The tone of both volumes is cautious. The greatest problem for climate history, it was determined, is the shortage of precise evidence. There can be no substitute for abundant and reliable instrumental records, and these are unavailable before the nineteenth century. One cannot use instrumental readings taken in England or Holland in the seventeenth century to draw conclusions about Germany or Scandinavia. Ambiguities inevitably emerge. Climate historians agree that there was a Little Ice Age, but there is considerable disagreement over its dates.[29] For all the shortcomings of data on Western Europe, it is the best documented region of the world since 1500. English experts argue that there will never be enough reliable evidence for most areas of the globe to permit precise evaluations of the relationship between climate and human society.[30]

Historians require evidence on climate that can be dated with precision. Field data may yield valuable information, particularly for ancient periods, but some of it is difficult to date precisely. As one scholar observed, "approximate dating of plus or minus fifty years, although marvelously precise on the scale of geological time, does not satisfy the needs of most historians."[31] Even chronicles, diaries, and journals that allude to weather episodes with precise dating tend to focus on specific events, usually disastrous ones, and offer little information about routine weather conditions.[32] A serious danger for climate historians, M. L. Parry observes, is that in their frustration over the shortage of precise and reliable evidence they are tempted to draw conclusions from the mere synchronism of climatic and economic events. Such arguments establish no more than a time-space coincidence.[33]

A deleterious shift in climate that shortened the growing season and created food shortages for humans and their animals would require adjustments at many levels. But people do adjust. The historian should no more assume that society is a constant to be impacted by climatic change than that climate itself is a constant. Jan de Vries stresses human adaptability in past times, noting that Dutch farmers substantially increased the planting of buckwheat, a hardy crop with a short growing season, during the cool sixteenth century. Other farmers in Europe substituted barley, oats, and rye for wheat during the Little Ice Age.[34] Acknowledging mankind's extraordinary adaptability, Le Roy Ladurie, who reconstructed French climate history from the timing of annual grape harvests, concluded that "in the long term the human consequences of climate seem to be slight, perhaps negligible, and certainly difficult to detect."[35]

Some historians of climate object to Le Roy Ladurie's minimalist conclusions, but few of them advocate grand climatic determinism.[36] Recent scholarship has deflated Braudel's hopeful supposition, uttered in 1967, that climate might provide the key to understanding universal trends in world history. At the same time, research has demonstrated the importance of climatic variables on a modest scale. On some issues, the jury is still out. We do not know for certain the extent to which cold phases—either during the last centuries of antiquity or the Little Ice Age—may have influenced human demography, nor do we fully understand the relation between meteorological stress and epidemic disease.

EPIDEMIC DISEASE AS AN ENGINE OF CHANGE

As an independent variable, disease may provide a better vehicle than climate for explaining universal rhythms in world history. For this insight we are indebted to William H. McNeill, a pioneer world historian who, among his many provocative and perceptive contributions to the field, has shown that epidemic disease operates in predictable patterns and that those patterns provide discernable contours for much of world history. His book, *Plagues and Peoples* (1976), forms the basis for much of the following discussion.[37]

All living organisms are parasites. As humans devour plants and beasts, so viruses, bacteria, and multi-celled creatures attach themselves to human tissue as a source of food. Some microparasitic organisms reside in their human host and cause no apparent damage. Some produce infections that diminish vigor without endangering the life of their host. Still others provoke acute disease that either kills their human host or induces an immunity reaction.[38] A disease organism that quickly kills its host must confront its own crisis of survival: unless it can find another host who will provide it nourishment and keep its reproductive chain intact, the organism may perish. Therefore, disease organisms and human or animal hosts commonly achieve a level of mutual adaptation that permits both to survive.

Viral and bacterial infections can achieve stable accommodation in human hosts only when the human population is fairly dense. Measles provides an example. In modern urban communities, measles propagates in a wave-like pattern that crests at roughly two-year intervals. To sustain this pattern, there must always be seven thousand persons susceptible to the disease. In light of modern birth rates and socialization practices, the minimal population required to sustain measles in a modern urban complex is around half a million.[39] Other diseases require different densities. It was not, however, until circa B.C. 3000 when stable, relatively sophisticated agricultural communities were established in the river valleys of Asia that human society provided the required population density to sustain many forms of epidemic disease.

Each of the widely separated civilizations that arose throughout Eurasia after circa B.C. 3000 was attacked by different diseases. Each achieved its particular adaptation to them. Diseases that arrived with lethal force were accommodated, in time, by immunity reactions. They became the "childhood diseases" of the stable civilizations, serious but only occasionally fatal. Because these diseases retained their full destructive power when introduced to unexposed populations, civilized societies with their acquired immunities possessed a potent weapon in dealing with alien peoples on their frontiers who lacked those immunities. The expansion of early civilized states is intelligible only in light of these epidemiological realities, McNeill argues.[40]

By the beginning of the Christian era, four "divergent civilized disease pools" had come into being—one in the Roman Mediterranean, others in the Middle East, India, and China. When trade and travel between these civilizations became regular and organized, as it did in the centuries from

B.C. 200 to A.D. 200, the interpenetration of disease from one pool to another was inescapable. The Antonine Plague, A.D. 165–180 took a heavy toll in Rome, as did a succeeding epidemic in 251–266. McNeill speculates that these episodes marked the entry of measles and smallpox to Europe, precipitating secular demographic decline in the Roman Empire. We have less specific knowledge of epidemics in other civilizations, although severe die-offs are known to have occurred in China after 161 and 310. Bubonic plague descended upon the Mediterranean in 541, upon China in 610. In both places, it cut recurring swaths of death for about two hundred years.

The tenth century was a watershed in the disease history of the Eastern hemisphere. By then, plague had disappeared, and people from Europe to China finally achieved what McNeill describes as a "successful biological accommodation" to the infections that had assailed their forefathers.[41] A homogeneous disease pool had been established across the hemisphere. As a result, population growth resumed everywhere. Economies expanded, and in succeeding centuries Europeans, in particular, would experience the cultural efflorescence of the High Middle Ages.

How might the disease patterns mentioned thus far have specifically affected historical developments? McNeill thinks the impact of new infections upon a Roman population that lacked established immunities contributed to civil disorder as well as to secular population decline in the second and third centuries. Agreements permitting German tribesmen to settle inside the Roman frontier as well as the laws of Diocletian (285–305) forbidding cultivators from leaving the land suggest that Roman population was falling sharply. Such a fall would have affected the volume of commerce throughout the Empire and the flow of tribute to the imperial treasury. Epidemic disease may also have assisted the rise and consolidation of Christianity. Care of the sick was for Christians an established religious duty. When normal social services broke down in periods of heavy die-off, the provision of nursing—even such simple practices as distributing food and water—would likely have endeared survivors to Christianity.

The plague of Justinian that struck Constantinople in 542 prevented the emperor from pursuing his plan to restore imperial unity. Recurrences of bubonic plague through the seventh and eighth centuries help to explain why Roman and Persian armies were ineffectual in resisting the advance of Moslem forces that erupted out of Arabia after 634. Pirenne argued that the shift of Christian civilization away from the Mediterranean was a result of Moslem conquests and political fragmentation around the inland sea. Is it not equally plausible that the shift was a deliberate turning from bubonic plague, which remained confined to the Mediterranean and its immediate hinterland?

McNeill is swift to point out parallels in China. Population fell sharply after the second century. Imperial administration faltered with the end of the Han Dynasty in A.D. 220. Invasions from the steppes followed, and the country was fragmented into as many as sixteen rival states. The height of this fragmentation coincided with the arrival of either measles or smallpox. Buddhism, an import from India in the first century, offered the type of care and comfort associated in the West with Christianity. It too taught that death was a release from pain and that believers could be reunited with loved ones in a sublime afterlife. Buddhism gained official dominance at court in the third century. While no cause-effect relationship between disease and these developments can be proven, McNeill finds them "intrinsically persuasive."[42]

After the tenth century, two major disease crises occurred that require attention: (1) the Black Death, and (2) the epidemiological decimation of the American Indian population. Both demonstrate how a severe disease episode triggers reaction and change across the spectrum of human activity. Both had an effect upon the growth of capitalism, and both were significant in the rise of Europe to world hegemony.

The Black Death

The Black Death has been treated in some detail in Chapter 4. There it was observed that bubonic plague erupted all across the Eastern hemisphere in the fourteenth century. If, as I have argued, there was no necessary connection between prevailing population pressure in Europe and the onset of plague, then the Black Death constitutes a thoroughly exogenous force. Nothing specific to European society triggered the disease. There was nothing that Europeans could have done to prevent it, and there was nothing they could have known that would have moderated its impact.[43] No prior trends in Christian civilization—economic, social, or demographic—significantly weakened or intensified the plague's depradations.

All societies invaded by plague—Egyptian, Chinese, European— suffered many of the same social consequences. At the same time, each culture responded to aspects of the crisis somewhat differently as its particular material and cultural circumstances dictated.[44] Everywhere, the price of foodstuffs fell (depopulation reduced demand) and the price of manufactures rose (labor costs increased). Landowners suffered losses of income. Merchants died in large numbers; cities wilted; and the volume of commerce fell. Still, if the demographic blowout of the fourteenth and fifteenth centuries reduced commercial activity in Europe, it accelerated social changes that facilitated the growth of capitalism by undermining what Marxists have defined as the feudal mode of production.

Fourteenth- and fifteenth-century die-offs in Europe are an important element in both the demographic and Marxian analyses examined in Part I of this book. In both cases, the fourteenth century was a time of crisis, and population pressure was central to that crisis. For neo-Malthusians, excessive population was expected to trigger a Malthusian check. That check, by reducing population, would have restored balance between land and people. Marxists considered the crisis a result of an exploitative social system that extracted surplus from serfs but discouraged production efficiencies that would have increased food production and sustained a larger population. Logically, a stand-off between classes would have produced class warfare.

Several things could have happened in fourteenth-century Europe. A Malthusian check, however unpleasant, could have improved the land/labor ratio and permitted peasants to subsist more easily despite continuing demands by their lords. Class warfare could have erupted, or significant technical innovations could have increased agricultural productivity, permitting the conflictive lord-peasant relationship to persist at a somewhat higher material level. Conceivably, the lords could have eased their extractive pressure to a level commensurate with the ability of the serfs to survive.

Any of these was possible. Only one, class warfare, would have posed an immediate threat to the prevailing feudal order. Yet none of these possibilities materialized. At least, none of them fully ran its course. Instead, Europe was "blind-sided" by an exogenous biological force, the Black Death, that hastened the dissolution of the feudal mode of production. As we have seen, massive die-offs altered bargaining power between peasants and lords, permitting the former to escape serfdom throughout Western Europe. Altered demographic conditions and the manifold dislocations caused by recurring pestilence provided opportunities for the most ambitious and long-lived peasant families to accumulate lands and local influence—to become "kulaks" or "cocks" of the villages. Their successes in acquiring rights to the land displaced other peasants, transforming the latter into landless (or virtually landless) wage workers available for hire in agriculture or manufacturing. The new organization of land was considerably more conducive to agricultural innovation. If, as Marxists argue, the structural adjustments required to produce capitalism were first achieved in the countryside, it was the awesome depradations of plague that promoted those adjustments.

Epidemic Disease and the Native American

The impact of epidemic disease upon the American Indian population may be likened to the first encounters of early civilizations with epidemic scourges or to the interpenetration of diseases between major civilizations in Eurasia at the beginning of the Christian era. It is probably the most devastating disease experience on historical record. Native Americans migrated to the New World during the Ice Age when the formation of glaciers had lowered sea levels and exposed a land bridge between Siberia and Alaska. Global warming restored the Bering Straits by B.C. 10,000, permanently separating the continents. By B.C. 9000 scattered bands of hunters had occupied the Americas from the extreme north to Tierra del Fuego. In the millennia that followed, they became more isolated from the rest of humanity than any other population except aboriginal Australians, who also walked to their new continent during the Ice Age. Genetically, Amerindians were exceptionally uniform. From southern Canada to the tip of South America, over 90 percent of the population carried blood type O. By contrast, blood types in the Eastern hemisphere are highly variant.[45]

The disease history of the Native American was also different. America was not a disease-free paradise. Pre-Columbian skeletal and mummified remains and studies of fossilized fecal matter from archaeological site: give evidence of infectious diseases such as pneumonia and tuberculosis as well as the presence of intestinal parasitic infestations. Still, the initial passage of Old World migrants through Siberia and across the Bering land bridge probably provided a "cold filter" that prevented the survival of many disease organisms that thrive in warm climates.[46] It stands to reason that Native Americans had no experience of and no immunity to the epidemic diseases that became endemic in settled Eurasian societies during the four millennia after B.C. 3000.

They paid heavily for their epidemiological innocence. After Columbus united the hemispheres, contact between Europeans and Native Americans commonly exposed the latter to epidemic disease. The English settlement at Roanoke generated pestilence among natives. Disease, probably contracted from European fishermen and fur traders, swept through New England in 1616–1617, clearing the way for the early Massachusetts settlements. The most monumental depradations of epidemic disease occurred in territories occupied by the Spanish. Historians have been all too inclined to attribute demographic devastation among the Indians to the cruelty of conquistadors. Cruelty there was. The Bahamas and many of the Lesser Antilles were stripped of their populations to feed the mines of Hispaniola and the pearl fisheries of Venezuela. On Hispaniola, the site of Columbus's first settlement, natives were brutalized and enslaved, but their precipitous decline was accelerated by disease. With the limited evidence at our disposal, it is impossible to offer precise numerical estimates for the Amerindian "contact" population of Hispaniola. Although scholarly estimates for the island range from 100,000 to eight million, most scholars consider one million an entirely reasonable, if not modest, figure.[47] By 1548, just a half-century after the Spanish landings, Gonzala Fernandez Oviedo, a contemporary historian, asserted that surviving descendants of the original population numbered about 500.

Smallpox was not among the early killers of Hispaniola Indians. It arrived in epidemic form in 1519 and finished off a thoroughly weakened population. The disease invaded Puerto Rico and Cuba with similar effects, then vaulted to the mainland with or before Cortez's hardy band of conquistadors. That the mighty Aztec Empire of Central Mexico should fall to several hundred Spaniards in two years is attributable more to disease than to valor. Smallpox raged in the Aztec capital for sixty days before Cortez launched his final successful attack. A similar fate would befall the Inca Empire of upland Peru.[48]

All through tropical and subtropical America, Indian populations were decimated, authority structures were dissolved, and native confidence was broken as Americans repeatedly witnessed the agonizing deaths of their fellows while Europeans, protected by their immunities, survived unscathed. Although estimates of the contact population are highly speculative, all the figures offered by scholars bear grisly witness to the tragedy. Focusing on Central Mexico, William Sanders estimated the Indian population in 1520 to have been 11.4 million. Sherburne Cook and Woodrow Borah, spokesmen of the California school of historical demographers, argued for 25–28 million, Henry Dobyns for 30 million.[49] What we know with some certainty is that the native population of Central Mexico in 1600, eighty years after the conquest, was scarcely above one million. If we adopt Sanders's comparatively low estimate, the demographic collapse in Central Mexico exceeded 85 percent.

There is little doubt that Europeans would have overcome the resistance of Amerindians even if the latter had not been decimated by diseases of the Eastern hemisphere.[50] European penetration of the densely populated and culturally more developed East Indies and India testifies to that. White men had weapons of steel and cannons that wrought terror and destruction. They had horses for mobility, sailing ships to deliver soldiers along the coast, and technical skills that awed primitive opponents who faced their assailants with little more than obsidian-tipped spears, arrows, and clubs. Yet who would deny the tenacity or ferocity of healthy Iroquois, Sioux, or Apache warriors? Against a healthy native population, European conquest would have been long and arduous. Charles I (1516–1556), Cortez's sovereign lord, had no troops to spare for America. His reign and that of his son, Philip II (1556–1598), were consumed by struggles with the French, Turks, and Protestants. Even with so formidable an ally as disease, Europeans did not swarm to the open spaces of the New World before the nineteenth century. In 1800, North America, the most hospitable region for European settlement, had only five million whites. Central America, South America, and the West Indian islands contained far fewer.

Without the social, demographic, and psychological ruination caused by disease, Native Americans would not have surrendered their gold and silver so readily, nor would they have permitted, without heavy casualties, great tracts of tropical and semi-tropical land to be absorbed by plantations of sugar, coffee, tobacco, and rice. Europe's "windfall" in America would have been much more painfully earned, much more costly in manpower and money, and much slower to materialize. The timing and the contours of Western capitalism would have been different. Certainly, Professor Wallerstein would have had fewer reasons to contemplate a capitalist world-system in the sixteenth century.

Disease in Animals

Animal disease, though rarely treated by historians, has exercised important influence in human affairs. One example will suffice. In 1889, on the eve of European conquest in East Africa, rinderpest, an alien cattle disease, was introduced to the region with animals brought from Asia to provision Italian soldiers. Rinderpest spread quickly to all parts of East Africa, killing up to 90 percent of the herds of pastoral peoples. Starvation followed. As many as two-thirds of the Masai died of famine, and great tracts of grazing land lay vacant. The ecological balance was disturbed, and the range of the tsetse fly, carrier of deadly sleeping sickness, expanded in the region. Authority structures collapsed, and regional political balances were altered. As for the political balance between Africans and Europeans, Lord Lugard, speaking for the British, drew these conclusions: "Powerful and warlike as the pastoral tribes are, their

pride has been humbled and our progress facilitated by this awful visita-
tion. The advent of the white man had else not been so peaceful."[51]

ECOLOGICAL IMPERIALISM

The overseas expansion of European animal species—vermin, domes-
ticated animals, and the diseases of both—constitutes a further dimension
of environmental history. Alfred Crosby has documented what he calls
ecological imperialism, the invasion of Australia, New Zealand, Southern
Africa, and the Americas by Europe's fauna and flora as well as its
people. Prior to Columbus, there were no cattle, horses, pigs, goats, or
sheep in the Americas. There were no sheep in Australia or New Zealand,
although by 1974 New Zealanders were grazing 55 million sheep. Rabbits
did not arrive in Australia until 1859. Less than a century later, the rabbit
population was estimated at around 500 million, and rabbits had become
serious competitors with cattle and sheep—both European imports—for
the continent's natural grasses. To everyone's dismay, Europe has
exported its weeds—notably, for the suburban lawn-keeper, the dandelion
and the plantain. Across the pampas of Argentina, only about a quarter of
the grasses now growing are native to America. The intercontinental transfer of plants is an important element of environmental history, one that has
direct bearing on the modern explosion of population. If Europeans introduced wheat, wine grapes, sugar cane, olives, the banana, and various
fruits to America, they received, in return, maize, potatoes, tomatoes,
peanuts, manioc, cacao, various types of beans, pumpkins, and squashes.
Maize and potatoes provide comparatively high caloric output per acre, the
latter being particularly suited to the cool, often damp climate of the North
European plain extending from Germany to the Urals. When the potato
was introduced to this region, it generated four times the caloric value per
acre of rye, the only reliable grain crop in that climate. Because it could be
planted on fallowed fields needed for the successful cultivation of rye, the
potato supplemented without reducing the production of grain.[52] During
Europe's nineteenth-century population explosion, the potato dominated
the diet of the poor.[53]

CONCLUSION

Among the topics treated in this chapter, disease provides a better
prospect for understanding universal developments than climate, although

the secular rhythms of climate and disease exhibit considerable similarity in pre-modern European history. The ebb and flow that demographic historians have attributed to Malthusian forces coincides with the patterning of epidemic disease in Europe. Falling population in the latter centuries of the ancient world can be attributed to the interpenetration of Eurasian disease pools, compounded in the sixth century by plague. The consolidation of a homogeneous pool across the Eastern hemisphere by the year 1000 permitted a general resumption of population growth until the second universal assault of plague arrived in the fourteenth century. Growth returned everywhere in the sixteenth century—except in America, where European conquest and Indian collapse were largely a function of disease. Demographic and economic decline in the final centuries of the ancient world coincided with a cool climatic phase. The period of growth from the tenth to the fourteenth century occurred in a warm phase. The fourteenth-century crisis was experienced during a period of climatic variability that led, by the sixteenth century, to the Little Ice Age. The extent to which all these phenomena may be linked is, as yet, undetermined.

Environmental history is all-embracing. No single historian can possibly master every aspect of the field, and apart from sweeping (albeit unverifiable) hypotheses like Lovelock's Gaia hypothesis, it is difficult to comprehend how anyone or any group could generate a governing model that would effectively encompass climate, disease, demography, culture, and everyday politics. Yet, as inhabitants of an endangered planet, we can no longer ignore the environmental implications of everyday politics, nor can we dismiss the political implications of population pressure, infectious disease, or global warming. No orientation to history is more sensitive to human interdependence in the global village than environmental history, nor is any more conscious of the mutual dependence of humans and other creatures—whether wild or tame, of land or of sea. Environmental history raises our sights to another level—beyond commercial, class, or demographic analysis. It does not supplant these forms of analysis. It enlarges them. It alters our perspective and compels us to seek creative methodologies that will enable us to integrate more effectively the *longue durée* and *l'histoire événementielle*.

NOTES

1. Fairfield Osborn, *Our Plundered Planet* (Boston, 1948).
2. William Vogt, *Road to Survival* (New York, 1948), p. 28.
3. Rachel Carson, *Silent Spring* (Boston, 1962), pp. 2, 16–17, 263–275.

4. Barbara Ward and René Dubos, *Only One Earth: The Care and Maintenance of a Small Planet* (New York, 1972), xviii.

5. A distinguished body of scientific and intellectual leaders from 58 countries served as consultants to Ward and Dubos, who had been commissioned to prepare a report on the United Nations Conference on the Human Environment, May 1971.

6. J. E. Lovelock, *Gaia: A New Look at Life on Earth* (New York, 1979), p. 9.

7. Lovelock observed: "The chemical composition of the atmosphere bears no relation to the expectations of steady-state chemical equilibrium. The presence of methane, nitrous oxide, and even nitrogen in our present oxidizing atmosphere represents violation of the rules of chemistry to be measured in tens of orders of magnitude." Ibid., p. 10.

8. Ibid., pp. 120–121.

9. This argument was affirmed by a group of Russian scholars who adopted a position not unlike that of Lovelock. N. N. Moisseiev, Yu. M. Svirezhev, V. F. Krapivin, and A. M. Tarko, "Biosphere Models," in Robert W. Kates, Jesse Ausubel, and Mimi Berberian, eds., *Climate Impact Assessment: Studies of the Interaction of Climate and Society* (New York, 1985), p. 494.

10. In particular, see Frederick Jackson Turner, *The Frontier in American History* (New York, 1920), and Walter Prescott Webb, *The Great Plains* (Boston, 1952).

11. First entitled *Annales d'histoire économique et sociale*, the journal's name was changed in 1946 to *Annales, Economies, Sociétés, Civilisations*. It is closely linked to the Sixth Section of the Ecole Practique des Hautes Etudes, founded in 1947 in Paris as an interdisciplinary center for scholarship in the social sciences.

12. George Iggers, *New Directions in European Historiography* (Middletown, 1975), p. 57. Iggers offers a comprehensive treatment of the *Annales* tradition.

13. There are numerous historiographical analyses of the *Annales* tradition. See Maurice Aymard, "The *Annales* and French Historiography (1929–72)," *Journal of European Economic History* 1 (1972): 491–511; Robert Forster, "Achievements of the *Annales* School," *Journal of Economic History* 38 (1978): 58–75; J. H. Hexter, "Fernand Braudel and the *Monde Braudelien* . . . ," *Journal of Modern History* 44 (1972): 480–539; Lynn Hunt, "French History in the Last Twenty Years: The Rise and Fall of the *Annales* Paradigm," *Journal of Contemporary History* 21 (1986): 209–224; Samuel Kinser, "*Annaliste* Paradigm? Geohistorical Structuralism of Fernand Braudel," *American Historical Review* 86 (1981): 63–105; H. R. Trevor-Roper, "Fernand Braudel, the *Annales*, and the Mediterranean," *Journal of Modern History* 44 (1972): 468–479; Traian Stoianovich, *French Historical Method: The Annales Paradigm* (Ithaca, 1976).

14. Fernand Braudel, *The Mediterranean and the Mediterranean World in the Age of Philip II*, vol. 1, trans. Sian Reynolds (New York, 1972), p. 21.

15. This weakness may explain the reluctance of other Annalistes to work on so vast a scale. Most of Braudel's successors have focused on individual regions, provinces, or cities.

16. For a detailed statement of historiographical architecture of environmental history, see Donald Worster, "Doing Environmental History," in Worster, ed., *The Ends of the Earth* (Cambridge, 1988), pp. 289–307.

17. See, for example, Jennifer Robinson, "Global Modeling and Simulations," in Kates, Ausubel, and Berberian, eds., *Climate Impact Assessment*, pp. 469–492. Cultural anthropologists have provided environmental historians a reservoir of engaging

theoretical formulations about man and nature that serve as interesting points of departure. For example, Marvin Harris employs a model he calls "cultural materialism" to explain similarities and differences in the thought and behavior of diverse human groups. All groups of people are constrained by the need to produce food, shelter, and tools, and by the necessity to reproduce their numbers. The parameters within which humans struggle to satisfy these basic requirements are dictated by environment. "For cultural materialists," writes Harris, "the most likely causes of variation in the mental or spiritual aspects of human life are the variations in the material constraints affecting the way people cope with the problems of satisfying basic needs in a particular habitat." In effect, aesthetics; moral values; religious beliefs; political, legal, and social institutions—however important—are largely derivative of humans' encounter with the material and biological realities of their environment. Marvin Harris, *Culture, People, Nature: An Introduction to General Anthropology,* 3d ed. (New York, 1980), pp. 5, 116–119. For a full elaboration of this thesis, see Marvin Harris, *Cultural Materialism: The Struggle for a Science of Culture* (New York, 1979).

18. Braudel wrote:

> The 'little ice age' . . . during Louis XIV's reign was more of a tyrant than the Sun King. Everything moved to its rhythm: cereal-growing in Europe and the rice fields and steppes of Asia; the olive groves of Provence and the Scandinavian countries where snow and ice, slow to disappear in normal circumstances, no longer left the corn sufficient time to ripen. . . . Natural disasters also multiplied in China in the middle of the seventeenth century—disastrous droughts, plagues of locusts—and a succession of peasant uprisings occurred in the interior provinces, as in France under Louis XIII. All this gives additional meaning to the fluctuations in material life, and possibly explains their simultaneity.

Fernand Braudel, *Capitalism and Material Life 1400–1800,* trans. Miriam Kochan (New York, 1975), p. 19.

19. Robert S. Lopez, *The Commercial Revolution of the Middle Ages, 950–1350* (Englewood Cliffs, 1971), p. 12.

20. Reid A. Bryson and Thomas J. Murray, *Climates of Hunger: Mankind and the World's Changing Weather* (Madison, 1977), p. 64.

21. F. Kenneth Hare, "Climatic Variability and Change," in Kates, Ausubel, and Berberian, eds., *Climatic Impact Assessment,* p. 63.

22. Reid A. Bryson and Christine Padoch, "On the Climates of History," *Journal of Interdisciplinary History* 10 (1980): 589.

23. Bryson and Murray, *Climates of Hunger,* pp. 49–55, 67.

24. For a discussion of the methods mentioned in this paragraph, see H. H. Lamb, *Climate, History and the Modern World* (London, 1982), pp. 67–100.

25. John D. Post, *The Last Great Subsistence Crisis in the Western World* (Baltimore, 1977), xii.

26. M. M. Postan, leading scholar of the demographic school, had acknowledged that famines in early fourteenth-century England were touched off by heavy rains and cold weather, but Postan preferred a Malthusian to a climatic explanation. Utterström tied population movements directly to climatic fluctuations, and he chastised the demographic school for failing to do the same. Gustaf Utterström, "Climatic Fluctuations and Population Problems in Early Modern History," *Scandinavian History Review* 3 (1955), reprinted in Worster, *The Ends of the Earth,* pp. 39–79. Utterström's position

is forcefully argued in H. H. Lamb, *Climate, History and the Modern World*, pp. 6, 187.

27. Braudel, *Capitalism and Material Life*, p. 18.

28. Theodore K. Rabb and Robert I. Rotberg, eds., *Climate and History: Studies in Interdisciplinary History* (Princeton, 1981). Papers presented in this book first appeared in the *Journal of Interdisciplinary History* 10 (1980). Thomas M. L. Wrigley, Martin J. Ingram, and Graham Farmer, eds., *Climate and History: Studies in Past Climates and Their Impact on Man* (Cambridge, 1981).

29. H. H. Lamb, who uses the most conventional dating, 1550–1850, notes that other scholars do employ other dates: 1300–1900, 1430–1850, 1550–1700. Lamb, *Climate, History and the Modern World*, p. 276. See also Lamb and Ingram, "Climate and History," p. 138.

30. H. H. Lamb and M. J. Ingram, "Climate and History," *Past and Present* 89 (1980): 138. This article was a report on the International Conference on Climate and History, Norwich, England, July 1979.

31. David Herlihy, "Climate and Documentary Sources: A Comment," *Journal of Interdisciplinary History* 10 (1980): 713.

32. Proxy evidence may also be fraught with imprecision. Le Roy Ladurie and Christian Pfister have compiled long runs of the dates when grape harvests were initiated in France and Switzerland. The earlier the start of harvest, the warmer the summer season, it is assumed. But the process of selecting the day to begin harvesting did not lie exclusively with the growers, nor was it based entirely upon when the grapes were mature. The decision was taken by government authorities in order to regulate economic enterprise and to prevent one group of growers from gaining comparative advantage over others by harvesting their crops early. Political influences must have penetrated the process as upland growers whose grapes would have ripened more slowly vied for influence against lowland growers who might have sought an early beginning of harvest. Herlihy, "Climate and Documentary Sources," pp. 716–717.

33. M. L. Parry, "Climatic Change and the Agricultural Frontier: A Research Strategy," in Wrigley, Ingram, and Farmer, eds., *Climate and History*, p. 321.

34. Jan de Vries, "Measuring the Impact of Climate on History: The Search for Appropriate Methodologies," *Journal of Interdisciplinary History* 10 (1980): 625.

35. Emmanuel Le Roy Ladurie, *Histoire du climat depuis l'an mil* (Paris, 1967), revised and translated into English as *Time of Feast, Time of Famine: A History of Climate since the Year 1000* (New York, 1971), p. 119. For strong confirmation of this, see J. L. Anderson, "Climatic Change in European Economic History," *Research in Economic History* 6 (1981): 1–34.

36. For an excellent overview of the state of climatic history from someone who is more optimistic than Le Roy Ladurie, see Robert H. Claxton, "Climate and History: From Speculation to Systematic Study," *The Historian* 45 (1983): 220–236.

37. For an abbreviated but highly stimulating presentation of many of the arguments lodged in *Plagues and Peoples*, see McNeill's *The Human Condition: An Ecological and Historical View* (Princeton, 1980).

38. William H. McNeill, *Plagues and Peoples* (Garden City, 1976).

39. Ibid., p. 60.

40. Ibid., p. 73.

41. Ibid., p. 137.

42. Ibid., p. 123.

43. The plague bacillus, *Pasteurella pestis,* was not discovered until 1894. Under pressure of an outbreak of plague in the Far East and India (six million deaths occurred in India in a decade), teams of scientists working at the beginning of the twentieth century gradually revealed the etiology of bubonic plague.

44. For a comparison of Christian and Moslem religious reactions, see Michael Dols, *The Black Death in the Middle East* (Princeton, 1977), pp. 122–124, 297.

45. Alfred W. Crosby, Jr., *The Columbian Exchange: Biological and Cultural Consequences of 1492* (Westport, 1972), pp. 2–29.

46. John W. Verano and Douglas H. Ubelaker, "Health and Disease in the Pre-Columbian World," in Herman J. Viola and Carolyn Margolis, eds., *Seeds of Change* (Washington, 1991), pp. 210–215.

47. See, for example, David Henige, "On the Contact Population of Hispaniola: History as High Mathematics," *Hispanic American Historical Review* 58 (1978): 217–237; R. A. Zambardino, "Critique of David Henige's 'On the Contact Population of Hispaniola,' " ibid., 700–708; Henige, "David Henige's Reply," ibid., 709–712.

48. For a thorough account of the disease exchanges occasioned by the merger of hemispheres, see Crosby's *The Columbian Exchange,* pp. 35–63, 122–164.

49. Woodrow Borah and Sherburne F. Cook, *The Aboriginal Population of Central Mexico on the Eve of the Spanish Conquest* (Berkeley, 1963), pp. 1–5, 88–91; Borah and Cook, *Essays in Population History: Mexico and the Caribbean,* vol. 1 (Berkeley, 1971), p. 115. William T. Sanders, "The Population of the Central Mexican Symbiotic Region, the Basin of Mexico, and the Teotihuacan Valley in the Sixteenth Century," in William M. Denevan, ed., *The Native Population of the Americas in 1492* (Madison, 1976), pp. 85–150. Denevan's book incorporates numerous articles and statistics dealing with all areas of the Americas.

50. Smallpox, chicken pox, measles, and cholera were brought to America by Europeans. Malaria, yellow fever, typhus, and typhoid may have been of African origin. Murdo J. MacLeod, *Spanish Central America: A Socioeconomic History, 1520–1720* (Berkeley, 1973), p. 16. Of America's native diseases, only venereal syphilis had any profound impact upon the Old World.

51. Quoted in Helge Kjekshus, *Ecology Control and Economic Development in East African History: The Case of Tanganyika, 1850–1950* (Berkeley, 1977), p. 131.

52. William H. McNeill, "American Food Crops in the Old World," in Viola and Margolis, eds., *Seeds of Change,* pp. 46–50.

53. The potato offers adequate nutrition for humans with minimal need of supplement. See William L. Langer, "Europe's Initial Population Explosion," *American Historical Review* 69 (1963): 1–17, and Langer, "American Foods and Europe's Population Growth, 1750–1850," *Journal of Social History* 8 (1975): 51–66.

Part IV
Summation

9

The Continuing Pursuit of Order

I began this book by observing that different people perceive the logic of history in different ways. If this is true of contemporaries, as I have repeatedly stressed, it is doubly the case for historians who have written in different centuries. Medieval writers considered history to be the slow, steady unfolding of God's will. In our time, no historian of renown, whatever his or her religious conviction, explains historical causation by reference to on-going divine intervention. Because we live in a materialist century, we commonly explain the process of change by reference to materialist forces—and these differ.

Our geographic focus has also shifted. In recent centuries, Europe led the world in the arts of civilization. Europe acted, the rest of the world reacted. It appeared entirely logical, therefore, for Western scholars to pursue the inner dynamic of history in the context of European experience. With the waning of European influence and the rise of a "global village" mentality, Western historians have begun to employ models of change that have a more universal application.

In the post-industrial world, change occurs at an alarming rate. Our way of life may be more remote from that of George Washington, Thomas Jefferson, and Andrew Jackson than theirs was from ancient Romans. The dynamics that underlie Western man's transition from a profoundly religious agrarian society regulated by customary practice and personal relationships to a secular, urban, industrial society regulated by bureaucracy are infinitely complex. The models examined in this book represent attempts by historians to fathom that process. Most of the historians treated here identify key changes in Western society between the tenth and eighteenth centuries with the rise and evolution of capitalism. Of course, "capitalism" is an abstraction, an omnibus term that means different things to different people, and the unwary student who stalks "capitalism" through the pages of numerous histories will find himself in pursuit of a perpetually moving target.

HISTORIANS AND THE RISE OF CAPITALISM

How one defines capitalism depends largely on one's theory of change. Still, everyone can agree on certain fundamentals. Capitalism involves the exchange of moveable goods for the purpose of earning profit in markets that employ a money economy. This definition suffices for some, not for others. Marxists contend that capitalism is primarily a mode of production that supports a particular set of class relations. Wallerstein insists that the inception of capitalism required the evolution of a trans-hemispheric world-system. Weber took a less structured view. For him, capitalism was a way of life, an orientation derived from particular religious foundations that inspired rational economic behavior and a dutiful orientation to profit making.

Since capitalism is variously defined, historians offer different timetables for its inception and development. With his relatively uncomplicated market orientation, Henri Pirenne located the origins of capitalism in expanding European towns of the twelfth century. Weber acknowledged the importance of markets, the evolution of an urban proletariat, and the improvement of business techniques in the late Middle Ages, but capitalism as a way of life did not take hold, he thought, until the Protestant Reformation of the sixteenth century. For quite different reasons—notably, the discovery of America and the exploitation of its mineral resources—Wallerstein also assigned a sixteenth-century date to the rise of capitalism. Marxists admit that the feudal mode of production was largely defunct by the sixteenth century. Nevertheless, the class structure of feudalism lingered in Europe during the Age of Absolutism, and the transition to capitalism, achieved in England in the seventeenth century, did not occur on the continent, Marxists argue, until the eighteenth century.

The late Fernand Braudel, possibly the most esteemed historian of the twentieth century, closed the interpretive ring by combining world-system analysis with the old commercial model. In a three-volume masterwork, the luxurious product of a lifetime of scholarship, he scanned the entire range of interpretive opinion from Pirenne through Wallerstein.[1] Although he borrowed Wallerstein's core-periphery concept, he rejected his notion that European capitalism waited upon the exploitation of Peruvian bullion. Braudel challenged every pillar of Marxist explanation except its materialism. Having minimized the importance of agrarian developments in the evolution of capitalism, he recoiled from the Marxist definition of capitalism as a system of production, and he dismissed the proposition that historical time should be or can be measured by successive changes in mode of production. History is too complicated for that, Braudel wrote: every mode of production coexists with every other in ways that enhance the power of the elite at the core. Similarly, Braudel discounted demographic explanations. It was improvements in agricultural technology and the demand pull of the towns that generated demographic change in pre-modern Europe, not the reverse.[2]

Concurring with almost every social-scientific scholar who has pursued these matters, Braudel judged modernity to be synonymous with capitalism. With Adam Smith, he believed that capitalism was rooted in commerce, that the size of the market determines division of labor, and that division of labor has given rise to the modern economy. In effect, Braudel returned to the place where we began, to the commercial division of labor model, but he presented that argument with a different perspective. For him, capitalism was more than large-scale exchange in a market economy. It was the *exclusive* realm of great financiers. Like birds of prey, they hovered above the economic landscape, diving opportunely to swoop up carefully selected rewards. Theirs was the exercise of raw money power.

They moved money freely from trade to state loans to manufacture. They intervened where they chose, how they chose, when they chose, and for as long as they chose, always in the interest of profit. If, as Wallerstein argued, the capitalist world-economy encompassed a spatial hierarchy of economic zones, the economy of the core area was also hierarchically divided. At its top resided the capitalists, and they controlled it all.

While achieving a marriage between the commercial and world-system theories, Braudel imparted a very different emphasis to Wallerstein's model. Where Wallerstein, true to his Marxist origins, concentrated on production, Braudel emphasized commercial forces and focused on circulation. He saw great concentrations of money power reaching out and setting in motion the productive systems of the periphery.[3] Where did this money power come from? From the early trade of towns, Braudel argued. Echoing Pirenne, he agreed that money power achieved its highest level of concentration among long-distance traders who earned extraordinary profits by exploiting the price differentials prevailing in widely separated markets. Europe's political structure did not inhibit the accumulation of great wealth in private family dynasties, and by the thirteenth century significant private holdings had given rise to the mentalities and instrumentalities of capitalism. Everything was in place, he wrote: "bills of exchange, credit, minted coins, banks, forward selling, public finance, loans, . . . colonialism—as well as social disturbances, as a sophisticated labour force, class struggles, social oppression, and political atrocities."[4] Two evolving nodes of capitalist development—one in the Low Countries, the other in northern Italy—were united at the Champagne fairs. Thereafter, Europe was bisected by a Venice-Bruges-London axis. A "string of glittering towns" prospered astride that axis (Augsburg, Nuremberg, Regensburg, Ulm, Basle, Strasbourg, and Cologne, to name a few), and the first capitalist world-economy, a coherent, interdependent, and largely autonomous economic network, came to life.

Where Wallerstein emphasized regions of the world-economy, Braudel concentrated on cities. Each world-economy, he argued, possessed a single urban metropole, and each metropole was distinguished by its command of the money supply, credit, and comprehensive exchange facilities. A capitalist world-economy centering on Venice was in being nearly three centuries before Wallerstein's sixteenth-century Atlantic-oriented model took form. Moreover, the mantle of leadership shifted with some frequency—from Venice to Antwerp around 1500; thence to Genoa after 1568; to Amsterdam after 1627; subsequently to London and New York.[5]

Braudel's emphasis on long-distance trade, a market-determined division of labor, and the vital role of cities—"like yeast in some mighty dough"—has reshaped and revitalized the commercial orientation that dominated historical explanation in the years between the world wars. Like Pirenne, Braudel located the roots of capitalism in early medieval Europe, although Braudel's more refined and hierarchical definition of capitalism confines it to Europe's predatory rich at the summits of economic life. Like earlier proponents of a trade-based model, Braudel is progressivist. Occasional mention is made of a fourteenth-century crisis or a fifteenth-century recession, but such references fail to daunt his upward and onward orientation to European economic history.

The Braudelian interpretation may have closed the interpretive circle, but his model is certain to generate as much skepticism as the other theories examined in this book. Braudel is exceedingly vague about the internal geographical hierarchy of the world-systems he describes. Even though he accepted Wallerstein's contention that the wealth of the core could be achieved only at the expense of the periphery, he made no attempt to specify core-periphery distinctions in terms of the production of primary as opposed to secondary goods. Most important, the internal dynamic that shaped relationships between tiers of the Braudelian world-economy is not clear.

EXPANDING USE OF WORLD-SYSTEM THEORY

Braudel is one of many scholars to embrace the core-periphery concept. André Gunder Frank, having accepted Wallerstein's elaboration upon his own dependency theory, has stridently advocated world-system analysis as a means of structuring world history over the past five thousand years.[6] The dean of world historians, William McNeill, has also offered his blessing. McNeill has reaffirmed his faith in "civilization" as the chief organizing principle in world history, and he continues to defend cultural diffusion as a motor of historical change. But these, he argues, are no longer sufficient. Because advanced civilizations intersected, overlapped, and interpenetrated, historians should employ a higher organizational model to identify and explain significant trans-civilizational developments. After B.C. 1700, McNeill declares, a world-system emerged in the Middle East. For a time, it was "preserved within ever-widening boundaries of a succession of great empires—Egyptian, Hittite, Assyrian, Babylonian, and Persian"; later, it encompassed the entire continental land mass from the Mediterranean to the Pacific.[7] The societies of ancient Greece and India, until now studied as distinct civilizations, should be integrated as elements of an expanding Middle Eastern world system. Special efflorescence passed from region to region within this ancient world system, McNeill asserts: from Hellenic civilization (B.C. 500–A.D. 200) to Indic (200–600), to Muslim (600–1000), to Chinese (1000–1500). Then, with European penetration of America, the mantle of world hegemony passed to the West.

Histories of the kind proposed by McNeill have already begun to appear. In 1989, Janet Abu-Lughod described the complex operation of a thirteenth-century Middle Eastern world-system. Its range extended from northwestern Europe to China.[8] Abu-Lughod is intent to show that Wallerstein's sixteenth-century capitalist world-system was not the first of its kind and that European society had no inherent qualities that rendered it exceptionally capable of achieving the breakthrough to capitalism. Except for the peculiar sequence of events that dissolved the thirteenth-century world-system, writes Abu-Lughod, modern capitalism might have developed outside of Europe. The rise of the West, she concludes, was preceded and facilitated by the fall of the East.

Applying the world-system model before 1500 is problematic. Premodern links between regions of the Afro-Eurasian ecumene were relatively thin, and evidence of them is difficult to unveil. Abu-Lughod's conceptualization of a thirteenth-century world-system is founded on her conclusion that interregional commerce in both primary and manufactured goods increased significantly after 1250. Her world-system comprises an "archipelago of cities"—among them Bruges, Venice, Cairo, Baghdad, Samarkand, Calicut, Canton—where rich merchant communities conducted inter-regional commerce with the aid of sophisticated exchange institutions that involved credit, the pooling of capital, and the sharing of risks.

What Abu-Lughod describes as a "system" has no single hegemon, no central core, no overarching hierarchy, and no clear geographical configuration. There is no explicitly defined interregional division of labor in her thirteenth-century world-system, nor does the "system" appear to require geographically differentiated methods of production for its efficient operation. Abu-Lughod has identified a far-flung network of commercial exchange that affected peoples from Bruges to Canton, but skeptics will ask whether the definition of this network as a system is not a case of academic hyperbole. No one, not even Braudel, has been as rigorous as Wallerstein in defining and integrating the numerous components of the world-system model. For Abu-Lughod, the core-periphery concept is more an organizing principle than a comprehensive theoretical model, and there is every reason to expect that Wallerstein's exacting criteria for what constitutes a legitimate world "system" will be diluted in forthcoming premodern world histories.

Wallerstein's work poses a dilemma for Third World historians as well as for world historians who write about the pre-modern era. His appealing and highly integrated analysis of capitalist development during the sixteenth century links Europe with the Western hemisphere, but it excludes Asia and Africa, thereby leaving three of the world's four great civilizations—China, India, and the Near East—outside of his formulation on the origins of capitalism. Abu-Lughod and others contend that the rise of capitalist modernity need not, as Wallerstein's model suggests, have occurred in the West. The fact remains, however, that capitalism *did* arise in the West. And the most compelling historical question of our time is, why? Why Europe?

COMPARATIVE WORLD HISTORY: WHY EUROPE?

Among the theorists treated in this book, only two, Max Weber and Immanuel Wallerstein (Weber more than Wallerstein), have undertaken the type of comparative analysis needed to address that question. Weber considered it myopic to engage in elaborate causal analysis of the rise of capitalism in Europe before careful study had been undertaken of other great civilizations. For all we know, he insisted, the factors and forces that Eurocentric historians consider to have been evocative of capitalism in Europe could have been amply present in other civilizations as well.

In an exemplary book, Eric Jones addresses the question—why Europe?—through comparative analysis of the four great civilizations. Jones is a world historian, an economic historian, an environmentalist. He is not an exponent of world-system theory, although clearly he has been influenced by Wallerstein. His topic is universal. It requires a universal framework, a common basis upon which to evaluate political, economic, social, and religious developments in four widely separated regions of Eurasia. Ignoring the possibility raised by Sombart that the ability of different peoples to sustain complex forms of civilization is biologically (therefore genetically) determined, Jones concludes that environment— physical habitat, climate, and disease—has been a most formidable influence upon the cultural habits and institutions of human beings. If all peoples encounter their environments with the same biological endowments, then environment itself must constitute the principal variable evoking diverse cultural responses.

By 1500, Jones argues, Europeans had the highest real wages of any of the world's most civilized peoples. Europe ranked third, behind China and India, in aggregate biomass (the total weight of humans and animal livestock), but Europeans had more working capital per head, more meat in their diets, more draught animals, more timber per person, more iron, higher literacy per capita, a more equitable distribution of income, and a better ability to obtain what they lacked through trade.[9] In substantial part, these advantages were the reward of environment. Europe was not troubled by schistosomiasis and worm infestations common to hot climates where irrigation agriculture prevailed and human excrement was used as fertilizer. Endoparasitic infestations that reduced human energy levels narrowed the real manpower gap between Europe and Asia. Watered by rainfall, European soils generally yielded less than the soils of Asia. Still, Europeans did not attempt to maximize crops by sowing all areas in which arable farming was possible. They persistently held population below the maximum and kept land back for livestock husbandry and woodland use.

Population control in Europe was achieved through the nuclear family, a family system that discouraged marriage until a couple could acquire sufficient land or goods to establish an independent household. If Europeans married late, Asians married early, maximizing family size. One effect of maximizing population was the need for irrigation farming. This, in turn, required the construction and coordination of large hydraulic works, projects that promoted the establishment of despotic, authoritarian regimes. Maximization of population in Asia was deliberately calculated to provide families with enough male children to facilitate recovery from environmental disasters. Because the environment of India and China was particularly susceptible to "shocks," males were favored over females and cows were venerated over oxen. Males offered greater physical strength, and cows served as essential breeding stock during post-disaster recovery (also, in a pinch, cows could function as draught animals).

Jones considers risk environment the crucial determinant of social behavior. An Asian was thirty times more likely to die in an earthquake than a European. Floods, drought, and famine were more frequent and more severe in Asia. Locusts were a recurring problem in Asia, not in Europe. Of all shocks, war was the most profound. Jones believes that the human costs of war were higher in Asia and that the loss of capital equipment was heavier still. Capital equipment in Europe was atomistic in nature— fences, roads, houses, livestock. Except in the Netherlands, there was little hydraulic agriculture with costly dykes that were vulnerable to destruction in time of war.[10] Because risks were greater for Asians than Europeans, the former attempted to maximize their numbers as an adaptation to the mortality peaks caused by environmental catastrophes and war. Enjoying a more stable environment, Europeans were able to limit fertility so that despite their lower soil yields, they accumulated capital more rapidly and were "in the *very* long term slightly but significantly better off than their Asian counterparts."[11]

A vital aspect of Europe's evolution toward capitalism, the consistent onward drift of technology, does not lend itself to environmental explanation. Nor can this drift be explained by market forces or by demography alone, since advances in technology often accompanied price recessions and demographic retreat, as in the fifteenth and seventeenth centuries. Europe's propensity to modernize through technology was not occasioned by a shortage of raw materials. In fact, this forward technological drift does not even appear to have been strongly driven by economic forces. Although many of the most important technological innovations embraced by Europeans were borrowed from Asia—the compass, printing, and gunpowder from China; others from the Middle East—Europeans commonly refined those borrowed technologies to a degree beyond that of their Asian originators. This was as true of gunpowder as it was of printing. When the composite effect of these new technologies had ignited "the fires of modernization," those fires "burned quickly to the fringes of this European system," wrote Jones. There they stopped, at the frontiers of Islam. Moslems showed no sign of response and no inclination to emulate the West.[12]

It was advancing technology combined with sheer energy that carried European power to America. What is most important and most characteristic about the exploitation of America is Europe's ability to rationalize and develop New World resources.[13] Like Wallerstein, Jones contends that Europe's ecological windfall in the New World stimulated unprecedented system-wide economic growth. Also like Wallerstein, Jones contends that the most important factor in the rational exploitation of America was Europe's political plurality—a states system that was decentralized, flexible, and intensely competitive.

After Rome, there was no successfully constructed empire across the whole of Europe. Europe developed a system of states that was maintained through balance of power. To some extent at least, political plurality was a product of environment. The core areas around which several of the most important states took their rise—the Paris basin, the Thames basin, the Po valley, and Flanders—were areas of good soil and relatively high productivity. In effect, they were areas that offered a relatively large base for taxation. As late as the fourteenth century, there were up to 1,000 polities in Europe; by the fifteenth century, 500; by the nineteenth century, 25. The core areas of most surviving states are traceable to a fertile heartland that amply supported its occupiers in extending their sway over neighboring lands. Jones is not an environmental determinist, and he acknowledges that environment alone did not dictate the shape of European states. Environment interacted with human personality, dynastic marriage, luck in battle, and other variables, but it was a major factor in the process.[14]

Along with Wallerstein, Jones characterizes large imperial states as economically inefficient, subject to corruption, and prone to taking economic decisions for political reasons. The European states system produced a spirit of competition that encouraged the diffusion of sound economic practices. If one state excluded or expelled disfavored groups of entrepreneurs, other states having different attitudes readily admitted them. The states system, wrote Jones, was "an insurance against economic and technological stagnation."[15] It was not sufficient cause for Europe's extraordinary economic development, but it was a necessary cause of the particular form of development that occurred.[16] The key to the European economic miracle is to be found in politics.

Of the other three great civilizations, only pre-modern China had any prospect of achieving an early breakthrough to capitalism, Jones argues. The Ottoman Empire of the Middle East, with a relatively small population (less than 30 million), was a "plunder machine." It operated an economic system that relied on "confiscation, displacement, and a total, calculated, insecurity of life and property."[17] The Mughal rulers of India were as oppressive and despoiling as the Ottomans. Although taxes were burdensome, taxes secured the people no real help against disasters. As Max Weber had noted, caste imposed endless restrictions on human interaction in the labor market, serving thereby as a formidable impediment to economic development. Hindu religious scruples, including taboos against the killing of rodents and insects, contributed to disease problems. The subcontinent had few navigable rivers, and inland communications were difficult.

China is a more difficult case. The Chinese had the technology, economic sophistication, and infrastructure to upstage the West, but Ming overlords (1368–1644) systematically promoted agriculture at the expense of industry. In the fifteenth century, Chinese armadas ventured as far as Zanzibar, but such seaborne adventurism (as impressive as that of either the Portuguese or Columbus) was abruptly terminated by political authorities in the interest of continental defense. In all the world's great civilizations, kings and emperors were extractive. Asian rulers were especially plunderous and given to arbitrary violence upon their subjects. No Asian civilization experienced an ecological windfall on the scale of America, but Europe's conquest of America did not occur until the sixteenth century, and by then, as Jones has noted, Europeans already enjoyed a higher average standard of wealth than the peoples of China, India, or the Middle East.

Jones's work tackles the most compelling historical issue of our time— why Europe? It is rooted in theory, creative in the questions it asks, and courageous, though not reckless, in the interpretations it offers. Such macrohistory cannot be written without sound, defensible theory. Historians who work within narrow time frames in regional or national histories might question whether comparative history on the scale attempted by Jones is feasible. Certainly, the data available from different cultures, though massive, is uneven. That which merited the attention of record-keepers in one age or one society may have been of little interest in others. Because the documentary record between civilizations is skewed, vast comparative analyses, like that undertaken by Jones, cannot even pretend to be definitive. This caveat does not negate the value of asking big questions. The importance of historical questions bears no necessary relationship to the availability or consistency of historical data, and no history, whatever its scale, can pretend to be entirely definitive. To grapple with big questions, one must often disregard regional experience. But the importance of regional history is not thereby diminished, for the ultimate value of large-scale patterns and of the macrohistorical models they inspire rests upon their ability to accommodate large numbers of diverse regional histories.

In his comparative history, Jones draws upon many of the models examined in this book without formally adhering to any. In fact, he questions whether historians should even seek the breakthrough to capitalist modernity in positive forces such as commercial innovations, demographic behavior, or Protestant ethics. On the contrary, Jones suggests, we should be attentive to negative factors, to the political, economic, religious, and environmental conditions that impeded economic development. Everywhere people tried to maximize material gains, and all the major civilizations exhibited considerable creativity and energy. But some were subject to more stringent constraints than others. Negative environmental constraints do not, in themselves, explain why Europe achieved an economic breakthrough and Asia did not, but they do help us to understand how and why political distinctions arose between the Orient and Occident. In this way, environmental factors provide powerful reinforcement to a theory of comparative history based fundamentally on political criteria.[18]

Jones's book makes comparative judgments that will be tested and retested by scholars working in the several geographical regions he surveyed. Although his work builds on a generation of scholarship in world history, it represents a fresh, almost breathtaking invitation to apply grand theory on a vast scale. If Braudel closed the circle on the theories of change commonly employed to explain historical developments in European history, Jones widens our range of inquiry and deftly employs universal environmental criteria in an attempt to answer universal questions. His work is a prime example of the degree to which both the complexity and the scale of historical inquiry have evolved in this century.

All the great theoreticians studied in this book have attempted to understand the past by discovering the process through which meaningful change occurs. The facts of history have significance only when they are integrated into an organic concept of change. In this regard, the historian's attempt to fathom the mysteries of history may be likened to the mental process of a great chef who is challenged to devine the recipe of an elaborate and many-layered cake by savoring a mere sliver of it. The great chef, his tastes acute, subtle, and refined, might with little difficulty recognize the chief ingredients of the cake, just as a historian might fathom the chief ingredients of a historical situation. But having identified ingredients, neither the chef nor the historian would have proceeded beyond the most preliminary stage of his assignment. If the chef is to reproduce the cake, he must determine how much of each ingredient was used, in what order the ingredients were joined, for how long, and at what temperature they were baked. Then, and only then, can he posit a recipe. Only by a similar endeavor can the historian posit an organic explanation of change, a model. In reality, neither the truly great chef nor the truly great historian is ever likely to get it entirely right.

REVISING THE FRAMEWORK OF HISTORY

In Part I of this book I examined the framework of history, the subdivision of time into historical periods. It was observed that periodization is one of the most pervasive and influential theoretical properties of history, one that determines how we derive images, draw associations, and perceive the beginning, middle, and ending of things. Historical periods, it was noted, assume a life of their own, being nurtured from generation to generation in the structure of university departments, the training of graduate students, the focus of professional journals, and the writing of texts. We continue to use a tripartite division of European historical time—ancient, medieval, modern—with watershed dates around 500 and 1500. These dates reflect concepts of continuity and change embraced by our intellectual forefathers. Not only have historians persisted in them, but they have adopted 1500 as the principal divide for the study of world history. Do the rhythms of world history so conform to those of Europe that the two periodizations actually harmonize? Have our historical priorities and the theoretical concepts we employ to explain historical dynamics not undergone change since tripartite periodization was adopted? Is it time to reconsider periodization?

How do the dynamic models of change that are examined in this book challenge or confirm existing modes of periodization? For the commercial division of labor model, it is partly a question of focus. Should we concentrate on social elites or on the commonalty? In drawing an epochal frontier around 1500, we have subscribed to an elitist position, for in 1500, substantial material change was experienced almost exclusively by people of wealth, education, and influence. As has been noted on several occasions, there was no significant growth in per capita income in Europe until the nineteenth century. Commercial institutions, business techniques, and division of labor were developing (with occasional setbacks) from the twelfth century, but a major change in consumer behavior did not occur until the eighteenth century. Neil McKendrick has shown that in England the consumer revolution of the eighteenth century occasioned a momentous historical discontinuity that sharply interrupted the gradual commercial gestation of earlier centuries:

The eighteenth century marked a major watershed. Whatever popular metaphor is preferred—whether revolution or lift-off or the achievement of critical mass—the same unmistakable breakthrough occurred in consumption as occurred in production. Just as the Industrial Revolution of the eighteenth century marks one of the great discontinuities in history . . . so . . . does the matching revolution in consumption.[19]

There is little doubt that the Industrial Revolution constitutes one of the great watersheds in human experience. There is equally little doubt that it was vastly more than a revolution in technology. Historians have tended to concentrate on production in the Industrial Revolution. Of late, however, scholarly attention has shifted to the other side of the equation, to demand and to such subjects as consumerism. Although the basic institutions of capitalism (banking, bills of exchange, and the like) were in place by 1500, the trade-based division of labor model more emphatically points to the eighteenth and early nineteenth centuries as the critical time when old continuities were eroded and new continuities established.

The demographic explanation offered by neo-Malthusians achieves comfortable accommodation with standard epochal frontiers. The demographic cycle that commenced in the tenth century reached its apogee in the fourteenth. A Malthusian crisis compounded by the Black Death drove down population for a century and a half, but by 1500 a new growth phase was under way. The moment of transition from one demographic cycle to the other commenced around 1500. However, if demographic shifts, whatever their origins, constitute the main engine of change in history, the eighteenth century offers a much more emphatic point of departure for the modern world than the sixteenth. Figures on population before the industrial age are speculative, and different authors provide different numbers. All demographers agree, however, that European population, followed closely by world population, shot upward at an unprecedented rate after the eighteenth century. In Europe, population rose as much as 80 percent in the century between 1750 and 1850. This rate of growth was more than double that of any preceding hundred-year period, and scholars appropriately identify it as the "vital revolution." Humankind reached the one-billion population mark in 1850. Seventy-five years later it added the second billion; thirty-five years thereafter, the third.[20] Currently, world population stands at around 5 billion. It is expected to reach 6.2 billion by the year 2000 and 8.5 billion by 2025. Before leveling off at the end of the twenty-first century, world population could soar to 10 billion, a 1,000 percent growth in a mere 150 years![21] Whether we are experiencing a third great demographic cycle since the year 1000—and where in that cycle we might be—cannot be said for certain. What can be said is that this unparalleled upward thrust in population, the most remarkable and transforming demographic phenomenon in human history, began in the eighteenth century.

Like the practitioners of other materialist models, Marxists consider capitalism as a distinct morphological category requiring recognition as a separate epoch of history. Explaining the transition between the end of the feudal mode and the beginning of the capitalist mode of production has been a problem for them. Whatever explanation different Marxists have offered, they generally agree that capitalism as a new and dynamic mode of production did not come into being in Europe until the late seventeenth or the eighteenth century.

Surprisingly few historians have directly addressed the issue of periodization in the past half century. Those who have—Dietrich Gerhard, Geoffrey Barraclough, and Herbert Butterfield—have rejected standard tripartite periodization and the period break around 1500. Unlike the theoreticians we have studied, none of these authors has been primarily concerned with materialist phenomena. Barraclough, a medievalist, expressed the common outrage of his colleagues over popular misapprehensions that the Middle Ages was a dark and catastrophic time. He urged the adoption of a four-part periodization for European history after the fall of Rome: (1) European prehistory, to 800 or 900; (2) the age of the formation of European societies, 900–1300; (3) the "Middle Ages" of Europe, 1300–1789; and (4) the modern period from 1789 to the present. What gives coherence to this scheme is Barraclough's personal judgment that each of these four periods possesses continuities in ideas and attitudes. Modern attitudes—what Troeltsch called the modern outlook—did not arrive in Europe, he argues, until the eighteenth-century Enlightenment.[22]

Butterfield agreed that continuity prevailed "in the texture of history" between 1400 and at least 1660. He too rejected 1500 as a meaningful watershed, and he too was interested primarily in ideas. Butterfield considered the Scientific Revolution of the seventeenth century the intellectual progenitor of the Enlightenment and a new beginning for European civilization. While his essay is learned, his advocacy of the Scientific Revolution as a leading sector of historical change is idiosyncratic and episodic, being altogether unattached to any broader argument involving an unfolding intellectual process in history.[23]

Gerhard offers an aggregate view. Before 1000, he writes, "one cannot speak of *European* history."[24] For the centuries after 1000 he posits a perpetual dialectical confrontation between two conflicting orientations to civil life. On one side stood tradition, privilege, social stratification, corporate organization, and regional and local attachments; on the other, the desire for change, for equality, and for centralized power and authority. All European history from 1000 to 1800 is encompassed in this struggle. The forces of change gradually eroded the forces of tradition, and the French Revolution constituted the culminating climactic event in the transition from old Europe to modern Europe.[25] Gerhard's dialectical tension is not driven by an overriding force, as in the case of Marx's class struggle. Nor are his periods distinguished by conditions as specific as modes of production. By coincidence and happenstance, various social and institutional orientations appeared to jell in the eleventh century. In the eighteenth century those orientations were finally overwhelmed by others. The tension between them provided continuity to the interim centuries.

None of these writers employed sophisticated methodology in defining period frontiers. Exercising personal priorities, each identified the existence of significant forms of change, but none probed beneath those forms to determine whether a powerful and pervading undercurrent propels the process of change, thereby creating major transitional moments. Nevertheless, each of them offered important suggestions that resonate well with the process models we have examined.

In forming historical periods, it is imperative that we reject any specific date, whether 1000, 1300, 1500, or 1789, as denoting the end of one epoch and the commencement of another. Major discontinuities involving multiple aspects of civil life do not happen suddenly. Transitional eras must be seen as *eras*, extended periods of time having numerous significant moments when old continuities are displaced and new civil coherencies become established.

Two such eras stand out in post-Roman European history. The first lies between the ninth and eleventh centuries, much as Barraclough and Gerhard have suggested. It is the time when Viking, Saracen, and Magyar invasions ended, permitting greater division of labor, encouraging trade and the formation of towns, and facilitating the consolidation of feudal government. In church, state, and economy, it was an era when new foundations were laid or secured. Historical demographers declare this era the beginning of three centuries of population growth, the first leg in a macrohistorical demographic cycle. Marxist study of the transition from ancient slavery to the feudal mode of production is still in its infancy, but it has a rich beginning in the work of Perry Anderson, who contends that the transition was slow, that it made its way incrementally across the continent, and that it was not solidified until the tenth and eleventh centuries.[26] A period break in the tenth and eleventh centuries is consistent with all the models we have examined, the individual judgment of scholars who have addressed periodization, and the longstanding practice among medievalists of dividing the early from the high Middle Ages roughly at the year 1000.

The second great discontinuity occurs in the eighteenth century. More emphatically than any other division of time, an eighteenth-century period break possesses logical consistency with the models we have considered. Butterfield's advocacy of the Scientific Revolution does not confute this dating. The evolution of Western science was gradual, and the consolidation of what might be called a European scientific community may only have been achieved in the early eighteenth century.

The interim period, as Gerhard has argued, is characterized more by continuity than discontinuity. Our problem with it, for practical historians, is how to accommodate this eight-century span of time to the requirements of academic specialization and to the organization of the history curriculum.

Can a periodization contrived by Europeans for the study of European history provide a meaningful structure for the study of world history? World historians appear to think so. Periodizing on a global scale, they have, ironically, affirmed, not dismissed, epochal divisions created for European regional history. The consensus among world historians is that a major global discontinuity occurred around 1500, and this view is powerfully strengthened by the ecological and epidemiological studies of Alfred Crosby, Jr. Having measured the botanical implications of the merger of the hemispheres after 1492, Crosby offered the following sober conclusion:

> Not for a half a billion years, at least, and probably for long before that, has an extreme or permanent physical change affected the whole earth. The single exception to this generality may be European man and his technologies, agricultural and industrial. He has spread all over the globe, and non-European peoples have adopted his techniques in all but the smallest islets. His effect is comparable to an increase in the influx of cosmic rays or the raising of whole new chains of Andes and Himalayas.[27]

The theoretical requirements of global historians are not identical with those of regional historians. World historians must identify conditions and forces that provide common denominators for all regions of the globe. Regional historians are concerned primarily with continuity and change in a particular region of the world. What is theoretically valid for one may or may not be valid for the other. If the world was integrated (commercially, biologically, and in other ways) as a result of the fifteenth- and sixteenth-century discoveries of Europeans, that integration occurred incrementally in the various regions affected. The great era of discontinuity for Native Americans was the sixteenth century; for Indonesian subjects of the Dutch, the seventeenth century; for the Indians of South Asia, the eighteenth century; for the Chinese and for many African peoples, the nineteenth century. After 1500, all peoples would encounter what McNeill called the "restless, disturbing ways" of the Europeans, but they would encounter them under different timetables. These differing timetables demand different regional periodizations. It is entirely fitting that regional historians of Amerindian civilization acknowledge a major discontinuity around 1500. For reasons that are not dissimilar, Chinese historians consider the Opium War of the 1840s the dawn of their modern era.

For global historians, the advent of world-system analysis has powerfully confirmed the sixteenth-century division between pre-modern and modern epochs. Also, it has intensified contemporary emphasis upon the primacy of materialist forces in driving the historical process.

For European history, a new division of time since the Roman era is needed. I concur with Gerhard and Barraclough, albeit for different reasons, that the tenth and the eighteenth centuries were times of major discontinuity in European society and that the centuries between 1000 and 1800 were distinguished more by their continuities than by their changes. An aggregate, episodic view of the tenth and eighteenth centuries would recommend them as watershed eras; indeed, medievalists and modern historians have traditionally subdivided their epochs at these junctures. More important, the theories of change that historians most commonly employ to explain process in history affirm these centuries as moments of fundamental transition and transformation.

Ironically, then, this study commends for world history the continued use of a period frontier, circa 1500, that was created for European history and the adoption of a different epochal structure for use in European regional history.

History is what we make of the past. It is our means, however feeble, of imposing rational order upon chaos. As our needs, our perceptions, and our priorities change, so must our history. Even if the data of the past were to remain the same—which it does not—the information we would attempt to derive from it would change. What determines the shape of historical knowledge is the questions we ask. Those questions are perpetually changing, and in each new phase of inquiry we must guard against purposeful teleological argumentation and undue subjectivity. At the same time, it is essential that those who write history reconstruct the past with some coherent and consistent theoretical orientation. Likewise, it is important that those who teach history and those who study it remain alert to the theoretical properties of historical literature. Good theory is no guarantee of good history, but bad theory or the contradictory employment of theory is a sure guarantee of bad history. Still, all historical theory has its limitations, as this book has attempted to demonstrate. No theory is gospel, nor is any ever likely to become gospel. We will never escape all the pitfalls that lay in wait for us. We will never entirely avoid teleology. We cannot extinguish our subjectivities, although to the extent that we are able, we should try to acknowledge them. History is not a pursuit of perfection. It is a pursuit of meaning. But the pursuers, if they are worthy, will seek diligently to avoid deceiving themselves as well as others.

NOTES

1. Fernand Braudel, *Civilization and Capitalism, 15th–18th Century:* vol. 1, *The Structures of Everyday Life;* vol. 2, *The Wheels of Commerce;* vol. 3, *The Perspective of the World* (New York, 1981, 1982, 1984).

2. Braudel, *The Perspective of the World,* pp. 94–96.

3. In Poland, Braudel wrote, "the western entrepreneurs first came knocking at their (the noblemens') door," luring them into the web of international capitalism. The

American plantations "were capitalist creations *par excellence*," the progeny of "money, credit, trade, and exchange." Braudel, *The Wheels of Commerce*, p. 272.

4. Braudel, *The Perspective of the World*, p. 91.

5. The shift from Venice was occasioned by the Portuguese discovery of the Atlantic sea route to India. Antwerp was dislodged by the Spanish bankruptcy of 1557, and Genoa's banking families were crippled, though not undone, by the Spanish bankruptcy of 1627.

6. André Gunder Frank, "A Theoretical Introduction to 5,000 Years of World System History," *Review* 13 (1990): 155–248; also (with Barry K. Gills), "The Cumulation of Accumulation: Theses and Research Agenda for 5,000 Years of World System History," *Dialectical Anthropology* 15 (1990): 19–42; and "A Plea for World System History," *Journal of World History* 2 (1991): 1–28.

7. William H. McNeill, "*The Rise of the West* after Twenty-Five Years," *Journal of World History* 1 (1990): 12.

8. Janet L. Abu-Lughod, *Before European Hegemony: The World System, A.D. 1250–1350* (New York, 1989).

9. E. L. Jones, *The European Miracle: Environments, Economies, and Geopolitics in the History of Europe and Asia* (Cambridge, 1981), pp. 3–5.

10. Ibid., pp. 24–41.

11. Ibid., p. 20.

12. Ibid., pp. 45–62.

13. Ibid., p. 80.

14. Ibid., pp. 106–108.

15. Ibid., pp. 118–119.

16. Ibid., p. 124.

17. Ibid., p. 187.

18. For an interesting defense of aspects of his approach, see E. L. Jones, "Disasters and Economic Differentiation across Eurasia: A Reply," *Journal of Economic History* 45 (1985): 675–682.

19. Neil McKendrick, John Brewer, and J. H. Plumb, *The Birth of a Consumer Society: The Commercialization of Eighteenth-Century England* (Bloomington, 1982), p. 9. See also Lorna Weatherhill, *Consumer Behavior and Material Culture in Britain, 1660–1760* (New York, 1988).

20. Philip M. Hauser, "The Population of the World: Recent Trends and Prospects," in Ronald Freedman, ed., *Population: The Vital Revolution* (Garden City, 1964), p. 18.

21. Richard N. Gardner, "Bush, the U.N., and Too Many People," *New York Times*, 22 September 1989.

22. Geoffrey Barraclough, *History in a Changing World* (Oxford, 1955), pp. 54–63.

23. Herbert Butterfield, *Man on His Past* (Cambridge, 1955), pp. 128–136.

24. Dietrich Gerhard, "Periodization in European History," *American Historical Review* 61 (1956): 903.

25. Dietrich Gerhard, *Old Europe: A Study of Continuity, 1000–1800* (New York, 1981), p. 139.

26. Perry Anderson, *Passages from Antiquity to Feudalism* (New York, 1978), pp. 128–172.

27. Alfred W. Crosby, Jr., *The Columbian Exchange* (Westport, 1972), pp. 218–219.

Bibliography

A book presenting macrohistorical theories that sweep across many lands and many centuries may invite interested readers to pursue, in greater detail, aspects of history or historiography that are only briefly touched in the text. This bibliography is designed to facilitate further study of the period from the tenth to the eighteenth century. With rare exception, it does not include titles on the Industrial Revolution or on economic and demographic developments since the eighteenth century. Similarly, it excludes studies using world-system analysis to interpret Western or world history over the last two centuries. The bibliography is divided topically in accord with the theories of change introduced in the chapters. Books and articles that defy easy categorization (e.g., the role of warfare in the process of change, or of printing, law, or concepts of time) are usually entered under the General Works section. In the case of publications that bridge two or more categories, I have attempted to achieve consistency in their placement. Works dealing with the aristocracy appear in the General Works section; those concerned with the rise of towns and the people of the city, the bourgeoisie, are listed in the Commerce, Capitalism, and Expansion section. Considerable attention has been given to publications in environmental history, an area that has received less attention than others in university courses to date, but one that will demand increasing consideration in the future.

HISTORY, THEORY, AND ACADEMICS

Acton, Lord (John Emerich Edward Dalberg Acton). *Essays in the Liberal Interpretation of History*. Chicago: University of Chicago Press, 1967.

Appleby, Joyce Oldham. *Economic Thought and Ideology in Seventeenth-Century England*. Princeton: Princeton University Press, 1978.

Ashplant, T. G., and Adrian Wilson. "Whig History and Present-Centered History." *Historical Journal* 31 (1988): 1–16.

Aymard, Maurice. "The *Annales* and French Historiography (1929–72)." *Journal of European Economic History* 1 (1972): 491–511.

Barraclough, Geoffrey. *History in a Changing World*. Oxford: Blackwell, 1955.

Billington, Ray, ed. *The Frontier Thesis: Valid Interpretation of American History?* New York: Kreiger, 1977.

Birnbaum, Norman. "Conflicting Interpretations of the Rise of Capitalism: Marx and Weber." *British Journal of Sociology* 4 (1953): 125–141.

Black, J. B. *The Art of History. A Study of Four Great Historians of the Eighteenth Century*. New York: F. S. Crofts, 1926.

Bodin, Jean. *Method for the Easy Comprehension of History,* trans. Beatrice Reynolds. New York: Columbia University Press, 1945.

Braudel, Fernand. "Personal Testimony." *Journal of Modern History* 44 (1972): 448–467.

Breisach, Ernst. *Historiography: Ancient Medieval, and Modern.* Chicago: University of Chicago Press, 1983.

Brumfitt, J. H. *Voltaire, Historian.* London: Oxford University Press, 1958.

Burckhardt, Jacob. *The Civilization of the Renaissance in Italy,* trans. S. G. C. Middlemore. London: Allen & Unwin, 1944.

Burr, George L. "How the Middle Ages Got Their Name." *American Historical Review* 20 (1914–1915): 813–814.

Butterfield, Herbert. *Man on His Past: The Study of the History of Historical Scholarship.* Cambridge: Cambridge University Press, 1955.

———. *The Whig Interpretation of History.* London: G. Bell and Sons, 1931.

Cahnman, Werner J., and Alvin Boskoff, eds. *Sociology and History: Theory and Research.* Glencoe: Free Press, 1964.

Cameron, Rondo. "The Logistics of European Economic Growth: A Note on Historical Periodization." *Journal of European Economic History* 2 (1973): 145–148.

Carr, E. H. *What Is History?* Harmondsworth: Penguin, 1970.

Clark, G. Kitson. "A Hundred Years of Teaching History at Cambridge, 1873–1973." *Historical Journal* 16 (1973): 535–553.

Clark, Terry Nichols. *Prophets and Patrons: The French University and the Emergence of the Social Sciences.* Cambridge, Mass.: Harvard University Press, 1973.

Cochrane, Eric. *Historians and Historiography of the Italian Renaissance.* Chicago: University of Chicago Press, 1981.

Cohen, Sande. *Historical Culture: On the Recording of an Academic Discipline.* Berkeley: University of California Press, 1989.

Coleman, D. C. *History and the Economic Past: An Account of the Rise and Decline of Economic History in Britain.* New York: Oxford University Press, 1987.

Cook, Albert. *History/Writing.* New York: Cambridge University Press, 1988.

Crafts, N. F. R. "Industrial Revolution in England and France: Some Thoughts on the Question, 'Why Was England First?' " *Economic History Review,* 2d ser., 30 (1977): 429–441.

Darnton, R. "The History of Mentalities." In R. H. Brown and S. M. Lyman, eds., *Structure, Consciousness and History.* Cambridge: Cambridge University Press, 1978.

de Roover, Raymond. "The Scholastic Attitude towards Trade and Entrepreneurship." *Explorations in Entrepreneurial History* 1 (1963): 76–87.

———. "Scholastic Economics: Survival and Lasting Influence from the Sixteenth Century to Adam Smith." *Quarterly Journal of Economics* 69 (1955): 161–190.

Duby, Georges. "L'histoire des systèmes de valuers." *History and Theory* 11 (1972): 15–25.

Elton, G. R. *The Practice of History.* New York: Crowell, 1967.

Ferguson, W. K. "The Interpretation of the Renaissance: Suggestions for a Synthesis." *Journal of the History of Ideas* 12 (1951): 483–495.

———. *The Renaissance in Historical Thought.* Boston: Houghton Mifflin, 1948.

Field, Alexander James. "What Is Wrong with Neoclassical Institutional Economics: A Critique of the North/Thomas Model of Pre-1500." *Explorations in Economic History* 18 (1981): 174–198.

Foster, Robert. "Achievements of the *Annales* School." *Journal of Economic History* 38 (1978): 58–75.

Frank, André Gunder. "A Plea for World System History." *Journal of World History* 2 (1991): 1–28.

———. "A Theoretical Introduction to 5,000 Years of World System History." *Review* 13 (1990): 155–248.

Frank, André Gunder, and Barry K. Gills. "The Cumulation of Accumulation: Theses and Research Agenda for 5,000 Years of World System History." *Dialectical Anthropology* 15 (1990): 19–42.

Gerhard, Deitrich. "Periodization in European History." *American Historical Review* 61 (1956): 900–913.

Gerschenkron, Alexander. *Economic Backwardness in Historical Perspective.* Cambridge, Mass.: Belknap Press of Harvard University Press, 1962.

Gibbon, Edward. *The Decline and Fall of the Roman Empire,* 7 vols. London: Methuen, 1909.

Giddens, Anthony. *Capitalism and Modern Social Theory: An Analysis of the Writings of Marx, Durkheim and Max Weber.* London: Cambridge University Press, 1971.

———. "Marx, Weber, and the Development of Capitalism." *Sociology* 4 (1970): 289–310.

Goldstein, Doris. "The Organizational Development of the British Historical Profession, 1884–1921." *Bulletin of the Institute of Historical Research* 55 (1982): 180–193.

———. "The Origins and Early Years of *The English Historical Review.*" *English Historical Review* 101 (1986): 3–11.

Gooch, G. P. "The Cambridge Chair of Modern History." In G. P. Gooch, ed., *Studies in Modern History.* Freeport: Books for Libraries Press, 1968.

———. *History and Historians in the Nineteenth Century.* London: Longmans, 1913.

Gottschalk, Louis, ed. *Generalization in the Writing of History.* Chicago: University of Chicago Press, 1963.

Green, William A. "Periodization in European and World History." *Journal of World History* 3 (1992): 13–53.

Harris, Marvin. *Cannibals and Kings: The Origins of Cultures.* London: Collins/Fontana, 1978.

———. *Culture, People, Nature: An Introduction to General Anthropology,* 3d ed. New York: Harper and Row, 1980.

Hart, B. H. Liddell. *Why Don't We Learn from History?* New York: Hawthorn, 1971.

Hartwell, R. M. "Economic Growth in England before the Industrial Revolution: Some Methodological Issues." *Journal of Economic History* 29 (1969): 13–31.

Hay, Denys. *Annalists and Historians: Western Historiography from the VIIIth to the XVIIIth Century.* London: Methuen, 1977.

———. "Flavio Biondo and the Middle Ages." *Proceedings of the British Academy* 45 (1959): 97–128.

Hexter, J. H. "Fernand Braudel and the *Monde Braudelien.*" *Journal of Modern History* 44 (1972): 480–539.

————. *Reappraisals in History*. Evanston: Northwestern University Press, 1962.

Hicks, Sir John. *A Theory of Economic History*. London: Oxford University Press, 1969.

Hirschman, Albert O. *The Passions and the Interests: Political Arguments for Capitalism before its Triumph*. Princeton: Princeton University Press, 1977.

Hirst, Paul Q. "The Necessity of Theory." *Economy and Society* 8 (1979): 417–445.

Hodges, Richard, and David Whitehouse. *Mohammad, Charlemagne, and the Origins of Europe: Archaeology and the Pirenne Thesis*. Ithaca: Cornell University Press, 1983.

Hollinger, David. "T. S. Kuhn's Theory of Science and Its Implications for History." *American Historical Review* 78 (1973): 370–393.

Hunt, Lynn. "French History in the Last Twenty Years: The Rise and Fall of the *Annales* Paradigm." *Journal of Contemporary History* 21 (1986): 209–224.

————, ed. *The New Cultural History*. Berkeley: University of California Press, 1989.

Huppert, George. *The Idea of Perfect History: Historical Erudition and Historical Philosophy in Renaissance France*. Urbana: University of Illinois Press, 1970.

————. "The Renaissance Background of Historicism." *History and Theory* 5 (1966): 48–60.

Iggers, George. *New Directions in European Historiography*. Middletown, Conn.: Wesleyan University Press, 1975.

Johnson, E. A. J. *Predecessors of Adam Smith: The Growth of British Economic Thought*. New York: Augustus M. Kelley, 1960.

Jones, Gareth Stedman. "From Historical Sociology to Theoretical History." *British Journal of Sociology* 27 (1976): 295–305.

Jordan, David P. *Gibbon and His Roman Empire*. Urbana: University of Illinois Press, 1971.

Keylor, William R. *Academy and Community: The Foundation of the French Historical Profession*. Cambridge, Mass.: Harvard University Press, 1973.

Kinser, Samuel. "Annaliste Paradigm? Geohistorical Structuralism of Fernand Braudel." *American Historical Review* 86 (1981): 63–105.

Kuhn, T. S. *The Structure of Scientific Revolutions*, 2d ed. Chicago: University of Chicago Press, 1970.

Kurzweil, Edith. *The Age of Structuralism: Levi-Straus to Foucault*. New York: Columbia University Press, 1980.

LaCapra, Dominick. *History and Criticism*. Ithaca: Cornell University Press, 1985.

Ladurie, Emmanuel Le Roy. "Motionless History." *Social Science History* 1 (1977): 115–136.

————. *The Territory of the Historian*. Sussex: Harvester Press, 1962.

Leff, Gordon. *History and Social Theory*. University: University of Alabama Press, 1969.

Link, Arthur J. "The American Historical Association, 1884–1984: Retrospect and Prospect." *American Historical Review* 90 (1985): 1–17.

Lloyd, Christopher. *Explanation in Social History*. New York: Blackwell, 1986.

Lowenthal, David. *The Past Is a Foreign Country*. Cambridge: Cambridge University Press, 1986.

Lyon, Bryce. *Henri Pirenne: A Biographical and Intellectual Study*. Ghent: E. Story-Scienta, 1974.

Malthus, Thomas. *An Essay on the Principle of Population*, ed. Philip Appleman. New York: Norton, 1976.

Marwick, Arthur. *The Nature of History*. London: Macmillan, 1970.

McClelland, Charles E. *State, Society, and University in Germany 1700–1914*. Cambridge: Cambridge University Press, 1980.

McClelland, Peter D. *Causal Explanation and Model Building in History, Economics, and the New Economic History*. Ithaca: Cornell University Press, 1975.

McNeill, William H. *Mythistory and Other Essays*. Chicago: University of Chicago Press, 1986.

———. "Mythistory, or Truth, Myth, History, and Historians." *American Historical Review* 91 (1986): 1–10.

———. "Organizing Concepts for World History." *Review* 10 (1986): 211–229.

———. *"The Rise of the West* after Twenty-Five Years." *Journal of World History* 1 (1990): 1–21.

Moore, Barrington, Jr. *Social Origins of Dictatorship and Democracy*. London: Allen Lane, 1967.

Mosse, George L. "History, Anthropology, and Mass Movements: Review Article." *American Historical Review* 75 (1969): 447–452.

Nisbet, Robert A. *Social Change and History: Aspects of Western Theory of Development*. New York: Oxford University Press, 1969.

North, Douglas C. "The Rise and Fall of the Manorial System: A Theoretical Model." *Journal of Economic History* 31 (1971): 777–803.

———. *Structure and Change in Economic History*. New York: Norton, 1981.

North, Douglas C., and Robert Paul Thomas. "An Economic Theory of the Growth of the Western World." *Economic History Review* 23 (1970): 1–17.

———. *The Rise of the Western World: A New Economic History*. Cambridge: Cambridge University Press, 1973.

Novick, Peter. *That Noble Dream: The "Objectivity Question" and the American Historical Profession*. New York: Cambridge University Press, 1988.

Parker, Harold T., and Georg G. Iggers, eds. *International Handbook of Historical Studies: Contemporary Research and Theory*. Westport, Conn.: Greenwood, 1979.

Pirenne, Henri. *Mohammed and Charlemagne*. New York: Norton, 1939.

Popper, Karl. *The Poverty of Historicism*. London: Routledge and Kegan Paul, 1961.

Poster, Mark. *Foucault, Marxism, and History: Mode of Production versus Mode of Information*. New York: Blackwell, 1984.

Preston, Joseph H. "Was There an Historical Revolution?" *Journal of the History of Ideas* 38 (1977): 353–364.

Reddy, William M. *Money and Liberty in Modern Europe: A Critique of Historical Understanding*. New York: Cambridge University Press, 1986.

Reill, Peter Hans. *The German Enlightenment and the Rise of Historicism*. Berkeley and Los Angeles: University of California Press, 1975.

———. "History and Hermeneutics in the Aufklärung: The Thought of Johann Christof Gatterer." *Journal of Modern History* 45 (1973): 24–51.

Rostow, W. W. *How It All Began: Origins of the Modern Economy*. New York: McGraw-Hill, 1975.

———. *The Stages of Economic Growth: A Non-Communist Manifesto*. Cambridge: Cambridge University Press, 1960.

Salomon, Albert. "German Sociology." In Georges Burvitch and Wilbert E. Moore, eds., *Twentieth Century Sociology*. New York: Philosophical Library, 1945.

Schumpeter, Joseph A. *Capitalism, Socialism, and Democracy*. New York: Harper, 1942.

Sherwood, John M. "Engels, Marx, Malthus, and the Machine." *American Historical Review* 90 (1985): 837–865.

Skocpol, Theda, ed. *Vision and Method in Historical Sociology*. New York: Cambridge University Press, 1984.

Smith, Adam. *An Inquiry into the Nature and Causes of the Wealth of Nations*, eds. R. H. Cambell and A. S. Skinner. Oxford: Clarendon Press, 1976.

Stern, Fritz, ed. *Varieties of History from Voltaire to the Present*. Cleveland: Meridian Books, 1956.

Stoianovich, Traian. *French Historical Method: The Annales Paradigm*. Ithaca: Cornell University Press, 1976.

Stone, Lawrence. "The Revival of Narrative: Reflections on a New Old History." *Past and Present* 85 (1979): 3–24.

Symonds, John Addington. *Renaissance in Italy*, 7 vols. London: Smith and Elder, 1875–1886.

Taylor, A. J. P. "Accident Prone, or What Happened Next." *Journal of Modern History* 49 (1977): 1–18.

Taylor, George Roger. *The Turner Thesis Concerning the Role of the Frontier in American History*. Boston: D. C. Heath, 1956.

Teggart, Frederick J. *Theory and Processes of History*. Berkeley: University of California Press, 1960.

Thompson, E. P. *The Poverty of Theory and Other Essays*. London: Merlin Press, 1978.

Tilly, Charles. *As Sociology Meets History*. New York: Academic Press, 1981.

————. *Big Structures, Large Processes, Huge Comparisons*. New York: Russell Sage Foundation, 1984.

Toews, John E. "Intellectual History after the Linguistic Turn: The Autonomy of Meaning and the Irreducibility of Experience." *American Historical Review* 92 (1987): 879–907.

Trevor-Roper, H. R. "Fernand Braudel, the *Annales* and the Mediterranean." *Journal of Modern History* 44 (1972): 468–479.

Tuma, Elias H. *Economic History and the Social Sciences: Problems of Methodology*. Berkeley and Los Angeles: University of California Press, 1971.

Turner, Frederick Jackson. *The Frontier in American History*. New York: H. Holt, 1920.

————. "The Significance of the Frontier in American History." In Ray Allen Billington, ed., *Frontier and Section: Selected Essays of Frederick Jackson Turner*. Englewood Cliffs, N.J.: Prentice-Hall, 1961.

Van Engen, John. "The Christian Middle Ages as an Historiographical Problem." *American Historical Review* 91 (1986): 519–552.

Wallerstein, Immanuel. "Fernand Braudel, Historian." *Radical History Review* 26 (1982): 105–119.

Webb, Walter Prescott. *The Great Frontier*. Boston: Houghton Mifflin, 1952.

Weeks, Jeffrey. "Foucault for Historians." *History Workshop* 14 (1982): 106–119.

White, Hayden. *The Content of the Form: Narrative Discourse and Historical Representation*. Baltimore: Johns Hopkins University Press, 1987.

———. *Metahistory: The Historical Imagination in Nineteenth-Century Europe*. Baltimore and London: Johns Hopkins University Press, 1973.

Wilcox, Donald J. *The Development of Florentine Humanist Historiography in the Fifteenth Century*. Cambridge, Mass.: Harvard University Press, 1969.

GENERAL WORKS

Abel, Wilhelm. *Agricultural Fluctuations in Europe from the Thirteenth to the Twentieth Centuries*. New York: St. Martin's Press, 1980.

Agnew, Jean-Christophe. *Worlds Apart: The Market and the Theatre in Anglo-American Thought, 1550–1750*. New York: Cambridge University Press, 1986.

Allmand, C. T. *Society at War: The Experience of England and France during the Hundred Years' War*. Edinburgh: Oliver and Boyd, 1973.

Appleby, Andrew B. *Famine in Tudor and Stuart England*. Stanford: Stanford University Press, 1978.

Aston, T. H., ed. *Landlords, Peasants and Politics in Medieval England*. New York: Cambridge University Press, 1988.

Aston, T. S. *Crisis in Europe 1560–1660*. New York: Doubleday, 1967.

Bairoch, Paul. "Europe's Gross National Product: 1800–1975." *Journal of European Economic History* 5 (1976): 273–340.

Baron, Hans. *The Crisis of the Early Italian Renaissance*, 2 vols. Princeton: Princeton University Press, 1955.

Barraclough, Geoffrey. *The Crucible of Europe: The Ninth and Tenth Centuries in European History*. Berkeley: University of California Press, 1976.

Basalla, George. *The Evolution of Technology*. New York: Cambridge University Press, 1988.

Bean, Richard. "War and the Birth of the Nation State." *Journal of Economic History* 33 (1973): 203–221.

Beik, William. *Absolutism and Society in Seventeenth-Century France: State Power and Provincial Aristocracy in Languedoc*. New York: Cambridge University Press, 1985.

Berman, Harold J. *Law and Revolution: The Formation of the Western Legal Tradition*. Cambridge, Mass.: Harvard University Press, 1983.

Bloch, Marc. *Feudal Society*. London: Routledge and Kegan Paul, 1961.

———. *French Rural History: An Essay on Its Basic Characteristics*, trans. Janet Sondheimer. London: Routledge and Kegan Paul, 1966.

Blum, J. *The End of the Old Order in Rural Europe*. Princeton: Princeton University Press, 1978.

Bolton, J. L. *The Medieval English Economy*. London: J. M. Dent and Sons, 1980.

Boorstin, Daniel J. *The Discoverers*. New York: Random House, 1983.

Boserup, Ester. *The Conditions of Agricultural Growth*. London: Allen & Unwin, 1965.

Braudel, Fernand. *The Mediterranean and the Mediterranean World in the Age of Phillip II*, 2 vols., trans. Sian Reynolds. New York: Harper and Row, 1972.

Breisach, Ernst. *Renaissance Europe, 1300–1517*. New York: Macmillan, 1973.

Bridbury, A. R. "Before the Black Death." *Economic History Review*, 2d ser., 30 (1977): 393–410.

———. "The Dark Ages." *Economic History Review*, 2d ser., 26 (1969): 577–592.

Britton, David. *The French Nobility in Crisis, 1560–1640*. Stanford: Stanford University Press, 1969.

Bush, M. L. *The English Aristocracy: A Comparative Synthesis*. Dover: Manchester University Press, 1984.

Cameron, Rondo. "A New View of European Industrialization." *Economic History Review* 38 (1985): 1–23.

Carter, Charles Howard. *The Western European Powers, 1500–1700*. Ithaca: Cornell University Press, 1971.

Chaussinand-Nogaret, Guy. *The French Nobility in the Eighteenth Century: From Feudalism to Enlightenment*. Cambridge: Cambridge University Press, 1985.

Cheyney, Edward P. *The Dawn of a New Era, 1250–1453*. New York: Harper and Row, 1936.

Childs, John. *Armies and Warfare in Europe. 1648–1789*. New York: Holmes and Meier, 1982.

Cipolla, Carlo M. *Before the Industrial Revolution: European Society and Economy, 1000–1700*. New York: Norton, 1976.

———. *Clocks and Culture 1300–1700*. London: Collins, 1967.

Clarkson, L. A. *The Pre-Industrial Economy in England, 1500–1750*. New York: Schocken Books, 1972.

Cochran, Thomas C. "The Business Revolution." *American Historical Review* 79 (1974): 1449–1466.

Coleman, D. C. *The Economy of England, 1450–1750*. New York: Oxford University Press, 1977.

Contamine, Philippe. *War in the Middle Ages*, trans. Michael Jones. New York: Blackwell, 1984.

Corvisier, André. *Armies and Societies in Europe, 1494–1789*, trans. Abigail T. Siddall. Bloomington: Indiana University Press, 1980.

Coulanges, Fustel de. *Histoire des institutions politiques de l'ancienne France*. Paris: Hachette, 1975.

Coulborn, Rushton, ed. *Feudalism in History*. Princeton: Princeton University Press, 1956.

Critchley, J. S. *Feudalism*. London: George Allen and Unwin, 1978.

Dahlman, Carl J. *The Open Field System and Beyond*. Cambridge: Cambridge University Press, 1980.

Davis, Natalie Zemon. *Society and Culture in Early Modern France*. Stanford: Stanford University Press, 1975.

Davis, Ralph. *The Rise of the Atlantic Economies*. Ithaca: Cornell University Press, 1973.

Davy, John. "The Great Bullion Famine of the Fifteenth Century." *Past and Present* 79 (1978): 3–54.

Deane, Phyllis, and W. A. Cole. *British Economic Growth 1688–1959*. Cambridge: Cambridge University Press, 1967.

de Vries, Jan. *The Dutch Rural Economy in the Golden Age, 1500–1700*. New Haven: Yale University Press, 1974.

————. *The Economy of Europe in an Age of Crisis, 1600–1750*. Cambridge and New York: Cambridge University Press, 1976.

Dickens, A. G. *Reformation and Society in Sixteenth-Century Europe*. London: Thames and Hudson, 1971.

Dopsch, Alfons. *The Economic and Social Foundations of European Civilization*. London: K. Paul, Trench, Trubner & Co., 1937.

Duby, George. *The Early Growth of the European Economy: Warriors and Peasants from the Seventh to the Twelfth Century*, trans. Cynthia Postan. London: Weidenfeld and Nicolson, 1974.

Duffy, Christopher. *Siege Warfare: The Fortress in the Early Modern World, 1495–1660*. Boston: Routledge and Kegan Paul, 1979.

Duhem, Pierre. *Medieval Cosmology: Theories of Infinity, Place, Time Void, and the Plurality of Worlds*, trans. Roger Ariew. Chicago: Chicago University Press, 1985.

Dyer, Christopher. *Lords and Peasants in a Changing Society: The Estates of the Bishopric of Worcester, 680–1540*. Cambridge: Cambridge University Press, 1980.

————. *Standards of Living in the Later Middle Ages: Social Change in England c. 1200–1520*. Cambridge: Cambridge University Press, 1989.

Eisenstein, Elizabeth. *The Printing Press as an Agent of Change: Communications and Cultural Transformations in Early Modern Europe*, 2 vols. London: Cambridge University Press, 1979.

Elias, Norbert. *The Civilizing Process: The History of Manners*. New York: Pantheon Books, 1978.

Elliott, J. H. "The Decline of Spain." *Past and Present* 20 (1961): 52–75.

————. *Imperial Spain, 1469–1716*. New York: Mentor, 1966.

————. "Self-Perception and Decline in Early Seventeenth-Century Spain." *Past and Present* 74 (1977): 41–61.

Elton, G. R. *The Tudor Revolution in Government*. Cambridge: Cambridge University Press, 1953.

Febvre, Lucien. *The Coming of the Book: The Impact of Printing 1450–1600*. London: New Left Books, 1976.

Ferguson, Wallace. *Europe in Transition, 1300–1520*. Boston: Houghton Mifflin, 1962.

Ferro, Marc. *The Great War 1914–1918*, trans. Nicole Stone. London: Routledge, 1973.

Flynn, Dennis O. "Fiscal Crisis and the Decline of Spain (Castile)." *Journal of Economic History* 42 (1982): 139–148.

Forster, Robert, and Jack P. Greene, eds. *Pre-Conditions of Revolution in Early Modern Europe*. Baltimore: Johns Hopkins University Press, 1970.

Ganshof, F. L., and A. Verhulst. "Medieval Agrarian Society in Its Prime: France, the Low Countries and Germany." In M. M. Postan, ed., *The Cambridge Economic History of Europe*: vol. 1, *The Agrarian Life of the Middle Ages*, 2d ed. Cambridge: Cambridge University Press, 1966.

Gaski, J. F. "The Causes of the Industrial Revolution: A Brief 'Single Factor' Argument." *Journal of European Economic History* 11 (1982): 227–233.

Gerhard, Dietrich. *Old Europe: A Study of Continuity, 1000–1800*. New York: Academic Press, 1981.

Gimpel, Jean. *The Medieval Machine: The Industrial Revolution of the Middle Ages.* New York: Penguin Books, 1977.

Godino, Vitorino Magãlhaes. *L'économie de l'empire portugais aux XVe et XVIe siècles.* Paris: S.E.V.P.E.N., 1969.

Gottfried, Robert S. *Bury St. Edmunds and the Urban Crisis, 1290–1539.* Princeton: Princeton University Press, 1981.

Goubert, Pierre. *The Ancien Regime: French Society 1600–1750,* trans. Steve Cox. New York: Harper Torchbooks, 1974.

———. *Louis XIV and Twenty Million Frenchmen,* trans. Ann Carter. New York: Pantheon, 1972.

Grigg, David. *Agricultural Systems of the World.* Cambridge: Cambridge University Press, 1974.

———. *The Dynamics of Agricultural Change: The Historical Experience.* New York: St. Martin's Press, 1982.

Guenée, Bernard. *States and Rulers in Later Medieval Europe,* trans. Juliet Vale. New York: Blackwell, 1985.

Haley, K. H. D. *The Dutch in the Seventeenth Century.* New York: Harcourt Brace Jovanovich, 1972.

Hallam, H. E. *Rural England, 1066–1348.* Brighton, Sussex, and Atlantic Highlands, N.J.: Harvester and Humanities Presses, 1981.

———. *Settlement and Society.* Cambridge: Cambridge University Press, 1965.

Hamilton, Earl J. "American Treasure and Andalusian Prices, 1503–1660: A Study in the Spanish Price Revolution." *Journal of Economic and Business History* 1 (1928): 1–35.

———. *American Treasure and the Price Revolution in Spain, 1501–1650.* Cambridge, Mass.: Harvard University Press, 1934.

———. "American Treasure and the Rise of Capitalism." *Economica* 9 (1929): 338–357.

Hartwell, R. M. *The Industrial Revolution and Economic Growth.* London: Methuen, 1971.

———, ed. *The Causes of the Industrial Revolution in England.* London: Methuen, 1967.

Harvey, P. D. A., ed. *The Peasant Land Market in Medieval England.* New York: Oxford University Press, 1984.

Hatcher, John. *Plague, Population and the English Economy, 1348–1530.* New York: Macmillan, 1977.

Hay, Denys. *Europe in the Fourteenth and Fifteenth Centuries,* 2d ed. London/New York: Longman, 1989.

Heaton, Herbert. *Economic History of Europe.* New York: Harper, 1948.

Heers, Jacques. "The 'Feudal' Economy and Capitalism: Words, Ideas and Reality." *Journal of European Economic History* 3 (1974): 609–653.

Helleiner, Karl F. "Moral Conditions of Economic Growth," *Journal of Economic History* 11 (1951): 97–116.

Hill, Christopher. *The Century of Revolution, 1603–1714.* Edinburgh: Nelson, 1963.

———. *Intellectual Origins of the English Revolution.* Oxford: Clarendon Press, 1965.

———. "Puritanism, Capitalism and the Scientific Revolution." *Past and Present* 29 (1964): 88–97.

———. *Reformation to Industrial Revolution: A Social and Economic History of Britain, 1530–1780*. London: Weidenfeld and Nicolson, 1969.

Hilton, R. H. *The English Peasantry in the Later Middle Ages: The Ford Lectures for 1973*. Oxford: Clarendon Press, 1975.

———. *A Medieval Society: The West Midlands at the End of the Thirteenth Century*. London: John Wiley, 1966.

Hobsbawm, Eric. "The General Crisis of the European Economy in the 17th Century," *Past and Present* 5 and 6 (1954): 33–53, 44–65.

Hodgett, Gerald. *A Social and Economic History of Medieval Europe*. London: Methuen, 1972.

Holderness, B. A. *Pre–Industrial England: Economy and Society, 1500–1750*. Totowa, N.J.: Rowman and Littlefield, 1976.

Howard, Michael. *War in European History*. Oxford: Oxford University Press, 1976.

Israel, Jonathan I. "A Conflict of Empires: Spain and the Netherlands 1618–1648." *Past and Present* 76 (1977): 34–74.

———. *The Dutch Republic and the Hispanic World, 1606–1661*. Oxford: Clarendon Press, 1982.

Jones, E. L. *Agriculture and Economic Growth in England, 1650–1815*. London: Methuen, 1967.

———. *Agriculture and the Industrial Revolution*. Oxford: Blackwell, 1974.

———. "English and European Agricultural Development 1650–1750." In R. M. Hartwell, ed., *The Industrial Revolution*. Oxford: Blackwell, 1970.

Jones, Richard Foster. *Ancients and Moderns: A Study of the Rise of the Scientific Movement in Seventeenth-Century England*. St. Louis, Mo.: Washington University Press, 1961.

Kaeuper, Richard W. *War, Justice, and Public Order: England and France in the Later Middle Ages*. New York: Oxford University Press, 1988.

Kamen, Henry. "The Decline of Spain: A Historical Myth." *Past and Present* 81 (1978): 24–50.

———. *The Iron Century: Social Change in Europe 1550–1660*. New York: Praeger, 1961.

———. *Spain 1469–1714: A Society of Conflict*. New York: Longman, 1983.

Kellenbenz, Hermann. *The Rise of the European Economy: An Economic History of Continental Europe from the Fifteenth to the Eighteenth Century*. New York: Holmes & Meier Publishers, 1976.

———. "Technology in the Age of the Scientific Revolution, 1500–1700." In Carlo M. Cipolla, ed., *The Fontana Economic History of Europe:* vol. 2, *The Sixteenth and Seventeenth Centuries*. London: Fontana/Collins, 1974.

Keller, Albert G., ed. *Earth Hunger and Other Essays*. New Haven: Yale University Press, 1913.

Kemp, Tom. *Economic Forces in French History*. London: Longman, 1971.

Kerridge, Eric. *The Agricultural Revolution*. New York: A. M. Kelley, 1968.

Kershaw, Ian. "The Great Famine and Agrarian Crisis in England, 1315–1322." *Past and Present* 59 (1973): 3–50.

Kjaergaard, T. "Origins of Economic Growth in European Societies since the Sixteenth Century: The Case of Agriculture." *Journal of European Economic History* 15 (1986): 591–598.

Lach, Donald. *Asia in the Making of Europe*, 2 vols. Chicago: University of Chicago Press, 1965, 1970.

Lambert, Audrey M. *The Making of the Dutch Landscape: An Historical Geography of the Netherlands*. London and New York: Seminar Press, 1971.

Landes, David S. *Revolution in Time: Clocks and the Making of the Modern World*. Cambridge, Mass.: Belknap Press of Harvard University Press, 1983.

Leff, Gordon. *The Dissolution of the Medieval Outlook: An Essay on Intellectual and Spiritual Change in the Fourteenth Century*. New York: New York University Press, 1976.

Le Goff, Jacques. *Time, Work, and Culture in the Middle Ages*. Chicago: University of Chicago Press, 1980.

Levy, Jack S. *War in the Modern Great Power System, 1495–1975*. Lexington: University of Kentucky Press, 1983.

Lewis, Archibald. *Nomads and Crusaders, A.D. 1000–1368*. Bloomington: University of Indiana Press, 1988.

———. *The Sea and Medieval Civilizations: Collected Essays*. London: Variorium Reprints, 1978.

Lewis, P. S. *The Recovery of France in the Fifteenth Century*. New York: Harper and Row, 1972.

Long, W. Harwood. "The Low Yields of Corn in Medieval England." *Economic History Review*, 2d ser., 32 (1979): 459–469.

Lynch, John. *Spain under the Hapsburgs*, 2 vols. Oxford: Blackwell, 1964.

Macfarlane, Alan. *The Origins of English Individualism: The Family Property and Social Transition*. Oxford: Blackwell, 1978.

MacKay, Angus. *Spain in the Middle Ages: From Frontier to Empire, 1000–1500*. London: Macmillan, 1977.

MacLeod, Murdo J. *Spanish Central America: A Socioeconomic History, 1520–1720*. Berkeley: University of California Press, 1973.

Mate, Mavis. "Medieval Agrarian Practices: The Determining Factors?" *Agricultural History Review* 33 (1985): 22–31.

Mauro, Frédéric. *Le XVIe Siècle Européen: Aspects Economiques*. Paris: Presses Universitaires de France, 1970.

McKay, Derek, and H. M. Scott. *The Rise of the Great Powers, 1648–1815*. New York: Longman, 1983.

McNeill, William H. "The Eccentricity of Wheels, or Eurasian Transportation in Historical Perspective." *American Historical Review* 92 (1987): 1111–1126.

———. *Europe's Steppe Frontier*. Chicago: University of Chicago Press, 1964.

———. *The Pursuit of Power: Technology, Armed Force, and Society since A.D. 1000*. Chicago: University of Chicago Press, 1982.

———. *The Rise of the West: A History of the Human Community*. Chicago: University of Chicago Press, 1963.

———. *The Shape of European History*. New York: Oxford, 1974.

Metcalf, D. M. "The Prosperity of North-Western Europe in the Eighth and Ninth Centuries." *Economic History Review*, 2d ser., 20 (1967): 344–357.

Meuvret, Jean. *Le Problème des subsistances à l'époque Louis XIV*. Paris: Mouton, 1977.

Michelet, Jules. *Histoire de France*, 16 vols. Paris: E. Flammarion, rev. ed., 1893–1899.

Miller, Edward, and John Hatcher. *Medieval England: Rural Society and Economic Change, 1086–1348.* London: Longman, 1978.

Miskimin, H. A. *The Economy of Early Renaissance Europe, 1300–1460.* London: Cambridge University Press, 1975.

Molenda, D. "Technological Innovations in Central Europe between the XIVth and XVIIth Centuries." *Journal of European Economic History* 17 (1988): 63–85.

Morris, Colin. *The Discovery of the Individual, 1050–1200.* London: S.P.C.K. for the Church Historical Society, 1972.

Mousnier, Roland. *Social Hierarchies: 1450 to the Present,* trans. Peter Evens, ed. Margaret Clarke. New York: Schocken Books, 1973.

Mundy, John H. *Europe in the High Middle Ages 1150–1309.* New York: Longman, 1973.

Musson, A. E. "Industrial Motive Power in the United Kingdom, 1800–1870." *Economic History Review* 29 (1976): 415–439.

Needham, Joseph. *Science and Civilisation in China:* vol. 2, *History of Scientific Thought.* Cambridge: Cambridge University Press, 1956.

Nef, J. U. *War and Human Progress.* New York: Norton, 1968.

Nelson, Benjamin. *The Idea of Usury.* Princeton: Princeton University Press, 1949.

Neuschel, Kristen B. *Word of Honor: Interpreting Noble Culture in Sixteenth-Century France.* Ithaca: Cornell University Press, 1989.

Oakley, Francis. *The Medieval Experience: Foundations of Western Cultural Singularity.* New York: Scribners, 1974.

O'Callaghan, Joseph F. *A History of Medieval Spain.* Ithaca: Cornell University Press, 1975.

O'Connell, Robert L. *Of Arms and Men: A History of War, Weapons, and Aggression.* New York: Oxford University Press, 1989.

Oliveira Margues, A. H. de. *History of Portugal,* 2 vols. New York: Columbia University Press, 1971–1972.

Olsh, John Lindsay. "The Growth of English Agricultural Productivity in the Seventeenth Century." *Social Science History* 1 (1977): 460–485.

Ortiz, Antonio Dominquez. *The Golden Age of Spain 1516–1659.* London and New York: Basic Books, 1971.

Outhwaite, R. B. "Progress and Backwardness in English Agriculture, 1500–1650." *Economic History Review,* 2d ser., 39 (1986): 1–18.

Ozment, Steven E. *The Age of Reform, 1250–1500.* New Haven: Yale University Press, 1980.

Parker, Geoffrey. *The Military Revolution: Military Innovation and the Rise of the West, 1500–1800.* New York: Cambridge University Press, 1988.

———. "The 'Military Revolution,' 1560–1660—A Myth?" *Journal of Modern History* 48 (1976): 195–214.

———. *The Thirty Years' War.* New York: Routledge and Kegan Paul, 1987.

Parker, Geoffrey, and Lesley M. Smith, eds. *The General Crisis of the Seventeenth Century.* London: Routledge and Kegan Paul, 1978.

Parker, William N., and E. L. Jones, eds. *European Peasants and Their Markets: Essays in Agrarian Economic History.* Princeton: Princeton University Press, 1975.

Phillips, Carla Rahn. "Time and Duration: A Model for the Economy of Early Modern Spain." *American Historical Review* 92 (1987): 531–562.

Pirenne, Henri. *Economic and Social History of Medieval Europe.* London: K. Paul, Trench, Trubner & Co., 1937.

Pocock, J. G. A., ed. *Three British Revolutions: 1641, 1688, 1776.* Princeton: Princeton University Press, 1980.

Polanyi, Karl. *The Great Transformation.* New York: Rinehart, 1944.

———. *The Livelihood of Man.* New York: Academic Press, 1977.

Postan, M. M. "The Chronology of Labour Services." In M. M. Postan, *Essays in Medieval Agriculture and General Problems of the Medieval Economy.* Cambridge: Cambridge University Press, 1973.

———. "England." In Chapter 7, "Medieval Agrarian Society in its Prime," in M. M. Postan, ed., *The Cambridge Economic History of Europe,* vol. 1, 2d ed. Cambridge: Cambridge University Press, 1966.

———. *Essays on Medieval Agriculture and General Problems of the Medieval Economy.* Cambridge: Cambridge University Press, 1973.

———. "Investment in Medieval Agriculture." *Journal of Economic History* 27 (1967): 576–587.

———. *The Medieval Economy and Society: An Economic History of Britain 1100–1500.* Berkeley and Los Angeles: University of California Press, 1972.

———. *Medieval Trade and Finance.* Cambridge: Cambridge University Press, 1973.

Pounds, N. J. G. *An Historical Geography of Europe 455 B.C.–A.D. 1330.* Cambridge: Cambridge University Press, 1973.

Pryor, John H. *Geography, Technology and War: Studies in the Maritime History of the Mediterranean, 649–1571.* New York: Cambridge University Press, 1988.

Rabb, T. K. "The Effects of the Thirty Years' War on the German Economy." *Journal of Modern History* 34 (1962): 40–51.

———. *The Struggle for Stability in Early Modern Europe.* New York: Oxford University Press, 1975.

Radding, Charles M. *A World Made by Man: Cognition and Society, 400–1200.* Chapel Hill: University of North Carolina Press, 1985.

Reynolds, Susan. *Kingdoms and Communities in Western Europe, 900–1300.* Oxford: Clarendon Press, 1984.

Richard, Guy. *Noblesse d'affaires au XVIIIe siècle.* Paris: A. Colin, 1974.

Richardson, R. C. *The Debate on the English Revolution.* New York: St. Martin's Press, 1977.

Riley, J. C. "The Dutch Economy after 1650: Decline or Growth?" *Journal of European Economic History* 13 (1984): 521–570.

Rosenberg, Nathan, and L. E. Birdzell. *How the West Grew Rich: The Economic Transformation of the Industrial World.* New York: Basic Books, 1986.

Russell, Conrad, ed. *The Origins of the English Civil War.* London: Macmillan, 1973.

Salmon, J. H. M. *Society in Crisis: France in the Sixteenth Century.* New York: St. Martin's Press, 1975.

Schalk, Ellergy. *From Valor to Pedigree: Ideas of Nobility in France in the Sixteenth and Seventeenth Centuries.* Princeton: Princeton University Press, 1986.

Schama, Simon. *The Embarrassment of Riches: An Interpretation of Dutch Culture in the Golden Age.* New York: Knopf, 1987.

Schwarzmann, Maurice. "Background Factors in Spanish Economic Decline." *Explorations in Entrepreneurial History* 3 (1951): 221–247.

Scoville, W. C. *The Persecution of Huguenots and French Economic Development 1680–1720*. Berkeley and Los Angeles: University of California Press, 1960.

Scribner, R. W. *The German Reformation*. Atlantic Highlands, N.J.: Humanities Press, 1986.

Shapre, J. A. *Early-Modern England: A Social History 1550–1760*. New York: Edward Arnold, 1988.

Simone, Franco. *The French Renaissance: Medieval Tradition and Italian Influence in Shaping the Renaissance in France*, trans. H. Gaston Hall. London: Macmillan, 1969.

Slicher van Bath, B. H. *The Agrarian History of Western Europe 500–1850*. New York: St. Martin's Press, 1963.

Solow, Barbara. "Caribbean Slavery and British Growth: The Eric Williams Hypothesis." *Journal of Development Economics* 17 (1985): 99–115.

Sombart, Werner. *A New Social Philosophy*, trans. Karl F. Geiser. Princeton: Princeton University Press, 1937.

Southern, R. W. *The Making of the Middle Ages*. New York: Penguin Books, 1970.

Spitz, Lewis W. *The Protestant Reformation, 1517–1559*. New York: Harper and Row, 1985.

Stavrianos, L. S. *A Global History of Man*. Boston: Allyn & Bacon, 1962.

Stone, Lawrence. *The Causes of the English Revolution, 1529–1642*. New York: Harper Torchbooks, 1972.

———. *The Crisis of the Aristocracy, 1558–1641*. New York: Oxford University Press, 1967.

———, ed. *Social Change and Revolution in England, 1540–1640*. London: Longman, 1965.

Stone, Lawrence, and J. C. Fawtier Stone. *An Open Elite? England 1540–1880*. Oxford: Clarendon Press, 1984.

Strayer, Joseph R. *On the Medieval Origins of the Modern State*. Princeton: Princeton University Press, 1970.

Tate, W. E. *The English Village Community and the Enclosure Movements*. London: Gollancz, 1967.

Thirsk, Joan. "The Common Fields." *Past and Present* 29 (1964): 3–25.

———. *English Peasant Farming: The Agrarian History of England and Wales*: vol. 4, *1500–1640*. London: Cambridge University Press, 1967.

Thompson, James Westfall. *Economic and Social History of Europe in the Later Middle Ages (1300–1530)*. New York: Frederick Ungar, 1960.

Tilly, Charles. *The Contentious French*. Cambridge: Belknap Press, 1986.

———, ed. *The Formation of National States in Western Europe*. Princeton: Princeton University Press, 1975.

Titow, J. Z. *English Rural Society, 1200–1350*. London: Allen & Unwin, 1969.

———. *Winchester Yields: A Study in Medieval Agriculture Productivity*. Cambridge: Cambridge University Press, 1972.

Trevor-Roper, Hugh. *The Rise of Christian Europe*. London: Thames and Hudson, 1965.

Van der Wee, Herman, and Eddy van Cauwenburghe, eds. *Productivity of Land and Agricultural Innovation in the Low Countries 1250–1800*. Leuven: Leuven University Press, 1977.

van Houtte, J. A. *An Economic History of the Low Countries, 800–1800*. New York: St. Martin's Press, 1977.

Vigarello, Georges. *Concepts of Cleanliness: Changing Attitudes in France since the Middle Ages*, trans. Jean Birrell. New York: Cambridge University Press, 1988 .

Vives, Jaime Vincens. *An Economic History of Spain*. Princeton: Princeton University Press, 1969.

Wallace-Hadrill, J. M. *The Barbarian West, 400–1000*, 3d ed. Oxford: Blackwell, 1989.

Watson, A. M. "The Arab Agricultural Revolution and Its Diffusion, 700–1100." *Journal of Economic History* 34 (1974): 8–35.

Watson, Alan. *The Evolution of Law*. Baltimore: Johns Hopkins University Press, 1985.

Weber, Max. *General Economic History*. New York: Free Press, 1927.

White, Lynn, Jr. "The Expansion of Technology 500–1500." In Carlo M. Cipolla, ed., *The Fontana Economic History of Europe: vol. 1, The Middle Ages*. London: Collins/Fontana, 1972.

————. *Medieval Technology and Social Change*. Oxford: Oxford University Press, 1962.

Whitrow, G. J. *Time in History: The Evolution of Our General Awareness of Time and Temporal Perspective*. New York: Oxford University Press, 1988.

Williams, Eric. *Capitalism and Slavery*. Chapel Hill: University of North Carolina Press, 1944.

Wilson, Charles. *England's Apprenticeship, 1603–1763*. New York: St. Martin's Press, 1965.

————. *The Transformation of Europe, 1558–1684*. Berkeley: University of California Press, 1976.

Winter, J. M., ed. *War and Economic Development*. Cambridge: Cambridge University Press, 1975.

Wittfogel, Karl A. *Oriental Despotism: A Comparative Study of Total Power*. New Haven: Yale University Press, 1957.

Wolf, Eric R. *Europe and the People Without History*. Berkeley: University of California Press, 1982.

Wolf, John B. *The Emergence of the Great Powers 1685–1715*. New York: Harper and Row, 1962.

Wrightson, Keith. *English Society, 1580–1680*. New Brunswick, N.J.: Rutgers University Press, 1982.

Wrigley, E. A. *People, Cities and Wealth: The Transformation of Traditional Society*. New York: Blackwell, 1989.

Wyman, W. D., and C. B. Kroeber, eds. *The Frontier in Perspective*. Madison: University of Wisconsin Press, 1965.

Yelling, J. A. *Common Field and Enclosure in England, 1450–1850*. Hamden, Conn.: Archon Books, 1977.

Zinkin, Maurice. *Asia and the West*. London: Chatto and Windus, 1951.

COMMERCE, CAPITALISM, AND EXPANSION

Andrews, Kenneth. *Trade, Plunder, and Settlement*. Cambridge: Cambridge University Press, 1984.

Ashton, T. S. "The Treatment of Capitalism by Historians." In F. A. Hayek, ed., *Capitalism and the Historians*. London: Routledge and Kegan Paul, 1954.

Ashtor, Eliyah. *Levant Trade in the Later Middle Ages*. Princeton: Princeton University Press, 1983.

Attman, Artur. *American Bullion in the European World Trade 1600–1800*, trans. Eva Green and Allan Green. Goteborg: Kungl, 1986.

———. *The Bullion Flow between Europe and the East, 1000–1750*, trans. Eva Green and Allan Green. Goteborg: Kungl, 1981.

———. *Dutch Enterprise in the World Bullion Trade, 1550–1800*, trans. Eva Green and Allan Green. Goteborg: Kungl, 1983.

Baechler, Jean. *The Origins of Capitalism*. Oxford: Blackwell, 1975.

Baechler, Jean, J. Hall, and M. Mann, eds. *Europe and the Rise of Capitalism*. Oxford: Blackwell, 1988.

Ball, J. N. *Merchants and Merchandise: The Expansion of Trade in Europe, 1500–1630*. London: Croom Helm, 1977.

Barbour, Violet. *Capitalism in Amsterdam in the Seventeenth Century*. Ann Arbor: University of Michigan Press, 1966.

Beaud, M. *A History of Capitalism*. London: Macmillan, 1984.

Beresford, M. W. *New Towns of the Middle Ages*. London: Lutterworth Press, 1967.

Berger, Peter. *The Capitalist Revolution*. New York: Basic Books, 1986.

Bergier, J-F. "The Industrial Bourgeoisie and the Rise of the Working Class 1700–1914." In Carlo M. Cipolla, ed., *The Fontana Economic History of Europe*: vol. 3, *The Industrial Revolution*. Glasgow: Fontana/Collins, 1973.

Bernard, Jacques. "Trade and Finance in the Middle Ages 900–1500." In Carlo M. Cipolla, ed., *Fontana Economic History of Europe*: vol. 1, *The Middle Ages*. London: Fontana/Collins, 1972.

Bogucka, Maria. "The Role of Baltic Trade in European Development from the XVIth to the XVIIIth Centuries." *Journal of European Economic History* 9 (1980): 5–20.

Boxer, C. R. *The Portuguese Seaborne Empire: 1415–1825*. New York: Knopf, 1969.

Boyajian, James C. *Portuguese Bankers at the Court of Spain, 1626–1650*. New Brunswick, N.J.: Rutgers University Press, 1983.

Braudel, Fernand. *Afterthoughts on Material Civilization and Capitalism*, trans. Patricia Ranum. Baltimore: Johns Hopkins University Press, 1977.

———. *Capitalism and Material Life 1400–1800*, trans. Miriam Kochan. New York: Harper, 1975.

———. *Civilization and Capitalism, 15th–18th Century*: vol. 1, *The Structures of Everyday Life*: vol. 2, *The Wheels of Commerce*: vol. 3, *The Perspective of the World*, trans. Sian Reynolds. New York: Harper and Row, 1981, 1982, 1984.

Brinley, Thomas. *Migration and Economic Growth: A Study of Great Britain and the Atlantic Economy*, 2d ed. Cambridge: Cambridge University Press, 1973.

Britnell, R. H. "Minor Landlords in England and Medieval Agrarian Capitalism." *Past and Present* 88 (1980): 3–22.

———. "The Proliferation of Markets in England, 1200–1349." *Economic History Review,* 2d ser., 34 (1981): 209–221

Burke, Peter. *Venice and Amsterdam: A Study of Seventeenth-Century Elites.* London: Temple-Smith, 1974.

Carus-Wilson, E. M. *Medieval Merchant Venturers: Collected Studies.* London: Methuen, 1967.

Chapman, Stanley D. "British Marketing Enterprise: The Changing Roles of Merchants, Manufacturers, and Financiers, 1700–1860." *Business History Review* 53 (1979): 205–234.

Chaunu, Pierre. *European Expansion in the Later Middle Ages.* Amsterdam: North-Holland Publishing, 1979.

Childs, Wendy R. *Anglo-Castilian Trade in the Later Middle Ages.* Manchester: Manchester University Press, 1978.

Cipolla, Carlo. *Guns, Sails and Empires: Technological Innovation and the Early Phases of European Expansion, 1400–1700.* New York: Pantheon, 1965.

———. *Money, Prices, and Civilization in the Mediterranean World: Fifth to Seventeenth Century.* Princeton: Published for University of Cincinnati by Princeton University Press, 1956.

Clark, Peter, and Paul Slack. *English Towns in Transition, 1500–1700.* London: Oxford University Press, 1976.

Coelho, Philip. "The Profitability of Imperialism: The British Experience in the West Indies, 1768–1772." *Explorations in Economic History* 10 (1973): 253–280.

Cohen, Jere. "Rational Capitalism in Renaissance Italy." *American Journal of Sociology* 85 (1980): 1340–1355.

Collins, J. B. "The Role of Atlantic France in the Baltic Trade: Dutch Traders and Polish Grain at Nantes, 1625–1675." *Journal of European Economic History* 13 (1984): 239–291.

Coornaert, E. L. J. "European Economic Institutions and the New World: The Chartered Companies." In E. E. Rich and C. H. Wilson, eds., *The Cambridge Economic History of Europe,* vol. 4. Cambridge: Cambridge University Press, 1967.

Cunningham, William. "Economic Change." In A. W. Ward, G. W. Prothero, and Stanley Leathes, eds., *The Cambridge Modern History:* vol. 1, *The Renaissance.* Cambridge: Cambridge University, 1902.

Curtin, Philip D. *Cross-Cultural Trade in World History.* Cambridge: Cambridge University Press, 1984.

Davies, K. G. *The North Atlantic World in the Seventeenth Century.* Minneapolis: University of Minnesota Press, 1974.

———. *The Royal African Company.* London: Longman, 1957.

Davis, Ralph. *English Merchant Shipping and Anglo-Dutch Rivalry in the Seventeenth Century.* London: H.M.S.O., 1975.

———. *English Overseas Trade 1500–1700.* London: Macmillan, 1973.

Debien, Gabriel. *Les engages pour les Antilles (1634–1715).* Paris: Société de l'histoire des colonies françaises, 1952.

de Roover, Raymond. *Business, Banking and Economic Thought in Late Medieval and Early Modern Europe.* Chicago: University of Chicago Press, 1974.

————. "A Florentine Firm of Cloth Manufacturers: Management and Organization of a Sixteenth-Century Business." *Speculum* 16 (1941): 3–33.

————. *Money, Banking and Credit in Medieval Bruges.* Cambridge, Mass.: Mediaeval Academy of America, 1948.

————. *The Rise and Decline of the Medici Bank, 1397–1494.* Cambridge, Mass.: Harvard University Press, 1963.

de Vries, Jan. *European Urbanization, 1500–1800.* London: Methuen, 1984.

di Corcia, Joseph. "Bourg, Bourgeois, Bourgeois de Paris from the Eleventh to the Eighteenth Century." *Journal of Modern History* 50 (1978): 207–233.

Diffie, Bailey W., and George D. Winius. *Foundations of the Portuguese Empire, 1415–1580.* Minneapolis: University of Minnesota Press, 1977.

————. *Prelude to Empire: Portugal Overseas before Henry the Navigator.* Lincoln: University of Nebraska Press, 1960 .

Ehrenberg, Richard. *Capital and Finance in the Age of the Renaissance,* trans. H. M. Lucas. New York: Harcourt, Brace, 1928.

Einzig, Paul. *The History of Foreign Exchange.* New York: St. Martin's Press, 1962.

Engerman, Stanley L. "The Slave Trade and British Capital Formation in the Eighteenth Century: A Comment on the Williams Thesis." *Business History Review* 46 (1972): 430–443.

Faroqhi, S. "The Venetian Presence in the Ottoman Empire, (1600–1630)." *Journal of European Economic History* 15 (1986): 345–384.

Goitein, S. D. *Letters of Medieval Jewish Traders.* Princeton: Princeton University Press, 1973.

Goldthwaite, R. A. "Local Banking in Renaissance Florence." *Journal of European Economic History* 14 (1985): 5–56.

Goodman, J. "Financing Pre-Modern European Industry: An Example from Florence 1580–1660." *Journal of European Economic History* 10 (1981): 415–436.

Gough, J. W. *The Rise of the Entrepreneur.* London: Batsford, 1969.

Grassby, Richard. "English Merchant Capitalism in the Late Seventeenth Century: The Composition of Business Fortunes." *Past and Present* 46 (1970): 87–107.

————. "The Personal Wealth of the Business Community in Seventeenth Century England." *Economic History Review,* 2d ser., 23 (1970): 220–234.

Hamilton, Earl, Jr. "Prices and Progress: Prices as a Factor in Business Growth." *Journal of Economic History* 12 (1952): 325–349.

Heers, Jacques. *Société et économie à Gênes (XIVe–XVe siècles).* London: Variorum Reprints, 1969.

Herlihy, David. "Treasure Hoards in the Italian Economy, 960–1139." *Economic History Review,* 2d ser., 10 (1957): 1–14.

Jeannin, Pierre. *Merchants of the Sixteenth Century.* New York: Harper, 1972.

————. "The Sea-Borne and the Overland Trade Routes of Northern Europe in the Sixteenth and Seventeenth Centuries." *Journal of European Economic History* 11 (1982): 5–59.

Kedar, Benjamin Z. *Merchants in Crisis: Genoese and Venetian Men of Affairs and the Fourteenth Century Depression.* New Haven and London: Yale University Press, 1976.

Keynes, John Maynard. *A Treatise on Money,* 2 vols. New York: Harcourt Brace, 1930.

Kindleberger, Charles P. *A Financial History of Western Europe*. London: Allen & Unwin, 1984.

Konetzke, Richard. "Entrepreneurial Activities of Spanish and Portuguese Noblemen in Medieval Times." *Explorations in Entrepreneurial History* 6 (1953): 115–120.

Landes, David, ed. *The Rise of Capitalism*. New York: Macmillan, 1966.

Lane, Frederic C. "The Mediterranean Spice Trade: Further Evidence of Its Revival in the Sixteenth Century." *American Historical Review* 45 (1939–40): 581–590.

———. *Venice. A Maritime Republic*. Baltimore: Johns Hopkins University Press, 1973.

Lane, Frederic C., and Reinhold C. Meuller. *Money and Banking in Medieval and Renaissance Venice:* vol. 1, *Coins and Moneys of Account*. Baltimore: Johns Hopkins University Press, 1985.

Lewis, A. R. *The Northern Seas: Shipping and Commerce in Northern Europe, A.D. 300–1100*. Princeton: Princeton University Press, 1958.

Liss, Peggy K. *Atlantic Empires: The Network of Trade and Revolution 1713–1826*. Baltimore: Johns Hopkins University Press, 1982.

Lloyd, T. H. *Alien Merchants in England in the High Middle Ages*. New York: St. Martin's Press, 1982.

———. *The English Wool Trade in the Middle Ages*. Cambridge: Cambridge University Press, 1977.

Lopez, Robert. *The Commercial Revolution of the Middle Ages, 950–1350*. Englewood Cliffs, N.J.: Prentice Hall, 1971.

———. "The Evolution of Land Transport in the Middle Ages." *Past and Present* 9 (1956): 17–29.

———. "The Market Expansion: The Case of Genoa." *Journal of Economic History* 24 (1964): 445–464.

Maddison, Angus. *Phases of Capitalist Development*. Oxford: Oxford University Press, 1982.

Malowist, Marian. "The Economic and Social Development of the Baltic Countries from the Fifteenth to the Seventeenth Centuries." *Economic History Review* 2d ser., 12 (1959): 177–189.

———. "Poland, Russia and Western Trade in the Fifteenth and Sixteenth Centuries." *Past and Present* 13 (1958): 26–39.

———. "The Problem of the Inequality of Economic Development in Europe in the Later Middle Ages." *Economic History Review*, 2d ser., 19 (1966): 15–28.

Marchant, Alexander. *From Barter to Slavery: The Economic Relations of Portuguese and Indians in the Settlement of Brazil, 1550–1580*. Baltimore: Johns Hopkins University Press, 1942.

Mauro, F. *Le Portugal et L'Atlantique au XVIIe Siècle 1570–1670*. Paris: S.E.V.P.E.N., 1960.

McKendrick, Niel, John Brewer, and J. H. Plumb. *The Birth of a Consumer Society: The Commercialization of Eighteenth-Century England*. Bloomington: Indiana University Press, 1982.

McNally, David. *Political Economy and the Rise of Capitalism: A Reinterpretation*. Berkeley: University of California Press, 1989.

McNeill, William H. *Venice, the Hinge of Europe, 1081–1797*. Chicago and London: University of Chicago Press, 1974.

Miskimin, Harry A. *Money and Power in Fifteenth-Century France*. New Haven: Yale University Press, 1984.

———. *Money, Prices and Foreign Exchange in Fourteenth Century France*. New Haven: Yale University Press, 1963.

Moore, Ellen Wedemeyer. *Alien Merchants in England in the High Middle Ages*. Brighton: Harvester Press, 1982.

———. *The Fairs of Medieval England: An Introductory Study*. Toronto: Pontifical Institute of Medieval Studies, 1985.

Mundy, John H., and Peter Riesenberg. *The Medieval Town*. Princeton: D. Van Nostrand, 1958.

Nef, John. *The Conquest of the Material World*. Chicago: University of Chicago Press, 1964.

Newman, K. "Hamburg in the European Economy, 1660–1750." *Journal of European Economic History* 14 (1985): 57–94.

Ormrod, D. *English Grain Exports and the Structure of Agrarian Capitalism, 1700–1760*. Hull: Hull University Press, 1985.

Palliser, D. M. "A Crisis of English Towns? The Case of York, 1460–1640." *Northern History* 14 (1978): 108–125.

Parker, William N. *Europe, America, and the Wider World: Essays on the Economic History of Western Capitalism:* vol. 1, *Europe and the World Economy*. Cambridge: Cambridge University Press, 1984.

Parry, J. H. *The Age of Reconnaissance*. New York: Menton, 1964.

———. *The Discovery of the Sea*. Berkeley and Los Angeles: University of California Press, 1981.

Penrose, Boies. *Travel and Discovery in the Renaissance 1420–1620*. Cambridge, Mass.: Harvard University Press, 1952.

Phillips, J. R. S. *The Medieval Expansion of Europe*. New York: Oxford University Press, 1988.

Phythian-Adams, C. *Desolation of a City: Coventry and the Urban Crisis of the Late Middle Ages*. Cambridge: Cambridge University Press, 1979.

Pike, Ruth. *Aristocrats and Traders: Sevellian Society in the Sixteenth Century*. Ithaca: Cornell University Press, 1972.

———. *Enterprise and Adventure: The Genoese in Seville and the Opening of the New World*. Ithaca: Cornell University Press, 1966.

Pirenne, Henri. *Medieval Cities: Their Origins and the Revival of Trade*. Princeton: Princeton University Press, 1925.

———. "The Stages in the Social History of Capitalism." *American Historical Review* 19 (1913–1914): 494–515.

Power, Eileen. *The Wool Trade in English Medieval History*. London: Oxford University Press, 1941.

Prawer, Joshua. *Crusaders' Kingdom: European Colonialism in the Middle Ages*. New York: Praeger, 1972.

Pryor, John H. "Commenda: The Operation of the Contract in Long Distance Commerce at Marseilles during the Thirteenth Century." *Journal of European Economic History* 12 (1984): 397–440.

———. "The Origins of the *Commenda* Contract." *Speculum* 52 (1977): 5–37.

Pullen, Brian, ed. *Crisis and Change in the Venetian Economy in the Sixteenth and Seventeenth Centuries.* London: Methuen, 1968.

Rabb, Theodore K. *Enterprise and Empire: Merchant and Gentry Investment in the Expansion of England 1575–1630.* Cambridge, Mass.: Harvard University Press, 1967.

———. "The Expansion of Europe and the Spirit of Capitalism." *Historical Journal* 17 (1974): 675–689.

———. "Investment in English Overseas Enterprise, 1575–1630." *Economic History Review,* 2d ser., 19 (1966): 70–81.

Rapp, R. T. "The Unmaking of the Mediterranean Trade Hegemony." *Journal of Economic History* 35 (1975): 499–525.

Raynal, Abbé (Guillaume-Thomas). *Histoire philosophique et politique des établissemens et du commerce des Européens dans les deux Indes.* Geneva: Jean-Leonard Pellet, 1782.

Reynolds, Robert L. "In Search of a Business Class in Thirteenth-Century Genoa." *Journal of Economic History* 5 (supplement) (1945): 1–19.

Reynolds, Susan. *An Introduction to the History of English Medieval Towns.* Oxford: Clarendon Press, 1977.

Rodinson, Maxime. *Islam and Capitalism.* Austin: University of Texas Press, 1978.

Rorig, Fritz. *The Medieval Town.* London: Batsford, 1967.

Scammell, G. V. *The First Imperial Age: European Overseas Expansion 1400–1715.* Winchester: Unwin Hyman, 1989.

———. *The World Encompassed: The First European Maritime Empires, c. 800–1650.* Berkeley and Los Angeles: University of California Press, 1981.

See, Henri. *Modern Capitalism: Its Origins and Evolution.* London: Noel Douglas, 1928.

Sheridan, R. B. "The Plantation Revolution and the Industrial Revolution, 1625–1775." *Caribbean Studies* 9 (1969): 5–25.

———. "Planters and Merchants: The Oliver Family of Antigua and London, 1716–1784." *Business History* 13 (1971): 104–116.

———. "Simon Taylor, Sugar Tycoon of Jamaica, 1740–1813." *Agricultural History* 45 (1971): 285–296.

———. *Sugar and Slavery: An Economic History of the British West Indies, 1623–1775.* Baltimore: Johns Hopkins University Press, 1974.

———. "The Wealth of Jamaica in the Eighteenth Century." *Economic History Review,* 2d ser., 18 (1965): 292–311.

———. "The Wealth of Jamaica in the Eighteenth Century: A Rejoinder." *Economic History Review,* 2d ser., 21 (1968): 46–61.

Smith, Woodruff D. "The Function of Commercial Centers in the Modernization of European Capitalism: Amsterdam as an Information Exchange in the Seventeenth Century." *Journal of Economic History* 54 (1984): 985–1006.

Solow, Barbara L., and Stanley L. Engerman, eds. *British Capitalism and Caribbean Slavery: The Legacy of Eric Williams.* Cambridge: Cambridge University Press, 1987.

Sombart, Werner. *Der Moderne Kapitalismus,* 2 vols. Leipzig: Duncker and Humblot, 1902.

———. *The Jews and Modern Capitalism.* Glencoe: Free Press, 1951 (first published 1911).

————. *Luxury and Capitalism.* Ann Arbor: University of Michigan Press, 1967 (first published 1913).

————. *The Quintessence of Capitalism.* New York: Howard Fertig, 1967 (first published 1915).

Spufford, Peter. *Money and Its Use in Medieval Europe.* New York: Cambridge University Press, 1987.

Supple, B. E. *Commercial Crisis and Change in England, 1600–1642.* Cambridge: Cambridge University Press, 1959.

Sweezy, Paul M. *The Theory of Capitalist Development.* New York: Oxford University Press, 1942.

Thirsk, Joan. *Economic Policy and Projects: The Development of a Consumer Society in Early Modern England.* Oxford: Clarendon Press, 1978.

Thomas, Robert Paul. "Sugar Colonies of the Old Empire: Profit or Loss for Great Britain?" *Economic History Review,* 2d ser., 21 (1968): 30–45.

Tribe, Keith. *Geneologies of Capitalism.* Atlantic Highlands, N.J.: Humanities Press, 1981.

Unger, Richard. *The Ship in the Medieval Economy, 600–1600.* Montreal: Croom Helm, 1980.

Usher, A. P. *The Early History of Deposit Banking in Mediterranean Europe.* Cambridge, Mass.: Harvard University Press, 1943.

van der Wee, Herman. *The Growth of the Antwerp Market and the European Economy, Fourteenth–Sixteenth Centuries,* 3 vols. The Hague: Nijhoff, 1963.

van Houtte, J. A. "The Rise and Decline of the Market of Bruges." *Economic History Review,* 2d ser., 19 (1966): 29–47.

van Stuijvenberg, J. H. *The Interactions of Amsterdam and Antwerp with the Baltic Region, 1400–1800.* Leiden: Martinus Nijhoff, 1983.

Verlinden, Charles. *The Beginning of Modern Colonization. Eleven Essays with Introduction,* trans. Yvonne Freccero. Ithaca: Cornell University Press, 1970.

————. "From the Mediterranean to the Atlantic: Aspects of an Economic Shift (12th–18th Century)." *Journal of European Economic History* 1 (1972): 625–646.

————. "Italian Influence on Iberian Colonization." *Hispanic American Historical Review* 33 (1953): 199–211.

Vilar, Pierre. "Problems of the Formation of Capitalism." *Past and Present* 10 (1956): 15–38.

Weatherill, Lorna. *Consumer Behavior and Material Culture in Britain, 1660–1760.* New York: Routledge, 1988.

Webb, Walter Prescott. *The Great Plains.* Boston: Ginn, 1931.

Willan, T. S. *Studies in Elizabethan Foreign Trade.* Manchester: Manchester University Press, 1959.

Zins, Henryk. *England and the Baltic in the Elizabethan Era,* trans. H. C. Stevens. Manchester: Manchester University Press, 1972.

POPULATION HISTORY AND THE DEMOGRAPHIC IMPERATIVE

Anderson, Michael. "Historical Demography after *The Population History of England.*" In Robert I. Rotberg and Theodore K. Rabb, eds., *Population and Economy:*

　　　Population History from the Traditional to the Modern World. Cambridge:
　　　Cambridge University Press, 1986.

Appleby, Andrew. "Grain Prices and Subsistence Crises in England and France, 1590–
　　　1740." *Journal of Economic History* 39 (1979): 865–887.

Bois, Guy. *Crise du Féodalisme.* Paris: Editions de la Maison des sciences de l'homme,
　　　1976.

Borah, Woodrow, and Shelburne F. Cook. *The Aboriginal Population of Central Mex-
　　　ico on the Eve of the Spanish Conquest.* Berkeley: University of California
　　　Press, 1963.

————. *Essays in Population History: Mexico and the Caribbean.* Berkeley: Univer-
　　　sity of California Press, 1971 .

Boserup, Ester. *Population and Technological Change: A Study of Long-Term Trends.*
　　　Chicago: University of Chicago Press, 1981.

Bridbury, A. R. "The Farming Out of Manors." *Economic History Review,* 2d ser., 31
　　　(1978): 503–520.

Campbell, Bruce M. S. "Agricultural Progress in Medieval England: Some Evidence
　　　from Eastern Norfolk." *Economic History Review,* 2d ser., 36 (1983): 25–
　　　46.

————. "Population Change and the Genesis of Commonfields on a Norfolk Manor."
　　　Economic History Review, 2d ser., 33 (1980): 174–192.

Chambers, J. D. *Population, Economy, and Society in Pre-Industrial England.* London:
　　　Oxford University Press, 1972.

Cipolla, Carlo M. *The Economic History of World Population.* Baltimore: Penguin
　　　Books, 1962.

Cowgill, George. "On Causes and Consequences of Ancient and Modern Population
　　　Change." *American Anthropologist* 77 (1975): 505–525.

Denevan, William M., ed. *The Native Population of the Americas in 1492.* Madison:
　　　University of Wisconsin Press, 1976.

Fleury, Michel, and Louis Henry. *Des registres paroissiaux à l'histoire de la popula-
　　　tion: Manuel de dépouillement et d'exploitation de l'état civil ancien.* Paris:
　　　Editions de l'Institut national d'études demographiques, 1956.

Flinn, M. W. *The European Demographic System.* Baltimore: Johns Hopkins Univer-
　　　sity Press, 1981.

Freeman, Ronald, ed. *Population: The Vital Revolution.* New York: Anchor Books,
　　　1964.

Gardner, Richard. "Bush, the U.N., and Too Many People." *New York Times,* 22
　　　September 1989.

Glass, C. V., and D. E. C. Eversley, eds. *Population in History.* London: Edward
　　　Arnold, 1965.

Glass, C. V., and Roger Revelle, eds. *Population and Social Change.* London: Edward
　　　Arnold, 1972.

Goody, Jack. *The Development of the Family and Marriage in Europe.* Cambridge:
　　　Cambridge University Press, 1983.

Goody, Jack, Joan Thirsk, and E. P. Thompson, eds. *Family and Inheritance: Rural
　　　Society in Western Europe, 1200–1800.* London: Cambridge University
　　　Press, 1976.

Gottfried, Robert S. "Bury St. Edmunds and the Populations of Late Medieval Towns,
　　　1270–1530." *Journal of British Studies* 20 (1980): 1–31.

Grigg, D. B. *Population Growth and Agrarian Change: An Alternative Perspective.* Cambridge: Cambridge University Press, 1980.

Habakkuk, H. J. *Population Growth and Economic Development since 1750.* Leicester: Leicester University Press, 1972.

Hajnal, J. "European Marriage Patterns in Perspective." In David Glass and D. E. C. Eversley, eds. *Population in History.* London: Edward Arnold, 1965.

Hallam, H. E. *Rural England, 1066–1348.* Atlantic Highlands, N.J.: Humanities Press, 1981.

Hanawalt, Barbara A. *The Ties That Bound: Peasant Families in Medieval England.* New York: Oxford University Press, 1986.

Helleiner, Karl F. "The Population of Europe from the Black Death to the Eve of the Vital Revolution." In E. E. Rich and C. H. Wilson, eds., *The Cambridge Economic History of Europe,* vol. 4. Cambridge: Cambridge University Press, 1967.

Henige, David. "On the Contact Population of Hispaniola: History as High Mathematics." *Hispanic American Historical Review* 58 (1978): 217–237.

Ho, Ping-Ti. *Studies in the Population of China, 1368–1953.* Cambridge, Mass.: Harvard University Press, 1959.

Hollingsworth, T. H. *Historical Demography.* Ithaca: Cornell University Press, 1969.

Houlbrooke, Ralph. *The English Family, 1450–1700.* New York: Longman, 1984.

Ladurie, Emmanuel Le Roy. "Family Structure and Inheritance Customs in Sixteenth Century France." In Jack Goody, Joan Thirsk, and E. P. Thompson, eds., *Family and Inheritance: Rural Society in Western Europe 1200–1800.* Cambridge: Cambridge University Press, 1976.

———. *The Peasants of Languedoc.* Urbana: University of Illinois Press, 1974.

Langer, W. L. "American Foods and Europe's Population Growth, 1750–1850." *Journal of Social History* 8 (1975): 51–66.

———. "Checks on Population Growth: 1750–1850." *Scientific American* 226 (1972): 92–99.

———. "Europe's Initial Population Explosion." *American Historical Review* 69 (1963): 1–17.

Laslett, Peter. *Family Life and Illicit Love in Earlier Generations.* Cambridge: Cambridge University Press, 1977.

———. *The World We Have Lost.* New York: Scribner, 1966.

Laslett, Peter, and Richard Wall. *Household and Family in Past Time.* Cambridge: Cambridge University Press, 1972.

Lee, Ronald Demos. *Population Patterns in the Past.* New York: Academic Press, 1977.

Lee, W. R., ed. *European Demography and Economic Growth.* New York: St. Martin's Press, 1979.

Levine, David. *Family Formation in an Age of Nascent Capitalism.* New York: Academic Press, 1977.

———. *Reproducing Families: The Political Economy of English Population History.* Cambridge: Cambridge University Press, 1987.

———, ed. *Proletarianization and Family History.* New York: Cambridge University Press, 1984.

Macfarlane, Alan. *Marriage and Love in England: Modes of Reproduction, 1300–1840.* Oxford: Blackwell, 1986.

Mate, Mavis. "Agrarian Economy after the Black Death: The Manors of Canterbury Cathedral Priory, 1348–91." *Economic History Review*, 2d ser., 37 (1984): 341–354.

McEvedy, Colin, and Richard Jones. *Atlas of World Population History*. Harmondsworth: Penguin Books, 1978.

McKeown, Thomas. *The Modern Rise of Population*. New York: Academic Press, 1976.

Meuvret, J. "Demographic Crisis in France from the Sixteenth to the Eighteenth Century." In David Glass and D. E. C. Eversley, eds., *Population in History*. Chicago: Aldine, 1965.

Miller, Edward. "The English Economy in the Thirteenth Century: Implications of Recent Research." *Past and Present* 28 (1964): 21–40.

Mols, Roger, S. J. "Population in Europe 1500–1700." In Carlo M. Cipolla, ed., *The Fontana Economic History of Europe:* vol. 2, *The Sixteenth and Seventeenth Centuries*. London: Fontana/Collins, 1974.

Palliser, D. M. "Tawney's Century: Brave New World or Malthusian Trap?" *Economic History Review*, 2d ser., 35 (1982): 339–353.

Poos, L. R. "The Rural Population of Essex in the Later Middle Ages." *Economic History Review*, 2d ser., 38 (1985): 515–530.

Postan, M. M. "The Chronology of Labour Services." In M. M. Postan, *Essays in Medieval Agriculture and General Problems of the Medieval Economy*. Cambridge: Cambridge University Press, 1973.

Pounds, N. J. C. "Overpopulation in France and the Low Countries in the Later Middle Ages." *Journal of Social History* 3 (1970): 225–247.

Razi, Zvi. *Life, Marriage and Death in a Medieval Parish. Economy, Society and Demography in Halesowen, 1270–1400*. Cambridge: Cambridge University Press, 1980.

Rotberg, Robert I., and Theodore K. Rabb, eds. *Hunger and History: The Impact of Changing Food Production and Consumption Patterns on Society*. Cambridge: Cambridge University Press, 1985.

————. *Population and Economy: Population and History from the Traditional to the Modern World*. Cambridge: Cambridge University Press, 1986.

Russell, Josiah Cox. *British Medieval Population*. Albuquerque: University of New Mexico, 1948.

————. *Late Ancient and Medieval Population Control*. Philadelphia: American Philosophical Society, 1985.

————. "Population in Europe 500–1500." In Carlo M. Cipolla, ed., *The Fontana Economic History of Europe:* vol. 1, *The Middle Ages*. London: Fontana/Collins, 1972.

————. "The Pre-Plague Population of England." *Journal of British Studies* 5 (1966): 1–21.

Schofield, Roger S. "Through a Glass Darkly: *The Population History of England* as an Experiment in History." In Robert I. Rotberg and Theodore K. Rabb, eds., *Population and Economy: Population and History from the Traditional to the Modern World*. Cambridge: Cambridge University Press, 1986.

Silver, Morris. "A Non-Neo Malthusian Model of English Land Values, Wages and Grain Yield before the Black Death." *Journal of European Economic History* 12 (1984): 631–650.

Thompson, John A. *The Transformation of Medieval England 1370–1529*. New York: Longman, 1983.

Thrupp, Sylvia L. "The Problem of Replacement-Rates in Late Medieval English Population." *Economic History Review*, 2d ser., 18 (1965): 101–119.

Tranter, N. L. *Population and Society, 1750–1940: Contrasts in Population Growth*. London: Longman, 1985.

Wrigley, E. A. "Family Limitation in Pre-Industrial England." *Economic History Review*, 2d ser., 19 (1966): 82–109.

———. *Population and History*. New York: McGraw-Hill, 1969.

Wrigley, E. A., and R. S. Schofield. *The Population History of England, 1541–1871: A Reconstruction*. Cambridge, Mass: Harvard University Press, 1981.

Zambardino, R. A. "Critique of David Henige's 'On the Contact Population of Hispaniola,' " *Hispanic American Historical Review* 58 (1978): 700–708.

MARXISM AND HISTORY

Adamson, Walter L. *Marx and the Disillusionment of Marxism*. Berkeley and Los Angeles: University of California Press, 1985.

Althusser, Louis. *For Marx*. London: New Left Books, 1977.

Althusser, Louis, and Etienne Balibar. *Reading Capital*. London: New Left Books, 1977.

Anderson, Perry. *Arguments within English Marxism*. London: Verso, 1980.

———. *Considerations on Western Marxism*. London: New Left Books, 1976.

———. *Lineages of the Absolutist State*. London: New Left Books, 1974.

———. *Passages from Antiquity to Feudalism*. New York: Schocken, 1978.

Aston, T. H., and C. H. E. Philpin, eds. *The Brenner Debate: Agrarian Class Structure and Economic Development in Pre-Industrial Europe*. Cambridge: Cambridge University Press, 1985.

Avineri, Schlomo. *The Social and Political Thought of Karl Marx*. Cambridge: Cambridge University Press, 1972.

Bober, M. M. *Karl Marx's Interpretation of History*. New York: Norton, 1965.

Bottomore, Tom, ed. *A Dictionary of Marxist Thought*. Cambridge, Mass.: Harvard University Press, 1983.

Brenner, Robert. "Agrarian Class Structure and Economic Development in Pre-Industrial Europe." *Past and Present* 70 (1976): 30–75.

Carver, Terrell. *A Marx Dictionary*. Totowa, N.J.: Barnes & Noble Books, 1987.

Cobban, Alfred. *The Social Interpretation of the French Revolution*. Cambridge: Cambridge University Press, 1964.

Cohen, G. A. *Karl Marx's Theory of History: A Defence*. Princeton: Princeton University Press, 1978.

Cohen, Jon S. "The Achievement of Economic History: The Marxist School." *Journal of Economic History* 38 (1978): 29–57.

Comninel, George C. *Rethinking the French Revolution: Marxism and the Revisionist Challenge*. New York: Verso, 1987.

Daniels, Robert V. "Marxian Theories of Historical Dynamics." In Werner J. Cahnman and Alvin Boskoff, eds., *Sociology and History: Theory and Research*. Glencoe: Free Press, 1964.

Dobb, Maurice. *Studies in the Development of Capitalism.* New York: International Publishers, 1984 (first published 1947).

Doyle, William. *Origins of the French Revolution.* New York: Oxford University Press, 1980.

Ellis, G. "The 'Marxist Interpretation' of the French Revolution." *English Historical Review* 93 (1978): 353–376.

Elster, Jon. *Making Sense of Marx.* Cambridge: Cambridge University Press, 1985.

Engels, Friedrich. *The Origin of the Family, Private Property and the State.* Chicago: Kerr, 1902.

Foster-Carter, Aidan. "The Modes of Production Controversy." *New Left Review* 107 (1978): 47–77.

Giddens, Anthony. *A Contemporary Critique of Historical Materialism.* Berkeley: University of California Press, 1981.

Goodman, David, and Michael Redcliffe. *From Peasant to Proletarian: Capitalist Development and Agrarian Transitions.* New York: St. Martin's Press, 1982.

Gottlieb, Roger S. "Feudalism and Historical Materialism: A Critique and a Synthesis." *Science and Society* 48 (1984): 1–37.

Greenlaw, Ralph W., ed. *The Social Origins of the French Revolution: The Debate on the Role of the Middle Classes.* Lexington: D. C. Heath, 1975.

Heller, Henry. "The Transition Debate in Historical Perspective." *Science and Society* 49 (1985): 208–213.

Hill, Christopher. *The English Revolution, 1640.* London: Lawrence & Wishart, 1955.

———. *Intellectual Origins of the English Revolution.* Oxford: Clarendon Press, 1965.

Hilton, R. H. *Bond Men Made Free: Medieval Peasant Movements and the English Rising of 1381.* London: Methuen, 1973.

———. "Capitalism—What's in a Name?" *Past and Present* 1 (1952): 32–43.

———. "A Crisis of Feudalism." *Past and Present* 80 (1978): 3–19.

———. *The English Peasantry in the Later Middle Ages.* Oxford: Clarendon Press, 1975.

Hilton, R. H., and T. H. Aston, eds. *The English Rising of 1381.* New York: Cambridge University Press, 1984.

Hilton, R. H., et al. *The Transition from Feudalism to Capitalism.* London: Verso, 1978.

Hindess, Barry, and Paul Q. Hirst. *Pre-Capitalist Modes of Production.* London: Routledge and Kegan Paul, 1975.

Johnson, Richard. "Edward Thompson, Eugene Genovese, and Socialist-Humanist History." *History Workshop* 6 (1978): 79–100.

Kaye, Harvey J. *The British Marxist Historians: An Introductory Analysis.* New York: Polity Press, 1984.

Kosminsky, E. "The Evolution of Feudal Rent in England from the XIth to the XVth Centuries." *Past and Present* 7 (1955): 13–36.

Kula, Witold. *An Economic Theory of the Feudal System: Towards a Model of the Polish Economy, 1500–1800.* London: New Left Books, 1976.

Laski, Harold J. *Harold J. Laski on the Communist Manifesto: An Introduction.* New York: Pantheon, 1967.

Lefebvre, Georges. *The Coming of the French Revolution, 1789,* trans. R. R. Palmer. Princeton: Princeton University Press, 1947.

Lichtheim, George. *Marxism*. London: Routledge and Kegan Paul, 1971.

Martin, John E. *Feudalism to Capitalism: Peasant and Landlord in English Agrarian Development*. Atlantic Highlands, N.J.: Humanities Press, 1983.

Marx, Karl. *Capital: A Critique of Political Economy*, 3 vols. Trans. Samuel Moore and Edward Areling, ed. Friedrich Engels. Chicago: Kerr, 1906–1909.

———. *A Contribution to the Critique of Political Economy*, trans. N. I. Stone. New York: International Library, 1904.

McLellan, David. *Karl Marx: His Life and Thought*. New York: Harper and Row, 1973.

Merrington, J. "Town and Country in the Transition to Capitalism." *New Left Review* 93 (1975): 71–92.

Richardson, R. C. *The Debate on the English Revolution*. London: Methuen, 1977.

Stone, Lawrence. "The Bourgeois Revolution of Seventeenth-Century England Revisited." *Past and Present* 109 (1985): 44–54.

Taylor, George V. "Non-Capitalist Wealth and the French Revolution," *American Historical Review* 72 (1967): 486–496.

Therborn, Goran. *Science, Class and Society: On the Formation of Sociology and Historical Materialism*. London: New Left Books, 1976.

Thompson, E. P. *The Making of the English Working Class*. New York: Vintage, 1966.

Trevor-Roper, H. R. "The General Crisis of the Seventeenth Century." *Past and Present* 16 (1959): 31–64.

Williams, Raymond. "Base and Superstructure in Marxist Cultural Theory." *New Left Review* 82 (1973): 3–16.

Willigan, Denis J. "Marxist Methodologies of History." *Historical Methods* 17 (1984): 219–228.

Wright, Erik Olin, et al. "The American Class Structure." *American Sociological Review* 47 (1982): 709–726.

Zagorin, Perez. "The Social Interpretation of the English Revolution." *Journal of Economic History* 19 (1959): 376–401.

Zaller, Robert. "What Does the English Revolution Mean? Recent Historiographical Interpretations of Mid-Seventeenth Century England." *Albion* 18 (1987): 617–636.

THE WEBER THESIS, RELIGION, AND HISTORY

Andreski, Stanislav. "Method and Substantive Theory in Max Weber." *British Journal of Sociology* 15 (1964): 1–18.

Ball, Donald W. "Catholics, Calvinists, and Rational Control: Further Explorations in the Weberian Thesis." *Sociological Analysis* 26 (1965): 181–188.

Bendix, Reinhard. *Max Weber: An Intellectual Portrait*. New York: Doubleday, 1960.

Bendix, Reinhard, and Guenther Roth. *Scholarship and Partisanship: Essays on Max Weber*. Berkeley and Los Angeles: University of California Press, 1971.

Bossy, John. *Christianity in the West, 1400–1700*. New York: Oxford University Press, 1985.

Burger, Thomas. *Max Weber's Theory of Concept Formation: History, Laws, and Ideal Types*. Durham: Duke University Press, 1976.

Cahnman, Werner J. "Max Weber and the Methodological Controversy in the Social Sciences." In Werner J. Cahnman and Alvin Boskoff, eds., *Sociology and History: Theory and Research*. Glencoe: Free Press, 1964.

Collins, Randall. *Max Weber: A Skeleton Key*. Beverly Hills: Sage, 1985.

———. *Weberian Sociological Theory*. New York: Cambridge University Press, 1986.

Eisenstadt, S. N. "The Implications of Weber's Sociology of Religion for Understanding Processes of Change in Contemporary Non-European Societies and Civilizations." In C. Y. Glock and P. E. Hammond, eds., *Beyond the Classics? Essays in the Scientific Study of Religion*. New York: Harper and Row, 1973.

———. "Some Reflections on the Significance of Max Weber's Sociology of Religions for the Analysis of Non-European Modernity." *Archives de Sociologie des Religions* 32 (1971): 29–52.

———, ed. *The Protestant Ethic and Modernization: A Comparative View*. New York: Basic Books, 1968.

Fischoff, Ephraim. "The Protestant Ethic and the Spirit of Capitalism—The History of a Controversy." *Social Research* 2 (1944): 53–77.

George, Charles H. "English Calvinist Opinion on Usury, 1600–1640." *Journal of the History of Ideas* 18 (1957): 455–474.

George, Charles H., and Katherine George. *The Protestant Mind of the English Reformation, 1570–1640*. Princeton: Princeton University Press, 1961.

———. "Protestantism and Capitalism in Pre-Revolutionary England." *Church History* 27 (1958): 351–371.

Gerth, H. H., and C. W. Mills. "Introduction: The Man and His Work." In H. H. Gerth and C. W. Mills, eds., *From Max Weber: Essays in Sociology*. London: Routledge and Kegan Paul, 1970.

Giddens, Anthony. *Politics and Sociology in the Thought of Max Weber*. London: Macmillan, 1972.

Green, Robert W., ed. *Protestantism and Capitalism: The Weber Thesis and Its Critics*. Lexington, Mass.: D. C. Heath, 1973.

Hansen, Niles. "The Protestant Ethic as a General Precondition for Economic Development." *Canadian Journal of Economics and Political Science* 29 (1963): 462–474.

Headley, John M. *Luther's View of Church History*. New Haven: Yale University Press, 1963.

Hennis, Wilhelm, ed. *Max Weber, Essays in Reconstruction*, trans. Keith Tribe. Winchester: Unwin Hyman, 1987.

Hill, Christopher. "Protestantism and the Rise of Capitalism." In F. J. Fisher, ed., *Essays in the Economic and Social History of Tudor and Stuart England in Honour of R. H. Tawney*. Cambridge: Cambridge University Press, 1961.

———. "Science, Religion and Society in the Sixteenth and Seventeenth Centuries." *Past and Present* 32 (1965): 110–112.

Hyma, Albert. "Calvinism and Capitalism in the Netherlands, 1555–1700." *Journal of Modern History* 10 (1938): 321–343.

Jedin, Hubert, et al. *History of the Church*, vol. 5, *Reformation and Counter Reformation*. New York: Seabury Press, 1980.

Kalberg, Stephen. "Max Weber's Types of Rationality." *American Journal of Sociology* 85 (1980): 1145–1179.

Kearney, H. F. "Puritanism, Capitalism and the Scientific Revolution." *Past and Present* 28 (1964): 81–101.

Kitch, M. J., ed. *Capitalism and the Reformation*. London: Longman, 1967.

Lachmann, L. M. *The Legacy of Max Weber*. London: Heinemann, 1970.

Little, Lester K. *Religious Poverty and the Profit Economy in Medieval Europe*. Ithaca: Cornell University Press, 1978.

Love, John. "Max Weber and the Theory of Ancient Capitalism." *History and Theory* 25 (1986): 152–172.

Luethy, Herbert. "Once Again: Calvinism and Capitalism." *Encounter* 22 (1964): 26–38.

Mandrou, Robert. "Capitalisme et protestantisme: La science et le mythe." *Revue Historique* 235 (1966): 101–106.

Marshall, Gordon. "The Dark Side of the Weber Thesis: The Case of Scotland." *British Journal of Sociology* 21 (1980): 419–440.

———. *In Search of the Spirit of Capitalism: An Essay on Max Weber's Protestant Ethic Thesis*. New York: Columbia University Press, 1982.

———. *Presbyteries and Profits: Calvinism and the Development of Capitalism in Scotland, 1560–1707*. Oxford: Clarendon Press, 1980.

———. "The Weber Thesis and the Development of Capitalism in Scotland." *Scottish Journal of Sociology* 3 (1979): 173–211.

Mason, S. F. "Science and Religion in Seventeenth Century England." *Past and Present* 3 (1953): 28–44.

McCormack, Thelma. "The Protestant Ethic and the Spirit of Socialism." *British Journal of Sociology* 20 (1969): 266–276.

McNeill, John T. *The History and Character of Calvinism*. New York: Oxford University Press, 1967.

Mitzman, Arthur. *The Iron Cage*. New York: Knopf, 1970.

———. *Sociology and Estrangement: Three Sociologists of Imperial Germany*. New York: Knopf, 1973.

Mommsen, Wolfgang J. "Max Weber as a Critic of Marxism." *Canadian Journal of Sociology* 2 (1977): 373–398.

———. "Max Weber's Political Sociology and His Philosophy of World History." *International Social Science Journal* 17 (1965): 23–45.

Moore, Robert. "History, Economics and Religion: A Review of 'The Max Weber Thesis.'" In Arun Sahay, ed., *Max Weber and Modern Sociology*. London: Routledge and Kegan Paul, 1971.

Nussbaum, Frederick L. *A History of the Economic Institutions of Modern Europe: An Introduction to Der Moderne Kapitalismus of Werner Sombart*. New York: Crofts, 1935.

Otsuka, Hisao. *The Spirit of Capitalism: The Max Weber Thesis in an Economic Historical Perspective*, trans. Masaomi Kondo. Tokyo: Iwanami Shoten, 1982.

Prades, J. A. *La Sociologie de la Religion chez Max Weber*. Louvain: Editions Nauwelaerts, 1969.

Prestwich, Menna, ed. *International Calvinism 1541–1715*. New York: Oxford University Press, 1985.

Rabb, Theodore K. "Puritanism and the Rise of Experimental Science in England." *Cahiers d'Histoire Mondiale* 7 (1962): 46–67.

————. "Religion and the Rise of Modern Science." *Past and Present* 31 (1965): 111–126.

Razzell, Peter. "The Protestant Ethic and the Spirit of Capitalism: A Natural Scientific Critique." *British Journal of Sociology* 28 (1977): 17–37.

Riemersma, J. C. *Religious Factors in Early Dutch Capitalism, 1550–1650*. The Hague: Mouton, 1967.

Rotenberg, Mordechai. *Damnation and Deviance: The Protestant Ethic and the Spirit of Failure*. New York: Free Press, 1978.

Roth, Guenther, and Wolfgang Schluchter. *Max Weber's Vision of History*. Berkeley and Los Angeles: University of California Press, 1979.

Samuelsson, Kurt. *Religion and Economic Action*. London: Heinemann, 1961.

Schluchter, Wolfgang. "The Paradox of Rationalization: On the Relation of Ethics and the World." In G. Roth and W. Schluchter, eds., *Max Weber's Vision of History: Ethics and Methods*. Berkeley and Los Angeles: University of California Press, 1979.

————. *The Rise of Western Rationalism: Max Weber's Developmental History*, trans. with introduction by Guenther Roth. Berkeley and Los Angeles: University of California Press, 1981.

See, Henri. "Dans quelle mesure Puritains et Juifs ont-ils contribué aux progrès du capitalisme moderne?" *Revue Historique* 155 (1927): 57–68.

Sprinzak, Ehud. "Weber's Thesis as an Historical Explanation." *History and Theory* 11 (1972): 294–320.

Strauss, Gerald. *Luther's House of Learning: Indoctrination of the Young in the German Reformation*. Baltimore: Johns Hopkins University Press, 1978.

Sutton, F. X. "The Social and Economic Philosophy of Werner Sombart: The Sociology of Capitalism." In Harry Elmer Barnes, ed., *An Introduction to the History of Sociology*. Chicago: University of Chicago Press, 1965.

Tawney, R. H. *Religion and the Rise of Capitalism*. Harmondsworth: Penguin, 1972 (first published 1926).

Tenbruck, Friedrich H. "The Problem of Thematic Unity in the Works of Max Weber." *British Journal of Sociology* 31 (1980): 316–351.

Turner, Bryan S. *Weber and Islam*. London: Routledge and Kegan Paul, 1974.

van der Sprenkel, Otto B. "Max Weber on China." *History and Theory* 3 (1963): 348–370.

Wagner, Helmut. "The Protestant Ethic: A Mid-Twentieth Century View." *Sociological Analysis* 25 (1964): 34–40.

Warner, R. Stephen. "The Role of Religious Ideas and the Use of Models in Max Weber's Comparative Studies of Non-Capitalist Societies." *Journal of Economic History* 30 (1970): 74–99.

Weber, Marianne. *Max Weber: A Biography*. London: John Wiley, 1975 (first published 1926).

Weber, Max. *Ancient Judaism*, trans. Hans H. Gerth and Don Martindale. Glencoe: Free Press, 1952 (originally published in *Archiv für Sozialwissenschaft und Sozialforschung*, 1917–1918).

————. "Anticritical Last Word on 'The Spirit of Capitalism,' by Max Weber." *American Journal of Sociology* 83 (1978): 1105–1131 (first published 1910).

———. *Economy and Society,* 3 vols., trans. Ephraim Fischoff and others, eds. Guenter Roth and Claus Wittich. New York: Bedminster Press, 1968 (first published 1922).

———. *The Methodology of the Social Sciences,* trans. Edward A. Shils and Henry A. Finch. New York: Free Press, 1969 (previously published 1904, 1906, 1917–1918).

———. *The Protestant Ethic and the Spirit of Capitalism,* trans. Talcott Parsons. New York: Scribner, 1958 (first published 1904–1905).

———. *The Religion of China: Confucianism and Taoism,* trans. Hans H. Gerth. New York: Free Press, 1951 (originally published in *Archiv für Sozialwissenschaft und Sozialforschung,* 1916).

———. *The Religion of India: The Sociology of Hinduism and Buddhism,* trans. Hans H. Gerth and Don Martindale. Glencoe: Free Press, 1958 (originally published in *Archiv für Sozialwissenschaft und Sozialforschung,* 1916–1917).

DEPENDENCY AND WORLD-SYSTEMS

Abu-Lughod, Janet L. *Before European Hegemony: The World System, A.D. 1250–1350.* New York: Oxford University Press, 1989.

Amin, Samir. *Unequal Development: An Essay on the Social Formation of Peripheral Capitalism.* New York: Monthly Review Press, 1976.

Arrighi, G., Terence Hopkins, and Immanuel Wallerstein. "Rethinking the Concepts of Class and Status-Group in a World-System Perspective." *Review* 6 (1983): 283–304.

Blomstrom, Magnus, and Bjorn Hettne. *Development Theory in Transition: The Dependency Debate and Beyond—Third World Responses.* London: Zed, 1984.

Bousquet, Nicole. "Esquisse d'une théorie de l'altérnance de périodes de concurrence et d'hégémonie au centre de l'économie-monde capitaliste." *Review* 2 (1979): 501–517.

Brenner, Robert. "The Origins of Capitalist Development: A Critique of Neo-Smithian Marxism." *New Left Review* 104 (1977): 25–92.

Cardoso, Fernando H. "The Consumption of Dependency Theory in the United States." *Latin American Research Review* 12 (1977): 7–24.

Cardoso, Fernando H., and Enzo Faletto. *Dependency and Development in Latin America.* Berkeley: University of California Press, 1979.

Chase-Dunn, C. *Global Formation: Structures of the World-Economy.* Oxford: Blackwell, 1989.

Chilcote, Roland H. "Dependency: A Critical Synthesis of the Literature." *Latin American Perspectives* 1 (1974): 3–29.

———, ed. *Dependency and Marxism: Toward a Resolution of the Debate.* Boulder: Westview, 1982.

Chirot, Daniel, and Thomas D. Hall. "World-System Theory." *Annual Review of Sociology* 8 (1982): 81–106.

Dodgshon, Robert A. "The Modern World-System: A Spatial Perspective." *Peasant Studies* 6 (1977): 8–19.

DuPlessis, Robert S. "The Partial Transition to World-Systems Analysis in Early Modern European History." *Radical History Review* 39 (1987): 22–27.

Flynn, Dennis. "Early Capitalism Despite New World Bullion: An Anti-Wallerstein Interpretation of Imperial Spain." Paper presented at meeting of Social Science Historical Association, Washington, D.C. 1983.

Foster-Carter, Aiden. "Neo-Marxist Approaches to Development and Underdevelopment." *Journal of Contemporary Asia* 3 (1973): 7–33.

Frank, André Gunder. *Capitalism and Underdevelopment in Latin America: Historical Studies of Chili and Brazil*. New York: Monthly Review Press, 1967.

———. "Dependence is Dead, Long Live Dependence and the Class Struggle." *Latin American Perspectives* 1 (1974): 87–106.

———. *Dependent Accumulation and Underdevelopment*. London: Macmillan, 1978.

———. *Latin America: Underdevelopment or Revolution*. New York and London: Monthly Review Press, 1969.

———. *Lumpenbourgeoisie: Lumpendevelopment, Dependence, Class and Politics in Latin America*. New York: Monthly Review Press, 1972.

———. *Sociology of Development and Underdevelopment of Sociology*. London: Pluto Press, 1971.

———. *World Accumulation, 1492–1789*. London: Macmillan, 1978.

Garst, Daniel. "Wallerstein and His Critics." *Theory and Society* 14 (1985): 445–468.

Goldfrank, Walter L., ed. *The World-System of Capitalism: Past and Present*. Beverly Hills: Sage, 1979.

Gulap, Haldun. "Frank and Wallerstein Revisited: A Contribution to Brenner's Critique." *Journal of Contemporary Asia* 11 (1981): 169–188.

Hopkins, Terence, and Immanuel Wallerstein, eds. *Process of the World-System*. Beverly Hills: Sage, 1980.

———. *World-System Analysis*. Beverly Hills: Sage, 1982.

Inikori, Joseph. *Forced Migration: The Impact of the Export Slave Trade on African Societies*. New York: Africana, 1982.

Jewsiewicki, Bogumil. "The African Prism of Immanuel Wallerstein." *Radical History Review* 39 (1987): 50–68.

Kaplan, Barbara H. *Social Change in the Capitalist World-Economy*. Beverly Hills: Sage, 1978.

Kay, Geoffrey. *Development and Underdevelopment: A Marxist Analysis*. London: Macmillan, 1975.

Leys, Colin. "Underdevelopment and Dependency: Critical Notes." *Journal of Contemporary Asia* 7 (1977): 92–107.

Palma, Gabriel. "Dependency: A Formal Theory of Underdevelopment or a Methodology for the Analysis of Concrete Situations of Underdevelopment." *World Development* 6 (1978): 881–894.

Petras, James. "Dependency and World-System Theory: A Critique and New Directions." In Ronald H. Chilcote, ed., *Dependency and Marxism: Toward a Resolution of the Debate*. Boulder: Westview, 1982.

Prebisch, R. *The Economic Development of Latin America and Its Principal Problems*. New York: United Nations, 1950.

Ragin, Charles, and Daniel Chirot. "The World System of Immanuel Wallerstein: Sociology and Politics as History." In Theda Skocpol, ed., *Vision and*

Method in Historical Sociology. Cambridge: Cambridge University Press, 1984.

Rodney, Walter. *How Europe Underdeveloped Africa*. London and Dar es Salaam: Bogle-L'Ouverture Publications, 1972.

Seers, Dudley. *Dependency Theory: A Critical Reassessment*. London: Frances Printer, 1981.

Skocpol, Theda. "Wallerstein's World Capitalist System: A Theoretical and Historical Critique." *American Journal of Sociology* 82 (1977): 1075–1090.

Smith, Alan. "Where Was the Periphery? The Wider World and the Core of the World-Economy." *Radical History Review* 39 (1987): 28–49.

So, Alvin Y. *Social Change and Development: Modernization, Dependency, and World-System Theories*. Newbury Park, Calif.: Sage, 1990.

Stern, Steve J. "Feudalism, Capitalism, and the World-System in the Perspective of Latin America and the Caribbean." *American Historical Review* 93 (1988): 829–872.

Taylor, John G. *From Modernization to Modes of Production: A Critique of the Sociologies of Development and Underdevelopment*. Atlantic Highlands, N.J.: Humanities Press, 1979.

Thompson, William R. *Contending Approaches to World-System Analysis*. Beverly Hills: Sage, 1983.

Trimberger, Ellen Kay. "World Systems Analysis: The Problem of Unequal Development." *Theory and Society* 8 (1979): 101–126.

Wallerstein, Immanuel. *The Capitalist World-Economy*. New York: Cambridge University Press, 1979.

———. *The Modern World-System I: Capitalist Agriculture and the Origins of the European World-Economy in the Sixteenth Century*. New York: Academic Press, 1974.

———. *The Modern World-System II: Mercantilism and the Consolidation of the European World-Economy, 1600–1750*. New York: Academic Press, 1980.

———. *The Modern World-System III: The Second Era of Great Expansion of the Capitalist World-Economy, 1730–1840s*. New York: Academic Press, 1989.

———. *The Politics of the Capitalist World-Economy*. Cambridge: Cambridge University Press, 1984.

———. "Underdevelopment Phase-B: Effect of the Seventeenth-Century Stagnation on Core and Periphery of the European World-Economy." In Walter L. Goldfrank, ed. *The World-System of Capitalism: Past and Present*. Beverly Hills: Sage, 1979.

———. "World-System Analysis." In Anthony Giddens and Jonathan H. Turner, eds., *Social Theory Today*. Stanford: Stanford University Press, 1987.

Weaver, James, and Marguerite Berger. "The Marxist Critique of Dependency Theory: An Introduction." In Charles K. Wilber, ed., *The Political Economy of Development and Underdevelopment*. New York: Random House, 1984.

Worsley, Peter. "One World or Three? A Critique of the World-System Theory of Immanuel Wallerstein." In David Held, ed., *State and Societies*. New York: New York University Press, 1982.

ENVIRONMENTAL HISTORY

Bailes, Kendall E., ed. *Environmental History: Critical Issues in Comparative Perspective*. Lanham, Md.: University Press of America, 1985.

Bennett, John W. *The Ecological Transition: Cultural Anthropology and Human Adaptation*. Elmsford, N.Y.: Pergamon, 1976.

Bertrand, Georges. "Pour une histoire écologique de la France rurale." In Georges Duby, ed., *Histoire de la France rurale*. Paris: Seuil, 1975.

Bilsky, Lester J., ed. *Historical Ecology: Essays on Environment and Social Change*. Port Washington, N.Y.: Kennikat Press, 1980.

Blouet, Brian, and Frederick C. Luebke, eds. *The Great Plains: Environment and Culture*. Lincoln: University of Nebraska Press, 1979.

Bolton, Geoffrey. *Spoils and Spoilers: Australians and Their Environment, 1788–1980*. Sydney: Allen & Unwin, 1981.

Burton, Ian, Robert W. Kates, and Gilbert F. White. *The Environment as Hazard*. New York: Oxford University Press, 1978.

Cantor, Leonard. *The Changing English Countryside 1400–1700*. New York: Routledge, 1987.

Carson, Rachel. *Silent Spring*. Boston: Houghton Mifflin, 1962.

Clark, Andrew H. *The Invasion of New Zealand by People, Plants, and Animals: The South Island*. New Brunswick, N.J.: Rutgers University Press, 1949.

Cronon, William. *Changes in the Land: Indians, Colonists, and the Ecology of New England*. New York: Hill & Wang, 1983.

Crosby, Alfred W. *The Columbian Exchange: Biological and Cultural Consequences of 1492*. Westport, Conn.: Greenwood, 1972.

———. *Ecological Imperialism: The Biological Expansion of Europe, 900–1900*. New York: Cambridge University Press, 1986.

———. "Virgin Soil Epidemics as a Factor in the Aboriginal Depopulation in America." *William and Mary Quarterly* 33 (1976): 289–299.

Ekirch, Arthur A., Jr. *Man and Nature in America*. New York: Columbia University Press, 1963.

Ellen, Roy F. *Environment, Subsistence and System: The Ecology of Small-Scale Social Formations*. Cambridge: Cambridge University Press, 1982.

Elton, Charles. *The Ecology of Invasions by Animals and Plants*. London: Methuen, 1958.

Fleure, H. J., and Margaret Davies. *A Natural History of Man in Britain: Conceived as a Study of Changing Relations between Men and Environments*. London: Collins, 1970.

Geertz, Clifford. *Agricultural Involution: The Process of Ecological Change in Indonesia*. Berkeley and Los Angeles: University of California Press, 1971.

Glacken, Clarence. *Traces on the Rhodian Shore: Nature and Culture in Western Thought from Ancient Times to the End of the Eighteenth Century*. Berkeley and Los Angeles: University of California Press, 1967.

Goudie, Andrew. *The Human Impact on the Natural Environment*, 2d ed. Cambridge, Mass.: MIT Press, 1986.

Hancock, William Keith. *Discovering Monaro: A Study of Man's Impact on His Environment*. Cambridge: Cambridge University Press, 1972.

Harris, Marvin. *Cultural Materialism: The Struggle for a Science of Culture.* New York: Random House, 1979.

Herlihy, David. "Ecological Conditions and Demographic Change." In Richard L. De Molen, ed., *One Thousand Years: Western Europe in the Middle Ages.* Boston: Houghton Mifflin, 1974.

Hoskins, W. G. *The Making of the English Landscape.* London: Hodder and Stoughton, 1977.

Hughes, J. Donald. *Ecology in Ancient Civilizations.* Albuquerque: University of New Mexico Press, 1975.

Jacobs, Wilbur. "The Great Despoliation: Environmental Themes in American Frontier History." *Pacific Historical Review* 47 (1978): 1–26.

Jones, E. L. "Disasters and Economic Differentiation across Eurasia: A Reply." *Journal of Economic History* 45 (1985): 675–682.

———. "Environment, Agriculture, and Industrialization in Europe." *Agricultural History* 51 (1977): 491–502.

———. "The Environment and the Economy." In Peter Burke, ed., *The New Cambridge Modern History:* vol. 13, *Companion Volume.* Cambridge: Cambridge University Press, 1979.

———. *The European Miracle: Environments, Economies, and Geopolitics in the History of Europe and Asia.* Cambridge: Cambridge University Press, 1981.

Kjekshus, Helge. *Ecology Control and Economic Development in East African History: The Case of Tanganyika, 1850–1950.* Berkeley and Los Angeles: University of California Press, 1977.

Lauwerys, J. A. *Man's Impact on Nature.* London: Aldus Books, 1969.

Leeds, Anthony, and Andrew P. Vayda, eds. *Man, Culture, and Animals: The Role of Animals in Human Ecological Adjustments.* Washington, D.C.: American Association for the Advancement of Science, 1965.

Levins, Richard. *Evolution in Changing Environments.* Princeton: Princeton University Press, 1968.

Loomis, R. S. "Ecological Dimensions of Medieval Agrarian Systems: An Ecologist Responds." *Agricultural History* 52 (1978): 478–483.

Lovelock, J. E. *Gaia: A New Look at Life on Earth.* New York: Oxford University Press, 1979.

McNeill, William H. *The Human Condition: An Ecological Perspective.* Princeton: Princeton University Press, 1980.

Meinig, D. W. *The Shaping of America: A Geographical Perspective on 500 Years of History:* vol. 1, *Atlantic America: 1492–1800.* New Haven: Yale University Press, 1986.

Moran, Emilio F. *Human Adaptability: An Introduction to Ecological Anthropology.* North Scituate, Mass.: Duxbury Press, 1979.

Nash, Roderick. "Environmental History." In Herbert J. Bass, ed., *The State of American History.* Chicago: Quadrangle Press, 1970.

Opie, John. "Frontier History in Environmental Perspective." In Jerome O. Steffen, ed., *The American West: New Perspectives, New Dimensions.* Norman: University of Oklahoma Press, 1979.

———. *Wilderness and the American Mind,* 3d ed. New Haven: Yale University Press, 1982.

Osborn, Fairfield. *Our Plundered Planet.* Boston: Little, Brown, 1948.

Parsons, Howard L., ed. *Marx and Engels on Ecology*. Westport, Conn.: Greenwood, 1977.

Passmore, John. *Man's Responsibility for Nature: Ecological Problems and Western Traditions*. New York: Charles Scribners' Sons, 1974.

Petulla, Joseph. *American Environmental History: The Exploitation and Conservation of Natural Resources*. San Francisco: Boyd & Fraser, 1977.

Post, J. D. *Food Shortage, Climatic Variability, and Epidemic Disease in Preindustrial Europe: The Mortality Peak in the Early 1740s*. Ithaca: Cornell University Press, 1985.

———. *The Last Great Subsistance Crisis in the Western World*. Baltimore: Johns Hopkins University Press, 1977.

Richards, John F. "World Environmental History and Economic Development." In William C. Clark and R. E. Munn, eds., *Sustainable Development of the Biosphere*. Cambridge: Cambridge University Press, 1986.

Roll, Eric C. *They All Ran Wild: The Story of Pests on the Land in Australia*. Sydney: Angus & Robertson, 1969.

Russell, W. M. S. *Man, Nature and History: Controlling the Environment*. Garden City: Natural History Press, 1967.

Salaman, Redliffe (with revisions and new introduction by J. G. Hawkins). *The History and Social Influence of the Potato*. New York: Cambridge University Press, 1985.

Sauer, Carl O. *Seventeenth-Century North America*. Berkeley: Turtle Island, 1980.

———. *Sixteenth-Century North America: The Land and People as Seen by the Europeans*. Berkeley and Los Angeles: University of California Press, 1971.

Seymour, John, and Herbert Girandet. *Far from Paradise: The Story of Man's Impact on the Environment*. London: British Broadcasting Corporation, 1986.

Steward, Julian. *The Theory of Culture Change: The Methodology of Multilinear Evolution*. Urbana: University of Illinois, 1955.

Stretton, Hugh. *Capitalism, Socialism, and the Environment*. Cambridge: Cambridge University Press, 1976.

TeBrake, William R. "Air Pollution and Fuel Crises in Preindustrial London, 1250–1650." *Technology and Culture* 16 (1975): 337–359.

———. *Medieval Frontier: Culture and Ecology in Rijnland*. College Station: Texas A & M University Press, 1985.

Viola, Herman J., and Carolyn Margolis, eds. *Seeds of Change: A Quincentennial Commemoration*. Washington, D.C.: Smithsonian Institution, 1991.

Vogt, William. *Road to Survival*. New York: Sloane Associates, 1948.

Walters, A. Harry. *Ecology, Food and Civilisation: An Ecological History of Human Society*. London: Charles Knight, 1973.

Ward, Barbara, and René Dubos. *Only One Earth: The Care and Maintenance of a Small Planet*. New York: Norton, 1972.

Weiner, Douglas R. *Models of Nature: Conservation, Ecology, and Cultural Revolution*. Bloomington: Indiana University Press, 1988.

White, Lynn, Jr. "The Historic Roots of Our Ecologic Crisis." *Science* 155 (1967): 1202–1207.

White, Richard. "American Environmental History: The Development of a New Historical Field." *Pacific Historical Review* 54 (1985): 297–335.

Wilkinson, Richard G. *Poverty and Progress: An Ecological Perspective on Economic Development.* New York: Praeger, 1973.

Worster, Donald. *Dust Bowl: The Southern Plains in the 1930s.* New York: Oxford University Press, 1977.

———. *Nature's Economy: A History of Ecological Ideas,* 2d ed. New York: Cambridge University Press, 1985.

———, ed. *The Ends of the Earth: Perspectives on Modern Environmental History.* New York: Cambridge University Press, 1988.

CLIMATE

Anderson, J. L. "Climatic Change in European Economic History." *Research in Economic History* 6 (1981): 1–34.

Bryson, Reid A., and Christine Padoch. "On the Climates of History." *Journal of Interdisciplinary History* 10 (1980): 583–597.

Bryson, Reid A., and Thomas J. Murray. *Climates of Hunger: Mankind and the World's Changing Weather.* Madison: University of Wisconsin Press, 1977.

Claxton, Robert H. "Climate and History: From Speculation to Systematic Study." *The Historian* 45 (1985): 220–236.

———. "Climatic and Human History in Europe and Latin America: An Opportunity for Comparative Study." *Climatic Change* 1 (1978): 195–203.

de Vries, Jan. "Measuring the Impact of Climate on History: The Search for Appropriate Methodologies." *Journal of Interdisciplinary History* 10 (1980): 599–630.

Herlihy, David. "Climate and Documentary Sources: A Comment." *Journal of Interdisciplinary History* 10 (1980): 713–717.

Huntington, E. *Civilisation and Climate.* New Haven: Yale University Press, 1915.

Jones, E. L. *Seasons and Prices: The Role of the Weather in English Agricultural History.* London: Allen & Unwin, 1964.

Kates, Robert W., Jesse H. Ausubel, and Mimi Berberian, eds. *Climate Impact Assessment: Studies of the Interaction of Climate and Society.* New York: John Wiley and Sons, 1985.

Ladurie, Emmanuel Le Roy. "Histoire et climat." *Annales, E.S.C.* 14 (1959): 3–34, translated as "History and Climate." In Peter Burke, ed., *Economy and Society in Early Modern Europe.* New York: Harper and Row, 1972.

———. *Times of Feast, Times of Famine: A History of Climate since the Year 1000,* trans. Barbara Bray. Garden City: Doubleday, 1971.

Lamb, H. H. *Climate, History and the Modern World.* London: Methuen, 1982.

Lamb, H. H., and M. J. Ingram. "Climate and History." *Past and Present* 89 (1980): 136–141.

———. *Climate Present, Past and Future:* vol. 2, *Climatic History and the Future.* London: Methuen, 1977.

Lambert, L. Don. "The Role of Climate in the Economic Development of Nations." *Land Economics* 47 (1971): 339–344.

Parry, M. L. *Climatic Change, Agriculture and Settlement.* Folkestone: William Dawson & Sons, 1978.

Pfister, C. "Climate and Economy in Eighteenth Century Switzerland." *Journal of Interdisciplinary History* 9 (1978): 223–243.

————. "The Little Ice Age: Thermal and Wetness Indices for Central Europe." *Journal of Interdisciplinary History* 10 (1980): 665–696.

Post, John D. "Climatic Change and Historical Discontinuity." *Journal of Interdisciplinary History* 14 (1983): 153–160.

————. "The Impact of Climate on Political, Social and Economic Change: A Comment." *Journal of Interdisciplinary History* 10 (1980): 719–723.

————. "Meteorological Historiography." *Journal of Interdisciplinary History* 3 (1973): 721–732.

Rabb, Theodore K., and Robert I. Rotberg, eds. *Climate and History: Studies in Interdisciplinary History.* Princeton: Princeton University Press, 1981.

Titow, J. Z. "Evidence of Weather in the Account Rolls of the Bishopric of Winchester, 1209–1350." *Economic History Review,* 2d ser., 12 (1960): 360–407.

Utterström, Gustaf. "Climatic Fluctuations and Population in Early Modern History." *Scandinavian Economic History Review* 3 (1955): 3–47.

Wrigley, T. M. L., M. J. Ingram, and G. Farmer, eds. *Climate and History: Studies in Past Climates and Their Impact on Man.* Cambridge: Cambridge University Press, 1981.

DISEASE

Alexander, John T. *Bubonic Plague in Early Modern Russia: Public Health and Urban Disaster.* Baltimore: Johns Hopkins University Press, 1980.

Appleby, Andrew B. "The Disappearance of Plague: A Continuing Puzzle." *Economic History Review,* 2d ser., 33 (1980): 161–173.

————. "Epidemics and Famine in the Little Ice Age." *Journal of Interdisciplinary History* 10 (1980): 643–663.

————. "Famine, Mortality, and Epidemic Disease: A Comment." *Economic History Review,* 2d ser., 30 (1977): 508–512.

Bean, J. M. W. "The Black Death: The Crisis and its Social and Economic Consequences." In Daniel Williman, ed., *The Black Death: The Impact of the Fourteenth Century Plague.* Binghamton: Center for Medieval and Early Renaissance Studies, 1982.

Biraben, J. N. "Current Medical and Epidemiological Views of Plague." In *The Plague Reconsidered: A New Look at Its Origins and Effects in Sixteenth and Seventeenth Century England.* Cambridge: Cambridge Group for the History of Population and Social Structure, 1977.

————. *Les Hommes et la peste en France et dans les pays européens et méditerranéens,* 2 vols. Paris: Mouton, 1975.

Biraben, J. N., and J. Le Goff. "La Peste du haut moyen age." *Annales E.S.C.* 24 (1969): 1484–1510.

————. "The Plague in the Early Middle Ages." In R. Foster and O. Ranum, eds., *Biology of Man in History.* Baltimore: Johns Hopkins University Press, 1975.

Bridbury, A. R. "The Black Death." *Economic History Review,* 2d ser., 26 (1973): 577–592.

Cipolla, C. M. *Public Health and the Medical Profession in the Renaissance.* Cambridge: Cambridge University Press, 1976.

Clarkson, Leslie. *Death, Disease and Famine in Pre-Industrial England.* Dublin: Gill & Macmillan, 1975.

Courtenay, William J. "The Effect of the Black Death on English Higher Education." *Speculum* 60 (1980): 696–714.

Dols, Michael W. "Al-Manbijti's 'Report of the Plague': A Treatise on the Plague of 764–65/1362–64 in the Middle East." In Daniel Williman, ed., *The Black Death: The Impact of the Fourteenth-Century Plague.* Binghamton: Center for Medieval and Early Renaissance Studies, 1982.

―――. *The Black Death in the Middle East.* Princeton: Princeton University Press, 1977.

Evans, Richard J. "Epidemics and Revolutions: Cholera in Nineteenth Century Europe." *Past and Present* 120 (1988): 123–147.

Flinn, M. W. "Plague in Europe and the Mediteranean Countries." *Journal of European Economic History* 8 (1979): 131–148.

Gottfried, Robert S. *The Black Death: Natural and Human Disaster in Medieval Europe.* New York: Free Press, 1983.

―――. *Epidemic Disease in Fifteenth Century England: The Medical Response and the Demographic Consequences.* New Brunswick, N.J.: Rutgers University Press, 1978.

―――. "Population, Plague, and the Sweating Sickness: Demographic Movements in Late Fifteenth Century England." *Journal of British Studies* 15 (1977): 12–37.

Hackett, L. W. *Malaria in Europe: An Ecological Study.* Oxford: Oxford University Press, 1937.

Hirst, L. Fabian. *The Conquest of Plague: A Study in the Development of Epidemiology.* Oxford: Clarendon Press, 1953.

Hopkins, Donald. *Princes and Peasants: Smallpox in History.* Chicago: University of Chicago Press, 1983.

Howe, George Melvyn. *Man, Environment and Disease in Britain: A Medical Geography of Britain through the Ages.* Newton Abbot: David & Charles, 1972.

Kahan, Arcadius. "Social Aspects of the Plague Epidemics in Eighteenth-Century Russia." *Economic Development and Cultural Change* 27 (1979): 255–266.

McNeill, W. H. *Plagues and Peoples.* Garden City: Anchor Press/Doubleday, 1976.

Mullett, Charles Frederic. *The Bubonic Plague in England: An Essay in the History of Preventive Medicine.* Lexington: University of Kentucky Press, 1956.

Norris, John. "East or West? The Geographic Origins of the Black Death." *Bulletin of the History of Medicine* 51 (1977): 1–24.

Patterson, K. David. *Pandemic Influenza 1700–1900: A Study in Historical Epidemiology.* Totowa, N.J.: Rowan and Littlefield, 1986.

Post, J. D. "Famine, Mortality, and Epidemic Disease in the Process of Modernization." *Economic History Review,* 2d ser., 29 (1976): 14–37.

Riley, James C. "Insects and the European Mortality Decline." *American Historical Review* 91 (1986): 833–858.

Shrewsbury, J. F. D. *History of Bubonic Plague in the British Isles.* Cambridge: Cambridge University Press, 1970.

Slack, Paul. "The Disappearance of the Plague: An Alternative View." *Economic History Review*, 2d ser., 34 (1981): 469–476.

Twigg, Graham. *The Black Death: A Biological Re-Appraisal*. New York: Schocken, 1984.

Zinsser, Hans. *Rats, Lice, and History*. Boston: Little, Brown, 1935.

Index

Absolutism, 97–98, 159–60
Abstractions, 8, 10, 25, 38, 111, 146, 154, 160, 194
Abu-Lughod, Janet, 197–99
Acton, John Emerich Edward Dalberg, Lord, 27–28, 32 n.31
Africa, 131–33, 147, 183–84
Alberti, Leon Battista, 119
Althusser, Louis, 92, 97–98, 208
America, 145, 149, 157–58, 173, 181–83, 184; European expansion to, 53–54, 156, 161, 201. *See also* New World
American Indians, 181–83
Amsterdam, 55, 196
Anachronism, 4, 36, 84, 91–92
Anderson, Perry, 97–98, 208
Annales school, 170–71
Antonine plague, 178
Antwerp, 55, 100, 196
Argentina, 184
Armstrong, Neil, 130
Asia, 23, 73, 131–32; comparison with Europe, 43, 199–202
Australia, 144, 184
Azores, 51
Aztec Empire, 182

Bahamas, 182
Baltic Sea region, 46, 51, 153, 159
Banking, 50
Barcelona, 45
Barraclough, Geoffrey, 206–8, 209
Base-superstructure model, 86, 88–90
Bible, 20–21, 25, 111
Biondo, Flavio, 22
Biosphere people, 130–31

Birabin, Jean-Noel, 73–74
Black Death, 18, 37, 52, 62–63, 66–67, 73–75, 80 n.28, 95, 155, 179–81, 205. *See also* Bubonic plague
Bloch, Marc, 170
Bodin, Jean, 23
Borah, Woodrow, 182
Boserup, Ester, 75–77
Bourgeoisie, 26, 48, 50, 87, 94–95, 98, 100, 117, 119–20, 135, 136, 138, 152–53
Braudel, Fernand, 36, 157–58, 170–72, 175, 176, 195–97, 198
Brazil, 156, 164 n.38
Brenner, Robert, 97, 158–59, 165 n.45
Britnell, R. H., 68
Bruges, 100
Bruni, Leonardo, 22
Bubonic plague, 62–63, 173, 178–79, 189 n.43. *See also* Black Death
Buddhism, 179
Bullion, 53, 110, 145, 158, 160, 164 nn.41, 44, 195. *See also* Gold; Silver
Burckhardt, Jacob, 26
Business techniques, 47–48, 54, 196, 205; bill of exchange, 48, 57 n.21; commenda, 47; joint stock company, 54; regulated company, 54
Butterfield, Herbert, 39, 206–9
Byzantine Empire, 42, 44, 62

Calvin, John, 116
Calvinism, 116–19
Cambridge Ancient History, 28
Cambridge Medieval History, 28

Cambridge Modern History, 27–28, 32
  nn.31, 32, 39, 52
Cambridge University, 27
Capitalism, 35, 49, 52–54, 87, 107–8,
  139, 146, 151, 160, 194–97;
  definition of, 36, 84, 94–95, 108,
  144–45, 157; environmental
  degradation of, 131; Marx's
  analysis of, 85–88; rise of, 35, 51,
  117, 149–50, 198; "spirit" of, 108,
  112–16, 120
Carson, Rachel, 167
Cassiodorus, 20
Castiglione, Baldassare, 49
Causation, 120
Cellarius (Christof Keller), 24–25
Champagne fairs, 51, 196
Charlemagne, 42
Chemical pollution, 168–69, 186 n.7
China, 73, 76, 114, 115, 172, 177–79,
  198, 200, 202, 209
Chloroflurocarbons, 169
Church of Rome, 43, 48, 55, 119,
  121–23; Catholics and capitalism,
  118–19, 123
City-states, 43–46
Class, 86–87, 91–92, 97
Class struggle, 85–87, 90–93, 99, 139,
  155, 180
Classical economists, 109
Climate and history, 150, 172–76
Cold War, 84–85, 132–34
Collins, Randall, 122–23
Colonization. *See* European expansion
Columbus, Christopher, 12, 27, 31
  n.17, 51, 130, 132, 144–45, 181–
  82, 184, 202
Communism, 37, 87, 89, 132–33
Consumer revolution, 205
Contingency, 13, 15 n.16, 159
Cook, Sherburne, 182
Copernicus, Nicolaus, 27
Cortez, Hernan, 113, 132, 182–83
Coulanges, Fustel de, 42
Courtly life, 49–50
Crisis of the seventeenth century, 72,
  75, 80 n.22
Crop yields, 79 n.12

Crosby, Alfred W., Jr., 29, 184, 208–9
Crusades, 45, 95
Culturism, 92

Daniel (Biblical Book of), 20
Daniels, Robert, 85
Dasmann, Raymond, 130
Davis, Ralph, 147
Deductive reasoning, 9
Defoe, Daniel, 119
Demesne lands, 47, 57 n.19
Dependency theory, 136–40
Determinism, 12–13, 86, 88–90
de Vries, Jan, 176
Dialectic materialism, 86–87
Diffusion, 133, 136, 197
Diplomatic history, 13
Disease in history, 176–85, 199–200
Dobb, Maurice, 94, 96–97, 101, 105
  n.18
Dobyns, Henry, 182
Dopsch, Alfons, 42
Dubos, René, 168

Ecosphere people, 130
Ecosystem, 168–70
Elton, Geoffrey, 10–11
Empires (modern European), 131–33,
  144–45
Engels, Friedrich, 85, 88, 90–91, 98
England, 45, 66, 68–69, 96, 99–102,
  132, 146, 151–53, 173; civil war
  (1642–1649), 103; economic status
  of, 70; population of, 63, 70
Enlightenment, 10, 24, 207
Entail, 40, 56 n.6
Environmentalists, 129–31, 167–69
Erasmus, 22, 27
Europe, 12, 54–55, 69, 131–32;
  comparison with Asia, 199–202;
  economy of, 52–53, 60; European
  marriage patterns, 77; population
  of, 62–65; states system, 201–2
European expansion, 50–51, 69, 131–
  32, 156; in Africa, 183–84; in East
  Elbia, 51, 149–50, 154, 159; in
  New World, 53–54, 150
Evolutionary theory, 134, 137

Fallow (long and short), 76
Family, 200
Febvre, Lucien, 170
Feudal mode of production, 87, 94–96, 138, 180
Flanders, 45–46
Flinn, Michael, 62, 74
Florence, 48, 123
Flynn, Dennis, 164 n.44
Foucault, Michel, 84
France, 26, 49, 52, 66, 70–71, 98–99, 132, 146, 152–53; population of, 63; revolution (1789), 10–11, 87, 103, 106 n.35
Frank, André Gunder, 136–40, 141 n.17, 151, 154, 160, 197
Franklin, Benjamin, 114–17, 119, 146
Free will, 12–13
Fronde, 98
Functionalist theory, 134, 137

Gaia hypothesis, 168, 185
Gatterer, Johann Cristof, 25
Generalizations in history, 6
Genoa (Genoese), 45, 48, 50–51, 100, 123, 196
Gerhard, Dietrich, 206–9
German Historical School, 109, 124 n.7
Germanic invasions, 20, 40, 42, 172
Germany, 42, 51–52, 108–9, 153; eastern expansion, 51; population of, 63
Gibbon, Edward, 24
Gold, 145, 157, 164 n.37, 183
Göttingen University, 25
Greenland, 173
Grigg, D. B., 65

Hamilton, Earl J., 145, 164 n.40
Hanseatic League, 51–52
Hegel, Georg Wilhelm Friedrich, 18, 85
Henry the Navigator, 53, 132, 155, 157
Hicks, Sir John, 40, 43–44
Hill, Christopher, 103
Hinduism, 122
Hispaniola, 157, 182

Hitler, Adolf, 12
Holland. See Netherlands
Humanists, 21–23, 26
Hume, David, 24, 31 n.19
Hundred Years War, 48, 52

Ice Age, 174
Iceland, 173
Inca Empire, 182
India, 122, 199–200, 202
Inductive reasoning, 7, 9
Industrial Revolution, 28, 55, 71, 92, 103, 108–9, 146–47, 161–62 n.11, 162 n.13, 205
Italy, 5, 26, 44–45, 52, 151, 196; economic status of, 69; humanists, 20–21; population of, 63

Jews, 110–13
Jones, Eric, 199–203
Jones, Gareth Stedman, 15 n.19
Just price, 43, 56 n.12

Keller, Christof (Cellarius), 24–25
Keynes, John Maynard, 146, 164 n.40
Kipling, Rudyard, 132
Krakatoa volcano, 169
Kulaks, 96, 99, 103, 180. See also Peasants

Ladurie, Emmanuel Le Roy, 70–71, 73, 176
Language, 5–6, 38
Languedoc, 70–71
Latin America, 129, 132, 135–39, 151
Lefebvre, Georges, 103
Little Ice Age, 173–76, 187 n.18, 188 n.29
London, 60, 196
Lopez, Robert, 172–73
Lovelock, James, 169, 185
Low Countries, 76, 152, 196. See also Netherlands; Flanders
Lugard, Frederic, Lord, 183–84
Luther, Martin, 12, 27, 30 n.12, 119, 125 n.13
Lutherans, 22–23

Madeira, 51
Maize, 78, 184
Malthus, Thomas Robert, 36, 60–62, 68, 71–73, 78
Malthusian trap (Malthusian check), 66, 70–71, 72–75, 180
Markets, 51–52, 68–69
Marseilles, 45
Marx, Karl, 8, 9, 11, 18, 37, 84–91, 102, 107–8, 115
Marxism, 84–90, 154; transition from feudalism to capitalism, 93–103
Marxist historians, 6, 20, 36, 84, 90–104, 117, 119, 139, 150, 155, 180, 194–95, 206
Massachusetts settlements, 181
McKendrick, Neil, 205
McKeown, Thomas, 62
McNeill, William, 133, 176–79, 197, 209
Measles, 177–79
Mediterranean Sea, 39, 42–45, 54, 56 n.13, 62, 153, 178
Merchants, 44, 47–50, 53, 100–101. *See also* Bourgeoisie
Meuvret, Jean, 73
Mexico, 157, 182
Modelling, 8–10, 204
Mode of production, 18, 20, 85–87, 91, 100, 139, 158, 160, 195
Modernization, 134, 136–37
Monarchs, 53, 96; courtly life, 49–50; political power relationships, 48–49, 67, 97–98, 101. *See also* Absolutism
Money economy, 47, 55, 60
Morocco, 157
Moslems, 42–45, 62, 178, 201
Mousnier, Roland, 105 n.14

Neo-Malthusians, 65–69, 73, 75, 77–78, 150, 155, 180, 205
Netherlands, 151–53, 200; economic status of, 70; population of, 63, 69–70
New England, 181
New World, 12, 100, 150–51. *See also* America

New York, 196
New Zealand, 144, 184
Nisbet, Robert, 5
Nobility, 87, 96, 153; feudal landlords, 46–47, 67, 94–95; political power relationships, 48–49, 67, 97
North, Douglas, 70, 73
Norway, 173

Orosius, 20
Osborn, Fairfield, 167
Ottoman Empire, 202
Oviedo, Gonzala Fernandez, 182
Ozone, 169

Paine, Thomas, 10
Papacy, 49
Parry, M. L., 176
Parsons, Talcott, 134
Peasant revolts, 67, 96, 99–100
Peasants, 67, 91, 95–96, 99
Periodization, 18–20, 204–10; aggregate theory, 19; four-monarchy scheme, 20–21, 23, 30 n.12; leading sector theory, 19; Marxian mode of, 87, 89; tripartite scheme, 17–18, 24–25
Peru, 157
Pirenne, Henri, 36, 41–43, 51, 83, 100, 117, 178, 194, 196
Pizarro, Francisco, 113
Poland, 60, 154; economic status of, 158–59
Population, 200; estimates for Europe, 62–63; estimates for Mediterranean basin, 62; estimates for world, 79 nn.10, 21, 206; trends in Europe, 65, 69–70, 206
Portugal, 156–57, 164 n.37
Post, John, 174–75
Postan, M. M., 59–60, 73–74, 187 n.26
Potato, 78, 184
Predestination, 116, 123
Price revolution, 145, 151, 160
Primogeniture, 40, 56 n.5
Proletariat, 46, 87, 94–95, 99–100
Protestants, 116

Putting-out, 101

Quine, Willard, 14

Raab, Theodore, 118
Raynal, Guillaume-Thomas, Abbé, 40
Reformation, 22–23, 116–17, 119–20,
    194
Reification, 10, 159–60
Renaissance, 5, 25–26, 31 n.25, 32
    n.27
Rinderpest, 183
Roanoke settlement, 181
Robertson, William, 24, 31 n.19
Rodney, Walter, 140
Roman Law, 46, 49, 97–98
Rome, 20–22, 24, 29 n.2, 40, 172,
    177–78, 201
Rostow, W. W., 135, 138–39
Rousseau, Jean-Jacques, 10
Russell, J. C., 62
Russia, 132
Russian Revolution, 88

Sanders, William, 182
Scientific Revolution, 207
Second serfdom, 150, 154
Serfdom (serfs), 46–47, 57 n.17, 97;
    commutation of labor services, 60;
    end of serfdom, 67, 155, 180
Sheridan, Richard, 148
Silver, 52, 145, 151–52, 157–58, 164
    nn.41, 44, 183
Slavery (slave trade), 45, 50, 147, 150,
    162 n.13
Sleeping sickness, 183
Smallpox, 178–79, 182
Smith, Adam, 20, 37, 40–41, 46–47,
    60, 72, 83, 108–9, 154, 195
Social scientists, 7, 9, 13, 15 n.19
Sombart, 37–38, 49–50, 107–12, 122,
    124 n.7, 199; identity with
    Nazism, 124 nn.6, 7; in relation to
    Weber, 113–14, 118, 123
Soviet Union, 84
Spain, 12, 53, 151–53; economic sta-
    tus of, 69, 158; population of, 63
Stavrianos, Leften, 133

Structuralism, 5–6, 14 n.6, 92–93
Subinfeudation, 95
Subjectivity, 4–7, 20, 210
Sugar, 51
Sumner, William Graham, 145

Tawney, R. H., 119, 121, 123
Taylor, A. J. P., 15 n.16
Technology, 66, 77, 200–201
Teleology, 11–12, 93, 139, 159, 210
Theory, 7–8, 14, 17, 20, 93
Theory-hypothesis-data method, 9–10
Third World, 72, 133–35, 138, 148,
    168
Thirty Years War, 23, 63
Thomas, Robert Paul, 70, 73
Thompson, E. P., 91–92, 99
Tomboro volcano, 174
Towns, 41, 44–47, 51, 69, 198; early
    European towns, 44–47, 196; East
    European towns, 51
Toynbee, Arnold, 146
Transaction costs, 44, 70
Tsetse fly, 183
Tuma, Elias, 9
Turner, Frederick Jackson, 143–44,
    170
Tuscany, 76–77

United Nations Conference on the
    Human Environment, 129, 168
United Nations Economic Commission
    for Latin America (ECLA), 135–37
United States, 132, 135, 143–45, 167
Universities, 19, 24–25, 27, 41
Usury, 43, 52, 56 n.11, 111, 118, 125
    n.13
Utterström, Gustaf, 175

Venice, 44–45, 55, 100, 111, 123,
    151, 196
Vikings, 45, 173, 208
Vilar, Pierre, 164 n.40
Vogt, William, 167
Voltaire, 3, 24, 26, 30 n.12

Wallerstein, Immanuel, 140, 148–61,
    183, 194–96, 198–99, 201

Ward, Barbara, 168
Warfare, 95, 158, 200
Weaponry, 48–49, 102
Webb, Walter Prescott, 144–45, 148,
    151, 157, 160, 161 n.6, 170
Weber, Max, 36–38, 107–8, 133, 145–
    46, 155, 194, 199, 202;
    Calvinism and capitalism, 116–
    17; response to critics, 120–24;
    "spirit" of capitalism, 112–16, 120
West Indies, 12, 146–47, 182
Westerly winds, 173

White, Hayden, 5
White, Lynn, Jr., 52
Williams, Eric Eustace, 146–48, 160,
    162 n.13
World history, 133, 209
World-system theory, 129–30, 148–55,
    197–99; challenges to, 155–60
World War I (1914–1918), 13, 15 n.16
Worster, Donald, 130
Wright, Erik Olin, 90–91

Zanzibar, 202

ABOUT THE AUTHOR

WILLIAM A. GREEN is Professor of History at Holy Cross College. He is author of *British Slave Emancipation: The Sugar Colonies and the Great Experiment, 1830–1865* (1976). He has also contributed to six books in European and imperial history and has written many articles for professional journals, including *Comparative Studies in Society and History, The Economic History Review, The Journal of British Studies, Victorian Studies, Albion, The Journal of African History, The Journal of Interdisciplinary History,* and *The Journal of World History.*

2984

Praise for
The Christmas Spirits on Tradd Street

"If you prefer your holiday tales with bit of a ghost story, look no further than *The Christmas Spirits on Tradd Street*. It's perfect for fans of *A Christmas Carol* and *Hamilton*, blending a tale of spectral rumors and American Revolutionary history."　　　　　　　　　　*—Entertainment Weekly*

"What a treat to open up a new Tradd Street book by Karen White and disappear into her witty, wonderful, and haunted world. . . . No one does ghosts better than Karen White, and this is one of Tradd Street's best."
　　　　　　　—New York Times bestselling author M. J. Rose

"While this is the sixth in White's Tradd Street series, it can be read on its own, but make time after the holidays to binge read the previous five for more adventures with these characters. . . . A cliff-hanger ending and promise of another book will please avid fans."　　　　　*—Library Journal*

"This is a fun-filled, festive, and witty read—a welcome, suspenseful story at a busy time of year!"　　　*—Connecticut Post*

"Full of history and details of the American Revolution; White continues her streak of entertaining, well-paced, and expertly told stories of the town of Charleston."
　　　　　　　　　　　　　　　　　　—The Nerd Daily

"Overall, an entertaining read. The Christmas theme is very secondary in the book, making it a good read for any time of the year."　　　　　　　　　—Girly Book Club

"This page-turner is a little bit spooky and a whole lot of fun."　　　　　　　　　　　　　　　　*—Grand Strand*

"Series fans will enjoy spending the holidays with Melanie Trenholm. The plot threads move pieces of this long-running saga forward, and the ending suggests that there's more to come."
                                                            —*Booklist*

"Christmas spirits from the past come alive in this festive supernatural tale. . . . Adventure meets mystery in this seasonal page-turner."
                                                            —*Woman's World*

Also by Karen White

The Color of Light
Pieces of the Heart
Learning to Breathe
The Memory of Water
The Lost Hours
On Folly Beach
Falling Home
The Beach Trees
Sea Change
After the Rain
The Time Between
A Long Time Gone
The Sound of Glass
Flight Patterns
Spinning the Moon
The Night the Lights Went Out
Dreams of Falling
The Last Night in London

Cowritten with Beatriz Williams and Lauren Willig

The Forgotten Room
The Glass Ocean
All the Ways We Said Goodbye

The Tradd Street Series

The House on Tradd Street
The Girl on Legare Street
The Strangers on Montagu Street
Return to Tradd Street
The Guests on South Battery

THE
CHRISTMAS SPIRITS
ON TRADD STREET

KAREN WHITE

BERKLEY
New York

BERKLEY
An imprint of Penguin Random House LLC
penguinrandomhouse.com

Copyright © 2019 by Harley House Books, LLC
Readers Guide copyright © 2019 by Penguin Random House LLC
Excerpt from *The Shop on Royal Street* copyright © 2021 by Harley House Books, LLC
Penguin Random House supports copyright. Copyright fuels creativity, encourages
diverse voices, promotes free speech, and creates a vibrant culture. Thank you for buying
an authorized edition of this book and for complying with copyright laws by not
reproducing, scanning, or distributing any part of it in any form without permission.
You are supporting writers and allowing Penguin Random House to continue to
publish books for every reader.

BERKLEY and the BERKLEY & B colophon are registered trademarks of
Penguin Random House LLC.

ISBN: 9780593099452

Berkley hardcover edition / October 2019
Berkley trade paperback edition / October 2020
Berkley mass-market edition / September 2021

Printed in the United States of America
1   3   5   7   9   10   8   6   4   2

This is a work of fiction. Names, characters, places, and incidents either are the product
of the author's imagination or are used fictitiously, and any resemblance to actual persons,
living or dead, business establishments, events, or locales is entirely coincidental.

If you purchased this book without a cover, you should be aware that this book is stolen
property. It was reported as "unsold and destroyed" to the publisher, and neither the author
nor the publisher has received any payment for this "stripped book."

*To the real Rich Kobylt, who allows me to use his name,
and who actually wears a belt.*

CHAPTER
1

S moky silhouettes of church spires stamped against the
bruised skies of a Charleston morning give testament to
the reason why it's called the Holy City. The steepled skyline at dawn is a familiar sight for early risers who enjoy a
respite from the heat and humidity in summer, or appreciate the beauty of the sunrise through the Cooper River
Bridge, or like hearing the chirps and calls of the thousands
of birds and insects that populate our corner of the world.

Others, like me, awaken early only to shorten the night,
to quiet the secret stirrings of the restless dead who wander
during the darkest hours between sunset and sunrise.

I lay on my side, Jack's arm resting protectively around
my waist, my own arm thrown around the soft fur of General Lee's belly. His snoring and my husband's soft breathing were the only sounds in the old house, despite its being
currently inhabited by two adults, three dogs, a teenage
girl, and twenty-month-old twins. I never counted the myr-
iad spirits who passed peacefully down the house's lofty
corridors. Over the past several years I'd extricated the
not-so-nice ones and made my peace with the others, who
were content to simply exist alongside us.

That's what had awakened me. The quiet. No, that
wasn't right. It was more the absence of sound. Like the
held breath between the pull of a trigger and the propulsion
of the bullet.

Being careful not to awaken Jack or General Lee, I
slowly disentangled myself from the bedsheets, watching

as General Lee assumed my former position next to Jack. Jack barely stirred and I considered for a moment whether I should be insulted. I picked up my iPhone and shut off the alarm, which was set for five a.m.—noting it was four forty-six—then crossed the room to my old-fashioned alarm clock, which I kept just in case. Jack had made me get rid of the additional two I'd once had stationed around the room. He'd accused me of trying to wake the dead each morning. As if I had to try.

Since I was a little girl, the spirits of the dearly departed had been trying to talk to me, to involve me in their unfinished business. I'd found ways—most often involving singing an ABBA song—to drown out their voices with some success, but every once in a while, one voice was louder than the others. Usually because a spirit was shouting in my ear or shoving me down the stairs, making it impossible to ignore regardless of how much I wanted to.

I stumbled into my bathroom using the flashlight on my phone, silently cursing my half sister, Jayne, and my best friend, Dr. Sophie Wallen-Arasi, for being the cause of my predawn ramblings. They had taken it upon themselves to get me fit and healthy after the birth of the twins, JJ (for Jack Junior) and Sarah. This involved feeding me food I wouldn't give my dog—although I'd tried and he'd turned up his nose and walked away—and forcing me to go for a run most mornings.

Although I was more a jogger than a runner, the exercise required lots of energy that shouldn't be provided by powdered doughnuts—according to Sophie—and made me sweat more than I thought necessary, especially in the humid summer months, when bending down to tie my shoes caused perspiration to drip down my face and neck.

Barely awake, I pulled on the running pants that Nola had given me for my last birthday, telling me that they had the dual purposes of being fashionable *and* functional, sucking everything in and making one's backside look as if it belonged to a lifelong runner. I tried to tell Jayne and Sophie that these wonder pants made the actual running part unnecessary, but they'd simply stared at me without blinking before returning to their conversation regarding lowering their times for the next Bridge Run, scheduled for the spring.

I tiptoed back into the bedroom, noticing as I pulled down the hem of my T-shirt that it was on inside out, and paused by the bed to look at my husband of less than two years. My chest did the little contracting thing it had been doing since I'd first met bestselling true-crime-history author Jack Trenholm. I'd thought then that he was too handsome, too charming, too opinionated, and way too annoying to be anything to me other than someone to be admired from afar or at least kept at arm's distance. Luckily for me, he'd disagreed.

My gaze traveled to the video baby monitor we kept on the bedside table. Sarah slept neatly on her side, her stuffed bunny—a gift from Sophie—tucked under her arm, her other stuffed animals arranged around the crib in a specific order that only Sarah—and I—understood. I'd had to explain to Jack that the animals had been arranged by fur patterns and colors, going from lightest to darkest. I'm sure I did the same thing when I was a child, because, I'd explained, it was important to make order of the world.

In the adjacent crib, Sarah's twin, JJ, slept on his back with his arms and legs flung out at various angles, his stuffed animals and his favorite whisk—even I couldn't explain his attachment to this particular kitchen utensil—tossed in disarray around his small body. My fingers twitched, and I had to internally recite the words to "Dancing Queen" backward to keep me from entering the nursery and lining up the toys in the bed and tucking my little son in a corner of the crib with a blanket over him.

It was a skill I'd learned at Jayne's insistence. She was a professional nanny, which meant—I suppose—that she knew best, and she insisted that my need for order was borderline OCD and not necessarily the best influence for the children. There was absolutely nothing wrong with my need for order, as it had helped me survive a childhood with an alcoholic father and an absent mother, but I loved my children too much to dismiss Jayne's concerns completely.

I would not, however, retire my labeling gun and had taken proactive measures by keeping it hidden so it wouldn't "disappear" as my last two had.

As I stared at my sweet babies on the monitor, my heart constricted again, leaving me breathless for a moment as I considered how very fortunate I was to have found Jack—or, as he insisted, to have been found by him—and then to have these two beautiful children. An added and welcome bonus to the equation was Jack's sixteen-year-old daughter, Nola, whom I loved as if she were my own child despite her insistence on removing my three main food groups—sugar, carbs, and chocolate—from the kitchen.

"Good morning, beautiful," Jack mumbled, two sleepy dark blue eyes staring up at me. General Lee emitted a snuffling snore. "Going to work?"

Before I was married, I'd always risen before dawn to be the first person in the offices of Henderson House Realty on Broad Street. But now I had a reason to stay in bed, and he was lying there looking so much more appealing than a run through the streets of Charleston. Of course, spending the night in the dungeon at the Old Exchange building was also more appealing than a run, but still.

"Not yet. Meeting Jayne for a run." I stood by the bed and leaned down to place a kiss on Jack's lips, lingering long enough to see if he would give any indication that he wanted me to crawl back in. Instead his eyes closed again as he moved General Lee closer to his chest, giving me an odd pang of jealousy.

I quietly closed the bedroom door and paused in the upstairs hallway, listening. Even the ticking of the old grandfather clock seemed muffled, the sound suffocated by something unseen. Something waiting. The night-lights that lined the hallway—a leftover from when Jayne lived with us and a concession to her crippling fear of the dark and the things that hid within—gave me a clear view of Nola's closed bedroom door.

She'd been sleeping in the guest room, as I'd decided right after the twins' first birthday party in March that her bedroom needed to be redecorated. I felt a tug of guilt as I walked past it to the stairs, remembering the shadowy figure I'd seen in Nola's bedroom window in a photograph taken by one of Sophie's preservation students, Meghan Black. She was excavating the recently discovered cistern in the rear garden and had taken the photograph and shown it to Jack and me. We'd both seen the shadowy figure of a man in old-fashioned clothing holding what looked to be a piece of jewelry. But I'd been the only one to notice the face in Nola's window.

Having recently dealt with a particularly nasty and vengeful spirit at Jayne's house on South Battery, I hadn't found the strength yet to grapple with another. Despite promises to be open and honest with each other, I hadn't told Jack, bargaining with myself that I'd bring it up just as soon as I thought I could mentally prepare myself. That had been eight months ago, and all I'd done was move Nola into the guest room and then interview a succession of decorators.

I stifled a yawn. *Just one more week,* I thought. One more week of working every possible hour trying to make my sales quota at Henderson House Realty, trying to put myself on the leaderboard once more. It was important not just for the sense of pride and accomplishment it gave me, but also because we needed the money.

Then I'd have enough energy and brain cells to be able to figure out who these new spirits were and to make them go away. Preferably without a fight. Then I'd tell Jack what I'd seen and that I'd already taken care of the problem so he wouldn't have to be worried. He had enough on his plate already, working with a new publisher on a book about my family and how Jayne had come to own her house on South Battery.

I entered the kitchen, my stomach rumbling as I reached behind the granola and quinoa boxes in the pantry for my secret stash of doughnuts. But instead of grasping the familiar brown paper bag, I found myself pulling out a box of nutrition bars—no doubt as tasty as the cardboard in which they were packaged. Taped to the front was a note in Nola's handwriting:

> *Try these instead! They've got chocolate and 9 grams of protein!*

Happy visions of running upstairs and pulling Nola from her bed earlier than she'd probably been awake since infancy were the only reason I didn't break down and weep. The grandfather clock chimed, telling me I was already late, so I gave one last-minute look to see if I could spot my doughnut bag, then left the house through the back door without eating anything. If I passed out from starvation halfway through my run, Nola might feel sorry enough for me to bring a doughnut.

I stopped on the back steps, suddenly aware that the silence had followed me outside. No birds chirped; no insects hummed. No sounds of street traffic crept into the formerly lush garden that my father had painstakingly restored from the original Loutrel Briggs plans. When an ancient cistern had been discovered after the heavy spring rains had swallowed up a large section of the garden, Sophie had swooped in and declared it an archaeological dig and surrounded it with yellow caution tape. Several months later, we were still staring at a hole behind our house. And I was still feeling the presence of an entity that continued to elude me but haunted my peripheral vision. A shadow that disappeared every time I turned a corner, the scent of rot the only hint that it had been there at all.

Walking backward to avoid turning my back on the gaping hole, I made my way to the front of the house, tripping only twice on the uneven flagstones that were as much a part of Charleston's South of Broad neighborhood as were wrought-iron gates and palmetto bugs.

"There you are!" shouted a voice from across the street. "I thought you were standing me up."

I squinted at the figure standing on the curb, regretting not putting in my contacts. I really didn't need them all the time, and not wearing them when I ran saved me from seeing my reflection without makeup in the bathroom mirror this early in the morning.

"Good morning, Jayne," I grumbled, making sure she was aware of how unhappy I was to be going for a run. Especially when I had a much better alternative waiting for me in my bedroom.

I was already starting to perspire at the thought of the four-mile jog in front of me. Despite its being early November, and although we'd been teased by Mother Nature with days chilly enough that we'd had to pull out our wool sweaters, the mercury had taken another surprise leap, and both the temperature and the dew point had risen, as if summer was returning to torture us for a bit.

Even though Jayne had already jogged several blocks in the heat and humidity from her house on South Battery, she was barely sweating and her breath came slowly and evenly. We'd only recently discovered each other, our shared mother having been led to believe that her second daughter, born eight years after me, had died at birth. Jayne and I had grown close in the ensuing months, our bonding most likely accelerated by the fact that we shared the ability to communicate with the dead, a trait inherited from our mother.

"Which way do you want to go this morning?" she said, jogging in place and looking way too perky.

"Is back inside an option?"

She laughed as if I'd been joking, then began to jog toward East Bay.

I struggled to catch up, pulling alongside her as she ran down the middle of the street. Dodging traffic this time of day was easier than risking a turned ankle on the ancient uneven sidewalks. "Will Detective Riley be joining us this morning?" I panted.

Her cheeks flushed, and I was sure it wasn't from exertion. "I don't know. I haven't spoken to him in a week."

"Did you have a fight?"

"You could say that." Her emotions seemed to fuel her steps, and she sprinted ahead. Only when she realized she'd left me behind did she slow down so I could catch up.

"What . . . happened?" I was finding it hard to breathe and talk at the same time, but I needed to know. I'd introduced Jayne to Detective Thomas Riley, and they'd been a couple ever since Jayne, our mother, and I had sent to the light several unsettled spirits who'd been inhabiting her house earlier in the year.

"I told him I wanted to go public with my abilities to help people communicate with loved ones. He said it was a bad idea because there are a lot of crazies out there who'd be knocking on my door."

I looked at her askance. "Funny, he didn't . . . seem to . . . have such qualms . . . when he asked me about some of his . . . unsolved cases." I'd recently considered working with Detective Riley on a case involving a coed who'd gone missing from her College of Charleston dorm room in 1997.

"That's because you're working incognito. I want to advertise. And Mother said she'd be happy to work alongside me. She thinks you should also go public and work with us." She sprinted ahead again, but this time I was sure it was because she didn't want me to respond. Not that I could have since my lungs were nearly bursting.

I doggedly pursued her, turning left on East Bay and almost catching up as we neared Queen Street, dodging the fermenting restaurant garbage waiting for pickup on the sidewalk. My feet dragged, the humidity seeming to make my legs heavier, and my breath came in choking gasps. My stomach rumbled and I quickly did a mental recalculation of my route. In an effort at self-preservation, I took a left on Hasell, not even wondering how long it would take Jayne to notice I was missing. With my destination in mind, I jogged toward King Street and took a right, my steps much lighter now as I headed toward my just reward.

Catching the green light on Calhoun, I nearly sprinted across the street toward Glazed Gourmet Donuts, almost expecting Jayne to show up just as I reached the door and yank me away. Instead I was merely greeted by the heavenly scent of freshly made doughnuts and the delicious smell of coffee gently embracing me and inviting me inside. I stood in the entryway for a moment, inhaling deeply, until I heard a cough from behind me.

I turned to apologize for blocking the doorway but stopped with my mouth halfway open. Not because the tall, dark-haired man standing behind me was a contender for *People* magazine's Sexiest Man Alive, or because he was smiling at me with more than just casual interest, his dark brown eyes lit with some inner amusement. Nor was it because he wore tight-fitting running clothes that accentuated his muscled chest and that he breathed slightly faster than the average pedestrian—although, like Jayne, he appeared to be barely perspiring. I stared at him because I'd seen him before. Not just that morning, not just in the doughnut shop, but around town several times in the past few weeks as I jogged down the streets of Charleston or ran errands or traveled to various house showings in the city.

It hadn't struck me as odd until right at that moment, when we were standing only inches apart. Charleston was a small city, and it was inevitable that I'd run into the same person occasionally. But not every day. I blinked once, wondering what else about him captivated my attention, and realized what it was just as the door opened behind the man and Jayne appeared, looking flustered and not a little bit annoyed.

"I knew I'd find you here," she said, walking past the man to stand in front of me and no doubt try to intimidate me. Which was hard to do considering we were the exact same height.

I looked at the man again. "Are you related to Marc Longo?" I asked, half hoping he'd say no. Marc was my cousin Rebecca's husband, and Jack's nemesis after having stolen Jack's book idea. We were still trying to recover from the financial and professional setback it had caused Jack. Marc was also a boil on the behind of our collective well-being, as he was currently trying to get us to allow in

our house on Tradd Street the filming of the movie based
on the novel he'd stolen from Jack. Because he was that
kind of insufferable jerk. The fact that I'd once dated him
didn't endear him to Jack, either.

"I am," he said, a shadow briefly settling behind his
eyes. He held out a slim hand to me. "I'm Anthony Longo,
Marc's younger brother. And you're Melanie Middleton."

"Melanie Trenholm now," I corrected. I hesitated for a
moment before placing my hand in his.

He grinned. "Don't worry. The only things my older
brother and I share are our last name and our parents."

Turning to Jayne, he said, "And you two beautiful
women must be related. Twins?"

I almost smiled at the compliment but didn't. Because I
was certain he already knew exactly who we were to each
other. Being in the same family wasn't the only thing Anthony Longo shared with his brother.

Jayne lifted her hand to shake his. Her lips worked to
form words, and before I could clamp my hand over her
mouth, she said, "You have very dark hair. It's brown." She
blinked rapidly before dropping her hand. "I mean . . . yes,
you have hair. Well, it's nice to meet you." Her face flushed
a dark red. Turning to me, she said, "I'm going to get us
some coffee and doughnuts."

"Sorry," I said, watching her departing back. "My sister,
Jayne, hasn't had a lot of experience with the opposite sex.
She seems to get tongue-tied when dealing with attractive
men."

He laughed, a deep, chest-rumbling sound. "I accept the
compliment, then."

I took a step back, as much to put distance between us
as to allow a couple to enter the shop. I was reserving judgment, wanting to hate him on sight, but there was something likable about him. He was charming, like Marc, but
without the smarmy self-love that Marc exuded from every
pore. I met Anthony's forthright gaze. "Have you been following me?"

His eyes widened, and I wondered if I'd taken him by

surprise with my candor or if he was just pretending. Instead of answering, he said, "Why don't we sit so we can chat?" He held out his hand toward an open table, and I led the way.

We sat just as Jayne approached with a bag and two coffees. Anthony immediately stood and took the coffees from her while Jayne clutched the doughnut bag close to her. "You don't eat doughnuts?" she said to Anthony, then quickly shook her head. "I mean, you don't have doughnuts."

He grinned warmly and I wanted to kick him to tell him being attractive and charming wasn't going to help matters.

"I've got a delicious protein shake waiting for me at home, so I'm good, thanks."

"She won't share," Jayne forced out, clutching the bag even tighter. We were going to have to work harder on social interactions with men. I'd thought that her relationship with Thomas Riley was a good sign that she'd been cured of acute awkwardness, but I'd been wrong. It apparently was on a man-to-man basis.

Anthony's smile faded slightly as he glanced at me, as if needing reassurance that Jayne wouldn't bite.

"She's probably referring to me. I don't share my doughnuts, and if anyone tries to take one, he will lose a finger." I didn't smile, trying to show him that I wasn't joking.

I took a sip from my coffee while eyeing the bag expectantly, but Jayne kept it clenched closely to her chest, no doubt planning to hold the doughnuts for ransom until I finished the run. "So," I said, "why have you been stalking me?"

Anthony quirked an eyebrow. "'Stalking'? Hardly. More like looking for an opportunity to approach you that wouldn't be noticed by any of your friends, family, or coworkers. It's very hard to do. You're a moving target."

I glanced around, glad we were in a public place and that Jayne was with me. Alarm bells were starting to go off inside my head, the same ones that rang out when Sophie or my handyman, Rich Kobylt, asked to talk to me. It was usually something bad—like wood-boring beetles in the dining room floor—and always something I didn't want to hear, such as the cost of the repair.

"So why did you want to see me?" I asked.

"I'd like to make a deal with you."

"A deal?" Jayne repeated.

Anthony leaned forward. "You may or may not be aware that I own Magnolia Ridge Plantation—or, as it's known now, Gallen Hall. It was formerly owned by the Vanderhorst family—the same family who once owned your house on Tradd Street. It was purchased at auction by my grandfather back in the twenties, sold shortly afterward, and then bought by Marc a few years ago. My grandfather was the man found buried beneath your fountain, if you recall."

Like I could forget. I kept still, trying not to remember the menacing ghost of Joseph Longo, or how his body came to be buried in my garden along with that of former owner Louisa Vanderhorst. "Okay," I said, not sure where this was heading but fairly certain I didn't want to go there.

"You may also recall that Marc and I started a winery venture together a few years ago, using the land around the plantation."

"Vaguely." The alarm bells were getting louder now. Jack had recently read to me—somewhat gleefully—an article in the *Post and Courier* about a Longo family member accusing Marc of swindling and threatening legal action.

"Yes, well, my dear brother knew the land wasn't good for a vineyard—a fact he kept from me when he told me from the goodness of his heart he was going to allow me to buy out his share and give me a good deal." His hands formed themselves into fists. "A good deal on worthless land."

"That wasn't very nice," Jayne said, her tone similar to the one she used when settling disputes between the twins. And Jack and me. She was a nanny, after all.

"You could say that," Anthony said, giving Jayne an appreciative grin.

She blushed, then resumed her deliberate breathing.

"So what does that have to do with me? He's married to my cousin, but we're not close."

"I know. Which is why I was thinking we needed to talk." He leaned very close. "It seems we both have a bone to pick with my brother."

"We do? If you're referring to Jack's career, he just signed a new two-book deal and is hard at work on the new book. Marc gave us a setback, but that's behind us."

"Is it? I thought Marc wanted to film his movie in your house."

"He does. And I believe Jack told him where he could file that idea."

Anthony smiled smugly. "I'm sure he did. I've never had the pleasure of meeting your husband, but I've heard Marc rant about him often enough to know they're not friends."

Jayne coughed.

"You could say that," I said. "Which is really why we're putting all of that in the past and moving forward."

"Yes, well, too bad Marc didn't get that memo."

The alarm bells were now clanging so loudly I was sure everyone in the restaurant could hear. "What do you mean?"

He leaned in a little closer. "Marc has lots of . . . connections. Has a lot of influence, even in the publishing world. Jack's new contract might not be as ironclad as you'd like to think."

"That's ridiculous," I hissed. "He's signed it and received the advance. He's working on the book now and his publisher has big plans for it."

Anthony shook his head slowly. "Doesn't matter to Marc. He has . . . ways to get what he wants."

"And what does he want?"

"Your house."

"My house? We're not selling. Ever. We've gone through quite a lot for that house." I thought of the ghost of Louisa Vanderhorst, who watched over us, the scent of roses alerting us to her presence. Of old Nevin Vanderhorst, who'd left the house to me in his will, knowing long before I did that the house and I were meant to be together for as long as I lived. Or, as Jack had said at our wedding in the back garden, perhaps even longer.

Anthony smiled, but it wasn't friendly. "Tell me, Melanie. Would you be financially solvent if it weren't for Jack's income? I'm sure he's getting royalties from his earlier books, but without a new book, sales of his older books peter out, don't they?"

I thought of how we'd had to borrow money from Nola, who had made a few lucrative sales of music she'd written, to keep the house. It was a loan, and we were still working on paying it back.

I started to say no, but Jayne kicked me under the table. "It's none of your business," she said, speaking slowly as if to make sure the right words came out.

"Right," I agreed. "It's none of your business." I stood, and Jayne stood, too.

Anthony slid his chair back and stood as well, blocking our way to the door. "What if I said I could help you out-maneuver Marc and make a lot of money at the same time?"

"What do you mean?"

"Marc found something that's convinced him that there is something valuable hidden in the mausoleum at the Gallen Hall cemetery. He can't get access, though."

"Why?" I asked, although with the mention of the mausoleum, I was afraid I knew why.

His voice very quiet, he said, "I know that you can speak to the dead."

Jayne inhaled quickly, but I kept my eyes on Anthony. "I don't know where you heard that. . . ."

"Rebecca, of course. I know she has premonitions in her dreams—she's even told me of a few she had about me. But she said your powers are much stronger, that you can actually talk to the dead."

"Well, she's mistaken." I slid my chair up to the table so I could inch my way around Anthony to access the door and saw Jayne do the same thing. "I've got to go. Sorry I can't help you."

We'd made it only a few feet before he said, "I heard about that cistern in your back garden—how several grad students assigned to the excavation refuse to return to the site. I was curious, so I did some digging. Do you know where the bricks came from?"

A chill pricked at the base of my neck as I recalled the apparition of the man in the photograph standing by the edge of the gaping hole and holding what appeared to be a piece of jewelry. And the menacing aura that had pervaded my house and yard ever since the cistern was discovered. "No," I said, my voice wavering only a little. "And I don't care."

We'd made it to the door when Anthony called out to us, "They're from an older mausoleum in the Gallen Hall cemetery. I thought you'd want to know. Just in case."

I turned to face him. "Just in case what?"

"Just in case you find something . . . unexpected in your cistern."

Jayne pushed the door open, then propelled me into the warm morning air with a gentle shove to my back. I turned around to see whether Anthony would follow us out and found myself staring at the glass door of the shop. Except instead of seeing my own reflection, I saw the clear specter of a gentleman in what appeared to be an old-fashioned cravat and jacket staring back at me with black, empty sockets.

CHAPTER
2

I had just finished drying my hair in the bathroom when Jack walked in, his pajama pants riding low on his slim hips, his defined abs under smooth skin making me almost drop the blow-dryer. His dark hair stuck up in a tousled fashion that I'm sure models had to work at, his beard stubble making him the perfect dictionary picture for the definition of *devastating*.

He turned on the shower and slid off his pants, his gaze in the mirror's reflection never leaving mine as he walked up behind me. Lifting my hair, he pressed a warm kiss to the back of my neck. "Could this gorgeous creature really be my wife?"

It took me a moment to find my voice. "You like my dress?" It wasn't what I'd planned on saying, but Jayne had apparently rubbed off on me.

"Mmm," he said, burying his nose in my hair as his hands skimmed over the red fabric that clung to my hips. "I like what's in it the best."

I gasped as his teeth found my earlobe. "You better not be practicing dialogue for your book."

He continued nibbling at the delicate skin of my ear. "I do like to re-create dialogue as authentically as possible." He used his hands to press me back against his chest, his interest in things other than dialogue apparent.

Although most of my brain cells were rapidly jumping ship, some of them clung to the memory of my earlier conversation with Anthony Longo. "So, the book's going well?"

His tongue did interesting flicking motions that he knew I loved against the area behind my ear. "Uh-huh."

"No more writer's block?"

"Nuh-uh," Jack said, blowing warm air on the damp skin, which nearly undid me. But, like a dog with a bone, I couldn't let go of Anthony's words.

"So, no problems with your new agent or publisher?"

He lifted his head, turning me around to face him. "Why are you asking?"

"Because . . ." I searched for something that was as close to the truth as possible so I couldn't be accused of avoidance later if this conversation ever came back to haunt me. "Because I was thinking this morning how happy I am to be living in this house with you and our family, and with my parents and your parents so close by. How I can't wait to see our children grow up in this house. I was just wanting to know if we're okay financially. I mean, I have a fairly good idea of what's in the bank accounts and what we have in investments, but I just want to make sure I'm not missing something. I don't know if I could take another scare like we had before, and I don't want to ask Nola to bail us out again. It's not fair to her."

Jack's eyes became serious. "Since we agreed to be completely honest with each other, I'll tell you that we're doing okay. If we keep to the budget you and I worked out, and this book does as well as my publisher expects, we might even be able to get ahead. My mother insisting on paying for Nola's tuition at Ashley Hall has been a huge help, and those two big sales you made last month were instrumental in putting us solidly in the black. You know you are more than welcome to go in my desk drawer where I keep all of our financial records. Honesty, remember?"

I nodded, my gaze slipping down to his lips, both because I couldn't meet his eyes and because his lips were so much more interesting than the conversation. "So we wouldn't need the money Marc's throwing in our faces for us to agree to film his movie here."

"Not right now. That could change, of course, but I'd rather have all the unpleasant ghosts you've gotten rid of come back to rattle their chains than agree to that."

My eyes shot back to meet his. "Don't say that out loud. You never know who might be listening."

Cocking his head to the side just like JJ did when watching Sarah babble at shadowy corners, Jack said, "Is there something you're not telling me?"

"Maybe."

He quirked an eyebrow. *Just one more week,* I thought to myself. Just one more week of domestic peace and contentment. One more week to get my life in order before I would attempt to discover what was lurking in my backyard. And who, or what, had taken up residence in Nola's bedroom.

"'Maybe'?" Jack repeated.

"I can't tell you about your Christmas present. Or am I not allowed to keep it a secret?"

He kissed me softly on the lips. "You can try. But I have ways of finding out all of your secrets."

"Do you, now?" I asked.

His phone, left on the counter, beeped. He glanced at it expectantly before turning back to me, but not before I'd seen the shadow of disappointment cloud his eyes.

"Who was it?" I asked, although what I really needed to know was who it *wasn't.* Right before we'd discovered that Marc had stolen Jack's book idea and had already signed a huge publishing deal, Jack's agent and editor had stopped returning his phone calls. For the second time that day, alarm bells began clanging inside my head.

He paused for a moment before answering. "It was my mother. I'll call her back."

"Were you expecting someone el—" I began, my words swallowed by his kiss.

"Let's find out if this dress is waterproof." His words were muffled against my neck as he dragged me into the shower, my senses perilously close to abandoning me completely, but still clinging to me enough to make me wonder what he was avoiding telling me.

∞

Women's voices came from inside my mother's Legare Street house as I pushed open the front door. The house had belonged to her family for generations, our ownership interrupted for a few years by a Texas junkyard millionaire following my parents' divorce. My formerly estranged mother, retired opera diva Ginette Prioleau, and Sophie were still working hard to erase the "creative touches" inflicted on the house by the previous owner, but at least the house was now back in the family. My mother had remarried my father on the same day I'd married Jack, and my parents now appeared to be living in marital bliss in the home in which I was born and had lived for the first six years of my life.

I followed the voices to the front parlor, where the glorious floor-to-ceiling stained glass window sparkled in the morning sunshine. A few years before, Jack and I had discovered the secret hidden in the glass that led us to unraveling an old family mystery, but now all I could see was the beauty of the window and the way it seemed to draw me into the parlor. Or maybe it was because of the sudden drop in temperature or the slight scent of Vanilla Musk.

There were about fifteen women seated in the parlor on the sofas and chairs, the furniture recently having been rescued from the leopard and zebra prints it had been forced to wear by the former occupants and now re-covered in historically accurate (and contemporarily expensive) damask and silk upholstery in shades of cream and pale blue.

I knew I'd find Veronica Farrell in the group even before I caught sight of her red hair. The presence of her dead sister's perfume had already alerted me that she'd be there, although I was surprised to find her at the Ashley Hall Christmas Progressive Dinner fund-raiser meeting. Her daughter, Lindsey, was a close friend and classmate of

Nola's, but ever since I'd flat-out refused to help her communicate with her deceased sister, Adrienne—and then had been more or less threatened by her husband, Michael, to let it be—I hadn't seen her. Even at school functions, we always seemed to be on opposite sides of the room, although I could never be sure by whose design.

"Mellie," my mother said, her trim figure floating toward me in a sea of blue silk chiffon, looking much younger than her sixty-six years. She and Jack were the only two people allowed to call me Mellie. It had once grated on my nerves, which was why Jack had adopted it, but now I found it endearing. She kissed me on the cheek as my mother-in-law, the perpetually elegant owner of Trenholm Antiques, Amelia Trenholm, stood and greeted me with a warm smile.

The two women had been friends since childhood, both attending Ashley Hall, so it made sense that they'd be on the committee. What didn't make sense was the way they had each taken hold of one of my arms as if they were afraid I might escape. I smelled cinnamon and coffee, and I wondered if they were trying to keep me from bolting toward the refreshments set up on a Chippendale mahogany sideboard.

All gazes were fixed on me as my mother began to speak. "Ladies, may I please have your attention? Now that my daughter is here, I thought we'd go ahead and get started with a major announcement."

I gently tried to pull away, but the two women held me tight. I wondered if escaping would be worth the scene and the comments I'd hear for years.

My mother continued. "Melanie's dear friend Dr. Sophie Wallen-Arasi, a professor of historic preservation at the college, couldn't be with us today, but she has graciously volunteered both herself and her expertise, along with my daughter Melanie, to be in charge of the wreath-making workshop this year."

She paused for the surprised gasps from the audience, mine being the loudest.

Mother continued. "She has also agreed to spearhead the decorations for the host homes for the dinner, promising to ensure that all materials and methods for both the wreaths and the decorations will be authentic and period-specific to the Revolutionary War era, which is our theme for the progressive dinner this year. As you all know, the workshop was a major fund-raiser last year, and with these two talented ladies at the helm, we expect to double our proceeds."

I turned to my mother to express my true feelings regarding historic wreath making but my words were drowned out by the round of applause. I'd never suspected that such slender and well-coiffed women could make that kind of noise.

The arrival of another latecomer turned everyone's heads. My cousin Rebecca Longo wore her signature pink—pink dress, pink shoes, and pink eyeglasses frames. I was pretty sure she didn't have a prescription inside the frames but was using them merely as a fashion statement. In her arms, and dressed in a coordinating pink dress, was her dog, Pucci. Pucci and General Lee had had a short-lived yet torrid affair that had resulted in a litter of puppies, two of which—Porgy and Bess—now belonged to Nola. They technically belonged to Jack and me, since they were a wedding gift, but when Nola was home they devoted their lives to following her around as if she'd bathed in beef broth and they never let her out of their sight. They even went into a mini mourning period each day when Nola left for school.

"Sorry I'm late," Rebecca announced. "I had to cook three filets mignons before I found a temperature Pucci would eat. I'm exhausted and it's barely ten o'clock!" With a heavy sigh she gracefully took a seat on one of the new sofas, smiling brightly at the women around her.

"Any alumnae could sign up for the committee," Amelia said quietly, anticipating my question.

I sent a weak smile in Rebecca's direction and she beamed back at me. I found some satisfaction in the pallor of her skin, caused by the sun shooting orange light through the stained glass and transforming Rebecca's blond hair to rust.

My mother turned to me. "Why don't you get seated so we can start going over the subcommittees and deciding who will head the entire fund-raiser?"

"I nominate Sophie," I said through gritted teeth.

"Sadly, she never attended Ashley Hall," my mother said, pushing me toward a settee.

I was already in front of it before I realized the other occupant was Veronica Farrell, and it was too late to change directions and find another seat without appearing rude. I liked Veronica and wouldn't have minded sitting next to her. It was the spectral form of her sister standing behind her that made me want to sit anywhere except that corner of the room.

Amelia began walking around the room handing out sign-up forms. "Please write your name on the top of the page if you're interested in being in charge of the fund-raiser. Then, at the bottom, please put your name beneath your three top choices of committees that you would like to participate in, and add an asterisk if you'd like to be the committee head. We already have two fabulous committee heads for wreath decorating, but I'm sure they would appreciate your help. And we expect everyone to sign up for at least two—even if you're the chair of one." Amelia smiled at me, her eyes focused on the middle of my forehead, as if she was afraid to meet my eyes and acknowledge that she'd been a part of my railroading. I was sure it was all my mother's machinations, but I held Amelia guilty by association.

Veronica leaned over to me. "I'm going to sign up to be the decorating committee chair, so if you sign up for that committee, I'll make sure you have the easier tasks. I know how busy you are." She smiled and I smiled back, hoping she wasn't being nice to me because she wasn't done asking for my help.

"Thanks," I said.

A strong whiff of Vanilla Musk wafted over us. Veronica's head jerked up, so I knew she smelled it, too. I quickly looked down at the paper in my lap, pretending to study it.

"She's here, isn't she?" Veronica whispered. "Whenever I smell her perfume, I know she's near."

"Who's here?" I asked, trying to sound uninterested.

Veronica simply stared at me, a look of reproach in her eyes. After a moment, she said, "You probably already know this, but your sister, Jayne, has been talking with Detective Riley to help with the reopened investigation into Adrienne's murder. As a mother and a sister, I'm sure you understand why I'm doing this. I can't accept not knowing what happened—not if there are other avenues out there to solving this crime." She smiled softly. "I just wanted to tell you that because I didn't want any awkwardness between us. Our daughters are good friends, and we'll be seeing a lot of each other. I'd like us to be friends, too."

"I'd like that, too," I said, sensing the presence moving away, and resisting a huge sigh of relief. "So," I said, eager to change the subject, "I guess I'll sign up for the decorating committee, then. Although wouldn't you think being in charge of the wreath-decorating workshop is punishment enough?"

Her laugh came out as a snort, bringing back memories of working together on a history project in college. I remembered I'd liked that about her, the fact that she could have such an ungracious laugh, but one that other people couldn't help but smile at because it showed real joy and happiness. I remembered, too, envying her that laugh, because at that point in my life I hadn't had a lot of reasons to laugh.

I tried to focus on the rest of the meeting, wondering how soon I would be free to mastermind a devious plot to get back at Sophie for volunteering me for the workshop. My mind wandered as I considered putting laminate over the wood floors in my dining room. Or giving her a litter of puppies.

My mother's voice interrupted my reverie. "Anyone else

want to volunteer to host one of the dinner courses?" She looked pointedly at me, but I pretended I hadn't heard the question. She knew how a lot of activity in the house could sometimes cause the spirits to become restless. And there were two spirits I wasn't eager to awaken.

Veronica raised her hand. "My house is a Victorian on Queen Street. I'd be happy to open it up for one of the courses."

Amelia made a note on her clipboard, smiling her approval at Veronica. "Thank you. That gives us five houses. We just need one more house to host the main course. Perhaps one of the grander and restored homes. It would sell more tickets, and the more tickets we sell, the more money for Ashley Hall."

There were murmurs of assent, and I could feel more than one set of eyes on me. I concentrated on recrossing my legs and straightening my skirt, trying not to be obvious as I scanned the side tables for where the coffee cake might be hidden, having already checked on the sideboard and seen only coffee cups and the tall coffee server. Veronica's half-eaten piece sat on the coffee table in front of us, and it took all of my willpower to resist reaching over with my fingers and popping it in my mouth.

Rebecca stood. "Marc and I would like to donate twenty thousand dollars to the fund-raiser." She smiled broadly as she turned to accept the applause, her gaze finally settling on me. I began to feel sick. "With just one condition."

She waited for a prolonged and very uncomfortable moment while my stomach roiled.

Without moving her gaze from mine, she said, "We will donate the money provided that the Trenholms will agree to host one of the courses. Not to put the burden all on Melanie, I promise to help her with the decorating."

There was another surprisingly loud round of applause amid murmurings about Rebecca's generosity and how such an offer would be impossible to refuse. I didn't know what I found more horrifying—the idea of pink garlands festooning my beautiful Adams mantels and a pink-frosted

Christmas tree in the front parlor window for all the neighbors to see, or the idea of all the agitated spirits shaken awake.

"I . . ." I began, then stopped, realizing how futile protesting would be.

"Thank you, Melanie," my mother said, leading another round of applause, which sounded more and more like nails being hammered into a coffin.

She turned back to the room. "I believe that concludes our meeting, ladies. Please make sure I have all the committee forms, and please be checking your e-mail for the name of our new fund-raising chairperson and which committees you've been assigned to. Thank you all for coming."

As the other women began to gather their things and say good-bye while thanking Rebecca as if she'd just found a cure for cancer, I stayed where I was, torn between strangling my cousin and faking my death and moving to another country. Because where there was Rebecca being generous and kind, there were ulterior motives.

"You okay?" Veronica asked softly.

I sent her a grateful glance. "I will be. Just as soon as I find a way to make my cousin disappear."

She grinned wryly. "Yeah, I could probably help you with that. What's with all that pink?" She picked up her plate, and I watched as she crumpled the remainder of her cake into a napkin. Veronica continued. "I'm getting bad vibes about her decorating skills. Want me to volunteer to help?"

I nodded enthusiastically. "Please. Maybe I can hold her down while you put normal Christmas decorations that don't resemble cotton candy around the house."

She snorted, then abruptly stopped as Rebecca approached, her expression managing to appear chagrined. "Will you excuse us for a moment, Veronica? I need to speak with my cousin."

With a little smile, Veronica left, offering a reassuring pat on my shoulder.

Rebecca slid onto the sofa in the spot vacated by Veronica.

"I'm sorry, Melanie. I really am. But you've got that big, beautiful house just aching to be shown off. It's a historic icon—just ask Sophie. People will be buying tickets just to see inside."

I pulled back. "You're trying to get film people inside the house, aren't you? You just can't take no for an answer, can you?"

She looked deflated, unprepared for me to expect the worst from her. But she'd never shown me reason not to.

"I'm sorry, Melanie. I really am. But Marc's on my case about getting the movie filmed inside your house. He's obsessed! I figured if we could get some of the film people in the house to take pictures, they can re-create it in a set. And then we'll all be happy."

"Really, Rebecca? You think that would make Marc happy?"

Her shoulders sank. "I had to try. You know what he's like."

I frowned. "I met your brother-in-law. Anthony. He told me something very interesting."

She looked at me warily. "Yes?"

"He said that Marc wants our house." I leaned forward, resisting the impulse to press my index finger into her chest. "Please make sure he knows, in no uncertain terms, that I'd rather burn my house down to the ground than see him take possession of it."

Pucci whimpered, and Rebecca held the little dog's head against her chest. "I'm sure you don't mean that. Marc is my husband, remember."

"Oh, that's not something I'd forget."

I thought she'd jump up and leave in a huff, but she stayed where she was, an expression that I'd come to recognize on her face. A signal that she had something unpleasant to tell me.

"I had a dream," she said.

I almost stood and left right then. All of my life, avoidance had been my modus operandi. But ever since my marriage to Jack, I'd been trying to change. To be a more mature version of myself by facing unpleasant things instead of pretending they didn't exist. I still failed as many times as I succeeded, but Jack said that as long as I tried, it wasn't a complete loss. I took a deep breath. "And?"

"It was about Jack. He's in danger."

She had my full attention. "From what?"

"I'm not sure. There's another man—no one I recognized. And he was . . ." She stopped.

"And he was what?"

"He was burying Jack alive."

CHAPTER
3

I'd halfway opened the bottom drawer of my desk, my mouth already salivating at the thought of the leftover doughnut from Glazed still nestled all soft and sugary in its bag. I'd resisted it for a day and a half and knew I had to eat it now because it couldn't be expected to stay fresh forever.

At the sound of my phone beeping my hand jerked, bumping hard against the solid wood of my desk. I hit the intercom button. "Yes, Jolly—what is it?"

The receptionist's voice was hushed. "Someone is here to see you, but he doesn't have an appointment. I told him that you have a showing in half an hour and to make an appointment when you'd have more time, but he was very insistent." The disapproving tone brought my attention away from the sweet-smelling bag and back to the intercom.

"Did he say what he wanted?"

"Just that you were old friends and he'd explain when he saw you."

I sat up straighter. "What's his name?"

"Marc Longo. Should I send him back?"

I slammed my desk drawer. *Marc?* He was the last person I expected or wanted to see, and I briefly considered stealthily opening one of the windows in my office and escaping into the parking lot. But that's what the old Melanie would have done. The Melanie who used to hide from her problems and avoided confrontation at all cost. I was the new, grown-up version of Melanie who didn't do things like that anymore. Most of the time.

I picked up my cell phone to call Jack to come over but changed my mind. He was working on a book that meant a lot to his career, and I didn't want to distract him. It was the same reason, I kept telling myself, why I hadn't told him about the face in Nola's window. Or about Rebecca's dream. It had nothing to do with my insecurities and fears of abandonment, despite all of Jack's reassurances that he loved me and was with me for keeps, even if I was prone to distractions of the paranormal kind. Old habits, I'd found, are like a favorite pair of worn-out old shoes; you just can't toss them out. You allow them to linger in your closet until you're tempted into walking around in them again because you crave the comfortable and familiar.

"Thank you, Jolly. Send him back."

I stood, straightening my skirt and trying out several relaxed and non-posed poses. I was awkwardly perched on the edge of my desk when Marc walked into my office, but I was spared greeting him by the avalanche of my phone, agenda, and desk lamp cascading to the floor because of an accidental tug of the cord by the leg I nonchalantly tried to cross.

"Let me help you," he said, crouching down to pick up the lamp, which had miraculously survived the tumble.

"Just leave it," I said. "Really. I'd rather you just tell me why you're here and then go."

He placed the lamp in the middle of my desk, the shade completely askew, and he grinned at me when he caught me noticing. I clenched my hands into fists so I wouldn't reach over and right it, and somehow managed not to start singing ABBA songs backward.

"Is that how you talk to all your clients, Melanie?"

"Well, you're not a client so it doesn't count."

He sat down in one of the chairs where legitimate clients usually sat and smiled. The resemblance to his brother was apparent: the same coloring and build, the same sexy smile. Except where I'd detected warmth behind Anthony's eyes, Marc's were like cold, lifeless stones. All his attention and devotion were directed inward. I couldn't remember if they'd been like that when I'd dated him or if this was something new. Being married to Rebecca could do that to anyone, I supposed.

He stretched his long legs in front of him and crossed his Italian-loafer-clad feet at the ankles. "Oh, but I could be."

Having given up on a casual lean on my desk, I returned to my chair. "I doubt it." I made a big show of avoiding looking at the crooked lampshade and instead glanced at my watch. "I'm afraid I have an appointment—"

As if I hadn't spoken, he said, "I'd like to buy a house. A nice, big, old one south of Broad. And I'm willing to pay a lot more than what it's worth."

I suddenly recalled what Anthony had said about Marc wanting my house, and frigidity spread from the base of my neck to my toes. I squared my shoulders, preparing to do battle. "If you're referring to our house on Tradd Street, I'm afraid it's off the market and I don't anticipate it being available for purchase for at least another hundred years or so."

He propped his elbows on the arms of the chair and steepled his fingers. Tilting his head slightly, he said, "When we were dating, I don't remember you being quite so . . . unwilling."

He'd emphasized the last word, making it seem sordid, and I felt my cheeks redden. His smile widened, his strike intentional. I stood. "Seeing as how we have nothing else to discuss, I'd like you to leave. I've got a lot of work—"

Marc cut me off. "Did Jack tell you his editor was let go?"

"What?" I groaned inwardly, wishing I hadn't allowed him to take me by surprise.

"Ah, I see he hasn't mentioned it. Happened last week. Not to repeat hearsay, but the rumors had something to do with being too friendly with an intern. A relation of mine, actually—what a small world, right? And now other victims are crawling out of the woodwork, eager to add to the growing pile of accusations. With the current social climate regarding workplace harassment, the publisher had no choice but to let him go." He grinned again. "Regardless of whether it was warranted. High-profile companies just can't take the chance, now, can they?"

I shivered, either from the chill that wouldn't dissipate or from the way he looked when he said the accuser was related to him. Something Anthony said pinged at my brain. *Marc has lots of connections. Has a lot of influence, even in the publishing world.* I tried very hard to keep my voice even. "I'm sure the reason Jack hasn't mentioned it is because it has no impact on him or his work. There are lots of really good editors at his publishing house. I'm sure with such a valuable asset as Jack is to them, they'll make sure they match him up to someone who's a good fit."

Marc sat up, a look of mock concern on his face. "I'm not sure if you're aware, but when an editor who has been the single and loudest championing voice for a particular author or book is suddenly let go, the author is, effectively, orphaned. Sure, Jack will be assigned to a new editor. But it just won't be the same, will it? Not unless the new editor shares the same passion and enthusiasm for the book as the previous editor. And that, my dear Melanie, rarely—if ever—happens."

I walked to the door and held it open so my intent was obvious. "I'm sure Jack and his project will be fine. Sorry I can't help you."

"Ah, Melanie. Still so naïve." He stood but didn't move, instead taking his time examining the contents of the top of my desk.

My voice shook a little when I spoke. "I'm not naïve. I know Jack is a very talented author, with a solid track record, and his new publisher knows this. His new book idea is brilliant and will succeed with whatever editor he's assigned to. He's got a fabulous agent who believes in him and has his back. So stop making these stupid threats and go away. We're not selling our house, nor will your movie be filmed there. And there is nothing you can say or do that will make us change our minds. You think your big donation to the Ashley Hall fund-raiser might give you a loophole to get stills or shots or whatever it is filmmakers do, but I will fight you every step of the way. And you won't get a single scene shot anywhere near my home."

When he didn't move, I jiggled the doorknob to remind him that he was just leaving.

He wasn't smiling anymore. "I'm being nice now because you and I have a history. But this courtesy has a limited time span." He walked slowly toward me, and stopped so that he was definitely invading my personal space. I didn't step back. "I'm not a patient man, Melanie. And I always get what I want. One way or another."

"You didn't get the Confederate diamonds," I said, referring to the treasure hidden in the house by a former Vanderhorst owner at the end of the Civil War. Jack and I had found them before Marc could, much to Marc's ire. I hadn't meant to antagonize him, but I couldn't stop myself. His smugness on top of what he'd done to Jack—to *us*—was too much for me to let it slide.

His nostrils flared. "You can make this easy, or you can make this hard. Either way, my wife and I will be moving into Fifty-five Tradd Street in the very near future, and we will happily open our doors to a film crew who are champing at the bit to begin filming what I'm sure will be a huge blockbuster hit." He leaned closer so I could see hazel flecks in his eyes. "And you can tell your historic-house-hugging professor friend that I have all sorts of ideas of what I'd like to do in the house once it's mine and that there will be nothing she can do to stop me. Just know that it will involve the removal of most of the interior walls and all of those tacky wedding-cake moldings."

Of all the things Marc said, that hurt me the most. My back still ached when I thought about how I'd hand sanded the wood floors, banister, and spindles. My head hurt as I recalled how much money I'd spent on replacing the roof, and the time and focus it had taken Sophie to repair the antique silk Chinese wallpaper in the foyer. Most of all, I couldn't forget the beautiful garden my father had brought back from ruin, or the memory of walking with Nola down the grand staircase on my wedding day and then carrying the twins up to their nursery on their first day home from the hospital. What Marc was suggesting was pure desecration. Considering I'd never wanted the house in the first place, I was stunned at the ache in my heart at just the thought of Marc and Rebecca moving in and ruining *my* house.

I leaned forward so that our noses were almost touching. "Over my dead body," I hissed.

Something flickered in his eyes before he stepped back, a crooked grin splitting his face. "That could be arranged."

A small frisson of fear erupted inside of me, but I refused to look away or even blink. Marc Longo was a bully, and I wouldn't be cowed by him. "Get out," I said through my teeth. "And don't even think you or your film crew will get past the front gate."

He walked out into the hallway, then turned around to face me. "I made another rather generous donation to Ashley Hall and promised them that I'd have movie professionals document the progressive dinner so they can use it for promotion. I think you'll have a hard time telling them no. But that's really just to annoy you and Jack. Sure, I'll be able to get some great interior shots of the house, but I think I'll wait until my name is on the deed before I make plans for the real filming to begin." He scratched his chin as if deep in thought. "I'm thinking Emma Stone—she'd have to dye her hair again, of course—would be the perfect actress to play Rebecca, don't you?"

Something pinged again at the back of my brain, and my anger slipped away, replaced again by something that felt a lot like fear. I just needed to make sure he didn't see it. "Why do you want it so badly, Marc? There are plenty of other beautiful historic houses much grander than mine for sale. What is it about my house?"

He paused for a moment. "Simple, really. It belongs to Jack. And you. But not for long." He raised his eyebrows before turning on his heel and walking away.

I watched him until he disappeared around a bend in the

corridor, a sense of unease settling in the pit of my stomach. Marc was a businessman. Everything he did had to be a means to make money or get ahead in some way. Marc had originally purchased the Vanderhorst plantation because he'd thought the Confederate diamonds had been hidden there. And then he'd lied to his own brother about turning it into a winery to extricate himself from a bad investment. He'd even professed his love for me just to access the house I'd inherited so he'd be in a good position to search for the diamonds.

There was something else about my house on Tradd Street besides jealousy that made Marc Longo want it. I just needed to figure out what it was before it was too late. I returned to my desk and sat down, knowing whom I needed to talk to. My finger was poised over the intercom button when Jolly tapped on the doorframe, her dragonfly earrings swinging. I could tell by the look on her face that she'd heard every word.

"He is not a nice man," she said, a deep crease between her brows. "He has a black karma cloud that hovers around him, but I think you have to be a psychic like me to see it." She gave me a sympathetic stare.

"I'm sure." Jolly was convinced she had psychic abilities and had begun taking classes to learn how to use them. So far, she'd had more misses than hits and had arrived at the firm conclusion that I had no abilities of my own. I was more than happy to have her continue to believe that.

"Would you like me to call Jack for you?" Her green eyes were wide with concern.

He probably was the first person I should call, but I couldn't. Not yet. If it was true that he'd lost his editor and hadn't told me, he had enough to worry about. "No. But I do need you to find a number for me. For Anthony Longo."

Jolly raised her eyebrows in question.

"Yes, Marc's brother. I believe he's local. I seem to recall Marc once telling me that his younger brother owned a house downtown. Hopefully he has a landline."

"Would you like me to put the call through if I can get him on the line?"

I shook my head. "No. Just get me the number. Please."

She nodded, then left my office, and I reached over to straighten the lampshade because I couldn't take it anymore. My iPhone buzzed and I looked down at the screen and saw a text from Rebecca.

I dreamed of a man in old-fashioned clothes with empty sockets for eyes. He said he was coming for you. And Jack.

I quickly hit CLEAR before leaning back in my chair and closing my eyes, wondering how, once again, my formerly orderly world had suddenly become everything but, and why the restless dead never seemed to want to leave me alone.

CHAPTER
4

When I walked in the front door after work, the smell of Mrs. Houlihan's Christmas cookies baking in the oven wafted from the kitchen, drawing me to the room like a cat to catnip. Or a dog to, well, baking cookies, since General Lee, Porgy, and Bess were all camped out in front of the kitchen door, gazing at the solid wood surface as if just the weight of their stares might open it.

It was still November, but Mrs. Houlihan insisted on stuffing the freezers with sugary holiday treats way in advance of any Christmas company we might have. I personally thought she did it to torment me, especially because only she and Jack had the keys to the large freezer in the carriage house and it was always locked. I knew because I checked. Daily.

I joined the dogs in their vigil, holding my breath to listen for any signs of movement from the other side of the door. I'd recently been banned from the kitchen while my housekeeper, Mrs. Houlihan—inherited along with General Lee and the house—did her Christmas baking, following the infamous cookie-cutting incident in which I was showing the children how to use cute winter shapes on the rolled-out cookie dough. I'd been eating all the leftover dough to make cleanup easier, ensuring the children didn't see me because Jayne said raw dough wasn't good for them. I'd eaten raw dough my entire life without issue, so I was sure Jayne's ban hadn't included me.

Mrs. Houlihan had been upset when she discovered she

didn't have enough dough for a second batch and gave me a warning, not seeming to care that I was hungry or sugar deprived—or that I paid her salary. When her stash of red and green M&M'S, which were supposed to be the snowmen's buttons, mysteriously disappeared, she threatened to quit if I didn't leave, and I had no choice but to exit the kitchen in defeat. Even the twins had watched my departure with what looked like disappointment in their eyes.

Pressing my ear against the door, I could hear Mrs. Houlihan bustling about inside. With a sigh, I turned to the dogs. "Sorry. We'll have to wait until she leaves, and then I promise to sneak us something to sample."

"I heard that!" Mrs. Houlihan called out from the other side of the door. "Just be aware that one of my pies and three dozen of the cookies were made from recipes Dr. Wallen-Arasi gave me with all vegan, gluten-free, and sugar-free ingredients. And I'm not going to tell you which ones they are."

I found my mouth puckering with the memory of some of Sophie's culinary recommendations and gave an involuntary shudder. I squatted to scratch behind three sets of furry ears. "Don't worry. I promise to stop by Woof Gang Bakery tomorrow and bring you home something tasty."

They resumed their vigil as I carefully hung up my coat in the small cloak closet. It took me longer than it should have because no one had buttoned and zipped up their coats or hung them all in the same direction, so I had to fix them. I made a mental note to bring it up with Nola and Jack during dinner. I was halfway to the stairs to head up to the nursery when I heard JJ's squealing laughter followed by Jack's deep-chested chuckle coming from behind me. I followed the sound toward Jack's closed office door, then carefully opened it before thrusting my head into the opening.

Jack's computer screen was dark, and he was lying faceup on the rug in front of his desk, JJ sitting on top of his chest. They both wore cowboy hats, Jack's stuck under his head on the floor, and Jack was bouncing his son up and down in a good imitation of the movement of a horse. All my insides melted as I watched them, wondering what I'd done to be so lucky. Not once during my own difficult childhood had I imagined this life. But now that it was mine, I clung to it with both hands like a squirrel in a hurricane might cling to a palmetto trunk.

My gaze slid to the corner of the room where Sarah sat in a shaft of sunlight, waving her hands and babbling as if in conversation. Which she was, I realized, although I couldn't see anyone. But I could smell the faint scent of roses, the telltale indicator that Louisa Vanderhorst, former resident of the house and planter of the Louisa roses in our garden, was nearby. Although she was a gentle maternal spirit, and one who only periodically visited, I felt a small shock of alarm. Because Louisa stopped by only when she felt we needed her protection.

I turned back to a now hatless Jack, who'd sat up and placed JJ in his lap. "Where's Jayne?" I asked, bending down to kiss Jack on the lips, then loudly blow a raspberry on JJ's cheek before swooping up Sarah into my arms. She smiled at me, her blue eyes bright and sparkling as she kissed my nose, then turned to wave her pudgy fingers at the empty corner.

"I sent her home." Jack didn't meet my eyes as he stood, intently focusing on lifting JJ onto his shoulders.

"You sent her home? But I thought you said you needed as many writing hours as you could get to turn your book in by the deadline."

"Did I?" he asked, starting to trot around the room, JJ's giggles bursting from his tiny chest like bubbles.

I almost allowed myself to let it go. Not to let harsh realities intrude on this sweet family moment. To pretend that I didn't know that my husband had heard bad news and had chosen not to share it with me. But if there was ever a moment when I needed to be the new Melanie I was intent on becoming, this had to be it.

"Jack," I began, ready to tell him about my conversation with Anthony, my run-in with Marc, and Rebecca's dreams—and maybe even the unwanted visitors I'd seen in the house.

"Mellie," Jack said at the same time, preempting me. Despite my good intentions, I was completely happy to let him go first. I smiled encouragingly at him, trying not to be obvious that I was holding my breath.

"My editor was let go. Patrick took a huge chance on me and was my main advocate at the publishing house, so it's a little devastating. They've assigned me to one of the newer editors—a young woman not much older than Nola, I think. Her name is Desmarae." He grinned, but it was a poorly executed replica of his usual smile. "Not that being so young is necessarily a bad thing, but she admitted when we spoke on the phone that she'd not only never read any of my books, but she also had no idea who I was when they assigned her to me."

My heart burned at the indignation. "Then I guess she's been living under a rock." Forcing a bright smile, I said, "You still have your awesome agent, who believes in you almost as much as I do."

He didn't even try to force a smile this time. "Desmarae did say she loved my author photo on the back of my last book."

I remembered that picture. It was what had convinced me to go out with him. I tried not to think of another woman looking at the picture and having the same thoughts I did. I cleared my throat. "So you still have a contract and a book deadline."

"Affirmative," he said, jostling JJ on his shoulders and making our son squeal with delight.

"Then why would you let Jayne go home early? So you could wallow in self-doubt?"

He stared back at me for a long moment. "Yeah, probably." He slid JJ from his shoulders and handed him to me.

"I'm going to feed and bathe the children and get them ready for bed while you write. Do not leave this room until you have finished at least three more pages. I'll have a little surprise waiting for you when you're done." I gave him our special look to show him just what kind of a surprise I had in mind, hoping, as I said it, that it wasn't Nola's turn to host her study group at our house that night.

Not that it would matter, I thought as Jack's face became serious and he returned to his desk chair.

"I can always try. It will probably all be crap because my brain's not in it right now, but writing is rewriting, as my ex-editor used to say." He jiggled the wireless mouse on his desk, and his computer screen came to life. He read the lines on the screen, his brows squeezed together in concentration.

With a child in each arm, I began to back out of the room, apparently already forgotten.

"What were you about to say—before, when I interrupted you?" Jack kept his fingers poised over his keyboard but turned around to face me.

"Nothing important." I smiled, and he began typing. I could still hear the clacking of his fingers on the keyboard as I began to nudge the door behind us with my foot.

Without slowing down the pace, he said, "And I haven't forgotten what you said about a surprise if I write three more pages. I'm going to hold you to it."

I smiled at the back of his head, feeling an odd mixture of relief and guilt grab me in a choke hold. I started to take a step toward him, to tell him everything, to be the Melanie I'd promised myself I was capable of. But each click on his keyboard was like a tap on the nails in the coffin of my resolve, convincing me that the best choice at that moment was to let him work.

I stood in the doorway for a long moment, battling with my conscience, but then JJ began to squirm and Sarah rubbed her eyes. Looking at Jack's head bowed over his keyboard, I said, "I love you."

He continued typing without looking up, already lost in his own world. I put the children down, then gently closed the study door.

∞

General Lee walked docilely on his leash beside me while Porgy and Bess, on a separate double leash, both seemed determined to head in opposite directions. If they weren't so innocent-looking, I would have suspected them of trying to kill me. Behind us, Jayne pushed the double running stroller with JJ and Sarah buckled inside and bundled up against the sudden drop in temperature, unperturbed by the bumps and jars of the uneven sidewalk as we headed down Tradd Street toward East Bay and my meeting with Anthony Longo.

"Remind me again why you need an entourage for this meeting?" Jayne asked.

I kept my gaze focused ahead of us. "For moral support."

"And it has nothing to do with the reflection of that guy in the doughnut shop window."

I jerked my head around to stare at her and immediately tripped over one of the dogs. When I'd righted myself, I said, "You saw him?"

"Of course, Melanie. I see dead people, too, remember?"

"Right," I said, a surprising jab of jealousy invading my psyche. Although I'd always hated my "gift," it had always belonged to me and me alone. It had separated me from the proverbial crowd. And now, suddenly and unexpectedly, I was supposed to share it. It was as if I'd been downgraded to less than special. Which wasn't how I really felt at all. Really.

"I mean," Jayne continued, "it would seem that whoever or whatever that was in the window is somehow connected to Anthony, right? Except I've seen the same spirit at the cistern in your backyard." Our eyes met as we both stopped.

I shivered, and I wasn't sure it was due to the cold wind. "Anthony said that bricks from a mausoleum at the Vanderhorst plantation cemetery were used in the cistern."

"It could be a coincidence," she said.

Our eyes met again. "Except there's no such thing as

coincidence," we said in unison, echoing Jack's favorite saying. And he'd yet to be proved wrong.

A wild barking came from a pretty Victorian behind a Philip Simmons gate, making General Lee pull at his leash, nearly separating my shoulder from its socket. I had no choice but to follow him to the gate, where a small white terrier mix with teddy bear ears and a sweet face was jumping up to greet General Lee.

"This is Cindy Lou Who," Jayne explained, bending down to offer a scratch behind a small furry ear through the fence railing. She straightened to allow General Lee to take her place in ecstatically greeting his canine friend. "I always walk the children past this house, and Cindy Lou Who always rushes over to the gate to say hello. I think she has a thing for General Lee."

"I think the feeling's mutual," I said. "I don't think I've seen her before. Should I tell her that he's already fathered puppies from another relationship?"

"Her family just moved here from California. I've met the mom—Robin. Very nice lady. I let her know that General Lee wasn't fixed yet but that you'd take care of it very soon so the two of them could play on the same side of the fence."

I pulled on General Lee's leash, feeling terrible at the looks of anguish he and Cindy Lou Who gave each other as they were separated. "I know—you're right. I'll get it taken care of. That would be a terrible way to welcome new neighbors to the street."

We continued walking down Tradd, each block a nod to a different architectural period, the houses ranging from brick-fronted Colonials to Greek Revivals and double-piazza single houses. Growing up in Charleston, I'd never noticed the veritable treasure trove of historic houses that made up the landscape of my childhood. I'd been too preoccupied with ignoring the spirits who beckoned me from each doorway and window, in every alley, and behind every tree. It had taken years to learn how to block them out so I could traverse the brick streets of my hometown. But now, with Jayne and me together, our light shone too brightly, a lighthouse beacon to the restless dead in a sea of perpetual night.

Since my sister and I had found each other, there were several things I'd learned about her. Like me, she loved all things with sugar, small children and dogs, and the sound of St. Michael's bells. Her favorite color was blue, always worn when she felt she needed confidence; she was very shy around men, especially good-looking ones, disliked onions, and preferred wearing flats to heels. We both could see dead people, but whereas I could pretend not to see them, Jayne, eight years younger than I, and not as jaded, sometimes found it difficult to ignore them. Growing up, she'd found ways to mentally block them, but now that we were together, she was finding it more difficult.

I watched as Jayne stopped in front of a Neoclassical Revival (according to Sophie) where two young boys, about eight and ten, sat on the porch steps. The children looked real except for the sickly yellow pallor of their skin and the fact that the steps they were sitting on no longer existed.

"Come on, Jayne. There's nothing we can do without a full intervention, and that's just not going to happen."

"But they're children."

"I know," I said firmly, my resolve as much for her as it was for me. "But if you start paying attention to every spirit you see, more will follow, and they'll never leave you alone. In your waking or sleeping hours. So let them be."

She began backing away from them, turning away only after they vanished, a plaintive wailing disappearing with them. We were silent as we walked past the house whose new owners had sold the Philip Simmons gate for scrap metal, prompting Sophie to cross the street to the other side whenever she walked past it. I'd thought I'd seen her spit on the ground in front of the modern gate a few times.

When we reached East Bay, we turned right toward Battery Park and the gazebo. The day had turned blustery, whipping the Cooper River into white-frothed tips like a mad chef with too much meringue. I spotted a pirate ship with a hole blasted in its side slowly sinking beneath the waves, and when I glanced at Jayne, I knew she'd seen it, too.

We needed to come up with a way to block the proverbial target with the arrow pointing at us for all restless spirits to follow. Maybe I could buy her another ABBA CD so she'd learn all the lyrics and we could shout them together in a mutual effort to discourage hangers-on. I'd already gifted her with several CDs, but Jayne had a way of accidentally stepping on them or misplacing them. I made a mental note to ask Nola for help in downloading a playlist for Jayne to listen to on her phone so there would be nothing to step on and break. Or lose. It was the least I could do.

Jayne spotted Anthony leaning on the railing of the gazebo at the same time I did. "He's wearing clothes," she said. "I mean, he's here, and he has on a warm jacket."

I rolled my eyes. "Remember you're here for moral support, so please don't say anything unless you have to, and only after you've rehearsed it several times in your head. All right?"

She nodded as Anthony smiled, then walked down the steps to greet us. "Good morning, ladies. I was only expecting Melanie, but I have to admit that seeing Jayne, too, has made my day."

I wanted to roll my eyes again, but there was real warmth in his eyes as he looked at my sister. Jayne's cheeks reddened, not entirely due to the wind, and she quickly bent over the stroller to make sure the children were still bundled like little fat sausages.

Anthony shoved his bare hands into the pockets of his jacket. "I have to admit I was surprised to hear from you so soon."

"Yes, well, I surprised myself. But your brother paid me a little visit to not only make an offer on my house, but also to threaten me if I didn't comply. I remembered what you'd said about him having influence everywhere, and I realized that I need to be proactive."

"Good move," he said, distracted by a metal whisk hitting him in the shin.

"Sorry," Jayne said, then quickly picked it up, wiped it off with a cleansing cloth she'd conveniently attached to the stroller's handle, and gave it back to JJ. "Whisk," she said, as if that explained everything.

Anthony leaned forward and made a face at the children, and they both giggled. "Is his name 'Whisk'?" he asked JJ.

"Whisk," JJ repeated, throwing it at Anthony, who quickly intercepted the kitchen utensil before it beaned him.

He handed it back to JJ, then stepped out of throwing range. "When I was a little boy, I had a special attachment to a yellow bath sponge." His face sobered. "Until Marc cut it into shreds and soaked the pieces in black paint."

"That explains a lot," Jayne said slowly, and I wondered how long she'd had to practice in her head before speaking out loud.

"So, what do we do now?" I said, directing my attention toward Anthony.

"I need you to come out to the Vanderhorst plantation. To help me gain access to the mausoleum. If there's a treasure buried there, we need to find it before Marc does."

"But doesn't the property belong to you, and Marc's digging would be trespassing?"

He looked uncomfortable. "Marc doesn't always ask first. He just does. To be honest, I'm a little afraid to tell him no, regardless of how clear it is he's in the wrong. But there are certain . . . elements that are barring both of us entry to the mausoleum. Which is why I need your help. I was hoping we could set up an appointment to meet there as soon as possible."

I shivered inside my heavy sweater. "Why couldn't you just tell me this on the phone?"

"Because I can't be completely sure Marc hasn't found some way to intercept my calls and texts."

Remembering my encounter with Marc in my office, I

couldn't say Anthony's concerns were without merit. I started to tell him more details about Marc's visit when I noticed what looked like black smoke forming behind him inside the gazebo. "Is there a fire . . . ?" I began. Jayne grabbed my arm, stopping me as she noticed the billowing dark cloud.

I didn't smell anything burning, and despite the strong wind, the black shape didn't waver, its edges appearing to pulsate with radiant heat. Aware that we were staring at something behind him, Anthony turned around just as the plume of dark smoke began to take on an almost human form, a dense shadow with distinct arms and legs and a head, its sex undeterminable.

Anthony took a step up the stairs toward it, his hands clenched in fists as if ready to do battle. "Don't!" I shouted, but I was too late. His head jerked backward, and then an unseen punch to his midriff had him buckled over. He turned to escape down the stairs, but something was holding him back. His feet slipped on the top step of the gazebo, his arms flailing as he tried to stay upright. I moved toward him with my arms raised to push him back as Jayne shoved the stroller out of harm's way.

I thought I imagined a low laugh that sounded like distant thunder right before the weight of Anthony's body hit me, crumpling us both to the ground. My head hit the packed earth and for a moment I saw stars behind my eyelids, the air deserting my lungs. When I'd found my breath, I opened my eyes to find Anthony's face only inches above mine, his look of surprise mirroring my own, the dogs barking hysterically.

"So," drawled a familiar voice above us. "Did my invitation to the party get lost in the mail?"

I blinked and saw Jack peering down at us with a bemused expression, the tattered remains of the smoky cloud dissolving in the air above him, leaving behind only the foul stench of rotting flesh.

CHAPTER
5

I quietly closed the door of the nursery after helping Jayne put the children down for their naps, pausing with my ear to the door just in case JJ was faking being asleep. Amelia said that at the same age, Jack would wait until the door was closed before wreaking havoc in his bedroom, which had once included removing all of the stuffing from his mattress and shoving little balls of it into the heating vents in the floor.

"He's asleep, Melanie," Jayne whispered. "We can go. Besides, you have the video monitor. But you won't need it."

I gave her a leveling stare. "He's still Jack's son." I pressed my ear against the door one last time, then felt my sister tug on my arm.

"How's your head?" she asked.

"Just a little bump. Mrs. Houlihan gave me an aspirin. And a cookie. I'm feeling much better now." I rubbed my head.

She was silent for a moment as she looked at me. "Did you tell Jack everything?"

"Mostly. I told him why I was there to meet Anthony and about my conversation with Marc."

"And the figure in Nola's bedroom?

I studied a spot on the wallpaper. "Sophie said this is all hand painted. Did you know that?"

"Melanie." Jayne's voice was full of warning. "You need to tell him everything. And if you don't, then I might have to. I don't like the energy I feel when I pass by Nola's bedroom. We need to take care of it soon, and Jack will have to know."

"I know, and I agree," I said, realizing her hand was still on my arm. "I'm just trying to figure out where to begin. And I really don't want to bother Jack with any of it until I know something for sure. The spirits are not showing themselves to me, like they don't want to talk to me."

"Or they don't know they're dead," Jayne suggested.

"Or that. At least I know Louisa is here, protecting the children while I try to sort everything out. I promise to tell Jack everything when we're ready to deal with it, all right? He's got a lot on his mind right now."

I ignored her sideways glance as she kept her hand gripped firmly in the crook of my elbow, leading me down the stairs and in the direction of the parlor. "I think he'd rather know than be caught by surprise. Like finding you flat on your back in front of the gazebo in Battery Park with another man sprawled on top of you."

I couldn't argue with her logic, but I was distracted by the firm tug on my arm. "Where are we going?" I asked, suddenly aware that I was being led for a reason.

"Both of your parents are here, and Nola and Jack are with them in the parlor. They'd like to have a little chat." Despite my digging in my heels at the mention of an apparent audience waiting to talk with me, she'd managed to pull me into the doorway of the parlor, where everyone had gathered, drinking coffee and tea and snacking on a plate of what looked like Mrs. Houlihan's holiday fudge. Each piece was decorated with green marshmallow-covered Frosted Flakes and tiny cinnamon drops to make them look like holly. They were my favorite, and Mrs. Houlihan had been keeping them under lock and key. I headed in their direction, but Jayne pulled me back.

"Hello, Mellie." My mother smiled and stood, followed by my father and then Nola. Even the three dogs, previously asleep in front of the fire, stood and faced me.

I eyed them all suspiciously, my gaze settling on Jack as he approached. "Is this an intervention?"

"Funny you should use that word." Jack stopped in front of me and smiled. It wasn't one of his devastating ones, which I was used to. This was the smile of a man about to have teeth pulled. Without anesthesia.

"Why is it funny?" I hedged, looking for a way to snag a piece of fudge en route to my escape.

Jack seemed to be speaking from behind gritted teeth. "Because only someone who thinks they might need one would ever assume that a gathering of loved ones might be an intervention."

"Well, no one's died, so I know it's not a funeral," I said, crossing my arms.

"Mellie. Sweetheart," he said, placing his arm around my shoulders and pulling me toward him. I tried to retain my indignation, but the scent of him, that "Jackness" that I couldn't name but could always identify, made me almost lose track of why I was supposed to feel indignant.

"Mmm," I mumbled into the soft cashmere arm of his sweater, enjoying the feel and smell of him but keeping my body rigid.

"How old are you?"

I jerked back. "Excuse me? Are you about to make some dig about how you're younger than I am?"

"I would never," he said solemnly. "It's just that while you were upstairs, we've been having a conversation where we all agree that you're old enough to know who to trust. And that would be everyone in this room."

"I have no idea what you're—" He stopped me with a firm kiss on the mouth that erased my next words.

"Get a room," Nola grumbled.

He grinned his Jack grin. "Glad that still works. As I was saying, you should have told me and the rest of us about your meeting with Marc and your decision to meet with Anthony. We're all in this together, remember? We're a family. We love you. We love this house and everyone connected to it. Well, most of them. Your problems are our problems. And we solve them together."

"But with your deadline, you don't need any distractions—"

He put his finger on my lips, stopping me. "You, your safety, and our happiness are never a distraction."

"Mellie, dear," my mother said. "Your father and I divorced all those years ago because we didn't communicate and because we each thought we knew what was best for the other. And look where that led us."

I stepped away from Jack so I could gather my thoughts. It was hard to think with him standing so close. "I understand your concern. I do. And I thank you. But I decided to do it myself not because I don't trust you. It's because I thought I could handle it on my own. Maybe I was wro . . ." I couldn't finish the word. I tried again. "Maybe I moved a little too fast and maybe I should have waited before agreeing to meet with Anthony. And I did tell Jayne," I said in a small voice.

"Right before we left, before I could get reinforcements," Jayne added with look of admonishment.

I stepped over to the couch and sat down. "Well, I'm still not convinced that I can't handle it. I was just a little blindsided by . . ." My gaze slid to my father. "By an unexpected visitor."

One of the reasons for my parents' divorce had been my father's unwillingness to accept or try to understand something he couldn't see. In the years since our reconciliation, he'd learned to tolerate the unexplained events that seemed to follow my mother and me, but he'd never accepted them. While no longer openly hostile to the improbable idea that speaking with the dead might be a viable thing, he simply turned his head the other way so he didn't need to confront it, like an ostrich with its head stuck in the sand: If he couldn't see it, then it must not be there.

"Mellie," my mother said with a warning in her voice. "You should still have told us about Marc's threats. You could have put yourself in danger. Remember, we're always stronger together."

I knew she was referring not only to the members of our new family unit currently surrounding me, all of them responsible in part for the happiness, the house, and the family who lived within its ancient walls, but also to the mantra we'd used before and since Jayne came to us to bind our strength together to fight angry spirits. Although being together made our beacon brighter, it also made us much, much stronger.

I watched as Nola snuck a piece of fudge from the side table next to her and shoved it in her mouth. I frowned at her, but she looked up at the ceiling—something she'd probably learned from my father.

"I realize that now," I said slowly. I'd been independent of all family connections for so long that it was still hard for me to believe I wasn't expected to do it all on my own. Maybe, deep down, I missed that part of the old Melanie. Despite some of her quirks, which I was trying very hard to bury, my independent nature wasn't going to go down without a fight. Perhaps I didn't want it to. Perhaps I only wanted to temper it, to meld the old Melanie into the new to create a stronger me who was fiercely independent but also needed the love and support of others. I apparently didn't have a clue as to how to make that happen.

I chewed on my lip as I thought for a moment. "So, I guess this means I'm supposed to bring someone with me to the mausoleum at the Vanderhorst plantation cemetery? Although I don't see—"

"I'll go!" Nola stuck her hand up as if she were in a classroom.

"I believe you have school." Jack sent his daughter a stern glance before directing his attention back to me. "Obviously, if a Longo is involved, I need to go with you. They're like sand fleas—you don't realize they're about to swarm and bite until it's too late."

I threw up my hands. "See? Another distraction from your writing! Exactly what I was trying to avoid."

"I'll go with you," Jayne offered. "If Mother could watch the children, of course. It's probably not a good thing if the three of us go together."

I wasn't sure which part of her comment made me more uncomfortable—the fact that she understood already the complexities of our abilities or the fact that she'd moved from "Ginette" to "Mother." It wasn't that I'd expected her to ask for my permission, but for more than forty years, I'd believed myself to be the only person in the universe authorized to call her Mother.

"Or you can stay here with the children and Mother will come with me. Just like old times." I felt everyone looking at me.

My father cleared his throat. "Jayne said the last time Ginny encountered unpleasant spirits, it took her nearly a month to fully recover. So if Jayne wants to go with Melanie, then I'll go, too. For protection. Jayne's kind of new to all this."

I jerked my head in his direction. "Who are you, and what have you done with my father?"

He had the decency to appear abashed. "While Jayne and I have been working in the garden, we've had some long and interesting chats. I still think there has to be some scientific explanation for everything, but Jayne has made me understand that if it's real to her, then I should give her and you and Ginny the benefit of the doubt and go along with it. At least until I can offer an explanation."

I saw a serene smile of mutual appreciation pass between Jayne and my mother, leaving me with the familiar feeling of being picked last for a team in gym class. The new Melanie was grateful that my parents and sister now had a close relationship despite having been separated for most of Jayne's life. But the old Melanie felt the hurt and abandonment smoldering like a banked fire, sparking bits of burning ash into the room.

I smelled chocolate and turned to find Nola holding out the dish of fudge to me. I smiled gratefully and took a piece, more relieved than I cared to admit that I wasn't the only person who recognized the weirdness of what had just happened. I took a bite and chewed, glad for the excuse not to have to speak immediately.

"Then it's settled," my mother said. "You'll let us know when you're meeting after you speak with Anthony Longo?"

Before I could tell her I needed to consider my options, the doorbell rang. The dogs began their alarm barking, alerting us that a threat from potential marauders had invaded the piazza. It was never clear what sort of protection the dogs might offer other than ferocious licking around the ankle area, but they were serious about their role as our protection detail.

"I'll get it," Jack said, touching my shoulder on the way to the front door.

We heard the door open and then: "Jack—it's been ages!" Rebecca's voice carried through to the parlor as those remaining let out a collective groan.

"Rebecca, so good to see you. Feels like yesterday that we saw you last. You and Marc are like a stain we can't rub out completely."

"Oh, Jack," she said, standing on her tiptoes to air-kiss his cheek. "Always the joker."

"Am I?" he asked, his tone one of mock innocence.

I hurried after Jack so I could stop him before he said something so direct that she might actually get it, and then I'd have to spend hours making her feel better. My mother would insist, since Rebecca, by some horrendous twist of fate, was a cousin. A distant one, I kept reminding myself, but still a cousin.

She turned her attention to me, a crease between her brows. "Did you tell Jack about my dreams?"

I quickly shook my head and was lifting my index finger to my neck in a close approximation of slicing it to make her stop, but Jack turned too quickly and saw it.

"Really, Mellie? There's more to what you haven't told me?"

Before I could think of an appropriate response, Rebecca

said, "Oh, come on, Melanie. Surely your marriage is strong enough that you can tell each other everything—even the bad things. Right?"

"Apparently not," Jack said.

"Of course," I said simultaneously.

Jack met my gaze, his eyebrows raised expectantly.

Rebecca cleared her throat. "I had two dreams: one where a man without eyes and wearing old-fashioned clothes was after you and Melanie, and the other was of an unidentifiable person—I think it was a man—trying to bury you alive."

"I see," he said slowly. "Well, then, thanks for letting me know that I should avoid strange men and open graves. Just wish I'd heard it from my wife."

To my relief, Sophie appeared from behind Rebecca carrying a large box stuffed to the brim with piney-smelling greenery. Her face was covered but I knew it was her from the bright blue braids of hair that crisscrossed her scalp like she'd been attacked by a runaway sewing machine.

Blowing a pine bough away from her mouth, she said, "There are a bunch more boxes in the back of Veronica's SUV if someone could help bring it all in."

"I'll get it," Jack said. He took the box from Sophie, setting it down in the vestibule before turning his most charming smile on me. "We'll talk about this later."

I started to say something that might sound like an apology, but I was distracted by the small bag that Rebecca clutched in her pink-gloved hand. "What's in there?" I asked.

"Contraband." Sophie stepped in front of us, her hands on her hips. "I've already explained several times that all the decorations in the progressive dinner homes have to be authentic—as in what people would find in houses during the Revolutionary War period."

Rebecca looked outraged. "That's only because the colonists didn't have bedazzling guns back in the day!" She held aloft what looked like a small laser gun with a dangling electric cord. "But if they did, I'm sure all of their pineapples and mobcaps would have been bedazzled."

Sophie took a step toward Rebecca. "If you don't put that thing away, it won't be fruit and caps getting bedazzled!"

"Stop!" I shouted, grabbing the gun from Rebecca's hand. "I'm sure we can speak rationally about this later. Right now, let's get everything inside to see what we have and decide where it's going to go, all right?"

An icy wind blew through the door, even colder than the chilly November day, and I looked up to see Veronica and Jack entering the vestibule, followed by Veronica's husband, Michael. I smelled Vanilla Musk perfume before I saw the blob of light hovering behind them, announcing a familiar presence.

I greeted the newcomers, hoping Michael would leave as soon as he'd deposited the bags he'd brought into the house. Ever since our uncomfortable confrontation in which he'd told me in no uncertain terms that I was to have nothing to do with helping his wife in her quest to find out what had happened to her sister more than twenty years before, I hadn't spoken two words to him. I hoped he was as eager to avoid me as I was to avoid him.

I turned toward Veronica and smiled. "Glad to see you're wearing black and white, as I have a feeling we might need to play referee with Rebecca and Sophie." I picked up several bags containing dried oranges and cloves and brought them to the dining room table to be artfully displayed by someone besides myself, hoping by the time I'd returned, Michael would be gone.

"Hello, Melanie." Michael's voice was close to my ear, making me drop one of the bags on the smooth dark wood of the table, spilling oranges, which began to roll. I was on the opposite side of the table and couldn't reach them before they fell off the edge, my view blocked by the ginormous centerpiece of flowers and greens from the garden that Mrs. Houlihan changed almost daily. I stood frozen, waiting for the sound of the oranges splatting on the floor.

When all I heard was the sound of General Lee licking himself under the table, I walked slowly to the other side and was brought up short by the sight of six plump oranges lined up in a neat row like soldiers, perched precariously at the table's edge.

"How did you do that?" Michael asked, his voice a little higher than usual.

I searched the room for Adrienne, Veronica's spectral sister, wondering why she was hiding from me. But I knew she was there. I could smell her perfume as if it had just been sprayed in the air in front of me.

I met his gaze. "Magic," I said.

He didn't smile. "I don't believe in magic."

"I don't think you need to believe in magic to see it."

He picked up one of the oranges to examine it, perhaps hoping to find a squared bottom. Without looking at me, he said, "I'm glad Veronica has found something to occupy herself with other than the pointless search for her sister's murderer. I hope you remember what I said before—about how important it is to me that you don't get involved with Veronica's little . . . obsession. It will go away a lot faster if it's not validated."

I tried to keep my temper in check. "I don't find the desire to solve her sister's murder an 'obsession.' I think it's a reasonable quest. As for me helping her, she hasn't asked."

He was still holding the orange as his gaze shot back to meet mine. "And if she does? I know she wants you to channel—or whatever it is you say you do to speak with dead people—Adrienne. Would you say yes?"

"I've never claimed to communicate with the dead." This, at least, was true. Denial was my best friend when it came to my special "gift." "But I'd like to think I could help Veronica in other ways to deal with her grief, and if she asks, I'd say yes."

Very carefully and deliberately, he put the orange down in the middle of the table. He held his hands out, palms up, his face a mask of desperation. "I don't know what to do, Melanie. Veronica talks about nothing else, like she believes finding out who killed Adrienne will make her come back. I really fear for Veronica's mental health." He closed his eyes for a long moment. "Please, Melanie. Don't get involved. You won't be helping her, and you might actually be hurting her. Veronica needs to move on with her life, and this is just holding her back." He stopped speaking for a moment, but I could tell he had more to say; he just wasn't sure how much or if he should continue at all.

Finally, he said, "It's affecting Lindsey in a negative way. She can barely sleep at night and her grades at school are slipping." He pursed his lips. "It's ruining our marriage."

I folded my arms across my chest. "I'm sorry, Michael. I really am. But all I can do is promise not to encourage her. I can't do any more than that."

"Then you'll probably regret it. I'm sure Nola wouldn't be thrilled if Lindsey were forbidden from seeing her. Or if your talents were advertised in a public way."

His mouth twitched as he held back either anger or tears; I couldn't tell which. His voice was very quiet when he spoke. "I want our lives back, and I see you as a potential interference to that happening. Please, Melanie. Please don't encourage her."

"I won't. But assuming I could help, don't you want to know the truth of what happened?"

He shrugged. "We already do—Adrienne's boyfriend killed her and his fraternity brothers helped give him an alibi and cover it up so he got away with it. Veronica thinks this necklace she found means someone else was involved, but I think it's just wishful thinking. Even Detective Riley can't find any connection." Michael shook his head. "I wish we'd never found that stupid necklace."

I began leading him from the dining room. "Yes, well, maybe this will run its course. Anyway, I'm sure we'll be busy with the decorating tonight, so no time to speak of murder or supposed evidence, all right? We'll be happy to drive Veronica home, so no need to stick around."

A solid thud from behind me made me spin around in

time to see an orange plop to the ground at Michael's feet,
a red splotch covering the spot where the fruit must have
collided with his jaw.

His eyes were wide as he looked from me to the orange,
then quickly turned to examine the room, as if expecting to
see someone else.

"Sorry about that," I said. "They're supposed to be dried.
A fresh one must have slipped into the box." I pretended that
that was the only thing weird about the flying fruit.

"How did you do that?" he asked, holding the orange
and looking around the room.

"Magic," I said with a lot of force, as if that might make
him believe it. With a smile, I left the room, Michael's footsteps hurrying after me, the scent of Adrienne's perfume
following close behind.

CHAPTER
6

My father picked up General Lee before reluctantly placing him inside my car and then sliding in next to him in the backseat. "Is this really necessary?" he asked, moving closer to the dog and giving him a firm scratch behind his ears.

"Yes," Jayne said, buckling her seat belt next to me. "There are plenty of dogs looking for homes, and we don't want to be part of the problem. Porgy and Bess are going in for their procedures next week, so this is good practice for all of us."

By the time I pulled out onto the street, General Lee was panting heavily, his eyes wide with anxiety. I glanced accusingly in the rearview mirror at my father. "Did you tell him where we were going?"

"I might have mentioned it. Seemed like a man-to-man talk was necessary."

I rolled my eyes. We were on the way to the mausoleum to meet Anthony, and since we were passing the veterinary clinic, Jayne had made an appointment to have General Lee neutered. When I'd inherited him, having never had a dog before and knowing nothing about dogs, I'd had no idea how old he was or that all of his equipment was intact until Porgy and Bess came along. Both Nola and Jayne had been badgering me ever since to get him "taken care of," but every time I'd asked him about it, he'd seemed less than enthusiastic. The night before, Nola had made a special dessert in General Lee's honor consisting of mixed nuts

rolled into sugarless and vegan cookie dough and rounded
into the shape of small balls. They were delicious. But
maybe I was just desperate for a cookie.

I turned up the heat in the car, then opened a rear window a bit so General Lee could stick out his head, one of
his favorite activities. But he ignored the beckoning window, remaining stoic and looking straight ahead like a soldier heading into battle.

When we dropped him off, I gave him a kiss on top of
his head, then waited as the nurse led him away. I called
after him, "Remember, sweet boy, that we have a playdate
with Cindy Lou Who when this is all over!"

General Lee looked back once and gave a low *woof* before moving in front of the nurse toward the door, his tail
and head held high. I was embarrassed to find I had tears in
my eyes and quickly wiped them away before I returned to
the car.

We headed south on Highway 17 over the Ashley River
Bridge toward Highway 61. Although it wasn't as scenic as
the Ravenel Bridge over the Cooper, which allowed drivers
to admire the skyline of the Holy City and the spires of the
many churches that gave Charleston its nickname, I almost
enjoyed the views of the Ashley and the marshes more.
Most likely because I heard Sophie's disparaging voice
every time I spotted a cruise ship in the Port of Charleston
as I crossed the Ravenel Bridge.

There was still a lot of mumbling among residents about
the height of the cruise ships that docked there, overwhelming the historic buildings that crouched in their shadows
like rabbits sighting a hawk. Sophie's voice had taken up
residence in my brain as my conscience, it seemed, as I also
heard it when I searched for mass-produced wallpaper to
replace the hand-painted strips in the dining room, or used
an electric sander to take off stubborn paint on the nursery
door.

As we turned off Highway 17, Jayne pointed at a bill-
board advertising visits to the USS *Yorktown*, docked at
Patriots Point in Mt. Pleasant. "Oh, look—an aircraft car-

rier," Jayne said, tapping on the window. "Since Mother said she's free all day to watch the children, maybe another day the three of us could . . ."

I looked at her in horror. I'd made the mistake of once joining Nola's class on a tour of the ship, embarrassing myself by having to leave only fifteen minutes after boarding. I should have assumed that many of the men who'd served on the ship over its long history might never have left and might have been waiting all this time for someone to talk to.

Before I'd been politely escorted off the ship, Nola told me that I'd been singing ABBA's "Take a Chance on Me" so loudly that no one could hear the tour guide. I hadn't remembered that part, my attention focused on the crush of wounded men calling my name and moving toward me, and the sight of one man in uniform smiling, half of his face missing, telling me his name was John and he needed to get home to see his girl, Dolores. I remembered gasping for air, and breathing in the stench of unwashed bodies and fresh blood, and hearing my name being repeated over and over.

"No." I shook my head to emphasize the word. I didn't look at her, hoping my abrupt answer would be all she needed.

My father leaned forward from the backseat. "Probably not a good idea, Jayne. I mean, besides a cemetery or hospital, I'd pick an old aircraft carrier that's seen wartime as being a pretty busy hotbed of paranormal activity, if such a thing existed. According to our conversations, that would make sense, right?"

Jayne sent him a warm smile. "You're absolutely right. Thanks."

I stole a peek at my father just to make sure this wasn't a joke. I was happy he was finally beginning to listen to someone on a subject that had always been taboo with us. And I was even happier that Jayne had been completely accepted by him. But, like a tiny splinter stuck beneath the skin, his ease with listening to Jayne and trying to see her point of view bothered me. A small annoyance that could easily be brushed aside. Or left to fester. Or, my favorite, ignored long enough that it went away on its own. I deliberately focused my attention on the passing landscape to distract myself from recalling all the times that strategy had failed dismally.

Autumn in the Lowcountry is not so much about the variable temperatures or the fact that we sometimes get four seasons in the space of a single week. Instead, the change of seasons is marked by a gradual shift in light and the leaching of colors from the tall sea grass and trees. Only the live oaks and southern magnolias clung to their greens, while all else faded to hazy golds and browns. New England's claim to fame for its beautiful fall foliage was rightfully earned, but fall in the Lowcountry wore its own jeweled crown. It was one of the growing reasons why I loved calling this place my home. I'd probably love it a lot more if it wasn't so full of restless spirits, but at least the scenery was nice.

Jayne read the directions Anthony had given me, although they'd been so simple I hadn't really needed to write them down. Drive about ten miles on 61, then take a right on an unmarked road, then turn at the red arrow on a wooden marker.

I missed the arrow the first time and had to make a U-turn. We bumped along an unpaved road for a short distance before coming to a large wooden sign nailed to an ancient tree, and I was glad Sophie wasn't there to see it. The blue paint had faded, but the large lettering was easy to read. GALLEN HALL PLANTATION.

Jayne looked at me. "Gallen Hall? I thought the Vanderhorst plantation was called Magnolia Ridge."

"It's actually the same place—just a different name. It's a convoluted story, so I'll tell you later—but I'm glad Anthony thought to mention it so I wouldn't be driving all over looking for the wrong plantation. Apparently, things change slowly in South Carolina, because most people around here still refer to it as Magnolia Ridge even though the name change happened two hundred years ago. If I'd driven around asking for Gallen Hall, we might still be looking."

We both turned back to the sign. Beneath the plantation's name were the edges of black letters that were visible over deep and repeated gashes in the wood that appeared to have been made with a sharp stick. Or a knife. Clearly, someone was trying to obliterate whatever had been written there. I wondered if it had something to do with the failed winery. I could imagine that kind of treachery between brothers might lend itself to the force and violence needed for that kind of damage.

We passed through an open iron gate set between brick pillars, each with a concrete pineapple perched on top. According to Sophie, it was the symbol of hospitality in Charleston, hence the two dozen pineapples she'd ordered for my house for the progressive dinner. I'd told her that I hated pineapple and had given her a few specific suggestions as to what she could do with the leftovers after the tour. She hadn't been amused.

As I drove down the long road edged with old-growth trees, my father leaned forward, peering through the windshield from the backseat. "So, this used to belong to the same Vanderhorsts who owned your house."

I nodded. "Although it had passed out of the family by the time Nevin Vanderhorst left Fifty-five Tradd Street to me." We all jerked as I swerved to miss a large rock in the middle of the road. "Joseph Longo owned it for a short time in the twenties, and more recently Marc Longo purchased the plantation, believing the Confederate diamonds were hidden here, and when he discovered that they weren't, he tried to buy my house, believing—correctly, as it turned out—that they were there. Not that we allowed him to find them first."

My father sat back in his seat. "Almost makes you feel sorry for the guy."

"No, it doesn't," Jayne and I said in unison.

"Especially because he's still not done trying to own my house," I added. "But as our lovely librarian, Yvonne Craig at the Historical Society Library, has said, he'll get what's coming to him. Her only wish is that we're all there to witness it."

Almost under his breath, my father said, "Vanderhorst. Vanderhorst." He tapped his fingers against the leather back of my seat.

"What is it, Dad?" I asked.

"I know I recently read something about the Vanderhorsts. Yvonne's been helping me find old plans and articles in the archives about the gardens at our house and yours, so I've been reading a lot about the Vanderhorsts." He scratched his head. "Something you said about the diamonds is ringing a bell." He was silent for a moment, and when I glanced in the rearview mirror he was pursing his lips. He continued. "I remember making a copy of the article for you and sticking it somewhere, and then I promptly forgot all about it. I was distracted by a sketch I'd found of the parterre garden from our house on Legare and got all excited."

I shared a glance with Jayne. "Yes, well, we found all the diamonds in the grandfather clock, remember? Still, I'd be interested in seeing the article. I've been working on a scrapbook for Nola, and I think a copy of it might have a place in the section on what our lives were like before she joined us. I don't have a lot of material for when she was a baby and little girl, so I thought miscellanea of Jack and me and our lives before she came to live with us might be fun for her. I mean, the whole mystery of the Confederate diamonds is how Jack and I met."

"I'll look for it," he said. "And we can ask Yvonne. She has a memory like an elephant's."

Yvonne was probably in her eighties but looked and acted like someone two decades younger. She had a terrible crush on Jack, with whom she'd been working for years on his book research, but I forgave her because I understood all too well how irresistible Jack's charms were. It's one of the reasons he had three children, none of them planned.

We came to an intersection and I stopped the car. A directional sign lay faceup, dirty and stained from the elements, half of a wooden stake still in the ground, its top half jagged and splintered where it had been decapitated. The letters on the sign were barely legible: GALLEN HALL WINERY.

"Anthony said the cemetery and mausoleum were near the house, so I'm guessing it must be this way." I drove in the opposite direction of the defunct winery. I assumed we were heading in the direction of the Ashley River, as most river plantations had direct access to the river for shipping crops and for basic travel. I'd learned all that and more, apparently by osmosis, from hanging around Sophie. I'd even found myself using terms like *curtilage* and *fenestration* and wondering out loud if a particular paint color was historically accurate for a specific neighborhood when discussing a real estate listing.

The tall pines fell away, revealing an alley of magnolias, a leftover from the founding Vanderhorsts. I knew they weren't the original trees, the life span of a magnolia being only eighty to one hundred and twenty years, although some were reported to be at least ten times older than that. But these were at least one hundred years old, their dark trunks thick and winding, giving the appearance of open hands with fingers holding bowls of wayward branches with shiny leaves. I imagined it was glorious to travel through the alley when the magnolias were in bloom in the spring. Yet a heavy feeling of dread that seemed to saturate the air as we drew closer made me hope that I wouldn't be coming back.

"You feel that?" Jayne asked quietly.

I nodded, the hair on the back of my neck pricking at my skin like sharp fingernails. A large house loomed at the end of the alley, and directly to the left of it, separated by an enormous live oak surrounded by benches in its generous shade, lay the cemetery. An elaborate and rusted iron fence with a closed gate would have informed any visitor what it was, but I knew because of the cluster of people in fashions from past centuries that were pressed against the inside of the gate, looking directly at us.

I started singing a loud rendition of "Knowing Me, Knowing You" while Jayne did her best to recall enough of the lyrics to sing along with me as we both tried to drown out the sound of multiple voices speaking at once.

"Stop!" my father shouted from the backseat. "What are you doing?"

I slammed on the brakes, jerking us all forward in our seat belts. "Sorry," I said, keeping my face averted from the cemetery so they'd take the hint that we didn't want to talk. "I thought before we went inside I'd tell you what Sophie told me about the house."

"I thought you already did." I met my father's annoyed gaze in the rearview mirror.

I swallowed, relieved to hear the voices receding but needing more time to get them to stop before I was prepared to get out of the car. "Yes, but not about the architecture." I gave him a shaky smile. "As you can probably tell, it's not Greek Revival. The original house was built by a bachelor and was a simple farmhouse. By the time his grandson inherited the property in the early half of the nineteenth century and got married, the plantation was much more profitable. It was his wife who insisted on something grander, in accordance with their place in society, and she wanted what was all the rage in England at the time, and that was Italianate."

I wasn't exactly sure what features were required to make it fit in the Italianate category, but I was going only on what Sophie told me and that it looked nothing like Tara in *Gone With the Wind*. I just needed a reason not to have to continue on the road, mostly due to the British soldier in full redcoat uniform who was at that moment standing in the middle of the alley and pointing his musket directly at us.

A quick intake of breath let me know that Jayne saw him, too, but my father appeared unaware of the soldier or his gun as he continued speaking. "Was she the one who changed the name of the plantation from Magnolia Ridge to Gallen Hall?"

"No," I said, the tremor in my voice almost imperceptible. "That was done around the time of the British occupation of Charleston during the Revolution, not that long after the first house was built. But all of the older maps and even some of the new ones still refer to it as Vanderhorst–Magnolia Ridge Plantation. I wonder if it bothered the subsequent owners that people still referred to it that way—as if the Vanderhorsts had never left."

"Maybe they haven't," Jayne said, half under her breath.

I gave her a sharp glance, noticing how she was sitting up straight, her gaze focused on the road ahead of us.

I continued. "Sophie wasn't able to find out the reason for the name change but thinks it might have had something to do with a family rivalry the Vanderhorsts had with the Draytons. The Draytons' Magnolia Plantation was established around the same time, but the Vanderhorsts wanted the name for their own plantation, so they just added the word *Ridge* to differentiate. Someone eventually saw reason and changed the name to avoid confusion. To make sure that everyone knew which plantation they were visiting, the Vanderhorsts added real peacocks to the lawn, where they flourished until the Civil War."

As I stared out the windshield, the specter of the soldier began to shimmer as waves of light rose from the ground like steam, before he disappeared completely.

"What happened to the peacocks?" Jayne's voice was stronger than mine had been, but I could still detect a slight quaver.

"They ate them." We exchanged a glance. "It was during the war and everybody was starving." I frowned as the sun glinted off of what could have been a part of a musket that was no longer there. "On a happier note, according to Sophie, a peacock symbol has been used on everything that ever originated from the plantation since the name change, including rice barrels and all of the furniture. I bet it was one of the first uses of a logo."

"Can we keep going?" my father asked impatiently. "I'm speaking at the gardening club at our meeting tonight, and I'd like to be able to go over my notes first."

"Of course," I said, reluctantly putting my foot on the gas again and moving forward down the lane. The full house had just come into view when we heard the sound of a siren behind us. I moved my car to the side for the unmarked car with the flashing dashboard light to pass, blowing up dirt onto my car before it came to a squealing stop in the circular drive right at the front steps of the house. Not sure what I was supposed to do, I followed, parking my car behind it.

Detective Riley, wearing dark sunglasses and a jacket and tie, stepped out of the driver's-side door and looked back at us with an obvious frown. Jayne tensed beside me. "He's tall. His shirt is blue."

My father had already stepped out of our car and was walking toward the man with an outstretched hand and smiling with familiarity. I grabbed my sister's shoulder and shook it gently. "Come on, Jayne. Get it together. We've been practicing, remember? It's Detective Riley. Thomas. We know him. You've been on dates with him. He's a nice guy."

I watched as she swallowed, nodding. "I can do this."

"Yes," I said, opening my door. "You can. Unless you want to pretend you're a dumbstruck teenager meeting Elvis for the first time."

We walked together toward the detective, who greeted us both with a perfunctory nod, reminding me that Jayne said they'd had a fight. "So good to see you, Thomas," I said with a smile, unused to his brusque greeting. "Why are you here?"

His gaze moved to Jayne and then back to me. "I was about to ask you the same question."

Jayne spoke up before I could. "We're meeting with Anthony Longo." Her words were slow and deliberate, but at least they were coherent.

His frown deepened. "Well, I'm afraid he's not here."

"He's not? Because we have an appointment." I paused. "And how would you know he's not here?"

"Because he's in the hospital. Someone tried to run him off the road on the Crosstown. He'll be okay, but his car is totaled."

"Thank goodness," I said, the skin of my neck prickling even more. "What happened?"

He was silent for a moment, as if deciding how much he could say. "It's not clear, although witnesses say it appeared to be a single-car accident. He wasn't exactly . . . coherent. Kept talking about someone hiding in his backseat and causing him to wreck. And then he said he was meeting someone out here at the winery and that he was afraid the same person might be here to harm them. I thought I should check it out. Imagine my surprise to find it's you."

While we'd been talking, my father had begun heading toward the cemetery, walking with a limp I knew he didn't have.

"Dad? Where are you going?"

He continued walking toward the cemetery gate as if he hadn't heard me.

Jayne began moving toward him. "Dad?" she called, but I was too worried about him to be annoyed at her use of the word Dad. "What's wrong?"

As he approached the gate, it swung open with a loud squeal of rust and old iron.

"Stop!" I yelled, the temperature plummeting.

He stopped, then slowly turned around, but it wasn't him. Not really. It was the same salt-and-pepper hair, the same strong jaw and crooked nose from having been broken several times in bar fights before he'd gotten sober. But it wasn't my father. Whoever it was had distorted his features, making them run together like ink in rain.

I stopped ten feet in front of him, the scent of something vile sliding off of him in waves. Bile rose in my throat. "Daddy?" I said, using the name I hadn't called him since I was six.

His mouth twisted and his eyes went hollow. "Go! Away!" The voice was loud and booming and definitely not his. His knees began to buckle, but I couldn't move. It was as if someone was holding my arms behind me. Thomas sprinted forward and reached my father before he could hit the ground.

CHAPTER

7

I stood in the back garden watching Sophie's graduate students—the few who agreed to come back—excavate the cistern, staying far enough back so that the whispers of unseen people remained unintelligible. Her graduate assistant, Meghan Black, wore cute bow-shaped earmuffs and what appeared to be a pink tool belt over a quilted Burberry jacket while she bent over a row of muddy bricks with a small brush. I could only wonder what her monthly dry-cleaning bill must be. Maybe her mother paid for that, along with the clothes.

I recalled what Anthony had said about the cistern's bricks having come from the mausoleum at Gallen Hall and knew he was right. Ever since I'd seen the specter of the man holding the piece of jewelry standing by its edge, I'd known something besides buried pottery and silverware was causing the air in the back garden to beat like the wings of a bird. I'd just ignored the truth, something at which I was very proficient. I wasn't sure if the dark shadow in Nola's room was related to the cistern, too, or simply something unpleasant brought forth during an unfortunate (and hopefully isolated) Ouija board game Nola had played with her friends Lindsey and Alston. Or maybe they were connected somehow, the energies of three teenage girls summoning the dark spirits that lurked in all shadows, waiting for an opportunity to invade our lives.

"You sure look sexy when you're thinking."

I didn't startle, having sensed Jack's presence from the

moment he entered the garden, my awareness of him like that of the ocean's tides for the moon. Or, as he'd once told me, like the wrong paint color for the Board of Architectural Review. He wasn't wrong.

He kissed the side of my neck, then slid his arm around my shoulders. I hadn't thought to put on a coat, and I was grateful for his warmth. "Aren't you cold?" he asked, pulling me against him.

"I didn't plan to be out here very long. I'm waiting for another designer to interview and thought I'd come check on the progress while I waited. I'd really like this to be done before the progressive dinner. It's such an eyesore."

"Well, even if it's still here, I'm sure your dad can make it look like it was designed to be here by Loutrel Briggs himself. Speaking of which, how is your dad? When I spoke with him last night, he said he was fine by the time he was loaded back into the car and denies any memory of what happened."

"Yep," I said. "Only now he's insisting that he might have blacked out because his blood pressure dipped. And he's still not speaking to me because I insisted that he stay in bed and miss his gardening club meeting yesterday."

"That's pretty serious. Did you have to lock him in his bedroom and bolt the windows? Either that or he really was hurting. That's the only thing that would make him listen."

"Exactly what I thought. You know he loves his gardening club. The only thing that pacified him was Jayne's assurance that she would speak for him at the meeting since she was already familiar with his notes on the subject matter. They apparently spend a lot of time together in the garden."

"Thank goodness for Jayne, then," he said.

"Yeah. Thank goodness." The white-hot seed of *something* that had implanted itself in my stomach yesterday when Jayne had made her offer and my dad had accepted seemed to explode in fireworks of heat as I relived the conversation. I turned my head to look up at Jack. "Aren't you supposed to be writing?"

He averted his gaze, studying the activity inside the cistern with great interest. "I'm just taking a break—I'm allowed breaks, aren't I?" His voice held an unfamiliar edge to it.

"Of course. But I heard you playing with the children in the nursery, so I was just wondering. Everything all right?"

"It's fine," he said quickly. "Just working through a scene with Button Pinckney and her sister-in-law," he said, referring to the former owners of Jayne's house on South Battery. "It's tough creating dialogue for real people, that's all."

"I'm sure it is," I said. "But I have every confidence your book will be the next *Midnight in the Garden of Good and Evil*. Isn't that what your editor said?"

"Former editor," Jack corrected, his expression solemn.

My gaze traveled behind him to Nola's bedroom window, and I wondered if the passing shadow had been my imagination. *It's now or never.* I took a deep breath and did a proverbial girding of my loins. "I need to show you something."

He quirked an eyebrow and gave me a lascivious grin. "Me, too. Do we have time?"

I gave him a playful shove, wondering if he'd ever grow up and hoping that he wouldn't. "That's not what I meant. I have a picture that Meghan took of the back of the house. There's something in it you need to see."

He glanced over at Meghan, happily brushing mud off of what looked like an old stick. "She just came back to work today after having her cast removed. When did she take the picture?" His eyes narrowed as he regarded me.

"Hello?" A tall man wearing an immaculate gray suit stood on the path that led from around the side of the house. "Your nanny was on the front porch with two of the most adorable babies and she told me I could find you two back here." He walked closer with his hand outstretched. "I'm Greco."

I was too relieved by my temporary reprieve to be startled by the stranger's appearance. He shook both of our hands as we introduced ourselves, then waited for us to speak. When we didn't, he prompted, "The designer. We had an appointment?"

I looked at him with confusion, taking in the yellow silk Hermès tie and the coordinating pocket square in his jacket. He was very tall with intelligent eyes and a warm smile and, even better, came without any spiritual hangers-on. "Yes," I said, "but I was expecting someone named Jimmy—a friend of our handyman, Rich Kobylt. Did I misunderstand?"

He laughed. "My last name is Del Greco, but my first name is James—or Jimmy, according to my friends and family. My sister was the one who said that Greco sounded more like a designer."

Jack grinned, clearly amused. "Can't argue with that. So you and Rich are good friends, huh?"

Greco nodded. "We've been best friends since grade school. We were even roommates at Clemson. Stayed in touch even after I left for nursing school. I'm an RN and MSN, but after all my friends and family started asking for my design help, I realized I was in the wrong profession."

Jack nodded in understanding. "I sometimes wonder the same thing. Mellie has said more than once that I'm always the person to go to when it comes to placing the stray ottoman or accessorizing a bookshelf."

Greco looked at Jack with appreciation. "It's a skill everybody thinks they have, but few actually do."

"Yes, well," I said, leading him toward the kitchen door and wondering if it would be appropriate to ask him what he and Rich Kobylt had in common, since it apparently wasn't fashion.

General Lee, wearing his cone of shame, stood facing the wall when we walked into the kitchen. Even though the cone was clear, he acted as if he couldn't see through it and nobody could see him. Except for eating and drinking and going outside briefly to relieve himself, he'd stayed in that position, stoically accepting his fate. It was sad and sweet at the same time, and I gave him extra treats when no one was looking and gave him a countdown to when he could see Cindy Lou Who. I wasn't sure which perked him up more.

"Good heavens," Greco said, coming to a full stop when he spotted the dog. "Do you do that to everyone who offends you?"

I was a little resentful that he addressed his question to me.

I frowned and Jack came to my rescue. "That's General Lee. He's just had his little procedure."

General Lee moved his head long enough to give us a deep, soulful look before resuming his examination of the wall paint.

"Poor little guy," Greco said. "I'd pet him, but I get the feeling he'd rather be alone right now."

Jack nodded. "He's holding up well, under the circumstances, but he keeps shooting me warning glances not to get in the car with Mellie and allow her in the driver's seat."

Greco raised his eyebrows but, being an apparently intelligent man, kept silent.

After he declined my offer of refreshments, I led the way up the stairs while he took his time eyeing the foyer with obvious appreciation. "So," Greco said as we walked, "have you met with any other designers?"

Jack coughed. "Only about a dozen or two. Mellie is . . ."

"Particular," I offered.

"Picky," Jack said at the same time.

I frowned at Jack. "By 'picky' he means that I like things . . ."

"Her way," Jack offered. "Besides impeccable taste and the ability to work within a budget, any designer we hire will also need to have some knowledge of psychology—especially obsessive-compulsive disorders."

My elbow contacted with Jack's hard stomach, eliciting a satisfying *oomph*.

"And probably self-defense," Jack continued. "It's a

good thing you have a nursing degree—that's definitely in your favor. Do you know how to use a labeling gun by any chance?"

Turning my back on Jack, I faced Greco. "Ignore him. He's a writer and lives in a fantasy world most of the time, so you really never know what's going to come out of his mouth next."

"Good to know," the designer said, looking refreshingly unfazed. Several of the other designers I'd interviewed had left before we'd even climbed the stairs, so I took this as a good omen.

The bedroom door was shut, as it had been since we'd moved Nola into the guest room in March, when I'd seen the face in her window and sensed the dark shadow hovering in the upstairs hallway. It was still there, waiting. And watching. I just wasn't sure for what. Or for how long.

When I'd given the excuse of needing to redecorate Nola's room to move her out, I'd had the worry of not having the money to spend on a major redo. But I'd been saved by my mother and Amelia agreeing it was a great idea since Nola was a young woman now and her bedroom should reflect her growing maturity. They'd been so enthusiastic that they'd decided to split the cost as a Christmas gift to Nola.

"So," I said, turning around to face the two men. "This is Nola's room. She just started her junior year at Ashley Hall and we'd like to give her a room that not only reflects her eclectic tastes for her to enjoy now, but will be a warm and comfortable retreat to come home to once she starts college."

We stood smiling at each other in the hallway for a long moment before Jack coughed. "Maybe we should go inside and take a look?"

"Yes," I said. "Of course." I put my hand on the door-knob and turned. Nothing happened.

"Is it locked?" Jack asked, stepping in front of me to try.

"I hope not," I said, "since there's only one key and it's

usually kept on the inside of the door." Our eyes met in mutual understanding.

Greco chimed in. "These old houses usually have a skeleton key. Maybe your housekeeper knows where it is?"

"Yes," I agreed, "but I don't think it's locked. It's just . . . stuck."

Jack tried turning the knob again, pushing hard against the door with the side of his body. I could see it give, the outline of light peeking out from around the frame. It definitely wasn't locked, then. But something was holding it closed from the other side.

The front door downstairs opened and closed. "Hello?" Nola called. "Anyone home?" I bit my lip, not wanting her to see the struggle and understand the reason for it. I heard the sound of her book bag being dropped at the bottom of the stairs—I needed to talk to her about that again—and then her feet running up the stairs, and knew I was too late to stop her.

"Need help?" she asked, moving toward her bedroom.

"It's all right . . ." I began, but she'd already squeezed in front of Jack, assessed the situation, and turned the knob. The door swung open. We stood staring into the space, unsure of what to say.

The first thing I noticed was the scent of horse and leather, along with the lingering odor of gunpowder. I wrinkled my nose, wondering why it seemed so familiar when it shouldn't, and recalled that I had smelled it recently. The second thing I noticed was that all the remaining furniture and bedding had been stacked on the rug, a teetering stepladder that reached the top of the posts of the antique bed. What looked like dried mud had been smeared on the walls and at first glance appeared to be random strokes and shapes. But when I looked closer I could see the individual letters formed a single word, splashed on the wall with fury and anger, the mud thick with hate. *Betrayed*.

"Well," Greco said, stepping purposefully into the room,

hands on hips, and then turning around to inspect the carnage. "It looks like we have a lot of work to do here."

Jack, Nola, and I shared surprised looks before turning our gazes back to the designer. "You're hired," I said, and then, without thought, I hugged him.

CHAPTER
8

I sat in a plastic folding chair in an empty listing, passing the time with a box of dried oranges, jabbing cloves into them in the pattern Sophie had dictated for the pomander balls she wanted strewn in every wreath and centerpiece in every house for the progressive dinner. It was taking me longer than expected because getting the cloves evenly spaced was more challenging than I'd thought it should be, even using the pocket-sized ruler I thankfully had in my purse. It was also possible that I was dragging out the chore because of the extra pleasure I got in envisioning each orange as a voodoo doll of my former best friend.

I was in no hurry to finish, since Sophie had so kindly stuffed the backseat of my car with boxwood cuttings that needed "conditioning" before we could use them in our Colonial-wreath-making workshop. "Conditioning" meant a lot of cutting, scraping, recutting, and soaking—four steps too many, in my opinion. I was hoping I'd have time to stop by a craft shop and buy plastic ones. A lot less trouble and they'd last forever. Hopefully, Sophie wouldn't be able to tell the difference.

This house was on State Street and belonged to a client whose listing I'd accepted only because I'd already sold them another home on Gibbes. I usually didn't do open houses because even when I was supposed to be alone in the house, I never really was, and I found it awkward trying to explain my sudden outbursts of singing to unsuspecting home browsers.

But this house was a relatively new (circa 2002) estate home—or, as Sophie referred to it, an aberration of architectural and historic sensibilities—built to loosely resemble the house that had originally been on the lot before being abandoned and then condemned by the city. I remembered how Sophie had dressed in black and wept whenever she passed the empty lot, then became openly hostile when she saw the opulent home being built in its place. It was a Charleston double house on steroids, according to Sophie, whose chief complaint was that the house was new. The owners, my clients, were a nice middle-aged couple from Boston who'd been happy in the house for several years until they heard that the most desirable location to own a home in Charleston was South of Broad. I didn't agree, but a double commission wasn't something I could ignore. Especially not now.

I heard the front gate close and I stood to look through the window, expecting another Realtor and her clients for a second showing. I waited until I heard footsteps on the porch, then opened the door before they had a chance to hear the doorbell chime "Dixie." The owners had thought it cute and that it might make their neighbors warm up to them. It hadn't.

"Anthony!" I said in surprise, taking in the crutches he was using because of a sprained ankle, the bruises on his face, and his arm in a sling—all apparently from the car accident.

"Sorry," he said. "I probably should have let you know I was coming. I called your office, and that nice Miss Jolly told me you were here."

Our receptionist was usually a better gatekeeper, but I was sure Anthony had used his considerable charm. I stood back and held the door open for him, watching as he looked around as if hoping to see someone.

"Is your sister here?"

"No—she's watching my children. She's our nanny."

He looked chagrined. "Of course. I was just . . . Never

mind. I came to apologize for the other day, and hopefully make another appointment for us to visit the mausoleum."

I shuddered at the memory of my father and the dark voice that had erupted from his mouth like bile. "I'm not sure. . . ."

"Someone messed with my car, Melanie. I know I won't be able to prove it, but my steering wheel was like something possessed. I couldn't control it—it was like it had its own mind. Like someone was controlling it remotely."

"What has this got to do with me going to the mausoleum?"

"It's Marc—don't you see? He's somehow found out what I'm up to, and he's desperate for us not to find whatever might be hidden there."

I wished I could see, because then I wouldn't have to consider the other very real possibility of what had happened to Anthony's car. "No, I don't. Marc is a jerk, but he's your brother. I doubt very much that he would try to physically harm you."

Despite the chill outside and in the empty house, beads of perspiration dotted his forehead. I led him to the lone chair and he sat down heavily.

"Sorry," he said. "This whole thing has me . . . spooked."

Me, too, I almost said. "Can I get you some water?"

He shook his head. "But thanks. I'll really feel better if you say you'll still help me."

I crossed my arms. "I think you need to tell me more than just 'meet me at the mausoleum.' I need you to tell me the whole story, okay?"

Anthony placed his crutches on the floor, then leaned back in his chair and stretched his legs out in front of him. "When Marc bought the plantation, it was because he thought that's where the Confederate diamonds were hidden."

"I knew that, but not why. What made him think that?" I asked, settling my gaze on one of the oranges and noticing that the spacing on the cloves was off.

"Same reason everyone did at the time, I guess—all those rumors about the Vanderhorst Confederate ancestor who supposedly hid the diamonds. But when Marc was doing research for his book on our ancestor Joseph Longo, he discovered Joseph's business diary at the Charleston Museum in the archives. Since he knew Jack was working on the same subject for a book, he tore out the pages. . . ." He stopped, a look of chagrin settling on his features. "And destroyed them, but there was enough there to make Marc believe the diamonds were somewhere on the plantation— or had been at some point before they were moved to your house."

Unable to stop myself, I picked up the orange with the errant cloves and pulled out my ruler. Anthony stopped speaking, and when I looked at him, I realized he was staring at me. "These are decorations for the progressive dinner. Haven't you ever seen cloves stuck into oranges to make pomander balls?"

He nodded slowly. "Sure. Just never with such . . . precision."

I frowned at him. "You were saying something about why Marc thought the diamonds were hidden at Gallen Hall."

"Right," he said, forcing his gaze away from what I was doing. "Joseph had copied into his diary what looked like some kind of weird drawing, almost like a doodle. Apparently while at a party at the Vanderhorst home on Tradd Street, Joseph did some snooping and found a really old piece of paper with these odd scribblings in Mr. Vanderhorst's desk, and Joseph copied them into his diary. Marc only showed the copy to me once—and I thought it looked like hieroglyphics, but Marc said that was proof the Vanderhorsts had hidden something valuable on one of their properties. I mean, why go through the trouble of using codes if they weren't hiding something valuable, right? Marc assumed it was the diamonds because of the story of Captain John Vanderhorst being entrusted with the diamonds after the war and then turning up in Charleston without them."

"Yes, well, we now know that Marc did, actually, have the diamonds and he hid them in my grandfather clock. So why does he think there's something else that might be hidden in the mausoleum?"

"Because when Marc found out that Jack was working on another book, he thought it could be a sequel, and Marc wanted to make sure that he knew everything and that Jack wouldn't find anything new. So he went back to his notes and saw that on that same page in Joseph's diary, he'd also copied the words 'French treasure.' Not sure what the 'French' part means, but 'treasure' is certainly clear. Marc thought the same thing. The Confederate diamonds weren't from France, which is probably why he dismissed this particular notation when searching for the diamonds."

I bent down to look into the box of oranges, using my ruler to check the placement of the cloves. "And?" I prompted, feeling his eyes on me again.

He cleared his throat. "Marc hasn't figured out what the drawing means—I know that much. He didn't ask for my help, either, because then he'd feel obliged to share any treasure with me. But that didn't keep him from looking. He pretty much tore apart Gallen Hall and used metal detectors over all the floors and walls, looking for whatever might be a 'French treasure.'"

I'd finished with the oranges and begun to pace, picking up stray lint from the bare wood floor as I walked. "I'm afraid you've lost me. All the diamonds are accounted for. There's no more treasure. And you still haven't said what this has to do with the mausoleum."

He sat up and leaned his elbows on his knees. "You're wrong. Maybe not about the diamonds, but definitely about there being another treasure hidden somewhere."

"I don't . . ."

He held up his hand. "Before Marc and I had our falling-out, we were in the library at Gallen Hall, smoking cigars and drinking bourbon. Marc never could hold his liquor, which is the only reason I can think of for him telling me this—and I seriously doubt that he knows he did, or he'd have burned down the house and everything else once it all belonged to me." He stopped, rubbing his sore arm.

"So what did he tell you?"

"He said he had proof that there was more hidden treasure on Vanderhorst property."

I frowned. "So you think he found another diamond?"

"No. He would have gloated about that for weeks. Several months ago when he found out that Jack was already at work on another book, he went to the archives where he'd found Joseph Longo's diary and found personal correspondence belonging to the Vanderhorst family from 1781, which was during the occupation of Charleston, in case you weren't aware."

I just nodded, not wanting to show that I had no idea to what he was referring.

"He stole the letters from the archives, too, just in case they contained something Jack could use for his book. But when Marc read them, he found something else entirely."

I was seething now, on Jack's behalf. We'd always known Marc was a weasel, but we'd thought we'd seen the bottom of his depravity. Apparently, we hadn't. "What?" I prompted.

"It was a mention that a room needed to be prepared for an important visitor from France who wished to lay a wreath on the tomb of the Vanderhorsts' daughter, Marie Claire. Marc pointed out that the Vanderhorsts, like most of the colony of South Carolina at that point, were loyalists. And the French were bitter enemies of the British. So why would a Frenchman be visiting the Vanderhorsts? To lay a wreath on the tomb of a daughter who'd never existed?"

Anthony raised an eyebrow. "Marc showed me the family tree—he was quite obsessed with the idea of more treasure to find and had made his own very complicated drawing—and the Vanderhorsts had six sons, only two of whom lived to adulthood. And let's not forget the words 'French treasure' Marc had seen in Joseph's diary."

I blinked. "So, between the drawing and the letter with incorrect information, he thought a treasure was hidden somewhere on Vanderhorst property? It seems a bit of a stretch."

"Yeah—so did finding the Confederate diamonds in your house." He gave me a sardonic smile. "But there's more. Marc thinks there's a connection to the drawing with some of the bricks inside the mausoleum. Marc's already dug around the floor of the mausoleum and searched and searched but come up empty-handed. He wanted to tear the entire mausoleum down to do a better search, but the preservation people put a stop to it. Apparently, it's protected by the Archaeological Resources Protection Act, which requires federal permits for excavation or removal of material remains of past human life or activities. We can't touch it. Not legally, anyway."

"But you've searched, surely."

Anthony's eyes darkened. "I've tried. But there's someone . . . something . . . keeping me out. That's the weirdest thing—because I'd been inside the mausoleum many times in the past without anything strange happening. But then all of a sudden when I tried to enter to search one more time, things would . . . happen to me. I'd feel punches and scratches. And . . ." He stopped, giving his head a firm shake as if trying to remove a painful memory. "A stone lid on one of the crypts slid partially off and broke, and one of the pieces barely missed landing on my foot. Do you know how heavy those lids are? They don't just slide off. I wanted to believe that I'd imagined it all, but there were purple bruises all over me." He looked away for a moment before forcing his gaze back to me. "And I had bloody scratch marks on my back. Under my clothes. Like someone had raked their fingernails over bare skin."

I didn't even try to pretend I had no idea what might have been responsible. "When was this?" My voice shook.

"It started around the time we had all those heavy rains this past spring, remember?"

Of course I did. That was when my back garden sank, revealing the hidden cistern. Unburying what had been covered for at least a century.

I nodded, my thoughts running a marathon down different paths, trying hard to avoid the most obvious. "And you somehow found out that the nineteenth-century Vanderhorsts used some of the bricks from the mausoleum and old cemetery wall to build the cistern at their Tradd Street house."

"Yeah. By accident. Apparently, Marc hadn't destroyed all the documents and letters he stole from the archives. He left a bunch of them in a shoebox in a garbage can. Luckily, when I discovered I was the hapless owner of a failed winery and took possession of the premises, I found the can in the carriage house. Apparently, whoever was in charge of taking out the garbage had forgotten this one bin."

He shook his head wearily, and I felt sorry for him, for having grown up with a brother like Marc Longo. He continued. "Feeling angry, and wanting some kind of evidence that Marc was doing something illegal, I went through the papers. There was a lot there, all stolen by Marc from the archives—nothing to do with him or any of his business dealings, sadly—and ready to go out in the trash. Which explains why I couldn't find anything about the plantation when I tried to do my own research. That's how I found out about the bricks. I read through everything—but it was just a bunch of ledgers with costs of all the building materials and furniture for both Vanderhorst properties, and a housekeeper's journal about how much tea and sugar she measured out on a daily basis. The only thing interesting I learned was that there'd been an older mausoleum on the same site as the one that's there now, but for some reason it was torn down and then rebuilt within two years of the original. They also replaced the brick wall that surrounded the cemetery with an iron fence at the same time. The Vanderhorsts were building a house on Tradd Street at the time—probably an earlier version of your house now—and the demolished mausoleum and wall would have been a cheap source of bricks."

I raised my eyebrows. "Why would they have done that? Is the new one bigger?"

Anthony shook his head. "No. That's the thing—they used the same blueprint both times. And it was practically brand-new. There were only three bodies interred at the time—all placed there in the same year: 1782."

I stopped pacing. "Please tell me that you still have the shoebox."

He picked up one of the oranges and began to examine it, and it took all my restraint not to ask him not to touch any of the cloves. "Of course—I'm not like Marc. I could never destroy a historical document. That's just . . . wrong."

I decided that I liked Anthony Longo a lot. "Can I see the shoebox?"

He began tossing the orange from one hand to the other, and I clenched my teeth. "So this means you're still in?"

I was pretty sure I didn't have a choice. There was no doubt in my mind that what was going on in his mausoleum was somehow connected to my cistern and the specter haunting Nola's bedroom. I unclenched my jaw. "Yes. I suppose I am."

He smiled, then stood. "I'll get out of your way, then. I'll bring the box to your house whenever it's convenient. Or I can drop it by your house now if Jayne's there."

I frowned. "Why don't you just bring it by my office? You can leave it with Jolly. She's completely trustworthy."

He looked disappointed, but I owed it to my friendship with Thomas Riley not to encourage another suitor for Jayne.

"And, Anthony?"

He looked at me expectantly.

"Don't tell anyone I'm helping you with this. It's not something I want people to know."

He gazed at me silently for a moment. "All right," he said with a nod before hoisting himself up with his crutches, then walking toward the front door in the octagonal entranceway. Its scale wasn't of the right period, in contrast with the rest of the house. I almost bit my tongue when I realized I'd started to think like Sophie.

"I wouldn't eat that orange if I were you. It's been dried," I said, eyeing the fruit he still held in his hand.

"Oh, right," he said, tossing it to me.

I somehow managed to catch the orange. "And one last thing."

He looked at me expectantly.

"Be careful. I'd stay away from the mausoleum for now until I can figure out a plan."

We said our good-byes and I watched him exit, closing the door behind him. When I turned around to resume my task, all the oranges from the box were now on the floor, neatly lined up to make a perfect X.

CHAPTER
9

As I locked up my clients' house, juggling the box of oranges and satisfied with the precisely arranged cloves sticking into their skins, I heard my name being called. I turned around and spotted Veronica's daughter and Nola's friend, Lindsey Farrell, and her father, Michael, walking what appeared to be a snowball white husky puppy.

"Need some help?" Michael called as he rushed up the steps to take the box.

"Thanks," I said. "My car's right over here—if you can just stick the box in the back, I'd appreciate it."

I used my remote to pop open the trunk, and while he was fitting the box inside, I turned to greet Lindsey. "It's nice to see you—Nola didn't mention that you got a new puppy."

I bent down to scratch the ball of fluff behind the ears, his gorgeous blue eyes happily staring into mine while his little pink tongue lolled. Ever since getting my own dog, I'd become hyperaware of other dogs. I couldn't walk down the street without smiling at them or asking to pet them, and I would be humiliated if Jack ever found out, because my official line was that I wasn't a dog person. Even though I now owned three and one of them slept on my pillow. I wasn't a person who wanted to advertise that she'd relaxed any of her personal rules.

"He was a birthday surprise from my mom." Lindsey leaned over and whispered conspiratorially, "My dad isn't too happy, but I've always wanted a dog. His name is Ghost."

I looked at her, startled. "Ghost?"

"Yeah. You know. Like from *Game of Thrones*."

I stared at her blankly.

"Like in the HBO series based on the books by George R. R. Martin," she prompted.

I could tell she wanted to roll her eyes when I showed no recognition, but because I was Nola's stepmom and an adult, she resisted. "Yes, well, I don't have a lot of extra time nowadays with the twins and work."

"And the house," she said. "My dad says keeping up with a historic house is like living with a persistent and fat mosquito with a hole in its stomach that keeps sucking you dry."

I pretended to be appalled, trying to forget how I'd once thought much the same thing. And still did on occasion, like when Sophie announced we had wood rot on the front piazza and we needed to restore the wood rather than replace it with something less vulnerable to the elements. Like with anything that wasn't wood.

"You got that right," Michael said as he approached. He jerked his chin in the direction of the car. "Doing more magic tricks with oranges?" His tone was light, but his eyes weren't, and I knew he was remembering the orange thrown at him in my dining room.

I feigned ignorance. "Actually, those are for progressive dinner house decorations. Since your house is one of the dessert course houses, I was about to call Veronica to see if I could get into your house now since it's so close. Sophie wanted me to measure the fireplaces so she would know how much garland we'd need, and also to look around to get an idea of what else we might need for the house. Yours is a Victorian, so it will be a little different than the rest. I'm not really sure how different, but I told her I'd take pictures with my phone and let her figure it out."

"I can do that," Michael said. "Or Veronica. No need for you to take up more of your day."

I was more than eager to agree, knowing I had just enough time to stop by Glazed for a doughnut and latte before an appointment I had at the office. But the sudden scent of Vanilla Musk made me close my mouth. "Actually, Sophie will just make me come back and do it, so I might as well get it taken care of the way she wants it the first time." I forced a big grin, recalling something Jack had once said about me. "You know how some people are— everything has to be just right, and done exactly as they would have done it, or it's just not good enough."

"Mom's not home, but the front door is unlocked if you don't want to wait for us to finish walking Ghost," Lindsey offered.

Michael started to protest, saying something about coming with me, but I spoke over him. I still couldn't put a finger on why I didn't want to be alone with him, and settled on the memory of the orange being thrown across the room at him. "Don't be silly—I don't want to be a bother or interrupt your family time. I promise to be quick, and I probably won't even be there when you get back. Nice to see you both," I said cheerily, trying to ignore the icy touch of the hand on my arm.

I walked the three blocks to the yellow Victorian on Queen Street. I'd passed it many times, even remembered hearing speculation about it going on the market after the former owners, Veronica's parents, had moved to an assisted-living community. Veronica and Michael had moved in instead, making it a home for their only child, Lindsey. I hadn't known any of this at the time, of course, having not yet reconnected with my old college classmate, but I remembered the house.

It was a pretty Queen Anne complete with an asymmetrical façade and a dominant front-facing gable. Until I'd met Sophie, I'd just called this style of house old and would have shown it to every buyer who stopped in my office looking for a piece of Charleston history regardless of which period they specified. Most buyers hadn't known much more about historic architecture than I did, the only impediment to their purchase usually the asking price. Despite many houses requiring extensive renovations, the prices were still higher than that for a four-bedroom new build in Poughkeepsie. But the desire to own a historic house in the Holy City kept me in business, which I was very grateful for even if I did not exactly understand it.

I walked through the front gate and up the steps to the wraparound porch. It didn't matter if the door was unlocked or not because it opened before I reached it, the heavy scent of Vanilla Musk saturating the chilly air. This was the house Veronica and her sister, Adrienne, had grown up in. Although Adrienne had been murdered while living in a dorm at the College of Charleston, it would make sense that this house, where she'd had so many happy memories, would be the place to which she'd return.

Victorian architecture, with its accompanying interiors and emphasis on dark wood, heavy fabrics, and clashing patterns, was my least favorite in my repertoire of old houses. As I stood in an arched doorway leading from the small entry hall into the front parlor, I couldn't tell if the look was intended to appear old or was simply dated. Beneath the lingering scent of Vanilla Musk, the pervading air of the room was of stale emptiness. Any past warmth or hint of comfort and family had long since vacated the premises.

I remembered from one of my earlier conversations with Veronica that Michael wanted to sell the house, saying that the renovations and repairs were too much. But after a box containing the contents of Adrienne's dorm room at the time of her death had been discovered in the attic, along with a new clue in the form of a necklace, Veronica couldn't let it go.

I pulled out my measuring tape—always carried alongside my ruler because one should always be prepared—and iPhone to measure the mantels and take pictures according to Sophie's directions, glad I had Nola as my personal technology manager. I'd never been good with any kind of electronic equipment, mostly because the devices always seemed to die or lose power when I came too close to lonely spirits wanting my attention. But even Nola had faith that I could manage the camera function on my phone and that even if my camera died, the photos would be put on a cloud somewhere so I wouldn't lose them. I figured I didn't need to know how things worked, but should just be happy that they did.

I stepped into the parlor and, after quickly measuring and jotting down the width of the mantel, aimed my camera at the heavily carved fireplace with the wavy mirror above it. A marble urn stood on each end of the mantel, and I hoped they didn't contain ashes, because Sophie would want me to stick greenery in them along with an orange or two for decoration.

A definite presence accompanied me as I walked through the open pocket doors to the dining room and then to the woefully outdated kitchen. Shiny floral wallpaper covered the walls, matching the harvest gold and avocado green appliances and laminate countertops. Although it needed a complete kitchen gut job and some cosmetic fixes, there would still be potential buyers lined up outside the door hoping to be able to call this address home. Invariably, they'd ask if the house was haunted—some enthusiastically and others less so—and I'd give a soft laugh to show them that I was in on the joke, because of course ghosts weren't real.

I sniffed the air, smelling the familiar perfume. I wondered why Adrienne chose not to show herself to me. I speculated whether it had to do with the other presence I sensed, the one that wasn't so friendly. The one whose dark and angry voice had come through my mother's mouth when she'd held the necklace found in the attic. My mother would say Adrienne was saving her energy in case she needed it to protect me.

I continued to measure and snap photos of the downstairs, my Realtor's brain automatically doing the calculations necessary for updating the house, not just for more comfortable modern living, but also for resale. As I passed through the small foyer toward the front door, I found myself hesitating at the bottom of the stairs. The wide steps were covered in dark wood and a somber-hued floral pattern. The heavy wooden balustrade jutted up alongside the steps before turning at the landing under a brilliant stained glass window and then continuing to the upper floors and the attic.

It was neither inviting nor welcoming, yet I felt a firm push on my back, nudging me forward, and when I tried to turn around, I found my way blocked by unseen hands.

"Fine," I muttered. "Go ahead and show me whatever it is you want me to see, but I can't promise anything other than I will tell my sister and my mother so they can help you if they can. That's it."

Jayne had told me that her argument with Detective Riley had come from her insistence that she advertise her abilities, and he had said it would only bring the crazies out of the woodwork to harass her. I happened to agree with him, which sidelined this investigation and any other cold cases for which he'd hoped to solicit our help. I had enough going on in my life anyway, so I didn't miss being involved. Not that the ghosts were paying any attention to my time-out.

Slowly, I climbed the stairs, holding tightly to the balustrade as I remembered other stairs on other occasions, and a solid push that could send a person hurtling to the bottom. I wasn't eager to repeat the experience. The old wood risers creaked under my feet, lending an uneasy feeling of foreboding and making me long for the creaking floors in my own house, which sounded more welcoming than frightening.

The upstairs hallway with its dark rose runner and mauve walls lent the effect of a funeral home, and, following a cursory glance to show Adrienne I'd done my best, I made to head back down the stairs. But the entity walking with me continued to forcefully guide me toward the stairs leading to the attic door.

I climbed the last flight of steps, then stood staring at the wooden door panels and the ceramic doorknob, hoping the door was locked so that I could turn around and leave. Not that it mattered, as the door swung open in front of me and I was pushed into a musty space. The rainbow of muted colors descending from the dirty stained glass windows on either side of the large room did nothing to dispel the darkness and gloom of the attic.

Hulking shapes of furniture draped with sheets were pushed against the walls, along with a child's miniature kitchen, grocery store, and baby stroller complete with Raggedy Ann doll strapped inside, sightless eyes reflecting the stained glass. The room echoed with what sounded like a sigh, an exhalation of memories and time. It weighted the air, the single sound carrying all the loss and grief of a life cut short. I closed my eyes for a moment, then jerked them open again as I felt a small shove on my shoulder.

I stepped forward, my foot colliding with the side of a cardboard box. Packing tape had been ripped from the top seam and lay curled against the box, the flaps stuck beneath one another to keep it closed. As if knowing what I was supposed to do, I leaned forward and pulled open the flaps, recognizing immediately that this was Adrienne's box. A sorority scrapbook sat pressed against one side, and photographs and invitations to various events were sprinkled like confetti over a small heart-shaped throw pillow and a College of Charleston Cougars baseball hat.

I rifled through the mementos of a college freshman, trying to determine what Adrienne wanted me to see, knowing this was the box Veronica and Detective Riley had already gone through. Frustrated, I straightened. "You've brought me all the way up here, but you've got to be more specific. They found the broken chain and charm already. We're just not sure what it means—if anything."

I felt a small stab of panic. After my mother had touched the necklace and the dark voice had come from her, I'd taken it away. I just had no recollection of what I'd done with it. I remembered putting it somewhere so special that even I couldn't remember exactly where. Or maybe subconsciously I'd known then that I hadn't wanted anything to do with it.

"I have to go, Adrienne. I'll let Jayne know I was here. Maybe she can find out more—"

I was cut off by the sound of the front door slamming shut and a dog barking. "Hello, Mrs. Trenholm." Lindsey's voice traveled up the stairs. "We're back!"

I stood frozen, staring at the door and wondering how I'd explain my presence in the attic. I contemplated hiding there until everyone was asleep and then sneaking out but quickly dismissed the idea. If I was caught, the headlines would be worse than any recounting my ghost-seeing abilities.

I was in the middle of calculating how long it would take me to get down to the second floor when something soft struck me in the back of the head. I looked down to where the object had landed at my feet and picked it up. It was the heart-shaped pillow, covered in red felt with a ruffled edge. The sound of running feet, heavier than Lindsey's, came from the stairway, and before I could think of what I was doing, I shoved the small pillow into my tote bag.

"Melanie? Are you up here?" It was Michael, sounding as if he'd already reached the second floor. I listened as his footsteps, slower now, approached the attic door.

Still immobile, I heard something else, something small and delicate, clatter against the floor at my feet. I looked down at the broken chain and the charm that Veronica had found in the box, the interlocking Greek letters offering a clue we'd yet to understand.

Panicking, I watched as the doorknob turned, then quickly scooped up the necklace and dropped it into my tote before Michael opened the door.

I registered his look of surprise as I walked past him with a smile. "Thank you," I said. "I think I've got all the pictures I need. Tell Veronica I'll give her a call."

I hurried down the stairs as fast as my high heels could

take me, gave Lindsey a quick good-bye and the dog a pat on the head, then exited the house as fast as I could, trying to decipher the look on Michael's face. It wasn't until I'd reached my car and met my gaze in the rearview mirror that I realized what it had been. *Grief.*

CHAPTER
10

When I got home, Jack's minivan wasn't in its space in the carriage house. It was dinnertime for the twins, so I doubted that Jayne had taken them out. Usually when Jack was knee-deep in a book, he didn't leave the house in the middle of the day unless there was an emergency. Or he was procrastinating. I frowned as I stepped out of my car, contemplating the possibilities.

The sound of squealing brakes followed by a revving engine brought my attention to the street. I walked to the end of our driveway and peered out to see Jack's minivan hurtling in my direction before coming to an abrupt stop about twenty feet away in the middle of the road.

The driver's-side door flung open and a very annoyed Nola emerged and began stomping toward the house. "I didn't want to know how to drive anyway," she shouted over her shoulder just as Jack exited from the passenger-side door.

"Good," Jack shouted in reply. "I'm sure the entire world will thank you."

Nola burst into tears and ran past me and up the steps to the piazza. I could hear her feet pounding to the front door as her sobs carried back to us on the street.

"Jack?" I'd never heard him raise his voice to his daughter, ever.

There was no remorse on his face as he stared back at me. "She's a menace to society when she's behind the wheel of a motor vehicle."

"Still, that's no reason to yell at her." I pointed to the house. "Go inside and apologize. I'll park the car since I don't think either one of you is capable of doing it right now."

I didn't wait for him to respond as I got behind the wheel and put the car in drive, then parked it in its space next to my car. After waiting long enough for Jack and Nola to have a heart-to-heart, I entered the house through the front door, avoiding the back garden and cistern. It had become such a habit that I'd forgotten what the back door looked like.

I paused in the foyer, listening to Jayne in the kitchen with the twins and trying to hear Jack's or Nola's voice. Instead I heard the distinctive clink of ice in a glass from the direction of the parlor, and I cautiously walked in that direction, my breath held.

Jack stood in front of the bar cart, usually filled with empty decanters. Because Jack and my father both were recovering alcoholics, we kept the decanters empty except when we had company. As I watched, Jack leaned down and, after hesitating for a brief moment, opened the cabinet door. Despite having a brass key in the lock, it had never been locked. Because there'd been no reason to lock it.

Jack reached inside to the back of the cabinet and pulled out what looked like a full bottle of Glenfiddich. Having grown up with an alcoholic father, I recognized the bottle like an old friend. I continued to hold my breath, not daring to move even though I wanted nothing more than to back away and pretend I hadn't seen him.

He held the bottle with both hands, looking at it for a long time, as if it might be the face of an old lover. I guess, in some ways, it was. And then, without a word, he leaned down and put the bottle back where it had been.

"Jack?" I said softly.

He started at the sound of his name but didn't turn around. "I thought you'd go check on Nola."

I moved to stand next to him, staring pointedly at the open door of the cabinet. "And that would give you time for what?" I found myself very close to tears. "What's going on?"

His beautiful eyes bored into mine, but there was none of the humor or love I usually saw in them. They weren't empty, but there was definitely something missing. "'What's going on'?" he repeated. "What's going on besides my career getting flushed down the toilet?"

I took his hand, and being unaccustomed to having our roles reversed, I led Jack to the sofa, pulling him down next to me. "What's happened?" I asked.

He jumped up and began pacing the room, keeping his distance from the bar cart. "Oh, just the usual in the life of a writer trying to resurrect his career. I write ten pages, then delete nine of them, and after I rewrite them I realize it's all total crap. So I went for a run because fresh air and exercise are supposed to help creativity, but as I'm running down Legare I practically trip over Rebecca and that little dog of hers—with ears dyed pink now, I kid you not—and she asked me how I am in the way somebody asks a person with some life-threatening disease, and then tells me she's sorry, and she seemed surprised that I had no idea what she was talking about or why she should be sorry and then wouldn't meet my eyes. So I rushed back home to check my messages and sure enough, there's one from my agent."

I took a deep breath, preparing myself for what I knew was not going to be good news. I wanted to suggest a time-out so I could find a doughnut or two to bury my worries in and to distract me from the looming problem. But that was what the old, single Mellie would have done. Now I was a married and responsible adult and mother of three. And I loved Jack. I had for even longer than I'd known. I needed to slap down the old Mellie and figure out a way to get us through this. That's what marriage was. We were a team. And if it was my turn to be the strong one, then I'd better figure out how. Even if I had no clue as to how to start.

My voice was a lot stronger than I felt. "And what did he say?"

Jack stopped in front of the grandfather clock, staring at

it as if it might still be holding on to secrets. "I didn't get to speak with him—just his assistant. She said my agent's taking early retirement; he's already gone. She said I would be given the option of working with another agent inside the agency or I could find my own."

If Rebecca had known bad news was coming, then there was only one place she could have heard it. I pushed the thought from my head, unwilling to go there, and swallowed, tried to put on a relaxed smile. "Well, that's good news, isn't it?"

He turned around and looked at me with wild eyes. "No—of course it's not. A literary agent is not the same as a real estate agent. They're not interchangeable."

I stood quickly, my temper pushing aside my attempt at being the rational adult. "Excuse me? I'll have you know that not every real estate agent is the same. . . ."

He held up his hand. "I know, I know. I'm sorry. That's not what I meant. I wanted to say that it's a personal connection between a literary agent and an editor and the writer. There has to be a strong belief in the writer's abilities for them to be able to work together. I can't just be handed off to someone who doesn't know anything about me or my books. Like Desmarae, my new editor. Did I tell you that she actually suggested we should aim for a younger audience with this book—the same book that she still hasn't read the first chapters of yet so she has no idea what it's about—and ask Kim Kardashian for a cover blurb?" He slapped his palm against his forehead so hard it left a red mark.

"Oh, Jack." I moved to his side, reaching up to touch his shoulder, hard and tense beneath my hand. "I'm so sorry. I know this is all sudden, and unexpected, and certainly not welcome when you're trying to finish your book. But maybe this will be a positive change. Maybe your new agent will be even more enthusiastic and energetic. And will be happy to tell Desmarae exactly where to put her Kim Kardashian blurb."

Jack frowned. "He or she might have to wait on that—

first I need someone to tell Desmarae that we can't wait another year before publication, which is what she's telling me now. Apparently, they're revisiting their publishing schedule and my previous slot has been given to a historical erotica series."

"But—"

"I know. We need the money. I've already spoken with my publisher directly, who was less than receptive to my idea of keeping me where I'm scheduled, so I'm hoping my new agent—whoever that's going to be—will have better luck."

"Do you think . . ." I paused, ready to suggest grabbing the children and taking them for a walk. It was procrastination, sure, but playing with the children was always such a stress reliever, and it was certainly easier than figuring out what we should do.

He quirked an eyebrow. "Were you going to ask me if I think it's a coincidence that Rebecca knew before I did?"

Our eyes met. "Because there's no such thing as coincidence," we said in unison.

"Exactly," Jack said. "And I don't have a doubt in my mind that Marc is behind this somehow."

I didn't want to agree, even though I had a sinking feeling that he was right. It was just too awful to think about right now. I distracted myself by looking at the red mark on Jack's forehead. Touching it gently with my thumb, I said, "Does it hurt?"

His eyes met mine, and a little spark passed between us. He nodded. "A little."

I stood on my tiptoes and kissed it.

"It hurts here, too," he said, pointing to his cheek.

Without question, I placed my hands on his shoulders and reached up to give him another kiss, feeling the bristles of his beard tickle my lips. I stepped back. "Better?"

"A little. It hurts here, too." Jack pointed to his mouth.

Pulling him closer, I happily obliged, ignoring the nagging thought that he was distracting me for a reason. His arms wrapped around me, his hands snaking under my blouse as he pressed me into him. I felt his fingers unfastening the hooks on my bra as he trailed small kisses across my cheek until he reached my ear. His hot breath fanned the bare skin on my neck as he whispered, "I think I need a little stress relief right now."

"Me, too," I whispered back, my hands fiddling with the button on his jeans.

There was a slight clearing of a throat behind us, and we both dropped our hands like teenagers caught in the backseat of our parents' sedan. We turned to see Greco standing in the entranceway, his head nearly touching the top of the molding. I'd forgotten that he was supposed to be at the house, taking inventory of the furniture in Nola's room and the attic to see what he could reuse or salvage for the redo.

"Sorry to interrupt," he said, looking around the room at everything but us. "I can come back at a more convenient time."

"No, no—it's perfectly fine," I said, smoothing my blouse and skirt, hoping that at least one of the hooks in my bra was still intact.

Greco smiled at a spot over our heads. "If you have a moment, I wanted to show you something upstairs."

I groaned inwardly, wondering if he'd found a skull hidden under a floorboard or a human femur behind loose wainscoting. In my world, anything was possible. I feigned a relaxed smile as Jack and I followed the designer up the staircase, going over all responses to whatever it was he wanted to show us that would placate him enough so he wouldn't quit. *Why, yes, I do believe that looks like an ax mark in the back of that skull you found in the air duct. That Nola—such a prankster!*

I realized Greco was speaking and I shut down my inner voice.

"The architectural details in this house, including Nola's room, are really quite spectacular. And the antiques are top-notch. Not that I don't appreciate the business, but except for a few cosmetic changes, I don't think there needs to be the kind of massive redo we originally spoke about."

Jack and I exchanged a glance. Clearing my throat, I said, "Well, when Nola moved in a few years ago, my mother-in-law did a refresh of the room with new fabrics and wall colors. The bed was here—it's too big to be moved unless we cut a hole in the wall and lower it with a crane into the back garden, in which case my house-hugging friend would throw me in the marsh with a cinder block attached to my ankle. But we added an antique desk Jack's mother found in the attic here, along with a few occasional pieces."

"Like the jewelry chest?" he asked, a small hitch in his voice.

We reached the top step and stopped. "Yes," I said. "I thought it needed to be refinished, but Amelia liked it the way it was—said it added 'character' to the piece."

Greco was frowning, and I didn't want the jewelry chest to be the reason he quit. I was ready to agree to painting everything neon green and adding a Harry Styles mural on the ceiling if that's what it would take to retain him. "But it doesn't have to stay if you don't like it. And I like Harry Styles." I was proud that I knew who that was, if only because Jack had taken Nola and me to see *Dunkirk* and she'd mentioned that the actor sang, too.

Greco smiled, looking a bit confused, but it didn't erase the frown lines over his nose. "No, it really is a beautiful piece and if your daughter likes it, we can certainly incorporate it into the new design. It's just . . ."

Jack walked toward the bedroom and grabbed the doorknob. "It's just such a tangled jumble of chains and baubles that you can't see how she can find anything?" He pushed open the door, then stepped back for us to enter.

We stopped at the threshold. Nola and I had scrubbed the walls clean, leaving only faint traces of the muddy letters that had appeared and had, thankfully, remained gone. But the jewelry cabinet, emptied by Nola when she'd moved to the guest room, stood in the corner now with every drawer open, the lid pulled all the way back like a gaping mouth.

"You want to use it more as a sculpture than a jewelry cabinet?" Jack suggested helpfully.

I smiled pleasantly as if that had been exactly what I'd been thinking, too, instead of what Greco was about to tell us.

"I appreciate your creativity," he said to Jack. "But there seems to be something wrong with it. I'll close all the drawers and the lid and turn my back, and the next thing I know, everything's opened again."

"How strange," Jack and I said in unison.

Greco crossed his arms and regarded us under lowered brows. "Something tells me that it's not."

Jack took a step toward the jewelry chest and pulled a drawer in and out as if testing it. "You know how these old houses are, with uneven floors and varying humidity. . . ."

Greco held out his hand palm up to stop Jack from continuing. "Please. Don't. Ever since my first visit here, I've been getting weird vibes from the whole house—and this room in particular."

I held my breath, preparing myself for his words of resignation.

"I kind of like it," he said. "I find it rather creatively inspiring. I actually grew up in a house on Broad that always had things that went bump in the night. I found it more interesting than frightening, and since I couldn't see whatever it was causing the ruckus, nothing really bothered me."

"Is that so?" I asked noncommittally, feeling a little jealous that the odd sounds never bothered him because he couldn't see anything. Until I'd learned how to block out all the sights and sounds, I'd spent my childhood sleeping with my eyes open. "Well, this is an old house, and Charleston is supposed to be one of the most haunted cities in the world, so I suppose it wouldn't be out of the question that there might be the odd spirit here or there."

"Phew," he said, doing a mock swipe of his forehead. "I was afraid I would scare you. Glad to know you're not easily scared."

Jack put his arm around my shoulder and pulled me close. "Who, us? Never."

"Good. Because I found something else you might find . . . interesting." He walked over to the large four-poster bed, the intricate rice carvings winding their way up to the acorn finials. Lowering his tall frame, he pointed at the ball-and-claw foot, tapping his finger against something near the bottom edge.

As usual, I wasn't wearing my glasses and couldn't see what he was pointing at no matter how much I squinted.

Jack shook his head at me before leaning forward to see. "A carving of a peacock."

"A peacock," I repeated, trying to recall why that seemed significant.

The designer straightened to his full height. "I'm not sure if it's connected, but the peacock was a secret symbol used here in the Carolinas during the Revolutionary War. I do a bit of Revolutionary War reenacting—on the British side—which is how I know this factoid. Of course, it could be something else entirely."

"What do you mean by 'secret symbol'?" Jack asked. He was wearing the expression he used when dissecting reams of information to boil down into something he could write about.

"A spy ring. From what I've read, it was as instrumental in leading us to an American victory as the Culper spy ring, but far less known. Mostly because to this day, historians aren't really sure who the major players were and, of the ones whose identities are known, what side they were on."

"Really?" Jack asked, and I could almost hear the wheels whirring in his brain.

Greco nodded. "I know you said this bed has been here for a long time, but do you know where it originally came from?"

I began shaking my head, then stopped. "The Vander-horsts were the original owners." I smiled at my own cleverness. "And they also owned Gallen Hall Plantation. My mother-in-law said a lot of the furniture in this house was most likely brought here from the plantation house, since so much of it predates this house. And I bet it was all made on the plantation, too, since it has the peacock mark."

Greco lifted his eyebrows. "Well, then, this would make sense. So it probably doesn't have anything to do with the spy ring at all."

Jack bent down to get a closer look at the carving, touching it with deference. He turned his head to look up at me and smiled, his eyes dark. "Or maybe it does."

Because there's no such thing as coincidence. Neither one of us said it out loud, but we didn't have to.

I had a sudden recollection of the smells that had pervaded the room when we'd discovered the word *Betrayed* smeared on the walls, as well as the scent of horse and leather, along with the lingering odor of gunpowder. Recalled now where I'd smelled it before. It had been at Gallen Hall when Jayne and I had seen the British soldier pointing a musket at us. Right before the cold, dead voice had erupted from my father's mouth.

I leaned against the bed, feeling suddenly weak. "Oh, it definitely does," I said, sinking down into the mattress and wondering if the cold breath across my cheek was only my imagination.

CHAPTER
11

Our mother stood between Jayne and me in the nursery, wearing a red-and-green silk sheath dress instead of the black-and-white referee's shirt she should have donned for a war of wills.

I held a contented Sarah wearing a red velvet dress with a white lace Peter Pan collar and intricate smocking on the chest. White stockings with tiny candy canes covered her chubby legs, and very small black patent leather Mary Janes were neatly buckled on her plump feet. Every so often, she'd stroke the soft velvet of her dress and smile, even twisting around to see the enormous bow I'd spent a good half hour tying to perfection.

A very unhappy JJ was in the midst of a tantrum, complete with head thrown back and all four limbs rigid, as if he couldn't bear the feel of his red velvet pantaloons or matching vest with lace cravat. His beloved whisk was clutched tightly in a small fist like a defective light saber.

Our mother was speaking in a very calm voice, making it hard to hear her over JJ's screaming. "They don't have to match, Mellie. They're twins but very separate individuals. Let him wear what he wants."

"But it's for the Christmas card photo," I protested. "They're supposed to match."

Jayne looked at me with what appeared to be her last thread of patience. "No, not really. And as long as it's not a matter of the child's safety or completely inappropriate— which does *not* include wearing colors besides red and green—he should be allowed to choose what he wants to wear."

I looked in horror at the outfit JJ had chosen and Jayne had placed on the blue glider. "Jeans? And sneakers? For our Christmas photo?" I didn't mention the ridiculous price I'd paid for the pantaloons and vest. If I did, I was afraid we'd all be throwing our heads back and screaming.

Jayne's smile was more like a grimace as she placed JJ on the floor before she might drop him because of his squirming. He immediately lay facedown on the rug and began beating the floor with his hands and feet and whisk. Jayne raised her voice slightly to be heard. "The bulldozer on the sweater is red, all right? So he'll fit right in. And we can borrow Sarah's red shoelaces for his sneakers. That way, we'll all have a cohesive look."

Sarah reached for my mother, no doubt wanting to touch the opera-length pearls that GiGi—what Sarah and JJ called their grandmother—wore around her neck. They had belonged to my grandmother, also named Sarah, and when my daughter played with the necklace, she'd gibber in a language I couldn't understand but definitely had the cadences of conversation. She'd pause at the appropriate times as if another person was speaking to her and would grin and laugh at intervals. I'd accepted this about Sarah, and so had Jack. But that didn't mean I was happy about it.

My mother looked over the large bow barrette on Sarah's head. "It's a Christmas card photo, Mellie. Not an audition for *Southern Charm*—not that I'd allow it, but you know what I mean. This is supposed to be fun, not torture. The twins couldn't look bad if we dressed them in potato sacks. I have to agree with Jayne that we should allow JJ to wear what he wants or we're all going to lose our hearing."

"Fine," I said, looking at my pitiful son thrashing about on the floor like a fish on a hook. "Maybe you can find a hay bale to bring into the foyer in front of the Christmas tree, too, so that blue jeans won't appear out of place."

My disappointment dissipated as I knelt on the floor next to JJ and placed my hand on the back of his head, feeling the heat of his exertion beneath his dark hair. "Sweetheart? Would you like to wear your doh-doh sweater?" He'd been calling bulldozers "doh-dohs" ever since he'd learned to speak, and the word had somehow inundated the vocabulary of the entire family.

He stilled at my touch, his sobs turning to hiccups, before flipping over onto his back, his appendages and whisk spread out so he looked like a beached starfish who liked to bake. His blue eyes—Jack's eyes—stared back at me with hurt and righteous indignation as tears dripped down his round cheeks. "And boo jeans?"

"Absolutely," I said, scooping up my son and feeling his arms wind around my neck, pressing his sodden cheek into my neck and making my heart melt. "I'm sorry you didn't like the outfit I picked out. Maybe next time I'll bring you with me and we can decide together."

"Daddy pick!" JJ said, pulling back with a wide grin, as if five seconds before he hadn't been tearing at his clothes like a penitent in sackcloth. It reminded me a little of Jack's abrupt transformation the day before from crazed writer on the verge of drinking to seductive man with a mission. Maybe there was more to DNA than eye color and face shape. Or maybe the Trenholm men knew how to manipulate women to simply distract or to get what they wanted. I shook my head, trying to erase the thought.

"We can talk about that later." I looked over at where my mother and Jayne were already pulling out the red shoelaces from Sarah's sneakers and replacing the white ones in JJ's. Behind them, I could see into the twins' closet to the shelf where I kept their accessories—hair bows and headbands on the right for Sarah, and bow ties and suspenders on the left for JJ. All neatly labeled by me, for which I'd yet to hear a word of appreciation from anyone. "What about a red bow tie . . . ?" I began.

"No," Jayne and my mother shouted in unison.

"Okay, fine," I said. "At least General Lee and the puppies don't mind dressing up."

As if on cue, the door opened slightly as the three dogs

came into the room, walking slowly instead of their usual jackrabbit bounding and general high spirits, followed by Jack.

"Daddy!" both children squealed, reaching out their arms to him.

Jack scooped up both children as I remained on the floor, patting my lap for the dogs to approach. They stared at me with an unfamiliar look in their eyes, their plumed tails, which normally draped proudly over their backs, now touching the ground by their hind legs, their heads held low. They didn't move, no matter how much I slapped at my lap or told them to come.

"I think they're boycotting their outfits," Jayne said.

"What do you mean? They look adorable!"

General Lee wore a knit Santa Claus outfit complete with pom-pom hood and shiny black belt. Porgy and Bess had matching reindeer outfits in green, but their hoods had antlers with Christmas lights draped around them.

"Oh, wait. I know the problem." I reached over to each puppy and found the switch on the battery pack to light up the antlers. "There!" I said. "Isn't that better?"

With a sharp yelp, General Lee bolted out of the door, quickly followed by Porgy and Bess.

"I think you have your answer," Jack said, the hint of a smile in his voice.

"*Et tu, Brute?*" I stood slowly, recognizing defeat. "Fine. I'll go take off their outfits and apologize. Although I think if we all told them how adorable they looked, they might be more excited about wearing their costumes."

I directed this last bit at my mother and Jayne, but they were both shaking their heads sadly, as if *I* were the delusional one. I continued. "We might as well take our Christmas card photo in July or October, because apparently it doesn't matter that we're not all dressed according to a Christmas theme."

"At least the photo can't be used as evidence against you when the animal-cruelty people show up," Jack said with mock seriousness.

I picked up the discarded red velvet pantaloons and threw them at his face, knowing that he couldn't catch them because he was holding a child in each arm.

"I'm going downstairs. Let me know if you all change the theme entirely and I need to put on a bathing suit and flip-flops for the photo."

When I reached the bottom of the staircase, the dogs were nowhere to be found. Either Mrs. Houlihan was giving them a treat in the kitchen or they were avoiding me. I sensed a movement from behind me in the upstairs corridor. I turned to look, but despite the sudden chill, the hallway was empty. At least I knew the dogs weren't hiding from *me*.

Taking a deep breath of what I hoped was courage, I turned and began climbing the steps, taking care not to disturb the draped magnolia-leaf garland Veronica had helped me throw together that morning for the photo. It was filled with plastic pomegranates, lemons, mixed pinecones, and cinnamon sticks so that the plastic stems of the magnolia leaves weren't noticeable. I'd made Veronica promise not to tell Sophie that the fruit was all fake and we'd used superglue to attach it all. I'd at least stopped at using a hammer and nails on the antique banister, knowing that Sophie would have thrown me into the cistern if I'd put one single tiny hole in the wood. Personally, I didn't care how Colonials had decorated their staircases. I wasn't interested in smelling rotting fruit wafting about the house for a month.

"Hello? Is anybody there?" I waited for a moment, and when I didn't hear anything, I started back down the stairs, relieved that I'd done my duty and could report to Jayne and our mother that whatever was lurking in the upstairs hallways didn't want our help.

A cold breath on the back of my neck made all the hairs on my arms stand at attention. I clutched the banister, getting ready for the inevitable shove from behind. Instead a woman's voice, as piercing and cold as ice, blew into my left ear. *Lies.* The "S" sound reverberated in the air like the hiss of a snake.

I jerked my head around, almost losing my balance. A woman stood on the top step looking at me with angry eyes, the color of them obscured by shadow. She wore a low-cut emerald green ball gown with a corseted waist and voluminous skirts indicative of the late eighteenth century. Her rich brown hair was unpowdered, coiled in long curls around her face, and swept high on top of her head with a flourish of entwined ribbons that matched her dress. A large brooch in the shape of a peacock, its eyes and feathers sparkling with colorful jewels, gleamed from the bodice of her dress, and I had the distinct impression that she wanted me to notice it.

As I watched she turned her head until it dipped at an odd angle, allowing me to see her small, perfect ear, the long expanse of her neck. And an angry welt standing out in crimson relief against her pale skin.

"Who are you?" I whispered.

The front door opened behind me, and the vision of the woman wavered, then vanished, but not before I saw the anger in her eyes soften to sadness. And noticed again the raw red welt that encircled her neck like a noose.

"Melanie?"

My father's voice called from behind me. I gripped the banister because I was too shaky to trust myself not to fall as I turned around. "Hi, Dad," I said, walking slowly down the stairs, accidentally dislodging a pomegranate. It fell over the stairs, landing with a hollow *thwack* as it hit the floor below, then rolled for a few feet before stopping.

He didn't smile back. "What's wrong?" he asked, looking behind me at the stairs.

"Nothing," I said. "Just arguing with JJ over what he should wear for the photo." Ever since the incident at the plantation mausoleum, my father had been staring into dark corners and paying more attention to Sarah's babbling. I just wasn't convinced that he was becoming a true believer; I thought he was either deciding that his family was destined for a freak show or just gathering enough evidence to debunk our psychic gifts completely. Despite any sincerity he'd shown Jayne by listening to her explanations, I still couldn't completely exonerate him for my lifelong embarrassment and reluctance to admit my abilities. I still saw them as a flaw, an ugly scar I wasn't eager to show the general public. Or lifelong disbelievers like him.

"Well, you're pale as a ghost." He smiled as if he'd made a joke. "I'm allowed to say that, right?"

"Why wouldn't you be?" Still shaken by my encounter, I wasn't yet ready to let go of my resentment. Eager to change the subject, I asked, "Where's the photographer?"

As if in answer, there was a brief knock on the door. When my father opened it, I was surprised to find our handyman, Rich Kobylt. "Sorry—I rang the doorbell a couple of times, but I don't think it's working again." He looked past my father's shoulder to meet my eyes. "I'd be happy to take a look at it again. . . ."

"No," I said abruptly. He'd already adjusted it several times, at a cost that would have bought me about one hundred new, modern doorbells if Sophie would allow it, but I knew there was something wrong with the doorbell that couldn't be fixed by ordinary means. And I suspected that Rich knew it, too. He'd once admitted to me that he had a little bit of a sixth sense, and I continued to humor him without revealing that he was absolutely right.

I looked at him now with dread. "Why are you here? Did I forget to pay an invoice?" There were so many from Hard Rock Foundations, it wouldn't be impossible that one could have been overlooked, despite my intricate and involved filing system that ensured every bill was logged and slotted for payment on the appropriate date. Jack had once complimented me on my system, saying the planning of the D-Day invasion paled in comparison.

He hitched up his pants. "No, Miz Trenholm. Not tonight. Your daddy was looking for a photographer, so I volunteered my services."

I looked at my dad, not trying to hide the horror on my face. "You said you were hiring a buddy of yours who's a professional photographer!"

"I did—and he called me this morning and told me he's got the flu and didn't want to get anyone sick. I happened to mention it to Rich, and he said he could help."

Rich cleared his throat. "Yes, ma'am. I'm the official photographer at all my family's gatherings—including weddings. I take a pretty good picture, if I do say so myself."

I tried to block out the image of a roomful of Kobylts all with baggy pants and no belts and felt myself involuntarily shudder. I attempted a smile, the last hope for a beautiful Christmas card photo completely obliterated by images of blurred faces and mismatched outfits. "Well, then, I'm glad you could step in. I'm not sure if I could get us all dressed and together in one place again."

"I hear you," Rich said. "It's a real production with a big family, especially if little kids and pets are involved. My sister-in-law even dresses up her dogs in the most ridiculous outfits for their Christmas card photo. They look so depressed I've refused to take their picture anymore. Unhappy dogs don't say a lot about my picture-taking capabilities, you know? I told her next time she did that to those dogs, I was calling the ASPCA."

The three dogs chose that moment to emerge from their hiding place in Jack's office, running toward Rich as if he were coming to spring them from prison. Nola, dressed in a red velvet dress that was a grown-up version of Sarah's— I'd known better than to push for a hair bow or Peter Pan collar—followed close behind as Rich gave me an accusing look. "Now, that's just pitiful." Three sets of sad canine eyes looked at me as if the dogs were practicing for those ASPCA TV commercials. I almost expected Rich to burst out singing, "In the arms of the angel . . ."

Nola bent down to remove the dogs' outfits. "I think Mr. Kobylt might have a point, Melanie. How about I ask Dad to put that stuffed round red reindeer nose on your front car bumper and antlers on the side windows and we'll call it a day, all right? I can't imagine your car will complain."

"It probably should," Rich muttered as he lifted a large

backpack off of his back and began pulling out camera equipment and setting it on the foyer floor.

Feeling completely defeated and not a little irritated, I crossed my arms. "I thought we'd take the picture by the Christmas tree next to the stairs. It's the tallest and the prettiest, in my opinion. It's also the only one of the six I'm supposed to have that's completely decorated for the progressive dinner. Of course, my opinion doesn't seem to matter around here, so if you'd prefer to take it in the middle of the cistern, have at it."

"No," Rich said a little forcefully. "I mean, I think the Christmas tree next to the banister with all that garland will look perfect. Don't you think, Mr. Trenholm?"

I turned around to see Jack on the landing, a child in each arm as he descended. He stopped next to me and kissed me gently on my temple. "If that's what my lovely wife wants, then that's what we should do."

Feeling slightly mollified, I said, "Just make sure no one leans against the banister. It's a pain to glue that fruit onto the garland."

Nola's eyes widened. "Glue?" She said it with the same inflection some people use to say the word *murder.* "Does Dr. Wallen-Arasi know?"

I was saved from responding by the sound of my phone's "Mamma Mia" ringtone coming from the parlor. "I'll get it," Nola said, racing across the foyer. By the time she returned, it had stopped ringing, but she was looking at it as her fingers tapped wildly on the screen.

Without looking up, she said, "It was Dr. Wallen-Arasi. She sent you a text asking you to look at the photos you sent her from Lindsey's house."

I frowned. "How did you know my password?"

She looked up at me to roll her eyes. "Seriously? You use the same password for everything: 1-2-2-1. Although even if I didn't know that already, I could have guessed it since you're such an ABBA freak." She stopped walking and looked down at my phone, her eyebrows raised. "Wow. That's seriously messed up."

I took the phone from her and looked at the photo on the screen. It was the one I'd taken of the mirror over the fireplace at the Farrells' house on Queen Street. Behind me, in the room where at the time I was completely alone, was a filmy cloud that vaguely resembled a human figure. I squinted, trying to discern any facial features or anything at all that would definitely identify what we were looking at.

"Is that a finger?" Nola asked, pointing to something that appeared to be a human hand floating behind the cloudy form.

I nodded. "I think it is. It's pointing up the stairs." I remembered the attic, and being led to the box against the wall. And the necklace being dropped at my feet.

"Can I tell Lindsey?" she asked quietly.

"No. I mean, not yet. Let me show this to her mother and she can decide."

Nola faced me. "It's her dead aunt, isn't it? Does this mean you're going to help them find out who killed her?"

I looked pointedly at Rich, who was pretending very hard to be focusing on setting up his camera equipment, while listening to every word. "Let's discuss this later," I said, handing her my phone before running after JJ, who now careened toward the banister, his focus on a prominent pomegranate.

"Melanie?"

Distracted from my pursuit, I turned at the odd note in Nola's voice.

"What's this?" She walked toward me with my phone held up to me, the screen filled with tiles of photos I'd taken not only of Veronica's house, but also of Nola's room to document the before and after of the redo.

She made one of the photos bigger and put it closer to my face as Jack came to stand next to me. I'd simply taken the photographs without looking at them, figuring I didn't need to see them until after the project was completed. I squinted, already knowing what she was seeing, and felt my stomach clench.

"Looks like a guy in really old-fashioned clothes standing

by the antique jewelry chest," Jack said. "And correct me if I'm wrong, but he doesn't appear to have any eyes in his eye sockets."

I felt Nola, Jack, and Rich staring at me.

"Did you know about this?" Nola asked in a strangled voice.

My answer was drowned out by the sound of JJ squealing as he pulled the pomegranate from the garland, yanking the rope of magnolia leaves off of the banister and sending plastic fruit and greenery cascading to the foyer floor. They rolled in an oddly uniform pattern, all coming to a stop in a perfect circle around me, as the sound of a sibilant "S" curling like a rope around my neck rang in my ears.

CHAPTER
12

I shoved the small shopping bag from the Finicky Filly farther under one of the folding tables set up in the stables of the Aiken-Rhett House museum on Elizabeth Street so Sophie wouldn't see and know why I was late to our scheduled session to organize the wreath workshop supplies before the big event. Sophie wanted to make sure we had enough materials before the actual workshop, and it was my goal to ensure she saw only the boxes of the real stuff and not the faux fruit and garland I'd supplied.

After the previous day's Christmas photo session debacle, I'd been in dire need of retail therapy, and the lovely people at my favorite clothing-and-accessories store had been more than happy to oblige. Despite wanting to buy half the store, I'd had to keep reminding myself that I was on a strict budget and that unlike in my single days, I now had other people to consider before whipping out my credit card. In the end, I'd chosen an on-sale skirt as a present for my mother, a cute pair of inexpensive earrings for Jayne, and an incredibly cheap pair of shoes for me that were marked down so far they were practically free. I felt a lot better when I left the store.

I began sorting through the boxes of Christmas-wreath-making materials, noting with aggravation that many of the oranges donated by other volunteers had randomly spaced cloves and that none of the pomegranates was of uniform size or shape.

"How did the Christmas photo turn out?" Sophie asked

as she appeared next to me. I tried not to stare at her en-
semble, which looked as if her toddler, Skye, had chosen it.
And made it. If she hadn't, then I imagined Sophie must
have raided a defunct circus-costume stash to come up with
the color-blocked balloon pants with elastic at the ankles
(to better display her Birkenstocks) and clashing floral cardigan with oversized buttons of varying colors. Neon green
toe socks poked out of her sandals. I'd tried for years to
tell her that a pair of Keds or really any other kind of
shoe besides sandals would keep her feet warm. I'd finally
given up.

"How far did you have to run to get away from the
clown once you took his clothes?" I asked, grabbing two
more oranges, trying not to shudder at the unevenly spaced
cloves.

Sophie picked up some pomegranates and began laying
them out on the table to count. "The photo session was that
bad, huh? Guess you won't end up on the cover of *Parents*
magazine now."

"Better than being on the cover of *Circus Life*," I said
under my breath. Louder, I said, "It was awful, if you must
know. We ended up taking the photo in Waterfront Park
near the Pineapple Fountain so we wouldn't catch any dead
people in the pictures, and because it was cold outside, we
all wore our coats, which hid our mismatched outfits—JJ
and the dogs refused to wear their Christmas clothes, and
it was a disaster. Taking the photos outside was a stroke of
genius on my part."

"A true disaster," Sophie said. "I don't know how you
manage. You're a real survivor, Melanie."

I couldn't tell if she was being serious or not, and I didn't
get the chance to ask her before she bent over one of the
boxes with the fake boxwood branches I'd found at a wholesale club for ninety-nine cents per branch. She pulled out a
bunch and raised it to her face and gave it a big sniff before
turning back to me. "Melanie!"

"Don't they look real?" I asked enthusiastically. "By
the way, did I tell you that I have an appointment at the

historical archives to return old Vanderhorst letters that
someone tried to throw away?"

She threw the branches on a table, my transgression
temporarily forgotten. "Really? Who tossed them?"

"Marc Longo. He stole them from the archives. And
then, instead of returning them, he just tossed them. Luckily, his brother found them and gave them to Jack and me
to look through."

Her eyes narrowed. "There's a special corner of hell for
monsters like that. Anything important in them?"

"I don't know. Jayne texted me while I was doing a little
Christmas shopping just now to let me know Anthony had
dropped them off. I asked her to leave them on Jack's desk
to go through first as a sort of apology."

"Why are you apologizing?" She held up her hand to
stop me from responding. "Let me guess—you labeled all
of his drawers again with color-coded labels."

She looked up, waiting for me to respond. When I didn't
she said, "Then you organized his desk the way you would
organize your own without any thought to how he would
want it?"

I kept silent and watched as her eyes widened. "Oh, no,
Melanie. Did you try to keep something from him again?"

I turned away from her, finally giving in to the urge to
pick up one of the oranges and fix it. "I really screwed up.
I feel like a complete failure as a wife."

She was silent for a moment, and I felt her gaze on me.
"Melanie." I looked up at the soft tone of her voice.

"You're not a failure, okay? Quirky, sure. Insecure?
Yeah, most of the time. But you're a pretty great person all
around. You're a great mother and a terrific friend. Remember how you watched Blue Skye when both Chad and I had
the flu even though you already had a full plate? You didn't
even think twice. And despite what you might think, you're
a great wife, too. You and Jack were really made for each
other, like Chad and me. Like peas in a pod." She smiled.
"Organic, of course."

Even I had to return her smile at that.

She continued. "But you need to remember that marriage isn't something you walk into knowing what to do. It's a learning process. So, yeah, you made a mistake. Just say you're sorry and that you'll try harder, and then move on."

"So you think I need to apologize?"

She gave me a look that didn't need any words.

"Okay. I get it. And thanks." I stared at her for a long moment. "Although I find it hard to listen to you when you're dressed like that."

"Forget what I said about you being a terrific friend. So," she said. "What didn't you tell him?"

I replaced the orange, then blew into my hands to warm them before emptying a box of pomegranates. "Just about the apparition I've seen in Nola's room. And the dark presence I've been sensing in the upstairs hallway that may or not be related to the strange man without eyes that I've seen at the cistern."

Her eyes narrowed. "What strange man?"

"I didn't ask his name, but he's wearing old-fashioned clothing and holding a piece of jewelry. Like a bracelet or something with different-colored stones."

"What kind of old-fashioned clothes?"

I shrugged. "I don't know—old."

She took a deep breath. "Was he wearing pants or knee breeches?"

I thought back, trying to remember an image I'd been desperately trying to forget. "Breeches. Definitely breeches."

"Okay," she said slowly. "What kind of shirt?"

I closed my eyes. "It had a high neck with lots of frills in the front, and a tied bow at his throat."

Sophie nodded. "Was the collar standing straight up or folded over a little?"

"Folded over," I said without having to think about it. There'd been a large dark spot on his shirt, and my gaze had lingered there. But I'd noticed the bow.

"Hmm," she murmured, nodding.

"'Hmm,' what?" I asked.

"Well, it's just that you told me that the bricks from the cistern came from the old Vanderhorst plantation, right?"

I nodded. "Yes."

"Before the plantation was turned into a winery, the graduate program at the college would use the mausoleum there to train the students on various cemetery preservation techniques—usually involving shoring up crumbling tombs and cleaning headstones. It was hard to get students to go back. A lot of them said they got bad vibes. But a few say they actually saw something." She grimaced. "You know how sometimes people think they see a shadow and then blow it all out of proportion, so others jump on the bandwagon and say they saw something, too? My students and I hang around a lot of old buildings and cemeteries, so I've learned to take it all with a grain of salt."

"And you never mentioned this to me?"

Sophie gave me the same kind of look I imagined she gave Blue Skye when her little girl pushed her plate of organic quinoa onto the floor. "Really, Melanie? Since when do you want to talk about ghost sightings? Like never."

"Whatever," I said, mimicking Nola. "So, what did they see?"

"Apparently it was a full apparition of a man wearing late-eighteenth-century clothing. None of them stuck around long enough to get a lot of details, but they saw it long enough to register that he was missing his eyes. Kind of hard to miss that detail, I'd guess. And there was something odd about his shirt. Like there was a big stain on it."

Small beads of cold sweat formed at the base of my neck. "Was he holding anything?"

Sophie thought for a moment. "I don't remember them saying anything about that—they might have and I just forgot. Or they ran away too fast to notice it. Meghan Black is one of the students who claim to have seen something—since she's working in the cistern, you can ask her. Just don't tell her I told you. I really don't want to give any credence to this kind of thing."

I frowned. "Why? Because you don't believe in ghosts?"

"No. Because I do. I've been your friend for too long to doubt their existence. See, Melanie? Some people actually do learn, change, and grow as they experience new things."

The alarm on my watch beeped. It was one of those new watches that did everything except make dinner and clean the dishes, but the only thing I'd mastered since Jack had given it to me for my birthday was setting the alarm.

"I'm sorry—I've got to go. I have just enough time to get the letters at the house before my appointment at the archives." I glanced around at the Ashley Hall moms hanging evergreen boughs and signs indicating the various wreath-decorating station stops. "Looks like you have plenty of volunteers, so you won't miss me."

"Hang on." Sophie pushed a clump of plastic stems in my direction. "Take these with you. I'll have my grad students condition the real boxwood clippings so we can use them for the workshop." She picked up a plastic stem and held it delicately between two fingers, as if it might be contagious. "Really, Melanie. Even for you, this is pretty pathetic. I should make you work with the students to condition the stems. It would be a good lesson for them to learn what happens when we take shortcuts."

She looked as if she might actually be serious. I spotted Veronica walking across the courtyard toward us and I eagerly waved her over. "Perfect timing—I think Sophie needs you."

I reached under the table and pulled out my shopping bag. "I'll send Jack over with the minivan later to retrieve the faux boxwoods—I saved the receipt just in case."

"Just in case I noticed?"

"I would *never*."

Sophie didn't return my smile. "Remind me sometime why we're still friends."

"Well, it's definitely not because we admire each other's style," I said, indicating her pants before backing away until I was a safe distance from being pelted with a pomegranate, then turned and left.

When I returned home, I stashed my shopping bag in the

dining room so it was out of sight until I could safely reclaim it and bury my new shoes in my closet. Not that I expected to fool Jack; he noticed everything about me. I couldn't part my hair a different way or paint my nails a new color without him noticing and saying something nice about it. Several of the women I worked with complained that they could paint their bodies blue and streak naked through their houses and their husbands wouldn't even look up. I supposed I should be grateful, especially when every compliment came with a kiss—or two—but I was always afraid that one day he would stop. Then I'd revert to the old insecure Melanie, who couldn't believe that Jack Trenholm had picked her.

I walked over to Jack's office door and hesitated for a moment before gently rapping on it. "Jack?"

"Come in."

I pushed the door open and was surprised to see him sitting on the floor with papers strewn all around him. He had a stack in his lap and was apparently sorting them. I closed the door and leaned against it. "Are you speaking to me yet?" Since the photo incident, we'd shared a bed but not much else. All our verbal exchanges had been excruciatingly polite, the aura of disappointment surrounding him as thick as the humidity before a hurricane.

He sighed and looked up at me. "I'm sorry, Mellie. I'm not trying to shut you out. I'm just trying to figure out what else I can do to make you trust me. To share everything with me. Even when you don't think it's the best timing."

"It's just that you don't need distractions right now. . . ."

He held his finger to his lips. "Stop. I don't want to rehash the same old thing. It won't get us anywhere."

The sound of screeching brakes outside followed by a quick acceleration brought our attention to the front windows. Jack stood and joined me at the window, both of us wincing as I spotted my dad's old Jeep Cherokee being tortured as it scooted down the street.

Jack turned away from the window. "I can't watch. It might give me nightmares. Your dad must have nerves of steel. Thank goodness Jayne is in the backseat. I think she'll give a calming influence."

A heat wave of some unidentifiable emotion flushed through me. "Jayne's with them?"

Jack nodded. "Your dad asked her, and Nola thought it a good idea. I guess she was looking for backup in case your dad threw himself out of the vehicle."

I watched for another moment before I, too, had to look away, but not for the same reason. "I wonder why Nola didn't ask me." I somehow managed to keep the hurt from my voice.

Jack regarded me, his mouth twitching as if he wanted to smile. "I can't imagine that ending well, can you? It could be very stressful for both of you if she put her seat belt on in the wrong order of things."

I frowned. "Well, there's a right way and a wrong way for everything."

"Exactly," Jack said.

I watched him for a beat, waiting for him to speak first. When he didn't, I asked, "So, are we okay?"

Jack faced me, his eyebrows raised, and didn't say anything.

I pushed myself away from the window and walked slowly until I stood in front of him, then forced myself to meet his eyes. "I'm sor—" I stopped. Swallowed. Remembered what Sophie had said, and that I was trying to be the more mature version of myself. The version of myself who knew how to apologize, regardless of whether I thought she'd done anything wrong. I tried again. "I'm . . . sorry. About not telling you about the apparition in Nola's room. I was just trying to—"

He silenced me with a slow kiss. When he lifted his head, he said, "Saying sorry was enough—I don't need to hear anything else. We're a team, Mellie. Always. I just need you to remember that before you decide again to keep something from me. There's a lot about you that drives me crazy, but that's the one thing that I just can't live with."

I pulled back. "There are other things about me that drive you crazy? Like what?"

"Where would you like me to start?" He kissed me again, his lips lingering on mine. "I didn't mean it in a bad way, since I find most of your craziness endearing. But I suppose we could start with the labeling gun. . . ."

There was a brief tap on the office door before it was opened by my father, looking flushed and rumpled, as if he'd just outrun a pack of wildcats, with wide eyes and hair standing up at attention. He clutched a manila folder stuffed with papers and his hands shook a little.

"Are you okay?" I asked, concerned about his pallor.

"I'll be fine in a moment."

We all turned at the screech of brakes outside. Jack rushed to the window. "You didn't leave her alone, did you?" he asked, his voice full of concern.

My dad shook his dead. "No. Jayne insisted she could handle it. I think she's destined for sainthood." He said it with a note of admiration, making that hot flush consume me again. I wondered if I might experiencing the change of life already and made a mental note to call my gynecologist the next day.

He looked down at the papers strewn on the floor. "What's all this?"

"From Anthony. He dropped by earlier with a shoebox full of old letters and documents he'd found in the garbage can at Gallen Hall, presumably stolen from the archives by Marc when he found out I was working on another book. Marc apparently tossed them instead of returning them when he discovered there was nothing interesting enough to write about. He and Melanie had hoped there might be some information in there regarding the mausoleum. Sadly, just a lot of receipts and lists—nothing helpful."

My father held out the manila folder. "Well, maybe this will have something for you. When Yvonne was helping me find information about the gardens here and at our house, we found some misfiled paperwork. Yvonne made copies and I stuck them in the back of one of my folders, then forgot all about it until we were on the way to Gallen Hall. Remember, Melanie?"

I nodded, wishing I could forget.

He continued. "They're newspaper clippings and architectural drawings all about the Vanderhorst plantation, but they had been stuck in with the Tradd Street garden papers. Easy to see how that would happen, since they're both Vanderhorst properties. Yvonne said they use a lot of volunteers and interns to do filing and to return papers to the archives after someone has checked them out. So it wouldn't be out of the question that they were simply returned to the wrong folder whenever the last person looked at them—which could have been decades ago."

Jack began thumbing through the papers, a smile growing on his face. "Which means Marc never saw these, or he would have kept them. Or thrown them away." He looked up at me with an excitement I hadn't seen in a long while. He paused, his eyes widening as he gently took a yellowed page from the stack. "Well, well, well," he said. "Looks like we just might have beaten Marc at his own game."

My father and I moved to either side of Jack, looking down at the fragile page in his hand. "Is that . . . ?" I began.

"Two architectural renderings of the mausoleum at Gallen Hall, I think," Jack replied, a wide grin on his face.

My dad started to say something, but his words were lost in the screech of skidding tires and crunching metal from the street outside, followed by the sharp barking of a dog and the incessant scream of a car horn penetrating the house and making my blood run cold.

Jack threw down the folder and grabbed my hand before running from the room, my father close behind. And from somewhere came the heady scent of roses, as sweet and redolent as a summer day, following us outside into the frigid late-November afternoon.

CHAPTER

13

Jack let go of my hand as he raced around the smoking wreck of the two vehicles to the Jeep's driver's-side door, calling Nola's name, while my dad rushed to the passenger side, looking for Jayne. My feet remained where they were, unwilling to listen to my direction, the mixed scent of roses and burnt rubber making me cough.

I watched as both doors opened easily despite the crinkled sides of the Jeep, which more closely resembled an accordion than vehicle panels, then stared as Nola and Jayne stepped out of the car looking stunned but unharmed. I exhaled loudly, my relief loosening my bones. I closed my eyes for a brief moment, only to notice upon opening them the filmy apparition of a woman wearing clothing from the nineteen twenties standing by the tree swing beneath the ancient oak in our front garden. She was gone so quickly that I thought I might have imagined her. Only the lingering scent of roses told me that I hadn't.

I turned toward the other car, recognizing Marc Longo's silver Jaguar, or what was left of it after Nola had apparently T-boned the back half of it in the middle of Tradd Street. Considering the street was one-way, it was difficult to imagine how it had happened, but I had witnessed Nola behind the wheel; anything was possible.

The distant wail of a siren reverberated in the chilly air as I ran toward the Jaguar, steeling myself for what I might see. On the driver's side Marc was hitting the inside of the door in a futile attempt to open it, a deflated airbag hanging limply from the steering wheel. He glared at me through the still-intact window as blood seeped from a deep gash on his forehead. I grabbed hold of the handle and yanked, but nothing happened. I shrugged to show Marc I hadn't had any luck. Panic bloomed in his eyes and he began beating on the window with his palms, yelling something that I was sure I didn't want to hear.

On the other side of the car, Jack had opened the passenger door and he and my father were pulling out a man who had blood dripping from his nose and an ugly scrape across his cheek and was dressed as if he'd been on his way to a pulsing dance club. He had the unwrinkled skin and small build of an adolescent, although when he waved his hands to knock away Jack's hold on him, the corded veins on his hands gave away his age. The shaved sides of his head and floppy wave of bleached-blond hair hanging over his forehead were more suited to a teen or twentysomething than to someone in his mid to late thirties or early forties, as this man probably was. His close-fitting white shirt revealed not only his lack of an undershirt, but also the presence of an impressive six-pack. The shirt was tucked into tight pencil jeans and I couldn't help but notice that he wore cowboy boots. My gaze moved to his face and was met with an ugly scowl that matched Marc's, and for a moment I wanted to ask Jack to put him back in the car and close the door.

He stepped away from Jack and my dad, shouting at whoever would listen. "I guess I shouldn't be surprised that this is how they drive down here in the South." Checking that his shirt was tucked in, he glanced around until he spotted Nola and Jayne huddled together on the sidewalk, Jayne's arm held protectively around Nola's shoulders.

As he moved toward them, I glanced behind him as Jack gave a halfhearted tug on Marc's door, unfazed by Marc's pounding on the window or the muffled shouting. Marc was neatly pinned behind the steering wheel, making it impossible for him to crawl out the other side.

"Sorry, Matt!" Jack shouted with an exaggerated shrug. He cupped his ear to indicate the sound of approaching sirens. "I'm sure the fire department will bring the Jaws of Life to let you out soon." He turned his back, and his smile quickly slipped from his face as he focused on the passenger from the car stalking toward his daughter.

The man stopped in front of the two women, jabbing an index finger in their faces. "Which one of you is the driver?"

Jayne put on her nanny face and spoke firmly and calmly to the man, keeping her arm around Nola. "There is no need to shout, sir. . . ."

"Like hell there isn't! I could have been killed!" He did a figure eight in the air with his pointer finger, moving from Jayne's face to Nola's and then back again. "Which one of you is the idiot who caused this accident?" When no one answered, he leaned closer. "Which one of you?" He was so close, I'm sure spit flew in their faces.

Nola responded by bursting into tears just as Jack reached them and pulled her into his arms, letting her sob against his chest. "You need to calm down, sir. You're all in shock right now. Can we just stop with the shouting until the police and emergency vehicles arrive? Let's just take a moment and be thankful that no one was seriously hurt."

I was standing next to Jayne and moved closer to put my arm around her, but I noticed that my father had reached her first and that she was now safely tucked against his side.

The man let out an expletive. Even though I was sure Nola had heard it before, Jack put his hands over her ears. I could tell that Jack's temper was on the verge of igniting, although he kept it in check as he spoke to the man again. "Really, sir. There is no need to use that kind of language."

Fortunately, the next two words out of the man's mouth, which were probably a suggestion of what Jack could do to himself, were drowned out by the simultaneous arrival of a fire truck, an ambulance, and two police cars.

Everyone began speaking at once as the police officers

approached to get statements, and two firemen approached
Marc's car, leaving me alone in front of the house, watching
everything as if it were unfolding like a movie. I stared at
the man as he elbowed his way in front of Jack and Nola to
give his statement first, his words carrying back to me.

"I'm going to sue the person responsible for everything
they're worth. I'm going to make them pay for this! I could
have been killed, or maimed, because of some moron who
has no business behind the wheel." He pulled out a cell
phone and began stabbing at the screen. "I'm calling my
lawyer and he'll be on the first flight out of L.A."

"Sir, may I have your name, please?" the officer asked
calmly.

He stopped barking into his phone briefly to address the
policeman. "It's Harvey Beckner, and I demand to have a
complete medical evaluation and I want that driver locked
up." He pointed vaguely in Jayne and Nola's direction, not
yet having ascertained who the driver had been and not,
apparently, overly concerned.

The name sounded vaguely familiar—not in a personal
way, but as a name I might have read in a magazine or
heard on the news. Jack's gaze caught mine, and I could tell
that his thoughts were running along in tandem with mine.
I glanced at the cowboy boots, the perfect physique, the
Botoxed face and mod hair—the entire package more at
home in Los Angeles than in Charleston. I darted my gaze
back to Jack as realization dawned on me. Jack's eyes widened and I knew he'd figured it out, too.

A scream of tearing metal brought our attention back to
the Jaguar, where a metal arm was prying the door from the
side of the car as two firemen freed Marc from his prison.
After they pulled him out he brushed them off, ignoring
their advice to lie down on the waiting gurney. He staggered toward the cluster of people surrounding the policeman, grasping Harvey Beckner's arm. The man was
currently yelling into his phone, presumably to his lawyer,
telling him that he was going to sue the person responsible
and the whole city of Charleston if he felt like it.

"Harvey," Marc said, attempting a smile. "Glad you're okay."

Harvey pulled the phone from his ear and looked at him as if he'd forgotten Marc even existed. He yanked his arm away, looking with disgust at the blood smear from Marc's hand. "Okay? Are you blind?" He swiped at the blood dripping from his nose, grimacing as dark red drops landed on his sleeve. "I think my nose is broken! And who knows how much therapy I will need? I'll probably have PTSD." He jerked his head in the direction of Nola and Jayne. "What I do know for sure is that I'm suing these yokels. They won't even know what hit them once I'm through with them."

As if suddenly registering our existence, Marc faced us, pausing for a moment before slowly turning his attention to Nola. His face relaxed into a cold smile. It was a ghostly shade of white—a hue I was overly familiar with—making the blood garish in contrast.

An EMT was trying to get his attention. "Sir, you've got a wound on your forehead and you might have internal injuries. You need to lie down. . . ."

He brushed the EMT aside, his grin wider now. "So, Nola, you were driving? You've got your permit, right?"

I wanted to tackle her to the ground, anything to keep her quiet. But she was already nodding, no doubt lulled by the false sense of security of Marc being familiar to her.

"This is perfect," he said, fully smiling now, the sight odd beneath the blood oozing from his forehead.

"You know these people?" Harvey asked, his tone only slightly less belligerent than before.

"Very well, I'd say. Actually, we're related. Aren't we, Cousin Jack?"

Jack smiled, and I wondered if anyone else could see the tension in his jaw or the odd light in his eyes. I assumed they hadn't, or they'd all be moving back to a safe distance.

"No, actually, we're not. *Matt*." He emphasized the name he'd been calling Marc since they'd met.

Marc swayed a bit on his feet, but his grin remained. "No matter." He turned to Harvey. "This is Jack Trenholm.

You probably haven't heard of him, so don't worry if the name doesn't sound familiar. But he and his wife own Fifty-five Tradd Street. The house where our movie is set."

Our movie. I knew for sure now. This was the producer of the film based on Marc's book. Or Jack's book, I corrected myself.

Harvey examined us now with interest, and I wanted to grab my entire family, run into the house, and bar the door before he came to the same conclusion that I had already reached, and that I was certain Marc and Jack had, too.

I took a step toward Nola so that Jack and I flanked her as Jayne and my dad looked on, realization dawning in their eyes, too.

Marc continued, his grin never dimming. "And that girl, the one who nearly killed us, is their daughter Nola."

"Is that so?" Harvey said. "So this is the family who've been denying us access to the house for filming?"

"That's right," Nola said, stepping forward, apparently not hearing my silent screams for her not to speak, to admit nothing. "I was driving, but it was an accident. I was just practicing backing out from our driveway and I didn't see you coming." She hiccupped, her voice coming between shallow breaths. "And Marc stole my dad's book idea, and that's why we will *never* allow that movie to be made in our house. *Never.* That's why Melanie said she'd dye her hair purple and restore another house if that ever happened—which means it never will."

She was shouting by the last word and I drew her to me so she could bury her face in my shoulder and catch her breath.

"Is that so?" Harvey said, his grin now matching Marc's. He leaned in close to Nola's ear. "Because I think never is going to be a lot sooner than you imagined." He straightened, focusing his attention on me. "And I sure hope Melanie likes purple."

Jack moved forward, blocking Nola and me. "Are you threatening my wife and daughter?"

Marc threw back his head and made a sound that could

have been a chortle, his pallor even worse than before. He ignored the two EMTs on either side of him trying to coerce him into lying on the gurney. "That wasn't a threat, Jack. I think he was just explaining that you lost. Again."

Jack's expression didn't change. "Don't count your chips yet, Marc. Because no matter how many times I might lose, you'll never be a winner."

Harvey was back to shouting to his lawyer on the phone, and the police had begun to take statements from Nola and Jayne. Which was why no one noticed when Jack hooked one of his feet behind one of Marc's. Marc slid to the ground like a kebab without its stick, landing with a small *oomph.*

The EMTs struggled to lift him off the ground and onto the gurney while Jack got the attention of one of the policemen. "Make sure you check him for alcohol. He didn't appear to be too steady on his feet."

Jack didn't wait for a response, instead returning to Nola and me, putting his arms around us both as Nola and Jayne made their statements to the police while I weighed which was worse: being sued for everything we had or learning to like purple hair.

∞

I sat on the floor of the master closet with my labeling gun, organizing the Christmas presents I'd already bought. Before my family had increased exponentially, I'd usually finished with my shopping and wrapping before Thanksgiving. But ever since the twins were born, I no longer seemed in complete control of my life. Not that I ever regretted having children—I couldn't imagine my life without all three of them. It was just that even with a nanny, two sets of grandparents who lived nearby and were involved in our lives, and a supportive husband, there never seemed to be enough hours in the day to do all of the things that had once filled my days.

Like decorating and labeling the new storage bins I'd bought to store gifts in my closet. Part of the problem had been that my labeling gun kept disappearing, but even my gift spreadsheet, where I listed gift recipients along with gift ideas, was still mostly blank, with only the headers along the top. My brain felt pulled in too many directions to settle on any one thing, so nothing seemed to get done, leaving a trail of half-finished projects in my wake.

I sat back and sighed. Despite its already being December, the bins were nearly empty and those gifts that were inside hadn't yet been wrapped. Jayne had bought four tickets for the King Street and Downtown Holiday Shop and Stroll for the following weekend, so I hoped I'd make a dent in my list. Assuming I ever finished making the list.

I rubbed my eyes, exhausted from watching two back-to-back Hallmark Christmas movies with Nola. We'd settled ourselves in front of the TV in the upstairs family room while Jack finished with the police and called the insurance company before driving my dad home. Nola had been resistant at first, but after five minutes she'd been hooked. Four hours and two bowls of extra-buttery popcorn later, she said she felt much better. But that if I ever told her friends what she'd just watched, she would make sure no doughnut would ever cross the threshold of my house again.

I felt Jack's presence before he joined me in the closet and pressed a kiss on the top of my head. He sat down on the floor beside me and smiled, although I could see the tense lines around his eyes and mouth. "You look so cute when you're organizing."

"Thanks. You might try it sometime. It's very relaxing."

His eyebrows rose. "Do you have an extra labeling gun?"

"Is the sky blue?" I leaned forward and flipped off the lid of a shoebox. Like all of my shoeboxes, this one had a photo of the shoes inside taped to the outside to make finding the right pair easier. Except this box had a photo of a pair of shoes I'd given to Nola last year. I reached inside and pulled out my spare labeler and handed it to Jack. "The last time it disappeared, I bought two."

He looked down at it with a frown.

"It's the old-fashioned kind," I explained. "Where you have to dial the disk at the top and click it with the trigger. They're harder to locate than the new digital ones, but I find the clicking very therapeutic." I gently elbowed him in the arm. "Go ahead and try it. Right now I need two sets of numbers one through ten. That's so I can label each of the presents for the twins so they get the same amount."

"Is that really necessary?"

"Yes. You and I were only children growing up so it didn't matter, but I want to make sure I'm always fair."

"But . . ."

I reached for the labeling gun. "And if you argue with me, it's not therapeutic anymore, okay?"

"All right, all right." He began twisting the disk to the number one. "I just got off the phone with Harvey Beckner's lawyer."

My throat tightened. "And?"

"And Beckner is apparently okay with forgiveness and a fat check from our insurance company in exchange for the rights to film in our house. In a surprising move, he also said he would still pay us the going rate for the use of the house. Which is a good thing since I won't see a penny of income for at least a year except for straggling royalties for my older books."

I looked over at Jack, clicking the trigger on the labeling gun with more force than required, lost in his thoughts. "I guess we're supposed to feel grateful, but I can't help but believe there's another shoe somewhere waiting to drop."

Our gazes met before he returned to the labeling gun.

"How's Nola doing?" I asked, eager to change the topic. Jack had knocked on Nola's door as I was leaving after the Christmas movie marathon, just as Rebecca called to let me know that both Marc and Harvey had been released from the hospital with only a few stitches. It was another thing for which I should be grateful, but I just couldn't manage.

Rebecca had started to say that maybe things were going to work out for the best after all, but I'd hung up on her before I could say that things working out for the best would be that the accident had rendered Marc sterile so that he couldn't spawn little Marcs.

"Nola's pretty shaken up," Jack said. "We're really fortunate that no one was killed or seriously hurt. I don't think she will ever voluntarily get behind the wheel of a car for the rest of her life. She told me that all she wants for Christmas is a prepaid Uber account."

I leaned over to my open laptop, where the Christmas spreadsheet was displayed on the screen, before typing "Uber gift card" under Nola's name. "I can't say I blame her. I once rear-ended a CARTA bus on Meeting Street because I'd been distracted by the cutest pair of shoes worn by a woman on the sidewalk—so it technically wasn't my fault, but it took me weeks to be comfortable behind the wheel again."

Jack blinked at me a few times without saying anything before returning to his labeling.

"Louisa was there," I said softly.

"Louisa Vanderhorst? I thought she'd gone to the light, or wherever it is you send restless spirits."

"She did. But she comes back whenever she thinks she needs to protect us. I saw her and smelled the Louisa roses. I've actually been smelling them a lot lately. As if she knows something we don't."

Jack frowned. "It would be helpful if she could be a little more specific. We might have seen this whole fiasco coming." Before I could explain to him that it didn't work that way, he continued. "They've suspended Nola's driving permit, so her not wanting to drive isn't really an issue right now anyway. She was definitely at fault since she was the one apparently speeding backward out of the driveway when Marc drove past, so the fine will be pretty hefty. She and I both agreed that it will come from her royalties from the Apple song commercial," he said, referring to her extracurricular hobby of writing music for other artists and for the occasional jingle. It's what had saved our Tradd Street house once before.

I took a deep breath, forcing myself to confront the elephant in the room. "So, that's it, then? They'll bring their film crews in and we won't lose the house, right?"

Jack put down the labeling gun and turned to me. "Do you remember what I told you outside in the garden on the day we were married?"

I nodded. "About how you wanted to live here for the rest of your life and see your children grow up here?"

"Yes. That's all I've ever wanted. You and me, our family, here. And I cannot—*will* not—allow Marc Longo to take it all away from us. I'd rather die than see that happen."

I grasped his hands. I had a sudden flashback of Rebecca telling me about her dream. Of an unknown man burying Jack alive. "Don't say that, Jack. Don't ever say that."

His lips twitched in a small grimace. "It's not that we couldn't continue our relationship, you know."

"Jack . . ." I said with warning.

"Yes, they're going to film Marc's movie in our house," he said grimly. "We don't have much choice. In the meantime, I've rescheduled our meeting with Yvonne for tomorrow. We're going to dig through every piece of paper and we will find something. I know we will. I've sent a copy of the mausoleum drawings to an architect friend of mine, Steve Dungan, to look at to see if there's something I can't see with my untrained eye. There's a different date at the bottom of each one, so I'm hoping he can compare them and tell us what's different, maybe explain why the first one was built and then rebuilt only two years later." He squeezed my hands. "We're a good team, Mellie. If we work together, we can't lose. In the meantime, we'll pretend our tails are between our legs and we've given up." He reached his hand behind my neck and gently drew me toward him. "Two can play this game, and things are about to get dirty."

I kissed him, but my thoughts remained on Rebecca's dream as an icy chill skittered across my skin like someone walking across my grave.

CHAPTER
14

I loved the way Charleston dressed up for the holidays. From the light-bedecked spans of the Ravenel Bridge and the wrapped trunks and fronds of the palmetto trees in Marion Square to the streetlights on King Street masquerading as gentlemen sporting wreaths with red bows around their necks, nothing put me in the spirit of Christmas more than walking through the streets of my city. I always waited with a child's anticipation for the giant Santa hat to be placed on top of the turret of the house on the corner of Tradd and Meeting Streets. But as Jack and I drove to our appointment with Yvonne downtown, I barely noticed the red bows and greenery sprouting from most doors and iron gates. I was much too preoccupied with spirits other than the Christmas kind.

As usual, Jack had no problem finding parking near the Addlestone Library on the College of Charleston campus, where the South Carolina Historical Society archives were now housed. Yvonne Craig, long past retirement age, had turned down incentives to retire and instead had moved the few miles to the new location along with her precious documents. When she'd announced her decision, Jack had told her that she was one of the most important treasures found in the archives, and followed the compliment with a kiss on her soft pink cheek. I'd thought she might pass out.

Jack carried the shoebox of documents we'd received from Anthony, and I held the folder of misfiled materials

Yvonne had given my dad. We'd already combed through all the papers, reading and then reading them again without seeing anything that caught our attention as being something we should investigate further. I supposed the cost of nails and sugar on an eighteenth-century plantation might have historical significance, but did not necessarily contain the seeds to overcome the goiter on the necks of our well-being, Marc Longo.

Neither Jack nor I was willing to believe that there wasn't anything in those files that might lead us to any more hidden treasure. Or at least something that might be valuable enough to protect us against Marc's next assault. We might be in a temporary truce now, but we weren't naïve enough to believe that Marc wasn't out there waiting to pounce like some feral cat outside a mousehole.

Our hopes were pinned on the indomitable Yvonne. She'd gleefully accepted the scanned documents Jack had sent her the previous day to go over before our meeting, just in case we'd missed something; she claimed that at her age she didn't sleep much anyway. Besides, she'd said, she was hoping she could be instrumental in showing karma the way to Marc's front door.

As we walked through the doors of the Addlestone Library, Jack's face was grim, the dark smudges under his eyes making them appear more blue. Along with the dark stubble on his unshaven jaw, those smudges made him look like a marauding pirate on a mission, and I was glad that I was on his side. And in his bed.

I could only wish I looked that good when I hadn't slept. Jack hadn't come to bed last night, wanting to go through the files one more time, and all morning he'd been so preoccupied that he hadn't even noticed the new labeling system I'd given his sock drawer during my labeling frenzy the previous day.

"There's one thing I don't understand," he said, pausing inside the enormous glass rotunda where the previous summer the full skeletal remains of a T. rex had been on display. I'd wanted to bring the children, but Jayne said they were too young, and Nola had added that Sarah would be petrified if it started talking to her.

"Just one?" I asked, not meaning to sound sarcastic.

Not that it mattered. Jack's face remained grim and I wasn't even sure he'd heard me. "We know Marc wants our house. He's admitted as much. So why not just sue us outright so we have to sell the house, and then they could film to their hearts' content? Why make us believe that they'll accept the insurance payout for the accident in return for the rights to film inside, and just let it go?"

We headed toward the third floor, where Yvonne said we'd find her in the historic archives' reading room. We walked slowly as we contemplated the implications. "Good point," I said. We stopped walking and our eyes met. I swallowed. "Unless he needs us."

Jack nodded. "Exactly what I was thinking. He must believe there's something valuable hidden in the house that he has yet to find. And he's hoping we'll lead him to it." His face darkened. "We just can't afford to let him get there first."

I nodded, the unease I'd felt before now blossoming into a full panic. There was no doubt in our minds that Marc had orchestrated Jack's current situation with his publisher, so he was aware how vulnerable we were. Nola's accident must have seemed like an answer to Marc's prayers.

I could almost see the pall of gloomy thoughts surrounding Jack as we entered the reading room, with its dark wood tables clustered in the middle, each one with a reading light. The white walls were crowded with black bookshelves, the tan carpet a sponge absorbing our footsteps.

I spotted Yvonne, wearing her signature rose petal pink and her rope of pearls, emerge from the other side of the room. It was odd seeing her in a place so modern, with lots of glass and concrete, instead of against the backdrop of the centuries-old Fireproof Building, where she used to work. She was frowning as she approached, something else I wasn't accustomed to, her hands outstretched toward me.

"Aren't you both a sight for sore eyes?" she said, accepting cheek kisses from both of us. "I don't think I've seen a person over twenty-five all week. I've actually begun to feel my age—especially against all this . . . newness."

The library was a recent addition to the campus and was a far cry from the elegant balustrades, Ionic columns, and fine architectural details of the Fireproof Building. "It certainly is newer," I agreed, pushing down the Sophie-like thought that the historical archives had no business sleeping beneath concrete and glass.

She sighed. "Yes, that's true." She grinned at Jack over the rims of her bifocals. "But as we all know, youth can be overrated."

Jack grinned back, and I was relieved to see a bit of the light return to his eyes. "And I hope you can prove that, Yvonne, by telling me you found something."

"I do believe I have," she said, leading us toward a table near the back of the room.

Jack let out a breath. "Thank goodness. Because if you didn't have anything new for us, we'd have to resort to our Plan B."

"We have a Plan B?" I asked.

"Not yet," he said, placing a hand on the small of my back as we followed Yvonne through the maze of mostly empty tables.

She indicated that we should sit down at one of them where a thick folder rested, causing my heart and stomach to jump in unison. Jack slid the shoebox toward Yvonne. "Here are the documents that were taken from the archives. We've already talked to our detective friend, who says that even though we're pretty sure Marc Longo took them, it's all circumstantial. But if I were you, I'd put his face with a line going across it on a poster near the entrance to the library."

"And these," I said, placing my own folder in front of me, "are copies of the papers you gave my dad that had been misfiled in the garden papers for the Tradd Street house. They're a jumble of things but include building plans for both mausoleums at Gallen Hall Plantation. The best thing about these documents is that we're fairly certain Marc Longo hasn't seen them because they were filed in error separately from the other documents."

I felt as if we were playing a game of poker, each of us carefully laying out our cards, with Yvonne our clever dealer. Beaming at us from behind her bifocals, she opened her own folder but kept her hand over the paper on top. "In addition to going through the documents you sent, I did a little digging on my own."

She slid the top page toward us like a dealer in a casino, still covering it with her hand. "From what Melanie told me on the phone, Marc has seen, and possibly destroyed, an appointment diary once belonging to his grandfather, Joseph Longo, and in it, a picture of a drawing Joseph copied from a letter he'd found in the Vanderhorst home during a party." She looked at me for corroboration, her eyes bright and shiny like those of a surgeon getting ready to cut.

I nodded.

"Marc's brother also told you that in the archives that Marc stole and then"—she paused, as if in remembrance of a dearly departed loved one—"destroyed, he found a letter dated 1781 stating that a French visitor was coming to lay a wreath on the tomb of the Vanderhorsts' beloved daughter, Marie Claire. I'll keep looking, but sadly, I can't find a copy of it or any other corroborating documentation about any visitors in 1781 to Gallen Hall. Either it doesn't exist or Marc has already found and destroyed it."

"But the Vanderhorsts at that time didn't have a daughter," Jack said.

"Precisely," Yvonne said, finally lifting her hand from the paper. "This next part was easy. Here in the archives we have several tomes dedicated to various Charleston families—the original land-grant Charlestonians, who many still believe are the only true Charlestonians. We're quite proud of our bloodlines, although some aren't as blue as we'd like to think." She winked. "Fortunately, the sheer number of sources makes it rather easy to find family trees and biographical information about them."

We looked down and saw a photocopy of a biography taken from what appeared to be an ancient textbook. "This young woman, Elizabeth Grosvenor—known as Eliza to her friends and family—wasn't a daughter but did live with the family at the time as Mrs. Vanderhorst's ward. Her mother and Mrs. Vanderhorst were distant cousins, and when young Eliza was orphaned, she came to live with the Vanderhorsts at their plantation known as Gallen Hall. She was still living there in 1781, the year the letter was written."

Jack reached for the shoebox and began riffling through the contents before he pulled out a thin piece of paper, holding it out triumphantly. "I knew I recognized the name. Eliza was the one who purchased the first peacocks on the plantation. This is a purchase order for three pair, and her name appears at the bottom."

"Well done," Yvonne said, smiling at Jack as if he were her protégé.

I looked down at the paper Yvonne had given us; at the top-left corner there was what appeared to be an image from an oil painting, but the copy had all but blacked out her face.

Yvonne saw what I was looking at and explained, "The original portrait of Eliza is hanging at Gallen Hall. Of course you can't see it here, but she was reputedly a real beauty. She left many broken hearts in her wake, both British and American."

"An equal opportunity heartbreaker," Jack said, examining the smudge of black ink as if to see beneath it.

"Hers was the first body to be interred in the second mausoleum," Yvonne continued. "The first mausoleum remained empty until it was demolished. The first of three bodies interred in the newly built one, all in the same year—1782. To this day, they are the only three bodies in the mausoleum, and there were no further burials in the

cemetery after that year, although the house was inhabited
for more than two centuries afterward."

"So sad," I said, squinting at the larger print of her birth
date on the bio: 1758. I recalled all the ways Sophie had told
me a person could reach an early grave back in the days
before antibiotics. "She was only twenty-three. Was it
illness?"

Yvonne shook her head. "There's nothing in the official
record—which made me curious, of course. So I went back
through the papers in the shoebox and found a letter from
Carrollton Vanderhorst, the owner of Gallen Hall at the
time, to the reverend at the local church about a substantial
donation in return for a favor."

Jack nodded eagerly. "I remember seeing that—
something about requiring a particular area in the cemetery
to be set aside for a new mausoleum, and asking the reverend if he could make it happen." He began flipping through
the papers again, finally pulling out a yellowed piece of
thin paper, delicate ink strokes scratched on one side. "Here
it is. 'In such circumstances, whereby church dictates a soul
cannot be buried in consecrated ground, my heartbroken
wife and I implore you to do whatever is necessary to allow
a place where a soul might find peace, despite an unholy
demise.'"

"When I read that," Yvonne said, "I could think of only
one thing."

"Suicide," Jack said quietly.

Yvonne nodded. "Yes, very tragic. Especially since she
was beloved by the Vanderhorsts enough that they would
make sure she was interred in the family cemetery. There's
nothing mentioning suicide anywhere, of course, because
that would have been a terrible scandal. There's simply no
reference to what she died from, but back then dying young
wasn't as rare as it is now."

"Why should Eliza be important to us?" I asked.

Yvonne said, "I wasn't sure at first, either, so I kept digging. Jack mentioned that there were two mausoleums built
in the same place, two years apart, and I saw the plans you

sent me. So far, I haven't seen anything that might explain why they tore down the first one, or what that cryptic message about a 'Marie Claire' might have meant. Except . . ." She slid another page in our direction.

Whoever had printed this page from what appeared to be an army supply journal had made sure that the font size had been blown up enough so I could read it. Not that it mattered, because it appeared to be only a list of four items: cognac, feathers of goldfinch, kitchen maid, Burgundy wine. "What is this?" I asked.

"Do you know who the Swamp Fox was?" Yvonne asked.

"Of course," Jack said.

"No clue," I said simultaneously.

We exchanged a quick glance before returning our focus to Yvonne.

"Francis Marion. During the Siege of Charleston he and his men used guerrilla warfare to attack the British. He was never captured and he managed to wreak devastating losses on the British and bolster the morale of the patriots. Many patriot sympathizers hid him in their houses as he moved through the Lowcountry. I'm assuming the Vanderhorsts must have been sympathizers since the name Gallen Hall was mentioned in his personal papers."

"And this list . . ." Jack began.

"Came from Francis Marion's personal documents from the war. I found it when I did an archive computer search using the words 'Gallen Hall.' It's amazing what computers can do these days, isn't it? And to think everything used to be in these little card files. . . ."

"Oh, I still use card files," I began, but Jack cut me off with a throat clearing before turning his attention back to Yvonne. "So, what did this list tell you?"

"Well, nothing at first. These items were apparently a shipment that originated in Virginia and was headed to Gallen Hall, and given to the Swamp Fox for safe transportation." She slid another page in our direction. "Which I might have overlooked, Jack, if you hadn't scanned those papers for me last night. Because this is from the house-keeping journal at Gallen Hall, showing a delivery of the exact same items on March 27, 1781."

Jack's brow furrowed. "And because there's no such thing as coincidence, this must mean something?"

"But of course," Yvonne said. "I haven't had a chance to go through everything you sent yet—I just need a couple more days to do a thorough job—but here's a few more things I think you might find interesting before we get back to our sweet Eliza." She slid three more pages toward us.

She pointed at the first one. "This is a timeline of the American Revolution. I wanted to know what was going on in Virginia in 1781, just in case that might shed some light on all this."

"The Siege of Yorktown," Jack offered.

I looked at him with surprise and admiration, wondering where he'd kept this nerdy side hidden from me and finding it rather sexy.

Yvonne looked at Jack like a teacher encouraging her favorite student. "And who was the commander in charge of the American forces there?"

Jack blinked for a moment, thinking, while Yvonne gave me a courtesy glance to see if I might be able to come up with an answer.

"Look at the list again, Jack. Not the typical list of necessities, is it? But if you had to guess a country of origin for at least two of the items, what would be your best guess?"

We both looked at the list. "France," I ventured.

"The Marquis de Lafayette," Jack said at the same time.

"You both get As." Yvonne beamed.

"Okay," Jack said slowly. "So what does this have to do with Eliza and anything valuable that might still be hidden on the property?"

Yvonne folded her hands primly in front of her. "As you know, the marquis was French and had the full support of the French king, as France had officially recognized American independence in 1778, most likely to thumb their noses at their enemies, the British. It is not documented, but there were rumors that the king of France, in addition to promising troops and ships to support the American cause, had also given the marquis something very valuable to support the Americans financially—namely, to fund spies. It wasn't easy to garner help from well-placed individuals who had so much to lose if caught. Priceless jewels or gold or even art would make a fine incentive.

"There is no official record of this happening, but there are certainly enough rumors and vague letters in various historical archives attesting to the probability that it did happen. However, if the treasure—and we still don't know what it might have been—did make it stateside, there is no record of what happened to it or where it might be today."

Jack slid the list closer. Almost under his breath, he read it out loud twice. "Cognac, feathers of goldfinch, kitchen maid, Burgundy wine. Those four items don't go together. I can almost buy that Lafayette would be delivering cognac and Burgundy wine to supporters in South Carolina, but a bird and a kitchen maid? I don't get it." His eyes widened. "There must be a code in there somewhere."

"Most likely," Yvonne said. "Although I must admit I haven't figured out exactly what yet."

I wanted to say that was exactly where my thoughts had been headed, but that would have been a lie. Instead, I said, "Do you think this is what Marc was looking for?"

Jack slowly shook his head as he regarded me. "It's possible, although there was nothing in the shoebox or the folder that mentioned it. Unless he read something in the papers he already discarded."

"There's more," Yvonne said.

We both looked at her, and it appeared Yvonne was enjoying the suspense just a little too much.

She slid an enlarged copy of a grainy photograph in our direction. I recognized the triangular shape of the mausoleum I'd seen at Gallen Hall Plantation. This was an old photograph of the front of it, showing the names and dates of the mausoleum's residents engraved on the granite.

I recognized Eliza Grosvenor's name, but the other two

names, Lawrence Vanderhorst and Alexander Monroe, were unfamiliar, except for the Vanderhorst last name, of course. The only thing that stood out was that all three had died in 1782, Eliza in July and the two men on different dates in October. "Do we know anything about the two men?" I asked.

"We do now," Yvonne said as she slid two more pages toward us, both apparently from the same book as Eliza's biography.

I squinted at the photograph of the mausoleum's plaque while I waited for Jack to read the two biographies. He was silent for a few minutes, then straightened. He took a deep breath. "Well, that's an unexpected turn of events."

"What?" I said without looking up, distracted by something in the photograph.

"Alexander was a British soldier quartered at Gallen Hall during the occupation of Charleston, which began in 1780. And Lawrence"—he paused for effect—"was engaged to marry Eliza."

That made me look up. "So what happened?"

"It's not really clear. It just says that Alexander was found floating facedown in the Ashley River. Cause of death was accidental drowning."

"And Lawrence?"

Jack's eyes narrowed. "He was found four days later, a pistol shot to the middle of his chest. According to the biography, no one was ever charged with his death."

"According to *that* source," Yvonne interrupted. "But in *this* source, an atlas of Revolutionary War spies published in the thirties, their deaths had something to do with a spy ring, and one of the men might have been a double agent, selling secrets."

Jack and I shared a glance, both of us recalling something Greco had told us about a spy ring. He'd been pointing to a peacock carving on the claw-foot of Nola's bed.

"What was the spy ring called?" Jack asked.

"There's not a lot of information on it," Yvonne said. "Some historians even doubt its existence because there aren't any existing rosters of member names. The only way they identified each other was in the use of a symbol shaped like a peacock."

I felt Jack looking at me, but I was focused on the photo in my hand. "I think the rumors were right," I said, not looking up from the photograph of the mausoleum, the graininess of the old photo making details hard to discern.

Jack stood behind me, his warm breath brushing the back of my head as I felt the tension in his body, the pent-up excitement that we might have found something, however obscure, that might help us break free of Marc's hold on us.

"Here," I said. "What does that look like to you?" I pointed to the scrolling design that edged the plaque, so many swirls and curls that it was easy to hide a picture inside the design. Unless you knew what you were looking for.

I heard the grin in his voice. "It looks like the eye at the end of a peacock's tail."

"I agree," I said, smiling back. "Of course, it could just be a nod toward Eliza's passion for the bird, since she's interred there. Or not."

He kissed me briefly on the lips. "I told you we make a great team."

Yvonne gently cleared her throat.

"The three of us make an *extraordinary* team," he corrected himself before turning back to me. "Looks like we need to head back to the mausoleum and see for sure," Jack said with enthusiasm. His smile dimmed a bit. "Although I'm not really sure what any of this means, or even *if* it means anything, but it least it gives me something to focus on other than Marc, and the book, and Desmarae, whose latest idea is for me to get new author photos of me shirtless. To attract that younger demographic."

"But does that demographic even know how to read?" I asked.

"I don't know. All I know is that I just want to be left alone in peace to write, and not have to deal with all of this."

I grabbed his free hand. "I know. Hopefully we'll hear back from your architect friend with something helpful soon. And in the meantime, I'll call Anthony and set up a time for us to visit the mausoleum and hopefully figure this all out," I said with a great deal less enthusiasm as I recalled with a sinking feeling the last time I'd been there, and the lingering stench of rotting flesh that had followed me home.

"Don't forget to let Jayne know, so she can come, too," Jack said, gathering up the photocopies Yvonne had given us before enveloping her in a hug.

"Of course," I said, forcing a smile as I gave Yvonne a kiss on the cheek and a good-bye hug.

Jack actually whistled to himself as we exited the library, despite angry looks from librarians and patrons alike. He took my hand and squeezed, and I willed myself to be just as thrilled as he was at our discovery, reluctant though I was to examine what it was that had dimmed my own excitement like a dark cloud scuttling in front of the sun.

CHAPTER

15

On my way to the kitchen the following morning to grab my coffee before work, I heard the twins' babbling voices coming from Jack's office. I peered around the door and spotted the children, still dressed in their matching Christmas footie pajamas, batting at a crumpled ball of paper while the three dogs looked on, mesmerized. There was a lesson to be learned here, I was sure, as I did a quick tally in my head of the money I'd already spent on presents for Sarah and JJ that would probably never be played with as much as this crumpled ball of paper.

Jack sat on the floor near them, snapping photos with his iPhone. He'd already had to upgrade to a new phone with more memory because of the sheer number of photos he took of his three children. Except for the times when he turned the camera on me, my heart squeezed with every click, making me love my husband even more. Assuming that was possible.

"Good morning," I said, moving forward to kiss Jack. "I was wondering where my babies were and why the clothes I'd laid out for them were still on the bedroom chair." I knelt in front of Sarah and JJ, kissing them on their soft cheeks while they made appropriate smooching sounds. They smiled at me but were quickly distracted by one of the puppies batting at the paper ball.

I frowned as I stood. "And where is Jayne? I would hope that by now she'd know that the children should be dressed before . . ."

"Hi, Melanie."

I swung around behind me, where Jayne stood with a cup of coffee, looking young and rested. Unlike me, who hadn't had my coffee yet and who'd been awakened three times in the middle of the night by Sarah babbling to someone I couldn't see. I'd smelled the roses, so I hadn't been frightened. Just annoyed that as a mother herself, Louisa Vanderhorst didn't recognize that I needed my sleep.

Jayne clutched her mug a little tighter, making me realize I'd been staring at it. "Sorry, Melanie—JJ and Sarah looked so absolutely adorable in their pajamas that I thought we'd have a jammie morning. It's so cold outside that I thought we'd bring pillows and blankets downstairs and piles of books and camp out in front of the fire. When it gets a little warmer this afternoon, I'll dress them and take them to the park."

She took a sip from her coffee, reminding me that I was still staring at it. I forced my gaze to her face. "Um, sure. That's fine." I tucked a strand of hair behind my ear, then quickly replaced it, aware of the sun streaming through the windows and probably highlighting the six layers of concealer I'd smeared under my eyes to hide the dark circles. "I guess I'll, um, go get my coffee and head to work. . . ."

Jack stood. "Wait. I've got some great photos of the kids you'll probably want for the album. Look." He put his arm around my shoulders to draw me nearer, then started swiping his thumb across the screen to show me photos of Sarah and JJ playing with the puppies and wearing their cute pajamas. Jack was right. They were great photos, and ones I'd probably include in their photo albums. Except in every single one, Jayne was there—either with the children in her lap or sitting between them or next to them. I wasn't sure why that bothered me. She was my sister. Their aunt. She belonged in our photo albums because she was part of our family. But the gnatlike whine and itch of an unnamed irritation plucked at my conscience, making it difficult for me to meet Jayne's eyes when Jack lowered the phone.

"You're right—they're all great." I began backing out of

the room, hoping that some caffeine was all I needed to slap down that persistent whine in the back of my head.

"And don't forget to call Anthony—I went ahead and told Jayne about what we learned yesterday with Yvonne. She's eager to return to Gallen Hall."

"Actually," I said slowly, looking at Jack, "I already spoke with him. He said later this week would work, and since I knew you didn't have anything on your calendar, I said we'd meet him on Friday at four o'clock."

"But Jayne will be watching the twins then," Jack pointed out.

"Oh, well," I started to say, but Jack spoke first. "I'm sure either your mother or mine will be happy to fill in."

"I'll call Mother and ask," Jayne offered. "Not sure if we should mention this to Dad, though. What do you think?"

Dad? "Um, well, assuming we don't want a repeat of what happened last time, I don't think that would be a good idea."

"Agreed," Jayne said brightly. She drained her mug and put it on Jack's desk before approaching, probably feeling it was safe now that her mug was empty. "While I was at the salon yesterday getting a mani-pedi, I did some thinking about everything that's been going on here at the cistern, and the connection with Gallen Hall and all of that history."

I curled my gnawed fingernails with raw cuticles into my palms so no one would notice how long it had been since I'd seen the inside of a nail salon. "Yes?" I said, forcing myself to listen.

"Remember the soldier we saw pointing the musket at us when we visited the plantation? Well, I find it interesting that one of Eliza's roommates at the mausoleum was a British soldier. Too much of a coincidence to be a coincidence, right, Jack?"

She looked at my husband for corroboration before continuing. "What's really interesting is that Alexander Monroe was a British officer billeted at the plantation during the occupation. So why would he be interred with a son of the household and his fiancée? They had the entire cemetery at their disposal—why not just bury him in a regular grave?"

"I've been thinking the same thing," Jack said, giving Jayne a look of admiration that made the gnat in my head buzz a little louder.

Jayne continued. "And remember that smell in Nola's room that happened when those letters appeared on her wall? It smelled like gunpowder and horses and leather, didn't it?"

I nodded. I'd thought the same thing but had kept it to myself, hoping to figure out what it meant first. Maybe if I'd had the time to get my nails done, I would have figured it out, too.

"Maybe it's Alexander," Jayne suggested. "Which means there's a definite connection to the cistern and the mausoleum. Although, I don't know." She shook her head. "I didn't get a negative feeling from him, but there's definitely a negative vibe in Nola's bedroom."

"There's a woman, too," I added, avoiding Jack's gaze. "I saw her on the stairs. Just once, and it was very quick. It was the day of the Christmas photo, and I only saw her that once. I didn't connect her to the mausoleum, probably because I saw her here, and . . ."

They were both looking at me with blank expressions, and I knew we were all remembering the argument I'd had with Jack that very afternoon when Nola had found the photos on my phone of the other spirit in her bedroom. The argument that had been about me not telling Jack everything. I swallowed. "It was very quick," I repeated. "But I think she said something—it wasn't very clear. I've been waiting to see her again so I could make sure I heard her right before I told anyone. I wanted to be sure."

Jack's lips pressed together in a tight line. "What did you think she said?"

I could still hear the "S" of the last consonant, slithering like oil inside my head. "Lies."

"Just that one word?" Jack's eyes narrowed.

I went to him and kissed him soundly on the lips, keeping

it G-rated on account of Jayne and the children being present. "Just that one word. I promise."

His hands cupped my shoulders. "Is there anything else you think you might want to tell me?"

I shook my head. "I don't tell you about every ghost I see because you might start questioning my sanity. I can't block them all." I looked over at Jayne for corroboration and she nodded. "I didn't think to mention the woman on the stairs because I thought it might be someone who'd followed me from outside and it was a onetime deal. It happens a lot. It might even have been something the girls conjured when they played with the Ouija board—there's really no way of knowing. But now, in context with what Yvonne told us, maybe the ghost is connected to the cistern."

"You look so sexy when you're being earnest," Jack said, his lips twitching into a reluctant smile. He pulled me closer to him and kissed me.

"Not to sound like Nola, but get a room."

We broke apart and looked over at Jayne, whose hands were firmly planted over her eyes, one on top of the other just in case there might be an opening she could peek through.

"Actually, I need to get to work," I said, my words dying as I recognized the Hard Rock Foundations truck pulling up in front of the house. "Did anyone else just hear the sound of a giant cash register sucking in all of our money?"

Jack followed my gaze. "Why is Rich Kobylt here?"

We heard the sound of Nola bounding down the stairs before coming to an abrupt stop outside Jack's office door. "Dad? Can you drive me to school? It's Mrs. Ravenel's turn to drive, but Alston and Lindsey have to be at school early and I don't so I said one of my parents could drive me instead."

Jack looked at his watch. "Don't you have to be at school in twenty minutes?"

She nodded. "Yes. So we have to hurry."

Jack sighed heavily as he reached for his car keys on his desk. "And you didn't think to mention this yesterday?"

"No, sorry. I forgot." She hitched her backpack higher on her back, pulling her long-sleeve purple polo out of the waistband of her gray uniform skirt, then turned to me. "And Dr. Wallen-Arasi stopped by yesterday afternoon to look at the dining room floor again and asked me to tell you that Mr. Kobylt would be here this morning to give you an estimate."

Jack and I exchanged a glance, an unspoken agreement to let it slide. We were still so grateful she'd emerged physically unscathed from the accident that neither of us wanted to call her out about being irresponsible. We'd save it for another time.

"Come on, Nola—let's get in the van." He gave me a brief kiss on the lips, said good-bye to Jayne and the twins, then left with Nola.

"Great," I said, sucking in my breath and mentally girding my loins. "I guess that means I need to go talk to Rich."

Jayne reached down to grab a hand of each toddler. "He went around to the back, so you might want to go through the kitchen. He probably wants to check on the progress of the cistern. Didn't you tell him that you want it filled in by Christmas?"

"Yep. Although I haven't told Sophie because I'm afraid of what she'll tell me." I kissed JJ and Sarah, then headed out through the kitchen, grabbing my coat and a cup of coffee on the way.

Rich Kobylt wore a thick sweater that was long enough to cover his waistband, something for which I was eternally grateful. I didn't think my stomach could handle the view of his backside without at least a cup of coffee in me.

"Good mornin', Miz Trenholm," he called out in greeting.

I closed the door behind me, my face stinging with the chill. "Hi, Rich." I noticed he wore a large metal cross on a heavy chain around his neck. I was pretty sure I hadn't seen it before. He must have guessed where I was looking, because he put his hand on it.

"My wife gave it to me," he said. "No offense, Miz Trenholm, but this garden gives me the creeps. You'd think finding a skeleton in the fountain and then again in the foundation would have sent me over the edge, but it's this cistern that just makes my skin crawl. I feel like someone's watching me whenever I'm in the backyard. My wife gave me this as a little extra protection." He jiggled the chain.

"That was nice of her," I said, not able to think of anything else to say. Was there a proper response for when someone starts wearing a religious icon to protect them from your backyard?

"Yeah, she's pretty thoughtful." Facing me again, he said, "So, I hear my friend Greco is working for you now. He's got a funny way of dressing, but he's a good guy."

I kept my face neutral. "He's great. Very nice to work with. And definitely not easily spooked."

Rich's eyes narrowed a little at my choice of words, and I bit my lip, wishing I hadn't said that out loud. He faced the cistern, where Meghan Black and two other students were diligently picking at the bricked sides despite the cold. "Between you and me, this is taking a lot longer than I'd thought. If they don't finish this week, there's no way I'm going to be able to fill this in and make it disappear before your big party."

"Could you just get a bulldozer in here and cover it all up and we'll call it an accident?"

He stared at me blankly. "You serious, Miz Trenholm? Because I don't think Dr. Wallen-Arasi would go for that." He emphasized his words by shaking his head. "As a matter of fact, she's nice and all, but I wouldn't want to get on her bad side."

As a frequent victim of her bad side, I had to agree. "No, you certainly wouldn't want to go there. So," I said, eager to get away from the cistern and the pervasive scent of dead, rotting things that lingered despite the cooler air and Sophie's assurances that anything dead would have disintegrated long ago. "You're here to look at the dining room floor?"

"Yes, ma'am. I understand you got some of those nasty wood-boring beetles."

"According to Dr. Wallen-Arasi, we do." I put my hand
on his arm and leaned closer. "Could you do me a favor,
please? If it's over a thousand dollars to get rid of them and
repair the floor, could you get me an estimate on laminate
floors? You know—the ones that look like wood but aren't
tasty to beetles?"

He pursed his lips. "Dr. Wallen-Arasi won't like that at
all. Not one bit."

I stepped back. "True. But she's not the one paying for
it, is she?" I narrowed my eyes at him. "And if you breathe
one word to her about what I just said, you're going to need
a lot more protection than that necklace. Do you understand?"

His eyebrows shot up. "Yes, ma'am. I understand."

"Good. You go on inside. I have a quick question for one
of the students first. I'll join you in a minute."

He didn't wait for me to tell him a second time. He'd
almost made it to the kitchen door before he bent down to
tie his shoe. I almost spit out my coffee and had to avert my
eyes.

Turning toward the cistern, I watched as Meghan Black,
in the same cute black bow earmuffs and pink tool belt I'd
seen her in before, bent forward with a tiny brush to wipe
dirt from a protruding brick in the cistern's wall.

"Hello, Meghan?" I called.

She continued with the brush and I noticed the wires
from her earbuds snaking beneath the earmuffs. I moved to
stand in front of her and waved my hands until she noticed
me. She reached up and pulled out the buds and smiled at
me. "Good morning, Mrs. Trenholm."

"Good morning." I took a sip of my coffee, the liquid
quickly growing cold. "So," I said, indicating the deep hole
in my backyard. "Are you all almost done here?"

She looked horrified. "No—far from it. We're finding
things every day, but it does take time to make sure nothing
is damaged when we excavate." She moved closer to me,
and I saw a pink and green Lilly Pulitzer coffee thermos on
the ground next to a white blanket, on which what looked

like junk lay in careful rows. "Look what we found this morning," she said with excitement as she held up what appeared to be a broken piece of china. "It's a broken piece of china!"

"Fascinating," I said.

"I know, right?" Meghan carefully replaced the shard next to a nearly identical piece. "I think we might have an entire cup and saucer." She moved her hand to something smaller lying on the blanket. "We found this bone, too," she said, holding up something small and white as my throat constricted.

Her smile fell. "Oh, don't worry, Mrs. Trenholm. Actually, we've found a lot of animal bones—mostly chicken bones. Probably from buried garbage. You know what they say—one man's trash is another man's treasure."

She said it with so much enthusiasm that I had to smile. "Do you have a moment? I wanted to ask you about that photo you took. And the man standing near the cistern."

A visible shudder went through her, and I was fairly sure it had nothing to do with the wind. "I deleted it from my phone. Along with the photo of the face in the window upstairs."

This didn't surprise me. I would have done the same thing if I didn't know for sure that the spirits wouldn't stay deleted. "No worries—you e-mailed them to me, so I have them on my phone, and you gave me printed copies, remember?"

She nodded. "Yeah. You should probably delete the photos and tear up the prints, too. It's not like I believe in that kind of thing, but it would seem to me that's not something you should have hanging around your house."

"No doubt," I said. "So, I don't know how much you recall about the photo, but was there anything you noticed that was memorable about the figure?"

"Apart from the fact that he wasn't there in person and only showed up in the photo? That's kind of hard to forget."

"Sure. But what do you remember about his clothing?"

"Oh. It was definitely late eighteenth century."

"Are you sure? Because in the picture, it appeared he wore a cravat with folded collars."

"A lot of people can't tell the difference between seventeenth- and eighteenth-century men's fashions unless they study that kind of thing—unlike women's fashions. You can always tell by the width of their skirts what decade of what century they're from. Cravats were worn for decades overlapping the two centuries. But I know it was eighteenth century because I distinctly remember his hair was pulled back, like in a ponytail, and not cut short. That's the main difference between the two centuries."

I'd been harboring a hope that this specter had nothing to do with the woman on the stairs or the soldier at Gallen Hall. Because then they would be separate entities, to be dealt with one at a time. But three eighteenth-century apparitions pointed in another direction entirely. "Was there anything else?" I asked, forcing myself not to hold my breath as I waited for her answer.

She began to shake her head, but stopped. "I've tried to forget it, but there was something about his eyes. At first I thought they were just hidden by shadows. But then . . ." She stopped, looked at me. "But after printing the pictures and looking at them closely, it looked as if they were . . . not there." Her brown eyes opened wide. "I hope I'm not scaring you, Mrs. Trenholm. It was probably just dirt on my iPhone. My mom has always said I have an active imagination, so I naturally made a smudge into a person. Because ghosts aren't real."

"So they say," I said. As if in afterthought, I said, "Did you ever do any work at the cemetery at Gallen Hall?"

"Oh, yeah. When I was an undergrad, we went out there a few times with the FARO laser scanner in our digital documentation class to document the headstones. It was really fun."

"Sounds like it," I said. "So, did you or any of your classmates ever . . . see anything there? Any dirt smudges on camera lenses that looked like a ghost?"

She went very still. "Maybe."

"Maybe, yes?" I prodded.

"Yeah. A bunch of us saw something once and everyone ran, including me. But I tripped—I'm a little clumsy—so I got a better look. He was standing by the mausoleum."

"Did it look like the same person that you saw here?"

She took a moment, then nodded. "Yeah—it was definitely the same . . . thing. I know because there was a . . . stain or something on his shirt, where you could see beneath his jacket. It must have been unbuttoned or something, because I could see the white shirt underneath." She rolled her shoulders as if to shake off the awareness of someone staring at her. "I don't talk about it because I'd rather just forget it."

I forced a bright smile. "Totally makes sense. If I'd seen something like that, I'd want to forget all about it, too." I finished my ice-cold coffee. "Well, thanks for speaking with me. I don't want to hold you up, so I'll let you get back to work. Have fun."

She nodded enthusiastically. "Don't worry—I will!" She replaced her earbuds as I stepped away from the yellow tape and made my way back to the house, the awareness of someone watching me making my skin crawl. I entered the kitchen without looking back, content with telling myself it had been Meghan.

CHAPTER
16

I held the step stool for Veronica so she could place the angel at the top of the dining room Christmas tree. I hoped no one would notice that half of the angel's yellow yarn hair and one of the felt wings were missing thanks to Sarah, who'd mistaken the angel-doll tree topper for a chew toy. I had no idea how she'd reached it since I'd had to put it in a closed box after she'd spotted it in the dining room, but it had managed to find its way into her crib. I wondered if Louisa might be exercising her indulgent-grandmother instinct postmortem.

"Perfect," Veronica said, stepping down from the stool. "I think all of the trees look lovely, but this is the prettiest in my opinion."

I stood back, admiring the effect of handmade dolls hanging from pine boughs, and strings of popcorn and pinecones wrapping around the tree. "My arms are so short. I'm glad you were here to hang the ornaments on the upper branches."

She smiled, but her eyes were sad. "Adrienne was five feet eleven inches by the time she was seventeen. She was always the go-to person for tree decorating or getting something off a high shelf. Everybody thought she played basketball or volleyball, but she wasn't athletic at all. She preferred to read and play the piano. It was really unfair— all that height wasted."

"I bet," I said, aware suddenly of her sister's perfume settling in the air around us. I pretended to continue studying the tree while I tried to decide if I should say something. "I, uh . . . When I was in your house taking photos for Sophie, I ended up in the attic."

She looked at me without surprise. It was almost as if we were challenging each other to see who could pretend the longest that they didn't see the elephant standing in the middle of the room.

"I know. Michael told me. He said he thought you were only planning on taking pictures of the first floor."

"I thought so, too. But your house is so beautiful, I couldn't stop. I hope you don't mind me being so nosy."

Veronica shook her head. "Not at all. I hope you got what you needed."

She kept her eyes leveled on me, and I knew she wasn't talking about the pictures. "I think so." I stopped, then found myself feeling the need to say more. "I found the box full of Adrienne's things."

"I know. I saw that her little heart pillow was missing."

My cheeks reddened. "I don't know why I took it. I just sort of . . . panicked when I heard Michael and Lindsey come in the front door, and it seemed the logical thing to do at the time. If you'll hang on a second, I'll go get it. . . ."

"No, please don't. I think Adrienne must have wanted you to have it. Unless you have a habit of taking things from people's houses." She smiled so I wouldn't take offense.

"No, not usually. I just felt . . . compelled to put it in my purse." I chewed on my lip for a moment, straightening a string of popcorn and pinecones. I wanted to get a ruler to make sure each strand was evenly spaced, but I was fighting the impulse. Jack said it was the only way I could get better, to fight that impulse for precision—unless I decided to become a Formula One mechanic or a brain surgeon.

"Was the pillow important to Adrienne?"

Veronica smiled. "Yes. Our mother made it for her before Adrienne went to college. Even though she was nearby, Mom said she wanted Adrienne to remember that she was loved."

The surge of perfume stung my eyes and I had to blink back tears. "Your poor mother," I said, thinking of Nola and how it would feel if something happened to her. I couldn't go beyond that thought.

"We were all devastated, of course, but especially our mother. I don't think she really ever recovered." Veronica brightened. "There was another box that we retrieved from her dorm room, full of clothes she'd made. She wanted to be a fashion designer—ever since she was a little girl. She was always making clothes for Mom and for me, and most of her friends. She was incredibly talented with a needle. I donated the clothes to a women's shelter, knowing Adrienne would approve. It's funny. . . ."

When she didn't continue, I prompted, "What?"

Veronica shrugged. "You know how you said you felt compelled to take the heart pillow? I felt the same thing when I saw that box of clothes. It was like Adrienne was speaking in my ear."

She probably was, I wanted to say.

"You still have the necklace, right?" she asked.

I couldn't tell her how I'd rediscovered it, so I just nodded.

Still looking at the tree, she said, "I've been meaning to ask you for it, but I thought . . ." She stopped for a moment, lifted her hand to touch a small wooden nutcracker ornament wearing British regimental red. "But I thought that as long as you held on to it there was a chance you would agree to help us."

"Us?"

Veronica met my gaze. "Adrienne and me. Michael just wants to put it behind us. But I can't move on." She lowered her voice to a near whisper. "I sense her near me all the time. I don't think she'll rest until we find out what happened to her. To punish the person responsible. Which means I can't give up. It's just that Detective Riley hasn't been able to turn up anything new despite the necklace and what it might mean. We're back to where we started before I found that box." She shrugged but I heard the hitch in her voice. "You were my last resort. I don't know where else to turn."

I turned back to the tree, focusing on a small robin's nest ornament, the single egg made from a wooden button. My cheeks heated as if she'd just scolded me, which, I suppose, she had. "So," I said. "Hypothetically speaking, if I were psychic, what would you ask me to do?"

"Hypothetically, if you were psychic, I'd want you to ask Adrienne who killed her."

I thought for a moment, remembering the apparition I'd captured on my phone while taking pictures in her house. But I didn't want to scare her. I paused, trying to find the right words. I cleared my throat and said, "From what I've been told, it never works that way. It's like the living and the dead still speak the same language but just use a completely different dialect. And there's, like, a . . . time delay. Remember what it used to be like speaking long-distance on a landline before fiber optics? Where one person asks a question, and by the time the other person hears it, they've already started asking their own question? So, no. It's never as easy as just asking."

I almost mentioned the Hessian soldier who'd once haunted my mother's house on Legare Street. I'd had complete conversations with him, and I hadn't understood why I'd been able to until my mother explained that he must have also been able to communicate with spirits when he was here on earth. But I couldn't tell Veronica that. Because I wasn't supposed to know what it's like to speak to the dead.

I realized Veronica was staring at me.

"So I've heard," I quickly added. "And a lot of times, the spirits aren't strong enough to convey an entire message. It takes a lot of energy just to make themselves seen." *Or smelled,* I almost added. "Then they have to find a way to deliver the message as quickly as they can, which usually lasts for a brief second. It's why so many messages from the other side seem coded. It's just quicker for them to say what they have to say."

"So you've heard."

I nodded. "Right."

"In that case, I'd ask you to keep the lines open, then pay close attention when she gives you a message. Like compelling you to walk upstairs to an attic where you hadn't planned on going."

"And if I did, and I somehow managed to figure out who did this to Adrienne, what would you do?"

"I'd tell Detective Riley and leave out any mention of your name in any publicity that might surround the story of solving a twenty-year cold case. I'd never find the words to adequately express my thanks, but I'd promise to never stop trying."

My eyes stung and I quickly blinked them. "That's good to know."

"So you'll help me?"

Our eyes met and I swallowed. "If I were a psychic, I'd find it very hard to say no."

Any response she had was lost as repeated loud knocks sounded on the front door. I rushed to open it, then wished I hadn't. Rebecca stood on the front porch looking flustered and a little disheveled, which, for her, consisted of a hair out of place and her pink hair bow slightly askew. She carried a silver flocked tabletop Christmas tree, complete with a bedazzled star tree topper and a pink feather garland.

I moved back to allow her and the tree inside the vestibule. "I don't know why you can't get that doorbell fixed, Melanie. I've been ringing and ringing and freezing to death outside. Did you forget I was coming?"

"Funny—it worked for Veronica. And, yes, I did forget. Veronica and I have been busy all morning finishing up all the fireplace mantels and we just completed decorating the last tree in the dining room."

Her pink-lipsticked mouth formed a pout. "But Sophie said I could put my tree in the dining room."

I shook my head, pretending to think. "No, I'm pretty sure she said laundry room. Since it's tabletop size, we all thought it would look best sitting on top of the washing machine."

Her lips pinched together. "Marc and I are donating a *lot* of money for this event. I would like to think that gives me *some* kind of bonus."

"Of course it does," Veronica said gently as she took the hideous tree from Rebecca so my cousin could take off her pink faux fur coat. "That's why we're putting your tree in the laundry room. It will be the centerpiece since no other decorations will be in there to compete with the beauty of your creation."

I wanted to high-five Veronica for not mentioning that the reason it would be the only Christmas-themed item in the laundry room was because the laundry room wasn't likely to be seen by any of the guests.

"Thank you," Rebecca said, sounding slightly mollified. Addressing Veronica, she said, "I've got a whole bag of ornaments in the shape of little dogs that I bedazzled in my car. If you'd like to go ahead and bring the tree to the laundry room, I'll go get them. You can help me put them on the tree."

"Will do," Veronica said, as I admired her ability to keep her eyes from rolling. "Oh, and please thank your husband again for that generous donation to Ashley Hall. I've already spoken with the school, and since I know Melanie is crazy busy this time of year with work and her family obligations, I told them I will be happy to host the film crew at my house for my portion of the progressive dinner so they won't have to bother Melanie. Can you please let him know?" She smiled brightly, then left, leaving Rebecca to just mutter, "Sure," as Veronica disappeared into the back of the house.

When Veronica was out of earshot, Rebecca put her hand on my arm. "How's Nola doing?"

I stiffened. "Physically, she's fine. Mentally, well, she says she's never going to drive a car again. Especially not after what that horrible Harvey Beckner said to her."

"I know." She leaned closer to me in a conspiratorial way. "He's not my favorite person, either. Marc's writing the screenplay, you know, because nobody else is really qualified to tell the story—"

"Except for Jack," I interrupted.

"Yes, well, be that as it may, Marc's working on the script and Harvey keeps on asking for more sex and violence and all sorts of things that weren't a part of the original book. He wants to show a love scene between Joseph Longo and Louisa Vanderhorst."

"What?" I said, horrified. "But she loved her husband. That never happened—never. That's just a horrible fabrication—and skews the whole story!"

"I know, I know. Poor Marc. He's really stuck between a rock and a hard place, isn't he?"

"Excuse me?" I asked, sure I'd misunderstood. "Are you saying Marc is the victim here?"

Rebecca's round blue eyes blinked slowly. "All I'm saying is that Harvey is being really unreasonable. Marc's book is perfection as it is—otherwise it wouldn't have hit so many bestseller lists, right? I don't know why Harvey is requesting so many changes. But, anyway, I've been worried about Nola and I'm glad to hear she's doing better."

"At least until the film crews arrive in January to start filming the movie. I think she's more upset about this deal than Jack and I are. She thinks it's all her fault."

"That's silly. Just tell her it would have happened sooner or later. Marc always gets his way."

"Really?" I said, crossing my arms. "Because he told me that he was going to own this house."

"I don't know why he wants this old, creaky house, but if he said he wants it, sooner or later he'll get it."

I waited a moment so she could let her own words sink in. "You do understand you're talking about my family home, right?"

"Sure—but you never really wanted it, remember? Didn't you use to refer to it as a goiter on your neck?"

"Yes, but that was before I married Jack, and before Nola came to live with us and the twins were born."

Rebecca looked skeptical. "All I know is that you never wanted this house. That you've always hated old houses. That's the only reason why I'm not fighting Marc on this. Because I know that it's really what you both want."

I was so angry that I couldn't find any words to argue. She must have taken my silence for agreement, because she put her hand on my arm again, and said, "I had another dream."

"About something bad happening to Jack? I'm starting to think you're making this all up just so we won't fight Marc anymore."

"No. This one wasn't about Jack."

She was scrutinizing me so closely that I had to step back. "Was it about me?"

Rebecca gave a quick shake of her head. "No. It was about Nola."

My stomach and heart squeezed. "Nola?"

"Yes. At least I'm pretty sure it was her. It was a young woman about her age, and she's the only person I know who fits that description, so I assumed it was her. There was . . ." She reached her hand up to her neck in a defensive gesture. "There was . . . there was a rope around her neck."

My breath came in shallow gasps as my hand slowly drifted up to my own neck, as if to make sure there was nothing there.

Rebecca patted me on my arm. "I know—it's hard to hear. But I also know you'll figure it out in time to protect her. I'll let you know if I have any more dreams." She flashed me a bright smile. "Right now, I'm going to get those gorgeous ornaments from my car and help Veronica set up my tree. It's going to be the most beautiful tree in the house, if not all the houses!"

I watched her leave, then stood where I was in the vestibule for a long moment, staring at the closed door. I'd heard

Nola come in from school about an hour before and had the sudden need to see her, to make sure she was all right.

I took the stairs two at a time, surprised to find her door open and voices coming from inside. I peered into the room to find Nola on the bed with a large and very thick book on her lap and her laptop in front of her, the three dogs perched at the foot watching her. Greco stood by the wall between the windows, impeccably dressed as usual in suit pants, shirt, and tie, his jacket draped neatly over a chair. His shirtsleeves were rolled up, and he appeared to be examining ten paint swatches on the wall.

He looked at me and smiled, then went back to frowning at the wall. "Who knew there were so many shades of gray?"

"I thought there were only supposed to be fifty," Nola said with a smirk.

"You're not supposed to know about that book," I said.

"There was a book? I only know about the movie."

"Actually there were several—of both. Maybe we should look at the convent school in Ireland your dad keeps talking about."

"But then you'd miss me too much." She gave me a grin, then returned to her laptop.

I stood next to Greco, trying to ignore the jewelry cabinet with its open lid and all the doors and drawers wide open. "I thought gray was just black and white mixed together."

"Sometimes," he said, tilting his head. "But in different light, some can appear to be more blue, or green, or beige. Miss Nola would prefer a strict black-and-white gray. And it is my job to make sure that's what gets put on her wall."

I looked over at Nola, who was reading something on her laptop. "Why are you in here, Nola? Don't you have a nice ergonomic desk and chair set up for you in the guest room?"

Without glancing up, she said, "Yes, but Greco is in

here, and he's the expert on the American Revolution, which is what we're studying now. He's a Revolutionary War reenactor. Did he tell you that?"

"He did," I said. "But he's not here to help with your homework."

"I'm rather enjoying it," Greco said. "I like talking about my favorite subject with such an interested and intelligent student."

I grinned with pride, as if he were complimenting me. But I couldn't take any of the credit where Nola was concerned. "Well, she does love history—which is a good thing since her father pretty much lives and breathes it."

"He should try reenacting."

Just the thought of Jack wearing a uniform did funny things to my stomach. "I'll mention it to him."

Greco picked up a sample quart of paint and screwed on the lid. "This one is definitely out. It's much too beige— and Miss Nola is just not a beige person."

As he spoke, Nola shifted her legs on the bed, making the three dogs adjust their reclining positions, resulting in the thick textbook beginning a nosedive off the side. I caught it midslide, slapping it against the bed on the page where Nola had it opened.

Nola pressed her hands against her heart. "Good save, Melanie. I hope it's not damaged. It belongs to Greco and it's really old."

"No worries," the designer said. "I've practically memorized it. It actually belongs to my great-uncle, a professor of history at Carolina back in the day. Quite well respected in his field. His expertise was focused on spies throughout American history, particularly during the Revolution."

I looked down at the splayed page and stopped, noticing the large picture at the top of the page. "That's Gallen Hall. Nola, did you know that it was owned by the same Vanderhorsts that owned this house?"

"Yes, Captain Obvious. You and Dad have only been talking about that nonstop for days."

Greco was saying something about blending two of the paint samples to make the perfect true gray, but I was listening with only half an ear as I read from the textbook. "This is interesting," I said, my heart beating a little faster as I saw the small picture beneath the one of the mansion. "Another reference book I saw also mentions that Lawrence Vanderhorst might have been a spy and was discovered shot in the chest, and that his killer was never found. But this is new." I stopped for a moment to find the part in the text again, and squinting so I could see it, I read out loud.

"'When Lawrence Vanderhorst's body was discovered on the morning of October twenty-eighth, the only thing clear about his death was that it had been caused by a single bullet to the chest. Several people from the house rushed outside at the noise but could only find footprints in the dew leading to and from the house, one set apparently being the victim's. All servants and family members were interviewed, but no clear evidence suggested that any of them were involved. His murder has never been solved.'"

I read it again to myself, thinking how strange it sounded that no one was arrested despite the evidence pointing to someone who'd been in the house at the time of the murder. I looked up to where Greco was painting another swatch of color on the wall, and then over at Nola, who was looking down at her laptop and absently rubbing her neck. I became aware of a scratching sound in the room, like a small animal trapped inside the walls, trying to get out.

"Do you hear that?" I asked.

"Hear what?" Nola looked up at me.

"That sound. That scratching sound."

Greco shook his head, but it was too late to pinpoint where it had come from, as it had already stopped. I placed the book back on the bed in front of Nola. "Could you please bookmark that page? I want to make a copy of it when you're done so I can show your dad. I have no idea if it means anything, but it couldn't . . ."

I forgot what I was saying. On the wall behind Nola,

above the headboard, the word *Lies* had been scratched into the paint.

Nola looked at the word, then back at me, her eyes wide. Slowly we both turned to Greco.

"Well," he said, smiling, "it's a good thing we're planning on painting the entire room."

CHAPTER
17

I stood at the threshold of Jack's office, listening as Nola plucked out a desultory tune on the piano. It wasn't the ideal spot for the instrument, but both Jack and Nola insisted being together in a shared space was good for their shared artistic vibe. It made my heart happy to watch them work in the same environment, knowing it was one of the reasons for their close father-daughter bond. Considering they'd been separated for most of Nola's life, their bond was no small feat. Nola and I were close, too, and I tried not to take offense that she never dared roll her eyes at her father, saving all that for me. Nor did she deprive him of his favorite foods. Nola insisted this was her way of showing me affection, but I wasn't convinced.

Jack huddled over his desk, poring over documents related to Gallen Hall and the three people buried in the mausoleum. He still hadn't heard back from his architect friend, Steve, and we were holding out hope that the architectural renderings would contain the one thing we needed.

As I entered the room Jack and Nola sighed in unison, pushing up the hair off their foreheads with the heels of their left hands as they stared down at their individual work spaces.

"You about ready to go?" I asked Jack.

It took him a moment to answer, as if he were unwilling to pull himself away. He moved his chair back before looking up at me. "Sure. Let me grab my jacket." He looked back at the papers on his desk, then slid his gaze over to

Nola. She'd had a doctor's appointment at noon and then managed to convince me afterward that she could just go home instead of back to school because all she had left were PE and music.

"Need to take a creative break?" he asked.

"Even if it's not creative, I need a break. I keep coming up with absolutely nothing new here. I've been adulting all day, and I'm done."

"'Adulting'?" I asked, pretty sure that if I looked that one up in *Webster's*, I wouldn't find it.

Both Jack and Nola looked at me with matching frowns.

"You know—being an adult," Nola said, speaking slowly as if explaining something to the twins.

"I don't think that's a real word," I said.

"It is." Jack stood and took his jacket off the antique coat rack behind the door. "If you watched any reality TV or subscribed to certain channels on YouTube, you'd know that."

"YouTube?" I asked, thinking I'd heard of it before—probably during carpool with Nola and her friends, which was generally a huge font of knowledge.

"I'll tell her in the car on our way to Gallen Hall," Jack reassured Nola. "If only so she won't embarrass you in front of your friends."

"Whatever." Nola dropped her hands from the keyboard and let her shoulders fall. "I need some creative inspiration. Are you sure I can't go with you?"

"Absolutely not," Jack said. "I'm sure you've got homework."

"It's Friday."

"Right," Jack said distractedly, as he patted his jacket and jeans pockets. "Has anyone seen my . . ." He stopped, then reached forward to grab his phone from his desk, pausing just a moment before picking up a piece of paper and walking over to Nola.

"Here," he said, holding it out to her. "You were so good figuring out Hasell Pinckney's snow globe puzzle, maybe you'll have better luck with this than I have. Feel free to search the Internet or any other source you can think of, although I'm pretty sure I've seen them all." He pointed to the books on the floor by his desk. "And there's a whole pile of books about ciphers going back to the Egyptians. Have at it."

Nola took the paper and stared at it, then read aloud, "'Cognac, feathers of goldfinch, kitchen maid, Burgundy wine.'" She looked up, her brow furrowed. "What's this supposed to mean?"

Jack gave her a grim smile. "We're hoping you can tell us. You said you needed a creative break, so you're welcome."

"Great," she said with a heavy sigh. "Can I invite Alston and Lindsey over to help?"

I nodded. "Sure. And you can order pizza. Just make sure it's not vegetarian and you save some for me. Jayne's coming with us, and the twins are with my parents, so your friends will be good company. They can spend the night if they want."

"I'm sure they'll come over, but they won't spend the night. They say our house after dark is creepy."

"Only after dark?" Jack asked.

I elbowed him. "That's fine. We'll be happy to drive them home when we get back—shouldn't be too late, if that makes you feel better."

"Finding out who that was in my bedroom window would make me feel better, but no pressure."

"We're working on it, Nola," Jack said as he bent to kiss the top of her head. He indicated the paper with his chin. "Maybe that will help. All we know so far is that it might connect a treasure from the king of France to the Americans during the Revolution."

"All right," she said, her fingers already flying on her phone as she texted her friends. "Have fun at the cemetery."

I grinned, finding it somewhat amusing that a comment like that in our house sounded perfectly normal.

We took my car, since Jack's minivan was full of baby toys, cracker crumbs, and spare diapers. He'd come a long way since his Porsche days, and he never seemed to have any nostalgia regarding the lost days of his bachelorhood. For his Christmas stocking, I'd purchased a bumper sticker that read REAL DADS DRIVE MINIVANS. Nola had been with me and had wanted to get one that read CONDOMS PREVENT MINIVANS, but I wouldn't let her.

Jayne was waiting outside her house on South Battery as we drove up, and she slid into the backseat.

"You ready?" Jack asked, looking at her in the rearview mirror.

"As ready as I'll ever be." She buckled her seat belt as Jack pulled out onto the street. "Mother gave me the rundown of what to do, so I feel confident that Melanie and I can handle whatever's waiting for us. And don't forget I have a little experience from that incident in my attic."

I felt Jack waiting for me to say something. "Yes. Absolutely. And Mother and I have faced enough evil spirits on our own that it's practically second nature now."

"I'll follow your lead," Jayne said with conviction.

Feeling a little embarrassed, I said, "As Mother says, we're stronger together. We just need to remember that."

"Good plan," Jayne said. "Speaking of Mother, have you thought yet about what to get her for Christmas?"

I turned slightly in my seat to get a better look at my sister. "Yes, actually. I already got her a skirt at Finicky Filly that I know she'll love. And she adores the Woodhouse Spa, so I decided to give her a spa-day gift certificate. The owner, Kim, is amazing and said she'd wrap it up in a gorgeous gift basket with candles and skin products."

"That's a great idea. How about I contribute and add stuff to the basket—maybe a whole weekend of pampering? Mother would love it."

My throat felt as if it had been coated in sawdust, and I couldn't speak for a moment, even though I could feel the weight of the silence in the car.

"That's a terrific idea, isn't it, Mellie?" Jack prompted. "Your mother has been so great with the twins and Nola— I think double the pampering from her daughters would be the perfect gift."

I nodded, trying to swallow the sawdust so I could speak.

"Great," said Jayne. "And for Dad, I thought we could arrange for a master gardener to give him personalized instruction in his own garden. Sophie said she knows someone from the college who would be perfect and she gave me his number—I just wanted to check with you first."

I finally managed to open my airway so I could speak. "Sounds wonderful. For both of them. I'll call Kim at Woodhouse if you want to take care of setting up the master gardener."

"Actually, I already did. And I have this great design software, so I made this really cool laminated poster that explains it all so we'd have something to wrap."

Jack poked me on the side of my leg. "Thanks," I managed. "That will save me a lot of time, and I'm sure he'll love it."

Thankfully, I was saved from coming up with anything else to say when Jack's phone rang. Jack looked at the dashboard screen. "It's Yvonne. I'll put her on speaker." He clicked a button on the steering wheel. "Hello, gorgeous. I'm in the car with my wife and sister-in-law, so don't say anything compromising."

Yvonne laughed, and I pictured her soft hands patting her white coiffure. "Oh, Jack Trenholm. You're incorrigible."

"Thank you. I try. We're on the way to Gallen Hall now. I hope you have good news for us."

"I'm not sure if it's good news, but it is interesting. I was out power walking this morning with my posse. . . ."

"Your 'posse'?" Jack asked with a grin.

"Yes, Jack. I've had to learn a whole new vocabulary since working here at the College of Charleston. They do say that studying a foreign language is the best way to keep your brain young."

"That they do. Please continue."

"Yes, well, remember when we were speaking I told you how I couldn't find anything regarding how Eliza died?"

"Yes," Jack said slowly.

"Well, the Charleston Museum has a huge collection of personal correspondence and photographs that they use interns to sort and file, so it's usually hit or miss. Plus, they get more and more documents each month as people empty attics and the like. So when I passed the museum this morning, I just had a feeling that I should go see if there was anything about the Vanderhorsts from Gallen Hall in there. I was pretty sure I'd found all there was, but it couldn't hurt to look again."

When she didn't continue, Jack gave me a sidelong glance, then said, "And?"

I could almost see Yvonne's pink cheeks and sparkling blue eyes. "I found something—it was filed with other documents from the Grosvenor family, which is probably why it was overlooked when Marc Longo was busy stealing the Vanderhorst letters."

She didn't say anything more, so Jack prompted, "And what did you find?"

"Well, I found a letter from the doctor who was called to the scene of Eliza's passing. It was addressed to his wife, which most likely explains his candor. In it he expresses his sadness at the loss of such a vibrant young woman, 'cut down in the bloom of her youth.' Those were his exact words. I wonder if the pun was intended, seeing as how she literally had to be cut down."

I leaned closer to the speaker, wanting to make sure I'd heard correctly.

"She hanged herself?" Jack said.

"Yes, sadly. According to the good doctor, Eliza hanged herself from an oak tree in the cemetery on the plantation grounds."

He rubbed his jaw, his face dark in thought. "It's very unusual today for females to commit suicide by hanging, or shooting or anything that violent. I wonder if it was different then."

"I would think it would have been less so," Yvonne offered. "Women were considered more delicate back then. Not that I've done the full research, but from what I recall from all my reading, of all the suicides and murders involving women in the last two centuries, women tended to favor poisons." Yvonne's voice brightened. "I read of an interesting case recently from the early eighteen hundreds where a nanny killed her mistress using oleander leaves—"

"Thanks, Yvonne," Jack said, cutting her short. "What are you thinking this might mean?"

"Isn't that your job?" she asked with a chuckle.

"Yes, but I always feel that I have a better chance of being right if you agree with me."

"Smart man. I knew there was a reason I liked you. And one thing that you've taught me is to go with my gut feeling. And when I read that letter about Eliza killing herself, and knowing that hanging is rare for female suicides, guess what I thought."

"That she hadn't killed herself at all," Jack said.

"Exactly."

Despite the seriousness of the subject, Jack smiled. "I sometimes wonder if we might have been separated at birth, Yvonne."

Yvonne clucked her tongue. "Now, Jack, don't be silly. Because then it would be wrong for you to have this tremendous crush on me."

Jack laughed out loud at that one. "So true. Thanks, Yvonne—this is definitely something to think about. We're headed to Gallen Hall now to see her tomb, so maybe we'll discover something new that will make sense."

"Keep me posted. Good-bye, everybody."

Jack clicked the button on the steering wheel to hang up. He reached for my hands, which I'd placed around my neck without being aware of it. "You okay?"

I nodded. "Yes. I'm fine. It's just . . ."

Jayne cleared her throat, as if to remind me of my promise to Jack to tell him everything.

"It's just that Rebecca told me about another dream."

Jack frowned. "What now? Were you being strung from a rope? Because I wouldn't trust anything Rebecca says. I'd bet that Marc is feeding her things to tell us."

"I know. I've thought that myself. But whatever Rebecca is, she's still family, and despite everything, she puts family first. Remember that she's the one who told us what Marc was planning after that horrible book-launch party. She's just kind of stuck in the middle because she's married to him. It's not in her makeup to harm us intentionally. But, no. It wasn't about me."

He gave me a sidelong glance, and I caught a glimpse of worry.

"It was Nola. At least she thinks it was—Rebecca said it was unclear, but it was a young woman around Nola's age." I recalled Nola sitting on her bed, doing homework, her fingers absently rubbing her neck. "Rebecca dreamed that . . . that Nola had a rope around her neck."

His jaw began to throb. Jayne reached from the backseat and put her hand on his shoulder. "We got this, Jack. Melanie and I are here. You figure out all the clues, and we'll talk to the dead people. We'll get to the bottom of this and won't let anything happen to Nola. All right?"

For the first time, I felt reassured by Jayne's presence, glad that Jack and I weren't tumbling into the abyss alone. I reached over and put my hand on top of Jayne's. "Stronger together, right?"

She nodded, then sat back in her seat. I did the same, watching the scenery go by as we crossed the Ashley River, resisting the impulse to touch my neck.

As we bumped over the road leading to the house, I was relieved that no specter of a soldier pointing a musket at us blocked our way, although an unsettled feeling, not unlike the one I'd felt the first time I'd been here, coated my skin like acid. I looked back at Jayne and knew she was feeling the same thing.

Jack parked the car in front of the steps, and we all exited. The first thing I noticed was the scent of gunpowder. The second thing I noticed was the underlying earthy odor of freshly turned dirt. I watched as Jayne held her hand over her nose, and once again I felt the nudge of reassurance that I wasn't doing this alone. Having Jack and his strength and brains with me was always helpful, but it wasn't the same as having a psychic sister. Although I wasn't sure I was ready to admit that out loud.

The front door opened, and Anthony stepped out onto the porch. He still wore a sling on his arm from the car accident and still needed crutches because of his sprained ankle, but he now sported a bandage across his nose and had two black eyes. "Thank you all for coming," he said, his eyes lingering on Jayne for a long moment before turning to me.

Jack reached out his hand to shake. "I hope the other guy looks worse than you."

Anthony reached for his nose as if he'd forgotten it was there. "Oh, right. Yes. Sadly, I wish I could say it was a valiant attempt to defend myself, but it was . . ." He stopped. "Actually, it was the oddest thing. I was standing on the steps leading to the wine cellar when I found myself tumbling forward. I was alone at the time, so I have no idea how that happened. I suppose I'm lucky I didn't break my neck." He held out a crutch. "This saved my life. It got stuck in the hand railing, preventing me from plummeting to the bottom."

Jayne and I exchanged a glance.

"We'll head to the cemetery in just a minute. I had no idea it was so chilly. Come on inside where it's warm while I go find my jacket."

He began leading us inside, but Jayne rushed to his side. "Can I get it for you? If it's not in your bedroom, I mean. Because that would be where you're not wearing clothes." She pressed her eyelids shut.

"I think she means to ask if she can get your jacket for you to save you from hobbling on your crutches."

Jayne's face had turned crimson, but she managed a nod.

A clearly amused Anthony nodded. "That would be nice. I do get tired hobbling around. There's a small coat closet under the stairs. Just pull on the knob—it gets stuck easily."

Eager to escape, Jayne walked away while Jack and I looked around us. Despite the Italianate exterior, the departure from architectural norms of the day hadn't influenced the interior. It was designed as a center-hall Colonial, with formal rooms on either side of the foyer, each separated from the one behind it with pocket doors. From what I could see of the parlor and drawing rooms, the furniture reclined within spectral sheets, ghostly inhabitants of an all-but-abandoned house. It reminded me of my house on Tradd Street the first time I'd seen it, complete with cobwebs and mold stains. *It's like a piece of history you can hold in your hands.* Mr. Vanderhorst's words always came back to haunt me just as my inner voice started tallying up all the repair costs when I entered an old building.

I was about to ask Anthony about his plans for the house and land when my gaze traveled up the wall along the circular staircase, where uncovered oil portraits of unknown people stared down at us from crumbling plaster. "Am I the only one who thinks by their expressions that we're not . . ." I stopped, my gaze having settled on the largest portrait, separated slightly from the others as it hung on the roundest section of the wall.

It was a portrait of a dark-haired woman wearing a green silk dress, her hair piled high on her head. She was young, late teens or early twenties. Her dark eyes seemed to gleam from the portrait, the kind of eyes that appeared to follow the viewer. But it wasn't her beauty or the skill of the painter that caught my eye. That made me stare. It was the jeweled peacock on her bodice that made it impossible to look away.

"Who is that?" I asked, although I was pretty sure I already knew.

Anthony shook his head. "I don't know—there's nothing on the frame or behind the portrait that indicates the subject of the painting. Although . . ."

Jack quirked an eyebrow. "'Although'?"

"Although I feel as if we know each other . . . intimately.

She has those eyes that follow me wherever I go. I find myself hurrying up the stairs at night just to get away from her."

I continued to stare at the portrait, recalling the woman I'd seen on the stairs at my house, the dark-haired woman in green with the peacock brooch. I remembered, too, the odd way she'd held her head, and the red welt that encircled her neck. When a person is hanged, Jack had once told me, most don't suffocate, as a lot of people think. If they're lucky, they die when their neck is broken by the fall, their bodies left dangling.

I turned to Jack. "I think that's Eliza. Eliza Grosvenor." And before I could stop myself, I raised both hands to my neck, just as Jayne walked up to me and whispered the word *lies*.

CHAPTER
18

I gaped at my sister, wondering if I'd imagined she'd just spoken that word out loud. "What did you say?" I asked Jayne.

Her eyes were dazed, like those of someone who'd just woken from a long sleep. "I said something?"

I nodded. "It sounded like you said 'lies.'" I looked back to where Anthony stood next to Jack. If he wanted our help, there was no point in sheltering him from any of the sinister aspects of what it meant to see dead people. "Which is what the woman said to me on my stairs at home before she disappeared."

I looked down at Anthony, surprised to find his demeanor more of anticipation than of apprehension. "Did you try to touch her?"

"Amateurs," I said under my breath. Jayne elbowed me, giving me a look of reproach.

Louder, so Anthony could hear, Jayne explained, "Usually, any sort of physical interaction will make them go away. Eventually, so will ignoring them—which is what Melanie likes to do—but that takes longer."

Dark brown eyes stared at me from the portrait as I crossed the foyer, and I tried to convince myself that it was the artist's talent that caused the effect. I climbed the stairs, stopping in front of the painting. I let my hands fall to my sides as I examined the woman in the green dress, her creamy skin contrasting sharply with her dark hair, the

delicate nose set in a slim face defined by high cheekbones
and sharp angles.

But her mouth couldn't be described adequately. Rosy
pink lips were half-open, as if she'd just finished speaking,
the corners of her mouth turned up in a *Mona Lisa* smile.
With those lips, coupled with her mesmerizing eyes, she
wouldn't have surprised me if she had stepped down from
the frame and continued down the stairs. I probably would
have been less surprised than the average person, but still.

"It's the woman in Yvonne's book," Jack said. "It was
a black-and-white copy, but it's definitely the same portrait. And am I the only one who sees the resemblance to
Mellie?"

"Not at all," I said, flattered but not convinced. Even
from the confines of a portrait, it was clear that the beauty,
elegance, and poise this woman possessed were inborn. If
I had any of those qualities, it could only have been accidental and only on my best days.

"No, he's right," Jayne said as she moved to the bottom
of the stairs. "It's not so much a physical resemblance per
se—although you both have those awesome cheekbones,
and there's something to the shape of the eyes. It's more
your expression. I see it on your face a lot—that look that
says you don't have a clue as to what you're supposed to do
next, but you're going to pretend that you do."

I frowned down at my sister, wanting to ask her when
she'd become such an expert on human behavior, but
stopped when I realized that she might not be too far from
the truth.

"You might be right, Jayne," Jack said, looking past me
at the portrait so he didn't see my annoyance. "And Yvonne
was right, too. Eliza was pretty hot."

I gave him the look I gave to other Realtors who insisted
their poaching of a client was accidental. "Really, Jack? Is
that how you'd want men to refer to your daughters?"

He cleared his throat. "I meant to say Eliza was a remarkably beautiful woman. Just like you. Probably intelligent, too."

We all turned to look at the portrait together, my eyes drawn to her neck and its lack of jewelry. And the absence of a red welt marring the perfect skin.

"That's definitely her?" Jayne asked, coming up the stairs to stand behind me. "The woman you saw on the stairs at home?"

The sound of Anthony's crutches crossing the marble floor echoed in the large space. "It was her ghost you saw?"

I met Jayne's eyes briefly before turning to look at Anthony. "Yes. I'm pretty sure it was her. She looked just like she does in this portrait. Except . . ." I paused, wondering what was different besides the missing ligature marks. My gaze traveled to the peacock brooch, the four multihued gems catching the light from an unseen source.

"'Except'?" Anthony prompted.

I frowned at the portrait. "I'm not sure. I saw her for such a brief moment that it's hard to recall. But I do remember her eyes. At first they were angry. And then, right before she disappeared, they seemed so . . . sad."

My eyes dropped to the brooch, and I had a sudden recollection of how I'd felt that she'd wanted me to notice it. To pay attention to it. "There's something about the brooch, I think. Something she wants us to notice."

Jack leaned closer, his eyes narrowing as he studied a thin gold chain that was wrapped around the ribbon and her dark curls, then he turned his gaze to the brooch. "Maybe it's the light the artist wanted to paint in, but it doesn't look like the metal in the brooch is gold, does it? The color is off—and definitely different than the gold chain in her hair."

"It looks almost orange," I agreed. "Not gold at all. And it's uniform throughout, with the same orangey color, so it doesn't appear to have been altered by whatever reflected light the artist might have seen and wanted to replicate."

"It looks like copper," Jayne and Anthony said together.

They looked at each other and Jayne smiled. "Jinx."

Anthony grinned back and I resisted the urge to roll my eyes at the cuteness of it. But my loyalty to Detective Riley held me back.

"Assuming those are real stones," Jack said, "I can't imagine why they'd use a less expensive metal than gold. Copper is a base metal, not a precious metal. It could be pinchbeck."

"'Pinchbeck'?" I asked, hoping I wasn't the only uninformed person in the room.

"It means a cheap imitation," Jack explained. "It's a mixture of copper and zinc and was originally used in costume jewelry and watchmaking. It's supposed to look like gold, but when you hold them up together, you can usually tell which is the real McCoy."

"Eliza wasn't a daughter of the family," Jayne said. "She was Mrs. Vanderhorst's ward. So maybe those are semiprecious stones set in pinchbeck."

"Then why is her portrait in such a prominent location?" Anthony asked. "If she wasn't considered a member of the family, I mean. From what I understand, nothing's been moved or changed since the Vanderhorsts owned the house, so these portraits have been here for a couple of centuries."

"Well, she was engaged to be married to Lawrence Vanderhorst, so she was soon to be a member of the family." Jack's gaze spanned the staircase wall. "It doesn't look like his portrait is here. The rest of the male portraits are from different eras." He climbed a few steps higher, stopping in front of two smaller oval portraits in gold frames. "Look at this. There's a whole story here—two men about the same age wearing Civil War uniforms. One is navy blue and the other gray—probably brother against brother. It's like the Vanderhorsts exist to give me book plots."

"True," I agreed. "And our house."

"For now," Jack said under his breath as he began to walk back down the stairs.

Before following him I paused for a moment, looking back at Eliza's portrait. Her gaze seemed to meet mine, and I had the sense that she was somehow disappointed in me. As if she were speaking loud and clear in a language I should understand, and I was still missing the point.

Quietly, I asked, "What lies, Eliza?"

I startled at Jack's hand on my arm. "We'll find out. Hopefully, it will lead us to whatever hidden treasure Marc Longo is after. And if not, to a bestselling book that gets made into a movie. I hear that happens sometimes."

"Yeah. I've heard that, too," I said, allowing him to lead me down the steps, feeling Eliza's eyes following us down the stairs.

As we headed out the door, Jack and I filled Anthony in on the details of what we'd learned so far from Yvonne, and then Jayne told him about my encounter with Eliza. She spoke calmly and concisely, which was why I allowed her to tell him about it, and because I wanted to make sure that Anthony knew Jayne had all her faculties. Not because I thought they should be dating, but because Rebecca was his sister-in-law, and I wanted to be sure he knew we weren't all crazy.

The late-afternoon sun slanted shadows across the drive, warping the shape of the house's shadow on the shell-and-dirt drive. What little warmth the sun offered disappeared as we walked toward the cemetery gates, the temperature dropping by degrees as we got closer.

The gates were closed but unlocked, and we stopped in front of them by unspoken agreement. Jayne and I shared a glance with each other, my concern mirrored in her eyes. I didn't smell anything or see anything unusual. But the chill in the air had nothing to do with the season. It worried me. Someone—something—was here, waiting and watching. And the absence of everything but the chill meant the unknown entity was storing its energy.

Jayne turned toward Anthony. "When do you normally sense you shouldn't go any farther?"

"Right here. As soon as I reach out to open the gate, I feel pressure on my chest. Like someone has a hand on me, holding me back."

"Is it just pressure, or a punch?" Jack asked.

"Just pressure—at first. But if I keep going farther, the force of whatever's holding me back becomes stronger, almost like someone's trying to protect me. But if I keep pressing forward, the pressure on my chest . . ." He stopped, taking a deep breath. "It becomes almost suffocating. Like I'm being squeezed between rocks. And the few times I was able to make it inside the mausoleum, it became full-blown punches and scratches."

We all looked toward the mausoleum as if expecting someone to step outside and challenge us.

"And Marc was able to go inside without a problem and dig around?" Jack asked.

Anthony nodded. "I was, too—up until recently."

"Around the time of the heavy rains," I said. "When the cistern collapsed in our backyard."

Jack looked at me. "I'm sure that's not a coincidence."

"Probably not," Jayne said. "Since the cistern's bricks came from here."

"And because there's no such thing as coincidence," I said sharply. I wasn't sure if it was the growing unease that made me snap at her or just her general air of confidence in almost every area of her life. I hadn't been that way when I was her age. I had doubts that I was that way now.

Her eyes met mine with understanding, which was even more irritating. I loved my sister; I did. I remembered being a little girl and telling whoever asked that what I wanted for all birthdays and Christmases was a sister. I was thrilled she was in my life. I just wasn't as thrilled to find her moving into it like Goldilocks into Baby Bear's bed.

Feeling ashamed at my own thoughts, I gave her a big smile. "According to Jack, I mean."

She smiled back, making me feel even worse. "And you're both right. Thanks for reminding me."

I caught Jack watching me with a questioning look and quickly turned toward Anthony. "I'm going to suggest that you wait here with Jack while Jayne and I try to get inside the mausoleum. Do you have the key?"

He shook his head. "I haven't been able to get close enough to relock it since the last time I was there. The gate is shut, but it shouldn't be locked."

I noticed for the first time the oak tree looming over the

fence on the opposite side of the cemetery. Its ropelike roots pushed up the iron spindles of the fencing, slithering under the ground like invisible snakes, forcing headstones to lean haphazardly and give the impression of crooked teeth.

"That's probably the tree," Jack said quietly.

I nodded, liking the way our thoughts often worked in tandem. I examined the circumference of the tree, the heavy elbows of the branches bent to hold drapes of Spanish moss, and I estimated the tree's age to be close to three hundred years old. "It's definitely old enough," I agreed.

"Old enough for what?" Anthony asked, his voice too loud.

"To be the tree from which Eliza hanged herself," Jayne said. Her voice was quiet, but it carried through the empty cemetery like a last breath.

Lies. I wasn't sure if I'd imagined the word whispered again in my ear. I looked at Jayne and she was staring back at me with wide eyes, and I knew she'd heard it, too. She reached for my hand and I took hers. "Stronger together, right?"

I nodded and we took a step toward the mausoleum. A breeze that scattered only the leaves on the ground but didn't stir the Spanish moss on the trees swirled around our legs, pushing at our backs and propelling us forward.

We took another step.

"Stop." We turned at the sound of Jack's voice.

"I don't feel right about sending you in alone. I'm coming with you." He took a step toward us, but I held up my hand.

"It's all right, Jack," I said. "We know what we're doing."

"We do?" Jayne spoke under her breath so Jack couldn't hear.

"Why don't you and Anthony examine the rest of the cemetery, look for anything unusual on any of the headstones?" I suggested.

"Some of Eliza's favorite peacocks are buried here,"

Anthony said. "But we'll stay close to the mausoleum so we can keep an eye out."

Jack frowned, torn between studying headstones—one of his favorite pastimes—and staying close to me, one of my favorite pastimes.

"I'll be fine," I said, sounding more assured than I felt. "You're close enough that if we need anything, you can be with us in seconds."

Wanting to get it over with before nightfall, I tugged on Jayne's hand, leading her toward the entrance to the mausoleum. As Anthony had said, the doorway gate, with a square wrought-iron design at the top, stood slightly ajar. We peered into the dark interior through the slats of the rusting bars, seeing nothing but the dim outline of a single crypt opposite the opening.

"The other two crypts must be on the sides," I said, noting the plaque on the front of the triangular structure listing Eliza's name along with the two men's. I held up my phone and snapped pictures of the plaque and the gate to study later. I wasn't interested in hanging out in this cemetery any longer than I needed to.

"Let's go," I said as we flipped on the flashlights on our phones. I shone my light inside the space, stopping short at a rustling noise like that of a mouse or a bird. Or a long dress sweeping across a stone floor.

"Did you hear that?" Jayne asked.

I nodded, peering inside and hoping I wouldn't see anything. The circular spots from our lights illuminated dusty bricks and thick mortar on the walls, then square stone tiles on the floor. In three alcoves stone crypts nestled in the brick walls, lying in supposedly quiet repose. The light from my phone allowed us to see a broken corner of one of the lids, then trailed down to the bricks beneath each crypt.

"Looks like hieroglyphics," Jayne said.

"Yeah, that's what Anthony said. And Marc thinks it's some kind of a code. Or it could just be fancy brick details because the bricklayer was feeling artistic."

"Do you really think so?" Jayne asked.

"Not really. I'm just wishing this were all a lot easier so we could make it go away faster. We'll take pictures to show Jack." I reached up to push the gate open, just as it slammed shut in front of my fingers, the sound as final as that of a crypt lid being slid into place.

I knew better than to blame Jayne for closing it and began to tug on the bars, hoping that common sense would prevail and the unlocked gate that had been ajar seconds ago would actually cooperate and open. It wouldn't. I began shaking it until Jayne placed her hand on my arm.

"Maybe what we need to see isn't inside." Jayne pointed at the complex design on the top half of the mausoleum gate, the swirls and lines as intricate and deliberate as those of a spiderweb. I lifted my phone and began snapping more photos.

The breeze had picked up, dead twigs and leaves now hurling themselves at us. I looked up at what had been a brilliant blue winter sky and saw instead an ominous black shelf cloud hovering over us like a grim smile.

Not completely convinced that we couldn't gain access to the mausoleum, I stuck my hand through the bars, hoping to find some kind of latch I could release from the inside.

I heard the crunch of running footsteps coming toward us, then Jack's voice behind me. "It's about to storm—we should get inside. . . ."

I didn't hear what else he said. Something yanked on my hand from inside the mausoleum, pulling so hard that my head banged against the iron gate. As spots gyrated in front of my eyes and my ears rang with a metallic echo, I heard a man's voice, deep and gravelly, shouting loudly inside my head. *Traitors deserve to die and rot in hell.*

"Mellie? Mellie!" Jack's voice was frantic, his hand grappling with the gate, trying to force it open. "Jayne— help me!"

Jayne's hand squeezed mine as my knees hit the concrete step in front of the gate, my arm now numb, my head bruised. The stench of rot filled my nostrils as the heavy stomp of boots thudded across the mausoleum toward me. I closed my eyes in terror, prepared for the worst. And then whatever had been pulling on my arm suddenly let go, sending me backward into Jack's arms. I looked up upon hearing the unsettling sound of squealing hinges as the gate of the mausoleum opened slowly. The specter of a British soldier in a bright red coat slowly faded into the dark abyss, leaving behind the scent of gunpowder and the unmistakable feeling of despair.

CHAPTER
19

The four of us stared at the opened gate leading inside the mausoleum as if it were welcoming us, as if it hadn't just moments before been slammed shut and locked in our faces, and as if something inside hadn't just been trying to rip my arm out of its socket. I looked at Jack, Jayne, and Anthony, their uncertainty about going inside apparent.

Glad we were all on the same page, I stepped backward, eager to leave. As soon as my foot hit the grass a bolt of lightning shattered the sky and the smoke-colored clouds above us opened up, dumping sheets of icy water over us and the graves, rain pelting us as drops ricocheted off the mausoleum's bricks.

I felt myself pushed from behind by Jayne. "Go on," she said, following me inside, then beckoning to the two men. "We'll be safe for a little while. What just happened took lots of energy, and it will take a bit for whatever that was to recharge."

She was right, but that didn't stop the shimmer of resentment I felt. Not because I really, really wanted to be high-tailing it out of there and already in our car driving home and she was ready to get back to work. I felt resentment because she'd said it first and hadn't hesitated to do the one thing none of us wanted to. What made it worse was that of the four of us, Jayne had the least at stake in this game. She was only there to help me. Somehow, that realization did nothing to soften the unwarranted bitterness burrowing into me like a wood-boring beetle planning a long stay in a dining room floor.

The temperature was a good ten or more degrees colder inside, owing—I hoped—to the brick walls. I shivered as we all flipped on our phone flashlights, water dripping from my hair onto my screen.

"Come here," Jack said, pulling me close. He was soaked, too, but gave off steady body heat that I wished I could find a way to market to others like me who remained chilled to the bone for most of the calendar year. It could be another source of income.

"Wow."

I enjoyed the rumble of his chest against my ear when he spoke, so that the word didn't register with me until Anthony said, "You're not kidding. I'm sure it means something, but I haven't got a clue."

I pulled away from Jack so I could see what he was talking about. Avoiding looking at the individual crypts, I studied the bricks on the lower half of the three beneath the alcoves. A stripe two bricks wide ran the width of each wall, with each brick inside the stripe carved with a swirly pattern that didn't appear to repeat.

"It does look like hieroglyphics," I said, squatting in front of one of the crypts. I ran my hand over one of the bricks, feeling the lines beneath my fingers. "But it's not."

"How do you know that?" Anthony asked.

"When I was in eighth grade I saw a movie about Cleopatra and decided to teach myself hieroglyphics. I'm not an expert or anything, but I know enough to know this isn't it."

No one said anything, so I turned around to find them all staring at me—including Jack, who was trying very hard not to smile. "Hey, I was a lonely kid. We didn't have Facebook to waste our time so we had to find other ways to entertain ourselves."

"Naturally," Jack said, giving in with a broad smile. "I just can't believe I didn't know that about you."

I sniffed as I turned back to stare at the bricks. "There's probably a lot you still don't know about me."

"Then I can't wait to find out."

Anthony cleared his throat. "I'd suggest you two get a room, but the bedrooms in the house are pretty dusty."

I slanted a look at Jack, then aimed my flashlight at the bricks in front of me.

"Where did Marc do his digging?" Jayne asked Anthony.

Anthony moved the beam of his light toward the crypt on the center wall with the broken corner on its lid. "According to the plaque, this is Eliza. For whatever reason, probably just a guess since she's in the middle, Marc began digging here after his scanning with a metal detector turned up nothing."

"Why did he stop?" I asked, shivering as I read ELIZABETH GROSVENOR on the plaque, her short life memorialized by the dates beneath her name.

"The same crypt cover that had slid off and almost landed on my foot before did the same thing to Marc—it barely missed him. That's why he tried later to have it demolished, but the preservation people stopped him." Anthony frowned. "The last time I was here, it was because Marc wanted help in opening the coffin. He figured once the lid was replaced, he'd never have a chance."

"Did you find anything?"

He gave me an odd look. "Not what we expected. When we returned, the lid was back on the crypt. The only thing that made me believe what Marc told me about it falling again was that the corner had been broken off and the broken piece was still on the ground." He pointed at a tile in the narrow border around the dirt floor in front of the crypt. "You can see where it hit—this tile is pretty much pulverized." An strange smile crept across his face. "You have no idea how refreshing it is not to have to try to explain the unexplainable."

We were all silent as we examined the odd markings, the sound of our fingers brushing brick melding with the splat of rain on the ground outside and the occasional sound of phone cameras clicking. I sat back on my heels for a moment, trying to pinpoint a stray thought. I tilted my head one way and then the next, and then again.

"If you want, I can hold you by your feet so you can see them upside down," Jack said.

I frowned at him, then looked back at the stripe of bricks. "It looks like one of those slide puzzles, doesn't it? You know—those square puzzles with the plastic squares inside with one missing space where you slide them around to make a picture?"

Jack nodded, a slow smile beginning to form. "Yeah—I used to get them in birthday party gift bags when I was a kid."

"I remember those," Anthony said. "And you're right. It's like every brick is in the wrong place, judging by how all of the lines on the edges don't match up with any of the adjacent bricks." He scratched his head. "I wonder if these were left over from something else, so it didn't matter what order they were placed in."

"Or they were put like that on purpose." Jack leaned closer, rubbing his fingers on the rough line of mortar between two bricks. "Considering this was built way before cameras, the only way to figure out the pattern—assuming it's intentional—would be to take out all the bricks and put them together."

"Have you heard back from Steve Dungan—your architect friend? Maybe he can shed some light on this," I asked.

"I'll call him as soon as we get home." He pulled out his phone. "In the meantime, let's each take a section of the wall and snap photos of the individual bricks. I figure we can enlarge them and print them out so we can lay them all out like puzzle pieces and see if they fit together."

I could hear the excitement in his voice, something that had become a rare thing in recent months. Even the trauma of being yanked through a mausoleum gate by an unknown entity made it worth it.

"Good idea," Jayne said. "I'll take this wall." She pointed

to the wall on the left. "Jack, why don't you take the one in the center, and Anthony, you take the one opposite mine?"

"What about me?" I bristled, feeling left out and being reminded yet again of the trauma of PE class when it was time to choose teammates for volleyball.

"You need to be on the lookout for any drop in temperature or weird breezes that might signal that our visitor is back. Your abilities are a lot stronger than mine."

Feeling mollified, yet guilty for being too quick to judge, I sent her a smile. "Good plan. And since it's stopped raining, I'll stand right outside the doorway. Just in case it locks again. I'd hate for all four of us to be trapped inside."

They all regarded me with wide eyes. "Smart," Jack said, his gaze not leaving the gate until I was safely on the other side.

I crossed my arms over my chest to hold in as much warmth as I could. The chill of the mausoleum seemed to have crept into my bones, unwilling to release me. I was glad, as it kept me alert, since I was unable to shake the feeling that someone—or something—was watching me.

"I'm freezing," I called inside the mausoleum. "I need to keep moving—I promise I won't go far."

I didn't wait to hear Jack telling me to be careful, and I took off in a sprint around the perimeter of the cemetery. I hoped my new smart watch was keeping track of my steps so they wouldn't be wasted effort. I slowed as I reached the oak tree, its sad limbs now dripping raindrop tears, and I felt a downward drift in the temperature. I wasn't afraid, though. The air had a softness to it, a sense of suspension, as if I were diving into the sea but my body was caught in midair. The smell of death and rot was gone, replaced with the scent of rain and wet grass. But I wasn't alone. Of that I was sure.

A movement caught my attention, nothing more than a shift of shadow, except no sun shone overhead. I didn't see her at first, her green gown blending into the overgrowth on the other side of the cemetery fence. As I continued to look, her form became less transparent, her face and clothing easily discernible. I felt my attention drawn again to the brooch worn on her bodice, the jewels in the peacock's tail and eyes sparkling despite the lack of sunlight. I wanted to step closer to see it better, but I was afraid of making her disappear. I wasn't wearing my glasses, so I couldn't see her in crisp detail, and for about the hundredth time I cursed my own vanity.

I recalled the first time I'd seen her, on the stairs at my house on Tradd Street, how I'd felt as if she'd wanted me to notice the brooch, and I remembered there was something about it that didn't look right. Maybe it had been the metal, which didn't look quite gold. I squinted to see better, then took a step backward as I realized her feet weren't touching the ground but were suspended at the level of the top of the fence. And when my eyes traveled upward, I saw the rope around her neck, the other end of the rope tied around a thick tree limb.

Her eyes never left my face, and her lips didn't move, but the word *lies* threw itself at me as if it had been shouted, startling two black crows from a tall patch of grass where they'd been hunting drowned worms. They flew away in a sharp flutter of wings just as I heard Jack, Anthony, and Jayne emerge from the mausoleum.

"Did you hear that?" I asked, staring at the empty tree.

Only Jayne nodded, reassuring me that I hadn't imagined it.

"Hear what?" Jack asked as he approached. He pulled me close and kissed the side of my head.

"Eliza was here. And I think . . ." I screwed up my eyes, trying to recall exactly what I'd seen.

"What?" Jack prompted.

"She definitely wanted me to notice her peacock brooch. I'm not exactly positive, but I'm pretty sure it's the same brooch in the portrait, with four jewels in the eyes and feathers."

"Let me guess. You weren't wearing your glasses so you can't say for sure. You know, Mellie, they have these things called contacts nowadays. . . ."

"I know, I know. It's just that my eyes get so dry and I find them uncomfortable. I've been meaning to make an appointment with my eye doctor, but haven't found the time. I will, though. Soon."

"Well, hopefully you'll run into her again when you're wearing glasses and can get a better look." Jack glanced up at the darkening sky. "We should get home. Nola's friends don't like hanging around after dark."

"Why's that?" Anthony asked. We all looked at him to make sure he wasn't joking.

"Same reason you run past Eliza's portrait," Jayne suggested. "This would all be so much easier if Marc was afraid of things that go bump in the night."

"Oh, he's afraid," Anthony said. "He just thinks that Rebecca has some kind of power over ghosts and can control them. Rebecca's happy to go along with it, too. But she only has premonitions, right? It's not like you and Melanie, where you can see and talk to them."

Jack was staring at him, but his thoughts seemed to be miles away. "No kidding," he said, turning to me. "I think we might have found Marc's Achilles' heel."

"What do you mean?"

"You once told me that bringing in a film crew might agitate some of the resident spirits. This might be a very good thing."

I frowned. "Since we've maybe found a way to make Marc less interested in stealing our house, are we giving up trying to figure out this puzzle?"

Jack shook his head. "Heck no. We will use every brain cell to figure this out and to make sure Marc never gets his hands on our house or any hidden treasure. Aggravating him while scaring his pants off will just be the icing on the cupcake."

∞

We dropped Jayne off at her house, then drove the short distance home, fighting over the radio station, more out of habit than out of any desire to listen to music. I didn't recognize the car parked at the curb in front of our house as Jack pulled into our driveway. "Is Lindsey or Alston driving already?" I asked as we walked around the house to the piazza.

"Not that I know of. They all just have their permits." Jack walked toward the unassuming sedan, stopping behind it to read the bumper sticker. His lips pressed together in a firm line. "Citadel," he said curtly.

I knew to tread lightly. Alston's older brother, Cooper, now a senior at the Citadel, was a frequent visitor to our house, but always with his sister or a group of friends. His visits had been less frequent over the last year due in part, I was sure, to Jack's frostiness. I actually liked Cooper. He was tall and good-looking, and he was also polite, smart, and nice to his sister and his mother. I'd always thought the latter was an indicator of good-husband material, my opinion solidified by watching Jack with his mother. Not that Nola was looking for a husband, or that Jack would allow her to date before she was thirty, but I was fairly confident that Nola was safe with Cooper. The craziest thing they'd ever done together was binge-watch all eight episodes of the *Star Wars* franchise over a weekend in our upstairs TV room. Jack had insisted on leaving the door open and then brought up fresh popcorn and drinks at regular intervals to make sure they weren't sitting too close.

"Cooper probably drove Alston and Lindsey—he's a good brother, you know."

"Humph." Jack stomped up the piazza steps. "He's a guy. That's all I need to know."

I rolled my eyes, waiting until he unlocked the front door and held it open for me. As we stood in the foyer, taking off our coats, we heard Nola's laughter from upstairs, followed by a male voice. We waited for another moment, anticipating hearing the sound of other female voices. When we didn't, Jack took the stairs two at a time while I followed at a more sedate pace.

I passed the three dogs at the top of the stairs, staring at a corner of the hallway. Stopping short, I followed their gaze, hoping I wouldn't see anything, and then worrying because I didn't. General Lee let out a low growl to let the unseen intruder know who was boss, then immediately ran behind me, quickly followed by Porgy and Bess. It was a good thing they were cute, because they were complete failures as protectors.

I continued to stare at the corner, willing myself to see whatever it was, aware suddenly of the scent of roses. I relaxed slightly, knowing that whatever was there, Louisa was there, too, protecting us. "Thank you," I whispered, backing away slowly toward Nola's room and Jack's raised voice.

"You know the rules about closed doors, Nola."

I stood behind Jack in the doorway, his hands on his hips just like Mrs. Houlihan's when she'd find me in her kitchen stealing cookies. Nola sat on her bed with her laptop and scattered books, and Cooper stood in front of the armchair he'd apparently been sitting in before Jack threw open the door without knocking.

"The dogs were acting weird, but they didn't want to go out and weren't interested in any treats, but they kept distracting us, so I just shut the door."

"Distracting you from what?" Jack asked. I couldn't see his face, but I imagined his eyes were narrowed in a perfect interpretation of the avenging father.

Cooper offered his hand to Jack. "Good to see you, sir. We were brainstorming about those words you gave Nola earlier, trying to see if we could interpret them."

After a brief hesitation, Jack shook the young man's hand. "Um-hm," he said. "I told her she could invite a few friends over for pizza."

"Yes, sir. But my sister wasn't feeling well, and Lindsey is in Pawleys Island this weekend with her parents. So I volunteered to come help and keep Nola company."

"Well, isn't that convenient . . ." Jack began.

I elbowed my way past Jack to greet Cooper. "That's wonderful. Thanks so much. And were you two able to figure anything out?"

Nola gave me a relieved look. "Nothing yet. We can't find anything that connects these things, so Cooper thought that we should make identifying lists of each object, starting with color, since three of them—just not *kitchen maid*— can be identified with specific colors."

Jack looked at Cooper with grudging admiration. "I hadn't thought of that. You might be onto something— although I have no idea where *kitchen maid* would fit into that equation."

"That's the same conclusion we reached, sir. But until we think of something else, we're creating four lists—since we're working with four items—of descriptive words, beginning with colors, to see if we can come up with anything. It's a process. Like writing a book, I would assume."

Jack actually smiled at Cooper. "Yes, you could certainly say that."

"Did you find anything at the cemetery?" Nola asked, looking a lot more relaxed now that Cooper and Jack had shared a cordial exchange of words.

"We're not sure," I said, pulling out my phone. "Jayne and Anthony will be sending me theirs, but basically we took lots of photos, including pictures of two rows of bricks with odd markings on them. If we print them individually, we should be able to put them together like a puzzle. It's going to take forever since I'll have to find a way to print every brick exactly proportionally and then find a surface large enough to put the puzzle together."

Cooper cleared his throat. "I might not be able to find the floor space for the actual puzzle, but I have access to some pretty cool software that should make the sizing-and-printing part a little easier. I'd be happy to take a look if you want to send the pictures to me."

Nola and I both beamed at Cooper, but Jack narrowed his eyes. "And what would you expect in return?"

"Dad!" Nola cried out as I punched Jack in the shoulder.

"Nothing, sir," Cooper said, his cheeks blazing red. "I'm just wanting to help. I think this whole puzzle thing is really cool—especially when I think it might end up in one of your books. I've read them all, by the way. I'm a huge fan."

"Hmm," Jack muttered.

I grabbed hold of his elbow and began pulling him out of the room before he could say anything else. "Thanks, Cooper," I called from the hallway. "I'll have Nola forward all of the photos to you to see if you can come up with anything. And we really can't thank you enough, can we, Jack?"

I yanked on his arm and dragged him down the hallway toward the stairs, aware now of pounding on the front door. We looked at each other before continuing down to the foyer, the dogs at our heels and General Lee growling. Jack stepped in front of me as if to shield me, then peered through the sidelights by the door. "Just when I think my day can't get any worse."

Before I could question him, he yanked open the door, revealing the smooth face and plucked eyebrows of Harvey Beckner. "It's about time someone came to the door! I've been ringing the doorbell for twenty minutes."

He made to step forward, but Jack blocked him. "The doorbell only rings when someone the house wants inside is ringing it."

Harvey sneered. "Right. Because houses have souls." He turned around to shout to a group of men unloading equipment from two vans illegally parked at the curb. It was street-sweeping day on Tradd Street the following morning, which meant a guaranteed tow, but I wasn't going to mention it.

Jack continued to block access to the house. "It's getting late, and we're about to have supper—"

"Perfect," said a voice from the door at the end of the piazza. "I'm starving."

Jack tensed. "Matt," he said, his jovial tone at odds with the set of his jaw. "Why are you darkening my doorstep?"

Marc moved to stand next to Harvey. "We need to get a few still shots of the interiors at night and test for lighting before it's time to begin filming. And Harvey hasn't seen

the inside yet, so he's brought his lighting people and location scouts to get their opinions."

"I don't know about this." Jack looked back at me. "Mellie, was this on your calendar?"

"No . . ." I began, feeling like a two-foot dam in the path
of a tsunami.

"I don't think you're in a position to argue, Jack," Marc
said. "It will go easier for all of us if you'll just let us get to
work."

"But I'm hosting a progressive dinner here in less than
two weeks," I protested. "Rebecca told me she'd worked it
out with you so that there wouldn't be any cameras and
equipment in the house until after Christmas."

Marc pushed on the door, but Jack was unyielding.
"We'll be out by Sunday. Until we're ready to begin filming
sometime around the first week of January. You'll need to
take down all this Christmas stuff by then." He frowned at
the magnolia garland that Veronica and I had spent hours
making. My blood began to heat at the affront.

"That's really not convenient . . ." Jack began, but he
stopped when I tugged on his arm.

I whispered in his ear, "Let it go, Jack. They've won this
battle. But not the war."

After a pause, Jack stepped back. "Then welcome to our
house," he said, graciously opening the front door as wide
as it would go. "So good of you to come."

Both Marc and Harvey eyed Jack suspiciously, and I
wondered if it had anything to do with the sudden chill in
the air that had nothing to do with the temperature outside,
or the sound of running footsteps across the empty foyer
behind us. I also wondered if either one of them was remembering what Harvey had said about houses having no
souls. And if they were about to find out how wrong he was.

"Please," Jack said, beckoning the men to enter. "Make
yourselves uncomfortable. My family and I will be sitting
down for a delicious meal in the kitchen and you are not
invited to join us. And just so you know, it's lights-out at

ten, sometimes earlier if our twins are here. Trust me, you don't want to be here after dark."

He said this just as the crew from the vans began to fill the vestibule. Jack put his hand on the small of my back and began guiding me toward the kitchen, where Mrs. Houlihan had left our dinner warming in the oven. He pushed open the door to the kitchen and allowed me to pass in front of him, giving a good impression of an evil Vincent Price laugh as the door swung closed behind us.

CHAPTER
20

I blew warm air into my gloved hands as I walked with Jack the short distance to Jayne's house on South Battery.

"Cold?" Jack asked, drawing me close to his side.

I turned my face toward his, sure he could see the trembling of my lips. "I'm at the point of turning numb, so I don't have to worry about feeling the cold anymore." I tried to smile, but the cold pierced my teeth. "I don't know why we couldn't take the car."

"Because there's only satellite parking for the Shop and Stroll, and we'd probably be walking just as far. I'm sure Jayne has hot chocolate to warm us, and there will definitely be plenty to eat and drink along the route once we pick up our tickets at the Francis Marion Hotel."

"If I don't die of hypothermia first," I muttered, attempting to wriggle my toes inside my shoes. I aligned my stride to his, pressing closer to him. "You're the best heated blanket a girl could ever ask for."

I could hear the smile in his voice. "Is that the reason why you married me?"

"One of them. I wouldn't say it's the number one reason, but it's pretty close to the top."

He kissed the crown of my head. "Mercenary."

"A girl's got to do what a girl's got to do." We'd reached Jayne's house, stopping at the bottom of the driveway. I stared at the wreath on the front door and the garland wrapped around the banisters that led up to the front portico. I squinted. "Are those . . . ?"

"Pink." Jack finished for me. "They're definitely a frosted pink. I'm guessing Rebecca's been here."

"Ugh. Just because she donated a lot of money to the Ashley Hall fund-raiser, she thinks she can do whatever she wants. At least she was able to talk Marc into filming the progressive dinner at Veronica's instead of at our house, so I guess I owe her one. But I certainly don't want to be here when Sophie sees this. I tremble to think what she'll do to retaliate."

"Take off Pucci's pink nail polish and sweater and make her look like a real dog, maybe?"

I glared up at him. "Okay, I agree that the polish is too much, but there's nothing wrong with dog sweaters."

"Let's just agree to disagree, shall we?" Jack asked as he led me down the front drive.

Speaking through chattering teeth, I said, "What on earth do you think Jayne's surprise is? She knew we had tickets for the Shop and Stroll tonight, so I hope it's something spectacular to justify our being thrown out in this weather longer than we needed to be."

"You know it's only about fifty degrees, right?"

I plastered an indignant look on my face. "To some of us, that's the same as freezing." I began climbing the steps. "Come on before I turn blue."

The door opened before I had a chance to ring the bell, my mother appearing in the opening. "What are you doing here?" I asked as we hugged. "Are you the surprise?"

"I've been here all afternoon with Jayne and your father preparing the surprise." She glanced behind me to where Jack stood. "Good job, Jack. I know how persistent Mellie can be when she suspects something's up."

I whirled to face my husband. "You know what it is?" I stepped forward into the foyer, barely recognizing the brightly lit space from when I'd first seen it right after Jayne had inherited the old house, every inch of it filled with cobwebs and peeling plaster. I knew Jayne had been working with Sophie to restore the house to its former grandeur, and after looking at the gleaming banister—peeking out from beneath a frosted pink garland—and mold-free walls, I had to grudgingly admit that Sophie knew what she was doing.

I spotted Jayne by the dining room door. "Please don't tell me you have a pink Christmas tree hidden somewhere," I said. "I just can't believe you let Rebecca do this to your house."

"I know, I know. But she was so upset when she came here. She knows that the laundry room at your house that you allowed her to decorate won't be seen, but she hid her disappointment from you because she knows you're dealing with 'issues' right now—her word, not mine. She said she had a lot of decorations left over and asked if I would allow her to decorate my house. Since it's still under renovation and I'm not hosting one of the courses for the progressive dinner, I agreed. She seemed really sincere."

I wasn't sure if I'd ever heard Rebecca's name and the word *sincere* uttered in the same sentence before. But the fact that she'd hidden her disappointment from me did loosen some of my resentment toward her. Just a little bit.

"Hello, Peanut," my father said, emerging from the dining room. I peered past him, almost expecting to see swaths of moisture-speckled wallpaper drooping from the cracked cornices. Instead, the walls were scraped clean, waiting for either paint or reproduction wallpaper. Knowing Sophie, I figured she'd probably brought artists from Italy to hand-paint the original wallpaper design, and Jayne had willingly allowed it.

"So, what's going on?" I asked while my father hugged me. I kept my gaze focused on the dining room, where I could see Jayne and the foot of another person standing at the dining table.

I stepped into the dining room and was met with a loud "Surprise!" from Jayne. I turned my head and was speechless for a moment as someone held up an iPhone to take my picture. "Cooper?"

"Yes, ma'am. Nola's babysitting, so she asked me to take a picture of you being surprised."

Before I could ask a question, my gaze was drawn to the surface of the enormous table and the neat rows of five-by-seven photographs.

"Are these . . . ?" I began, looking around at the faces now clustered around the table.

Cooper cleared his throat. "I pulled an all-nighter to get them all downloaded, then sized so they're all the same, and then printed them. Nola brought me breakfast, though, so it was worth it."

I could feel Jack glowering at Cooper, so I said, "I'm sure it was all vegan and gluten-free, so no chance she was out to impress anyone."

Cooper shook his head. "Actually, it was a cinnamon bun with a side of hash browns Mrs. Houlihan made. She even drove Nola over to deliver it. Best hash browns I've ever tasted . . ."

As if sensing the tension, Jayne moved to stand next to me, straightening one of the photos. "Mother told me about Marc and that horrible Harvey guy invading your house, so when Nola told me that Cooper had printed out all of the photographs, I thought bringing them to my house would be safest. That way, Marc can't snoop."

"Brilliant idea," I said, meaning it, although a tone I hadn't expected emerged.

Jack nodded. "Jayne also suggested that I clear out my office for the same reason. She offered her house to store everything for the time being."

"Jayne certainly thinks of everything," I said, tapping lightly on one of the photographs. "Can't imagine how we survived before she came to Charleston." I looked at the single photograph, then picked it up, studying it closely. "I think this goes in one of the corners—you can tell from the design because only two sides have finished patterns, and the other two have truncated lines that must continue onto other bricks."

I looked up to find all sets of eyes focused on me. Except for one—Jayne's. Her eyes were blinking rapidly, her bottom

lip clenched between her teeth. She jerked her gaze up to
the table and to the photograph I held pinched between my
fingers. She swallowed. "I think you're right, Melanie.
Good job—now we have a place to start." She began clearing one corner of the table, then pointed to the empty spot.
"I think you should have the honor of putting the first piece
here." She smiled at me and I felt as if I'd been kicked in
the stomach.

"Actually," I said, feeling the looks of censure from
around the table, "you should do the honors. You're the one
who had the foresight to set up the puzzle in your dining
room." I handed her the photograph. "Here."

She hesitated just for a moment before taking the picture. "Thanks," she said, putting it in its place of honor in
the corner of the table. "I want you all to feel free to come
here at any time and work on this puzzle. When I'm at
Melanie's looking after the twins, just stop by and get my
key. The more, the merrier, I say."

An antique carriage clock chimed from the fireplace
mantel, making me glance at my watch. "I don't want to be
late picking up our tickets at the Francis Marion. It will cut
into our shopping time."

Jack was eyeing the table, and I knew he was thinking
his time would be better spent playing with the puzzle than
Christmas shopping on King Street. "Jack," I said with
a warning in my voice, "you know they have a special
service tonight to help men take care of their shopping. I'd
hate for you to miss that."

He looked up, surprised at being caught. "I just
thought . . ."

"Come on," I said. "Let's call an Uber or something. It
is way too cold to walk all the way to Calhoun." I glanced
around the room, aware of someone missing. "Where's Anthony? Isn't he supposed to be coming tonight?"

Jayne shook her head. "He's sick. He said he hasn't been
feeling well since he left the cemetery. I told him he should
come to his house in town just in case it's something at
Gallen Hall, but he said he was too sick to move. I asked if

I could call his doctor, but he said he'd be fine by morning.
I'll check in then."

I exchanged a glance with my mother but didn't want to
say anything in front of Cooper about how Anthony should
stay away from stairs and open windows while alone at the
plantation house.

"And if it's all right with you, Miss Smith, I'd love to
stay here for a bit and work on the puzzle. Just for an hour
or two." Cooper looked at Jack. "I mean, if that's all right
with you, sir."

"As long as you're here, and Nola's not, I'm fine with
that arrangement."

"Jack . . ." I started to say, but I was interrupted by the
ring of the doorbell.

We watched as Jayne walked across the foyer to open
the door. There was a slight pause and then: "Thomas," she
said, her voice an octave higher than it had been five seconds ago. "What are you doing here?"

Detective Riley stood in the doorway, his tall figure filling the space. He looked behind Jayne and met my gaze.
"Sorry. I didn't know you'd have company. I just wanted to
stop by and see how you were doing." He grinned. "And if
your house is behaving."

Cooper and my dad looked confused, but the rest of us,
who'd witnessed the spirit cleansing in Jayne's attic, understood.

"It's doing fine," Jayne said, pulling the door open wider.
"And you have shoes; please walk them inside."

Feeling the need to rescue my sister, I placed my hand
on her shoulder and squeezed, a reminder to take a deep
breath before trying again. "So great to see you, Thomas.
We're getting ready to leave for the Shop and Stroll, but
come in for a minute to warm up. If that's all right with
Jayne?"

I glanced at my sister and she gave one decisive nod.

"I really don't want to intrude. I can come back later . . ."
Thomas began.

"Don't be silly. We're all old friends here." I pulled him

inside and closed the door behind him. There was an awkward silence, filled with Jayne's deep breathing, as we all looked at one another.

My dad clasped his hands together. "What are we thinking? We have a trained detective in our midst and a whole mystery spread out on the dining room table." He indicated the dining room. "Would you like to take a gander, Detective?"

I thought I saw a bright gleam in Thomas's eye. "I'd love to," he said, following my dad and stopping in front of the table. "Wow. It's like a giant jigsaw puzzle. Are these bricks?"

"From the inside of the mausoleum at Gallen Hall," Jayne said slowly, considering each word. "There was a horizontal design two bricks wide encircling the interior, but none of them matched."

"And you figured out that the lines on the bricks might match up if you could separate them into individual puzzle pieces." Thomas looked at Jayne as if she were Einstein himself standing in the dining room.

"Actually, it was my other daughter," my dad said, beaming. "I sure hit the lottery with three brilliant women in my family."

Other daughter? I smiled and nodded appreciation, unable to feel truly grateful at his compliment. I didn't scrutinize my feelings, fairly confident that I was certain I knew the exact reason.

Thomas began unbuttoning his coat. "This actually looks like fun. Although it could be that these were just leftover bricks and don't have any connection to each other at all."

"Oh, we've definitely considered that possibility," Jack said. "But we're determined to remain hopeful."

Thomas leaned over the table to get a better look. "I see someone's found a corner piece already. Nice going."

"That was me," I said, a little too eagerly, because apparently I thought I was still in kindergarten and required approval and reassurance for every small task.

"Yes, it was," Jack said, rubbing my back and making me feel even more like a child. I turned to express my annoyance and was immediately met with a gentle kiss on my lips.

"Has anyone considered staying in tonight and working on the puzzle?" Thomas looked around for collaborators, his eyes hopeful.

"Yes," Jack said at the same time I said, "No."

My mother stepped forward to intervene. "We have an extra ticket for the Shop and Stroll, Thomas. Why don't you join us?"

Both Jack and Thomas looked longingly at the photographs. Turning his head back to address my mother, Thomas said, "That sounds like fun. I've got all those nieces and nephews I have to buy gifts for, so the Shop and Stroll could be just what I need."

"And they have a service just for men, to help them select gifts," my mother said as she sidled up to my dad. "Although I must say that some men don't need any help at all."

I started to roll my eyes but stopped when I saw Jayne looking at them with adoration. I was thrilled my parents had found each other again and were so much in love. And, yes, our relationship with each other had a difficult past, but we'd moved so far beyond those old resentments and hurts. Or we should have. Even I recognized this. Maybe negative emotions were like bad habits, and I needed a twelve-step program to cure myself so I could move forward without all that baggage tethered to my ankles that kept me firmly planted in the past. I made a mental note to add that to the top of my New Year's resolutions spreadsheet.

"Great," I said. "Everyone get bundled up. I'd rather take an Uber, but I don't feel like arguing with Jack, who apparently enjoys the cold. We've got a long walk in the frozen tundra, but I understand there are warm drinks waiting."

"It's not that cold," everyone said at once as I wrapped my scarf around my neck twice and tucked my hair and ears under my knit cap.

"Humph," I said, shoving my gloved hands into the pockets of my coat and leading everyone out the front door.

We'd made it only to the end of the drive before Jack's phone rang. He looked at the screen and groaned. "It's Harvey. I'm going to let him leave a message."

We'd left him and his crew at the house for the second night in a row, the previous night being a complete wash because none of their equipment would work for some reason. Nola and the twins had been forced to camp out at my parents'—a small price to pay, according to Nola.

I frowned. "I think you should answer it. Maybe he's just telling you he's leaving forever and wants to know how to set the alarm."

Jack frowned back at me but hit ANSWER on his phone. I couldn't hear what was being said, but the growing smile on Jack's face told me it was good news. When he'd hung up, he put the phone back into his jacket pocket.

"Are they done?" I asked.

"Nope. First of all, he needed to complain about the man with his crack showing above his pants who was working in the dining room and wouldn't leave."

"That's Rich Kobylt," I said. "He wanted to finish the dining room floor before Christmas so he could spend time with his kids, who will be home from college, and I told him he could take as long as he needed." I grinned at the success of my plan.

"And then he said the power kept going off but that the breakers were still in the on position and none of the other houses on the street were without their lights." He sounded practically jovial now. "Then he said most of his crew ran out of the house after the lighting guy said he saw a woman standing behind him in the mirror in the front parlor, but when he turned around no one was there."

"Go figure," I said, my smile matching his.

He looked up into the clear night sky and put his arm around me, pulling me close. "Have I ever mentioned what a brilliant team we make?"

"I think so. But I don't think I'd ever get tired of you saying it."

We stopped on the sidewalk, allowing the others to walk around us as Jack bent his head to kiss me. "I think we're on the home stretch now, Mellie. I think we're right on the cusp of getting Marc Longo out of our lives forever." He kissed me again. "We're going to bury him alive."

He pulled me close to his side, walking fast to catch up to the rest of our group. "Still cold?" he asked.

I nodded, unable to tell him that the trembling of my lips had nothing to do with the air temperature, and more to do with remembering Rebecca's dream and how it hadn't been Marc being buried alive.

CHAPTER

21

We stood in the elegant lobby of the Francis Marion Hotel beneath antique crystal chandeliers, soaring ceilings, and tall columns with gilt acanthus leaves on their capitals. The hotel had undergone a face-lift in the late nineties, winning a twelve-million-dollar restoration award from the National Trust for Historic Preservation and, more important, the approval of my friend (and sometime nemesis) Dr. Sophie Wallen-Arasi. The restoration team had brought the hotel back to its nineteen-twenties elegance, which, although beautiful, was one of the reasons I usually avoided this particular hotel.

"Do you hear that?" I asked Jayne.

"The twenties music?" She nodded. "Have you spotted the girl dancing the Charleston in midair where a table must have once been?"

I almost didn't turn, not wanting to attract the spirit's unwelcome attention, but couldn't stop myself. There was something about seeing unadulterated history as it had been lived, even in brief snippets, that was the one and only part of my sixth sense that I didn't hate.

The girl, not much older than Nola, had blond, bobbed hair peeking out of a net cap with dangling pearls over her ears. Her drop-waist dress and long ropes of pearls swung in sync with her kicking legs as she danced the Charleston, the low heels on her ankle-strapped shoes making soft thudding noises each time they landed on the invisible table.

I wanted to turn away, but I couldn't, because now her dance movements had slowed as she became aware that someone was watching her. That someone could see her. She stopped completely and slowly turned toward us so that we could see her entire face, including the dark bruise that covered one cheek and the red blood dripping from her nose and lips.

We watched each other for a long moment, as if each was expecting the other to make the first move. "We should go," I said softly to Jayne, who was also unable to turn away from the sad eyes of the flapper.

"We could help her, you know," Jayne whispered back. "Not right now, but later. We could ask the hotel to allow us access so we can find out what's keeping her here and send her on her way."

"Send who on her way?" Thomas appeared at our sides with a glass of wine from the lobby's corner bar in each hand.

"No one," I said, accepting a glass and taking a gulp. I felt Jayne's gaze and recalled that her breakup with Thomas had been due, in part, to his insistence that she shouldn't go public with her abilities. Doing a ghost cleansing in a public hotel lobby wasn't a good way to keep our light under a bushel, I was fairly certain. I glanced back to where the flapper had been and saw only the beautiful lobby, filled with warmly bundled holiday shoppers eager for a fun evening in Charleston.

"Rebecca," Jayne said in answer to Thomas's question, raising her own glass to her lips.

"If she were here, I would definitely want to send her on her way," I said, taking another sip, which I almost spit back into my glass when our cousin appeared as if conjured, looming behind Jayne in a pink fur coat and matching pink Uggs.

"I didn't expect to see you here," I managed to say after I choked down my wine. "Seeing as how you need to get up so early tomorrow for the wreath-making workshop. I know how you like your ten hours of beauty sleep."

"True," she said. "I like it but don't need it, thankfully. No worries—I'll be bright-eyed and bushy-tailed tomorrow morning at eight sharp." She gave a little salute while I furtively glanced around for any sign of Marc.

"Hello again," Thomas said to Rebecca. "I don't think I've had the pleasure of seeing you since we met at Cannon Green, at your husband's book-launch party." He gave a show of scanning the crowd. "Speaking of which, is Marc here?"

I wondered if he was trying to give us a head start to find Jack, my parents, and our tickets before making a beeline out the back door.

"Sadly, no. He was supposed to be, but he's at Melanie's house trying to calm down Harvey Beckner. Seems they're experiencing a lot of equipment failure and they can't get anything done. Harvey thinks it has something to do with inferior Southern infrastructure."

"I hope he said that out loud so anyone listening could hear," I said.

"Interesting." Jayne's face was expressionless. "What did Marc tell him?"

Rebecca shrugged. "I'm not sure. He's been having issues with the battery on his phone—it keeps dying right after it's charged. I could hear that Rich person in the background shouting at Harvey to keep his equipment off the newly repaired dining room floors, and then it cut out."

Jayne and I shared a glance. "So, Rebecca," I said. "Don't you think this is a sign that Marc's not meant to be filming in my house?"

"Oh, I don't think he really cares about filming. . . ." She stopped talking, her eyes widening as she realized whom she was speaking to and what she'd just said.

"So what does he care about?" I asked, stepping closer to her so that I could almost feel the pink fur tickle my nose.

"It's nothing—I didn't mean to say that. Of course he wants to—"

"Rebecca." I cut her off. "If all the stuff you say about

family being the most important thing to you is true, then you need to tell us what Marc is up to."

Her bright blue eyes filled with moisture. "But Marc is my family, too. And I love him. He's kind and gentle, and not anything like the monster you think he is. He's my husband."

Bile rose in my throat but I swallowed it down. "Well, the fact that you actually married him is your fault. And now his actions are partly your responsibility. Marc is trying to ruin my life—destroy my husband's career and steal my house. I think it's clear where your loyalty needs to lie."

She began tugging on the fingers of her pink knit gloves in a nervous gesture.

"If he's doing anything illegal," Thomas said gently, "then you could be an accessory to a crime and punished accordingly. I don't know if you watch television, but *Orange Is the New Black* is something you should be watching to prepare yourself for women's prison. Where wearing pink isn't an option. And I don't think orange is your color."

Her eyes widened as her skin blanched. "You don't need to threaten me."

"I'm not threatening you. I'm just giving you a heads-up." Thomas crossed his arms as the three of us stared at Rebecca, waiting for her to break.

She tucked her chin like a turtle taking a defensive stance. "It's not illegal to take something that once belonged to you, is it?"

"Like what?" I narrowed my eyes at her.

She looked around discreetly before leaning closer and whispering, "A piece of paper."

"What kind of paper?" I asked, growing impatient. Behind her shoulder I spotted my parents and Jack crossing the lobby, and I was fairly sure Rebecca wouldn't be as forthcoming in Jack's presence.

"Something he'd thrown in the trash at the plantation. But when he went to get it, everything was gone."

"You mean the papers from the historical archives that he stole and then threw away?"

She drew her shoulders back defensively. "I don't know anything about that, but I'm sure Marc wouldn't have stolen anything from the archives. Maybe it was an accident and when he went to return them he saw that they were gone."

We all stared her down with the same dubious expression. "They were found in a garbage can, Rebecca." I glanced behind my cousin to see that Jack and my parents had been stopped by a middle-aged couple and were chatting. I looked back at Rebecca. "Can you be more specific about the paper he's looking for? Maybe I know where he can find it."

Rebecca pressed her lips together, contemplating, her eyes moving from me to Jayne to Thomas, then back to me. "It's a drawing. The design matches what he thought was some kind of drawing in Joseph Longo's diary. It was one of a bunch of papers in a folder he'd *borrowed* from the archives. He didn't realize it the first time he saw it, but when he saw the copy of the diary drawing again recently, he was pretty sure it was a match."

"Where did he see it again?" Jayne asked.

Rebecca sucked in a deep breath. "Marc thought he'd accidentally thrown out a bunch of the notes he'd gathered at the archives to research his next book." She looked at us to see if we knew that he'd gone to the archives only because he'd learned Jack was working on a new book.

We remained expressionless as she continued. "Anyway, the drawing and several other papers must have fallen behind his desk, because there they were when we had to move it when I decided he needed shiplap in his office. It's all the rage now on that HGTV show—"

"Rebecca . . ." Jayne interrupted, and I saw her watching my parents and Jack resume their approach behind us.

"Anyway, he didn't find anything he thought was important in those papers he'd borrowed from the archives, which is why he'd *misplaced* them, meaning to return them to the archives later, but when we found his own research papers behind his desk and he saw the diary drawing again, he had second thoughts. So he went back to the plantation to retrieve the box of papers from the archives and found it was missing."

"What kind of drawing?" I asked.

Rebecca shrugged again. "It was weird—lots of scrolls and lines."

"Can you show it to me?" I asked quickly, but Rebecca had already stepped back and was smiling and greeting my mother while keeping a wary eye on Jack.

"Rebecca," Jack said. "Where's your dog?"

"It's so cold out that I felt Pucci would be more comfortable at home. It was so sweet of you to ask."

"I wasn't referring to Pucci," Jack said with a smile that could rival glaciers.

Rebecca frowned. "I just don't understand how the two men I've had the most meaningful relationships with don't like each other. I'm convinced that if we spent more time together—the four of us—we'd be the best of friends."

If her reminder that she and Jack had once dated hadn't brought up my lunch, this last comment certainly would have. I was suddenly very glad that I hadn't eaten anything yet, but the wine sloshed unhappily in my stomach.

Jack continued with his glacial smile, his eyes focused on the ceiling as if he were actually considering her suggestion. Finally, he said, "Or I could dip myself in oil and light myself on fire. I imagine the outcome would be the same in either case."

Rebecca's large eyes blinked slowly. Twice. "And what would that be?"

It was Jack's turn to blink. "Reaching the same level of fun."

Before she could think of anything else to say, Jack made a show of waving to someone across the room. "If you could excuse us, please? There's someone I'd like Melanie and me to say hello to." He smiled at the rest of the group. "We'll be right back. And I'm sure Rebecca has a Christmas list of new sweaters and accessories for Pucci she needs to go buy, and we don't want to keep her."

Without waiting for a response, Jack took my hand and

began leading me across the room, while I attempted to make eye contact with Rebecca to let her know that we weren't done talking. I had the distinct impression that she was avoiding my gaze, focusing her attention on rebuttoning her coat.

I ran into Jack's back when he stopped suddenly in front of an elegant older couple. The gentleman, wearing a proper felt hat like men had worn in the fifties, was helping a platinum-haired woman with her coat. After gently settling it on her shoulders, he handed her a soft-hued silk scarf from his own coat pocket and she smiled up at him as she placed it over her head.

"Yvonne," Jack said, and I did a double take, believing that Jack had been lying about seeing someone he knew so that he could get away from Rebecca.

"Yvonne?" I repeated, almost not recognizing her out of context. It was as if I expected her to be surrounded by thick and dusty reference volumes wherever she went.

"What a lovely surprise," she said, accepting a kiss on her cheek from Jack and then me. Facing the man standing next to her, she said, "Allow me to introduce my beau, Harold Chalmers." She glanced up at her date with sparkling eyes. "Harold, I'd like you to meet some of my dearest friends, Jack and Melanie Trenholm."

I was too surprised to speak for a moment as I realized that I knew very little about Yvonne's personal life. I looked up at the tall, elegant man, scrutinizing him more closely than was warranted, my curiosity winning out over my good manners. Harold Chalmers's eyes were a warm brown, the hair beneath his hat a George Clooney salt-and-pepper. There were lines in the corners of his eyes indicating that he probably laughed a lot and spent a good deal of time in the sun.

I gave him my hand and he took it in a warm and firm clasp. "It's a pleasure to meet you, Mr. Chalmers."

He chuckled, a low, deep rumble in this throat. "Please don't make me feel older than I am. It's Harold," he said, squeezing my hand. "And may I call you Melanie? I feel as if I already know you after everything Yvonne's told me about you. All good, I can assure you."

Jack pressed the heel of his hand against his heart. "But what about us, Yvonne? I thought we had something special."

Yvonne's cheeks pinkened, making her eyes sparkle even more. She slapped at Jack's arm with her gloves. "We do, Jack. But I think it's best if we just admire each other from afar, don't you?"

"That's probably best," Harold agreed. "I wouldn't want to challenge you to a duel for the lady's favor. They once did that a lot in Charleston. In lots of places, I imagine, but quite a lot nearby in Philadelphia Alley."

I smiled and nodded, familiar with the thoroughfare. I'd made the mistake of going down the narrow bricked walkway only once and found myself watching in horror as two men dressed in eighteenth-century clothing stood back-to-back before pacing away from each other, pistols drawn.

"No, sir," Jack said, extending his hand to shake. He was smiling, but I saw him shooting furtive glances at the crowd around us.

"Don't worry," I said. "Marc's not here. Rebecca said he was still at the house, taking the brunt of Harvey's anger over the sporadic power and equipment failures."

Jack gave me a slow, warm grin. "What a shame."

"That's exactly what I thought." I grinned back, sliding my hand into the crook of his elbow.

"Oh, speaking of Marc Longo," Yvonne said, her tone bitter enough that if she'd been anyone else I'd have expected her to spit on the ground at the mention of his name, "I've been doing more research about the Vanderhorsts and Gallen Hall in particular, trying to see if there was anything else that might help you find what you're looking for. I haven't had time to photocopy and e-mail you this yet because I had my appointment at the beauty parlor today and time got away from me." She patted her shining helmet of hair.

"Anyway," she continued, "I couldn't stop thinking about that note from the marquis to the Swamp Fox, and the rumors of a treasure from the French king to the Americans that was never found. I haven't even been able to find anything definitive that would clarify what the treasure actually was. However . . ." She closed her mouth, and her cheeks puffed out slightly as if they were finding it hard to contain the secret.

"Yes?" I prompted, afraid Jack might lose his mind if he had to drag out every word.

"So I decided to focus my search on specific treasurelike words, like jewels, gold, and metal."

Once again, her cheeks filled with anticipation, and even I had a hard time restraining myself from shaking her a little to get the words to pop out of her mouth. "And?" I prompted.

"And," she said, drawing out the word in a way that would make any Charlestonian proud, "I happened to get a hit on something very unexpected. It might not mean anything, but then again, since there's no such thing as coincidence, it might." She winked at Jack. "I found an article in an ancient Charleston architecture text that focused on the various craftsmen and metalworks in and around the city. We do have the most beautiful iron gates and fences, don't we?"

We all nodded, but I could see the tic starting in Jack's jaw. "Anyway, I saw mention of a Samuel Vanderhorst, a respected metalworker in the city around the end of the eighteenth century. The name popped out at me, of course, so I did a little digging and found a small biography of him in the antiquated volume that also mentioned Elizabeth Grosvenor." She shook her head. "I shouldn't have missed it the first time I went through the book, except he didn't have his own listing, because . . ." She paused but quickly continued when she spotted the manic look in Jack's eyes. "Because Samuel was a freedman and former slave on the plantation and therefore was mentioned only briefly, his name tucked in amongst about twenty other craftsmen on the plantation. His owners freed him when they discovered what a gift he had for metalworking. All the gates and fences at the plantation, including the cemetery, were designed and made by him. I might not have taken note of his name and occupation, except that the listing mentioned that he also made jewelry." She raised her eyebrows and I fully expected her to waggle them for effect, but she didn't. "Aren't you going to ask me what keyword I used in my search that ended up on the listing?"

With a tight smile, Jack said, "Yes, please. I don't think I can take any more suspense."

"Pinchbeck! After the Revolution, Samuel left the plantation and set up shop in Charleston, where most of his work involved forging gates and fences in and around the city. But in his spare time, he also made costume jewelry for less affluent clients, most of it with pinchbeck."

Jack and I stared at each other. "The brooch," we said simultaneously.

"It wouldn't be out of the realm of possibility that he made the peacock brooch Eliza Grosvenor is wearing in her portrait at Gallen Hall," Jack finished.

"Does that help?" Yvonne asked.

"I hope so," Jack said. "I don't know, but I'm sure it's a piece of the puzzle. I'm just not sure yet where it fits." He looked up at Harold. "Is it all right if I hug Yvonne?"

"Go right ahead. I think she'd be disappointed if you didn't."

Jack hugged the older woman and kissed her on the cheek. "Have I told you lately how wonderful you are?"

"Now, hush, Jack. Harold can hear you," Yvonne said, giggling.

We all laughed, then said our good-byes, with Yvonne promising that she'd e-mail the photocopies of what she'd discovered.

As Jack and I walked across the lobby to join our group, I looked around to make sure no could hear, then said,

"Rebecca just told me that Marc is looking for one of the papers we found in the box Anthony gave us. It's a drawing, and apparently Marc has one that matches it—it's the one copied by Joseph Longo at the Vanderhorst house. All Rebecca knows is that Marc believes they're connected. Do you think he has any idea what he's looking for?"

Jack stopped walking and met my gaze. "I doubt it. The only thing I *do* know is that Marc doesn't know anything more than we do—yet. Meaning we're probably still a few steps ahead of him. I think the brooch is important—you said that Eliza wanted you to notice it. Regardless, we need to find it before Marc does. Remember how Anthony said that Marc had used a metal detector on the floor of the mausoleum? A metal detector can't detect pinchbeck—it's made of copper and zinc, which are both nonferrous metals."

"Meaning?"

"Meaning that there'd have to be a heck of a lot of it to be detected with a metal detector. And the amount of pinchbeck used in a brooch wouldn't be enough. It also means that Marc doesn't know what he's looking for." He was thoughtful for a moment. "Do you think you could ask Eliza about her brooch?"

"You know it doesn't work that way . . ." I began.

"I know. But I thought you could maybe try, see where it goes. I'm sure Jayne would love to help, too."

I swallowed. "Sure," I said. "Because Jayne's always happy to help."

Jack gave me an odd look.

"She is," I said, squirming under his gaze. "That's a good thing, right? And don't say what you're thinking."

Jack held up his hands in surrender. "I didn't say anything."

"You didn't have to." I began walking toward the group, my pace quickening as I spotted the young Charleston dancer moving toward me from the other side of the room, her bruised and bloody mouth open as if she were trying to speak.

"Come on," I said, sliding my arm into Jayne's. "Let's go—we're missing out on some Christmas shopping." I hurried toward the exit without turning back, feeling the disappointed gaze of the dead woman following me out the door.

CHAPTER
22

The high heel of my shoe got stuck for the third time in the dirt courtyard of the Aiken-Rhett House museum as I moved among the various wreath-decorating stations set up inside the carriage house and around the courtyard. As I twisted my foot back and forth to remove it from the rocky soil, I looked up to see Sophie standing by the coffee and doughnut table watching me before dipping her head and staring pointedly at her own Birkenstock-clad feet.

I hobbled toward her, intent on diving into the box of doughnuts on the table in front of her; I had ordered them from Glazed, making sure there were plenty of my favorite flavors, the Purple Goat and tiramisu. I'd already placed two in a napkin and hidden them inside my purse beneath the table.

"Sure," I said, "you might be more comfortable, but at least I don't have to worry about being mistaken for someone needing a handout. You should probably put a glass jar in front of you—you can always give the proceeds to Ashley Hall." I eyed her mom jeans with the tapered ankles and high waist circa 1990, the turtleneck with tiny whales all over it that was definitely a 1980s holdover but had been subjected to Sophie's tie-dyeing obsession, and the leather-fringed vest that was more circa 1880.

When Sophie had told me her parents were downsizing and her mother was sending her a bunch of clothes from her closet, I'd tried to prepare myself. But the sheer scope of Sophie's windfall had been worse than I'd thought. I'd tried to tell my friend that just because her mother had given her all those clothes didn't mean she actually had to wear them, but Sophie was as dedicated to reusing and repurposing everything as she was to restoring old homes. Unfortunately.

"It's a nice turnout," I said, looking around at the groups of people standing at each wreath-making station. I leaned down and reached beneath the red-draped table. "Thank goodness for the good weather—maybe we'll raise enough money today that we can skip the progressive dinner."

Sophie blew out of her face a strand of green-streaked hair that had slipped from its braid. "Right. And that would happen just after they cancel Christmas."

I pulled out a small shopping bag from Sugar Snap Pea and handed it to Sophie. "Against my better judgment, I bought this for Skye. I was in the store looking for yet another replacement for Sarah's favorite book, *If I Were a Lamb*—JJ keeps tearing off the covers—and I saw these and had to get them."

Sophie opened the bag and peered inside. With a happy exclamation, she pulled out a small yellow knit cap with peace signs stamped all over it in neon colors. "I have one just like this!" she said.

"I know. But I thought it would look cute on Skye anyway."

"Thank you!" she said, taking me by surprise and hugging me. "I've always known you're not the curmudgeon you pretend to be."

"Humph." I looked across the courtyard to where Veronica was at the orange-and-clove station, helping customers attach the fruit to their boxwood wreath frames before they moved on to the holly-berry station.

"Aren't you supposed to be helping Veronica?" Sophie asked, pouring coffee from an industrial percolator into a recyclable paper cup for a customer.

"I was, but then she said she could handle it by herself, so she sent me to Jayne, who's at the ribbon station, and she said the same thing. So I came over here to see if you needed any help."

We looked over at the growing lines in front of Veronica's and Jayne's stations, where it was obvious they needed another pair of hands. Sophie faced me. "You were reorganizing all their supplies, weren't you?" She looked pointedly at the stack of cups I'd picked up and was placing on the opposite side of the table.

"Maybe," I said slowly. "Is there something here I can help you with?"

"Sure. Why don't you organize the sugar packets in the little basket by expiration dates printed in tiny writing on the back of each pouch, oldest in front?"

I would be lying if I said the thought didn't excite me. I replaced the cups and reached for the sugar. "All right," I said. "Although it looks like my talents could be used elsewhere." I indicated the growing lines now spilling out into the courtyard.

I looked at the milling crowd, wishing Rebecca would hurry up and get here so I could ask her more about the drawing Marc had. I'd told Jack what Rebecca had told me the previous evening, and we'd gone through the papers from the archives after we'd returned from the Shop and Stroll, eventually finding the photocopied page of what Rebecca had described as lines and scrolls. It meant nothing to us, and I'm sure Marc had reached the same conclusion about his drawing. But we needed to see it, just in case it did mean something. All I needed to do was to make Rebecca show it to me.

"Dr. Wallen-Arasi?"

Sophie and I looked up to see Meghan Black standing in front of us. I might not have recognized her out of context, except she wore her usual pearls and Burberry quilted jacket, her hair in a high ponytail. She didn't have on the cute earmuffs, but I recognized the J.Crew pants and flats from a recent shopping expedition with Nola.

"Meghan!" I said. "Good to see you out of the cistern. I was starting to think you were only three feet tall. Here to make a wreath or two?"

"I might—I live in a carriage house on Rutledge and the

door isn't visible from the street, but I bet my mom in Atlanta would like one. I'm actually here because Nola mentioned this is where I could find both of you this morning." She looked around for a moment, then stepped a little closer. "Is Mrs. Longo here?"

I shook my head. "My cousin won't be here for at least another hour. She said her husband came home late last night and woke her up, and it took her a while to get back to sleep. She's exhausted." I forced my expression to remain neutral as I recalled the two trips to the nursery I'd made the previous night, one because JJ's whisk had fallen through the slats of his crib, and the second one because Sarah was babbling so loudly I thought someone was in her room. She'd settled down by the time I'd reached her, the sweet smell of roses telling me it had been Louisa. The third time, Jack had gone and I'd fallen back asleep immediately so I had no idea who or what had caused the interruption to my sleep, and at that point I'd ceased to care.

Meghan nodded, her brown eyes wide. "Don't take this the wrong way, but I'm not sure she should hear this." She leaned in a little closer. "I found something in the cistern yesterday that I thought you both might want to see. That film guy and Mr. Longo were hanging around a lot, asking questions and requesting that if we find anything we show it to them first. Please don't take offense, but I'm not sure I'd want them around anything fragile or historically important. I don't think they appreciate the importance of old things, you know?"

Sophie and I nodded emphatically. I'd liked Meghan from the moment I'd first met her, and now I understood why. "We couldn't agree more," I said, peering at the Anthropologie shopping bag she held in her hand, balls of newspaper shoved inside and around a newspaper-wrapped object. "What did you find?"

Glancing around one more time, she placed the bag on the ground next to her, then took out the newspaper-wrapped package before placing it on an empty corner of the refreshment table. It was rectangular, but thinner than a brick, and seemed lightweight. "It's not super fragile, but it's old, so be careful when you open it." She slid it toward Sophie.

"I don't have gloves."

Meghan smiled. "I always carry extras." She reached into her coat pocket and pulled out a clear surgical pair.

Sophie snapped them on her hands, then began to unfurl the newspaper while Meghan and I played lookout. Two older women approached and I poured coffee for them without charging them just to make them leave faster.

"Oh." Sophie's head was bent over the paper and I joined her to peer into the opening.

"I know, right?" Meghan said. "It's amazing that it's so well preserved. Probably because it's made of mahogany, which is naturally bug and moisture resistant, but also because it found its way inside a leather traveling bag with a wad of what we think might have been a fabric coated with linseed oil that made it partially waterproof. It's what floor mats were originally made of, and it's just our luck that one may have been discarded around the same time this ended up in the cistern. It's amazing what really old garbage we can salvage because it was accidentally thrown away with something that worked to preserve it." She sounded as excited as I imagined a bride would when discovering the perfect wedding dress.

A small slab of wood, about the size of my car's rearview mirror, lay in the middle of the newspaper. One side was finished in the remains of a dark stain, the wood dull and split from years of being buried. Sophie flipped it over, the wood lighter and unstained on this side, and in worse condition without the protection of the stain and varnish of the front. On one of the short sides, a mottled brass square that might have been a hinge hung precariously to its spot near the top, two small nail holes near the bottom showing where a second hinge might have been. "It looks like a tiny door," I said.

Meghan nodded. "That's what I thought, too. I brushed it clean before wrapping it so Dr. Wallen-Arasi could have a better look. It's so different from all the pottery fragments and animal bones that I thought it was unusual enough to make sure I brought it to your attention."

"Nice work, Meghan," Sophie said, making the young woman's cheeks pinken. Sophie leaned a little closer. "What's this?"

I wasn't wearing my glasses—no surprise there—and when I squinted it appeared that there was just a dark smudge of dirt in the corner.

"I saw that, too," Meghan said. "So after I got it cleaned up, I got out my magnifying glass and took a look. It's a carving of a peacock. With its tail feathers opened. I have no idea what it might mean."

Sophie and I met each other's gaze. "It probably means that whatever piece of furniture this came from—and I'm assuming it's part of a piece of furniture because of the fine wood—was made at Gallen Hall Plantation." Sophie ran her finger over a small indentation at the top corner, her finger fitting neatly into the space. "I'm thinking this might have been one of those hidden doors we find all the time inside old desks and dressers. This door would have been flush against the back or side of a drawer opening and could be opened with a single finger." She flipped it over in her hands again. "This would have been a fairly small place to hide things. Most likely letters or documents." She glanced briefly at me. "Definitely something small."

"So not gold bricks?" Meghan asked.

"Definitely not." Sophie shook her head. "What makes you ask that?"

"Several times Marc Longo has come out to the cistern to check our progress, asking us whether or not we've used metal detectors to find anything metal." Meghan rolled her eyes. "Like we don't have better equipment than that." She held up a foot, now without a cast, to remind us of the XRF machine that had fallen on it earlier in the year. "The thing is, I overheard him saying something to that producer guy. I didn't mean to eavesdrop, but you know how loudly he talks."

I nodded, encouraging her to continue.

"Anyway, I was in the dining room and Mr. Kobylt was showing me the repairs he was doing to the floor in there, and Mr. Longo was telling the producer guy something about how he was sure the Confederate gold was on Vanderhorst property." Meghan rolled her eyes again. "Which is kind of ridiculous, really. There has been so much research on the subject and the conclusion is that the bulk of it was stolen from federal troops in 1865 by unknown persons and disbursed." With an insider grin, she said, "And we've all read about the Confederate diamonds found in your grandfather clock, Mrs. Trenholm. They're all accounted for, so I guess Mr. Longo just wants to believe that the gold must be there, too." She tilted her head in question. "They are all accounted for, right?"

I nodded. "Yes. We know what happened to all of the diamonds, and found the remaining ones that hadn't been given away or sold. I wish there were more." I hadn't meant to say that, at least not out loud to an almost stranger. There was just something about Meghan's open and eager face that encouraged confidences.

"Are you sure?" she asked.

"Very," I said slowly. "Why do you ask?"

She continued to look speculative. "Well, there was a reporter from the *Post and Courier*—Suzy something—who came by yesterday. She's writing a story on hidden historical treasures that might be found in the Lowcountry. She mentioned the pirate treasure supposedly buried on Sullivan's Island, the Confederate gold and diamonds, and the connection of the last two to your house. I told her you would be the best person to ask about that because all I knew was that I was supposed to be excavating the cistern and so far had only discovered broken bits of pottery and bones."

"That's all, then? She didn't say anything else?"

"Actually, she did. Something about another treasure— from the American Revolution. Something given to the Americans by the king of France maybe? She said there are plenty of rumors about what the treasure might be, but no-body knows for sure. She wanted to know if I'd heard any-thing about that, or if you'd mentioned it to me."

My mouth went completely dry. I had had a dozen or so phone calls and texts from Suzy Dorf, which, as usual, I'd ignored. She'd been nothing but a thorn in my side since I'd inherited the house on Tradd Street. Besides being nosy and too inquisitive about the rumored possibility that I could speak to the dead, her worst fault was being friends with Rebecca. Now I wondered if I should have been so hasty with the DECLINE button on my phone.

"I see. And was Mr. Longo there when she stopped by?"

Meghan shook her head. "No. He'd been sent out to get more batteries and lightbulbs since everything was losing power and every time they flipped on a light, the bulb would explode." She raised her eyebrows, as if she expected us to reassure her that this was perfectly normal. Which it was, of course. For us.

"Interesting," Sophie said, her tone indicating that the subject was anything but. "Did she happen to mention why she thought Mrs. Trenholm would have any knowledge about the French treasure?"

Meghan shook her head again. "She didn't, and I didn't ask. It was getting dark and I still had a lot more work to do in the cistern while there was still daylight. None of us like to be there after the sun goes down." She didn't need to explain that the reason was only partially because it was hard to excavate without full light.

"That's fine," Sophie said reassuringly. "You're doing a great job, by the way." She indicated the wooden door rest-ing on the newspaper. "And thanks for bringing this to me—I'm sure it's important; I just can't figure out why yet."

"Yay," Meghan said, giving a little clap with her hands. "You'll let me know when you figure it out, all right?"

"Absolutely," Sophie said. "Now, go make a wreath for your mom and have fun. Nola and her friends are here to help get you started. . . ." Her words trailed off as we fol-lowed her gaze to the first table in the opened carriage house, where Nola, Alston, and Lindsey were supposed to be welcoming the participants, taking tickets, and explaining how the whole process worked. Instead, the three girls were sitting at the table with their heads bowed over a thick textbook that was opened between the three of them while people milled about in front of them trying to figure out where they should start.

I exhaled a deep breath. "Hang on—let me go find out what's going on with those three Gen Zers."

"Hey, don't knock millennials—we're not all bad!" Meghan looked genuinely upset.

"Sorry," I called as I walked across the courtyard to where the girls sat at a long table under one of the arched openings, my heels slowing me down as I tiptoed over the dirt in an attempt to save my shoes. I stopped in front of the table, waiting for one of the girls to look up. When no one did, I cleared my throat.

"Oh, hi, Mrs. Trenholm," Lindsey said sweetly. "We didn't see you standing there."

"Or the other twenty or so people who are looking for a little guidance here." I frowned at the three of them, wearing matching black Ashley Hall cardigan sweaters with long-sleeved purple polo shirts, plaid skirts, and black tights. They never intentionally coordinated what color polo or tights they were going to wear, as allowed by the school, but somehow they always ended up looking like fraternal triplets. Personally, I liked that they always matched. Maybe because I was the thwarted mother of twins who preferred things to match but whose efforts were never appreciated.

Nola sat back heavily in her chair. "Sorry. It's just that Lindsey reminded me this morning that our art history teacher told the class on Thursday that we were having a quiz on Dutch painters on Monday and I forgot to bring my art history book home. It's going to be a big part of our final exam, too, so we have to know it."

"I forgot my book, too," Alton said. "And it's like ten

percent of our grade, so we need all the time we can get to study."

I glanced down at the thick book with shiny pages and a photograph of a painting of a woman wearing a Dutch cap and a bright blue apron, pouring what looked like milk from a pitcher. I frowned, remembering how obsessive I'd been about grades at that age, and even felt a small tug of panic in the pit of my stomach. I glanced at my watch. "You're supposed to be here for two more hours. How about I relieve you for an hour so you can go study? But only an hour. I've got work to do today, too." I didn't mention that part of that work would involve solving the photo puzzle on Jayne's dining room table.

The girls shot up from their seats at once. "Thanks, Melanie," Nola said, giving me a quick hug. "I'll dedicate my A in the class to you."

Nola scooped up the heavy book with both hands, and the three of them took off toward the house. I hoped they were aware that the Aiken-Rhett House was preserved and not restored—a distinction drilled into my head by Sophie—and that there was no furniture they'd be allowed to sit on. I turned away, intent on allowing them to figure it out.

I smelled coffee and turned to find a recyclable cup held in front of me. I smiled up at Veronica and accepted the cup. "Thank you. You must be a mind reader," I said.

"I needed a coffee break and figured you probably did, too." She took a sip from her cup. "I wish you'd been here earlier when we had a customer demanding plastic greens for her wreath so that she could keep it up as long as she wanted to without it turning brown. I thought Sophie might have a heart attack."

I laughed out loud. "I can't believe I missed that. I didn't get a lot of sleep last night, so I'm moving slowly this morning."

Veronica nodded. She didn't say anything, although I could tell by her air of anticipation that she wanted to. I remained silent, sipping my coffee, and waited.

Eventually, she said, "Should I be concerned if the attic door opens on its own all the time now?"

"Are you asking if you think there's something structurally wrong with your house? I'd say probably not. Although I'm not an expert on that sort of thing."

"Adrienne's trying to tell me something, isn't she?"

I closed my eyes for a moment, smelling the dark coffee and enjoying the warmth on my bare hands. "Probably. Especially if this is something new."

"It is, and I don't think it's a coincidence. It started the night Michael said he wanted to put the house on the market."

I looked at her. "When does he want to do that?"

"After the first of the year." She met my gaze. "He gave me an ultimatum. Either him or the house. He said if I valued our marriage, I'd sell and allow us to start over." She took a sip of her coffee. "I'm afraid that if we move out, we'll lose Adrienne forever. And I'll never know what really happened to her."

I stared into my cup, tilting it in my hand and making my reflection swirl on the dark liquid. "I'm crazy right now with all this Christmas stuff and the filming going on at my house—not to mention the excavation in my backyard."

Veronica's face fell, and I briefly thought she might cry. "I don't know what to do."

I thought for a long moment of the young dancer in the hotel the night before. Of all the times I'd been forced to sing ABBA songs to block out cries for help. I took a deep breath. "I might be able to help you—or at least buy you some time. Why don't you call my office and set up an appointment with me? I can certainly list your house, just as I can certainly make it go as slowly as possible." My boss, Dave Henderson, would kill me for hanging on to an unproductive listing, but I couldn't tell Veronica that I couldn't help her. Besides, I wasn't promising that I could find out what Adrienne was trying to tell her. All I was saying was that I could buy her some time.

Veronica grabbed my free hand and squeezed, her

eyes moist. "Thank you, Melanie. Thank you so much. I don't care what Rebecca says about you—I think you're wonderful."

I opened my mouth to ask her what she meant, but a group of mothers I recognized from the school had approached the table and were already busy chatting to me and asking questions. I drained my coffee and turned my attention to them, all the while aware of the faint scent of Vanilla Musk perfume and the ribbon of icy air that caressed my cheek, leaving no doubt that the new activity in Veronica's attic had nothing to do with coincidence.

CHAPTER
23

I woke up to a single ring of the landline telephone that I was no longer plugged in but remained on my bedside table for occasions like this. I sat up quickly, not wanting to disturb General Lee or Jack, and held the receiver to my ear. "Hello?"

The snap and crackle of empty space filled my ear. I pressed the phone closer, hoping to hear my grandmother's voice. She'd been dead for years, but she still preferred the phone to communicate with me. And only when she thought I might be in trouble. "Grandmother?" I whispered into the receiver, my stomach feeling as if multiple rubber bands were wrapped tightly around it. My greeting was met only with the electric sizzle of an ancient telephone line that shouldn't be making any noise at all.

"Grandmother?" I said again, still straining to hear. I waited for another moment, then slowly pulled the receiver away from my ear but stopped; the sound was as strident as a baby bird's cry, beaming its way to me as if from another galaxy.

Jack.

"What?" I pressed the phone against my ear again. "Did you say 'Jack'?"

Another moment passed, and then I heard it again. *Jack.*

"What about Jack?" My question was met by silence, even the crackling sound fading. "What about Jack?" I repeated. But the phone had gone completely dead; there were only the sounds of the old house and General Lee's snoring for company.

I hung up the phone and turned around to see if Jack was awake. A sliver of moonlight cut across his pillow, accentuating the white of his empty pillowcase. "Jack?" I said out loud, looking at the bathroom door for any light from beneath it. But the door yawned wide, an empty black shadow indicating no lights were on inside.

I slid out of bed, making General Lee snuffle and adjust himself on my pillow, then go back to sleep. I glanced at the video monitor, but the nursery was empty except for the two sleeping babies in their cribs. Sliding on my slippers, I grabbed my robe and thrust my arms into it before hurrying out the door, the rubber bands around my stomach squeezing tighter. My grandmother never called just to chat.

I hurried down the corridor and paused at the top of the stairs. A light was on downstairs, and a few of the rubber bands slid off my insides. When Jack was writing, he often woke up in the middle of the night with a story idea that couldn't wait until morning. I placed my foot on the top step, then stopped, aware of an odd sound coming from Nola's bedroom behind the closed door. She was still sleeping in the guest room as Greco continued with his redo of her room, the paint and sawdust from the new built-in bookshelves and window cornices making it nearly unlivable. The restless spirits, too, if one wanted to count them as disrupters of sleep.

After a quick glance toward the light downstairs, I moved slowly down the hall to Nola's bedroom, brushing past the two miniature Christmas trees filled with tiny children's-toy ornaments—one for a girl and one for a boy—that Sophie had insisted we needed. One shook and nearly toppled when my robe snagged on it, and I had to grab it by the stuffed teddy bear tree topper to keep it upright. I promised myself for the millionth time that next year we were going on a cruise and skipping the holidays completely.

I paused a moment to flip on the upstairs hallway lights, and was not completely surprised when nothing happened. One of the screaming phone calls Jack had received from Harvey that past evening had been about these exact same lights. Apparently, there was something wrong with the Southern wiring (his words, not mine, and he used a few more descriptive adjectives before the word *Southern*) that was causing the lightbulbs to blow out as soon as the switches were flipped.

I thought for a moment about getting Jack but stopped myself. If he was writing, that would be a good thing, and nothing I wanted to interfere with. I was an adult. And a mother of toddler twins and a teenage girl. There shouldn't be anything left that could scare me. Surely I could handle whatever was behind that door. And if not, I could close it and then go get Jack.

I gingerly touched the door handle, for some reason thinking it would be hot. The brass felt cool to the touch, so I wrapped my fingers around it, then pressed my ear to the door. I couldn't identify the sound at first, probably because it seemed so out of context in my house in the dead of winter. A buzzing, like a man's electric razor several decibels louder than it should have been, vibrated through the door, traveling from my head to my fingers and making them tingle.

With a deep breath, I turned the handle, then pushed the door open enough for me to peer inside. Moonlight filled the unadorned windows, lighting the room with a blue-white glow. I reached around the doorframe for the light switch and flicked it on. Nothing happened.

The buzzing was louder now, unbalanced, the source concentrated on one side of the room. The dusty scent of gunpowder drifted toward me and I glanced furtively into the dark corners for the musket-carrying British soldier I'd seen twice before. Except for the moonlight, the corners were empty, the room bare.

Pushing the door as far as it would open, I stepped a little farther into the room, listening as the buzzing took on a new rhythm, a *thud-thump, thud-thump*. Like a beating heart. I swallowed, unwilling to let go of the doorknob just in case I needed to make a hasty retreat and needed to find the door. My eyes gradually adjusted to the moonlight, my gaze moving from one side of the room to the other, stopping when it reached the bed.

Greco had stripped it of all its bedding and had been draping fabric samples over it for Nola and her grandmothers to pick and choose from. But the noise wasn't coming from the mattress. It was coming from higher up. I looked at the foot of the bed, where the two carved bedposts jutted toward the ceiling like fat fingers. I blinked, my eyesight even worse in the dark, but good enough to tell that one of the posts was different from the other. It was thicker at the top, it seemed. Rounder. I blinked again. *Moving.*

I stepped back quickly, my heels bumping into the edge of the open door. Taking a deep breath, I looked at the top of the bedpost again, trying to decipher what I was seeing, hoping against all hope that it wasn't those flying palmetto bugs that were terrifying when they were solo. I had no word to use for when they traveled in packs.

But they were buzzing. Like bees. Forcing myself to let go of the doorknob, I stepped closer to the bed to get a better look. One flew in front of my face as if on reconnaissance, and to my relief it was much smaller than a palmetto bug and most likely a bee. It buzzed and jerked, then flew back to join the cluster of buzzing insects swarming along the entire length of the bedpost.

I walked across the room to examine the windows, wondering if one had been left open. Then I remembered. It was December. From what my father had explained to me about bee behavior, during the winter months bees stayed in their hives, keeping the queen warm until spring. There was another reason there would be a swarm of bees inside my house in December. An unnatural reason. My grandmother had once told me that bees were messengers from the spirit world. How appropriate, then, that I would have just received a phone call from her. As I stared through the hazy darkness at the buzzing, swarming mass on Nola's bedpost, I wished she'd simply told me on the phone what she wanted me to know instead of sending bees. Apparently, *simple* wasn't a word anyone in my family was familiar with.

A shape drifted across the cistern below, a fall of light followed quickly by darkness. I stepped back, not wanting to be seen, and waited for whoever it was to show up on the other side. I squinted, wondering if it was an intruder of the flesh-and-blood type or of a ghostlier sort, unsure which one I'd prefer. I waited for whatever it was to emerge, but the night remained still and dark. But I knew there was someone—some*thing*—out there. I felt malevolent eyes on me, like sticky tar that clung to my skin.

I backed away quickly, unwilling to wait for whatever it was to show itself. I continued to walk in reverse until I reached the doorway, not brave enough to turn my back on the window. I saw her then. Eliza. She stood by the bedpost, staring at it as if she were as surprised by the bees as I was.

I remembered Jack telling me to ask Eliza about her brooch. I knew it didn't usually work that way, but I was tired of waiting for the message to come to me. I wanted to be left alone, to focus on Jack and our family and my career again. To resume normal lives that didn't involve swarming bees, specters haunting the backyard, and reporters asking questions I didn't want to answer.

Eliza was more shadow than light, but the green of her dress gleamed like an emerald in the moonlight, the sparkle of the jeweled brooch on her bodice winking at me. "Eliza." I kept my voice light, mingling it with the buzzing of the bees, not wanting to scare her into vanishing.

She looked directly at me. At least I sensed that she was looking at me. I wasn't sure—her face and body were swathed in shadow—but I felt her gaze on me. Despite the darkness that enshrouded her, the jewels on her brooch seemed lit from within, small beacons of light. I felt compelled to look at it, to notice something. I squinted out of habit but was close enough to see the shape of the bird, the fanned tail. The four stones seemed to mock me as I struggled to understand what Eliza was trying to tell me.

"What is it?" I whispered. "What do you want me to see?"

Lies. For a moment it was if the buzzing of the bees had mimicked the sound, the cold breath of a corpse washing over me as the word swirled around the room telling me that it hadn't been.

"Eliza?" I whispered, but she was gone, along with the bees and the buzzing and the smell of gunpowder. I waited for a moment, attempting to catch my breath, and then, with trembling hands, I reached for the door and left the room, gently latching the door closed behind me. I spotted the light in the foyer and ran down the stairs, knowing Jack was on the other side of that light and could make it all better.

Jack's study door was open, the green-shaded banker's lamp on his desk giving pale light to the room. I stopped on the threshold, breathing heavily, not seeing Jack at first. Yet I definitely smelled . . . pipe smoke? "Jack?" I called, hoping another ghost wasn't waiting for me. One per night was more than enough.

"Over here."

My gaze followed the voice, stopping at the corner behind the piano where Amelia had placed a lovely leather Chesterfield chair and ottoman, for times when he wanted to read quietly or just think in his office. I rarely saw him use them, as he did most of his thinking either walking around the room or sitting at his desk. But he was sitting in the chair now, in the near dark, his feet on the ottoman. And smoking a pipe.

I had so many questions that it was hard to pick one to start with. "Why are you smoking a pipe?" I managed.

He took it from his mouth and looked at it as if surprised to see it. "I know you disapprove of cigarettes, and cigars stink, but I thought you'd be okay with a pipe. My grandfather left me his collection when he died, and

Mr. Vanderhorst was kind enough to leave several tins of tobacco in the freezer."

"But you don't smoke."

He shrugged. "No, I really don't. But I didn't want to start drinking again, and smoking was the next best thing. And it worked for Sherlock Holmes—he always smoked a pipe when solving complex puzzles. Besides, after I'm gone, the pipe smoke will let you know that I'm hanging around." He offered a half smile.

"Don't say that, Jack." I wasn't sure if my concern was more over him mentioning his death or over his need for a drink. I walked across the room and stopped near his chair. "What's happened?"

A crease formed above his nose as if he was trying to remember. "Well, for starters, when I woke up at three in the morning, the first thought in my head was that I needed a drink." He took a long puff from his pipe, then coughed a little. "It's been years since I had that thought first thing." His eyes met mine, and I felt the heat of his gaze. "I usually have better things to think about when I wake up."

A flash of heat spiraled up from my core, nearly making me dizzy as it reached my head. He'd had that effect on me since we'd first met. I took a deep breath. "Has something happened?"

"Do you want the good news or the bad news first?"

"Let's start with the good news," I suggested, thinking in the back of my head that maybe I could distract him from telling me the bad news.

"I heard from Steve Dungan, my architect friend. He finally looked at the building plans for both mausoleums, examining all the measurements, comparing the width and length of all the walls, the angles of the triangle that forms the structure, looking for any differences." He sucked on the pipe, his eyes closed briefly. When he blew out the smoke, I smelled a not-unpleasing mixture of sweetness and spice.

"And?" I prompted.

"He found only two changes from the original. The first

is that the original mausoleum had spaces for ten crypts, not just the three that are there now. The other thing he noticed is that the second mausoleum is exactly two brick widths taller than the first."

I thought for a moment. "The row of bricks with the strange markings is two bricks wide. Which tells me that the whole purpose of rebuilding the mausoleum was to add that double row."

"Yeah, so that might be the reason why the first mausoleum was demolished and replaced with a nearly identical one two years later. Hopefully we'll figure out what the reason was when we finish the puzzle on Jayne's dining room table." He raised his eyebrows. "Maybe you can ask the ghost of Sherlock Holmes for help on that one for me?"

I frowned. "You do know he's a fictional character, right?"

Jack leaned his head against the back of his chair and looked at me through half-closed eyes. "Sure. Just trying to keep my fantasy world intact so I can still write books." He tilted his head slightly. "You look real sexy with your hair like that—all rumpled from sleep."

I smiled, glad not only that distracting Jack was going to be easier than I'd thought, but also that I didn't have to listen to the bad news. I took a step closer, his eyes following me.

"And then there's the bad news," he said, and I stopped.

He lifted his head. "I made the mistake of checking my e-mail instead of trying to go back to sleep. My brilliant editor, whom I'm beginning to believe really must be a twelve-year-old boy in disguise, told me that in a marketing meeting where all the powers that be discuss what to do with problem children—books they don't know how to market, that is—the brilliant suggestion had been made to convert my next book into a graphic novel."

"A graphic novel? What's that?"

"Basically? A cartoon. They're going for that younger market."

"But your book is about a mentally ill mother with

Munchausen syndrome by proxy who kills her daughter. Not sure how that would translate into a cartoon."

"Bingo. You don't know how refreshing it is to hear the voice of reason. It's rare in the publishing business, apparently."

"But they can't do that if you don't agree to it, right? And if you don't, you'll just find another publisher."

He barked out a laugh, a dark, ugly sound. "If it were only that easy. If there's such a thing as being blackballed, that's what would happen to me. Nobody is taking my phone calls or returning my e-mails. I couldn't find a new agent right now unless I could prove I was the reincarnation of Margaret Mitchell. It's like I'm the plague and nobody wants to be infected."

I sat on the edge of the ottoman, unsure of my role. He was always the one with the answers. The first person I ran to. It was hard to reconcile the accomplished man with the chiseled face and piercing eyes with this man referring to himself as an infectious disease. For an instant I considered looking past this moment to the next, of closing my eyes to a problem I had no idea how to solve and telling him what I'd just seen upstairs, hoping that answering the question of Eliza would make him forget about his own.

But I couldn't do any of those things. Because Jack needed me. Needed me to be strong and to shoulder some of the problem solving on my own. I had a small fantasy where I figured out what Eliza was trying to tell me tonight and it was the key to everything. I imagined solving it all and handing it to Jack and him immediately turning it all into a bestselling novel. Maybe that's why my grandmother had called. To tell me I needed to take care of things, to protect Jack while he dealt with his personal demons.

Placing my hands on his leg, I leaned forward and said, "This is all temporary, Jack. You've got a great book already written, and the idea for another one—you're not out of the game. Not by a long shot. You've got a respected body of work and that alone speaks volumes."

He blew out a puff of smoke, temporarily obscuring his

face. "I want to believe that. You have no idea how much. But, Mellie, my career is my identity. I'm a writer. A best-selling author. Without that, who am I?"

I leaned closer. "You're a father, a son, and a husband. And you're damned good at all three of those roles, and those are a heck of a lot more important than anything else." I tried to think of what else might jolt him from his despondency, but I was woefully lacking in the ability to give a pep talk. As an only child and a single woman for most of my adult life, I hadn't learned that skill. Maybe, just this once, I'd revert to the old Mellie and pretend that Jack's despondency didn't exist. It was simple, really. I just wouldn't allow it.

"Do you mean that?" he said, his voice smoky.

I stood, took the pipe from his hand, and placed it in a crystal ashtray on the table next to him. Then I straddled his lap, his hands moving under my robe and resting on my waist. "I do. I couldn't pick a better father for my children. I am also hopelessly and ceaselessly in love with you, Jack Trenholm. Whatever profession you choose."

His hands caressed my sides through the thin fabric of my nightgown, doing wild things to my nerve endings. "Show me," he whispered in my ear.

So I did.

CHAPTER

24

When I got home after work the next day, I threw open the door to the piazza, intent on rushing upstairs to Nola's room to see any lingering evidence that Eliza or the bees had been there the previous night. I'd been running late for work that morning and both Sarah and JJ had been out of sorts, begging to be held, and I hadn't had the time to investigate. I stopped short at the sight of Greco hanging a Christmas wreath on the front door. I walked more sedately toward him, then stood back so we could both admire it.

"What happened to the wreath that was there? I made it, you know. At the workshop I ran benefiting Ashley Hall."

Greco stepped forward to rearrange a strand of holly berries and adjust the enormous, intricately knotted red velvet bow. "Oh, it's in there. I loved your color scheme—you did a nice job of that. It just needed a bit of . . . zhushing."

"'Zhushing'?"

He nodded. "It's a technical term designers use that means 'adding to' or 'expanding.' In layman's terms, it's taking something skimpy and inelegant and re-creating it as something a client might actually be proud to have in her home. Or to hang on her front door."

I probably should have been offended, but he was annoyingly right. Compared to this elegant and gorgeous confection, mine had been a puny impostor. Even Jack had had a difficult time coming up with a convincing compliment. Nola had just called it sad.

I peered closely at it. "So my wreath is somewhere underneath all this . . . zhushing?"

He nodded. "Yes. Somewhere very deep." He turned around to indicate the glass hurricane lamps that lined the perimeter of the piazza. "And I switched out your luminaries. I didn't think paper bags were the best look, and the fake candles inside looked, well, fake. I found these electric candles that not only appear real but aren't nearly as tacky as some of those less expensive ones."

I started to protest, but he held out his hands. "My treat. Your mother and mother-in-law are being so generous with the redo of Nola's room that I felt I needed to up my game a bit. I hope you don't mind."

I looked at the hurricane lamps, each one spotless and sporting an ivory candle in a brass candlestick. It was impossible to tell the candles weren't real. "Do the flames flicker like actual candles?"

Greco looked offended. "Of course. They're also on timers so that they turn on at dusk and turn off at sunrise. The best part is that Dr. Wallen-Arasi approves. She says they look like the sort of lighting they had during Colonial times, so they will be appropriate for the progressive dinner—and safer than real flames. She actually likes them so much that she wants more to be placed throughout the entire house so there won't be a need for more obviously electric lights the night of the dinner."

"Great," I said, picturing diners stumbling around my house in the near dark, the spirits rousing due to the lack of bright lights to deter them. I looked up at him. "Did you say Dr. Wallen-Arasi? Did you see her?"

"She's inside. She arrived about twenty minutes ago and I let her in. I hope you don't mind. She didn't see the replacement window brochures on the hall table, if that's what you're worried about. Although I'm not sure I shouldn't have mentioned them to her, since everyone knows repairing your historic windows is much more economical in the long run."

"Thanks, Greco. And if you'd like to pay for the repairs,

I'll ask Nola to start one of those GoFundMe accounts and let you know."

He picked up two shopping bags from Hyams Garden and Accent Store, several boughs of fresh pine poking out of the tops. "I'm going home to make potpourri with these, and I'll bring it tomorrow inside some of my vintage silver pomander balls—all very kosher, as I explained to Dr. Wallen-Arasi. Nothing on the inside or outside of my potpourri isn't authentic to the Colonial period."

"That's a relief." I pretended to wipe sweat off my brow. I was fairly certain that Greco knew about my lukewarm feelings toward authenticity when it came to the bottom line. I was all about the bottom line and convenience. I think he appreciated this and might even have been enjoying his role as referee between Sophie and me. "Did they even have potpourri back in the day? I thought that was more of a modern invention by stores like Abercrombie & Fitch to get people to come inside."

He stared at me for a long moment, and I wondered if his eyes looked funny because he was trying very hard not to roll them. "No, actually. Potpourri has been around since early civilizations. I think its usage correlates to the level of hygiene practiced by humans of the time period. In Colonial days, with no running water and certainly very rarely heated, people didn't bathe much, especially in the winter. Try to imagine body odor on top of that of wet wool, and you can perhaps come close to what it must have smelled like in the average home. Hence potpourri."

It was my turn to stare at him. "I didn't know that, and I might even have been happy continuing in my ignorance, but thank you."

"You're welcome." He twisted a blue cashmere scarf around his neck. "By the way, that word that was scratched into the wall that I sanded out is back again. I wanted to let you know that I'm aware of it, and I'm on it." He smiled, touched his forehead in a mock salute, then walked toward the piazza door.

"Thank you," I said to his retreating back, amazed that

he was more concerned about concealing the word than why it was there or what it might mean.

I glanced at my watch, then hurried through the front door, letting it slam behind me. I had quickly taken off my coat and hung it up, buttoning every single button because that's the way it should be done, when I turned around and nearly ran into Jayne.

"Sorry!" I said. "I was running a bit late and then stopped to chat with Greco outside. But I'm here, so you can leave now. Twins good today?" I thrust my hand into the closet and grabbed her coat, having to unbutton only the top button.

"Little angels, as usual. That Sarah is running all over the place and babbling up a storm. JJ prefers to be carried everywhere and to build stuff with whatever he can find. Hard to believe they're related, except they both look like Jack."

"Hard to believe," I repeated, placing my hand on her shoulder and gently propelling her to the door.

"They're catnapping in their cribs, so they should be good for another thirty minutes or so." She looked at my hand on her shoulder, then into my eyes. "Why are you so eager to get rid of me?"

I looked past her toward the small carriage clock on the table in the foyer and walked a little faster. "I'm not trying to get rid of you, but didn't you say you had to leave a little earlier today? That's why I rushed back."

She stopped. "It's not an emergency or anything, Melanie. I'm just going to see Anthony in the hospital."

I paused with my hand on the doorknob. "He's in the hospital?"

"Yeah—they're not sure what's wrong with him. It's some kind of virus, they think, but they can't figure it out. He can't keep down any food or liquid, so he's hooked up to an IV."

I met her concerned gaze. "And he's been that way since we were all in the cemetery?"

She nodded. "I think he's . . . susceptible to evil spirits. Remember his car accident?"

"But I thought Marc had done something to his car."

"Could be, but he did tell Thomas he saw someone or something in his backseat right before the accident, and then he was pushed down the stairs when he was alone in the house, and now this. I can't imagine how Marc could cause Anthony to be this sick. I'm thinking the negative presence we keep sensing is having an effect on Anthony because he's trying to dig for answers that whatever it is doesn't want him to find." She took a deep breath. "I'm going to tell Anthony he should move into my house when they stabilize him enough to release him from the hospital. It's a big house, and I'll be there to make sure nothing happens to him. And he'll be away from the cemetery."

"You want him to move in with you?"

"No, not like that. It's to protect him, and only until he's one hundred percent better."

I peered closely at her. "Was this your idea or his?"

Her gaze slid to the space behind me. "It was sort of both of ours." She paused. "Although he may have mentioned it first. I think he's scared. And this way, someone will be home to work on the puzzle all day long. We've only got about one-quarter of it done. There are way too many bricks with nearly identical patterns, with only tiny swirls or lines to make them unique. I'm beginning to wonder if there's an intentional design at all."

I'd had the same doubt but had been keeping my thoughts to myself. It was as if I really believed that if I didn't say anything out loud, it couldn't be true. Instead, I said, "I don't think Thomas is going to like this very much."

Jayne pressed her lips together. "I don't think he has any say in the matter."

The carriage clock chimed, and I yanked open the front door. "I don't want to keep you—tell Anthony I said hello and call me later and let me know how he's doing." I closed the door, then waited until I could hear her retreating footsteps.

I raced to the dining room window and peered out, looking for my mother on the sidewalk. When I didn't spot her,

I ran up the stairs, taking them two at a time, and hurried into Nola's room.

Sophie looked up from where she knelt in front of the jewelry cabinet. "Is there a fire I should know about?"

"No, sorry. Jayne just left and my mother's not here yet, so I only have a few minutes to come see Nola's room."

She looked confused. "I have no idea how those three things are supposed to be related to each other."

I sighed. "My mother and I are supposed to take JJ and Sarah to Hampton Park this afternoon. The weather's so nice. . . ." I paused, wondering at the expression on her face.

"And you didn't want Jayne to go with you?"

I closed my mouth, realizing that, yes, not wanting Jayne to accompany us had been the reason I'd been rushing around, making sure she was out of the house before our mother arrived. I swallowed. "Maybe."

"Don't be ashamed to admit it, Melanie. It's understandable. You've only recently rediscovered your mother and built a strong relationship. You never thought you'd have to share her, and now you do. And nobody asked you first."

It felt as if a bowling ball had been lifted from my chest. I took two deep breaths, enjoying the new sensation of lightness. "I hadn't really put it into words, but, yes. You're right. And this afternoon I just wanted it to be my mother and me. Not because I don't like Jayne or don't want us all to have a good relationship; it's just that I wanted some alone time with my mother and the twins. Is that so wrong?"

Sophie shook her head. "Of course not. And admitting to yourself what you need is the first step toward building stronger relationships with others."

"Thanks," I said. "I appreciate you telling me things I need to hear. Most people don't have the nerve." My gaze took in her crazy green-streaked hair, her 1980s Benetton sweater with enormous shoulder pads, the same mom jeans she'd worn to the wreath-making workshop, and her Birkenstocks. "So, despite your questionable style sense, you still qualify as my best friend."

"Ditto," she said, using the bedpost to help her stand. "And remind me to pick up some chakra stones for you. You seem stressed."

"Gee, really? I can't imagine why." I walked toward the bed, recognizing the rectangular piece of wood Meghan Black had found in the cistern; it was still resting in a nest of newspaper. "I guess this has something to do with why you're here? Besides dispensing advice, that is."

She grimaced. "And deflecting nosy reporters, too, apparently. That Suzy Dorf was here looking for you. Seems she went to your office but was told you weren't there, either."

"Good to know that Jolly at the front desk is doing her job. What did you tell her?"

"That you weren't here and I had no idea when you'd be back. She did have one question for me, though."

I raised my eyebrows.

"She wanted to know why we're friends. I told her I have no idea."

I gave her a half grin. "Me, neither."

"You know, Melanie, you should probably speak with her. Find out what she knows about the French king's gift. Because it's only a matter of time before she finds out everything we've discovered so far and tells Rebecca. Then Marc will swoop in for the kill like a palmetto bug on a bread crumb."

I sighed. The last thing I wanted to do was speak with the inquisitive and diminutive Suzy Dorf. But Sophie was right. As usual. "Fine. I'll reach out to her tomorrow." I indicated the piece of wood. "So, did you find out anything?"

"Yes and no." She walked over to the jewelry chest, the drawers and lid all open. "I'm pretty sure I know where that small secret door is from." Putting down the newspaper, she removed the top drawer of the chest and placed it on the floor before flipping on her iPhone flashlight and beaming it inside. "Look on the right-hand side here—there's still a broken hinge clinging to the wood of a small cavity, and the size of it matches the holes in the piece Meghan found. When I held up the piece of wood, it was an exact fit." She looked at me, and our gazes locked. "It appears it was ripped off its hinges. It's not lockable, so there'd be no reason to rip it off to get to the contents of the narrow cavity."

"Unless someone was in a big hurry."

Sophie nodded.

"But the cavity is empty?"

"Yep." She picked up the drawer and placed it back inside the jewelry chest. Facing me again, she said, "Do you remember where the chest came from? Is it possible it came from the Vanderhorst plantation?"

"It came from the attic—it's full of Vanderhorst furniture. It's like a time machine up there. I don't think the family ever threw away anything." I remembered the peacock Greco had shown me on the bed, and the story of how everything made on the plantation had been marked with the peacock icon. I indicated the claw-foot at the bottom of the bedpost. "Does the peacock carving match the one on the little door?"

"Yep. But that only means that they were both made at Gallen Hall, and most likely used as furnishings there before being moved here. This house isn't as old as Gallen Hall, and the carpenters and craftsmen would have been making the furniture for that house first." She gently kicked at something on the floor. "Any idea why there are so many dead bees in here?"

I stepped closer to get a better look, the sole of my shoe crunching something beneath it. I looked down and saw a cluster of dead bees, their wings and legs frozen in eternal flight. "They were here last night. Swarming around this bedpost but nowhere else. The windows were closed, and it's been too cool for the bees to be out of their hives anyway."

She tapped her chin. "I'm sure there was something hidden in that jewelry chest. I'm not certain how that little door ended up in the cistern, but it was probably considered garbage after it was broken off and discarded. That's

how most things end up in a cistern. Now, it's anybody's
guess as to where whatever that chest was hiding might be
now, but if this bedpost has the same carving, and they're
both made in the same period style and wood, meaning it's
possible they were created to be in the same room, and
there were bees buzzing around this post last night, inside,
in the dead of winter, I'd bet here would be a good place to
start."

Being careful not to step on any of the bees, she leaned
over and knocked on the post in several places, her expression not changing. "Pretty solid." Without a word, she slid
out of her Birkenstocks and climbed on top of the bed,
moving aside a lilac drapery panel with her foot. Standing
on her tiptoes, she reached toward the pineapple finial at
the top of the post and lifted it off. "These finials are re-
movable on all antique four-poster beds so the canopy can
be attached in the winter for warmer bed hangings." Smiling down at me, she stuck her fingers into the opening and
swished them around. "Nothing," she said, frowning. "I'd
be lying if I said I wasn't disappointed. Were the bees only
around this post?"

"Yes—definitely. The finial was as big as a basketball,
there were so many bees."

"Hmm." She stuck her fingers inside the bedpost one
more time before replacing the finial, then gingerly stepped
around the mattress to check the other three. With a grunt
of defeat, she lowered herself to the floor. "Sorry, Melanie.
I don't know what to tell you. I could have sworn that small
door cover would lead us somewhere."

"Me, too. Thanks, anyway, for trying."

She began wrapping the piece of wood in the newspaper.
"Let me know what the reporter says, okay? Or if you
would like help replacing all the plastic fruit on the stairway garland."

I was saved from responding by the appearance of my
mother, looking beautiful and elegant and not nearly old
enough to be my mother. "Sorry to barge in, but the door

was open, so I just walked right in. You know, Mellie, it's not a good idea to leave the door open."

"I didn't." I met her gaze, then waited for her and Sophie to greet each other. "Are you ready to go? I just need to get the children up from their naps and put their sweaters on."

She wasn't listening, her eyes focused on the bed behind me. "There's something . . ." She stopped, shook her head. "There's something here we can't see. I'm being drawn to this bedpost for some reason." Looking down on the floor, she spotted the pile of bee carcasses. "Oh."

"Exactly," I said.

"They were swarming around the bedpost last night," Sophie explained. "I've already looked inside the top of each post and knocked on the rest to see how solid they are, and found nothing."

"And," I added, "Eliza was here last night. Briefly."

Our eyes met. "Did she say anything?"

I hesitated a moment. "'Lies.' She's said that before."

My mother stepped closer to the bed, then held her gloved finger to her lips before pressing her ear up against the wood of the bedpost. "I hear something. Someone. A woman." She pressed her ear against the bedpost again and closed her eyes. "It's too garbled. I can't hear her clearly." She began to peel off her gloves, finger by finger.

I moved forward to grab her arm, to stop her, but she'd already wrapped her hand around the post. Her body went rigid and her face contorted as if in pain, before her chin dipped to her chest and I couldn't see her face anymore.

"Mother . . ."

Her head jerked back and for a moment I didn't recognize the mottled face that glared at me now, with bulging eyes and bloody skin. The voice that erupted from my mother's small body made Sophie and me step back as if we'd been struck, but neither of us could look away.

Traitors deserve to die and rot in hell!

The putrid stench of rotting flesh leached in through the floor and plaster walls, and my stomach roiled, but I couldn't leave, no matter how much I wanted to. "Mother!" I screamed, reaching for her hand and peeling her bare fingers off the bedpost, feeling what seemed like an electric current pulse against her skin.

Her eyes widened as she looked into my face, her expression of confusion softening slightly as she seemed to recognize me. "It's me, Mother. It's Mellie."

She nodded, letting me know she heard me. I held on tightly to her arms as her body relaxed and I led her to the bed. Just before we reached the edge, her eyes jerked wide, and, as clear as air, my grandmother's voice shouted from my mother's mouth. *Jack.*

CHAPTER
25

The following morning, I stepped around the small frosted Christmas tree in the middle of the lobby at Henderson House Realty and stopped at the tinsel-bedecked receptionist's desk, surprised to find it empty. "Jolly? Jolly Thompson? Are you here?"

"Right here," called a voice from beneath the desk. "I'll be right with you."

I moved around to the back of the desk and spotted our receptionist wearing yoga pants and a bright blue tunic, sitting cross-legged in the knee well. Her eyes were closed, allowing me to admire her turquoise eye shadow and sparkly mascara. "What are you doing?"

Her eyes snapped open. "Hang on." She rolled over onto her hands and knees and crawled out from under her desk. She reached out her hands and I helped her to stand. She shook her head as if to clear it. "Sorry—just trying to do more homework for my online psychic class. It's about channeling, so I was giving it a try."

"Any luck?" I asked.

"Not yet. I'm not really surprised, though. I think my strength is intuition. And touch." She rubbed her hands together. "Like right now, I felt nothing when you pulled me up. There was no tingle or anything, which just confirms my suspicions that you have no psychic powers whatsoever."

"Really?" I said. "How interesting." Her psychic statements were more miss than hit, so I tried not to encourage

her, despite the fact that a few times she'd come eerily close
to hitting the nail on the proverbial head. I peered at the top
of her desk. "Any messages? Cancellations?"

I was hoping that Veronica would call and cancel our
morning appointment. I'd told her I would help her buy
time, but I knew that sooner or later I'd need to confront the
ghost of her sister and find out what was keeping her here.
I just couldn't manage adding one more thing to my over-
flowing plate without my head exploding.

Jolly leaned over her desk, her dragonfly earrings temporarily replaced for the season with light-up Christmas
bulbs. "You have two new appointments for showings—
both with out-of-towners—and Veronica Farrell called to
confirm an appointment at nine o'clock regarding a new
listing. And . . ." She drew out the word slowly for dramatic
effect. "That Suzy Dorf stopped by yesterday while you
were at a house showing and then called twice after you left
for the day. I don't know how much longer I can hold her
off. She has a hard time taking no for an answer."

I recalled what Sophie had said, how I needed to speak
to Suzy and find out exactly what she knew. I blew out a
heavy sigh. "Fine. Send me the call next time. Maybe that
will make her stop pestering us."

"Only if you're sure," Jolly said, her disappointment at
my apparent caving showing on her face. She was enjoying
being my gatekeeper maybe just a little too much.

"I'm sure."

She picked up one of her never-ending lists—she made
lists for everything, which was one of the reasons we got
along so well—and crossed something off. "Well, then,
here you go." She handed me the messages. "Oh, and one
more." She reached for a pink memo pad and tore off the
top note. "Your mother called. She said instead of the park
at noon, to meet her and the children at Belmond Place to
see the Christmas tree and the toy train in the lobby. The
weather has turned a bit nasty for a walk in the park."

I nodded, recalling my mother's collapse the previous

afternoon and the aborted trip to the park. "Did she mention if Jayne would be joining us?"

"No, she didn't." Jolly lowered her chin, looking at me over the top of her glasses. "Does that make a difference?"

I waved a hand in dismissal. "Of course not. She's my sister."

"Um-hm," Jolly said, looking like someone who knew way more than she should and probably attributed it to her "psychic powers." I wondered for a moment if I might be mentally broadcasting my mixed feelings about Jayne, and made a note to think only about babies and puppies while in Jolly's presence.

I forced a smile, eyeing the coffee and doughnut on the credenza behind her; they were almost hidden behind a giant Santa Claus that would say, *Ho, ho, ho* and ring his bell if a person clapped. She saw where I was looking and blocked my view of the doughnut. "I'll be in my office," I said. "Let me know when the Farrells get here."

"Will do."

I began to walk toward my office but stopped when Jolly called me back. I turned around. "Yes?"

"When that adorable husband of yours stopped by yesterday to drop off your glasses, I saw that man again standing behind him."

"That man?"

"Yes, remember? A while back, I told you both I'd seen a dark-haired man holding a piece of jewelry standing behind Jack. But then I said he had a mustache, and now I'm not so sure. I think he just has a dark shadow like he hasn't shaved in a few days."

"Yes, of course." I did remember, mostly because Meghan Black had managed to capture a photo on her phone of a man standing by the cistern and matching the same description. "Tell me again what he looked like?" I asked, hoping she'd say something completely different this time.

She closed her eyes. "Well, like I said, he had dark hair,

which I could see because he wasn't wearing a hat. And his clothes were old-fashioned, with those short pants men used to wear that ended at the knees." Her eyes popped open. "He was holding something, too. I think the first time I saw him, I thought it was a bracelet, but this time I saw it wasn't a bracelet at all."

"So what was it?" I pressed.

"Some kind of a bird, I think. With four really big jewels, which was why I thought it was a bracelet at first. But this time I could tell it wasn't. Maybe a pendant?"

"Or a brooch?" My voice cracked.

"Yes! I think that's it." She nodded to emphasize her realization. "And whoever it was must have come from wherever Jack had just been, because he followed Jack out when he left."

I didn't mention that Jack had been at home working, or that I knew where the spirit had come from. Nor did I mention that I had no idea why.

"Did you tell Jack about the apparition?"

"Of course." Jolly chewed on her bottom lip. "Especially because there were some definite unfriendly vibes coming from the man. And when I looked at his face, his eyes were just dark, hollow circles. So I thought Jack should know." Her expression was sympathetic. "I will admit that Jack seemed a little startled—not everyone expects to hear that they're being shadowed by an evil spirit."

I realized my jaw was nearly numb from clenching my teeth. I almost didn't recognize the sound of my own voice when the words finally tumbled out. "Did the spirit . . . say anything?"

Jolly's bright green eyes stared straight into mine. "Ghosts don't talk, dear. You've been watching too many reruns of *Ghost Whisperer*." She leaned forward, Christmas bulb earrings swinging. "It's more of a . . . mental connection with the spirit. And let me tell you, this was an angry spirit and I was pretty sure I didn't want to hear what he was saying. Except . . ."

"'Except'?" I prompted.

"Except I felt something beneath his anger. Something that felt a lot like . . . heartbreak. Not just a broken heart, but a *seared* heart. Like he was a man who'd been horribly betrayed by someone he'd deeply loved. So I decided to listen to what he was trying to communicate to me."

The phone rang, startling us both. "One moment," she said as she answered the phone, then placed the call on hold.

"And?" I asked impatiently.

She pressed her lips together. "I don't usually use this kind of language. . . ."

"Just tell me, please."

"I was pretty sure he was trying to say, 'Traitors deserve to die and rot in hell.'"

Icy fear dripped down my spine as I recalled the same words in my own head at the mausoleum, and then coming from my mother's mouth in Nola's bedroom. I swallowed. "Was that all?"

She paused, then shook her head. "No. There was a name, too. But I got the impression that he was thinking it was Jack's name, except it wasn't."

"What was the name?"

Jolly's green eyes widened. "I'm pretty sure it was Alexander."

There was only one Alexander I knew. Alexander Monroe. The name on one of the crypts in the mausoleum. The British soldier billeted at Gallen Hall during the occupation of Charleston.

"Hmm," I said, pretending that the name didn't mean anything. "Very interesting. And you told all this to Jack?"

"Yes, of course. I assumed he would mention it to you, although he did say you were under a lot of stress right now with the holidays and the film crew in your house and getting ready for the progressive dinner. Jack said you're hosting twenty-four couples for the main course? And all on top of you having two little ones and a teenager and a full-time job. I'm exhausted just thinking about it." She gave me a sympathetic smile. "That Jack is such a wonderful husband—so compassionate and caring. That's probably why he didn't bring it up. It's not an emergency or anything. I mean, it's not like ghosts can hurt you, right?"

I stared at her for a moment without comment. "Right," I said noncommittally. "Well, thanks for letting me know. And for these." I held up the pink message slips. Walking back to my office, I was left to wonder why Jack hadn't mentioned any of it to me. As I closed my office door, I felt a small surge of anger. It might be petty, but feeling left out was the one thing I couldn't live with and that always made me revert to the old Mellie. Even with that knowledge, the hurt didn't dissipate, making me decide that when Jack was ready to share what Jolly had just told me, I'd tell him about the bees in Nola's bedroom and what had happened when my mother touched the bedpost.

I hung up my coat on the coatrack, buttoning it up to the collar and checking the pockets even though I'd just checked them before I'd left the house. It was an old habit, started when I was a young girl taking care of my alcoholic father, checking his pockets for flasks or small bottles so I could destroy them before he remembered where they were. It was the kind of old habit that was difficult to break. Along with drawer labeling so my father didn't have to struggle in the morning picking between black and navy socks.

When Jack laughed at some of my quirks, I sometimes had the urge to explain why I did these things. But then I'd have to explain to him why I still did, even after all these years of my father being sober. If only I knew the answer, then maybe I could stop.

I moved to the Keurig machine—a birthday gift from Jack—on my credenza and was selecting which flavored coffee I wanted from the rack of alphabetized K-Cups when a flash of red caught my attention. Keeping my body still, I shifted my gaze toward my desk and froze. The heart-shaped red pillow that I'd taken from Veronica's attic sat on my chair, propped up so I couldn't help but notice it.

Putting down my coffee mug, I walked over and picked up the pillow, thinking—hoping—it was a different one. But because of how things worked in my neck of the woods, I knew hoping was a lot like planning on putting out a forest fire with a single puff of breath. I studied the pillow, noticing the neat hand-stitched seams along the ruffled edge, the nubby red material that appeared as new and vibrant as it probably had thirty years before. I brought it to my face and sniffed, recognizing the faint scent of Vanilla Musk perfume.

I pressed the intercom button on my desk phone and waited for Jolly to pick up. "Jolly, has anyone been in my office since I left it yesterday?"

"No, Melanie. Just the cleaning people. Why? Is something missing?"

I stared at the small pillow still clutched in my hand. "No, actually. It's—"

"The Farrells are here. I'm sending them back now."

"Thanks—" I started, but she'd already hung up, the sound of dead space quickly replaced with that of tapping on my office door. "Come in."

Michael opened the door and stepped back to allow Veronica to enter first, his hand solicitous on the small of her back. Veronica startled when she saw what I held in my hands, her eyes questioning. When Michael noticed it, too, I saw him do a double take, but otherwise he gave no sign that he recognized it.

I indicated the chairs in front of my desk. "Please, have a seat." Not knowing where else I could put the pillow, I tossed it on the seat of my chair, then sat on it, hoping I wasn't offending anyone. "Sorry," I said in explanation. "Bad back."

They both stared at me, expressionless. To break the awkward silence, I offered them both coffee, and when they declined I pulled out a brand-new yellow lined notepad from my top desk drawer. I had a laptop, a desktop, and an iPad, but nothing could beat plain paper and pencil. And whatever I wrote never disappeared into a cloud, or whatever that thing was where Nola continued to tell me I should be storing documents.

"So," I said, getting ready for my sales pitch. "I'm glad that my friendship with Veronica has brought you in today, but I also hope that you've done some research into my sales record to know that I'm the best agent to list your historic home."

"Of course," Michael said, uncrossing his legs and leaning forward with his arms on his thighs—what my boss, Dave Henderson, called the "power stance," meaning a client was ready to sign on the dotted line. Except I hadn't gotten that far yet. "So can we dispense with the chitchat and get the house on the market today?"

I placed my perfectly sharpened number two pencil on the pad and looked up at Veronica, who was staring at her lap. "Today?"

"Yes," Michael said. "I see no reason for delay. We think it will move fast, so we'd also like to look at options for a good family home to move into. We'll include Lindsey in the decision, of course, but it will be mostly Veronica's choice."

He put his hand on her arm, but she was now looking directly at me.

"I see." I picked up my pencil again. "So, let's start with that so I can begin thinking about available houses. Veronica, what would you like to see in a new house?"

Michael spoke before Veronica could open her mouth. "We're flexible on location—Mt. Pleasant and James Island are possibilities. Probably not downtown or South of Broad because we definitely want something more modern than what we have now." He smiled at his wife, oblivious to the fact that she was neither smiling nor nodding but sitting stoically and staring into space.

He continued. "We're both tired of the maintenance and upkeep on an older home. And with Lindsey going to college soon, we'd like to spend our downtime traveling and doing things together instead of spending all that time and money repairing things on the house." He pointed at the pad of paper. "Aren't you going to write that down?"

I looked up at Veronica to gauge her reaction, but she'd returned her gaze to her lap. I replaced the pencil on the pad with a decisive snap. "Look, why don't we work on this part later? I've already got about a dozen homes in mind—we'll narrow it down by location later. Right now, I think we should visit your house on Queen Street and make a list of things that might need to be changed or updated before putting it on the market, so you can get top dollar."

"Oh, please," Michael said. "There could be a gaping hole in the roof with rain pouring in and someone would still want to buy it because it's historic and in Charleston."

"Well, while there is some truth in that, if the house needs expensive repairs or major updates, it will be reflected in the sale price. And if you're wanting to replace it with another house in Charleston, you'll want as much money from the sale as you can get."

Veronica finally spoke. "She's right, Michael. I don't want to skimp on the new house, since we'll be there for a very long time. We have to think of the future, of possibly having grandchildren and making sure there's room for them and yard space. It won't be cheap."

His face softened, as if the mention of the word *grandchildren* had given him a new perspective. Or maybe it had been the words "it won't be cheap." "I see what you're saying. But that doesn't mean we should be dragging our heels."

"Of course not," I said. "But we need to make sure that we take enough time to do it right, however long that takes. Try to think of it in terms of money—the more move-in ready your house, the higher the asking price."

When Michael smiled, I realized we were finally speaking the same language. "Fine," he said as he stood. "Then bring your pencil and paper and let's head home so we can get started. Hopefully, it won't take too long."

Michael was already walking toward the door and didn't

notice Veronica's thumbs-up, which she gave me behind his back.

"Hopefully," I said, shoving the pad and pencil into my briefcase and retrieving my coat. "Just for good luck, let's all cross our fingers that there's nothing major that needs to be done on the house before we put it on the market."

Michael opened the door and held it for us, dramatically displaying his other hand to show his crossed fingers. "I got us covered."

Veronica exited in front of me, delivering a brief kiss to Michael's cheek and distracting him just long enough that he didn't notice the red pillow fly across the room and hit me in the back before falling to the floor.

Michael glanced behind me briefly as if the flash of color had caught his eye. Then he followed me out the door, pulling it shut with a soft snap.

CHAPTER
26

I took a pedicab from the Farrells' house on Queen Street to Charleston Place to meet my mother and the children because if I'd had to walk in my heels after exploring all three floors of the Farrells' Victorian, I would have had to self-amputate at the ankles.

I also had bruises on my rib cage and back from Veronica prodding me every time I said something was fine, and she'd continued poking me until I had ratcheted up the needed upgrade or repair to her satisfaction. By the time I left, my list was ten pages long, enough to keep the house off the market for at least a year unless Michael had his say. He certainly hadn't looked happy as he'd closed the front door, and I doubted he would go along with even half of the suggestions I'd made.

As I sat in the pedicab, I had the brilliant thought of calling Sophie and sending her over to Veronica's to make a few structural suggestions, along with dire warnings. She was a college professor and quite good at intimidation and wearing down those who disagreed with her regarding old-house restorations. Which was why I'd spent more money than I had ever thought possible on a new roof and foundation, along with hand-painted wallpaper and hand-sanded floors. All because I couldn't say no to Sophie, even though she dressed like a toddler who'd chosen her own clothes.

I plucked my phone from my purse just when it started to ring. There was no name next to the familiar telephone number because I was too optimistic in believing that I'd

never have a need to add her name to my contact list. I slid
my thumb across the screen, then held the phone to my ear.
"Hello, Suzy. This is Melanie."

"I can't believe I'm actually speaking with you! You're
a hard person to pin down."

"So sorry," I said, mimicking the bored tones I'd
heard my coworker Wendy Wax using with one of her ex-
husbands. "'Tis the season to lose one's mind, and all that."

"That's for sure." Suzy giggled, sounding like the
twelve-year-old girl she resembled. "I understand you have
a full house right now with a film crew, a decorator, and a
classroom full of preservation students in your backyard.
How *do* you do it all?"

"Is this an interview about my life? Because if it is, I can
save us a lot of time up front and tell you now that I'm not
interested."

She giggled again, setting my teeth on edge. "Oh, I'm
sure your day-to-day life is fascinating, Melanie, but I'm
calling about something else. Are you familiar with the
series I'm writing in the *Post and Courier* about lost treasures in the Lowcountry? It's a weekly serial in the Sunday
edition."

I was too embarrassed to admit that I only had time to
pull the real estate section from the paper and that, despite
promises to myself that I would read the rest and become a
better-informed member of society, the rest of the paper
would usually end up in the recycling bin unread. Jack usually read the whole thing cover to cover, but I'd noticed
recently he'd been too immersed in puzzle solving and going over the research materials that Yvonne would send
over on an almost daily schedule to find the time to read the
paper.

"I think our neighbor's dog has been taking our Sunday
paper, because we haven't received it for several weeks
now. Her name is Cindy Lou Who, and she's just the sweetest dog, but she does love a juicy newspaper."

I prepared myself for another giggle, and when I didn't

hear one, I pulled my phone from my ear to make sure the call hadn't been dropped.

"You know, Melanie, journalists and editors work very hard on the newspaper. We would all appreciate a little respect."

"Sorry. I didn't mean that Cindy Lou Who was chewing on it, Suzy. I was thinking she was probably taking it to read. She's a very smart dog." I wasn't sure why I said that, only that my feet were hurting and the woman annoyed me.

"Glad to know you have a sense of humor, Melanie. Rebecca says you're probably going to need it."

I sat up. "What do you mean?"

I could imagine the reporter shrugging her narrow shoulders. "You'll have to ask your cousin. Now, do you have a few moments to answer some questions?"

We were creeping down King Street, the traffic slower due to the heavy volume and the number of pedestrians doing their holiday shopping. "That would depend. About what?"

"Lost treasures. For my series."

"Right. I'm not sure if I have anything to add, unless you're referring to the cistern in the backyard. They've found lots of broken pottery, if that's what you're looking for. I'd suggest asking one of the grad students working on the excavation, named Meghan Black. . . ."

"I'm looking for something lost since the Revolution, something valuable given by the French king to the patriots, presumably to pay American spies."

I kept my voice even. "Well, we certainly haven't found anything valuable—"

"Yet," she broke in. "While doing research on buried pirate treasure along the coast, I came upon the story in the national archives of Barbados, if you can imagine, of a treasure given to the Marquis de Lafayette in 1781 by the king of France. You're probably wondering why Barbados—"

"No, actually, I'm not. Look, Suzy, I don't have any idea—"

She continued as if I hadn't spoken. "I was researching 'the Gentleman Pirate,' Stede Bonnet, who was born in Barbados and hanged in Charleston—or Charles Towne, as it was known prior to the Revolution. That's why I was looking in the national archives of Barbados, and there it was—an obscure article about missing treasures that included Blackbeard, Bonnet, and"—she gave a dramatic pause—"the Marquis de Lafayette!"

She paused again, apparently waiting for applause. When I didn't respond, she continued. "Anyway, the article claimed that the marquis had been entrusted with delivering the French king's gift to an unnamed American who'd been charged with the task of enlisting influential citizens in Charleston as spies for the patriot cause. Whatever it was must have been easy to transport and quite valuable, as most of the influential citizens in South Carolina at the time were wealthy landowners, and to be caught planning against the Crown would mean certain death in addition to the confiscation of all your property and leaving your family destitute."

We passed a storefront window, a cute dress catching my attention, so I missed the first part of Suzy's next sentence, my focus snapping back when I recognized the name Vanderhorst. "I'm sorry—what did you say? About a Vanderhorst?"

A heavy sigh reverberated in my ear. "I said that I also went through and read old records regarding the detainees at the Provost Dungeon during the British occupation in the early seventeen eighties. The records included depositions of accused American spies prior to their executions. One of the men who was about to be hanged thought to save himself by naming names and mentioned Lawrence Vanderhorst of Gallen Hall Plantation. You can only imagine how excited I was to hear that and to know that I had an in with the owner of a Vanderhorst property."

I wanted to tell her she was delusional if she considered me an in but kept my thoughts to myself. They were too busy running back and forth over Lawrence's name, the name of the third occupant of the mausoleum at Gallen Hall. Not that I had any intention of mentioning that to Suzy Dorf.

"For the record," she said, "Lawrence was known as a staunch loyalist and had turned in American spies, so his reputation was pretty clean. He was never arrested, so the prisoner was either making something up to get a lighter sentence or he got the name wrong."

"Okay," I said slowly. "I'm not really sure why you're calling me about this. I'm not really into history." We were approaching the intersection of Market and King, where I'd be getting out of the pedicab. I hoisted my purse strap onto my shoulder in preparation, eager to end the call.

"That's not what Rebecca Longo told me."

I stilled. "What do you mean?"

I imagined I could see her satisfied smile at getting my attention. "She said that you and your sister and husband were working with her brother-in-law, Anthony Longo, on something involving Gallen Hall Plantation. You can probably guess how thrilled I was when I read that deposition that mentioned Lawrence Vanderhorst. The accuser claimed Lawrence was a member of an American spy ring. Which was quite a blow, I'm sure, since the Vanderhorsts were supposedly such staunch loyalists. They even quartered British officers in their home."

She paused, as if waiting for me to agree or claim knowledge or even surprise. But I remained silent. I wasn't sure whose side she was on, and I wasn't about to give anything away that might filter back to Marc through Rebecca.

"Anyway," Suzy continued, "the name of the spy ring has been lost to history, but one thing I was able to clarify was that members used the peacock as their symbol when communicating with one another. There are a few wax envelope seals embossed with a peacock still in existence in the Charleston Museum, but nothing to show who sent them, so members of the spy ring cannot be confirmed. But Lawrence's family owned the only plantation on the Ashley River with a large population of *peacocks*"—she emphasized the word—"and my journalist's brain would not let me think that's a coincidence."

"Of course it is," I said brightly. "The world is full of coincidences."

"Funny you should say that, Melanie. Because Rebecca told me that your husband's favorite thing to say is that there's no such thing."

I swallowed, hoping she couldn't hear it over the phone. "He may say something like that from time to time. Regardless, we haven't found anything valuable in our cistern, and I know next to nothing about the American Revolution, the marquis, or the king of France, so I think you should find someone else to interview if you want something juicy to print."

"But you know about Eliza Grosvenor."

I paused, considering my next words, knowing that pretending to be completely ignorant would confirm that I was evading the whole truth. "I know she was engaged to Lawrence Vanderhorst. But why would you think I should know more?"

She giggled, and my teeth ground together. "When I came to your office a couple of weeks ago to see if you were available, that handsome husband of yours was there with the children and had placed a stack of photocopied documents on the receptionist's desk while he prevented World War III from erupting in the double stroller. I couldn't help but notice the biography of Eliza Grosvenor, where someone had helpfully highlighted both Lawrence's name and the words *spy ring*. If that's the story your husband is working on now, I can't wait to read it."

Despite all the evil spirits and vengeful ghosts I'd faced in my life, nothing put more fear in my heart than hearing those words come from Suzy's mouth. As casually as I could, I asked, "Did you mention that to Rebecca?"

"No. Not yet, anyway. Would you not want me to?"

The pedicab took a right on Market Street and stopped in front of Charleston Place. I held up my finger to indicate

I needed a minute. I closed my eyes, remembering Jack's face when he'd learned about Marc's subterfuge, and when Jack's book had been canceled and Marc's book on the same subject had been published to so much acclaim. I wasn't sure if either one of us could bear it for a second time. "No, Suzy. To be honest, I wouldn't want you to mention it to anyone, but especially not someone with the last name of Longo."

"I don't know, Melanie. That's a lot to ask a journalist who's trying to get answers."

"Hold on," I said, digging in my purse for money to pay the pedicab, thankful for the few moments it gave me to think. I was silent as I watched the pedicab leave, the phone pressed to my ear.

"Melanie? Are you there?"

"Yes. I'm here. What kind of answers are you looking for?"

"Oh, I don't know. Maybe exclusive access to whatever is going on in your backyard and how it connects to Gallen Hall. I know that the legendary treasure entrusted to Lafayette has some connection to the Vanderhorsts, and I want to be the first to know about it."

"But if there's no connection, and nothing to be found in the cistern or anywhere else?"

"Then I want to interview you. I want to witness you talking to the dead and I want to tell my readers. Or put it in a book. I've been working on one for a while, about interesting Charleston residents of the past and present, and I think you'd be a perfect fit. Anyway, I'd say access to you would be a fair trade for my not sharing any of this with Rebecca, don't you think?"

"Mama!"

I turned at the sound of the little voice, my heart softening when I spotted JJ and Sarah in their double stroller as my mother pushed them toward me on the sidewalk, two sets of chubby little hands reaching for me. "Look, I've got to go. Can we talk later?"

"Sure. Just don't wait too long. I've got deadlines, and I'll need to print something to keep my readers wanting the next installment."

I began walking toward my mother and the stroller, feeling a flash of anger at Suzy Dorf, this virtual stranger who could destroy everything I loved. "You're all heart, Suzy."

After a short pause, she said, "I'm just trying to do my job. For the record, I'm not a fan of Marc Longo, either. He ruined my brother, bankrupted him in a sour business deal. I know how he operates and I'd rather see you and your husband end up on top of this. But I've got newspapers to sell."

"I just need to think about it," I said as I reached the stroller, then bent down to look at my beautiful babies.

"You do that. And, Melanie?"

"Yes?"

"I wanted you to know that I saw Jack a couple of nights ago at the Gin Joint. He was by himself, and he only ordered ginger ale. But he kept looking at the menu again and again, asking the bartender lots of questions. And I don't think it was for book research. Just thought you should know."

Something that felt like a block of ice gripped my heart. "But he left without ordering anything, right?"

"Yeah. He did."

"Thanks, Suzy."

"You're welcome. Talk to you soon."

The call ended, and I immediately pressed my face against the soft cheeks of my children, smelling them and feeling their soft breath on my face. The overwhelming need to save Jack, to save our family, suddenly consumed me. I had to find the answers, even if I had to do it by myself.

"Are you all right, Mellie?" My mother's solicitous tone nearly brought tears to my eyes.

I straightened. "Let's go sit down in the lobby so we can chat and JJ and Sarah can see the train."

"Choo-choo," JJ screeched, waving his whisk in the air and making a young couple chuckle as they passed by us.

We headed into the beautiful lobby with the double staircase festooned with lush garlands, bows, and clusters of glass ornaments. Both children bounced up and down in their stroller as we neared the enormous display beneath the stairway, the fabricated snow-topped mountains surrounding an alpine village, the toy train chugging its way down the tracks and through a mountain tunnel. A row of poinsettias stood sentry before the magical scene and I could almost feel my blood pressure drop.

Even before I'd had children, I'd always thought the Christmas display at Charleston Place was magical, easily imagining that this miniature world of houses with actual lights, tiny people waving, and vehicles with open doors was real. Both JJ and Sarah were watching with wide eyes and open mouths, and I felt a little bit of the fear that had gripped me since my conversation with Suzy dissipate.

"Has something happened?" my mother asked.

I shrugged. "Yes and no. We're not getting anywhere with any of the information we've discovered—not with the mausoleum puzzle or the four words that Nola and Cooper have been working on every spare moment. Even the little drawer cover that Meghan found in the cistern turned up nothing. And Jack, well, he's understandably upset about what's going on with his publisher's plans for his book and very frustrated that he can't sink his teeth into this next book without a single clue to go on."

"Amelia mentioned something to that effect yesterday. Jack stopped by Trenholm Antiques to help his parents place all the new items from their recent European buying trip in the best spots in the store, and he said he had no opinion one way or another."

I raised my eyebrows. "This could be more serious than I thought." I'd meant it as a lighthearted comment but realized too late that it wasn't. The way Jack relaxed and de-stressed was to rearrange furniture and accessories. He had an excellent eye and always knew where the overlooked étagères belonged, or where to place the spare chinoiserie biscuit jar. He hadn't so much as dragged an ottoman across a room for weeks.

"There's more," I said. "Grandmother called me."

"Oh."

"Exactly. She only calls when there's trouble."

"I know. Did she say anything?"

I met her eyes and felt a sinking feeling when I recognized the fear and worry in them. I nodded. "She said Jack's name. Just like you did when you touched the bedpost in Nola's room. Right after you said, 'Traitors deserve to die and rot in hell.'"

She frowned. "I wish I could tell you why I said either thing, but I don't remember any of it." Softening her voice, she asked, "Is Jack drinking again?"

I leaned over the stroller handle to straighten the large red bow in Sarah's hair. "No. Not that I've seen, anyway. But Suzy Dorf said she saw him at the Gin Joint. He wasn't drinking, but I think it was pretty clear that he wanted to."

My mother straightened her shoulders, making her seem larger than her petite frame. "We need to tell your father. Jack is his sponsor, so it would make sense that he should be the one to confront him."

I shook my head. "No. Confrontation never works with Jack. We can definitely tell Dad; maybe he can just have conversations with him. But don't confront him. In the meantime, I'm trying to find some answers to this whole peacock–spy ring thing. If I could just gift Jack with something concrete for this new story idea, he should be able to find a new publisher who will publish him the way he deserves."

"I'm not sure that will help, Mellie. Jack prides himself on being the smartest person in the room. His whole career has been built on digging up and figuring out buried mysteries of the past. Being that man feeds his confidence and his ego. I'm not sure if handing him answers on a platter will help."

I bristled. I'd always hated being told what to do, or that

my thought processes might be wrong. Sophie said that was proof I was stubborn and too independent, a product of how I was raised. She also insisted they were bad characteristics I needed to shed. I wasn't completely sure I agreed with her, and being married had certainly taught me compromise. On some things. But not this. We were talking about Jack here, the man I loved almost to distraction. The man who, according to Rebecca, might be in serious danger. I had to do what I thought best.

"I can take care of this, Mother."

"Of course you can. But you shouldn't do it on your own. Your father, Jayne, and I are all here to help. You just need to ask."

I bristled again at the mention of Jayne's name. My mother must have noticed, because she placed her gloved hand on my sleeve. "Mellie, you do know that your sister is on your side, right? And that your father and I love you both equally. I realize her sudden appearance in our lives must have been a bit of a shock to you, but I think having a sister should be a good thing. I disliked the loneliness of being an only child. And Jayne is such a friendly and loving person. . . ."

I sent her a stony look and she stopped waxing poetic about my half sister.

She continued. "What I mean to say is that a little jealousy on your part is understandable. But you have so much in common and such potential to be close. I hope you recognize that and move forward accordingly. Remember, Mellie. We're stronger together."

Everything she said after the word *jealousy* evaporated quickly. "Me? Jealous?" The forced laugh sounded so odd that both children turned to look at me with apprehension on their little faces.

My mother regarded me with solemn eyes but didn't say anything.

I grabbed the stroller handle. "Let's go look at the Christmas tree. Maybe it will give me a few ideas on how to 'zhush' the trees in my house for the progressive dinner. They're looking kind of skimpy."

We walked in silence around the display toward the enormous tree, JJ fretting because we were leaving the choo-choo train behind, his frustration matching my own as the ability to identify and grasp the one thing I wanted evaded me.

"Mellie?" my mother said quietly.

I faced her. "Yes?"

"I know we didn't find anything in the bedpost. But there's something there. I felt it too strongly. Have you told Jack?"

I shook my head. "I didn't see a need since there was nothing there."

"I think you need to tell him. Maybe he can figure it out. Because there is definitely something there."

I nodded noncommittally, returning my focus to the Christmas tree and all the sparkling ornaments, pretending I couldn't sense my mother's stare of disapproval burrowing within me, where my conscience lay sleeping.

CHAPTER

27

I lay back on my pillow panting as Jack's bare arm pulled me against his similarly clad body. General Lee was burrowing somewhere in the room, having sought a quieter place to sleep earlier in the night. I'd forgotten the one form of relaxation and de-stressing that Jack enjoyed besides furniture arranging, and I was grateful that he'd remembered.

"Wow," he said, kissing my neck.

"I was about to say the same thing. I'm guessing that was enough aerobic exercise that I can skip my jog this morning, right?"

"Nice try." He gave my earlobe a nibble, sending shivers down my back. "It's almost six o'clock and time for my run. You could join me."

I turned my head and opened up one eye. "Are you trying to kill me?"

"Jayne said your stamina has really improved and you've increased your pace. You should be very proud of yourself. She says you're on track for the Bridge Run in April."

I turned away at the mention of Jayne's name, recalling my conversation with my mother. And Sophie. I wasn't saying that they were wrong, but I certainly wasn't agreeing that they were right. My feelings about Jayne were far more complicated than what they were implying, and something I needed to figure out on my own without everyone offering advice. "I'm thinking about taking up yoga instead."

Jack's chest rumbled against my back as he chuckled. "You tried that with Sophie, remember? Before the twins were born. You said every time you closed your eyes and tried to open your mind, some lost spirit would wander in."

"Yeah, well, at least it doesn't hurt my knees. I think I'm too old to run. Yoga's more my speed. Or maybe I'll try Pilates. I don't think that involves any meditation."

He was kissing my neck again, and I felt my brain slowly melting. "Pilates sounds good. It could make you even more flexible." The way he said the word *flexible* made it sound dirty.

I rolled in his arms to face him, placing my palms against his cheeks and enjoying the warm scratchiness of his beard. "I'm so glad you're feeling better."

He pulled away slightly, his eyes darkening. "Better? I wasn't aware that I was feeling poorly."

Too late, I realized my mistake. "I meant, I know how upset you've been with the whole publishing nightmare and Marc Longo bribing us to agree to film in our house, and the rest of it. You've been really down lately, but you don't seem to be in such a dark place this morning."

He let go of me and lay on his back, his arms folded beneath his head. "'Dark place'? Have you been watching *Star Wars* with Nola and Cooper?"

I could tell he was trying to dismiss my worry, but I was a mother now, my worry not easily waved away. "You've just been a bit down, that's all. And with your history . . ."

"As a drunk?"

I leaned up on my elbow so I could look him in the face. "That's not what I was going to say. You're a recovering alcoholic, and I know from my dad that it will be something you will need to confront every day for the rest of your life. But I'm here, Jack. If you feel the need to talk with someone . . ."

Before I was even aware of him moving, he'd flipped me over on my back, his frame pressing me into the mattress, his blue eyes staring into mine, and I was reminded again of his powers of persuasion and how he knew just what it took to distract me.

"I find you irresistible when you're trying to be serious."

"But I am serious," I said, trying not to focus on the heat of his bare skin against mine, or how I knew it was all intentional. "I'm worried that all this pressure is affecting you. . . ."

He nibbled on my neck, moving up to my earlobe with small kisses. "There's only one thing affecting me right now, Mellie, and that's you, naked, in my bed. I don't think I'll ever get tired of this."

I struggled to remain coherent. "Jack, please. Listen to me. Maybe you and I should go away for a long weekend— to Palmetto Bluff, maybe. To get away from everything."

He didn't lift his head as he continued his attention on every nerve ending in my neck. "We can't afford to get away, remember?"

I focused on my breathing, wondering if I should try to use the Lamaze techniques I hadn't had a chance to put into practice when the twins were almost born in the backseat of a minivan.

"Just promise me one thing, Mellie."

"Mmm?" I mumbled, unable to articulate a coherent word.

"Please don't think you need to solve all of our problems, all right? When you get it into your head that you and you alone can fix everything, your tendency is to react rashly and independently, and that never turns out well."

"But . . ." My words of protest were quickly forgotten as he moved his lips against mine, neatly erasing all thought and worry.

My blissful and oblivious satiation lasted until an hour later, when I was awakened from a deep sleep by the sound of Jack sitting down on the edge of the bed and lacing up his running shoes before closing the door gently behind him. The last thought I had before I fell back asleep was that he hadn't kissed me good-bye.

∞

"You might find this easier with your glasses on," Anthony suggested.

I glanced up at him over the top of Jayne's dining room table. Despite having been in the hospital for almost a week and not being able to eat any solid food, he looked surprisingly robust. His coloring seemed healthy and his hair was thick and shiny, the crutches and arm sling gone. Maybe it was a male thing. I remembered what I'd looked like following my hospital stay after giving birth, when I resembled an extra from *The Walking Dead* instead of a youngish new mother. I would have hated him if he hadn't been so affable.

I sighed, then reached inside my purse under my chair for my glasses. "I'm just not in the habit of wearing them."

Anthony nodded sympathetically. "So they're new?"

I considered lying, then changed my mind. It was stupid, really. "No. I've had them for a couple of years. I just haven't gotten in the habit of wearing them."

He smiled. "Well, for the record, I think you look just as beautiful with them on as you do without them. Just in case you were wondering. And you don't look like Jayne's older sister at all—more like her twin. But I suppose with a mother like Ginette Prioleau, it's in the genes."

There it was again, that little pang in my gut at the mention of Jayne. We'd just had a lovely tea party with the twins in the garden, taking turns pushing JJ and Sarah in the new double swing. I'd enjoyed being with her and loved the relationship my sister had with my children. It was clear she loved them, and the sentiment was returned twofold. But the ball of resentment lodged in my stomach wouldn't budge. Obviously, I was the worst person in the world.

I forced myself to smile. "If I didn't know any better, Anthony, I could swear you were buttering me up for something."

"Ha—got me," he said, standing up with one of the brick pictures and bringing it to my side of the table. "I want you to say nice things about me to your sister."

"I do that anyway."

He met my eyes for a moment. "Yeah, well, Jayne and I are just friends. I'm hoping we can move beyond the friend zone."

"Ah. Have you mentioned this to her?" I picked up a photograph and leaned over the table, holding it next to other photos to see if it matched.

"No. I can be pretty shy around women." A slight blush tinged his cheeks. "Marc was always the one who got the girls when we were growing up. Or maybe he just bullied me enough that I wouldn't go after the girls he wanted. And if I had a girlfriend he found interesting, he usually ended up dating her."

"Sounds like a wonderful big brother."

"You think? He certainly had the potential. He's always had the kind of personality that makes people do what he tells them to."

There was an odd note in his voice, one that I was beginning to recognize in my own when I talked about Jayne. Something that could be either love or hate. Something unexplainable. "Even now?"

He was silent for a moment, his eyes unable to meet mine. "Well, we don't speak anymore, remember? It's easier without him in my life."

"I'm sorry," I said, meaning it. Despite all my weirdness where Jayne was concerned, I couldn't imagine my life without her now.

He waved his hand dismissively. "Nah—don't be. Maybe when we're old men we'll reconcile enough to be chess partners in the same nursing home. Who knows?"

Before I could say anything else, he yelled, "Bingo! Got one." He slid one of the photos up next to another three, making it a perfect match on the top, bottom, and one side.

"Thank goodness. At this rate we'll be lucky to be done by the time we're all ready for the nursing home."

"So it's a good thing I'm living here for a bit while I recuperate. I intend to spend every spare minute working on it until we've found where all the pieces fit." Anthony's voice had a hard edge to it, and I wondered if it had to do with Jayne keeping him at arm's length.

"Yeah," I said. "It's a good thing. Because everything else we've discovered has led us nowhere in a hurry."

"Seems like it," he said. "Jayne's caught me up to speed on everything—thought that maybe I could help. Sadly, I can't offer anything new. Except . . . Well, did Jack find the drawing in the box of papers I gave him?"

"Yes, he did. But it means nothing to us. We need to see the one Marc copied from your grandfather's diary, put them together, maybe, to see if they form a picture or code or something that might make sense."

"Remember I told you that Marc showed it to me? I might remember it if I could see the other picture. It's a long shot, but worth a try, right?"

For the first time in a long while, I felt a glimmer of hope. "Yes," I said brightly. "It's definitely worth a try. I know Jack hid it, but I'm not sure where. I'd call him and ask, but I know he's working and I hate to disturb him, but I promise to ask him tonight. Not to worry—it's out of sight, so Marc can't find it. And if you can't offer any hints after you've seen it, I'll try to get Rebecca to help."

"Rebecca? Good luck with that. She's definitely drunk the Kool-Aid where Marc's concerned."

"Yeah, well, she's still my cousin. And they say that blood's thicker than water."

"So they say," Anthony said, already back to studying the photo in his hand, searching for where it might belong.

The doorbell rang, startling us both. "Maybe it's the UPS man," I said. "Jayne does a lot of online shopping." That was only half the truth. I actually did a lot of on-line shopping—or had before our financial situation had deteriorated—and had most of it delivered to Jayne's house so Jack wouldn't realize exactly how much.

I peered through the sidelights, surprised to see Meghan Black, holding her Kate Spade purse against her chest with both arms wrapped around it, the shoulder strap around the back of her neck. I pulled open the door and ushered her inside.

"Meghan! It's good to see you. But what are you doing here?"

"Your sister, Miss Smith, said I could find you here. I hope you don't mind, but I needed to see you right away."

Fear tiptoed its way down my spine. "Has something happened?"

She looked past me to the dining room, where she could see Anthony sitting at the table. He glanced up and waved. Her large brown eyes widened with concern. "Can we speak privately?"

"It's okay," I assured her. "He's on our side."

She nodded, but the look of concern didn't leave her face. Lifting the strap off her neck, she said, "We found something."

The scrape of the chair in the dining room announced Anthony's approach. "In the cistern?" he asked.

Meghan nodded. "It was actually my friend Rachel Flooring who discovered it. She wasn't sure what it was, so she showed it to me. I probably wouldn't have had any idea, either, except that I've seen that portrait of Eliza Grosvenor at Gallen Hall—back when we were doing work in the cemetery there, we were given a tour of the house. I remember how creepy the painting was, how the eyes kind of followed me around, you know?"

Anthony nodded emphatically. "I know exactly what you mean. I will admit to hurrying past it as fast as I can every time I need to use the stairs." Anthony reached out his hand. "Anthony Longo. Pleased to meet you."

Meghan's eyebrows shot up as she jerked her head toward me.

"He's Marc Longo's brother—but it's okay. Anthony doesn't see eye to eye with Marc on what he has planned for our house on Tradd Street and is trying to help us."

Meghan relaxed a little and shook his hand. "Good to know. But, yeah, that portrait with the scary eyes . . . Well, it's not something a person forgets. Especially that peacock brooch she's wearing. Something about it draws the eye. Like she's asking you to look at it." She began fumbling with the latch on her purse. "Speaking of which." After pulling a small bundle wrapped in cloth from her purse, she looked toward the dining room. "Can I put this on the table? You should probably see it under better light."

I led her into the dining room, Anthony following close behind. Meghan's eyes widened when she spotted the rows and columns of photographs. "Wow—what's going on here?"

"These are bricks from the mausoleum at Gallen Hall," Anthony said. "We think they're all supposed to fit together like some kind of a puzzle. It's a total guess, but as you can see we've already matched up quite a few, so it's possible we're not completely out of the park."

Meghan smiled. "It reminds me of a Nancy Drew book. I was obsessed with them when I was younger—I've read them all about a dozen times."

"Me, too," I said, liking Meghan more and more.

"So," Anthony said, reminding us of why we were there, "what did you find? The Confederate gold or another diamond?" His laugh sounded forced, and both Meghan and I looked at him.

With a serious face, Meghan said, "You know, Mr. Longo, all the diamonds were located and the story of how the gold is buried somewhere waiting to be discovered by some lucky person is a complete fabrication."

Anthony chuckled. "Yes, of course. Just making sure you'd done your homework."

I wasn't sure, but I thought Meghan might have rolled her eyes as she placed the wrapped item on an empty corner of the table, then carefully peeled back the layers. She stood back so we could see it under the light of the chandelier.

"Wow," Anthony and I said in union, our hands stretched at the same time.

"Please put these on before you handle it," Meghan said, pulling out a pair of gloves and handing them to me. "Sorry, Mr. Longo. I only have one pair, so you'll have to wait your turn."

I quickly slid on the gloves, then hesitated a moment.

"It's the brooch, isn't it? Eliza's brooch from the portrait." I carefully lifted it in one hand, fitting it inside my palm while I traced the outline of the peacock's head and body and the splayed tail feathers, as if to reassure myself that it wasn't my imagination.

Meghan nodded. "I pulled up a photo of the painting I took on my phone and compared it. It's definitely the same. Well, either an exact replica or the same one."

"But all four stones are missing," Anthony said, as if he couldn't quite believe it.

Meghan glanced up at him before redirecting her attention toward me. "We're pretty sure it's pinchbeck—that's why it didn't show up on any of our scans. And because pinchbeck was almost exclusively used for costume jewelry, we're assuming that the stones were glass or paste."

"Have you found any of the stones?" Anthony asked. "I mean, even if they're not valuable, it would be nice to put them back in the brooch. For posterity."

Meghan shook her head. "Not yet. But if they're in there, we'll find them. We're literally sifting through every ounce of dirt. We'll be lucky to be done by next Christmas." She laughed but stopped when she realized no one else was laughing with her. She cleared her throat. "Flip it over and look closely at the back of the bird's head."

I squinted and saw only blurry gold before holding it up for Anthony to see, and he did the same. Even with my glasses it was too small for me to read. This time I was sure Meghan rolled her eyes. Pointing toward a spot on the back of the brooch, she said, "The initials S.V. are engraved on the neck of the bird. So, even if it's pinchbeck and it's missing its stones, it could have some value just because of who the jewelry maker was."

"Samuel Vanderhorst!" I shouted, as if I were a contestant on *Wheel of Fortune*. "He was the metalworker who did all the gates in the cemetery at Gallen Hall, right? And later became famous as a freedman after the Revolution when he set up shop in downtown Charleston."

"Exactly," Meghan said. "It's further evidence that this

might be Eliza's brooch, since both she and Samuel lived at Gallen Hall around the same time. It's possible she commissioned it, or someone else did for her. Maybe he did it as a favor in return for his freedom."

"Why do you say that?" Anthony asked.

Meghan shrugged. "Well, it was unusual for a slave to be freed because he was good at something. His owner could make a profit from the slave's skills. Samuel Vanderhorst was incredibly skilled—and Carrollton Vanderhorst definitely knew it. It's curious, that's all. Something lost to history, I suppose. Or buried in a cistern."

"True," I said, gently placing the brooch on top of the cloth. "Have you shown this to Dr. Wallen-Arasi yet?"

"No. I wanted to get it to you as soon as possible, and I figured I'd let you show it to her." She glanced at Anthony again. "Marc Longo and that Harvey person were hanging around the dig again this morning, making sure we knew to tell them if we found anything interesting."

"Did they see this?" I asked in alarm.

"Nope. My Burberry jacket has these great, deep pockets so I stuck it in there as soon as Rachel showed it to me."

"Good job, Meghan," Anthony said.

"I agree. Thanks, Meghan. You've been a big help."

She beamed at us. "Anytime—happy to help." She glanced over at the dining room. "And if you think you need more help with that puzzle, please let me know. I'd love to work on it, and I bet my friend Rachel would, too."

I walked her to the door and opened it for her. "Thanks. I'll keep that in mind next time I've spent three hours at the table without finding a single piece."

We said good-bye and I closed the door behind her. Rubbing my hands over my arms, I walked back to the dining room, where Anthony stood looking down at the brooch. "A cold front's coming in. The weatherman said this morning there was a chance of snow by this weekend. I sure hope not. It's a rare occurrence, thankfully, but Charleston is worse than Atlanta when it comes to snow."

"Hmm," he said, making me wonder if he'd heard anything I'd said. "You should probably keep this here, just to make sure Marc doesn't see it."

"I thought about that, but I really need to show it to Sophie, get her expert opinion. Not to worry—I have a good hiding spot in mind. He'll never find it."

"Oh, sounds fascinating. Where?"

I carefully rewrapped the brooch in the soft cloth it had arrived in. "If I told you, it wouldn't be a good hiding spot, would it?"

He laughed. "No, I suppose not. Just hide it well. At least until Marc and Harvey are done."

"If they'll ever be done. They're having so many technical problems I've suggested they find a soundstage somewhere and make it look like my house. Because then they'd be out of my hair."

"Good plan," Anthony said, settling himself into a chair and picking up another photograph. "In the meantime, let's get this puzzle solved so we can all move on."

I regarded Anthony for a moment, his mention of moving on striking a chord with me. "Can I ask you a personal question?"

He peered up at me without moving his head. "I suppose. As long as it's not too personal."

"Well, maybe it's because this whole sibling thing is new to me, but have you ever considered what sort of permanent damage it might cause to your relationship with Marc when he finds out that you've been helping us?"

He looked down at the table, immersed in his study of the lines and circles on the photograph in his hand. "No," he said. Looking up to meet my eyes, he repeated, "No. If there's anything Marc has taught me, it's that to be successful, you need to be prepared to make enemies. Even if they're your friends. Or your brother."

I wasn't sure what I'd been expecting him to say, but I was pretty sure that wasn't it. I thought of Jayne, and despite any of the weird feelings I'd been experiencing where she was concerned, at least I knew I could never deliberately do her harm. Maybe that meant I wasn't the worst person in the world after all.

"Well," I said, "I've got to run by the office and pick up a set of keys for a showing tomorrow, so I'll leave you to it. Good luck."

He lifted his hand in a wave without looking up at me, and I backed out of the room, not wanting to interrupt his concentration. I pulled on my coat, scarf, gloves, and hat before stepping outside. I paused and looked up, the gray clouds seeming to shutter the bright blue sky of early afternoon, closing out the sun. A wind burst blew at me, making me shiver as I contemplated the difficult relationship between siblings and how I was grateful, for a moment, to have something to worry about besides Jack.

CHAPTER
28

Mrs. Houlihan peered out the window of the kitchen at the back garden, where my father and his friends from the gardening society were doing their best to decorate the black hole to make it look more festive for the progressive dinner. I'd hoped the gaping presence would have qualified my house for an exemption from the event, but Sophie had merely asked my father to do something with the cistern that would make it look in keeping with the holiday while not impeding the progress of the excavation.

Not that much was happening in that regard right now, anyway. The semester had ended and the students had returned to their respective homes for the holidays. Meghan had sent us a Christmas card with a photo of her and her dog, which was a doppelganger of General Lee. That's when I knew the excavation had lasted way too long. As had all the renovations in the house, since Rich Kobylt's Christmas card had arrived the same day and it hadn't taken me long to realize that the background behind his smiling family was my front garden.

I took advantage of Mrs. Houlihan's being distracted to pinch one of her famous ginger cookies cooling on a rack.

"I saw that." She hadn't turned her head, confirming the fact that the woman did, indeed, have eyes in the back of her head. "And if you take another, I'll tell you how many calories are in each one."

I finished chewing and wiped the crumbs from my mouth. "I don't know why you're insisting on doing all this baking. You do know the dinner is being catered, don't you?"

She shook her head in disgust, her jowls quivering with disdain. "In all the years I've worked for Mr. Vanderhorst and for your family, I have *never* seen the need to hire *outsiders* to bring food into my kitchen. I'm afraid I'm taking it personally."

"I'm sorry—I really am. Sadly, I don't seem to have any control as to what's going on in my house these days." I thought of the excessive number of Christmas trees and the over-the-top decorations, of the progressive dinner and of Harvey Beckner and his people, who continued to invade my home and refused to give up in their attempts to do the prefilming work that should have been accomplished in a single day. I wondered if they'd be here on Christmas morning and if I should get them gifts so they'd have something to open under the tree. I stared longingly at the cookies. "I can only hope we'll have our house back soon."

"Are they still planning on filming here starting in January?" Mrs. Houlihan asked.

"Not if I can help it."

She looked almost disappointed. "That's a shame. I heard George Clooney was signed up to play Nevin Vanderhorst's father, Robert, and Reese Witherspoon was to play his mother, Louisa. I'd already started planning my menus in my head."

The timer on the oven beeped and she slid on her oven mitts before sliding out what looked like her chocolate-and-mint holiday brownies. My mouth watered as I followed the movement of the pan, watching the housekeeper place it on a cooling rack. Mrs. Houlihan moved to the kitchen sink and began filling it with hot water and suds. With her back to me, she said, "Keep your fingers off of those brownies. Those are for Mr. Kobylt and his family."

I dropped my hand, sufficiently chastened.

There was a brief knock on the kitchen door before it opened, and I was glad I didn't have food in my mouth, because I probably would have choked. Standing in the doorway was a very tall man wearing a scarlet red British regimental uniform complete with shiny brass buttons, white breeches, and shiny black knee-high boots. I blinked a few times to see if he would disappear, eventually registering the iPhone he held in his hand.

"You better not be scuffing up my floors with those boots, Mr. Greco." A warm smile across Mrs. Houlihan's pudgy face eradicated her stern tone. "And if you just give me a sec, I'll have your favorite ginger cookies all wrapped up for you to take home."

"That's very kind of you, Mrs. Houlihan. Thank you."

"Greco," I said, my voice full of relief.

He must have seen the panic on my face, or maybe it was my hand pressed against my heart. "Melanie—I'm so sorry. I almost forgot I was wearing this." He patted the white crisscrossed straps across his jacket and chuckled. "Several of my reenactor friends and I have been hired for an event at the Old Exchange building tonight, but I needed a fabric swatch I'd left upstairs, so I figured I'd stop by on the way."

"No worries. I can't say I haven't seen stranger things in this house."

He raised his eyebrows but didn't say anything. He accepted a brown paper bag from Mrs. Houlihan—complete with a red satin ribbon she'd tied in a bow. "I promise to save these until after dinner, and only eat one at a time so I can savor it and appreciate your culinary talents as they should be appreciated."

She waved her hand at him. "Oh, don't be silly. I'll just make more for you. Eat as many as you like." Her smile was big enough to show the deep dimples on her cheeks.

I frowned at her, but she'd already turned back to the sink to wash dishes.

Greco cleared his throat. "Uh, Melanie. I was actually looking for you. Can you come upstairs to Nola's room for a moment?"

As I followed him upstairs, I kept picturing more words carved into the plaster walls, or a human skull protruding from a cornice. And wondering how much Greco would be okay with before he gave up and quit.

He held the door open for me and waited for me to enter before following me inside. He cleared his throat again. "So," he said. "When I came upstairs a short while ago, I could have sworn I heard, well, the sound long skirts make when a woman is walking across the floor. I knocked on the door twice, and when I didn't hear anything, I walked in and found the room empty."

I kept my expression neutral, not sure if I should mention that odd noises in empty rooms were part of my daily life. I spun around to verify that, yes, the room was actually devoid of people, especially women in long skirts. I followed his gaze to a new pile of bee carcasses clustered around the leg of the bed, the claw-foot nearly covered with them.

I made a show of checking the windows to ensure they were closed, flicking the locks to verify that the windows were, indeed, locked and couldn't accidentally slide open. "I guess we have a hive in the wall somewhere, so I'll have to call a bee removal specialist. You don't want to kill bees, you know—it's bad for the environment."

"It's also bad luck," Greco said, walking toward the bed. "But bees are dormant in the winter, which makes their presence in the room that much stranger." He knelt by the foot of the bed and began running his fingers around the back of the claw-foot, gently flicking the bees out of the way.

"My grandfather was a beekeeper," he explained. "That's how I know a little bit about bees and bee behavior. He always told me that a smart person listened to the bees because they always had something important to say. And this"—he indicated the pile of carcasses—"was telling me something. A pile of dead bees in the middle of winter clustered around one single area spoke to me. So I figured I should investigate."

He continued to move his fingers around the back of the claw-foot leg until I heard a small click. His eyes widened and I knew that he'd found what he'd been looking for. "I was just running my hands up and down over the wood until I felt something—and when I pushed it, a small door popped open right at the spot where the leg is attached to the footboard, to protect it from being seen when the bed-clothes are removed, and this fell out."

He stood and carried something to me in his closed fist. When he reached me, he slowly unfurled his fingers and revealed a gold ring with a flat top, with something engraved on it. Without a word, Greco reached inside his waistcoat and pulled out a pair of reading glasses. I slid them on, then picked up the ring to see it better.

I ran a finger over the flat top. "It's a peacock," I said, and I could hear the excitement in my voice.

"Indeed it is. And I do believe it was used as a wax sealer—I've seen them before. That's why it's flat on top. You don't have to take it off to dip in the wax."

"It's a peacock," I said again, not sure how else I could articulate how much I thought this was a Good Thing. I had no idea why, but I was pretty sure Jack would.

"I know," Greco said, his tone matching mine. "Remember how I mentioned the spy ring that had a peacock as its symbol? I think this ring must have belonged to a member, which is why it was hidden, to keep the owner's identity a secret." He reached over and gently flipped the ring over in my palm. "Look on the inside of the ring—there are two initials. I'm wondering if they're the owner's."

Leaning closer and squinting even with the reading glasses, I was able to make out the initials S.V. I met Greco's eyes. "I don't think these are the owner's initials—I think they're the initials of the man who made it, Samuel Vanderhorst."

Greco nodded excitedly. "I've heard of him! He's quite famous for his metalworking and jewelry designs, isn't he?"

"Yes. And he was a former slave at Gallen Hall Plantation, too, which is where this bed was mostly likely made." I looked at Greco's red coat as if noticing it for the first time. "Is your great-uncle—the one who was the American history professor at Carolina—is he still alive?"

"Absolutely. My mother says he'll outlive us all. My father suspects his longevity is due to the fact that he spends so much time studying dead people that it's convinced him that he's better off in the land of the living." He tilted his head. "Why? Is there anything you'd like me to ask him? I'm going to see him tomorrow at a living history encampment at the Camden battlefield. He interprets Major General Horatio Gates."

"Another redcoat?"

He looked offended. "Certainly not. Major General Gates led the American forces at the battle and was responsible for their resounding defeat. Ruined his military career, actually."

"Oh, of course," I said, although I'd never heard the name before. "If you're willing, that would be wonderful. When Nola was using the textbook she'd borrowed, there was a mention that Lawrence Vanderhorst had been shot. Was that because he was a spy? But if the Vanderhorsts were known loyalists, would that make him a spy for the Crown or for the Americans?"

"That's a very good question, and one I'm sure my great-uncle should be able to shed some light on. You might remember that was his expertise—spies during the American Revolution. Actually, if you're all right with me taking a few photos of the ring on my phone, I'd love to send them to Uncle Oliver."

"Absolutely." I held up my palm, showing the front, side, and back of the ring so Greco could photograph it.

"One other thing," I said as I slid the ring on my largest finger, where it was still loose, then folded my fingers over it so it wouldn't slide off. "There was a British soldier quartered at Gallen Hall Plantation, an Alexander Monroe. He was found drowned in the Ashley River four days before Lawrence was shot." I could almost hear Jack's voice in my head. *There is no such thing as coincidence.* "I have no reason to suspect they might be connected, but could you ask your great-uncle, just in case, if he knows anything about either death?"

"No problem—I'm sure Uncle Oliver will be thrilled to help. He lives for that stuff." He glanced back at the claw-foot and the bees; he was silent for a moment, as if contemplating his next words. "There's something else I should probably mention."

I waited in silence, just in case he was looking for a reason to change his mind.

Greco continued. "The weirdest thing about it all is . . . Well, I'm not sure how to explain this." He stopped and a small flush crossed his handsome face. "Although for some reason, I think you could take this better than most."

"What do you mean?" I asked, although I was pretty sure I knew.

He gave me a knowing glance before continuing. "When I found the ring I did what most people would do, I suppose, and I slid it on my pinkie finger. I figured that's where signet rings go, right? Anyway, it fit me perfectly, and just as I was thinking that exact thought, I felt someone—I'm pretty sure it was a woman. . . ." He paused, rubbed his hand across the back of his neck. "I felt someone kiss my cheek. It was definitely a kiss; I could feel it and hear it, you know? Except, instead of being warm, like from someone's lips, it was icy cold."

"And there was no one else in the room?" I was imagining Mrs. Houlihan trying to hide behind the door, since she had been the only other person in the house at the time.

"No. At least no one I could see." His gaze settled on me, and I was surprised it wasn't one of expectation. Like he didn't need any explanations from me, and I was fine with that.

"Hmm," I said noncommittally, eagerly filing away the information to use later.

He glanced at the screen of his phone. "Sorry—I've got to run. Let me go grab the fabric swatch and my cookies from the kitchen and I'll see myself out. I'll be in touch after I speak with Uncle Oliver."

"Thanks so much, Greco."

I listened to the sound of his boots heading down the

stairs as I began to scoop up the dead bees onto a paint-swatch board, disappointed that Greco had remembered he'd left his little bag of cookies in the kitchen. When I was done, I dumped the dead bees into an empty paint can being used as a trash receptacle and headed down the stairs, eager to share with Jack the signet ring and the brooch Meghan had found in the cistern.

A loud, hacking cough came from the direction of my bedroom. I ran back up the stairs and pushed on the partially open door. Jack lay huddled under the covers, his teeth chattering. I moved quickly to the bed and placed the back of my hand on his forehead.

"Jack—you're burning up!" I looked at the digital thermometer on the bedside table. "Did you already take your temperature?"

He nodded, his teeth continuing their chatter. "It's one hund-d- d-dred and f-f-four." He attempted a smile, but it looked more like a grimace. "I h-h-have a f-f-fever because you're st-st-standing so n-near."

Despite how horrible he looked, I smiled. "Right." I leaned forward and kissed him on the forehead, my lips burning where they contacted his skin. "I'm going to get something to give you to bring down the fever, then call your doctor. This could be the flu that's been going around, and I don't want to take any chances."

I took a wool throw from the back of one of the two armchairs and placed it on top of him, tucking it around him before sitting down on the mattress. "Is there anything else I can get for you? I could read to you. Or sing."

His eyes widened in alarm. "N-n-n-no. P-p-please." He widened his eyes hopefully. "Ch-ch-chicken s-s-soup?"

"Sure. I'll ask Mrs. Houlihan. If she can't make you some, I'll open a can for you."

He smiled, then closed his eyes. I kissed him again, then stood, absently wondering if I could stick a Santa hat on his head and leave him in the bed just in case he wasn't better in time for the progressive dinner. "I'll be right back. I'll leave the door open in case you need something, and you can shout. The bell I used when I was on bed rest with the twins somehow disappeared before they were born."

Jack began coughing again and I hurried from the room toward the stairs, my steps slowing as I reached the hallway outside Nola's bedroom. The door was open, although I was positive I'd closed it to keep the dogs out. I took a step forward to close it but stopped as my stockinged foot landed in a puddle of liquid.

I immediately thought of Bess, who still occasionally had accidents in the house when the weather conditions and temperature weren't to her liking and therefore not conducive to her using the outdoor facilities.

My gaze traveled past the threshold and into the room, where the puddles continued in a pattern. The kind of pattern wet feet would make. I looked down at where I'd stepped into one of the footprints, noticing how big and solid it was. Definitely not a bare foot, then. Most likely a booted foot, the narrower heel of each footprint making it clear that the wearer had been headed from the room toward the stairs. I thought for a moment I should call Greco and ask him if he'd stepped in anything, but I stopped when the unmistakable scent of gunpowder and leather saturated the air in the room.

"Alexander?" I whispered.

The only response was the buzz of a lone bee as it flew around my head before colliding with the window, its body plummeting to the windowsill, where it lay still and quiet.

CHAPTER
29

I searched behind all of the greenery draped around the front door of my parents' house on Legare Street for the doorbell. I knew it was there, just well hidden beneath the fruits of the zealous administrations of the decorating committee. I recognized the enormous and stunning wreath as the one my mother had made at the workshop, and I tried not to compare it to my own pathetic attempt. Of all the gifts I'd inherited from my mother, apparently talents for singing and wreath making hadn't been included. Not for the first time, I wished I'd been given a choice as to which genes I wanted. And which ones I didn't.

The sky sat leaden and ominous above us, the scent in the air unfamiliar to us Charleston natives. The meteorologists on every channel kept predicting snow, but the models weren't exactly clear as to when or how much. One even said it would miss us entirely and head straight to North Carolina. I just kept hoping the storm would hit hard Saturday so that the progressive dinner would be canceled and I could get back to work on figuring out what was hidden in the mausoleum.

When my finger finally found the doorbell button, I pressed it, then waited for the dulcet tones of the chime. After trying two more times and not hearing anything—typical in the damp and salty climate of the Lowcountry—I knocked. Then knocked again. Finally, I resorted to pulling out the key that my mother insisted I have and let myself in.

"Mother," I shouted from the foyer. Despite her constant reminders that this was my house, too, and I didn't need to make an appointment to see her, I'd sent her a quick text to let her know I was coming. Just in case she and my father were busy. Doing exactly what, I didn't want to know, but I did want to give them fair warning.

I walked through the foyer, which was bedecked, similarly to mine, in garland and fruit, my grandmother's furniture a warm and familiar backdrop to the decorations. She'd loved Christmas and had always made it a special time for me despite the tension between my parents. Her antique miniature English village had been set out on the center-hall table, the small figures of a caroling choir dressed in distinctive Victorian garb. I wondered if Sophie knew about this and had given her blessing. Not that it mattered. My mother had a way of doing what she wanted while making others think it was their idea. And Sophie, a huge opera fan, was always a little starstruck where my mother was concerned.

"Mother!" I called again, peeking into the front parlor with the stained glass window, then back through the foyer toward the dining room. "Mother!" I shouted, more loudly this time.

"Back here," called a small voice toward the back of the house.

I made my way through the kitchen and a narrow hallway into a glass-walled sunroom that my father had transformed into a greenhouse. My mother used it as a morning room to drink her tea and listen to her music, piped through brand-new speakers hidden within the walls according to Sophie's advice. The room had been a later addition to the house, but that was no reason to desecrate (Sophie's word) the integrity of a historic house with unsightly modern conveniences.

My mother, wearing a thick red velvet lounging robe and matching slippers, reclined on a chaise, delicately sipping from a teacup. "Hello, Mellie. I'm sorry—I didn't hear the doorbell."

"It didn't . . ." I began, then stopped when I realized she wasn't alone.

"Hi, Melanie." Rebecca sat opposite my mother in an upholstered armchair that had been my grandmother's but was recently re-covered in a gorgeous Liberty of London floral print. Rebecca looked small and wan within its brightly patterned cushions, and I wondered if she might be sick. Or if something had happened to Pucci, since her ubiquitous four-legged companion wasn't with her. Her eyes looked puffy and red rimmed and I wondered if she might have lost her favorite pair of pink gloves.

"Oh, hello, Rebecca. I didn't expect to see you here."

She gave my mother a quick glance. "It was sort of last-minute."

"Have some tea," my mother offered.

I removed my coat, then poured myself tea from my grandmother's antique Limoges pot into a matching teacup. Sitting on the edge of the armchair next to Rebecca, I allowed my gaze to move from one woman to the next, finally settling on Rebecca, noticing again how pale she was. "I've been trying to reach you ever since I saw you at the Francis Marion on the night of the Shop and Stroll. I didn't think we'd finished our conversation."

"Yes, well, I've been busy." She took a long sip from her tea, avoiding my gaze.

"I'm sure. A part-time job at the paper and no children must leave you exhausted by the end of the day."

My mother sent me a warning glance and I immediately felt ashamed. It made me wonder how old I'd have to be before that look no longer affected me. Or how long it would take before I'd no longer need it.

She cleared her throat and asked, "How is Jack, Mellie?"

"Still very sick. The doctor suspects it's the flu, so he's being quarantined in our room. I'm sleeping in the second guest room, which hasn't been updated or changed since Mr. Vanderhorst lived in the house. I'm giving Jack flu medication prescribed by his doctor and taking his temp at regular intervals. Mrs. Houlihan keeps him fed with her homemade chicken soup, and Cooper's been keeping him well stocked on all the spy-thriller movies that have been released in the last ten years so that at least he's entertained." I looked accusingly at Rebecca. "Not that he can stay awake very long to watch an entire movie. I think the stresses of the last year have really taken their toll on him and this is his body's way of telling him to slow down and recharge."

I didn't mention how Cooper was also bringing Jack every book he could find that Jack didn't own or hadn't already read on code breaking through the centuries. Jack was desperate to keep working on figuring out what Gallen Hall was hiding, but he barely had the strength to hold one of the books up for longer than it took him to fall asleep.

"I hope you're not using Jack's illness as an excuse not to fill him in on any developments," Mother said softly. "I know he needs his rest, but I'm sure he'd appreciate you keeping him in the loop."

"Of course," I said, making sure my indignant tone was loud and clear. I hadn't exactly shared everything with Jack, because he really was too sick. And the medication made him groggy, so that he was barely coherent anyway. As soon as he was better, I'd tell him everything. I would. "And I don't think this is the appropriate time to bring this up," I said, my eyes darting over to where Rebecca sat.

"Rebecca understands the importance of family, Mellie. Despite what you might think. We've just been talking about that very thing."

"Really?" I asked, turning my attention to my cousin. "So, about our unfinished conversation . . ." I began, then stopped when I noticed fat tears rolling down her pale cheeks. She grabbed a small tea napkin from her lap and dabbed at her eyes.

"I'm sorry," she said. "I came here to get some advice from your mother—she's much more worldly than my own mother, which is why I came to her first."

My mother *had* been a world-famous opera singer, but I couldn't imagine any of Rebecca's troubles needing any kind of worldly advice. I made a point not to roll my eyes, my gaze drifting instead to the antique Dresden desk clock on the side table by the chaise. I had a house showing in an hour and I still needed to speak with my mother.

"Maybe I can help," I suggested, trying to move the proceedings further along.

"Why don't you tell Mellie what you just told me?" Mother suggested gently.

I sat up in alarm. "Have you been having more dreams about Jack or Nola?"

Rebecca shook her head. "No. I can't. I'm . . . blocked, it seems."

I sat up straighter, remembering how that had felt when it had happened to me twice before. And the reasons why.

"Go on," Mother prompted.

"Are you sure? It's not like she's a fan of Marc's to begin with."

"That's true. But is anyone, really?" Mother smiled benignly, taking the sting out of her words. "Besides, Mellie understands discretion. Don't you, dear?"

"Of course."

"And we're all family here," my mother continued. "I'm sure we're all in agreement that blood trumps everything, correct?"

I waited until I saw Rebecca nod before I did the same.

With a small voice that I needed to strain to hear, Rebecca said, "Marc's cheating on me."

I couldn't even feign surprise at this revelation. He was such a cheat and a liar in all of his dealings, it would follow reason that he couldn't remain faithful in his marriage. Still, I felt a glimmer of compassion for her, recalling how tied up in knots I'd been the year before when I thought that Jack and Jayne were having an affair.

"Are you sure?" I asked.

She nodded. "He's been acting . . . weird lately. Not himself. I know this whole filming thing has been a huge distraction, and Harvey Beckner is good at making everyone around him miserable. But still . . ." She dabbed at her eyes again. "Last week, Marc fell asleep on the couch, and his phone fell to the floor. It dinged when I walked in the room, and I went to pick it up to see if it was important and if I needed to wake him. It was . . ." She shuddered. "It was a photo of a woman. A *brunette*," she said with distaste, apparently forgetting that she was in a room with two brunettes. "She barely had on a blouse—and definitely not a bra—and she was saying she couldn't wait to see Marc again, since the last time was so amazing." She stifled a sob with her balled-up napkin. "I felt so . . . defiled."

"You poor thing," my mother said, getting up to refill Rebecca's teacup.

"I didn't say anything, wanting to be sure first. So I did a little digging and found out she's a grad student at the college—in psychology or something. And they've been seeing each other for months. For *months*."

"Are you going to leave him?" I asked.

Her shoulders hunched forward as she began to sob and shake her head. "I . . . can't."

"But why n—" I stopped. Recalled what she'd said about how her dreams were blocked, and I remembered when that had happened to me. "You're . . . pregnant?"

Rebecca glared at me with reddened eyes. "You don't have to sound so surprised, you know. Marc is a very virile man."

I swallowed down the bile that rose in my throat. "I'm sure he is. But that doesn't mean you have to stay married to him, you know. If you have the right support system in place, it's possible to raise the baby on your own."

A fresh torrent of tears streamed down her face. "But I love him. I will never love another man as much as I love him." She slumped down so completely she was almost folded in half, looking as pathetic as a kitten in the rain.

I sat back in my chair, completely defeated. I would be lying if I said I wasn't thinking of using the situation to convince her to share with me the piece of paper Jack and I so desperately wanted to get a look at. But seeing Rebecca's desperation made me quash that idea. The mere thought of trying to make a life without Jack made me sick and crazy at the same time. It was inconceivable, really. I understood her pain, and I couldn't take advantage of it, no matter how much I wanted to. Or how much Marc deserved it.

"I'm so sorry, Rebecca. But like Mother said, we're family. We're your support system. We will help you get through this whether you decide to stay with Marc or not."

My mother moved to sit down on the arm of Rebecca's chair, pulling her close. "Mellie's right. We're here for you."

Rebecca's phone in her purse announced a text. Slowly, she pulled away from my mother and reached for it. She stared at the screen for a long moment, blinking only once and very, very slowly. I thought she might start to cry again, but then I saw her expression change to disbelief, then anger, and finally fury. Without responding, she threw her phone into her purse. "That was Marc. He said he won't be home tonight for dinner again. He's got a *business* meeting and said not to wait up."

She sat still, breathing deeply, her expression slowly returning to neutral while my mother and I watched, unsure what we should do. "Are you all right?" my mother asked.

Rebecca shook her head, a new, determined glint lighting her reddened eyes. "Not really. But I will be." She reached into her purse again, pulled out a piece of paper folded into a square, and held it close to her chest. "I put this in my purse right after I saw you at the Francis Marion, not really thinking I could go through with this. But Marc has left me no choice." After an exaggerated pause, she stood and handed me the paper. "Just in case you weren't aware that Marc has already ransacked your house looking for your drawing while he's supposedly helping Harvey. And don't worry—this is a copy. I could see you already worrying about how to tell Sophie about the creases."

I wished I could tell her she was wrong. Instead, I quickly opened it up and saw what looked like a page identical to what Jack and I had found in the papers from the shoebox. "Thank you," I said. "Won't Marc be angry?"

She slid her purse strap over her shoulder. "He won't find out, will he? I might still love him more than he deserves, and I will do what I can to fight to get him back, but that doesn't mean that I can't enjoy a little revenge for what he's done to me. And our baby." She rested her hand on her still-flat abdomen.

Rebecca embraced my mother. "Thank you both. Right now, I'm in dire need of a spa day and I'm headed to Woodhouse Spa. I'm charging it all on Marc's credit card. And then I'm going to figure out how to win him back—right after I find a way to punish him."

We said our good-byes and she left, saying she'd see herself out, and for once I didn't roll my eyes behind her back, regardless of how much she'd just reminded me of Scarlett O'Hara after Rhett Butler's departure. This was the first time since I'd known Rebecca that she'd demonstrated that she had more brains and gumption than the Barbie doll she closely resembled.

"Well," my mother said, "that was illuminating." She indicated the piece of paper in my hand. "Do you think that will help?"

I shrugged. "I have no idea. I'll compare it to the matching piece of paper that we have and see if it means anything." I looked down at the page, at the weird lines and swirls that resembled the bricks of the mausoleum but were somehow different. I'd have to put them side by side to know for sure.

I carefully refolded the paper and placed it in my purse. "I came over to discuss the schedule for Saturday night. I'll have Nola bring the twins and dogs over to Amelia's house—and remind her to make sure JJ has his kitchen whisk. She forgot it last time and Amelia gave him one from her kitchen, but he apparently can tell the difference. Anyway, I know you'll be busy doing one of the appetizer sessions here, but I was hoping you could hurry to my house before the dinner to help me with last-minute preparations since I won't have Jack."

My mother sat up and pulled her notepad from the side

table before adjusting her reading glasses on her nose. "Of course, dear. I'm sure your father can handle any stragglers so I can leave. And I'll make sure Mrs. Houlihan makes more of her gingerbread cookies just for Jack—they might cheer him up, and the ginger can't hurt. Did you know that she sent over a little gift bag of cookies for us? She's just the sweetest."

I looked at my mother to see if she might be deliberately tormenting me, but she was busy writing on her notepad.

My phone buzzed, alerting me that I had a text. I glanced at it to see who it was. "It's just Nola," I offered. "She's not supposed to be using her phone at school, but occasionally she'll text me about things she needs at the store or for a homework project. She likes to be prepared."

"Sounds familiar," Mother said as she bent over her notepad. "So, since yours is one of the dinner houses, you'll need to lay out the appropriate serving pieces for oyster stew and bone-in ham. I'll stop by your house later to get a count of dinner plates, but I'd suggest using the Vander-horsts' beautiful antique Imari china. All of that gold will look beautiful with the decorations, plus I know there are a ton of serving pieces."

The phone buzzed again, and I pulled it out to make sure the message was from Nola. As I yanked it out, it caught a purse strap, which caused the purse to tip over, spilling the contents.

My mother stood to help, but I held up my hand to stop her. "You don't want to touch something you might react to," I warned.

"What's that?" She pointed near the skirt of the chair Rebecca had just vacated.

I recognized the signet ring that Greco had found. I'd brought it to show Sophie when I met her for lunch and had thought it was secure in the pocket of my purse. I had planned to tell my mother that we'd found it and where but had no intention of actually showing it to her. "Don't touch it," I said. "It was in the bedpost, just like you suspected. Greco found it."

Ignoring my warning, she moved toward it, reaching it before I could get up off of my hands and knees. "Mother . . ."

"I didn't get bad vibes from it, Mellie. It was practically begging me to find it. I think it's okay for me to touch it." She bent down and picked it up, holding it tightly in her palm. I waited for her to scream or for some otherworldly voice to come from her mouth or for her face to become unrecognizable. Instead she closed her eyes serenely, her face softening as she tilted her head to the side as if she were listening to a voice that only she could hear. And then her other hand flew to her neck, pulling at something I couldn't see, and she began to cough.

"Mother!" I grabbed her hand, pulling at her fingers to get her to release the ring, but they were like steel straps, unwilling to let go of their prize.

I was wondering if I should call Jayne for help, when my mother stopped coughing and her breathing returned to normal. Her eyes moved under her eyelids like those of a person having a vivid dream, but she was no longer agitated.

She stayed that way for a full minute, until her hand relaxed and the ring fell onto the rug with a small thud. She opened her eyes as if to reorient herself, then sat back in the chaise. I went to her quickly, taking her hand and finding it surprisingly warm.

"Mother? Are you all right?"

"I'm fine—I promise. The whole process is just exhausting—and gets even more so the older I become." She gave me a reassuring smile. "But I'm fine. Really."

I bent down to pick up the ring from the floor, then slid it onto my finger so I couldn't lose it. "Did you see anything? Did you see the man it belonged to?"

She tucked her chin as if confused by my question. "The man?" She shook her head. "No, Mellie, it didn't belong to a man. It was a woman. Definitely a woman."

"A woman?" I said slowly, recalling what Greco had said. How when he'd slipped the ring on his finger, someone had kissed him on his cheek.

"Yes." She reached up and brushed her neck with her fingers. "She . . . couldn't breathe. She was choking. But she was hurting elsewhere, too." Her palm pressed against her chest where her heart was. "Not like the pain from a heart attack. More like . . . a broken heart."

We stared at each other while I tried to find room for this particular puzzle piece. "Is that all?"

Mother shook her head. "No. She kept repeating the same word, over and over. I believe she's said it before."

"What?" I asked, although I knew exactly what she was going to say before the word passed her lips.

"Lies."

CHAPTER
30

I hesitated on my mother's porch, the chilly wind buffeting me, the scent in the air definitely something odd. Something that smelled a lot like a word I dared not say out loud. Down south, where snow was treated with the seriousness of an erupting volcano and its subsequent lava flow, it was often referred to as a four-letter word.

I looked at my watch again. I'd already called Jolly and had her cancel lunch with Sophie and change my appointment, so I wasn't worried about being late. But I was torn between heading over to Jayne's house—where Jack had told me he'd moved the box of documents—to compare the drawing Rebecca had given me with the one from the archives, and going home to see how Jack was and to go over the most recent developments with him.

The wind hit me full on, so cold that my cheeks burned and I could no longer feel my nose. There was definitely going to be something freezing and cold dripping from the sky, so it simply made more sense for me to head to Jayne's first, so that if it did begin to snow, I could head home to hunker down and talk with Jack then. Assuming he was even up to any kind of discussion.

Telling myself I was doing this in Jack's best interest, I slid behind the steering wheel of my Volvo, glad I'd driven the short distance instead of walking. I'd learned my lesson that morning when I'd walked the dogs—Jack's usual duty—and I'd felt an odd sort of solidarity with the mushers racing the Alaskan Iditarod as the wind pierced my coat and three sweaters and froze my mascara.

I rang the doorbell of Jayne's house, even though I had her key, too. But with Anthony temporarily living there, it felt like an invasion of privacy to just walk in. He opened the door and smiled widely, in contrast with his bedraggled appearance and bleary eyes.

"You look like you've just pulled an all-nighter," I said as I stepped inside.

"That's because I have," he said, shutting the door behind me.

"Working on the puzzle?"

He nodded. "Yeah. It's a little obsessive, I know. But when I do find a brick that fits, I can't help but think the next one will be easier, and then off I go again."

"Well, it looks like you're doing much better—despite the exhaustion you look perfectly fine."

"You're right. Recuperating here at Jayne's was a very good idea. Nobody pushing me down stairs, at least."

"That's a good thing," I said as I took a step toward the dining room.

"Jayne's not here," he said quickly.

I stopped. "Of course not. She's at my house with JJ and Sarah. She's the nanny, remember?"

He gave a little chuckle. "Sorry, of course. I'm just exhausted, so I suppose my brain's not functioning completely."

"No worries—I go a little crazy after just ten minutes staring at the bricks. Did you get very far?"

"Not really. I think it's going to take another week."

I made a move toward the dining room and he stepped in front of me, so that for a moment I thought he was trying to block me. Realizing his mistake, he stepped aside, then followed me into the dining room. I stopped in front of the table, surprised at what I saw. "You've got more than seventy-five percent of it done. Surely it won't take that long to finish—especially since there are fewer pieces now."

Anthony scratched the back of his head. "Yeah, I guess

you're right. Cooper was here for a bit early this morning before class—I guess he did more than I thought."

"Why don't you go take a nap?" I suggested. "You'll be able to think more clearly once you give your brain a rest. And you'll want to be rested for the progressive dinner tomorrow."

"Is that tomorrow?"

"Yes, sadly. Unless it snows," I said hopefully. "Although knowing the organizers, they'll make it happen no matter what gets dumped on us from the sky."

He looked longingly toward the stairs, as if already envisioning his bed and crawling into it. "Are you here to work on the puzzle?"

"No, actually." I reached into my purse and pulled out the piece of paper. "Rebecca just gave this to me. This is the drawing Joseph Longo copied from Robert Vanderhorst's desk. I just need to compare it to the one you found with the other papers in the garbage."

Anthony followed me as I moved toward the front window with the large curved window seat. "Pretty clever hiding place, right? Even though it's not even locked. Jack figured that besides Jayne having an alarm system, Marc wouldn't have thought to look here." I slid off the seat cushion, then pulled open the lid. "And apparently he didn't figure it out."

I reached inside and pulled out the box.

"Wow. So it's been here the whole time? Very clever."

"Pretty much the only thing that hasn't been hidden is this." I held out my hand, where the signet ring sat on my finger. "I think this belonged to a spy in the peacock spy ring—but I'm not sure. Still so much we need to figure out."

Anthony was shaking his head. "So none of the pieces are coming together for you yet?"

"Not yet. As soon as Jack gets over this flu bug, I'm confident that he'll see the connection. It's how his mind works."

"But you both think it'll lead you to Lafayette's treasure."

"We certainly hope so. That would really be the answer

to everything for us. It would solve our financial issues, give Jack a brand-new book idea to start fresh with a new publisher and contract, and get Marc off our backs for good." I looked at him closely. "What about you, Anthony? What do you hope to gain?"

He looked uncomfortable. "I just want to see him not get what he wants for the first time in his life." He looked away, staring at the photographs on the table. "He's always gotten what he wanted, regardless of who he might hurt in the process." He indicated the box I was holding. "Let's see if this tells us anything."

I placed the box on the table and sat down. It took me only a few minutes to thumb through the documents until I found the drawing I was looking for. I pulled it out, then placed it on the table next to the one from Rebecca.

"They look the same until you see them together, don't they?" Anthony said.

I nodded, then moved them around, perpendicular and then parallel, to see if that changed the perspective. It didn't. I stared at them, knowing I'd seen something similar. Recently, even. Similar, but not the same. I was silent for a moment, trying to think of where I'd seen it, the memory dangling in front of me like a carrot.

I squinted, getting closer to the page from the archives, and saw something I hadn't seen before. I tapped on the spot with my fingernail. "Anthony—can you see this? Does this look like anything?"

He leaned over the drawing, then looked at me with a grin. "It's initials. S.V. Like on the brooch."

I nodded excitedly. "Exactly. Samuel Vanderhorst, the metalsmith at Gallen Hall. Maybe this was the pattern for something he was working on." I sobered a bit. "Which means it's probably not going to help us. He made all the wrought-iron gates and fences at the plantation, so it would make sense that his sketches would remain either in the archives or in a Vanderhorst desk. Which makes me wonder why Marc was so eager to find our drawing."

"Probably because he knew that our grandfather had

made a copy of something he saw in Robert Vanderhorst's desk, so it must mean something, right?" Anthony picked up the pages, moving them around like he'd done with the photographs in the brick puzzle. When none of the sides matched up, he placed one drawing on top of the other, then held them up to the chandelier, turning the one on top several times before stopping. "It appears to be something like a primitive map—just lines and angles," he said. "But they need to be converted to the same size so that they match up better. Maybe then we can figure out what it's a map of."

"It's just . . ." I closed my eyes, desperate to remember.

"What?" Anthony prodded.

"I know I've seen this pattern before—or one very similar. And recently."

"Where?"

I glanced up at the sharpness in his voice. "It'll come to me. I just need to stop thinking about it. My subconscious does a lot of my thinking for me."

"Right. Sorry—I really am so tired. Forgive me."

"I understand. I'm the mother of twins under the age of two, remember? I know what mental exhaustion is like."

Anthony nodded, his gaze moving past me to the stairwell behind me. "I think I'm getting delirious in my fatigue. I keep imagining I see Elizabeth, even though I'm not at home with her portrait. And I have the distinct impression she doesn't like me. I'm pretty sure she's the one who pushed me down the stairs."

"Really? And you're sure you didn't trip?"

"Positive. I had the bruises on my back to prove it—in the shape of a small woman's hands."

"Did Marc have any experiences while he was living there?"

"Nope. I seem to be the lucky one."

"Right. The lucky one. It's just odd that she's picking on you and no one else. She seems to be more of an insistent spirit than a malevolent one, from my experiences with her."

"Maybe I just remind her of someone she didn't like when she was alive."

"Maybe. It's been known to happen." My phone rang. I plucked it from my purse and looked at the screen, surprised to see it was Nola calling. She never called. I didn't think her generation knew their smartphones could actually be used to make phone calls. "Hang on," I said to Anthony. "It's Nola—it might be important."

I slid my thumb across the screen to answer, but before I could offer a greeting, she demanded, "Where are you? Didn't you read my texts?"

"I'm at Jayne's house, and no, I haven't read your texts yet. Is everything all right?"

"I'm at home. I figured something out, so I left school so I could get home to show you. But you're not here."

"You left school?"

"Melanie!" Her tone was part frustration and part exasperation. "So sue me—but trust me, this is important. Can you come home right now? I've already texted Cooper and he's on his way, too."

"I can be there in about five minutes. But can you first tell me what this is about?"

"The code!" She nearly screamed the word, and I had to hold my phone away from my ear. "Those four words, remember? In the letter from Lafayette that Dad gave me to work on? Cognac, feathers of goldfinch, kitchen maid, Burgundy wine? We were going over our Dutch painters quiz in my art history class—I got an A, by the way—and it hit me. I know what the words mean. And it's definitely a code."

∞

My fingers were so cold from my race down Jayne's driveway that I could barely fumble in my purse for my keys or pry the car door handle open. I'd almost managed to close the door when it was wrenched from my grasp. Anthony stuck his head inside the door opening. "Let me come with you. I can help."

"Thanks, Anthony, but we'll have Nola and Cooper and Jayne, and even Jack if he's up to it. Right now, I think you'd be most helpful finishing up the brick puzzle. You're really close."

He looked so disappointed that I almost changed my mind and sent him back into the house for his coat and shoes. But then my phone dinged again and I glanced at it on the seat next to me. The message was from Nola. PLS HURRY!

I shook my head. "Thanks—but we've got this covered. I'll check back with you later. Go inside now and take a nap."

"Fine, you're right. But keep me posted." He closed my door and shoved his hands into his jeans pockets, then stood watching me as I backed out of the driveway and onto South Battery.

I'd barely made it a block when I was met by flashing lights and a policeman rerouting traffic toward Water Street. It was apparently just a fender bender involving two cars, but it was enough to block traffic going in both directions. Biting back an expletive, I waited behind five cars to take the directed U-turn, drumming my hands impatiently on my steering wheel.

My phone beeped again. I glanced over at the seat again, expecting to see another text from Nola, but that wasn't what it was. Instead, my screen was rapidly scrolling through all of my stored photos, mostly of JJ, Sarah, and Nola, slowing down when it got to the photos I'd taken at the Gallen Hall cemetery. I started to get annoyed—now was not the time for my phone to go on the fritz. But then I noticed the photo it had stopped on and understood that my phone wasn't malfunctioning at all.

A car honked behind me, and I jerked my head to face forward, noticing the policeman waiting for me to make my U-turn. I smiled and waved, hoping he wouldn't stop me for texting and driving—not that that's what I was doing, but it might have looked that way. Beyond it being dangerous and stupid to text while driving, texting was a skill I could barely perform sitting at a desk and using two hands, much less using one hand while trying to control a car.

I smiled as I passed the officer, then hit the dial button on my steering wheel and called Anthony's cell. I skipped all formalities as I blurted, "It's on my phone—where I saw that pattern before!" I took a deep breath to slow down my words. "It's on the small square inside the larger wrought-iron gate in the mausoleum. I took a picture of it, and I've still got it on my phone."

"Can you send it to me right away?"

"I'll text the picture in just a minute—I'm not home yet."

Another text came from Nola. HURRY!!!!!

I found myself clenching my jaw and forced myself to relax. Ignoring the text, I said, "I was thinking that maybe you could convert the three patterns to the same dimensions and see if putting them together means something."

"Great idea, Melanie. And I'll absolutely do that. I'll keep you posted—and do the same with whatever Nola's discovered, too, all right?"

"Deal." I hit the disconnect button, then found myself detouring my way back to Tradd Street, the short distance taking forever because of all the one-way streets not going the one way I needed to.

When I pulled into the driveway, I immediately texted the photo to Anthony, then raced inside the house. Nola met me in the foyer and began pulling me back toward the kitchen. "I thought we'd work on the dining room table, but Mrs. Houlihan said you'd probably blow a gasket if we messed up any of your table settings for the party."

She dragged me through the kitchen door before I could defend myself, which was a good thing, since Mrs. Houlihan was probably right.

"Jack!" I said in surprise. He sat at the head of the table wearing his pajamas, robe, and slippers, with a thick blanket wrapped around him. A box of tissues sat near his right hand, a wadded tissue shoved in the collar of his pajamas. His hair looked like he'd been stuck in a wind tunnel, and he had three days of stubble on his chin, yet when he grinned at me, my heart beat a little faster and he was still the most devastatingly handsome man I had ever seen.

I raced over to his side of the table, but he held a hand up to block me. "Not too close, Mellie. You can't get sick, too."

I looked around the table and noticed how all the chairs were clustered at the other end. I greeted Cooper, then glanced around for Jayne and the children. I was a little addicted to two sets of pudgy arms around my neck and sloppy kisses on my cheeks when I came home each day. Even with the three dogs scurrying around my feet in greeting, it just wasn't the same. Still, I bent down to scratch behind each set of ears, spending longer on General Lee because he was the eldest.

"Jayne's upstairs with the twins, but when they go down for their nap she'll join us," Jack said. Despite wanting to see JJ and Sarah, I felt a tiny twist of relief that Jayne wouldn't be a part of this. I told myself that I would dissect my feelings later. When I had time.

Jack continued. "We were going to have the twins in the kitchen with us on their blanket with their toys and the dogs, but they kept wanting me to hold them. I don't know who this quarantine is harder on—them or me."

"It's pretty hard for me, too," I said, giving him a meaningful glance.

Nola sighed heavily. "Okay, you two. Can we focus, please?"

I moved to stand behind her while she opened the same art history textbook I recalled seeing her and her two friends with at the wreath workshop. Cooper pulled out a notebook and opened it to a blank page.

Nola began. "So, if you'll recall, when Dad first gave me those four words to make some sense out of, Cooper and I sat down to try to categorize them, see what they had in common." She looked around the table, meeting everyone's gaze, the blue intensity in hers just like her father's when figuring out a tangled mystery with obscure clues. It's what he did best, and apparently, he'd passed it on to his older daughter. Maybe his younger daughter, and son, too, but it was too early to tell.

"Melanie?"

I realized Nola had turned around to look at me, while I'd been staring at Jack and thinking about our children. "Yes?"

"Are you with us?"

I nodded. "Of course. Go on."

"So, Cooper and I made these columns and wrote down adjectives to describe each word and see if we could find any similarities. We did that for days, going over and over the columns, coming up with new words that I wouldn't even know existed if I hadn't used Google. Or had been working with someone besides Cooper."

They shared a glance and Jack frowned. Either he was getting better or his radar where Nola was concerned wasn't affected by the flu.

Nola continued. "The only thing we noticed was that three of them could be identified with a color—cognac is brown, goldfinch feathers are yellow, and Burgundy wine is often red. But that left us with the kitchen maid. Even back in the seventeen hundreds, they probably came in different colors. It made no sense, so Cooper and I just figured that we were pointed in the wrong direction."

Dramatically, she picked up the book and held it open for everyone to see, splay backed like a book an elementary school teacher was reading to her students. I recognized the painting showing a woman with a white cloth hat and what appeared to be a clay pitcher pouring milk into a bowl. "This is a famous painting by the Dutch artist Johannes Vermeer. Its official name is *The Milkmaid*. But"—she paused for dramatic effect—"perhaps because of what most people think a milkmaid should look like—a young woman out with the cows gathering milk, maybe—the painting is more commonly known as . . ."

She paused again, but instead of gritting his teeth, Jack smiled. *"The Kitchen Maid."*

"Bingo!" Nola's smile matched her father's. "I felt really dumb because we've been studying Vermeer all semester, so I knew a lot about him, so this should have clicked a long time ago. What was *really* interesting and caught my attention finally was his color palette."

Nola's arms were drooping from the weight of the book, so Cooper stood and took it from her while I took his vacated seat at the table. "Thank you," she said, and I hoped Jack couldn't see the look on her face when she smiled at the young man.

Nola's brows knitted. "Where was I?"

"Vermeer's color palette," Cooper said gently.

"Right. So each painter pretty much had their signature palette. During the seventeenth century, when Vermeer was painting, there were only about twenty pigments available to him, and he chose to work mostly with just seven." Her smile broadened as she used her index finger to indicate the background in *The Milkmaid*. "His palette was unusual because of the pigment he used to create shadows on whitewashed walls that were warmer than those created with black pigment used by other artists."

"And that pigment was . . ." Cooper announced like a master of ceremonies, and I wondered if I should do a drumroll on the table.

Jack and I stared blankly at Nola and then Cooper, as if waiting for them to turn the page and reveal the answer, because apparently we had no idea.

"Umber!" Nola shouted.

Cooper placed the book on the table. "So, basically, we now have four objects with identifiable colors: brown, yellow, umber, and red."

I sat up. "And that means . . . ?"

Cooper and Nola shared a glance before looking back at me. "We're not sure. That's why we were hoping we could brainstorm a little bit now."

Jack reached for the notebook and pen and Cooper slid them down the table. Across the top of a blank page, Jack jotted down the four words and their four corresponding colors. "What we need to do now is put this all in the context of the Vanderhorsts at that time. What they would have been familiar with and what connection to those four words and/or colors they might have had. A familiarity known by Lafayette so that his letter would be understood by them and hopefully not by any others."

"Our thoughts exactly, sir," Cooper said. "And since we're working on the premise that this might be connected to the French king's treasure, we've been looking at those four colors in that context."

Jack was still scribbling but looked up at Cooper. "And what have you found so far?"

"Nothing yet, sir. But I'm prepared to stay here all night with Nola and help figure it out."

Jack's eyes narrowed. "I'm sure that won't be necessary."

"Dad!" Nola shouted, her face a mask of mortification.

"No, sir," Cooper said, a pink stain on his cheeks. He cleared his throat. "We did figure out one thing, sir, in regards to the umber. Mrs. Vanderhorst was an avid art collector. There are actually quite a few paintings she acquired while living at Gallen Hall that were later donated by the family to the Gibbes Museum. It was well-known that her favorite artists were Rembrandt and Vermeer. So it would make sense that she'd know about Vermeer's preferred palette."

"And the marquis would have made it his business to know this," Jack said, thumping the end of his pen against the notebook before dropping it, then slumping back in his chair, his face taking on a waxy sheen.

"Jack—you need to rest." I stood and went to him. Cooper and Nola moved toward him, too, but I waved them back. "No sense in three of us getting exposed—I promise to be careful." I helped Jack stand, and I could hear his teeth chattering again. "Come on, let's get you into bed."

"I love it when you say that," he croaked.

"Dad!" Nola shouted again. "We're still here, you know."

Jack grinned through his chattering, then reached back toward the table. "I need my notebook. For later," he said after he saw my alarm.

Nola grabbed it and handed it to me, and I carried it

upstairs while my other arm was wrapped around Jack's shoulders. I gave him an Advil, then tucked him into bed, adding another blanket at his request.

"Put the notebook and pen here," he said, indicating the space where I usually slept in the bed. "For when I wake up and feel better."

"Sure," I said, "but don't work too hard. You really need to rest so you can get better." I sat down on the edge of the bed, smoothing the hair from his forehead. "Is there anything else you need?"

He raised his eyebrows in a familiar gesture.

"Jack—you're sick, remember?"

"Doesn't mean I'm dead," he muttered. "Anything else I can be mulling over while I'm stuck here?"

The word *dead* reminded me of something Anthony had said. "Maybe. Anthony and I were talking earlier, and he mentioned how he's pretty sure it's Eliza Grosvenor who pushed him down the stairs at Gallen Hall. He gets really bad vibes when he passes her portrait, so he thinks she hates him. He suggested that maybe he resembles somebody from her life that she didn't like."

"Or maybe she just hates men."

I shook my head. "No, I don't think that's it. It's only Anthony she seems to pick on. And she definitely doesn't hate men. I think she kissed Greco."

Jack lifted his head from the pillow, then immediately laid it back down. "When did this happen?"

I couldn't remember what I'd told him and what I hadn't. He still hadn't told me what Jolly had mentioned—the evil presence from the cistern that had followed Jack into my office. In a fit of pique I'd decided to keep the bee incidents and my mother's outbursts from Jack until he shared with me what he'd learned. It was childish and stupid, and I'd already decided that I was going to tell him everything. As soon as he was better, when he could process it all. That's what I kept telling myself, anyway. I looked down at my hand where I wore the signet ring and placed my other hand over it.

"He had to stop by to pick something up before heading out to a living history event and was dressed in his complete British regimental uniform. He was standing in Nola's room when he said he felt a woman kiss his cheek. I'm pretty sure it was Eliza—I sense her a lot in there."

Jack was thoughtful for a moment. "So, Alexander was the British soldier quartered at Gallen Hall, but Eliza was engaged to Lawrence, the son of the family." His eyelids were beginning to droop. "It's interesting that she'd kiss a British soldier, don't you think?"

I looked down at the signet ring again, remembering how Greco had told me he'd felt the kiss after he'd slipped it on his finger. And how my mother was certain the owner of the ring was a woman. I lifted my hand to show him. "Greco found this in the bedpost. . . ."

I stopped. Jack's eyes were closed, the muscles in his face relaxed, his breathing even. "Never mind," I said. "I'll tell you later." I stood, then leaned over the bed to kiss his forehead. "I love you," I whispered, watching him sleeping for a moment before quietly letting myself out of the room.

CHAPTER
31

On Saturday morning, the day of the progressive dinner, I was up early so I could steer the final preparations. The night before, Nola had helped me pack up the twins and move them and all their equipment to Jack's parents'. I'd argued at first that they wouldn't be in the way, until Nola reminded me of how much JJ loved to throw all round objects he could get his little hands on as if they were baseballs, and how Sarah had taken to climbing into the Christmas trees in search of the shiniest ornament. I'd quickly acquiesced.

Mrs. Houlihan, Nola, and Jayne would be on hand to help. Jack was still too sick to be out of bed, but Cooper said he'd be available if we needed extra help setting up the rented tables to accommodate the twelve couples who couldn't fit around the table in the dining room.

I'd printed out spreadsheets with a time schedule and tasks to be accomplished and by whom in the appropriate rows and columns. I labeled each one with the person's name and then printed extra copies just in case anyone lost theirs, which seemed to happen a lot. The main dining room table was already set with my grandmother's antique Belgian lace tablecloth and matching napkins and the Vanderhorsts' stunning Imari place settings, the brilliant gold, red, and dark blue standing out like jewels against the white tablecloth.

I hated to admit it, but the homemade centerpieces of oranges, pineapples, and pinecones that Sophie had forced

me to make were a festive and gorgeous touch. As were
Greco's hurricane lanterns on the piazza, which he had returned to festoon with evergreen sprigs of pine, sapphire
cedar, and boxwood. He'd even prepared enough to include
in the centerpieces of the smaller tables, so they were as
elegant as the main table.

My phone beeped and I saw a text from Greco, and I
was relieved that he texted like a real person and used full
sentences and punctuation.

> I heard back from Uncle Oliver with a bit of information for
> you. Lawrence V. and his father were basically estranged
> although living under the same roof. It was rumored in
> some circles that one of them supported the patriot cause
> while the other remained loyalist. Not clear which one was
> which as historical information is conflicting. Whatever the
> truth, he believes it's the reason Lawrence was killed.

While I was still attempting to text the word *thanks*,
another text popped up on my screen.

> You might also be interested to know that St. Gallen
> was the patron saint of birds. Uncle O. finds it interesting
> that the name change happened around the time of the
> Revolution and Eliza's purchase of the first peacocks.

He added a smile emoji to the end of that sentence and
then a fist-bump GIF.

Jayne was emerging from the dining room when I came
down the stairs. I showed her the text from Greco. Her eyes
widened. "The plot thickens," she said. "And the whole
Gallen thing—right under our noses."

"Apparently we weren't the only ones, since nobody
seems to have made the connection between Gallen Hall
and peacocks."

I read the text again, remembering what I'd read in
Nola's borrowed textbook, about the only footprints leading to Lawrence's body coming from the house.

"So who killed Lawrence?" Jayne asked, giving voice to my own thoughts.

"Someone close to him. Someone in the house. The only thing we know for sure is that it wasn't Eliza or Alexander, because they were already dead." I frowned. "But I know Eliza is connected somehow. She brought the peacocks to Gallen Hall, and then the name of the plantation was changed."

"Definitely not a coincidence," Jayne said.

I nodded. "All we know for sure is that she was engaged to Lawrence. But when Mother held the signet ring, she said the owner had been female."

"Then . . ." Jayne began but stopped as Mrs. Houlihan bustled past us clutching a feather duster on her way to the front parlor.

"Let's talk about this later—we've got a lot of work to do."

Jayne nodded, then held up what looked like an orange in her hand. "I found a bunch of these under the table and behind the draperies in the dining room. Are they part of the decoration?"

I remembered a few of them flying around the table when I'd been in there with Michael, but I thought I'd removed them all. "No, not exactly. I think Veronica's sister sent them to remind me that she's still here and waiting to move on. Or JJ was let loose with a bowl of oranges." I marched into the dining room and began to pick up the errant oranges.

"And?"

"And, what?" I lifted the long silk drapes and rescued two more oranges.

"And are you going to help her?"

I moved to the other window and checked under the drapes, finding one more piece of fruit. "I guess I'm going to have to. I told Veronica I would but that I couldn't it do it right now. Michael wants to put their house on the market now so they can move, but Veronica feels that if they move out of the house, they'll lose some vital clue to Adrienne's disappearance."

"So you agreed to help her?"

"Against my better judgment, I did—but not until after Christmas. I'm so insanely busy right now I just couldn't add one more restless spirit to my plate. I think I've thrown in enough brakes on the house sale so that we have until after the first of the year before I have to actually do anything."

"Maybe I can help you."

I didn't meet her gaze. "Maybe. Let's cross that bridge when we come to it."

I began walking around the perimeter of the room, searching for any missed fruit.

"She's right, you know," Jayne said. "About losing some vital clue. I see Adrienne, too, sometimes, and I feel that time is of the essence. I've seen her a few times when I've been working with Veronica. They must have been very close."

I stood and faced my sister. "I guess so. Veronica still misses her and it's been more than twenty years."

Jayne's face looked wistful. "It must have been nice to grow up with a sister, don't you think? Sharing confidences. And makeup. Clothes."

"And fights," I added. "Most sisters I know have always done a lot of fighting." I immediately regretted my words. For a brief moment I pictured Jayne and me with matching black patent Mary Janes having ice cream sundaes at the curved booth in the front of Carolina's with our grandmother. Grandmother would have known that we'd each want our own since even now as adults neither Jayne nor I ever shared a dessert with anyone. And we would have been aware of the silent spirits around us at the other tables and standing nearby, but we wouldn't have been afraid because we would have had each other.

I softened my tone when I saw her wounded look. "Yeah, it would have been nice not to grow up alone. And I'd rather have a sister than a brother. Especially for the sharing of clothes."

As if she'd heard only the first part, Jayne said, "I don't

think we would have fought." She peered behind the dining room door and plucked out an orange I'd missed. "Because you and I have this thing we share—this gift or whatever you want to call it. It would have bonded us together. Kind of like how it's bonding us now."

"True," I said, wishing I felt as reassured as I sounded.

She smiled and I smiled back, feeling only a little tinge of remorse that I couldn't completely agree with her.

I indicated the oranges we both held. "Why don't we put these in the kitchen for Mrs. Houlihan? She'll probably use them to whip up another batch of wonderful cookies that she won't let me have." I walked toward the kitchen to deposit the oranges in the bowl in the middle of the center island, Jayne right behind me.

Jayne grimaced. "Probably. I find it's easiest to resist sweets when they're not in the house."

The look I gave her made her quickly switch the subject. "I missed you on our run this morning. You're doing so well, and I feel it's my duty as a coach to keep you motivated."

We returned to the dining room, where I glanced out the window. "Yeah, well, I was more motivated to get this day over with than to get frostbite. It's really getting ugly out there."

"Oh, it was a little cold. But it's all about the proper gear. I was well insulated and I brought my little hand warmers to stick inside my running gloves." She considered me for a moment. "I think I know what I need to put in your Christmas stocking."

I forced a smile. "I like chocolate Santas, if anyone's asking. Dark chocolate and solid—none of that milk chocolate hollow stuff. I might as well eat tofu."

The doorbell rang, announcing the arrival of the party-rental people, and Jayne, Mrs. Houlihan, and I got busy directing the placement of the six extra tables in the front parlor, placing a white tablecloth on each. I began putting the centerpieces on the tables and attempting to zhush them as Greco had taught me, but I stopped when I realized Mrs.

Houlihan was going right behind me and redoing them. And making them look much better.

Wonderful baking smells wafted from the kitchen while we worked, making it hard to concentrate. Mrs. Houlihan had insisted on adding to the caterer's menu with her famed tomato bisque, topped with chilled shrimp that her husband had caught off of Edisto the past summer and she'd set aside and frozen "just in case."

She'd also persuaded me to allow her to gift our dinner guests with small bags of goodies, including her praline pecans, homemade truffles, lemon cranberry tarts, and spicy iced peppermint shortbread cookies. I'd yet to taste a single bite of any of it, as Mrs. Houlihan seemed to have a sixth sense where I was concerned, always facing the kitchen door as if expecting me each time I tried to sneak in for a sample. She claimed that I didn't know what a sample was and every time she'd allowed it in the past, she'd had to make another batch of whatever it was I'd sampled. I denied it, of course, blaming it on whoever else happened to be in the house, but she never believed me.

My mother arrived around ten, after going with my father to the gardening store for tarps for his beloved Daphne evergreen shrubs and camellias to protect them from snow. They were hardy, winter-sustainable plants, but Dad wasn't convinced that his Southern beauties would know how to handle icy rain or a thick coat of snow. I'd called him on his cell, asking him to get more tarps than he needed because Sophie was concerned about the cistern and exposing anything old to the frigid cold. I'd bit my tongue before I could make a comment about how it wasn't possible to make a piece of garbage less valuable, refraining from speaking when I reminded myself that we were friends.

Nola came downstairs around the same time my mother arrived. Nola wasn't an early riser, so I was impressed she made it downstairs before noon on a Saturday. Mrs. Houlihan placed a cup of tea in one hand and I put a spreadsheet in the other, and then waited another fifteen minutes for her to completely wake up and get to work.

She began with helping Mrs. Houlihan and me set the small tables with a mix of the Vanderhorst Imari and my mother's borrowed Cartier wedding china with the narrow gold edges, which blended beautifully with the other pattern. The mix and match had been suggested by Greco, and I shook my head in wonder at how I'd found him on a recommendation from his good friend Rich Kobylt of the low-slung pants and pickup truck.

I continued to keep an eye out the window as we worked, constantly checking the weather outside and on my phone and occasionally turning on the Weather Channel for corroboration that it wasn't going to snow before Sunday morning. My life's mantra was that if it was worth doing, it was worth doing three times.

Nola and I were folding napkins in elegant tepee shapes following Jayne's directions—she'd apparently learned how to fold any material into any shape in nanny school—when Jack appeared at the top of the stairs. "Mellie?"

I quickly dropped the linen square and took the stairs two at a time. He still looked pale and not at all well, but there was a little flush of color to his cheeks. "You shouldn't be out of bed."

"Probably not," he agreed, "but I think I just figured out what those colors mean." He leaned into me and I put my arms around his shoulders. His knees seemed to bend a bit and I struggled to keep him upright. Jayne ran up the stairs and stood on his other side, slipping her arm around his waist.

"Should I come up, too?" Nola called.

"No, your aunt Jayne and I can handle this."

"But I was the one—"

"Yes, you helped us figure out about the umber." It was hard to forget since she'd been bringing it into every conversation since the previous evening. "And we're grateful— but those napkins won't fold themselves. You can borrow my ruler to make sure the sides are all equal—I left it on the table next to you."

Jayne and I carefully led Jack back to bed, although I

had to move the notebook and about ten crumpled balls
of paper off first. I frowned down at him as I adjusted the
pillow beneath his head. "Did you work on this instead of
sleeping?"

The half grin he gave me was so devastatingly familiar
that my anger quickly evaporated, as I'm sure had been his
intention. "Maybe."

"Jack! How are you going to get better if you don't take
care of yourself?"

"All I need to do is look at your beautiful face, and I
immediately feel better." He looked behind me to where
Jayne stood, her arms folded. "How was that?"

Jayne attempted to hide a smile beneath her frown.
"Terrible. And Melanie's right, Jack. You need your sleep."

I gave her a quick nod of gratitude. "Now go to sleep and
we'll talk later. We've got to get ready for the party." I
reached for the lamp, but Jack put a hand on my arm. "Let
me show you first—and then I'll go to sleep. Promise."

I slid the notebook out from under the pile of rumpled
paper and handed it to him.

"See," he said, jabbing his finger at what appeared to be
a lot of gibberish. "My mistake is that I thought this should
be more complicated than it is."

"Like looking for zebras instead of horses," Jayne said.

"Exactly." Jack sent Jayne an appreciative glance.

As if guessing I had no clue what she was talking about,
Jayne explained, "I used to work for a doctor and her family, and she told me that new doctors are always looking for
the bizarre diseases when examining symptoms rather than
considering the everyday, common-cold-type thing."

"Ah," I said, looking at the jumbled words on the notebook.

Jack coughed and I handed him a glass of water I kept
filled on his nightstand. "So," he said, "I spent a couple of
hours going over all the code books I have to see if I could
break this out. It's only four words, and Nola had already
done the hardest part, figuring out the color connection, so

I figured I should be able to figure out the rest." Jack paused a moment to lay his head back against the pillow and catch his breath.

"Anyway," he continued, "after a lot of wasted time, I just went back to the most basic of all codes—letter substitution and first letters. Looking for horses instead of zebras, so to speak. It's pretty elementary, but I suspect that whoever came up with the original list of supplies thought it was a good enough coded hint that any additional cipher was just a precaution and didn't need to be as involved."

I followed his finger down the page, where I saw his attempts at making words using various letter orders, then watched as he turned the page, where a single word was written in shaky block print. R-U-B-Y. "Red, umber, brown, and yellow," I said out loud. "So simple, yet so diabolical when you're looking for something so much harder."

Jayne rubbed her forehead. "So the French king gave the Marquis de Lafayette a valuable ruby to secretly give to someone—possibly a spy—at Gallen Hall to support the American cause. And I'm only saying 'spy' since the Vanderhorsts were loyalists, correct?"

Jack nodded, as if the effort it took to speak was wearing on him. But I knew I couldn't stop him at this point. Being tenacious and smart was one of the things I loved the most about him, and I knew it would be pointless to make him stop talking now and relax.

The deep V above his nose suddenly cleared as his eyes widened with realization. "But not just one ruby," he said excitedly. "Four. And what place better to hide valuable jewels than in a piece of costume jewelry? Remember the brooch Eliza is wearing in her portrait—the peacock. I'm sure it's the same brooch I told you about from the vision Jolly had. It had four jewels in it."

Jayne nodded while I tried to keep relaxed. Jolly had told me about her vision of the man with the brooch following Jack, but Jack hadn't. Up until that moment, I'd still been waiting. But apparently he'd told Jayne. Part of me wanted to believe it was an oversight—he'd been sick and everything was so crazed right now—but part of me felt the old sense of being left out.

"The jewels weren't all red, though," I said, remembering the portrait and the times I'd seen Eliza. I sounded bossy and realized this might be my attempt to feel relevant.

"True," Jayne said. She looked at Jack. "They could have been disguised, right? Maybe some kind of stain or watercolor paint?"

Jack smiled with approval. "That's what I was thinking. Stick multicolored jewels into a pinchbeck brooch, and nobody would know what they were hiding."

"Then where are the four rubies?" I asked.

Jack shook his head slowly. "I know it has something to do with the mausoleum—the way it was destroyed and rebuilt two brick rows higher. It has to mean something. It can't be a coincidence that it was rebuilt the year after Lafayette supposedly brought the treasure into the country."

"And the three people interred there have to be connected, too," Jayne added. "Since they all died the same year that the treasure was supposedly delivered to Gallen Hall."

I sat down on the edge of the bed, suddenly aware of the signet ring I still had on my finger. It felt very warm, almost burning my skin with its heat. I remembered what my mother had said when she'd held it, the feeling of heartbreak, and the kiss Greco had received while wearing the ring. The wet boot prints after Greco had left. And I recalled, too, what Jolly had told me about the man following Jack, and the specter's own broken heart.

I looked up with a small gasp, knowing with certainty who the spy was. And the meaning of the word *lies*. More important, if I didn't know exactly where the rubies were hidden, I knew where to look to find them.

"What?" Jack asked, his eyes barely slits as he fought his exhaustion.

"It can wait. We have a party to get ready for." I stood

and tucked the covers around him. "You get some sleep. We'll talk more tomorrow."

"Mellie . . ." My name was a word of warning, but I pretended I didn't hear it as I bent down to kiss his forehead, then ushered Jayne out of the room.

"What was that all about?" Jayne asked as I led her to the stairs.

"What do you mean?"

"You gasped, and I don't know if it's because I'm psychic or because we're sisters, but whatever it is you're thinking, I don't have a good feeling about it."

"The only thing I'm thinking about right now is this party and getting everything ready before the first guest arrives. And then we can figure out where the rubies are."

Jayne right behind me, I continued my hurried pace down the stairs, aware of her worried gaze following my every step.

CHAPTER
32

I clasped my grandmother's pearls behind my neck, feeling odd to be doing it alone. Jack and my usual going-out ritual involved me lifting my hair and Jack lingering on the fastenings of my necklace, then finishing with a soft kiss beneath my ear. He was only in the adjacent bedroom, but I missed him as if he were in another country on an extended trip. I'd never seen him have so much as a cold, so to have him confined to bed for nearly a week was unsettling. It was as if the carousel we'd been riding had suddenly switched directions, and I couldn't quite get my bearings.

I stopped by the bedroom to see if Jack needed anything before I went downstairs. He was propped up on pillows so he could breathe better; pill bottles and a filled water jug sat next to him on the bedside table. He had a large textbook open on his lap, and I recognized it as Greco's great-uncle's book about spies.

He watched me approach, that gleam in his eye only partially clouded with medicine. "You look beautiful," he said.

I sat down on the edge of the bed, making sure I avoided the trash can that was halfway filled with used tissues even though I'd emptied it only a couple of hours before. "Feeling a little better?"

He nodded. "Mrs. Houlihan brought me up some of her tomato bisque and a plate of her cookies. I actually had enough of an appetite to enjoy them."

I looked around for the plate. "Did you eat them all? Or at least save me a crumb?"

"Sorry—I ate every last bite. I'm sure there are more downstairs."

"Oh, yes. Tons. I'm just not allowed to have any." I folded my arms.

"You do realize Mrs. Houlihan works for you, right?"

"Yes, but . . ." He was right, of course. Having been raised by a military father, I had an almost unnatural respect for authority, and going against her wishes always seemed a bit like insubordination. "It's complicated," I said. Changing the subject, I tapped the book in front of him. "Find anything interesting?"

"Not sure. I'm trying to determine who the major players were in the peacock spy ring. Carrollton Vanderhorst, Lawrence's father, was a known loyalist, but after the Revolution, he retained all of his lands on the Ashley River. Nothing was confiscated as punishment for supporting the wrong side."

"Interesting," I said. "What about Lawrence?"

"Defender of the Crown, through and through. A little fanatical about it—which could be why Carrollton kept his true beliefs secret from his son."

"Speaking of Carrollton, Greco's uncle, the historian, says that father and son were estranged. And apparently Lawrence's murderer came from Gallen Hall—two sets of footprints leading from the house, and only one returning. But no one was ever arrested."

Jack raised his eyebrows. "That certainly fuels the fire of the stories of how they were rooting for opposite sides."

I nodded. "And one more thing. St. Gallen was the patron saint of birds. I don't think that's a coincidence."

"Definitely not." He leaned across the bed and picked up a photocopied page. "Yvonne faxed this to me this morning—Nola brought it up for me so I didn't have to bother you. It's from an architectural design book she found in the archives about Charleston's cemeteries. There's quite a large section regarding the mausoleum at Gallen Hall."

He handed it to me, but when he saw me squinting, he took it back. "Should I just paraphrase?"

"My glasses are downstairs, just so you know. I was using them this morning to measure napkin folds."

He was silent for a moment before he continued. "Carrollton Vanderhorst was the one who had the original mausoleum built in 1780, as a family crypt, which is why there were ten niches in the original plan. But he's also the one who ordered it destroyed two years later and had his son, his son's fiancée, and the British soldier interred there. Carrollton planned the addition of the two rows as well as commissioned all of the wrought iron for the fence around the periphery, the front gate, and the mausoleum door gate. There were two more gates designed for the cemetery, but they disappeared after Hurricane Hugo in 'eighty-nine. The remaining iron fencing miraculously survived."

I squinted at the page, wishing I could see. "So there were three gates designed for the redo, but only the front gate along with the mausoleum door survived?"

Jack nodded. "Apparently. Samuel Vanderhorst designed and made all of them. But there's one last bit of info that I find the most promising."

He plucked his reading glasses off the collar of his pajamas and then reached under the heavy textbook to pull out a small leather-bound volume. "This rare gem was actually discovered by Cooper at the Citadel library. They have an impressive collection of books about South Carolinians with military backgrounds—of which Carrollton Vanderhorst was one. Apparently, he led several militias up in Virginia during the early years of the French and Indian War. George Washington himself referred to Vanderhorst as his 'great strategist.' When I read that, the next part started to make sense to me."

He flipped the book open to where a clean tissue was being used as a bookmark. "Carrollton died in January 1783 of a"—he paused for a moment to find the correct wording—"'bilious liver.' Apparently he'd been ill for several years, so his death wasn't unexpected. That's why he'd had the original mausoleum built to begin with, along with a brick wall to surround the cemetery." Jack's gaze met mine. "So, let's assume that Carrollton finds himself in possession of four valuable jewels for the patriot cause. But he's dying, and whoever the spy was isn't there to help him, and maybe he doesn't know who to trust with the jewels. After all, Alexander and Lawrence have been murdered by a person or persons unknown, so there's real danger if he's found with the rubies. Remember, the genius military commander Washington referred to Carrollton as a 'great strategist,' so I'm thinking he's pretty clever. So he figures a cunning way to hide the jewels and uses clues to lead the way just in case he dies before he can find out what to do with the rubies."

"Except maybe he was too clever, and no one did." I thought of the drawings I'd given to Anthony, along with the photo of the gate insert and how now would be the time to share what I knew. "I . . ."

Jack spoke at the same time, and I allowed him to continue. "Why would the ghost of a man holding the brooch—and I'm assuming it's Lawrence since of the three buried in the mausoleum, he's the only male who wasn't a soldier—be at the cistern? It's nowhere near Gallen Hall. Maybe he's there protecting the jewels."

"It's possible, I suppose. Even though this house wasn't built until the earlier part of the nineteenth century, there was another house here before it, owned by the Vanderhorsts. When they tore down the first mausoleum and brick wall at the Gallen Hall cemetery, Sophie believes they probably used some of the bricks to build this cistern. People reused bricks all the time back then simply because it was more economical. So, a spirit connected to the old cemetery could possibly feel a connection to the cistern because of that." I gave him a crooked smile. "Just because I see them doesn't mean I understand them."

Jack threw his glasses onto the bed beside him. "Marc's looked everywhere at the plantation for those jewels. I'm beginning to think they're in the cistern. Maybe hidden inside one of the bricks. I'm so tired of being sick, I've half a mind to get out of bed tonight and start digging myself."

I placed a restraining hand on his shoulder, sensing his renewed desperation and frustration. The New York publishing world virtually shut down in the month of December, so Jack was back in limbo land, stuck with stewing and mulling over the fate of his career. "Don't be silly, Jack. It's freezing outside and you're sick. And don't worry—I'm working on things while you're down for the count. I might be able to give you a nice Christmas surprise."

He narrowed his eyes at me. "Remember what I said, Mellie. Don't do anything rash."

"How can I?" I said flippantly. "I've got twenty-four couples coming to our house for dinner tonight. The only thing rash I can picture is me raiding Mrs. Houlihan's party bags so I can finally get a cookie."

Jack smiled, but he didn't look completely convinced. I wondered if he'd always been able to see through me, or if this was what marriage did to couples.

"Lawrence followed me one day, according to Jolly," Jack said. "Did I mention that to you? I might not have. That was around the time I was starting to feel sick, and I don't think I was thinking straight. And she's not the most reliable of psychics, you know? I might not have wanted to scare you. You've had a tough month."

"We both have," I said, taking his hand. "I think I'm getting really close to solving this, Jack."

"'I'm'?"

"We are," I corrected.

The doorbell rang downstairs. I glanced at my watch and stood. "It's the caterers. I've got to go and let them know where everything goes. Mother and Jayne left to get dressed, and Nola went to your mother's to help with bath time for the twins, and then she'll get changed and come here to help. I let Mrs. Houlihan go home an hour ago since the caterers can take over now, but someone still needs to be in charge."

"And you're so good at being in charge," Jack said, almost looking like his old self. "But what were you about to say? Earlier, before I interrupted."

The doorbell rang again. I leaned down and kissed him on his forehead. "I've got to get that. We'll talk later."

I put the TV remote in his hand and ran out of the room, pausing at the top of the stairs to text Anthony, asking him if he'd had any luck with the drawings and the photo of the gate panel. I had to do it twice because autocorrect kept translating it into something that looked like Swahili.

When I opened the door to let in the caterers, Jayne came in behind them. Her coat was open and we both stopped in the foyer to stare at each other. Finally, Jayne laughed out loud. "People are going to think we called each other to coordinate our outfits."

We both wore dark green velvet dresses with low V-necks and slightly flared skirts. "I saw this one in the window at the Finicky Filly and had to have it," I explained.

"Me, too," Jayne said, holding in a giggle. "It's my favorite store."

I didn't bother telling her that it was my favorite store, too. "I guess I'll go change," I said, heading for the stairs. "Tell the caterers not to do anything until I get back."

"Don't be silly," Jayne said. "I always wanted a sister so we could wear matching outfits."

I almost admitted out loud that I had, too, but stopped just in time. I looked behind her. "Where's Anthony?"

"I'm assuming he's on his way, because I've been trying to reach him, but I haven't heard back. Last time I spoke with him, he said to come on over without him because he was running late and had gone home to get dressed. He knows you've assigned him to hang up coats instead of going to the first house for appetizers, and he seemed okay with that."

I frowned. "I could have assigned him to toilet-paper-refill duty, but I didn't. I can still change the spreadsheet— I've got it open on my computer screen."

She grabbed my hands. "Did he call you? He said he would."

I looked down at my phone. No recent texts or phone calls from Anthony. "Nothing from him at all. What is it?"

"He finished the puzzle. Sometime last night. His bedroom door was closed when I got up, so I have no idea when. Let's go tell Jack—this will make him feel better."

"No. I mean, wait," I said, holding her back. "He's probably sleeping. But tell me—what does it look like? Does it tell us anything?"

She shook her head. "No. Not yet, anyway. But it must mean something, right?"

"Hopefully. Let's wait until we talk to Anthony—maybe he'll have more to tell Jack."

She looked at me dubiously, then down at her dress. "I have time to run home and change. Will you be okay without me for a little bit? I promise I'll hurry."

I looked at my watch, then back at Jayne. "I'm coming with you. Let me get the caterers situated, then text Mother and ask her to get here a little earlier than planned. I have to see the puzzle and I don't really think I can wait."

"Really, Melanie, I think it can—"

"I've got an hour and a half before the first guests arrive, and I'm dressed, and the house is ready, and Mother will be here. It will be fine."

Without waiting for her to respond, I ran to the kitchen to talk with the caterers, then texted both Nola and my mother to let them know where Jayne and I were and that we would be back in half an hour at the most. I grabbed my coat and purse, then ran out the door, stopping at the bottom of the piazza as I watched the freezing rain give way to small snowflakes that lazily glided their way between the streetlamps before settling on the ground below.

"It's not melting," Jayne said. "That's not good."

"At least it's not heavy. Maybe that means it'll stop."

She glanced at me, but I just shrugged before heading toward her car. "We have to take yours—mine's been blocked in by the caterer's van."

Jayne drove like an old woman, leaning close to her steering wheel as if that might help her see better.

"It's not even sticking to your windshield, Jayne, so you can definitely drive faster. Or I'll get out and walk and meet you there."

She pushed her foot just a little harder, creeping up to twenty miles per hour. If it hadn't been so cold out, I would have made good on my threat and hopped out.

I tapped my foot from cold and anticipation as I waited for her to unlock her front door, doing my best not to push her out of my way as I ran to the dining room. Jayne flicked on the wall switch to light up the chandelier, and we stood in the doorway looking at the table with awe.

"It's exactly how I thought it would look," I said. "When I said it reminded me of one of those puzzle squares. It's still a bunch of random designs, but look at how they all connect to each other."

"So this was intentional," Jayne said. "Whoever designed this wanted it to look haphazard."

I nodded. "Jack thinks it must have all been designed by Carrollton Vanderhorst, Lawrence's father. He fought alongside George Washington in the French and Indian War and Washington himself called him his 'great strategist.' He designed the cemetery and must have left clues as to where the treasure was hidden."

"But who was he hiding it from? Was he the patriot, since he was friends with Washington? And what about Lawrence and Eliza? What side were they working on?"

I began walking around the dining room table. "I'm not sure—and I don't know if we'll ever find out the whole story. But I think Lawrence was in love with Eliza, but Eliza was in love with Alexander, the British soldier." I told her about Greco being dressed in his reenactor's uniform, and the kiss he'd received when he'd slipped on the peacock signet ring. "Mother said the owner of the ring was a woman, and I'm fairly confident that was Eliza."

"And she wore the brooch, remember? She must have known what it was." Jayne was silent for a moment, thinking.

"So—she was the spy," Jayne said slowly. "And she and the British soldier had a thing. Maybe that's why he ended up buried in the mausoleum, too."

"Maybe, because Carrollton would have been the one to decide that. And the interment of the soldier. Even with his patriot beliefs, he must have known that Eliza would want to be buried with her beloved."

"And Lawrence, too. Or maybe he felt that Lawrence belonged there because he was Carrollton's son."

I leaned over the table, mesmerized by swirls and lines. "Jolly told me something interesting. That when she sensed the man following Jack—the man from the cistern holding the brooch, who I suspect is Lawrence—she sensed his heart was deeply wounded."

Jayne nodded. "I imagine if his fiancée was in love with another man, that would hurt. And that she was betraying him by being a spy for the other side would be a double betrayal."

I nodded. "Which is why I don't think she killed herself. That's why she keeps repeating the word *lies*. She wants people to know the truth."

"But what is the truth? That Lawrence killed her?"

I shrugged. "He's the spirit with the evil vibes, remember? The one who spoke through our mother saying that traitors deserve to die and rot in hell. I mean, there's a possibility that Alexander killed Eliza when he found out that she was using information she got from him to pass on to the patriots, but that's not the feeling I get from him at all."

Jayne nodded. "I agree. But whether Alexander was aware of what was going on and either helping Eliza or turned the other way is something lost to history."

I continued to walk around the table, studying the completed puzzle, occasionally reaching over to make an alignment of edges straighter. I slid my finger around the lip of the table, thinking out loud. "Since Eliza and Alexander died before Lawrence, it's entirely possible that he killed them both."

I stopped walking, feeling Jayne's wide-eyed gaze on

me. "And that brings us back to the question of who killed Lawrence."

"I suspect someone on the American side—maybe they thought he had the rubies."

"Or maybe they *knew* he had the rubies. Eliza had the brooch. Remember the door on the hidden compartment in her jewelry cabinet, how it had been ripped off its hinges as if in a hurry. Or in anger. And only the brooch was found in the cistern, discarded with the garbage. The one scenario that makes sense is that Lawrence found out about the jewels and somehow found out where she'd hidden them. Maybe he killed her out of anger, or revenge."

"Or a broken heart," Jayne added.

"And then he was killed trying to make his escape, and the rubies were saved. By whom, I don't know for sure. Everything's conjecture at this point. All I do know for sure is that Eliza didn't kill herself, and she wants the record to be set straight."

I returned to studying the maze, the lines and curves simple, like in an artist's original sketch before it's filled in with color. I could almost hear Jack speaking in my head about Carrollton Vanderhorst. *So he figures a cunning way to hide the jewels and uses clues to lead the way just in case he dies before he can find out what to do with the rubies.* A top and bottom of the puzzle were clearly identified now, the top two corners curved in opposite directions, like an arch. Just like the arch over the gate leading into the cemetery.

I jerked my head up, almost laughing at Carrollton Vanderhorst's cleverness. "Jayne, I really need to talk with Anthony."

Jayne looked down at her phone, then began dialing. She waited a moment before ending the call. "It went straight to voice mail."

I looked around the dining room, then walked quickly out to the foyer, toward the stairs. "Where's his room?"

"Melanie, that would be an invasion of privacy. . . ."

I didn't stop. "This is your house, Jayne, and he is a

guest. I'm looking for something specific—a couple of drawings I gave him earlier. They belong to me, so technically I'm only trying to recover my property."

"Fine," she said, walking past me down the hall. She stopped outside one of the bedroom doors and tapped. "Anthony?" After waiting a respectful moment, she pushed the door open and waited for me on the threshold.

The room was elegantly appointed with the furnishings of the late owner, Button Pinckney, Jayne's aunt. The bed was neatly made and the draperies open. The only thing missing was any sign of occupancy. "Didn't he bring a suitcase or anything?"

"Sure, but I don't know what was in it. I assumed it was full of clothes. I haven't been in here, Melanie, if that's what you're implying."

I rolled my eyes. "Did he bring a laptop or printer or anything so he could work while he was here?"

She nodded, her gaze traveling around the room. "He had both—I know that because I saw the laptop a few times and could hear the printer from this room." She walked to the closet and opened it. "Empty," she said, her voice hollow. "No printer, laptop. Or clothes. Maybe he just decided he'd already overstayed his welcome and, with the puzzle finished, figured it was time to head home."

"Maybe," I said. "Let me try to reach him again." I dialed his number, but the call went straight to voice mail. "Maybe his battery died. Doesn't matter—we'll see him when we get back to my house."

Avoiding her gaze, I knelt on the floor and lifted the bed skirt, then moved around the room, opening every drawer, finally stopping at the trash can tucked next to the chest of drawers. I eagerly plucked up the can and poured the balled-up papers out on top of the bedspread.

"What are these?" Jayne asked.

"These are multiple copies of the same thing—Anthony was just trying to get them all to be the same size." I opened a ball of paper and smoothed it on the bed, then began opening another, starting two different piles. "One is the copy of the drawing Joseph Longo made from a paper he found on Robert Vanderhorst's desk back in the twenties. The other is a page from the Vanderhorst family archives at the Charleston Museum—the ones Marc tried to throw out and Anthony found. And the third . . ." I held up a black-and-white copy on my phone.

"Is the little panel from the mausoleum door," Jayne finished, her eyes widening in understanding. She reached for one of the balled-up papers and began flattening it. "So these three pictures belong together and are some kind of clue?"

I nodded quickly, adding another paper to one of the piles. "The old cemetery fence was brick and was destroyed when the old mausoleum was rebuilt. Anyway, Samuel Vanderhorst designed the new wrought-iron fence and gates, as well as the mausoleum door. But the two gates were destroyed or lost around the time of Hurricane Hugo, so all that remains of them are these drawings."

"Oh, my gosh," Jayne said as she moved more quickly. "So if we get these all to fit together, they should show us something," she said excitedly.

"That's my theory, anyway," I said, my own excitement at having someone who understood the way I thought almost masking the unexpected twinge of annoyance that the person was Jayne.

When we'd divvied up all the wrinkled pages into their own piles, I spread them out into fans and began to sort through them, comparing those that seemed to match up best with ones from the other two. Catching on to what I was doing, Jayne pulled one from the third pile and held it up to the two I held. "I think this one works."

I nodded my thanks and took it, then held the three of them together up toward the light. "These aren't exact—I imagine Anthony would have the ones that are—but they will work."

I ran out of the room and toward the stairs. "Where are you going?" Jayne called from right behind me.

I didn't answer but led her to the dining room table.

"Hold these." I shoved the three pages into her hand, then pulled out a dining room chair to stand on. Holding my phone as high as it would go over the puzzle, I took a photo. "You have a printer, right?"

Before she'd finished nodding, I'd e-mailed the photo to her. "Go pull the photo up in the scrapbooking software you're always talking about, and make it fit in an eight-by-eight square so it matches the other three. And please make it black-and-white. While you're doing that, I'm going to try Anthony again. Failing that, I'll call Mother to see if she's at the house yet and if she's seen Anthony."

She was already running up the stairs by the time I'd finished speaking. I used the initials, S.V., to orient each picture, then pulled out my phone again. When Jayne returned fifteen minutes later, I shook my head in answer to her unasked question, then took the page she handed to me. "Perfect," I said, smiling at her. I placed the picture of the completed puzzle behind the other three sheets and then, after a shared look of anticipation with Jayne, held them up to the light as I remembered Anthony had done.

I wasn't sure who gasped louder, but I was suddenly very glad that someone was with me to share my discovery. With the three pictures held together, four distinct dark circles were clearly visible from the layering of the lines of each page. And each dark circle was now projected onto the puzzle made from the bricks.

"I'll go get a marker," Jayne said. She raced out of the room, and returned quickly with a black Sharpie.

"Good thinking." I continued to hold the pages up to the light while Jayne marked the back side of the last page with black marker. When she was done, I lowered them to the table and slid out the last page, using the marker to darken the spots that had bled through to the front of the puzzle page.

"It's a map of the cemetery, isn't it?" Jayne asked.

I nodded. "And I'd bet a fortune in rubies that these four spots show us where Lafayette's treasures were buried."

The hall clock chimed and our giddy smiles quickly turned to expressions of panic. "We've got to go," I said.

"But I haven't changed my dress yet."

"No time. We need to find Anthony. I'm hoping he'll be at the house by the time we get there."

"And if he's not?" Jayne asked.

"Then we've got a problem."

CHAPTER
33

The flurries had stopped by the time we left Jayne's house and headed back to Tradd Street, but when I checked the weather app on my phone, it looked like the break was temporary, the chance of frozen precipitation going from five percent to one hundred percent by two in the morning.

Jayne squeezed into the driveway behind the catering van, promising to move her car when they were ready to leave, unwilling to park blocks away and walk back in the cold. Nola had texted earlier to let us know that Cooper had brought sand to scatter on the walkway and steps, which I'd have to make sure Jack knew about so he'd stop scowling so much in the young man's direction.

The front door opened as we walked quickly down the piazza, and I held back a shout of surprise when I saw Anthony wearing a dinner jacket and holding two coat hangers. "Ladies," he said with a wide smile. "So glad to see you. We were wondering if you would get here before the guests."

"We've been calling you and texting," Jayne said, turning around so he could help her with her coat. "We noticed that you've moved out—weren't you going to tell me?"

"Sorry—I should have given you a heads-up. I figured I had imposed enough on you and that I needed to get back to my house. That's when I dropped my phone down your stairs this afternoon and it shattered. First thing tomorrow, snow allowing, I'm heading to the Apple store on King Street. I'm so sorry for making you worry—I didn't think to borrow someone's phone to let you know since I knew I'd see you here."

He placed her coat on a hanger, then reached to help me take off mine, pausing slightly when he noticed our dresses but making no comment. "Well," I said, "I'm glad you're here. We need to get to Gallen Hall—can you take me as soon as the dinner is over?"

His eyebrows shot up. "Why?"

I looked at him, surprised. "You didn't figure out the map?"

He shook his head. "What map? Of Gallen Hall?"

"No—the cemetery. I think there's something—" The doorbell rang, cutting me off. He sent it an annoyed look but didn't move to answer it.

I gave him a small shove on his back. "Guests are arriving, and I'd rather we speak in private. We'll talk later."

He looked as if he might argue, but then smiled as he opened the door to allow in a couple I'd seen at another Ashley Hall event. Several other couples followed, including a group of teachers from the school, and it quickly grew loud and crowded as guests began filling the foyer. Nola joined Anthony to help hang up the coats on the rented racks placed in Jack's study, even though I was pretty sure I hadn't assigned her that job on her spreadsheet.

They were kept busy hanging coats for half an hour as people trailed in at different times, most of them having hesitated leaving the appetizer houses until assured the snow would stop. Servers dressed in Revolutionary War–era clothing walked around with tankards of syllabub (made from Sophie's authentic recipe) to keep the party atmosphere going while we waited for everyone to arrive before we were seated.

I was eager to find time to speak with Anthony, but I had to play hostess and give guests the tour of the Christmas trees and discuss how I'd made the centerpieces and wreaths.

"Are these real?" The mother of one of Nola's classmates leaned over to study the oranges in the large bowl on the foyer table that Greco had been kind enough to zhush for me.

"Yes," I said. "All of the fruit in every decoration is real."

She put her hand to the side of her mouth to whisper conspiratorially, "You know, they sell fake ones now that look as good as the real ones, and they last a lot longer."

I kept the smile on my face, considering for a moment calling Sophie and asking the woman to repeat what she'd just said. "Yes, well, I've heard that, too, but we wanted this to be a more authentic experience for the attendees."

The woman moved on as I was approached by an older couple who remembered Nevin Vanderhorst and said they were happy to see the house dressed up for the holidays again. "You've done such a lovely job, my dear," the wife said, her green eyes matching her beautiful emerald earrings. "It certainly has the feeling of being a home again." She took my hand and patted it. "I'm sure Nevin and his mother would be thrilled to know what you've done."

"I'm pretty sure they know," I said, not meaning to say it out loud.

They both looked a little startled as the woman dropped my hand. "Yes, well, I just wanted to let you know that this house finally has the warmth of a home."

"Thank you," I said, feeling my chest puff with love and pride for this house that I'd never wanted to own and that I still had doubts about. But she was right. It was *home* for my family and for me. It was something worth fighting for.

As they walked away, they paused by the centerpiece bowl and I overheard the gentleman say, "I don't believe I've ever seen cloves placed so precisely on oranges in all of my years. . . ."

I hid my smile as I turned toward the front door, watching it open with the last of the arrivals. I knew that Veronica and Michael had been assigned to dinner at my house, so I wasn't surprised to see them, but I was quite certain that Rebecca and Marc weren't on my list. Especially because I'd ensured their names appeared on the dinner list at another house.

"Cousin!" Rebecca squealed as Anthony helped her with her coat. I said hello to Veronica and Michael before they headed into the room to greet Alston and Cooper's parents. I looked in dismay at Rebecca's green velvet dress, thankfully adorned with pink shoes and matching handbag so she, Jayne, and I wouldn't look like triplets. I'd already rethought my whole dressing-the-twins-alike mode in the three seconds it had taken to register that Rebecca was wearing the same dress as Jayne and me.

She hugged both of us before standing back and taking in our dresses. Despite her outward cheeriness, her eyes were slightly puffy and her peaches-and-cream complexion was sprinkled with small, angry bumps along her cheeks. Either pregnancy didn't suit her or her marriage didn't.

"Great minds think alike, right? And I hope you don't mind, but I changed house assignments with another couple so I could come here."

She looked so sad and pathetic that I had to smile. "Sure." I glanced behind her. "Is Marc with you?" I asked, resisting the impulse to cross my fingers behind my back.

Rebecca stuck out her chin. "No. He said he had important 'business' to take care of." She swallowed heavily. "It doesn't matter. I'm here to have fun with my family." She waved to my mother across the room, then smiled shakily at Jayne and me.

"I'm sorry," Anthony said, putting an arm around Rebecca's shoulders. "My brother's a jerk. He has been my whole life. Why don't you sit at our table so you won't have to sit next to strangers?" He looked at me. "Is that all right with you?"

Before I could say no or that I'd spent three whole days and two spreadsheets on planning the seating arrangements, he was headed to the front parlor, where I'd placed Anthony and Jayne at a table with two teachers from Ashley Hall, and I tried not to wince as I noticed him dragging an extra chair to his table. Rebecca leaned close to me. "I hope you were able to use the drawing I gave you."

"I was, actually. It was very helpful."

Jayne widened her eyes at me.

"Thank you," I added.

"So, what was it?" Rebecca asked.

I hesitated, not forgetting that she was Marc's wife. But I owed her. I couldn't have figured anything out without the one critical piece of information she'd given me. And, as she and my mother kept reminding me, she was family. "It's part of a map."

"A map?"

Jayne nodded. "Yes. Melanie figured it all out. The brick puzzle Anthony was working on is the actual cemetery at Gallen Hall, and the two drawings along with a photo Melanie took of the mausoleum gate are part of the same map."

Rebecca actually giggled. "Wow. Marc couldn't have figured that one out in a million years." She sobered quickly. "You won't tell him I said that, right?"

I rolled my eyes. "I have no intention of speaking with your husband ever again, so the answer is no."

She tilted her head to the side. "Never say never. Marc and Anthony will swear up and down that they hate each other, but Marc said he wants his brother to be godfather to our baby."

"Really?" Jayne and I said together.

We were interrupted by our mother approaching, looking elegant and regal in a dark violet silk chiffon dress and matching velvet pumps. "Mellie, darling, I think it's time for everyone to be seated."

With a quick glance at Rebecca, I moved away to find Nola to give her permission to ring the dinner bell; then Cooper appeared by her side to escort her to one of the smaller tables. She hadn't complained about being seated at one of the "children's tables," as she called them, when I told her I'd saved a seat at her table for anyone she cared to invite.

I helped guests find their place cards and take their seats, and I finally headed into the dining room to take my place at the head of the table just as the caterers began serving the soup course. I remembered my manners, taking turns to speak with diners on either side of me, happily answering questions regarding my connection to Ashley Hall, the house, my job, and whether I was wearing a uniform of some sort, which was why there were three of us all dressed alike. I smiled and ate and talked, all the while aware of something niggling at the back of my mind, as tiny and destructive as a termite.

Keenly aware of the time, I listened for the chiming of the grandfather clock in the parlor. As soon as the last guest left, I'd ask Anthony to take me to Gallen Hall. I was already envisioning dumping the rubies in Jack's hands, and then him kissing me, his anger at me easily pushed aside by his gratitude.

Dessert was served at different houses, so there wasn't much lingering after the guests had finished eating. I might have been too enthusiastic about pulling out people's chairs, removing plates, and bringing coats into the foyer in my haste for them to leave, but it had started flurrying again and I could hear an imaginary clock ticking in my head.

Despite a few stragglers wandering around the foyer chatting and examining the decorations, I went in search of Anthony to make sure he was ready to go as soon as the last guest departed. I found Jayne saying good-bye to Veronica and Michael at the front door.

Her smile faded when she saw me approach. "Where's Anthony?"

"I was coming to ask you the same thing. Wasn't he with you at dinner?"

"Yes, but right after the main course was served, he excused himself, saying that you'd asked him to come find you before the meal was over because you needed him for something."

I shook my head slowly. "No. I never said that." Our eyes met as a sick feeling, as viscous and dark as octopus ink, flooded my insides.

"He must be here somewhere," Jayne said, an unmistakable note of panic in her voice. "I must have misunderstood."

"I'm sure you're right," I said, although I had no such

certainty. Together we looked in all of the downstairs rooms including the kitchen and powder room, and even searched the back garden. We found our parents kissing under the mistletoe strung across the threshold of Jack's office. I coughed loudly as we approached, and they, mercifully, pulled away from each other. "Has either of you seen Anthony?"

My father nodded. "I was headed to the bathroom and saw him leave out the back door about forty-five minutes ago. I assumed you'd sent him on some errand."

"No. I didn't." I met Jayne's gaze. Without a word she ran toward the front door and threw it open, leaving it ajar as she raced down the piazza to the front walk. I met her at the front door on her return, her eyes wide and glazed.

"His car's not here." She looked at me. "His car's not *here*," she repeated, as if to convince herself.

I grabbed her hand and pulled her inside, closing the door behind us.

"This isn't good, is it?" she asked.

"No," I said. "It's not."

Our parents appeared with Rebecca, all three bundled for the weather. "We're going to take Rebecca with us, if that's all right. It was a lovely event," Mother said, and kissed me on the cheek.

I tried to act relaxed, as if my world hadn't suddenly been shaken like a snow globe. We said our good-byes and I watched them leave. Then I put my face close to Jayne's. "Did you talk about the map at dinner?"

She shook her head. "No," she said. "I didn't." A loud, choking sob erupted from her throat. "But . . ."

"But what?"

"But Rebecca did. She mentioned how you'd figured out everything with her help. I didn't stop her because it was Anthony. I didn't think I needed to. But she didn't say anything about how the three drawings and the brick puzzle have to be used together because she doesn't know about it. That's a good thing, right?"

"Oh, my gosh. Oh, my *gosh*." I squeezed my head between my hands as if that would somehow eradicate all the stupidity that apparently lived there. I remembered the niggling feeling at the back of my head that had started when Rebecca mentioned that Marc wanted Anthony to be the godfather to their baby. "Marc and Anthony—they're just pretending. They're not estranged."

"But why . . ." Jayne stopped, her eyes widening, her breath coming in short, hollow puffs. "They set us up." Her face lost color as the implications settled on her. "Everything Anthony said to us was a lie. He used us. All of us."

I nodded, thinking of snippets of all the conversations I'd had with Anthony, all the information that I'd shared that he'd told Marc. Beneath the shame and humiliation, I felt the rolling burn of anger. "I have no doubt that they're both at Gallen Hall now."

"But they don't know everything, right? They still need to figure out how you have to put them all together."

"They will, though." I closed my eyes, allowing the dismal dread of failure to swallow me. And somewhere, in the black darkness, I heard my grandmother's voice. *Jack.* I couldn't fail him now, not when he needed me the most. I opened my eyes, a renewed sense of determination flooding my veins. "We can't let them beat us. We just can't."

"But how—"

"Give me your car keys. The caterer is blocking me in and I don't have time to waste to ask them to move."

"Where are you going?"

"To Gallen Hall. To the cemetery. I've got to get those rubies before Marc finds them."

"But what if you run into Marc and Anthony?" Jayne asked, her eyes wide.

"I don't know," I said somberly. "I can only hope that they're still trying to figure out what to do with the map. Or that they're waiting until morning. And if not, then I'll think about that when I have to."

Jayne shook her head. "I'm going with you," she said, already marching toward the door. "So at least it's two against two if it comes to that."

"Absolutely not. You need to stay here. If I need help, I'll call you. Besides, it wouldn't do for both of us to get into trouble without backup. And I don't want anyone else knowing yet—they'll just try to stop me and then I'll be too late."

I could tell her resistance was weakening. "But what should I tell Jack?"

"You don't need to tell him anything. Let him sleep. I'll let him know when I bring home the rubies." I offered a hopeful smile that she didn't return.

"Melanie, I can't let you go alone. We're stronger together, remember?"

"I won't be alone. Eliza is there, and she's on our side. I now understand why she pushed Anthony down the stairs."

"And wrecked his car?"

I shook my head. "No. Now that I know that Marc and Anthony are cut from the same cloth, I wouldn't be surprised if he wrecked it himself to get our sympathy."

"But Lawrence is there, too, Melanie. Remember what happened at the mausoleum."

My arm hurt at the memory, but I couldn't let fear hold me back. There was just too much at stake. "Give me your keys, Jayne. Please. We're running out of time."

With a heavy sigh, she went to the makeshift coatrack and pulled her purse from a hanger. "For the record, I don't agree with what you're doing. I think this would be one of your decisions that Jack would call rash and un-thought-out. Just let me tell him—"

"No. He needs his rest. Let him sleep. I'll tell him everything when I get back."

"If you get back." She dropped her keys in my outstretched hand.

"What do you mean, *if*? It's not like Marc and Anthony are going to kill me or anything."

Her eyes widened. "I used to think Anthony wouldn't be capable of anything like that. Until tonight." She swallowed, and I thought for a moment she might actually cry. "Apparently, I'm not a very good judge of character."

Before I knew what I was doing, I'd put my arms around her for a quick hug. She looked as surprised as I felt. "Well," I said, "if it makes you feel any better, neither am I. At least this way we have a chance to beat them at their own game." I turned toward the demilune chest in the hallway and opened the doors to pull out a heavy pair of sweatpants and waterproof ankle boots. "I slip these on to take the dogs out," I offered in explanation. "They'll keep me warm and dry." I sent a paranoid glance toward the stairs, afraid that I'd see Jack and he'd tell me not to go. "I'll put these on in the car."

"Here, then," she said, diving into her coat pockets and pulling out a pair of thick gloves. "These are waterproof and fleece lined." I gratefully accepted them, knowing they'd be a lot warmer than my leather gloves. "And this." She placed a thick knit hat over my head, pulling it below my ears and tucking in my hair. "But it doesn't mean I'm agreeing that you should be doing this."

"I know. And if anybody asks, I'll let them know that you tried to stop me."

"I'll remember that." Jayne stepped forward to tuck my scarf into the collar of my coat. "I have a phone charger in the car, so plug in your phone so it'll have a full charge by the time you get to Gallen Hall. I want you to call me when you get there, and I'll want you to check in every fifteen minutes with a text. And if you don't, I'm calling Thomas."

"Really, Jayne, I don't—"

"That's the deal. Either agree or I'm going to tell Jack right now."

"Fine," I said, moving toward the door, making sure no one else was in the foyer to see me leave.

"Dad's shed is unlocked," Jayne said. "You'll want a shovel and a flashlight."

"Right," I said, embarrassed that I probably wouldn't have thought about either until I was almost at the cemetery. I pulled open the door and saw Greco's hurricane lanterns flickering brightly as white flakes blew across the piazza, dancing around the glass like fairies.

"My car has front-wheel drive," Jayne offered. "But if there's anything more than half an inch, you won't get any traction. Just remember to keep your phone charged."

I nodded, walking toward the door at the end of the pi-azza, afraid to look back just in case I changed my mind.

"I love you, Melanie. I'm glad you're my sister."

I just nodded as I let myself through the piazza door, unable to speak because of the sudden lump in my throat.

CHAPTER
34

Fat snowflakes were falling by the time I pulled onto the Ashley River Bridge. Only a few other drivers braved the roads, tempting fate and the potential closing of the bridges. I tried not to think about how I would get back with closed bridges and icy roads. Charleston hadn't had a significant snowfall since 1989, so, except for the northern transplants, not many of us knew how to drive in snow.

My hands hurt from clutching the steering wheel too tightly. I flexed my fingers, trying to make the blood flow back into the tips. I didn't dare take my eyes off the road to check on the status of my phone charge, but I'd plugged it in just as Jayne had instructed. Remembering her concern brought me a small comfort, making me feel less alone on my mission, the cord charging my phone like a lifeline.

I found the road to Gallen Hall after missing it the first time because of the snow. My father's gardening tools shifted in the trunk, clanking loudly as I slowly drove over the uneven dirt road, straining to see through the falling snowflakes. In addition to a battery-powered camping light I'd found in the shed, I'd brought a shovel, a spade, and a pick. I'd grabbed the latter at the last second, realizing that the ground would be rock-hard from the cold. I refused to consider that I might not be strong enough to swing the pick with enough force to even break the surface. Failure wasn't an option, not after I'd come this far. I thought of Jack and how much finding these rubies would mean for him both emotionally and professionally. I recognized, too, that I

wanted Jack back—the charming, smart, and capable husband and father I loved. With renewed determination, I
straightened my shoulders, then turned Jayne's car into the
deep, dark woods, where the trees seemed to swallow me
as I drew closer to the house.

When I neared the edge of the woods, I stopped the car
and switched off my headlights so I wouldn't alert anyone
who might be in the house. My plan was to slip into the
cemetery without being seen, do what needed to be done,
then head back home before the snowfall got heavy enough
to close the roads. It had seemed like a clear plan when I'd
left the house, and only now that it was too late could I spot
the giant leaps of faith it would take to successfully execute
it. I glanced at my phone, knowing one call from me for
help would be all it would take. But I had to try. And if I
failed, then I'd call.

I peered down the dark road, the snow reflecting the
ambient light from the sky like some celestial flashlight,
making it easier to see. With a sigh, I reached over to the
floor of the passenger seat and grabbed Jayne's umbrella.
Bracing myself against the cold and snow, I jumped out of
the car and began walking through the thin coating of
snow, stopping before I reached the horseshoe of the front
drive in an attempt to remain unseen.

With an exhalation of relief, I saw no lights on in the
house, nor did I pick out the shapes of a car or cars on the
front drive. Either Anthony and Marc had stayed in town,
not wanting to risk the weather, or they hadn't yet figured
out the final clue.

I felt lighter as I made my way back to the car. I flipped
on the headlights, then drove past the house toward the
cemetery, stopping in front of the main gate, the lights from
the car shining through the black bars and reflecting off the
fat snowflakes. I put the car in park, leaving the headlights
and wipers on before reaching under the seat for the drawings and the map that Jayne had placed there when we'd left
her house.

I pushed the seat back and placed the map on the steering

wheel to orient myself to where the four black Sharpie marks indicated the spots in the cemetery. I looked up at the gate and the adjacent fence sections, then back to the map, realizing that the edges of the drawings corresponded to the iron gate designs that edged the cemetery.

Like the red lights on the floor of a plane that led a passenger to the emergency exit door, the fence designs served the same purpose, instructing the treasure hunter how deep into the cemetery one needed to go before bearing left or right to each dot on the map. It was brilliant, really, and I turned my head to share it with Jack, too late remembering that I was alone.

I remembered Yvonne telling us that no burials had taken place in the cemetery since Eliza, Lawrence, and Alexander had been interred in the mausoleum in 1782. It had never occurred to us to wonder why, even though Gallen Hall had been inhabited for more than two centuries afterward and people had presumably died during that period. The moratorium on burials had been part of Carrollton Vanderhorst's great master clue, and we'd overlooked it completely.

Not wanting to get the paper wet, I pulled out my phone and took a photo of the map with the dots marked, then of the pattern of each section of fence I needed to find. Having the images on my phone meant I could make them bigger, making it easier to see the intricate designs.

I sent a text to Jayne to let her know I'd arrived, that there was no sign of Marc or Anthony, and that I was about to head into the cemetery. I made no mention of the fat blobs of snow now splattering quietly onto my windshield. I hit SEND, then slid the phone into my coat pocket. I'd deal with that later. Somehow. I popped the trunk, pulled Jayne's hat lower over my ears, then exited the car.

The smell of gunpowder permeated the air, the jangling of a horse harness ringing out in the quiet of falling snow. I quickly retrieved the camping light from the trunk, knowing with certainty that I wasn't alone. I held it aloft, turning around in a circle, seeing no one, dead or alive, but registering the scent of horses and leather now mingling with that of gunpowder.

"Eliza?" I called out, more because I needed to hear the sound of a human voice than because I expected to hear her answer. But she was there. I felt her presence, warm and comforting, as if she knew that I wanted to expose the truth about her death. And maybe even to let the world know that she'd been a patriot and had stayed true to her cause despite her heart calling her in another direction.

Using the camping light to see the way, I walked through the unlocked front gate, pulling out my phone to access the map and guide me to where the first spot was indicated. A dark shadow emerged from behind an ancient obelisk at the rear of the cemetery. I jerked the light up, trying to find out who—or what—it was. The blood rushed through my ears, my breath frosty puffs blowing out in quick succession. I stayed perfectly still for a long moment, my gaze trained on the spot, but nothing moved.

The sound of iron clanging made me jump. I swung the light toward the mausoleum, realizing it must have been the door swinging shut, briefly wondering why it had been open. The sound of whispering voices came from behind and in front of me, the snow seeming to blur the words, making it impossible to tell what was being said.

My feet crunched over the frozen grass and a thin layer of snow. I was careful to avoid the sunken spots where Sophie had warned me the oldest wooden caskets, some piled in as many as three or four layers, had disintegrated under the ground, making the earth above the concave spots treacherous to walk on. I shivered at the thought of slipping beneath the surface and being buried alive, out here alone where no one could hear me scream. At least no one who could help me.

I shone the light at the fence, studying the pattern on each panel and comparing it with the picture on the phone. The snow was falling faster now, and I had to continually wipe it off my screen. I had reached the halfway point in the fence when I matched the pattern to the edge of the brick puzzle, telling me that it was time to turn right and head into the middle of the cemetery.

The whispers, louder now, had the cadence of a taunt, or a threat. I stopped to listen, recognizing one word among the others, nearly smothered by the falling snow. *Traitors*. I swallowed down the fear and uncertainty. I wasn't by nature a brave person, but at that moment I had no other choice.

I walked around a slight indentation in the ground, then nearly ran into a headstone. I glanced down at my map to make sure I was at the right spot, then shone my light on the slate face of the headstone. The words were worn by the elements but still legible. Leaning closer, I read the name: HERA. I put the light closer, trying to find a last name or dates, but there was nothing. I squatted to see the bottom, scraping snow off to make sure I hadn't missed anything. I sat back, staring at a carving that would be easily missed by the casual observer.

It was of a peacock feather, long and slender, the eye clearly marked at its end. If I hadn't been so cold and afraid, I might have appreciated the cleverness of it all. I remembered Anthony mentioning that Eliza buried her favorite peacocks in the cemetery, and seeing about a dozen stones with only first names on them on my previous visit. Until the Civil War, when the last one had been eaten, the family had apparently continued to bury the birds here, either intentionally or inadvertently helping to hide the four gravesites I was sure were indicated on the map.

Encouraged by my success, I dug the heel of my boot into the ground in front of the stone, stirring up dead grass and dirt so I could find it again without using the map, assuming the snow stopped soon. Looking at my map again, my frozen fingers nearly dropping my phone twice as I remembered to text Jayne that I was okay, I found the other three graves, all with female Greek mythological names. I marked them with the heel of my boot as I'd done the first one, inordinately proud of myself.

I wanted to sink down onto the ground and cry with

relief. But I knew I couldn't or I'd risk hypothermia. I needed to keep going. Jack needed me to keep going, no matter how many times in my head I could hear him telling me not to think I could solve all of our problems by myself. But I was here, and I had figured out where Lafayette's treasure was buried. I needed to take care of this now, or risk our losing to Marc Longo one more time.

First, I needed to sit in the car with the heater blasting to defrost myself. I knew I probably had a candy bar some-where in my purse to give me a burst of energy I would definitely need. Then I'd grab the pick from the trunk and figure out what I was supposed to do with it.

I was so focused on getting to the car that it took me a moment to become aware of movement from the direction of the mausoleum. A violent shiver went through me that had nothing to do with the snow pelting my face and freezing my toes as I recalled my arm being pulled through the gate by an unseen hand.

A bright spotlight flipped on, blinding me, but not be-fore I'd had the chance to register who the two figures were standing behind it.

"Thank you, Melanie. Such a help, as always." Marc Longo moved forward to stand in front of me. "You must be freezing."

I clenched my teeth to keep them from chattering, and looked behind his shoulder to see Anthony. He wasn't cow-ering, exactly, but he seemed to want to hide behind his brother.

"I hope you're ashamed of yourself," I shouted at him, although the effect was muted by my stiff jaw.

"For helping his brother?" Marc offered. "He did the right thing. As you did, helping us find the treasure. For a brief moment, I thought Anthony and I should take the time to figure it out ourselves, and then I realized we didn't need to bother. You're such a worker bee, Melanie—we knew you'd be on it. We parked our cars out back and waited in the warm house for you to do all the work." He feigned a concerned expression. "We left hot chocolate on the stove for you, if you'd like it. And there's a fire going in the kitchen with a chair in front of it waiting for you."

I frowned. "What? And leave the treasure out here for you to find?"

Marc threw back his head and laughed. He held a can out toward me. "I've brought spray paint to mark the four headstones, so when it warms up in a few days and the ground has thawed a bit, we can go in at our leisure and dig up Lafayette's treasure. Except this time we'll remember to lock the gate against intruders and have someone standing guard."

It occurred to me then that he didn't know what the treasure was. And that it didn't matter to him. All he cared about was winning and crushing Jack and getting what he wanted. If he came into possession of a fortune, too, even better.

"But I found it." I sounded like a child on a playground, but I couldn't think of a better way to say it.

"Yes, you did. But you found it on Anthony's property. According to South Carolina law, it legally belongs to him. Sure, you could probably take us to court, but the process would be long and expensive and you and I both know that you can't afford it. Who knows what the stress might do to Jack? And because you're family, I'm not going to charge you with trespassing. This time."

An icy wind blew through the cemetery, slapping me in the face and forming small tornadoes of snow around us. I saw Anthony glance at them uneasily, and it occurred to me that the funnels might not be part of the natural world. The distinct clang of a horse harness made Marc spin around, taking the light with him. I blinked in the darkness, aware of the sparkle of a gold brooch against a dark form. And behind that was the man from the cistern photo—Lawrence, with the dark hollows for eyes, his white stockings bright against the night. And right before Marc's light blinded me again, I saw the bloody hole in his white shirt.

I was shaking with anger and cold and fear. I had lost everything, and I had no one to blame but myself. I had once loved my aloneness, my independence, which meant I didn't have to rely on anyone but myself. Even with the expansion of my family in the last years, I'd still seen myself as a separate entity—out of either habit or stubbornness, I didn't know, and it didn't matter anymore. Whatever the reason, it had been my undoing.

"But I found it," I repeated, incapable of expressing every emotion that was running through me. I cringed at how toddlerlike I sounded and was oddly relieved that it was so cold that my watery eyes disguised the fact that angry tears were streaming down my face.

"Like I said," Marc responded calmly, "it doesn't matter. Gallen Hall Plantation belongs to Anthony, and anything found on his property belongs to him."

"Not exactly," a voice called from the front gate.

"Jack?" I said, relief battling with horror in my voice.

Marc jerked around, shining his light in Jack's direction, illuminating three figures walking toward us.

"Jayne?" Anthony stepped forward, then stopped, as if realizing that she might not be happy to see him.

I squinted through the dark and the falling snow, recognizing the tall form of Detective Thomas Riley, my knees almost weak with relief that I was no longer alone.

Marc barked out a laugh. "Wrong again, Jack. Gallen Hall belongs to Anthony. Therefore, whatever is found here belongs to him." He nodded in Thomas's direction. "I'm glad you brought the police with you to help enforce the law. Although I'm hoping reasonable heads will prevail so we won't have to reduce ourselves to using force."

Jack now stood in the circle of light but didn't come stand next to me. He didn't look at me, either, and I told myself it was so he could stare Marc down. Keeping his voice low, he said, "You're right. Gallen Hall does belong to Anthony. But the cemetery doesn't. When Gallen Hall was sold all those years ago, the cemetery wasn't part of the deal. It was still owned by Vanderhorst descendants, until Nevin Vanderhorst willed it to Melanie. Which means that what is found in this cemetery belongs to her."

We all stared at Jack in stunned silence, until Marc struggled to find his voice. "You're lying."

"He's not," Jayne said. "After Melanie left tonight, I realized too late that Anthony might lay claim to the treasure and I wanted to know the legal implications." She shot a quick glance of apology in my direction. "So I told Jack everything, and he called Yvonne from the archives. She has access to several databases on her home computer and was able to look up the property deed to trace ownership. The cemetery wasn't included in any sale, remaining the property of the Vanderhorst family until Melanie inherited Nevin Vanderhorst's estate. She e-mailed me a copy, if you'd like to see it."

"This is ridiculous," Marc said, moving toward Jack just as Thomas took a step in Marc's direction. He fumbled with his words for a moment before a grin lifted his mouth. "You're still trespassing. To get to the cemetery you had to pass through private property and park your cars on land belonging to Anthony." He faced Thomas. "I want you to arrest these four people for trespassing."

"So much for family," I mumbled.

"So you'll have time to remove whatever is buried under those markers?" Jack said. "I think not."

Marc turned to Anthony. "Tell them, Anthony. Tell them that you want them off of your property now."

"Don't you dare," Jayne shouted, approaching Anthony with a raised hand. He didn't even bother to block her slap.

"Detective, that's physical assault," Marc shouted. "We are pressing charges and want her arrested."

"No." Anthony stepped away from where Marc was facing off with Jack. "We're not pressing charges. I deserved that."

He began to walk away, brushing roughly against his brother and making Marc stumble.

"Hey, what's your problem?" Marc said, rushing after Anthony and grabbing him by the shoulders. "You said it was easier than taking candy from a baby, remember?"

Anthony tried to pull back, but Marc wouldn't let go. He

tilted his head as he stared at his younger brother. "You didn't sleep with her, did you? I told you not to complicate things."

Anthony drew his fist back for a punch, but before he could swing, Marc flew backward, propelled by an unseen force and thrown twenty feet before landing flat on his back with a grunt.

Thomas was the only one to move, rushing over to Marc. Instead of taking the offered hand to help him up, Marc twisted in the opposite direction, pulling himself to stand and angrily dusting the snow from the sleeves of his jacket. "What the—"

Before he could finish the sentence, he was knocked down again, then dragged through the snow by his feet toward the mausoleum. He clawed at the ground, trying to find purchase, his face showing his terror. Jayne and I both moved forward to help, but whatever was pulling him was too strong and fast. Before we reached him, the mausoleum had swallowed him, his head bumping like a rubber ball against the brick steps, the gate slamming in our faces. We wrapped our fingers around the bars and shook them, but the gate remained unyielding.

"Marc!" Anthony shouted as he and Thomas ran up behind us. Thomas had grabbed Marc's light, and he shone it inside, moving from one crypt to another, then back, looking for Marc.

"Marc!" Thomas shouted. Slowly, he trained the light on the top of Lawrence's crypt and paused. The lid had been slid back unevenly, a corner of it hanging over the edge, the opening big enough for a man to fit through.

"Is there another entrance to this?" Thomas asked.

I half listened to Anthony's answer as I became aware of two black shadows in front of Lawrence's crypt. As Jayne and I watched, the shadows took on human forms. I told my feet to back away, to start running as fast as they could in the opposite direction, but I was frozen, forced to stay and watch whatever was about to unfold. Lying prone, the red spot on his cravat larger now, was the man I recognized as Lawrence, and standing over him was an older man with graying hair pulled back in a ponytail and wearing a heavy cape. He turned to look at me, his cape billowing open and revealing a pistol in his hand. His eyes were piercing, asking me for something I couldn't understand.

"Forgiveness," Jayne whispered from beside me.

I nodded, because I knew that was the word I'd heard inside my head. It was the reason I wasn't afraid. I understood that I wasn't meant to be. And when I looked down at the prone figure of Lawrence, I understood something else, too.

"It's his father," Jayne whispered. "It was Carrollton Vanderhorst who killed him. He didn't feel as if he had a choice."

I nodded, knowing she was right. "Neither did Lawrence." I closed my eyes, trying to hear the voices in my head, to decipher the words that sounded as if they were out of order, nodding when I finally understood. "He felt betrayed by Eliza for being a spy and for loving another man, so he killed them both." I looked at the spirit of the old man, his face a mask of old grief. "Tell Lawrence you forgive him for what he did," I whispered. "So he can forgive you, too."

A soft rumbling vibrated the earth beneath us and I heard Anthony swear behind me.

"It's okay," Jayne said. "Their souls are being released."

The ground trembled one more time as lightning flashed through the sky above us, showering us with the smell of burnt ions and filling the mausoleum with a bright, bluish white light. When it had faded, the mausoleum was empty, the only sounds a low moaning from the direction of the opened crypt and the click of the gate latch as the door slowly began swinging open.

Anthony pushed it fully open and entered, Thomas and Jayne close behind. I felt a soft tug on my arm and turned around, thinking it was Jack, but no one was there. "Eliza?"

A firm push propelled me away from the mausoleum. I grabbed my phone and turned on the flashlight, unsure

what had happened to my camping light. "Jack?" I called
out. I spun around with my light, looking for him. I'd begun
heading toward the front gate when a hard tug on my arm
propelled me in the opposite direction.

I had taken only three steps before I saw it was Eliza,
and where she was directing me. One of the soft dips that I
had just navigated around during my gravestone search was
now a gaping hole, a blemish on the pristine white ground.

"Jack!" I screamed. I ran to the edge of the hole and
stared down at the mix of dark soil and snow, Rebecca's
dream of Jack being buried alive playing like a movie reel
in my head. "Jack!" I screamed again.

Jayne came from behind and knelt next to me. "There,"
she shouted, pointing to something pale and still near the
bottom of the six-foot hole. "He's there."

I might have screamed again, the sight of Jack's closed
eyes and pale face at the bottom of a grave too surreal to
accept.

"I'll get help," Jayne said, moving to stand.

While she ran to get Thomas, I lowered myself into the
pit, no longer feeling the cold or the fear of the last few
hours. I didn't think about how I would get out of the pit or
even whether it was done collapsing. I had no idea how
many coffins had been buried here, or how deep. I didn't
care. If something happened to Jack, nothing else would
ever matter again.

His body was completely covered up to his nose with the
dirt and snow. I carefully crawled over, taking care to distribute my weight evenly, until my fingers could reach his
face and begin brushing the dirt off his chin and mouth.
"Jack, it's Mellie. Don't talk—I've got to get the dirt off
your face first. Just nod that you can hear me."

He didn't move or respond in any way, his face as still
and colorless as the moon as he lay at the bottom of the
grave, just as Rebecca had seen in her dreams.

Kiss him. I wasn't sure if the words had been spoken
aloud, but I looked up at the edge of the collapsed grave and

saw the British soldier standing next to Eliza, his arm around her. *Kiss him.*

I pinched Jack's nose closed and pressed my mouth against his and blew a deep breath. When nothing happened, I did it again, harder this time, imagining his lungs expanding with the air of my breath. He gasped, his eyes blinking open as he took a breath on his own, his eyelids fluttering until he caught sight of me.

"Oh, Jack. You're going to be okay. I'm here. It's Mellie. I found the rubies!" His eyes focused on me and I smiled. "I love you, Jack."

His eyes looked behind me to where Anthony and Thomas had replaced Eliza and Alexander and were peering at us from the top of the grave. Then Jack's eyes shifted back to me, and there was no warmth or light in them. "Go. To. Hell."

CHAPTER
35

The rest of the night was mostly a blur—the fire and rescue sirens, the ambulance, the trip to the hospital with
Thomas and Jayne in the detective's four-wheel-drive truck.
I remembered Jack turning his head away from me as they
loaded him into the back of the ambulance and strapped
him lying down into a bench seat, and I remembered the
shock of seeing Marc as they slid his gurney in next to Jack.
I didn't recognize him at first, and not because of the large,
swollen bruise on the side of his face. It was because of his
hair—his thick, dark brown hair had gone completely
white, incongruous with his black eyebrows and unlined
face. He asked me to call Rebecca, and I did, and that was
the last coherent memory I had.

When I awoke the following morning, I was at my mother's house. I vaguely recalled her picking me up at the hospital and telling me that Jack was fine except for some
bruising and a sprained ankle. They'd wanted to keep him
overnight for observation, and even though I'd been prepared to wait and bring him home the next morning, he'd
refused to see me and had requested someone else—anyone
else—to drive him. I'd been too stunned to cry and allowed
my mother to lead me from the hospital, as Jayne and
Thomas had offered to stay and chauffeur Jack when he
was discharged.

I sat up in my old bedroom, feeling disoriented, as if I'd
been standing on a moving sidewalk that had suddenly
stopped. I recalled Jack's hurtful words and could feel

nothing but shame, knowing I'd deserved them. I needed my babies, needed to see them and hold them and talk with Nola and confirm we were all going to be all right. That Jack would forgive me. I threw off the covers and pulled on the green velvet dress I'd worn to the party the night before, then ran downstairs in search of my mother.

She was just putting down her cell phone when I walked into the kitchen. She was dressed and perfectly made-up, but her gaze didn't falter as she took in my unbrushed hair and wrinkled dress. "That was Amelia. She said the twins have been perfect angels and she's happy to keep them a little longer if you need her to. She already asked Nola to bring over more supplies just in case your answer was yes."

I opened my mouth to say something, but all that came out was a loud sob that quickly become a torrent of tears I couldn't stop. She came over to me and enveloped me in a warm and sweetly scented embrace, bringing back old memories of when I was a little girl. The girl I'd been before she'd left me behind.

My mother brought me into the parlor and sat me down on the couch, where I continued to sob for five minutes, until I had no more tears left. She waited a moment before pulling back and lifting my chin with her fingers.

"So, what are you going to do, Mellie?"

"You know?" I sniffled.

She nodded. "When Jayne called me to tell me you were all at the hospital, she filled me in on what happened." She kept all judgment from her voice, making me so grateful that I cried a fresh torrent of tears.

When I was done, I wiped my eyes with the back of my hand, recalling what she'd just said. This wasn't how I'd anticipated the conversation going. I'd envisioned her commiserating with me, telling me that even though things hadn't turned out as planned, I'd been smart and resourceful and everything had worked out all right in the end. And then I'd sit and listen while she told me what I needed to do next. When she didn't speak, I asked, "So, what should I do now?"

"You've really hurt Jack, Mellie. And your marriage. The damage might even be irreparable."

I stood abruptly. "Why are you saying this? I thought you would be on my side."

"I *am* on your side. That's why I'm saying this. Because someone has to. You deliberately kept Jack in the dark so you, for reasons I've yet to determine, could solve a mystery and keep the glory all for yourself. Even though you'd promised Jack you wouldn't. You lied to him, Mellie, and now you expect him to applaud your cleverness. That's not how a good marriage works. I thought you'd already learned that, but apparently I was wrong."

I felt the strong impulse to find a disconnected phone and call my grandmother.

"She'd tell you the same thing." My mother looked at me with knowing eyes. "No, I can't read minds, but I know how you think. And finding someone to agree with you is not how you mature. Sometimes you remind me of a moth at a porch light, thinking that if it hits the light one more time it will get a different result. I'd like to think you're smarter than that."

I sat back down on the couch, deflated. "So what do I do?"

"What do you think you should do?"

She raised her brows as my eyes met hers. "Apologize?"

"That would be a good start. It won't be enough, but it's a start."

My heart jerked and skidded. "What do you mean, it won't be enough?"

"You've apologized before, remember? And made promises. But neither seemed to be important enough to you. You have to find a way to really mean it, and to make sure he knows it. Just realize that it won't happen overnight. Assuming he can forgive you." She took my hand. "Mellie, I know I'm partly why you are the way you are. I abandoned you, leaving you to be raised by your alcoholic father. To survive your childhood you decided to rely only on yourself. And I'm so proud of you, of how you've succeeded despite everything. I think your resistance to change is because you've never wanted to forget how far you've come since you were that lonely little girl. Or that you've done it all by yourself." She squeezed my hand. "But just because you might rely on someone else doesn't negate any of where you've been or what you are. You need to learn to accept that."

I shook my head. "I'm *not* resisting change. I want to change—I'm ready for it. I just need to let Jack know." I stood up again. "I'll go over there right now."

My mother let go of my hands with a sigh. I marched to the door and yanked it open. "Oh." The street was indistinguishable from the curbs or sidewalks under the white layer of snow, the points at the tops of the iron fencing less menacing with their caps of white.

Mother came from behind me and shut the door. "May I suggest a shower and hair brushing first? There are new toothbrushes and toothpaste in the linen closet in your bathroom, and you can use my makeup. I'll leave an outfit on your bed—something in a bright and cheerful color— and your snow boots are on the back porch steps and your coat is in the hall closet. Carry your heels so you can put them on when you go talk to Jack. Men do love high heels."

"And you think that will work?"

She shook her head. "No. But it can't hurt."

I frowned. "Maybe I should walk barefoot through the snow to let him know how sorry I am."

"It might be worth a try," Mother said, embracing me. Holding me at arm's length, she added, "Jack loves you so much, Mellie. And you love him, too. And you've got those two precious babies and Nola, who need you two to make this work. Love is a great foundation, but there has to be trust, too. Sadly, trust is a lot harder to maintain than love. You're going to have to work very, very hard to regain his trust." She stepped back, eyeing me up and down. "The only thing I know for sure is that looking like a hot mess isn't a good way to start. And it will give you time to think about what you want to say. You know how badly things can go when you act and speak rashly."

I hurried away up the stairs before I began to sob again.

∞

The winter wonderland I crossed on my walk home was something out of a storybook. Amelia texted me a photograph of the twins bundled up like Eskimos sitting in the snow next to a snowman with stick arms and a carrot nose and what looked like Oreo cookie eyes. The picture made me want to cry, so I slipped my phone back in my pocket and continued to trudge down the street.

The temperature had already begun to climb with the rising of the sun in a cloudless blue sky. The sound of dripping gutters and tree branches tittered along both sides of the street like happy birdsong. Children and adults alike were outside using anything they could find for sleds—including flattened cardboard boxes and inner tubes—spending most of their time looking for something that resembled a hill to slide down. I returned smiles and waves, but my heart felt as frozen as the snow beneath my boots.

My house on Tradd Street was oddly quiet when I opened the front door, only the sounds of the Sunday church bells from St. Michael's echoing throughout the vacant rooms. Someone—probably my dad—had moved the furniture back into position, the temporary tables and chairs already folded and stacked in the dining room to be picked up the following day by the rental company.

The house had the sad, empty air of finality, the laughter and chatter of so many people ushered outside leaving behind only silence. Even the wandering spirits that lived there were suddenly absent, either exhausted from all the activity of the party, or worried about what was going to happen next. Or maybe that was just me.

"Jack?" I called, slipping out of my boots and putting on my heels.

I heard movement from upstairs, but no one responded.

"Jack?" I called again, climbing the stairs quickly. I stood at the top, aware of the lightness in the air, as if it had just been cleansed.

I peered into Nola's room and spotted the jewelry cabinet, all the drawers and the top neatly closed. I thought of the hidden compartment and imagined Eliza bending forward and hiding the brooch with the four disguised rubies. I remembered examining it with Sophie, how she'd said the hinges were broken because the door had been ripped off as if by an impatient hand. I pictured Lawrence threatening Eliza to tell him where the rubies were, or spying on her to discover where they'd been hidden. He'd killed her regardless, making it look like suicide. And his own father had killed him as punishment or to get the rubies back; we'd never know. But they had made their peace with each other in the mausoleum, and Eliza and Alexander were gone, too, together finally for all eternity. Since they'd helped me find Jack, I'd no longer felt their presence. It felt good to know we'd helped one another, a connection through time that I was lucky enough to experience. I'd never thought of it that way before, and I felt my chest expand as I considered the implications.

I paused on the threshold, the white world outside bathing the walls in bright reflected light from the snow, and took a deep breath. It was as if the world was agreeing that it was time for a new start. A commitment to a new way of being. Feeling emboldened, I headed down the hallway to the bedroom I shared with Jack.

The door was slightly ajar, and I pushed it open, expecting to find Jack in bed with tissues in a wastebasket next to him. Instead, the bed had been made, and a suitcase was opened on top of it with several of Jack's sweaters, shirts, socks, and underclothes already packed neatly inside.

"Jack?" I called again, my voice thready.

He emerged from the bathroom carrying his dopp kit, limping on his wrapped ankle. He didn't even glance in my direction as he walked past me toward his suitcase.

"What are you doing?"

"I'm packing." He moved a few shirts around to make room for the dopp kit, then closed the case, the sound from the zipper horrifyingly final.

"Packing? But why? You're sick and you're hurt. You should be in bed."

"I will be. My parents' rental apartment on State Street is vacant and they're letting me use it."

The breath rushed from my lungs and I had to grab the bedpost to stay upright. "But . . . but you don't need to leave. I came to apologize. To tell you I know I was wrong, that I shouldn't have left on my own last night and without telling you what was going on. It was stupid and rash, and I did it anyway." I looked up at him imploringly. "But I've learned my lesson. I won't ever break your trust again. I've changed. I really have. Last night taught me that I have people in my life who love me and who I can rely on. I don't have to go it alone."

As if I hadn't spoken, he picked up his suitcase and walked out to the hallway and then down the stairs. I rushed after him. "Jack, stop. Please. I said I was sorry."

He stopped and looked back at me, his face devoid of all emotion except anger. "It's too little, too late. I'll let you know when I'd like to see JJ and Sarah so we can work out a visiting arrangement."

"'A visiting arrangement'? How long are you planning to be gone?"

He shook his head. "I have no idea. I need time away from you to think."

"To think? About what? I love you, and I said I'm sorry. I've changed—please give me a chance to show it."

"I've given you more chances than I can count. I just can't live this way anymore. I love you, but it's not enough. Not when I can't trust you."

He took his coat from the closet and put it on. I wanted to throw myself at him, cling to his lapels and force him to stay, regardless of how degrading that would be. I was already hollowed out, scraped clean, with only my empty shell remaining. I had no pride or shame left, just the sickening feeling that I had lost Jack, and I had no one to blame but myself.

"I'll be back this week while you're at work to get the rest of my things." He frowned. "Nola wants to stay here, although she says she's not taking sides. She says she's tired of acting like the only adult around here." His gaze traveled around the foyer as if seeing it for the last time. "How right she is."

He headed to the front door and opened it. I followed him, hoping for one gesture, one look that would tell me there was hope. He stepped over the same threshold he'd carried me over on our wedding day and met my eyes. I held my breath, waiting.

"Good-bye, Mellie." The door closed in my face with a gentle snap.

I stood there without moving, staring at the closed door and listening to the grandfather clock chime every fifteen minutes while the light outside grew dimmer and dimmer as I waited for the worst day of my life to be over.

CHAPTER
36

A week later I sat at Jack's empty desk in his study, attempting to address Christmas cards and trying not to notice that the framed photos of Nola and the twins were gone but the ones of me remained. I wasn't sure what hurt more—that or Jack's empty drawers and closet upstairs in the bedroom we'd shared. I stared at the happy photo of all of us that Rich Kobylt had taken at the Pineapple Fountain, the twins in their mismatched outfits and the dogs wearing nothing at all. And there was Jack, the center of all our lives, his arm casually thrown around me as I looked up at him with a wide smile.

I felt the familiar knot in my throat as I closed a card and shoved it into an envelope. I'd thought about not sending them this year, as if I might be perpetuating a lie. But the little stubbornness I clung to allowed me to believe that Jack would come back. I would give up coffee and doughnuts for life if I could be permitted to hang on to that one bit of stubbornness that made it possible to get out of bed each morning and face a new day.

My phone buzzed and I felt the thrill of anticipation as I looked at the screen to see if it was Jack. Even the short, terse texts regarding his scheduled visits with the twins gave me a lift, as these notifications were proof that he hadn't forgotten my existence. It was the best I could hope for right now.

This text was from Suzy Dorf, reminding me of our chat when she'd asked me to let her interview me about talking with ghosts. She'd offered that in exchange for not telling Rebecca what she'd discovered about the Vanderhorsts and the spy ring. Not that any of that mattered anymore. I wished she'd been in the cemetery the night Marc was dragged into the mausoleum. That might have killed two birds with one stone.

I slid my thumb across the screen to erase the text and pretended I hadn't seen it, promising myself that I would do the grown-up thing and call her back. Just not right now. I hadn't even put the phone back down when something soft struck me in the back of the head. I looked at the floor where the object had fallen and saw Adrienne's red heart-shaped pillow. It had been in my closet on the back of a shelf the last time I'd seen it.

I picked it up and was fingering the ruffled edge when the doorbell rang. My heart skittered, and I almost heard Jack's words in my head about there being no such thing as coincidence. I ran across the foyer to throw open the door, then stood staring at my visitors, forgetting to hide my disappointment that it wasn't Jack bringing back the twins himself instead of using Jayne as our go-between.

Instead Jayne, Veronica, and Rebecca stood on the piazza with bright smiles and what looked like a large doughnut box from Glazed, the sugary smell wafting toward me. When I didn't say anything, Veronica said, "We thought we'd stop by to cheer you up."

I tried to smile, to thank them for their kindness, but I failed miserably as my lips would only tremble. "Unless Jack is in that box, I don't think there's anything you can do to cheer me up right now." I blinked rapidly, embarrassed to find myself on the verge of tears. Again. I thought I'd reached the point of having none left, wishing I could stop so I wouldn't have to keep telling my work associates and clients that I had winter allergies.

"Oh, Melanie," Jayne said, stepping forward and enveloping me in a hug as the others moved past us into the foyer. "We—and the doughnuts—are here to get you through this. And you will get through this."

I sniffled into her shoulder. "But I don't want to get through this. I just want him back."

"Come with us," Veronica said, steering us all into the parlor.

Mrs. Houlihan appeared and greeted everyone, then returned shortly with a tray carrying coffee, cups, and a plate of her Christmas cookies, and placed it in front of me. She patted my shoulder as she left, either in commiseration or as an apology for depriving me all season of her baking confections. I smiled my thanks, although I knew I couldn't eat anything. She'd been tempting me with all my favorite foods, but I could barely find the energy or enthusiasm to do much more than rearrange the food on my plate to make it look like I'd eaten more than a bite or two.

Jayne poured my coffee, heaping in all the sugar and cream that she knew I liked, then filled a plate with a tiramisu doughnut and three of Mrs. Houlihan's cookies.

"Thank you," I said, then took a sip of the coffee and barely tasted it.

Veronica looked at the red pillow I'd placed on the coffee table. "Is that Adrienne's?"

I nodded. "It hit me in the head right before the doorbell rang."

The three of them exchanged glances. "Perfect," Rebecca said. I almost did a double take. She wasn't wearing pink, but a subtle shade of mauve. She caught me looking and said, "I felt the bright pink next to Marc's new white hair was too startling, so I've toned it down a notch. Plus, I think I'll save the brighter shades of pink for after our daughter is born."

"A daughter?" I took another sip of my coffee.

"I had a dream," she said, looking around at the other two women. "Before I was pregnant and got blocked." A small V appeared between her brows. "Around the same time, I had another dream." She paused.

"Go on," Jayne said gently.

Rebecca nodded. "I dreamed that the three of us were at

Veronica's house." She swallowed. "Adrienne was there, too, pointing at something around her neck. And there was someone else—someone in the attic. And the house . . ."

"The house was on fire," Veronica finished.

"So we thought . . ." Jayne started.

Rebecca continued. "That it meant we're all supposed to pool our resources and help Veronica find out what happened to Adrienne. To stop the fire, even. You did promise to help her, Melanie." Rebecca gave me the same look I usually reserved for the twins when they didn't eat their vegetables.

"How is this supposed to help me get Jack back?" I sounded as pathetic as I felt.

"Melanie," Jayne said softly. "Helping others is the best way to take our own worries away. And while you're thinking about something else is usually when the solution to your own problems starts untangling in your head. It's a win-win." She smiled at me, and I was ashamed of all the times I'd felt envious of, well, everything about her.

I looked up at the ceiling to stem the new flood of tears before turning back to her. "I'm glad you're my sister, Jayne. I can't tell you how much. And you have my permission to slap me if I ever forget that."

She laughed. "Well, if you could have seen the bruise on Anthony's face, you might change your mind. And, no, I haven't seen him—I have no interest in seeing him ever again—but Rebecca sent me a picture from her phone. I might have missed my calling. Be a prizefighter instead of a nanny."

"Although," Rebecca said, "I think you can call it even now. He hired security for the cemetery until he could find someone to dig up the peacocks' graves. He didn't even try to keep the rubies for himself."

Jayne sniffed. "Because that was the right thing to do. But I still never want to see him again as long as I live."

Veronica pinched a bite from a doughnut, leaving the rest on her plate. "I hope you have those rubies in a secure place, Melanie. Especially after all you've been through to get them."

"They're in a safe-deposit box at our bank until Jack and I decide what we're going to do with them." I'd refused to make any decisions regarding our windfall. I'd wait as long as it took to get Jack back, and then we'd decide together.

Jayne's eyes were warm as she took my hand. "But in the meantime, I want you to think about using your gift. There is so much good we can do. Even after we help Veronica and Adrienne. Thomas has files and files of unsolved cases. And let's not forget that flapper at the Francis Marion Hotel."

Rebecca leaned forward in her chair. "Since my gift is on hiatus for the next six months, I can put all my skills of attracting men to help you win Jack back."

"But . . ." I stopped, thinking about her own marital issues but not wanting to sound rude.

"I know. Marc and I have had our problems. But ever since the . . . incident . . . in the cemetery, he's been quite attentive. He barely leaves my side. I don't know if it's because he's decided he really wants to be with me and embrace impending fatherhood, or if he's just scared witless and doesn't want to be alone. Regardless, I do know a few tricks to keep a man interested and I'm willing to share everything I know with you."

I frowned at her. "What I'd really like you to do is talk Marc out of filming in my house. Then I'll believe he's changed."

Rebecca's large blue eyes watered as she regarded me. "It's not him, Melanie—it's that Harvey person. He won't be talked out of it. And because you and Jack signed the contract, you can't back out. I'm sorry."

I had to blink, feeling my eyes begin to water again.

Veronica turned to me. "You and Jack are the most perfect couple, Melanie. Anybody can see the love you have for each other and your children. This is a rough patch, but all good marriages have them, and they're stronger on the other side because of it. You will work this out—I'm sure of it. And you've got friends and family to help and support you. You know that, right?"

I nodded, unable to speak, as I'd started to cry again. We all ended up in a group hug, sobbing and laughing together, none of us really surprised when the red pillow flew up in the air and landed in Veronica's lap.

EPILOGUE

Post and Courier

December 21

by SUZY DORF

Dear Readers,

Many of you have written to thank me for my recent series on hidden treasures in Charleston and the Low-country, urging me to continue. I must confess that your enthusiasm alone would encourage me to write more, even if it weren't one of my favorite topics. And while we're talking of topics, please continue to send in your requests for future columns. One never knows what might be discovered by shining a light in a long-darkened corner.

Speaking of long-darkened corners, several of you have asked me about the hullabaloo at the Gallen Hall cemetery the night of the Big Snow. Apparently, much news coverage was dedicated to the five inches of white stuff that covered our city, so that other news was over-looked in the excitement. Some of you inquired as to whether the apparent owner of the land upon which the cemetery sits, and who has been mentioned in this column more than once, might have been involved. Let's just say that this story deserves its own column, with enough room for all the salacious details, of which, I assure you, there are many.

Please keep your eyes trained on this column each Sunday for new revelations and stories centered around our fair city and its citizens, both living and dead. And those in between. I am confident that there will be much material to be discussed in the near future, as a source close to most of the strange goings-on in the Holy City has recently experienced a change of heart that this writer is much excited about.

As for unfinished business related to my previous series on the historic homes in Charleston, please know that the cistern excavation at the former Vanderhorst residence on Tradd Street is still in progress, but an unnamed source has told me that there are more secrets hidden there, and there are bets going on in certain parts of our society on whether the owners of the house will be residing together in the home by the time the last treasure is revealed.

Until next time,
Happy reading

ACKNOWLEDGMENTS

I am full of gratitude for my editor, Cindy Hwang, and the other amazing people at Penguin Random House whose enthusiasm and dedication to all the steps in getting my books into readers' hands are so very much appreciated. I couldn't do this without you!

As always, thanks to my first readers, Susan Crandall and Wendy Wax, for gallantly reading every word I write and for constantly challenging me to be a better writer. Thank you for your friendship.

And a huge thank-you to James Del Greco, RN, MSN, for allowing me to use your name for one of my favorite new characters in this book. You won a raffle and were so kind to let me use my imagination to sculpt your character into one I'm sure my readers will love as much as I do. Note to readers: All aspects of the character (except physical description) are completely fictional and simply a figment of the author's imagination.

Last, but certainly not least, thanks to my readers who have fallen in love with Melanie and Jack and the rest of the characters who populate the Tradd Street series. The series was originally supposed to be only two books, but you have inspired me to make it seven. Yes, there will be one more! Sign up for my newsletter at karen-white.com so you'll get the scoop first.

THE
CHRISTMAS SPIRITS
ON TRADD STREET

KAREN WHITE

Questions for Discussion

1. We have seen Melanie grow up in so many ways throughout the series and in this book. Why do you think she allows her insecurity to get the best of her and her relationship with Jack?

2. Family can be wonderful but can also be tricky to deal with. In the case of Marc and Anthony, how do you think two brothers who were raised in the same home can grow up to be such different people?

3. Speaking of family, how would you describe the dynamic between Rebecca and Melanie? What caused their relationship to dissolve and what causes it to grow closer again? Is blood truly thicker than water?

4. Jack loves Melanie for who she is and accepts her faults. Why do you think Jack couldn't tell Melanie the truth about what happened to him, his editor, and his book? Do you think he was bound by the sense that he needed to support his family or to show the same level of independence that Melanie exhibits?

5. Melanie has the ability to see and interact with ghosts. Would you want that ability and would you do what

Melanie does to help enable the ghosts to rest in peace? Or would you ignore your ability?

6. Marriage plays a prominent role in the book, and we see many different aspects of it—the good and the rough parts. Did you like seeing both Melanie and Jack's tender moments and their moments of frustration? Could you relate to the ups and downs?

7. Why do you think Melanie feels she has to be the one to solve everyone's problems? Why is she unable to allow herself to accept help from others, including from her parents and Jack?

8. In the next (and final) book in the series, where do you expect to find the characters—especially Melanie and Jack?

Keep reading for an excerpt from
the first book in a new Tradd Street
spin-off series by Karen White

THE SHOP
ON ROYAL STREET

Available in spring 2022 from Berkley

Shadowy reflections of drooping banana leaves haunted the dirt-smudged windows of the old house. It made me think of the hidden memories of people and a past long since gone but still trapped within the walls of the crumbling structure, pressing against the glass in a vain attempt to escape. The roof of the front porch sagged, as if weighted with the gravity of the human experience that had once passed through the corridors before exiting out the doors and windows forever.

I stepped up onto the porch, my fingers brushing the rainbow-hued Mardi Gras beads dangling on the handrails and over the missing porch spindles that lent a grinning pumpkin look to the front of the house. Creeping vines claimed most of the three guillotine windows that lined the porch adjacent to the front door, completing the abandoned air and haunted look of the Creole cottage I'd already set my heart on buying. This dilapidated structure was a symbol. A call to arms for me. A new place to start after an impressive and unexpected stumble and a complicated knot of bad decisions, stupidity, and an alarming amount of unwarranted confidence that had almost derailed my life. And all despite the family whose love and support I wasn't convinced I deserved.

"Nola . . ."

Despite the worry and caution in my stepmother's voice, she stopped. We had both learned over the last six years that I needed to make my own decisions. And accept the consequences.

I played a slow hopscotch as I avoided broken boards and patches of termite-chewed wood, the lacelike sinews as dangerous as thin ice. Spots of faded fuchsia paint clung to the front door and corbels of the porch roof, contrasting with the inevitable haint blue paint of the ceiling and lime green of the clapboards. A line of dusty blue bottles sat atop the sash of one of the windows, a precarious position for something so fragile. Maybe whoever had placed them there believed in taking chances.

"It needs a little work," I said. "Mostly TLC. And maybe a few gallons of paint and linseed oil." I looked down at the sidewalk where my stepmother, Charleston Realtor Melanie Middleton Trenholm, stood in her high heels—despite my warnings about New Orleans sidewalks. Her face wore the expression of someone who'd just witnessed a train wreck. I would have laughed except she was looking at the house I wanted to buy.

She muttered something under her breath, something that sounded a lot like *oh, no, not again*. Louder, she said, "You know, Nola, speaking from experience here, I'd say this house needs more than paint and linseed oil. A wrecking ball or flame thrower might be more appropriate."

To distract her, I pointed past a cluster of debris piled on the porch, including a discarded surfboard—not completely out of place in the eclectic Faubourg Marigny neighborhood— toward a tall oleander plant, its clusters of white, funnel-shaped blooms drooping drunkenly in the heat. "The front and back gardens are a little overgrown but contain lots of gorgeous plants. I can't wait for Granddad to come visit and offer his expertise."

I said this with a grin, trying hard to transfer my need for her to see what I saw, the possibilities and hope that I imagined both the house and I required. The beauty and life that existed just under the surface if given the opportunity to shed our old paint. I looked around again, determined to be honest with myself. Maybe it did need more than TLC and touch-ups. But whatever it required, I was up to the task. I straightened my shoulders and returned my gaze to Melanie. One thing I was sure of: Our foundations were strong. The house and I were survivors.

"Nola . . ." Melanie began again, then stopped. She met my gaze, her eyes warming with understanding. She'd inherited an old house in Charleston despite a lifelong dislike of them. It wasn't the houses so much as the restless spirits of past residents who hadn't left and insisted on communicating with her—a gift she tried to deny for most of her life but seemed to have finally come to terms with. In the intervening years, as the "goiter on her neck"—as she'd once referred to the architectural relic she'd inherited—had become less of a burden and more of the warm and welcoming home where she lived with her husband, children, and multiple dogs, she'd earned a grudging admiration for old houses. I'd even heard her describe one to a client as "a piece of history you can hold in your hands."

Now, looking at me with dawning perception, I knew she was seeing this house as I saw it. As a chance to move on with my life, much as the inheritance of her own house had pushed her forward. Kicking and screaming, for sure, but still in a forward and positive trajectory. The light flickered in her eyes, and I hoped she wasn't hearing the sound of a cash register ringing in the back of her practical mind.

"Well, then," she said, carefully stepping up on the bottom porch step. "Let's have a look inside."

Relief unclenched my chest and allowed me to take a deep breath as I reached for the key inside the rusted metal mailbox nailed to one of the square columns holding up the porch.

"Is that really a good idea?" Melanie asked. "I mean, anybody could just walk in and steal everything."

"Uh, yeah. That. Luckily, there's nothing left to steal. Anything of value has been long since stolen or otherwise removed. Anyway, Alison said it would be a good idea for us to have access."

"Who's Alison? What happened to what's-his-name?"

"Frank? He resigned as my agent. Something about how he wouldn't show me another house if you were going to be there. I'm sure it's because he recognized that you're an accomplished real estate agent and that I didn't need both of you." I spared Melanie the adjectives Frank had used to describe her—pushy, overbearing, officious, and anal retentive. The rest of his descriptions weren't repeatable in polite company.

"Good. His presence was completely redundant. I'm glad he was gracious enough to admit it."

I hid my smile as I stuck the old-fashioned iron key into the lock and jiggled it the way Alison had instructed me over the phone. "He said the owner would stop by to answer any questions. Apparently, he must be made of stronger stuff and can't be cowed by a labeling gun." I bit my lip as I continued to jiggle the key, hoping Melanie hadn't noticed my slip.

"Excuse me? Did you look inside his briefcase? It was a disaster. He should be thankful that I organized it for him."

I was spared from responding by the door opening on its own, despite the fact that I hadn't felt the turn of the key or any release from the lock. I felt Melanie's gaze on me. "That was easier than I thought it would be," I said brightly. "Alison said the lock should be the first thing I replace because it took her forever to get it open. Guess I just have the right touch."

I stepped across the threshold, hearing the delicate tap of Melanie's heels following me inside, her gaze boring holes in the back of my head. I shut the door then turned to face her. "Remember our agreement. If you hear or see anything while we are touring this house, please keep it to yourself. I'm not the one who can talk to dead people. Except for that one time in Charleston, they don't have a reason to bother me and I remain blissfully oblivious if they're around. If I feel a connection to a house, I won't care if there is an army of wandering souls in its hallways—I won't hear or see them, so it won't keep me up at night.

Besides, there are no old houses in New Orleans without at least one lingering spirit. It's a given."

Melanie smiled tightly. "Of course."

We turned our attention to the interior of the house, neither of us speaking. Either the pictures Alison had e-mailed me had been taken a decade or two earlier, or someone was very skilled with Photoshop. Without furniture to hide behind, the scarred cypress floors glared up at us like an unbandaged wound. Splotches of colorful and unidentifiable stains of varying sizes dotted the old wood, and I promised myself that I wouldn't look too closely or try to identify the sources. Especially the ones that were definitely not water- or pet-related.

Like a woman in the throes of labor trying to imagine the happy outcome despite the agony, I said, "It could be worse."

"How?" Melanie walked toward the remains of a fireplace. The millwork had been removed with what must have been an ax, judging by the scars in the surrounding plaster that were deep enough to show the wood studs underneath. "Nothing that a match and some lighter fluid couldn't fix."

"Oh, come on. I know you don't really believe that. Not anymore, anyway. Just think of our house on Tradd Street. And your mother's house on Legare. You helped saved them both from the brink. Even you have to admit that in the end it was all worth it."

"I might. But they were only on the brink. This one has been completely pushed over it. And then trampled on. I think it would appreciate being put out of its misery."

"Look," I said, sticking my fingers through one of the holes in the plaster. "Imagine how beautiful these walls might be if we removed all the plaster and drywall to expose the beautiful wood beneath. And refinished the floors and fixed the millwork around the windows and doors. Just look at these high ceilings! Imagine the history in these walls."

As I spoke, her gaze traveled behind me toward the stairs with the missing balustrade, her eyes following something. Or someone. I didn't turn around. She forced her attention back to me and gave me another tight smile. "Are all the bedrooms upstairs?"

"Yes. Just three, but because they have to fit under the pitch of the steeply gabled roof, they're tiny according to the floor plan. I noticed two dormer windows which should at least let in a lot of light. I might have to knock out a wall to enlarge both bedrooms, as well as make the one full bath bigger. And more functional."

"More functional?"

I tried speaking too fast and too softly, in the dim hope that she couldn't hear me and would be too embarrassed to ask for me to repeat myself. She was highly sensitive about her age for no reason except for the fact that she was a few years older than my dad. This meant I should be safe from further scrutiny regarding the condition of the house and my sanity. "Alison mentioned that the toilet was missing. As well as a sink. But at least there's a half-bath down here. Although I believe the toilet doesn't actually flush."

"You do realize that despite my advanced age I have perfect hearing, right?" Melanie moved toward the stairs, turning around to take stock. "So, this room runs the length of the house and doubles as entryway and living room."

I followed behind her, smelling her rose perfume— something she'd started wearing my freshman year in college when I'd moved back home. "Right. The other front-facing room is the dining room, and behind it, facing the courtyard, is the kitchen."

"Which I'm sure is just as functional as the upstairs bathroom."

"No," I said, hating to admit she was right. "The kitchen has a sink."

Melanie glanced over her shoulder at me but didn't say anything.

As we climbed the stairs to the second level, the temperature changed as if the thermostat had abruptly dropped thirty degrees despite the hot sun streaming in unimpeded from one of the dormer windows. Except there was no air conditioner. Or thermostat. Melanie didn't say anything, but I saw her shiver.

We both ducked at the top of the stairs to avoid hitting the pitched ceiling, Melanie rubbing her arms as she looked around at the laminate wood panels covering the walls. Dust motes floated in front of the filthy windows, the musky scent of old houses—an oddly appealing mix of dust, ancient fabrics, and furniture polish—making me a little homesick.

This room was as long as the living space beneath us, but far less functional because of the ceiling slope. Still, it held a lot of charm and the same cypress floors as the first story. While getting my master's degree in historic preservation, I'd done a lot of floor rehab, and my fingers itched to see what a little sanding and linseed oil might do to these.

Melanie's gaze focused on a closed door at the top of the stairs, her mouth opening and then shutting immediately. I walked past her and turned the knob. "It's locked, and there's no key in the keyhole. I think it's just a closet. We can ask the owner."

"Do you smell that?" She stuck her neck forward, sniffing the air. "It's pipe tobacco. It's like someone just blew pipe smoke in my face."

"I don't smell anything. Just the house."

She nodded, her eyes remaining on the closet door. "I think . . ."

"You promised." I gave her a warning glance before going through an open doorway that led directly into one of the small bedrooms. Two other doorways opened up into the second bedroom and what must be the bathroom.

I stuck my head into the bathroom, and immediately pulled it back. "I don't recommend you look in there." I was grateful for the lower temperature, sparing us from the scent of heat-baked whatever had been left in the plumbing. I looked at the tall, sloped ceiling, at the original wood beams and dormer window surround, and a fireplace like the one downstairs, with its mantel intact. "I think if I just reposition these walls, we could have two decent-sized bedrooms. And . . ."

The familiar notes of "Dancing Queen" being loudly hummed behind me caught my attention. I shouldn't have been surprised. Loudly humming ABBA songs was Melanie's way of drowning out the restless spirits who wanted to talk to her. I assumed they found it as annoying as we did, which is why it worked. It was one of Melanie's quirks—definitely weird, but also surprisingly lovable.

I sighed. "Fine. I've seen enough up here, let's go back downstairs." As I turned, I spotted an unhinged door leaning against the wall. The wood tone and the top panel of frosted glass told me it hadn't come from the house, but it didn't tell me why it was there.

Melanie stopped humming long enough to lean down to look at the iron lock and doorknob. She touched it gently with her finger. "It has the initials MB embossed on the handle."

I leaned closer. "I've seen a few of these doors before. They're from the famous Maison Blanche department store building downtown. When the store and the offices on the upper floors were gutted to transform it into the Ritz Carlton in the late nineteen nineties, a lot of the unwanted interior was scavenged." I ran my hand along the privacy bubbles in the glass, admiring the thick wood of the door, a relic of a time when even basic office doors were made with skill and with longevity in mind. Straightening, I added, "Mostly by locals who wanted to keep something from an iconic New Orleans building and renovators who wanted a piece of history in their houses. I saw a lot of it in grad school—including a lingerie display counter refitted as a kitchen island in a house in the Quarter."

Melanie suddenly turned toward the window, her head tilted slightly as if listening to someone speaking. She shook her head then began humming again, this time "Waterloo." Without waiting for me, she marched through the doorway then down the stairs as I hurried to catch up to her, glancing over my shoulder only once.

I caught up to her in the kitchen, where she'd placed her bag on a scarred and pitted countertop with indeterminate stains the color of a sunset before a storm. We both studiously avoided discussing the elephant in the room—or whatever that had been upstairs—as I examined the peeling laminate floor, its lifted corners revealing the cypress floor planks beneath.

Melanie opened her bag and pulled out one of her infamous spreadsheets. "I've been looking at the comps in the Faubourg Marigny . . ."

I held up my hand to stop her. "You know how you grit your teeth when you're with a client who wants to buy a house in Charleston but doesn't know how to pronounce the street names? They phonetically sound out Legare and Vanderhorst and it's like fingernails on a chalkboard? So please. Locals here call it 'the MAR-i-nee.' No need to put 'Faubourg' in front of it because it means neighborhood so it's redundant. And while we're at it, it's a streetcar, not a trolley, and whatever you do, do *not* say 'New Orleans,' okay? It's all one word—'Newawlins.' Otherwise, people will have the same reaction you get when you overhear a tourist call Charleston 'Chucktown.'"

A shudder rippled through Melanie. "Got it. Since I imagine we'll be visiting you a lot, it's important that we fit right in."

At my look of alarm, she quickly amended, "I mean—not too much. You'll be busy with work, as will your father and I, and the twins have school, but I just thought . . ."

I put my hand on her arm and squeezed. Melanie, for all of her quirks and idiosyncrasies, had been my mother and fierce defender ever since I'd shown up unannounced on her doorstep at fourteen, lost and alone with only the name of my father—Jack Trenholm—as the one certainty in my life. Owing to her own shattered childhood, Melanie had recognized a kindred unmoored soul and had taken me in without reservation or conditions and proceeded to mother me long before she married Jack and the title became official.

"I'll miss you, too," I said softly. "And you and Dad and JJ and Sarah can visit as often as you like. And Aunt Jayne and all the grandparents. Just not too often, okay? I need to do this on my own."

Melanie nodded, her lips pressed together, her eyes bright, undoubtedly remembering the first time I'd moved to New Orleans as an undergrad freshman at Tulane, excited and nervous at this great new adventure. Seeing only my bright new future ahead of me. Until it had all gone spectacularly wrong.

I blinked my stinging eyes as I opened my backpack and pulled out my own spreadsheet on recent sales in the neighborhood, earning me a look of approval and a little bit of surprise. I hadn't meant to show Melanie, not wanting her to know that despite my adamant demands that I leave my home behind me, there were some things that I would need to hold on to. And because I'd realized that she might need the same thing.

"Let's just say that after living with you for so long, a few things might have rubbed off on me. I've found that spreadsheets can actually be useful in situations where organization of details is important. Like house searches. Or class schedules. But not the contents of my dresser drawers." I raised my eyebrows. "Or shoes."

"Um-hmm." That was the Melanie equivalent of letting me know that she was right and I'd figure that out eventually. "Anyway," she continued. "Even in the condition this house is in, it still appears to be structurally sound. Which is why I don't understand the listing price. It's way below market, even lower than other homes in worse condition that were sold before being rehabbed. I just can't figure out why. I was wondering if maybe this house sustained major damage during Katrina and that's scared off buyers?"

I shook my head, remembering all the research I'd done before accepting my new job as an architectural historian for a New Orleans–based civil engineering firm. I knew I needed to be fully armed to talk my parents out of all of their objections. "The section of the neighborhood on the Mississippi River side of Rampart experienced some wind damage, but the Marigny is at a high enough elevation to have escaped the flooding. Most of the nineteenth century–style raised houses are elevated enough so that the flood waters didn't do significant damage. I know you won't admit it, but older houses are just built better."

Melanie's forehead creased even more. "Then why hasn't it sold? It's been on the market for over a year, and the price is so below market that I'm wondering if they forgot a zero." She raised the worksheet closer to her face and squinted. "The average time on the market for this neighborhood is less than two months—even for those in need of rehab. And, according to my notes, it looks like this house has made it to escrow six times before the deal fell through." She looked at me. "Frank or this Alison person, if they truly consider themselves real estate agents, would have done their research and figured out why."

I kept my mouth closed, not wanting to mention that they probably had but had thought it best not to tell me. Before Melanie reached the same conclusion, I marched past her toward the back door. "Let's check out the courtyard."

I threw open the door and paused. "I found the toilet and sink!" Both had been planted along the fence line, a healthy sprouting of weeds spilling out of both and trailing down to the lichen-coated, brick-covered ground. Muppet hair–like spikes of grass poked out from between the worn bricks, many of them broken or missing corners. A pine coffin, questionably refurbished as a planter, sprouted surprisingly hardy miniature palm trees, while an impressive amount of something green and fuzzy covered it like five-o'clock shadow.

Melanie shuddered. "I noticed that the neighbor across the street has a coffin planter, too. Maybe they'd like a pair."

I looked at Melanie with alarm. "Do you think . . . ?"

She shook her head. "No. It's not been used for its original purpose. It's just . . . not all right."

"Actually, in the Marigny it's pretty much par for the course. Did you notice the goat with a rhinestone collar in the yard on the corner? I'm assuming that's what the homeowner uses as a lawnmower. I think the whole vibe here is cool. It's pretty eclectic, and I'm excited about the neighborhood music scene. I'd like to get back into writing music again, and I think I'd be a good fit here. And my office is downtown on Poydras, so it's an easy commute. I could even bike it."

At Melanie's look of alarm, I quickly added. "Or take the streetcar. Or even Uber it if it's dark."

She relaxed. "Or you could learn to drive. I'm sure . . ."

"No," I said, shutting her down. "I tried once and just missed getting killed and being sued for everything we own. No thanks."

I struggled to draw in a deep breath in the sticky air of a New Orleans July. I glanced at Melanie, whose hair had already frizzed out into alarming proportions. "Just like Charleston," I said, trying to wipe away the look of worry on her face.

She gave me her "mom look," the one that told me she knew that I didn't believe it, either. That despite the tropical climates that wilted less-sturdy souls, Charleston and New Orleans were merely distant cousins with traces of common ancestry apparent in their architecture built to accommodate scorching temperatures and the always-present threat of hurricanes.

Their separateness was evident in their respective monikers: the Big Easy and the Holy City. The aura of New Orleans was best described as feral; Charleston's refined and graceful. My new home embraced decay, painted it in neon colors and put it on the front porch. In Charleston, they threw a lace doily over it. Charleston had palmetto bugs. New Orleans had flying cockroaches. Each city had a place in my heart. One a place from which to return, and one a place to go.

"Hello? Anyone here?" A male voice came from the kitchen.

Melanie and I looked at each other. "It must be the owner," Melanie said as she delicately stepped across the broken bricks toward the kitchen. "We're out here!"

I held back, the voice vaguely familiar. And not in a good way.

"Oh," the voice said, this time from the doorway. "It's you."

"Oh," I repeated with the same lack of enthusiasm.

Melanie began to speak, stopping suddenly as her gaze fixed on something beyond the doorway, her eyes widening just before a loud crash erupted from somewhere inside the house. An icy blast of air whipped through us, raising gooseflesh over my entire body, as a woman's scream pierced the quiet afternoon.

NEW YORK TIMES BESTSELLING AUTHOR

KAREN WHITE

"This is storytelling of the highest order: the kind of book that leaves you both deeply satisfied and aching for more."

—*New York Times* bestselling author **Beatriz Williams**

For a complete list of titles, please visit prh.com/karenwhite